WITHDRAWN

THE MIDDLE EAST IN WORLD

The Middle East

in World Affairs

ттттттттттттттттттттттттттттттттттттттт

BY GEORGE LENCZOWSKI

University of California at Berkeley

SECOND EDITION

Cornell University Press

ITHACA, NEW YORK

First edition 1952

Second edition 1956

Second printing August 1957

Third printing July 1958

PRINTED IN THE UNITED STATES OF AMERICA BY THE

VAIL-BALLOU PRESS, INC., BINGHAMTON, NEW YORK

TO B. L. AND J. L.

Foreword

EXPERIENCE in the foreign service and in teaching has convinced the author of the need for a comprehensive study of contemporary politics and diplomacy in the Middle East. The aim of the present book is to fill this need by supplying politically relevant facts and interpretations to the general reader and student alike.

The Middle East between 1914 and the present day is the subject; however, an introductory chapter gives the diplomatic history of the Ottoman and Persian empires, especially in the nineteenth century. Readers will find little on the prewar history of the Arabs, but they are given an account of the Near Eastern question because, from the point of view of the political scientist, knowledge of it is essential to an understanding of contemporary politics. Geographically, attention shifts from the northwest (the Balkans and the Turkish Straits) in the period before 1914 to the south and east (Africa and Asia) after that date. Of course, there are exceptions. Thus, in the nineteenth century the impact of Napoleon's adventure in Egypt, the rise of Mohammed Ali, and French and British interventions in Lebanon and Egypt draw our attention to the African and Asiatic possessions of the Ottoman Empire. And recent developments in Turko-Soviet relations remind us that the old Near Eastern question is being revived under a different guise.

The structure of the book stems largely from the author's primary interest in political developments. The area is treated as a whole as long as it is largely included in the Ottoman Empire (Part One); following the Empire's dissolution and its transformation into a number of successor states, individual countries are studied (Parts

Two to Four). In the final portion entitled "Problems of War and Peace" (Part Five), questions that transcend the limits of single states are discussed. There particular stress is laid on the policies of the big powers regarding the Middle East as a whole.

Both primary and secondary sources have been used: the earlier the period chronologically, the more reliance has been given to the finished products of research. The author gratefully acknowledges his debt to monographs and other works treating individual countries of the Middle East. For more recent developments, more need was felt to use primary sources such as memoirs, firsthand reports, treaties, and other official documents. All these sources have been utilized against a background of personal observations made during the author's eight-year stay in the Middle East.

The system of transliteration of Middle Eastern names follows contemporary usage by leading English-language newspapers and periodicals. The practice of such papers as the *New York Times*, *The Times* of London, and *The Economist* has been generally adhered to. Although not perfectly consistent, this system has at least the merit of familiarity to the public.

The author would like to thank the following persons for their assistance during his work on the manuscript: Mr. David T. Wilder, formerly librarian of Hamilton College (now of the American University in Beirut), Miss D. M. Quackenbush and Mrs. Robert M. Browning, members of the Hamilton Library staff, for their help in securing materials through the interlibrary loan system; Miss Helen Gaffney, reference librarian at Hamilton, for her many unselfish services; Messrs. Donald C. Curry and William J. Schwarz, seniors at Hamilton College (1951–1952), for taking care of certain technical tasks, thereby enabling the author to concentrate on research and writing; Mrs. Harold Bodmer of Clinton, New York, for typing the manuscript; and Mr. Philip Oxley, assistant professor of geology at Hamilton, for drawing the maps. To his wife the author would like to acknowledge his warm debt of gratitude for her most helpful assistance in research.

G. L.

Berkeley, California
March, 1952

Contents

PART THREE. *The Fertile Crescent*

CONTENTS

CONTENTS

Appendix Tables, Bibliography, and Index

xiv

Maps

Introduction

NO UNANIMITY has so far been reached on a definition of the Middle East, and even the name has not been universally accepted. Scholars, statesmen, and journalists refer to the area sometimes as the Near East, sometimes as the Middle East. The Near East is the older term. In addition to southwestern Asia it comprises those areas of southeastern Europe which have in the past been under Turkish control. The term Middle East seems to be of more recent origin and owes its widespread acceptance in modern times to its official use by the British. In this study the modern practice has been followed, with the understanding that the Middle East encompasses all those countries of Asia situated south of the Soviet Union and west of Pakistan, and Egypt on the African continent as well. The Balkans have been excluded. In the few cases in which it was necessary to include Greece and the Aegean, the older term, Near East, has been employed.

The Middle East has a unique geographical position. It is an area situated at the junction of Europe, Asia, and Africa, and as such it commands the strategic approaches to these three continents. One is tempted to call it the hub of the Eastern Hemisphere. The shortest and most convenient air and water routes from Europe to Asia go through the Middle East. Every major empire in the history of the Old World has either been included in this area, in whole or in part, or has cast covetous eyes at it. At present the Middle East is located astride the imperial life line of the British Commonwealth; hence whatever happens to the area is bound to have an effect on the destiny of Britain.

Taken as a part of Asia (where it is chiefly located), the Middle East falls within the middle zone which extends the whole length of this gigantic continent, roughly between the 30th and 40th parallels. To the north of this middle zone lies the great land mass of Russia; to the south, those peninsular extremities of Asia which have until recently been directly controlled by the great powers of the West. The middle zone has traditionally been a contested ground between the land power of Russia and the naval power of the West. The Middle East has been and continues to be of particular importance to Russia as an area through which she might obtain access to the warm waters and major commercial routes of the globe. Moreover, Russia is particularly vulnerable to attack from the Middle East if we consider Soviet concentrations of industry in the Black Sea–Ural region.

Of all parts of the middle zone of Asia, the Middle East has been most exposed to penetration by naval powers, no doubt owing to its long and curved coast line, which is washed by the Black Sea, the Mediterranean, the Red Sea, and the Indian Ocean. It is less easily accessible by land from the north. This explains the fact that the West succeeded in obtaining a firmer foothold in the area than did Russia. Yet, there is no reason why the roles may not one day be reversed. Russia has progressed technologically; moreover, she has the advantage of being directly adjacent to the Middle East. The colonies of southern Asia, which formerly the West could freely use as bases, have recently been emancipated and have ceased to be a source of power to the West. In fact, Asia's middle zone, the zone of weak and independent states, has recently expanded southward to the detriment of Western strength. Under these conditions the balance hitherto maintained between Russia and the West on the Asiatic mainland has been seriously affected.

In addition to geographical uniqueness, the Middle East has several other distinctive features. Although inhabited by no more than ninety million people, it is the center of the Islamic world, a world of three hundred million souls. It contains the holiest places of Islam as well as the highest institutions of Islamic learning. The Moslem religion and culture have permeated the whole society of the Middle East and have imbued it with philosophical attitudes such that only radical revolution is likely to effect a change in its behavior. In the Holy Land of Palestine the Middle East possesses a focus of aspirations of Jews and Christians alike. Moreover, under the arid soil of some sections of the Middle East lies the greatest single reserve of oil, the black gold of nations. For these reasons its importance transcends its geographical limits. No intelligent foreign policy today can ignore the Middle East and its impact upon the rest of the world.

Politically and culturally the Middle East may be divided into two main regions, the Northern Belt and the Arab Core. The former differs from the latter in that it is ethnically non-Arab and that it has a direct boundary with Russia. These two traits have helped to shape its destinies and its present political complexion. Turkey, Iran, and Afghanistan may differ from one another in many respects, yet the overwhelming presence of the Russian giant north of their borders creates an invisible bond. Populated by about forty-eight million people, this Northern Belt separates and protects the Arab Core from Russia. As a defense line, it is uneven, the strongest link being Turkey; the weakest, Iran. To a certain extent its role can be compared to the historical role of Poland in Europe: like Poland, which was a rampart of Western Christendom against the hordes from the East, so Turkey, and to a lesser extent Iran and Afghanistan, have stood guard against Muscovy's southward expansion. And like Poland, the countries of the Northern Belt isolated their hinterland so effectively from the great power of Muscovy that the hinterland—just as the West—tended to minimize this power and acquire a false sense of security.

Peopled by forty-two million souls, the Arab Core of the Middle East can in turn be subdivided into the Fertile Crescent and the Red Sea Region. The Fertile Crescent comprises Iraq—the once-wealthy Mesopotamia or Land of Two Rivers—and the Mediterranean coast of Asia. The latter is the home of Syria, Lebanon, Israel, and Jordan. Despite the multiplicity of races and religions in its midst, the Fertile Crescent has certain features common to all of its component parts and, in the past, has been more than once unified under a single political power.

The Red Sea Region differs from the Fertile Crescent, but it contains tremendous contrasts within itself. On the east there is the vast and arid expanse of the Arabian peninsula, thinly populated, rich in oil, and steeped in Mohammedan tradition. Its way of life is still largely medieval, and wide tracts of desert separate it effectively from closer contact with the Fertile Crescent and the Mediterranean. On the west there is Egypt, a country living off the longest river in the world, with a teeming population in its lush and unhealthy delta. Egypt with her three crops a year, an abundant supply of water, and a fortunate location astride the great commercial routes has traditionally been the seat of culture and today is by far the most advanced of Arab countries.

It is practical and helpful to keep in mind this division of the Middle East. In the following pages a mass of detail may tempt one to see primarily diversity in the Middle Eastern scene. But one must never forget the basic unity of the Middle East as produced by the features of geography, culture, economy, and strategy common to the area as a whole.

‑‑ PART ONE ‑‑

THE FIRST WORLD WAR

AND THE PEACE

⊣ CHAPTER I ⊢

Historical Background

THE history of the Middle East up to the First World War is largely a history of two empires, the Ottoman and the Persian. It is difficult to understand the politics of this area in the last quarter of a century without knowing, at least in outline, the turbulent story of these two major powers. Of the two, the Ottoman Empire should receive priority for two reasons: first, because of the Empire's size, which extended to three continents, and, secondly, because of the involvement of practically every great European power in its foreign or domestic affairs in the course of the last three hundred years.

I. THE OTTOMAN EMPIRE

The Ottoman Turks first appeared in Asia Minor in the thirteenth century as a frontier tribe on the western confines of the Seljuk Sultanate of Rum (or Iconium). Better disciplined and organized than their immediate neighbors, they began to expand at the expense of the Seljuks and the Byzantines. The Seljuk sultanate, weakened by Mongol pressure, soon disintegrated into petty principalities which fell under the Ottomans. In the fourteenth century the Ottomans established themselves at strategic points in Greece (1399), Serbia (1389), and Bulgaria (1393). By the middle of the next century the Byzantine Empire was practically surrounded by Ottoman possessions and vulnerable to a major attack. This came with the conquest of Constantinople by the Turks in 1453. Emperor Constantine IX died defending the city. The mopping-up operations included the conquest eight years later of the tiny Empire of Trebizond and the subjugation of some recalcitrant Turkoman tribes.

[handwritten margin note: A. Rise (1299-1453)]

[handwritten margin note: B. Expansion (1453-1566)]

3

By 1473 Asia Minor was firmly under Ottoman rule. Under Mohammed the Conqueror (1451–1481) the Turks pushed their conquests farther into Europe and Asia.

By 1468 Greece, including Morea and Euboea, was subjected to Ottoman rule, largely at the expense of the Venetian Republic. Serbia was converted into a Turkish pashalik in 1459, and Bosnia and Herzegovina were annexed by 1465.

Having established their supremacy in Anatolia and in the Balkans, the Turks then turned to the northern shores of the Black Sea. In 1475 the Genoese colonies of Azov and Crimea surrendered to the Ottomans, and the Tatars accepted the suzerainty of the Sultan. Thus the Black Sea had become a "Turkish lake."

Under Mohammed's successors the Empire expanded to the East. Under Selim I (1512–1520), the Turks conquered northern Mesopotamia, Egypt, Syria, and Arabia. The conquest of Egypt was important because it ended the Abbassid caliphs. The story that the last Abbassid ruler transferred the title to the victorious sultan is not supported by historical evidence, but Ottoman rulers took the title. The caliphate implied spiritual and temporal authority over the Moslems.

The reign of Suleiman I, the Magnificent, Selim's only son, was the climax of Ottoman greatness both in foreign and in domestic affairs. Suleiman rounded out the Empire's European possessions by conquering Belgrade in 1521 and by subduing Hungary at the famous battle of Mohacs in 1526. In 1547 most of Hungary and Transylvania were incorporated into the Ottoman Empire. At the same time the Empire expanded toward the East. In a series of wars with Persia, Suleiman acquired large portions of Armenia and Mesopotamia, including the cities of Baghdad and Basra. Owing to his great sea power, he was able to extend his mastery to Aden and the southeastern coast of Arabia. Ambitious expansion in the Mediterranean, the Adriatic, and North Africa (Algiers acknowledged his suzerainty in 1516) completed Suleiman's impressive conquests.

At the time of Suleiman's death the Ottoman Empire stretched from the Danube to the Persian Gulf and from the Ukrainian steppes to the Tropic of Cancer in upper Egypt. It included the mastery of the great trade routes of the Mediterranean, of the Black and Red seas, and of parts of the Indian Ocean. It had an estimated population of fifty million as against some four million in England and embraced some twenty races and nationalities.

Suleiman's reign not only was the apogee of Ottoman glory, but it

4

opened a new chapter in the Empire's foreign relations. Until then the Empire had been expanding at the expense of Byzantium and of relatively minor European and Asiatic nations. Suleiman's reign marked the beginning of a prolonged contest with major powers. Two of them were European, the Habsburg Empire and Venice; one was Asiatic, Persia. The contest with the Habsburgs and the Venetian Republic lasted for about a century and a half and concluded in 1699. Thereafter Austro-Ottoman relations passed to a secondary plane.

Suleiman's reign also inaugurated a new era in the Empire's relations with France. This was a logical outgrowth of the contest which the Habsburgs carried on simultaneously with their eastern and western rivals. It was only natural that France and Turkey should look toward each other as friends and allies faced with the threat of the central-European power of Austria.

In 1535 a treaty was concluded between Suleiman I and Francis I of France. This was a treaty of friendship and collaboration, directed against the Habsburgs, in which the French were granted many far-reaching rights and privileges. These privileges, called thereafter *Capitulations* (from *capitula* or chapters of the treaty), extended to the French freedom of trade and navigation in Ottoman ports, reduced the customs duty to 5 per cent in their favor only, exempted French traders from Ottoman jurisdiction and placed them under French consular jurisdiction in matters both civil and criminal, guaranteed to French settlers full religious liberty as well as the custody of the Christian holy places (this, in turn, implied a quasi-protectorate of the French kings over Christians of Latin rite in Ottoman possessions), and extended to French subjects other valuable property and navigation privileges.

The treaty was the basis of a prolonged collaboration between France and Turkey, a collaboration which was to last for at least three centuries. It was confirmed several times, the most important confirmation being that of 1740 which followed a successful Ottoman campaign against the Habsburgs in Serbia. A strong Ottoman Empire was a conscious aim of France, and the maintenance of its integrity became an axiom of French foreign policy a long time before England gave thought to Turkish questions.

The contest with the Habsburgs was the main feature of Turkish history after Suleiman's death, the struggle with Venice being rather in the nature of a side show. Venice was a declining power. Only the aid of the Habsburgs and occasionally of other European powers

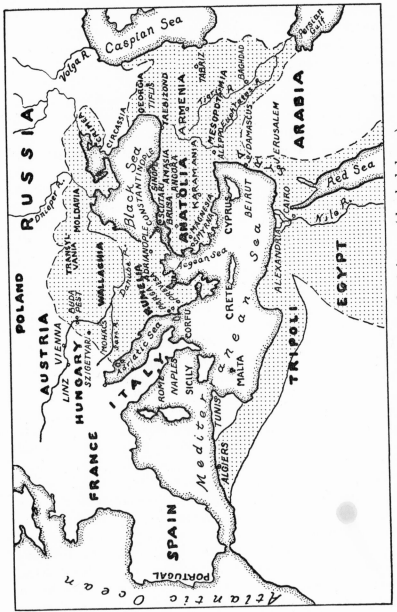

Map 1. The Ottoman Empire under Suleiman (the shaded area).

permitted the Republic of the Doges to hold its ground against the Turks for a relatively long time.

On the other hand, Ottoman might was also declining. This decline was primarily due to internal reasons. First of all, after Suleiman's death, the Empire was ruled by a succession of utterly degenerate sultans, often oblivious to the real needs of the Empire and as a rule cruel and incapable. Secondly, corruption crept into the administration and the tax-collecting processes. And, finally, the military organization of the Empire deteriorated appreciably. Here mention should be made of the special role played by the Janissaries. The Janissaries were an elite corps of the sultans, recruited among the young sons of the Christian subjects or captives of the Empire. Converted to Mohammedanism, these boys were brought up under very strict discipline and taught military arts. Uprooted and isolated from other social connections, the Janissaries constituted a formidable military order, pledged to personal service to the sultan and possessing the highest military efficiency. The position of the corps underwent a revolutionary change, however, when in 1566 its members were permitted to marry. This immediately produced two results: first, the growth of a hereditary caste feeling and, secondly, the softening of their military valor. This circumstance as well as the fact that the sultans personally participated less and less frequently in campaigns led to a decline in the Janissaries' standards and in their loyalty to their rulers. The effects upon the military power of the Empire were obviously detrimental.

In these circumstances of progressive weakening, the problem for the Empire was not so much to expand and conquer as to maintain its existing possessions. This is a somewhat oversimplified statement, of course, as the Turks were still capable of initiative in expansion. The struggle with the Habsburgs centered in the mastery of the valleys of the Danube and Sava rivers, and the contest with Venice was primarily over the mastery of the seas. The latter had its dramatic development when at the Battle of Lepanto (1571), at the entrance to the Gulf of Patros, a Christian armada organized by the Venetians and commanded by Don John of Austria, utterly defeated the Turkish navy. Although the Turks retained command of the seas for a long time to come, they were no longer considered invincible.

The deteriorating position of the Ottoman Empire was best illustrated perhaps during the Thirty Years' War (1618–1648), which threw Europe into unprecedented turmoil and considerably weakened the Holy Roman Empire. Instead of exploiting this weakness and pushing on toward Vienna, the Turks remained passive, a thing which would certainly not have happened in the earlier, more virile period of their history. New life was given the Ottoman Empire with the advent to power of the very able and strong-willed grand viziers of the Albanian family of Köprülü. Assuming the highest office of the Empire in 1656, the Köprülüs, one after another, were able during the next half-century to arouse the weakening giant to new and bold actions.

The most remarkable of these actions was the attempt to defeat Austria and conquer Vienna in 1683. The immediate cause of this campaign was a revolt against the Habsburgs of that part of Hungary which remained under their rule. The rebels made their cause the cause of the whole of Hungary and sought the support of the sultan. This support was not denied them. A magnificent Turkish army of 200,000 which had been gathered at Adrianople under the command of Grand Vizier Kara Mustafa (a relative of the Köprülü clan), proceeded toward the Hungarian plain and approached Vienna. Emperor Leopold sent envoys to Poland asking for help. King John Sobieski of Poland, believing that the fate of Christendom was at stake, decided to come to the rescue of the Emperor and personally assumed command of a strong Polish army of 40,000 men, organized into cavalry units. The defense of the city of Vienna, itself poorly fortified, was entrusted to Count Stahremberg, who had only 10,000 men at his disposal. Other imperial forces were commanded by Charles IV, duke of Lorraine, who withdrew from the city to await the Poles' arrival. The Ottoman army appeared before the walls of Vienna, in midsummer 1683, and began the siege which was to last sixty days. In September Sobieski, after a strenuous, two-week march from Poland, arrived at Vienna and replaced the duke of Lorraine as commander of the imperial forces. At the sight of the Poles panic seized the Turks. The charge of the Polish cavalry brought confusion and disorder into the ranks of the enemy. The once invincible army was completely routed. Leaving 10,000 dead, 300 guns, and enormous quantities of equipment on the battlefield, the Turks escaped toward Hungary. Vienna and central Europe were saved. Emperor Leopold returned to his capital. Sobieski and the Christian army continued to pursue the retreating Turks. The war between the Habsburgs and the sultan continued for another fifteen years. Led by the duke of Lorraine, by the Margrave Ludwig of

Baden, and by Prince Eugene of Savoy, the imperial armies inflicted many crushing defeats on the Ottomans. The Treaty of Carlowitz ended the war in 1699. Turkey was obliged to cede to the Habsburgs Transylvania, most of Hungary, and major parts of Slavonia and Croatia, and to restore parts of the Ukraine and Podolia to Poland.

From the Treaty of Carlowitz to the Treaty of Jassy

D. Fall (1699-1918)

The battle of Vienna and the Treaty of Carlowitz closed a chapter in the history of the Ottoman Empire. No longer were the Turks a formidable enemy threatening western Christendom. On the contrary, their obvious weakness resulted in an exchange of roles for the Empire and for Europe. Henceforth, it was Europe that threatened the integrity of the Ottoman Empire. Among the European powers the most ambitious in this respect was Russia. Austria, while never pro-Turkish, began to play a less prominent role, though she was ever eager to enlarge her possessions in the Balkans and to prevent Russia from becoming too strong at the expense of the Turks. This new diplomatic chapter in the history of Turkey lasted for over two centuries and came to be termed "the Eastern Question." It was a story of diplomatic moves designed, in the first place, to prevent the sudden and disorderly dissolution of the Ottoman Empire and, in the second place, in case of the inevitability of such a dissolution, to secure such equal distribution of the spoils as to prevent the upsetting of the balance of power. More concretely, the Eastern Question may be narrowed down to the maneuvering of various European powers to prevent Russia from encroaching too much upon the integrity of the Ottoman Empire.

Russia appeared on the horizon of Eastern politics in the ninth century. Toward the end of the fifteenth century Ivan III, grand duke of Muscovy (1462–1505), having married Sophia, niece of the last Byzantine emperor, considered himself an heir to the Byzantine heritage. He adopted the double-headed eagle as the emblem of Russia and called Moscow the "Third Rome." But there was little political action or direct friction between Russia and Turkey beyond these vague ideological generalities. This was mainly due to the physical separation of the two states, isolated as they were by the large and sparsely populated steppes of the Ukraine. In 1575, during Ivan the Terrible's reign, an armed clash occurred between the two states for control of Astrakhan. This isolated episode did not cause

9

any appreciable worsening of relations or any prolonged hostilities. Whatever warfare there was, was limited to the mutual raids of unruly border elements, Tatar and Cossack, upon each other. Neither the tsar nor the sultan was inclined to assume responsibility for these raids.

The situation changed appreciably with the accession of Peter the Great to the throne of Russia. Ambitious to "open the window on the Baltic" and to gain access to warm-water ports, the Tsar was determined to acquire a foothold on the Black Sea. At the time of the western offensive against the Turks, Peter in 1696, after dogged preparation, captured the fortress of Azov, which was subsequently ceded to Russia in a formal treaty concluded in 1702. In less than a decade Russia and Turkey were again at war, the result of complications in the Russo-Swedish war. Peter invaded the Ottoman Empire by way of Bessarabia in 1711 but found himself surrounded by superior Turkish forces. He was compelled to sue for peace. Actually it was a capitulation of the Russian forces, and the peace terms were damaging to Peter's foothold in and around the Black Sea. Azov and the adjoining territory were returned to the Ottomans, and the Russians had to agree to a number of restrictive measures. Because of the grand vizier's lack of foresight, the Russians managed to preserve the body of their army intact, and the great opportunity for the Turks to annihilate Russian military power was lost.

The peace concluded in 1711 was only temporary. Following the conclusion of an alliance with Austria in 1726, Russia repeatedly invaded Turkish possessions. The war of 1733–1739 resulted in the reconquest of Azov by the Russians. Catherine the Great's accession to the throne added new impetus to the policy inaugurated by Peter the Great. In fact, the Russian Empress devised grandiose schemes with regard to Turkey and freely used the technique of infiltration to prepare the Slavic and Orthodox populations of the Ottoman Empire for uprising in case of a Russian invasion.

The pretext for a new war was given Catherine by differences arising out of the Polish question. The war which broke out in 1768 abounded in Russian victories, both on land—in the Rumanian principalities—and on sea. The naval operations included the dispatch of a Russian flotilla around Europe to the Mediterranean, an operation which provoked a sensation all over the world.

The war was concluded in 1774 by the Treaty of Kuchuk Kainardji. The treaty was a milestone in Russo-Turkish relations and must be considered as a major political event in the history of Turkey and of Europe. The major provisions of the treaty can be divided into four categories:

1) *Territorial.* Russia gained direct access to the Black Sea, between the mouths of the Dnieper and the Bug. In addition, she obtained Kertch and Yenikale, i.e., control of the straits between the Sea of Azov and the Black Sea, as well as Azov, Kuban, and Terek, which gave her access to the northeastern shore of the Black Sea. Thus the Tatar khanate of Crimea was surrounded by Russian possessions. Furthermore the khanate itself was declared independent of Ottoman rule.

2) *Maritime and commercial.* Russia was allowed to establish consulates in Ottoman possessions; her traders were given freedom of trade in the Empire; and her merchant vessels obtained freedom of navigation in time of peace in the Black Sea and the Turkish Straits.

3) *Religious.* Russia was given the right to erect in Constantinople an Orthodox church administered by Russian ecclesiastics; her subjects were permitted to make pilgrimages to the holy places; the sultan promised to protect the Christian religion; and the Russian government was permitted to intervene in favor of the new church in the Ottoman capital.

4) *Political.* Russia obtained a protectorate over the Christian population of Moldavia and Wallachia.

The treaty obviously gave Russia enormous advantages and territorial accretions. It put an end to exclusive Turkish control of the Black Sea, and it gave some justification to the subsequent Russian claim of having the right of intervention on behalf of all Orthodox Christians throughout the Ottoman Empire. By declaring the Crimean Tatar khanate independent, it paved the way for its eventual annexation by Russia in 1783.

From that time on, Russia exercised relentless pressure on the Ottoman Empire, using the weapons of diplomacy, Pan-Slavism, Orthodoxy, and outright military aggression to achieve her ends. An additional stretch of territory on the Black Sea, between the Bug and Dniester rivers, was granted to Russia by the Treaty of Jassy after a five-year war ending in 1792. This treaty also secured Turkey's agreement to Russia's previous annexation of the Crimea.

As a result of these developments, Russia emerged as a first-rate Black Sea power. She constructed important naval bases and fortifications at Sevastopol and Odessa, and her navy achieved supremacy

11

in Black Sea waters. Russia's progress was not without effect upon the British, who slowly became aware of the dangers inherent in these Russian successes. The younger Pitt, in particular, attempted to arouse Parliament to take action against the threat to British interests implicit in Russia's policy. Before anything could be done, however, a new complication arose, which attracted Europe's attention away from the Russian danger. The spectacular rise of Napoleon, following on the French revolution, had a disturbing effect on the pattern of European politics and on the history of the Middle East as well.

Napoleon's Middle Eastern Adventure

Initially the outbreak of the French revolution gave a somewhat pleasant relief to Turkey, since it diverted the attention of Turkey's two enemies—Russia and Austria—toward France. Yet, ultimately, even the Ottoman Empire felt the disturbing effects of the developments in France. This may be attributed to two reasons: first, Napoleon's military campaigns brought him eventually into bodily contact with the Turks; secondly, the ideas of popular rights and nationalism engendered by the French revolution affected various subject races of the Ottoman Empire and produced disturbing consequences.

In 1798 Napoleon organized a military expedition to Egypt for the purpose of crippling British communications with India. This naturally meant an invasion of Ottoman territory, and after centuries of friendship put France at odds with the sultan. Notwithstanding a crushing naval defeat on August 1, 1798, Napoleon persevered in his Egyptian campaign, occupying the whole of Egypt, then ruled by the Mameluke viceroys, and advancing into Palestine and Syria. Despite the valor of his armies, Bonaparte failed to take the fortress of St. Jean D'Acre (Akka), and his army did not proceed beyond Sidon in Lebanon. The French expedition, while militarily spectacular, was perhaps more significant in the cultural sense. Napoleon brought with him a number of scholars, who promptly began to study ancient Egyptian monuments, language, and history. Their work left an indelible trace in Egypt and—together with subsequent French commercial penetration—laid a firm foundation for cultural links between France and the Land of the Nile. Politically and militarily Napoleon's expedition ultimately turned out to be no more than a transitional adventure, which failed to entrench France

12

in the East. It had, however, an important political effect in focusing British attention on the Ottoman Empire and on the latter's significance in the over-all scheme of the British imperial system. Russia's steady progress southward, both in Turkey and in Iran, was bound sooner or later to provoke British countermeasures, but Napoleon's intervention acted as a catalyst in this process. In 1799 Napoleon returned secretly to France, leaving his army behind in Egypt.

In 1801 the French in Egypt surrendered to the British. A temporary British occupation followed, but in 1802 the country was restored to the sultan. The evacuation of French forces from Ottoman territory made possible a gradual restoration of the traditionally friendly feelings between the two countries. French ascendancy in the Ottoman capital was re-established, and by 1806 Napoleon was able to induce the Porte to take arms against Russia, with whom France was then at war. The Turks, who hoped to get rid of the Russian danger by collaborating with the seemingly invincible French Emperor, were sorely disappointed when Napoleon, after spectacular victories over the Russians, concluded the Treaty of Tilsit with Tsar Alexander I in 1807. Napoleon's betrayal of his Turkish allies stemmed from his anxiety to gain Russia's collaboration in his continental blockade of Britain. To save appearances, he offered his good offices to restore peace between Russia and Turkey. Moreover, he firmly rejected Alexander's plea for control of Constantinople. Even to the continentally minded Bonaparte it was clear that Russian control of the Turkish Straits would gravely disturb the European balance of power. In his reputed exclamation: "Constantinople? *Jamais!*" he bore witness to the importance he attached to the preservation of Ottoman independence. His mediation brought about a temporary suspension of the Russo-Turkish hostilities, but in 1809 they were resumed. Finally, the war was ended in May of 1812 by the Treaty of Bucharest. By that time Franco-Russian relations had cooled off perceptibly, and in anticipation of a French invasion Tsar Alexander was willing to grant a respite to the harassed Turks. The Treaty of Bucharest marked another step in Russia's territorial progress at the expense of Turkey. Russia annexed Bessarabia, thus extending her hold on the Black Sea shore up to the Pruth River, and secured possession of an important military road linking the Caucasian Black Sea shore with Tiflis. The latter was acquired as a result of simultaneous operations against Persia.

The Near Eastern Question, 1812–1830

In 1812 Napoleon's ill-starred expedition to Moscow closed the chapter of forceful French intervention in the affairs of the Middle East, and the traditional story of Russia's southward expansion was resumed. At this time, however, the Eastern Question presented itself in a new light, owing to aroused British interest in this part of the world. Russia henceforth had to confront not only the opposition of the Turks themselves (with the jealousy of the Habsburg Empire) but also the power of the British, who emerged in the nineteenth century as Russia's principal competitor in Asia.

It now became an axiom of British foreign policy to uphold the independence and integrity of the Ottoman Empire, in order to prevent the undue strengthening of Russia and to protect the imperial life line. The acquisition of Malta by Great Britain at the Congress of Vienna in 1815 added to the British interest in the Mediterranean and its adjacent shores.

In France, weakened after the Napoleonic wars, England found a friendly power. With minor exceptions no major conflicts separated the two nations on Middle Eastern policy. Throughout the nineteenth century the two countries presented a common front against Russia's imperialism. This concerted attitude might have arrested further Ottoman disintegration if it had not been for the seed planted involuntarily by France herself. The concept of national and popular rights which was born at the time of the revolution, spread to the four corners of Europe in the wake of Napoleonic victories. The Christian subjects of the Ottoman Empire, particularly those living in compact national groups in the Balkans, did not remain unaffected by it. The story of the struggle for national independence by the Balkan nations is outside the scope of this work. It is sufficient to state here that, beginning with the Serbian war of independence (1804–1813), one by one the Balkan nations emancipated themselves from the rule of the Empire in the course of the nineteenth and twentieth centuries. Greece (1832), Rumania (1856–1878), Serbia (1834–1878), Montenegro (1878), and Bulgaria (1878–1908), all detached themselves and formed independent states.

In the liberation of the Balkan Christians, Russia played a decisive role. Her pressure on and wars with Turkey gave the Balkan peoples the encouragement and military opportunity to throw off the Ottoman yoke. The role of other European powers, in particular that

14

of England, was difficult and often complicated. On the one hand, Europe in general and England in particular strove to preserve the life of the Ottoman Empire. On this account they were bound to oppose both Russia's aggressiveness and the disintegrating tendencies in the Balkans. On the other hand, no European power could openly place itself athwart the desire of a Christian nation to attain freedom from the rule of the infidel Moslem Empire, corrupt and decaying. Out of the dilemma thus created, the British-inspired concert of European powers attempted for the most part to adjust itself to the realities of the Eastern situation without compromising too many of the vital principles underlying European diplomacy. Autonomy under Turkish suzerainty first, and later full independence, were reluctantly conceded to the Balkan nations at a series of congresses. At the same time, care was taken to prevent Russia from gaining sole credit for and undue political advantages from such developments, and to assure that this emancipatory process would be carried out without producing a collapse of the Ottoman Empire.

Much of this basic aim was accomplished. Yet it would be erroneous to conclude that the liberation of the Balkan nations was obtained in an orderly manner. Quite the contrary, there were a number of insurrections, wars, and diplomatic crises, which might easily have led to a major European conflagration.

The Greek war of independence (1821–1829) brought Russia into conflict with Turkey in 1828. The fighting, which took place in the Balkans and in the Caucasus, ended with the Russian conquest of Adrianople, less than 150 miles from Constantinople. The Treaty of Adrianople confirmed the Russian protectorate over the Danubian principalities, provided for Turkey's agreement to any proposed solution concerning Greece, and secured for Russia new territorial acquisitions on the eastern shore of the Black Sea. These gains included the ports of Anapa and Poti, the coastal region of the Caucasus known as Abkhasia, and the fortress of Akhaltsikh in western Georgia. This newly acquired territory, in conjunction with several annexations in the general area of the Caucasus at the expense of the Persian Empire, considerably strengthened Russia's position in the Black Sea region.

The Rise of Mohammed Ali

The Treaty of Adrianople brought the Turks only a temporary respite from Russian expansionism. Scarcely three years passed before

Russia scored a new success at the expense of Turkey. This time no war was necessary. Paradoxically enough, for the first and probably only time in the nineteenth century, Russia posed as a friend and ally of the Ottoman Empire. The circumstances leading to this unusual development had their roots in Egypt. Following the Napoleonic expedition, this fertile province of the Empire found itself under the rule of an Albanian adventurer, Mohammed Ali. His rise was spectacular. He appeared in Egypt for the first time in 1801. By 1805 he was a viceroy under the sultan's suzerainty. In 1818 he subdued the Wahhabi tribes in Arabia and subjected Mecca and Medina to Ottoman control. He conquered Nubia in 1822, and in the same year he obtained the governship of Crete in return for assistance that he extended to the Ottoman government during the Greek revolt. Mohammed Ali's co-operation in quelling the Greek insurrection was to have been repaid by control not only of Crete but also of the Peloponnesus. The Greek war of liberation, however, interfered with these plans. Denied Morea, Mohammed Ali demanded Syria. When this demand was refused, he declared war on the Porte in 1831 and sent an Egyptian expeditionary force to Syria under his son Ibrahim. His troops progressed victoriously through Syria, entered Anatolia proper, and in a major battle defeated the Turkish army at Konya in 1832. The sultan, by the Treaty of Kutaya, was forced to grant to his vassal the government of Syria and Adana. At this moment Russia proferred her services to the sultan, who, bitter and revengeful, was ready to accept any assistance against further threats by the Egyptian upstart.

The Treaty of Unkiar Iskelessi, concluded in 1833, marked the climax of Russia's success in Turkey and brought the Ottoman Empire very close to complete dependence upon its powerful northern neighbor. The treaty openly provided for a defensive alliance between the two countries; its secret clauses gave Russia a uniquely privileged position concerning the Straits. Turkey promised to close the Straits to any power at war with Russia, while permitting Russia full freedom of navigation in war or peace. The result of the treaty was a veiled Russian protectorate over the Ottoman Empire and caused much concern in British government circles. Thus ended the first phase of the Mohammed Ali episode.

The second phase opened with the renewal of war between the Porte and Egypt in 1839. Ibrahim Pasha achieved another resounding victory over the Turks at the battle of Nisib on the upper

16

Euphrates. The road to Constantinople lay virtually open to the ambitious Egyptians. At this time, however, the European powers intervened. This intervention, sponsored by the British government, was motivated by two factors: first, Europe was seriously alarmed by the extent of Russian influence in Constantinople, an influence which was bound to increase if the position of the sultan weakened as a result of Mohammed Ali's successes; secondly, Europe decided, under British leadership, not to permit the enfeebled Ottoman Empire to be replaced by a new empire headed by Mohammed Ali. France did not concur in this decision. Having established many commercial and cultural links with Egypt since the Napoleonic campaigns, the French viewed the rise of Mohammed Ali with favor and foresaw many advantages to them in the strengthening of his position. Eventually the intervention of the European powers took the form of an Anglo-Austrian naval blockade of the Syrian coast to cut Ibrahim's communications with his base. This was accompanied by an ultimatum demanding his withdrawal to Egypt. The Egyptians were forced to bow to this display of determination. At the Conference of London in 1840, Britain, Austria, Prussia, Russia—and also France—agreed upon a settlement by which Mohammed Ali was obliged to return Syria to the sultan. As compensation, he was made hereditary pasha of Egypt. Another part of the settlement, known as the Convention of the Straits (1841), ended the privileged position of Russia and set up an arrangement more agreeable to the other European powers. The London settlement, which quite clearly constituted intervention by outside powers into the domestic affairs of the Ottoman Empire, can be regarded as the establishment of a joint European protectorate over Turkey. As such, it replaced the exclusive Russian protectorate formulated under the Treaty of Unkiar Iskelessi.

Outwardly, it seemed that the London agreements had settled the Eastern Question for some time to come to the mutual satisfaction of most of the powers concerned. Soon, however, it developed that Britain and Russia were attaching different interpretations to these decisions. Britain was happy to see Ottoman integrity preserved and viewed with favor a reform movement in Turkey, which was bound to regenerate and strengthen the Empire. Russia, on the contrary, considered Anglo-Russian co-operation in solving Turkish domestic problems as a logical step toward further intervention and eventual partition of Ottoman territory. It was at this time that

17

Tsar Nicholas I made his famous statement about "the Sick Man of Europe," suggesting in conversation with British statesmen and diplomats that the Sick Man's estate should be divided in an orderly manner before his impending death.

From the Crimean War to the Treaty of Berlin

This difference as to interpretation provided the setting for the Crimean War (1854–1856). When events came to a head in 1854, Russia found herself opposed by a coalition of Turkey, Britain, France, and Sardinia. The immediate cause of the war was the quarrel between France and Russia over control of the holy places in Palestine. The local dispute between the French-supported Latin monks and the Russian-protected Greek ecclesiastics led to dispatch of a Russian diplomatic mission to Constantinople. In an ultimatum Russia demanded not only the recognition of her right to protect all Orthodox Christians in the Ottoman Empire (about twelve million souls), but also an alliance with Turkey. To support this ultimatum, the Russian army entered two Rumanian principalities. Last minute attempts by a conference of European powers to effect a settlement did not produce satisfactory results, and Turkey found herself at war with her northern neighbor. In the early spring of 1854 Britain and France declared war on Russia, to be followed by a similar declaration by the small but rising kingdom of Sardinia. Military and naval operations took place predominantly in the Crimea, at a heavy cost in human lives, primarily because of poor sanitary services. The death of Tsar Nicholas I, followed by the fall of Sevastopol, in 1855 led Russia, under Alexander II, to sue for peace. The resulting Treaty of Paris (1856) contained the following major provisions:

1) The Black Sea was to be demilitarized. This actually meant the termination of the Russian naval establishments and the destruction of shore installations and fortifications.

2) Navigation on the Danube River was to be free to all nations. This was to be a check on the Russian tendency to secure a monopolistic position there.

3) A Russian protectorate over the Rumanian principalities was to be ended. The latter states were in turn to be granted fuller autonomy under Ottoman suzerainty with a joint guarantee by the powers.

4) Southern Bessarabia was to be ceded by Russia to the Ottoman

18

Empire. This meant a physical separation of Russia from the banks of the Danube delta and, consequently, a check upon her control of the mouth of this important European river.

The Crimean War has often been termed utterly unnecessary. Its importance and profound consequences upon the future of the Ottoman Empire should not, however, be underrated. The defeat of Russia gave the Turks a new lease on life, and Russian expansion in the Black Sea and toward the Mediterranean suffered a serious check. The war closed a definite chapter in Ottoman history, a chapter of growing Russian influence and disquieting ascendancy in Constantinople, which started with the Treaty of Unkiar Iskelessi and was only partially checked by the London conventions of 1840–1841.

The period that followed eloquently illustrated the influence of domestic upon foreign affairs. Despite the successful outcome of the Crimean War, Turkey's troubles were by no means over. The growing nationalism of her Balkan subjects and the inefficiency and corruption of her administration were tinder for a new conflagration. Irked by the cruel exactions of the Turkish authorities, the people of Bosnia rose in revolt. The flames of insurrection soon spread to Bulgaria. Serbia and Montenegro showed solidarity with their Balkan brethren by declaring war on the Porte.

Turkish reprisals assumed cruel proportions, especially in Bulgaria, and aroused much indignation in Europe. The reaction in Russia was intense, and Moscow declared war on Turkey in 1877. As so many times before, the Russians were successful in their contest with the Turks and dictated a victor's peace in San Stefano. In this agreement, Russia annexed some territory and provided for the creation of a big Bulgarian state to extend from the Albanian mountains to the Black Sea, and from the Danube to the Aegean. Formal recognition of the independence of Serbia, Rumania, and Montenegro completed the main political provisions of the treaty. The huge state of Bulgaria, entirely dependent on Russian aid, was to constitute an outpost and an instrument of Russian influence in this region; this was to be the crowning achievement of Russian Near Eastern policy. The Treaty of San Stefano, however, was not destined to endure. Britain, Austria, and France, seriously alarmed at this new manifestation of Russian ambitions, protested. The ensuing Treaty of Berlin (1878), replacing the Treaty of San Stefano, deprived Russia of the major part of the spoils. It provided (1) for the creation of a small autonomous Bulgaria still under Turkish suzerainty, (2) for the independence of Serbia, Rumania, and Montenegro, (3) for the cession of southern Bessarabia to Russia, (4) for the cession of Kars, Ardahan, and Batum to Russia, (5) for the promise of more extended frontiers to Greece, (6) for the Austrian occupation of Bosnia and Herzegovina, and (7) for the British occupation of Cyprus.

Russia thus suffered a severe check in her Balkan diplomacy and resentfully felt that her military victory had been politically frustrated. Yet she had succeeded in enlarging her possessions at the expense of Turkey. On the other hand, with the avalanche of national liberation once set into motion, the Ottoman Empire could not avoid knowing that its domains would probably shrink again.

The Treaty of Berlin produced a new situation in Russo-Turkish relationships. Owing to the creation of an independent Rumania and of an autonomous Bulgaria, Russia lost her direct boundary with the Ottoman Empire in the west. Henceforth her territorial ambitions at the expense of Turkey had to be limited to the eastern boundary. There a pretext could be found in the Armenian people living in the Turkish vilayets. Russia was in a position to exploit this situation, and she was not hesitant about doing so. Otherwise, whatever further designs Russia might have had on the Ottoman Empire, they had perforce to be confined to political or military control of Turkey proper and of the Turkish Straits. In other words, the margin of justification of Russian imperialist actions—which in the past had been the liberation of Balkan Slavs and Christians—was now narrowed to a bare minimum. Trespass on this minimum was bound to pose the long-delayed basic problem of the existence of Turkey as an independent state. Thus the Treaty of Berlin constituted a definite landmark in Russo-Turkish relations.

On the other hand, the treaty illustrated the growing ambiguity of the attitude of the European powers. While attempting to check Russia's southward drive and while professing to desire the preservation of Ottoman integrity, they were not loath to secure advantages for themselves. The Austrian occupation of part of the Balkans and the British acquisition of Cyprus are cases in point. To this may be added the French quest for authority to occupy Tunisia and the revelation of Italian designs upon Albania and Libya. Germany was the only power that asked for nothing, a fact not without further political consequences.

It is perhaps time to turn our eyes from the main pattern of Russia vs. Turkey vs. Europe toward the oriental portions of the Ottoman Empire. The history of the Empire in Asia and Africa is politically less important than its history in Europe. Nevertheless, events that developed there in the fifty years between 1864 and 1914 deserve attention because they reveal a pattern of gradual penetration or outright imperialism on the part of western European powers at the expense of the Ottoman Empire.

Western Imperialism and the Ottoman Empire

Four countries appear as contenders for various advantages or territories: France, England, Italy, and Germany.

Despite the traditional alliance between the Ottoman Empire and France, the latter was not reluctant to take advantage of the Empire's weakness in those areas deemed important to French interests. And yet, although France extended her rule over Algeria (1830), Tunisia (1883), and Morocco (1906–1912), these moves could not be interpreted as anti-Turkish since the lands in question had been under only nominal and very remote control of the Porte. Egypt and Lebanon were the main areas where French interests came into direct contact or clash with those of the Turks. France's support of Mohammed Ali led to the entrenchment of her cultural and commercial influence in Egypt. This influence became obvious when the French explorer and engineer Ferdinand de Lesseps obtained in 1856, from the Egyptian viceroy (or khedive), Ismail Pasha, a concession for the construction of a canal through the Isthmus of Suez. The canal was opened for maritime traffic in 1869 in an impressive ceremony attended by Empress Eugenie, and it seemed that it would be important as a spearhead of French influence in Egypt. Subsequent events, however, radically changed the picture. With the purchase of Khedive Ismail's interest by the Disraeli government in 1875, the British assumed a decisive role in the affairs of the canal.

Another area of traditionally strong French influence was Lebanon. Inhabited by a Christian majority, this ancient stronghold of the Crusaders had always looked toward France for inspiration and protection. The anti-Christian riots and persecutions that occurred there in the early 1860's provoked French naval and military intervention. This in turn brought about a constitutional change.

Under the pressure of the powers, the sultan in 1864 was forced

21

to grant autonomy to the sanjak of Lebanon, which was to be governed by a Christian governor. France, to be sure, was not given any formal position of privilege as a result of these events, but she was regarded unofficially as a protecting power of the Lebanese Christians. This intervention was France's last major success in the Ottoman realm before World War I. Her defeat in the war with Prussia in 1870 weakened her and hence interfered with her ambitious designs in the Middle East. From that time on France's political influence was on the wane and she was a constant loser in the competition with Great Britain.

The British record in relation to the Ottoman Empire must at its best be described as ambiguous, and at its worst as insincere. While the preservation of the Ottoman Empire was an axiom of nineteenth-century British policy, this axiom was hedged with qualifications and practical reservations. As it was pointed out earlier, Britain, as a Christian country, was not in a position to oppose outright the struggle for national liberation of the Balkan Christians. Therefore, rather reluctantly (although it was enthusiastically at the time of Gladstone) the British supported the national aspirations of the Balkan peoples whenever their revolutionary action and corresponding Russian intervention made European intervention necessary.

Britain's interest in Ottoman integrity originated, of course, in her desire to protect her imperial line to the East. Protection of this life line sometimes demanded more than a mere negative hands-off-Turkey policy, addressed as it was to Russia. It required occasionally positive British penetration into Asiatic and African Ottoman possessions. Between 1833 and 1887 Britain was intensely interested in establishing an English-controlled land-and-river route through Mesopotamia to India. At the same time she manifested a prolonged and consistent interest in Egypt as a link in the chain leading from Gibraltar to Aden (Aden was acquired in 1839). The acquisition of Malta in 1815 and of Cyprus in 1878, the latter at the expense of the Ottoman Empire, reinforced this chain. Disraeli's decision to purchase the bankrupt khedive's interest in the Suez Canal was, therefore, a logical consequence of this policy. The 1870's witnessed a growing British commercial penetration into Egypt. When in 1882 native xenophobia caused Arabi Pasha to revolt both against the khedive and against foreign influence in Egypt, the British stake was deemed so high as to justify naval and military intervention.

British bombardment of Alexandria was followed by the battle of Tel el-Kebir and resulted in the occupation of the country.

In 1883 Sir Evelyn Baring (later Lord Cromer) arrived in Cairo officially as British consul general and diplomatic agent and unofficially as virtual ruler of Egypt. This benevolent rule lasted until his retirement in 1907 and elevated Egypt from a state of bankruptcy and chaos into the richest and best-developed country in the Middle East.

Britain's involvement in Egyptian affairs brought her logically to intervention in the affairs of the Sudan, at the time of the uprising of the Mahdi in that area. British forces were sent, alongside those of the Egyptians, to quell the rebellion. The Sudanese drama can be divided into two phases. The first, between 1882 and 1885, brought defeat to the British armies and death to General Gordon at Khartoum. Thirteen years of the Mahdi's rule followed. The second phase, highlighted by Kitchener's victory at Omdurman in 1898, resulted in the final overthrow of the Mahdi and the establishment of the Anglo-Egyptian condominium over the Sudan. The grip on the Sudan strengthened the British position in Egypt and, despite early assurances in 1882, the question of British evacuation from Egypt never seriously arose thereafter. These *faits accomplis* were given their diplomatic confirmation at the time of the formation of the Entente Cordiale in 1904. In return for the recognition of French preponderance in Morocco, France recognized the British position in Egypt. Thereafter British interests in the Middle East could be challenged only by Germany, a challenge which was by no means negligible.

Germany began to show serious interest in the affairs of the Ottoman Empire around 1880. In 1881 General von der Goltz was appointed head of the German military mission to reorganize the Turkish army. In 1889 Emperor William II and the Empress paid a state visit to Constantinople, inaugurating an era of friendship and close co-operation between Germany and Turkey. The growth of German prestige coincided with the waning of British popularity, which resulted from (1) Britain's grasping attitude toward Cyprus, (2) British support of Greece in the latter's irredentism, and (3) British occupation of Egypt in 1882. Moreover, British interests in the Middle East were not well served by Gladstone's policy in the 1880's. Gladstone was outspokenly anti-Turkish. The Armenian massa-

23

cres in Turkey (1897–1898) produced indignation and intervention on the part of the European powers, with the exception of the Germans, who remained cautiously aloof. As relations between Turkey and the other powers became more estranged, Germany's attitude became more cordial. During his second visit to the Ottoman Empire in 1898, the Kaiser made a simultaneous bid for the friendship of the Turks and of other Moslem peoples. "His Majesty, the Sultan Abdul Hamid and the 300 million Mohammedans, who reverence him as Caliph, may rest assured that at all times the German Emperor will be their friend," declared William II in Damascus. The effects of this diplomacy could soon be felt economically. German banking and business interests began to penetrate Turkey, and a series of concessions was awarded German firms. The most important of these, and one which caused violent international controversy, was a concession granted in 1902 to the German company of Anatolian Railways to construct the Constantinople-Baghdad railroad line. This line, if constructed, would link Berlin with Baghdad and eventually with Basra, and would serve the interests of German economic expansion. The project was deeply resented by the British, who spared no efforts to frustrate German initiative. By the turn of the century it became obvious that, in their Near Eastern policies, Berlin and Vienna worked hand in hand, the Austrians being the junior partner. Austria's role in this partnership could be described as the paving of the road to Turkey through the Balkans (where her ambitions focused). Germany would take upon herself the infiltration of Anatolia and other Asiatic domains of the Ottoman Empire. Internal developments in Turkey at this time contributed in no small measure to the success of these concerted Austro-German policies.

To complete this review of Western imperialism at the expense of the Empire, a word must be said of Italy. Ever since her emancipation as a united state, Italy had been casting covetous glances toward the northern coast of Africa, an area formerly controlled by the Roman Empire. British penetration of Egypt and French annexations in Tunisia and Morocco greatly stimulated Italy's interest in the intermediate zone of North Africa, situated as it was opposite to Italy's shores and deemed strategically important by Italian statesmen. It was the Moroccan crisis of 1911 which precipitated Italy's decision to seek a solution in Africa by the force of arms. In the fall of that year Italy declared war on the Porte and sent an expeditionary army to Libya. After thirteen months peace was concluded at Lausanne in October 1912. Partly by its terms and partly by their dubious legal interpretation Italy obtained control of Libya and of the Dodecanese Islands in the Aegean. As a result, the Ottoman Empire lost its last direct stronghold on the African continent.

Attempts at Reform: The Young Turks

Thus far we have paid little attention to Turkish internal developments, which are largely outside the scope of this study. A few facts, however, deserve mention, particularly those which affected Turkey's strength or weakness. In the nineteenth century, while Turkey's international and internal situation was steadily deteriorating, a few attempts were made at reform. Mahmud II (1808–1839), the greatest of the Turkish rulers since Suleiman the Magnificent, annihilated in one bold stroke the corps of Janissaries, whose influence had become detrimental to the welfare of the Empire. A series of internal reforms including military and administrative organization followed. These were interrupted, however, by constant warfare and by Mohammed Ali's rebellion and as a result never came to full fruition. The decade of the 1840's, following the settlement of the Egyptian question, brought the Empire an interlude of peace. During this period, under the rule of Abdul Mejid (1839–1861), the Turkish reform party headed by Reshid Pasha undertook a number of measures destined to strengthen and modernize the Empire. Following the issuance of the Charter of Liberties (or *Hatti Sherif of Gülhane*) in 1839, reforms were instituted in the fields of administration, taxation, justice, education, minorities, and military affairs. These reforms, however, were destined to be as unsuccessful as the previous ones, partly because of the domestic reactionary opposition and partly because of the new international complications which resulted in the Crimean War. Even the reaffirmation of the rights of minorities (in a decree known as *Hatti-Humayun* in 1856) did not materially change the picture. Under Abdul Aziz (1861–1876) sincere efforts for reform were exerted by an enlightened Turkish statesman of high repute, Midhat Pasha. His efforts also came largely to naught, because of the weakness of the sultan himself. Reform in the Empire could be accomplished either by having a very strong-willed ruler, who would think in terms of public interest and would command public obedience, or by carrying out a radical social revolution, which would change the theocratic character of the Empire and secularize it. As to the first alternative, the rulers of Turkey did not have the necessary

25

qualifications. Neither Sultan Abdul Aziz, well-intentioned but incompetent, nor his successor Murad V—both deposed on account of mental disorders—nor Abdul Hamid II (1876–1909), corrupt and reactionary, were the leaders to carry out reform. True enough, for a brief period after Abdul Hamid's ascension, the forces of reform seemed victorious. On December 23, 1876, Midhat Pasha succeeded in inducing the new sultan to proclaim a constitution which guaranteed civil liberties and provided for parliamentary government based on general representation. But this turned out to be no more than a brief liberal interlude. Jealous of his power, Abdul Hamid soon reverted to repressive policies, dismissed and banished Midhat Pasha, and, in 1877, prorogued the newly created parliament, suspending the constitution. Thereafter for thirty years he ruled as absolute monarch.

The other alternative remained, that of a radical change by revolution. The task of shaking the Empire out of its lethargy was taken up by the Young Turk movement. Composed of youthful and impatient elements, the Young Turk Party drew its inspiration from the West and wanted to remodel the Empire into a liberal constitutional monarchy. Their Committee of Union and Progress was successful in creating a strong conspiratorial organization and in enlisting many army officers. In the *coup d'état* of 1908, the Young Turks seized power, compelled Abdul Hamid to restore the constitution, and then forced him to abdicate. In its immediate effects, the Young Turk revolution produced further shrinkage of the Empire. Profiting from what they believed to be a sign of weakness, Austria annexed Bosnia and Herzegovina (under occupation since 1878), and Bulgaria proclaimed her full independence from the Empire. These acts, though they came as a shock both internally and internationally, were expected to happen sooner or later. More interesting was the effect of the Young Turk revolution on German-Ottoman relations. On the surface, it appeared that the forcible elimination of Germany's friend, Sultan Abdul Hamid, might produce a radical reorientation of Turkey's foreign policy. The Young Turks professed admiration for Western democratic liberalism and could hardly be expected to feel friendly toward Prussian military autocracy. History, however, reveals surprising shifts, and ideologies are often overshadowed by personalities. Enver Pasha, a leading member of the triumvirate that ruled Turkey after 1908, turned out to be definitely pro-German and anti-British. Consequently, he facilitated German penetration and did his utmost to put Turkey into a pro-German frame of mind as the great war approached. This frame of mind was not too difficult to create because the traditional friends of Turkey, the British and the French, effected a far-reaching rapprochement with Turkey's hereditary enemy, Russia.

As a result of the two Balkan wars (1912–1913) fought with her small Christian neighbors and largely caused by the controversial question of Macedonia, Turkey lost most of her European territory.

The outbreak of the Great War found the Empire reduced territorially. Of its European possessions, only eastern Thrace remained. Egypt was under British control and virtually detached. Internally matters were far from reassuring. The Empire's national minorities were resentful, and hence of doubtful loyalty. The Arabs were inclined toward nationalism. The Young Turks failed to institute the promised reforms, except in the military sphere. Here the expert advice of Prussian officers, combined with the virile characteristics of the Turkish race, made it possible to recreate the Ottoman army so that it could again be called a military factor on the international scene. German diplomatic ascendancy in Constantinople was manifest. Turkey was ready to plunge into a new war. This she did with incalculable consequences to herself and to all the rest of the Middle East.

II. THE PERSIAN EMPIRE

Another country whose history is relevant to understanding of the political changes in the Middle East prior to the First World War is the ancient empire of Persia. Established in the sixth century B.C. by Cyrus, who united Media with Persia, Persia knew glory under her Achaemenid dynasty. Persia's ancient civilization, her Zoroastrian religion, and her wars with the Hellenes left an indelible mark upon the history of mankind. The dynastic history of Persia reveals periods of rule under native kings alternating with those under alien rulers. Thus, the first and truly Persian dynasty of the Achaemenids (558–331) was succeeded by Alexander the Great and the Seleucides, to be followed by more than four hundred years of the Arsacid Parthian dynasty (250 B.C.–A.D. 228). The Parthian rule gave way, in turn, to a native Persian monarchy of the Sassanids (242–642). In 642, at the battle of Nehavend, Persia was defeated and conquered by the Arabs. Conversion to the Islamic religion

27

and rule by a series of viceroys of either Arab or Persian descent followed. Persia ceased to be a single political entity, being divided into
various principalities. This era came to an end with the Mongol invasion. The capture of Baghdad in 1258 by Hulagu opened a new
period of alien domination. The country rallied again under the native dynasty of the Safavids (1502–1753). Under Abbas I the Great,
Persia passed through a period of regeneration and experienced a
golden age in the development of her culture. The Safavi era was
followed by a period of uncertainty until the establishment at the
end of the eighteenth century of the Kajar dynasty, which was to rule
Persia until 1925. Despotic yet weak, the Kajars proved incapable of
protecting Persia against foreign encroachments.

In the course of the Kajar era, Persia entered modern world politics as a pawn in the big-power rivalry for control of the Middle
East. The principal actors in this historical drama were the Russians,
who, since Peter the Great, had wanted to expand toward the south.
Inasmuch as Russia's approach to the Persian Gulf threatened Britain's position in India, Britain consistently opposed this expansion.
Thus, the balancing of Anglo-Russian claims in Persia became a
permanent feature of nineteenth-century diplomacy and was upset
only when a third power threw its might on the scales. Such a situation occurred twice between 1800 and 1914. In the early 1800's and
in the early 1900's, Napoleonic France and Imperial Germany, respectively, succeeded in securing paramount influence in Persia. In
both cases, this interest was dictated by the basically anti-British
policies of the newcomers. Influence over Persia was not treated as
an end in itself but rather as a stepping stone toward the conquest of
India. When such intervention occurred, Britain was, as a rule, inclined to compose her differences with Russia, such turns of British
policy inevitably working to the detriment of Persia. This was so
because in opposing Russian southward imperialism Great Britain
acted as a virtual guarantor of Persian independence. Britain's Persian policy was dictated primarily by her concern for India, and
Persia was to be an independent buffer state or neutral zone between
the Indian and the Russian empires. Britain sought unimpeded commercial opportunity in Persia, and to this extent she was interested
in exercising moderate influence in the area. She was unwilling, however, to assume direct imperial responsibilities similar to those in
India. It was, therefore, in her interest to see Persia relatively strong
and capable of withstanding Russian pressure. It was largely due to

this British policy that Persia succeeded in maintaining her independence instead of falling under Russian domination.

This Russo-British rivalry could be described as almost chronic disease; it had an occasional crisis now and then, but it was essentially a disease to which the British government and public opinion were accustomed. The sudden appearance of Napoleonic France or Imperial Germany in Middle Eastern politics would throw this nicely balanced mechanism into confusion. Under such circumstances, Britain was willing temporarily to compromise with the chronic Russian danger in order to avert the more dynamic and immediate threat of the "unauthorized" adventurers. But such a compromise with Russia would obviously mean concessions at the expense of Persia. Persia's hope, in the long run, was that third-party intervention would not last too long and that the traditional pattern of Russo-British rivalry would be resumed. This fact, however, was not always recognized by the Persian rulers, who were inclined to think that the third party would give a mortal blow to both traditional protagonists and thus deliver Persia from obnoxious tutelage. Yet the uncontested historical fact is that Persia's independence in the nineteenth and twentieth centuries was gravely impaired only when, as a result of outside interference, Britain and Russia were willing to shelve their rivalry.

This picture must be kept in mind when one studies the apparently complicated policies in and over Persia from 1800 onward. Russian pressure in the direction of the Caucasus, working against Persia and Turkey, was obvious in the last decade of the eighteenth and the first decade of the nineteenth century. This threat Britain was anxious to eliminate, but her attention was temporarily diverted toward the new danger in the shape of Napoleonic imperialism. What followed was an intricate play of British and French intrigues at the shah's court in Teheran. In 1800 the British scored a diplomatic success by concluding with Persia the so-called Malcolm Treaty of Alliance. This treaty contained a French exclusion clause, and this point was of utmost importance to Britain at that time. To Shah Fath Ali, however, it was the British pledge to aid him in resisting external aggression which was of real significance. The external aggression which he most feared was that of Russia. Consequently, when it transpired that the British were lukewarm in assisting him at the time of the Russian aggression in 1802, the Shah was quite willing to abandon this alliance and turn toward France in his search for security. He first entered into negotiations with Colonel Romieu, who had arrived in Teheran to offer him an alliance and a subsidy; next he sent an envoy to Napoleon. The Franco-Persian Treaty of Finkenstein in May 1807 gave formal confirmation to the preliminary arrangements. It was followed by the dispatch to Persia of a French military mission under General Gardanne. Soon, however, Persia experienced a new disappointment. At Tilsit in July, barely two months after the Treaty of Finkenstein was signed, Napoleon and Alexander I of Russia came to terms.[1] Although no arrangements were made concerning Persia, it was clear that the latter's trust in effective French protection against Russia was to be betrayed. The French mission lost its original political usefulness and General Gardanne could do no more than offer mediation with Russia, an obviously inadequate proposal from the Persian point of view.

By 1805 it had become clear to the British that unless they recognized the primacy of the Russian danger, they would not be able to count on any stable relationship with Persia. It was futile to count on Persian collaboration against France, since France was viewed not as an enemy but as a potential ally by Teheran. In fact, some British critics maintained that any French threat to India was imaginary and that the only threat was apt to come from the north. In recognition of this new trend, Sir Hartford Jones in 1805 concluded the preliminary Treaty of Alliance with Persia, clearly directed against Russian expansion. Britain promised Persia arms, munitions, army instructors, and a subsidy. The Shah, in view of Napoleon's betrayal at Tilsit, was glad to avail himself of this assistance. With the conclusion of that treaty, the principle of the integrity of Persia became a corollary to the principle of Ottoman integrity in British foreign policy. Britain kept her word, the treaty provisions were carried out, and some British officers attached to the Shah's army came into contact with advanced Russian units on the Caucasian frontier.

Scarcely had this era of co-operation begun, when it was suspended by Napoleon's invasion of Russia in 1812. Britain, vitally interested in checkmating France, attempted reconciliation with Russia. The twofold effects of this policy were immediately visible in Persia. On the one hand, Britain disregarded her early promises of assistance and

[1] Napoleon's understanding with Alexander I thus revived an earlier friendship between Napoleon and Tsar Paul. In 1800 Paul and Napoleon had planned an invasion of India by the concerted action of the Russian and French armies.

offered instead her good offices in the Persian-Russian disputes; on the other hand, Russia, emboldened by Britain's softened attitude, increased her pressure and in October 1813 concluded with the Shah the Treaty of Gulistan, by which Persia ceded to Russia Derbend, Baku, Shirvan, Shaki, Karabagh, and part of Talish, renounced all titles to Georgia, Daghestan, Mingrelia, and Abkhasia, and agreed to domination of the Caspian by the Russian navy.

This suspension of the Anglo-Persian alliance was viewed in Great Britain as a temporary expedient only. As soon as the French threat was parried, the British hastened to conclude with Persia the "definitive" Treaty of Teheran (1814), which, under somewhat emasculated terms, confirmed the Jones treaty. But the effects of the temporary relaxation of vigilance proved to be more than provisional. The Treaty of Gulistan became the opening wedge for steadily rising Russian influence. The immediate aim of the Russians was to reach the boundary which they considered to be strategic between Russia and Persia, the Aras River. The complete subjugation of Persia, by one means or another, was Russia's long-range objective. A pretext for a new war with Persia was found in 1828. Britain's assistance to Persia was limited to a few subsidies. The Treaty of Turkomanchai, concluding the war in 1828, gave Russia coveted Persian territory (Erivan and Nakhichevan) up to the Aras River [2] and supremacy over the country. Russia obtained preferential economic treatment expressed in low customs duties and in other trading privileges; secured capitulations; and in return guaranteed Persian dynastic interests, which, in itself, amounted to a veiled protectorate.

Anglo-Russian Rivalry in the Nineteenth Century

Having suffered severe territorial losses in the Caucasian region, Persia sought compensation in the east at the expense of Afghanistan. The immediate object of Persian ambitions was the strategic fortress and province of Herat. Russia encouraged this expansionist policy because it diverted Persia's attention from her northern borders and, at the same time, indirectly threatened the British position in India. Britain considered Afghanistan another link in the protective chain around India and was determined to protect it from Russian or Russian-sponsored Persian encroachments. Persia's attempts to con-

---

[2] The boundary followed the Aras River up to the 48th meridian and then turned southeastward, putting the province of Lankoran and the town of Astara in Russia. This boundary has not changed since.

31

quer Herat in 1833 and in 1837–1838 ended in failure, despite expert advice given her by the Russians. When, however, in 1856 a Persian army succeeded in capturing the coveted fortress, Britain reluctantly declared war. British troops disembarked on the Persian Gulf coast, captured Bushire, Mohammera, and Ahwaz, and forced Persia to sue for peace. The Anglo-Persian Treaty of Paris (1857) provided for evacuation of Afghanistan and the recognition of Afghanistan's independence. The British, interested in cultivating Persian good will, displayed remarkable self-restraint and refrained from asking for territory, concessions, or indemnities.

The Anglo-Persian war over Afghanistan put an end to the adventurous policy of Persia in the east and again focused her attention on the chronic Russian danger in the north. Having acquired the naval base of Ashurada on the southern Caspian coast at the expense of Persia in 1840, the Empire of the Tsars now devoted its energies to the conquest of Central Asia—a process which was inevitably bound to affect Persian security. The three independent Central Asian khanates, Bukhara, Khiva, and Kokand, were conquered by Russia in 1868, 1873, and 1876, respectively. Simultaneously, Russia advanced in the Transcaspian region, conquering Krasnovodsk in 1869, capturing Geok Tepe, the Turkoman stronghold, in 1881, and subjugating Merv and Panjdeh in 1884. The latter operations affected Persia directly, inasmuch as she claimed rights over these regions. Furthermore, the subjugation of the Turkomans created a common boundary between Russia and Persia east of the Caspian. In 1881 Persia had to agree to the Atrek River boundary. Britain's worry about this advance caused a serious international crisis which brought the two protagonists close to war in 1885. Open rupture was averted by Britain's energetic stand and by the Russian decision not to cross into Afghanistan.

While Russia was thus expanding southward, the "nation of shopkeepers" attempted to secure economic advantages in Persia. In 1872 a naturalized British subject, Baron Julius de Reuter, obtained a sweeping seventy-year concession from Shah Nasser ed-Din, which gave him the right to construct a railway between the Caspian Sea and the Persian Gulf; to exploit all mines except those of gold, silver, and precious stones; to construct waterworks and regulate the rivers; and to organize street-car transportation in Teheran.

This concession was not destined to materialize. The Shah, who in 1873 made a tour of European capitals, was frigidly received at

St. Petersburg and decided, under Russian pressure, to cancel Reuter's concession. Reuter appealed to the British government for protection. In 1889, following lengthy diplomatic maneuvers, Persia, as compensation, granted two concessions to British interests: one for the "Imperial Bank of Persia" with the right to issue banknotes and one for "The Imperial Tobacco Corporation of Persia." To satisfy Russia, the Shah was compelled to allow her to establish a Russian discount and loans bank, as well as to construct a railway line in Azerbaijan. Even these concessions did not appease the northern neighbors; Russian agents skillfully instigated a popular movement against tobacco which ended in the cancellation of the British tobacco concession. This time the Persian government agreed to pay the aggrieved British investors half a million pounds sterling for damages.

At the time of Nasser ed-Din's violent death in 1896, Persia had an uncertain future and an empty treasury. The luxurious journey to Europe of his successor, Muzaffar ed-Din, did not ease the situation, and in 1900 Persia was compelled to seek a loan of twenty-two million rubles from Russia, followed by another two years later. These loans deepened Persia's dependence upon the tsar, who enjoyed his monopolistic role as creditor and who took care to ask for Persian customs revenues as a guarantee.

During this period of Russian ascendancy the first oil concession was granted to William Knox D'Arcy, an Australian financier, in 1901. This concession covered all of Persia, except the five northern provinces adjacent to Russia. Following intensive exploration in the southwest, oil was discovered in 1908, and the Anglo-Persian Oil Company, heir to D'Arcy's concession, was created. The company became a major supplier of the British navy. In 1914, shortly before the outbreak of the First World War, the British Admiralty purchased the controlling stock in this company.

Persia between 1905 and 1914

During the first decade of the twentieth century, Persia was in political ferment, partly due to the crying need for reform and partly due to the echoes of the Russian revolution of 1905. Whereas Russia supported the reactionary rulers in Teheran, Great Britain identified herself with the Democratic Party, which struggled for some semblance of political liberalism. In 1906 the crisis came to a head. Five thousand Persian merchants, representing the democratic bourgeois trend, closed their shops in the bazaar and massed together in the spacious gardens of the British legation in Teheran. Determined to resist the Shah by pressure, they encamped for several days in the legation's compound. The Democrats eventually forced the Shah to grant a constitution, which provided for a Westernized parliamentary form of government under a limited royal authority.

The success of the Democrats was intensely resented by the Russians, who felt that it was engineered by the British and considered it a threat to their own ascendancy in Persia.[3] Taking advantage of her rapprochement with Britain, which occurred in 1907, Russia encouraged Shah Mohammed Ali to repudiate the constitution in the *coup d'état* of 1908. The Shah's success was short-lived. In 1909 the opposition, led by the chieftains of the southern Bakhtiyari tribe, marched on Teheran and deposed the ruler. Mohammed Ali first sought refuge in the Russian legation and then, seeing that his position was untenable, fled the country. Under his minor son, Sultan Ahmed Mirza Shah, the constitutional government was restored and the Democratic Party slowly returned to power.

Ironically enough, after all this turmoil the Persian Democrats became anti-British. This change of heart on the part of the new Persian government resulted from the Anglo-Russian agreement of 1907. Russia and Britain, fearful of the rising might of Germany, finally decided to compose their differences in Asia and, for that purpose, reached a comprehensive settlement concerning Iran, Afghanistan, and Tibet. Russia promised to respect the *status quo* in Afghanistan (which implied the recognition of British ascendancy there), and both countries agreed to consider Tibet a no man's land, with whose affairs neither party would interfere. Persia was divided by this treaty into three zones. A Russian zone of influence was to extend over the five provinces in the north and was to embrace the central area including such cities as Qum, Kashan, Isfahan, and Yazd. Teheran was deep in the Russian zone. The British zone was to be limited to the southeastern area of Persia (Seistan and Baluchistan). The southwestern part of Persia was to constitute a neutral zone.[4]

[3] Readers may well ponder the similarity between Persian constitutional reform in 1906 and the adoption of a liberal constitution by the kingdom of Poland in 1791, just prior to the second partition. Both documents were designed to rescue their respective countries from anarchy and to strengthen them through much-needed governmental reform. In both cases Russia forcibly intervened to prevent such reforms from materializing.

[4] The British oil concession was situated in the neutral zone.

Although the signatories declared solemnly that they were determined to respect the political independence of Persia, the publication of the agreement caused understandable anger among the Persians. The Democrats, initially pro-British but now profoundly disillusioned, turned to the Germans, who were eager to exploit this change of heart to their best advantage. Gradually Germany succeeded not only in penetrating Persia commercially but also in securing great political influence over the Democratic politicians within and without the Persian government. This new friendship did not, however, relieve Persia from the constant pressure of the Russians, who, following the 1907 agreement, became bolder in their actions in the northern section. Thus, when the Persian government made another attempt, in 1911, to restore order and stability within Persia's political fabric by engaging an American financial expert, Dr. Morgan Shuster, Russia promptly sabotaged the appointment. Frustrated, Dr. Shuster was compelled to leave Persia, his task unfulfilled. His book, *The Strangling of Persia,* presents an eloquent account of this situation.

While Persia was thus frantically—and unsuccessfully—trying to shake off foreign interference and to reform her internal affairs, the chasm between Germany and the Entente powers was deepening. Under these circumstances, minor agreements negotiated between 1910 and 1914 among the rival powers proved to be of little significance. The first attempt to reconcile Russian and German interests in Persia was made at Potsdam in November 1910, during the conference between Tsar Nicholas II and Emperor William II, but no formal agreement emerged at that time. Less than a year later, however, on August 19, 1911, Russia and Germany signed a treaty at St. Petersburg by which Germany implicitly recognized the Russian sphere of influence in Persia in return for the right to extend her Baghdad railway system into northern Persia under certain circumstances. The treaty gave Russia nothing of value while conceding important advantages to Germany. It could, therefore, be interpreted as a unilateral Russian appeasement move, and as such it was viewed with uneasiness in Great Britain. But this concern proved to be ill-founded. The basic incompatibility of German and Russian ambitions in Europe drove them inexorably toward war, and their agreements concerning a minor area of competition could not avert the final clash.

In 1914, when the war broke out, Persia's independence was severely curtailed as a result of Russo-British co-operation. Russian troops were stationed in several parts of Persia's northern provinces, and minor British-Indian detachments guarded the oil fields in Khuzistan. The only two efficient military formations—the Persian Cossack Brigade and the Gendarmerie Corps—were officered by the Russians and the Swedes, respectively, and were subject to foreign influences. The powerful nomad tribes in the provinces were armed, and to a marked degree remained independent of the central government. Shah Ahmed, barely sixteen years old, was too young and too weak to conduct the affairs of the state with wisdom and determination. Under these conditions, Persia's officially proclaimed neutrality meant little and could not deter the big powers from using her territory as a battlefield should their interests so dictate.

CHAPTER II

War in the Middle East

AT THE outbreak of the First World War on August 2, 1914, the Ottoman Empire was ruled by Sultan Mohammed V, over seventy years of age and in frail health. The Sultan, who had been held prisoner in a palace in Constantinople for thirty-two years by his predecessor, Abdul Hamid II, and who had been placed on the throne by the Young Turks, was a nominal ruler only. The real power rested in the hands of the triumvirate of Young Turkish leaders: Enver Pasha, Talaat Pasha, and Jemal Pasha. Even the grand vizier, the Egyptian Prince Said Halim, was no more than a convenient front for these three leaders. Enver, thirty-two years of age, was minister of war and chief of the General Staff, but his influence far exceeded these functions and eventually he emerged as the real master of Turkey at war.

Prior to the outbreak of the war, German influence in the Ottoman Empire had grown out of all proportion to the influence of the other powers. It was especially noticeable in the military field. In 1914 the Ottoman army was trained and instructed by a mission of forty-two German officers under the command of General Liman von Sanders.

On August 2, 1914, Germany and Turkey concluded a treaty of alliance and a military convention, both secret. Despite these agreements, Turkey continued to maintain neutrality for some time. This neutrality was outward only. On August 11, the Porte permitted two German battleships, the *Goeben* and the *Breslau,* to enter the Dardanelles and granted them refuge in Turkish territorial waters. These ships were being pursued by the British navy. The same privilege was refused to a British naval squadron under Admiral Trubridge. Upon Britain's protest the Porte accused the British of failing to supply Turkey with two battleships previously ordered in British shipyards and paid for. (The ships had been requisitioned at the last moment by British authorities.) Furthermore, the Porte officially "purchased" the two German ships and engaged their personnel to serve in the Ottoman navy. The German commanding admiral, Souchon, was given command of the Ottoman naval forces, replacing the British admiral, who was dismissed. The last link with Britain was severed, and the German hold on the Ottoman defense establishment became complete. Thus inexorably by virtue of the treaty with Germany and as a result of these violations of neutrality, Turkey was heading for war. The Turkish cabinet, however, was not unanimous on this issue, and some ministers manifested either pro-Western or neutral attitudes. Among them were Jemal Pasha (one of the members of the triumvirate), the minister of finance, Javid, and three others. The grand vizier, Said Halim, played a double role; although sympathetic to the peace party, he hesitated to antagonize the war party headed by Enver. It was Enver's influence that eventually tipped the scales in favor of the entry into war.

Whatever hesitation the Porte had was cut short by the *Goeben* and *Breslau* incident. On orders from Enver, who acted in connivance with the Germans, these two ships, renamed *Sultan Selim* and *Medilli* but manned by their German crews, left Istanbul and on October 29 attacked the Russian fleet in the Black Sea. Russia declared war on the Ottoman Empire on November 4. This was followed by similar declarations by Britain and France one day later.

WAR AIMS AND POLITICAL STRATEGY OF GERMANY

The decisive battles of the First World War were fought in Europe, and European problems had priority in the considerations of the belligerents. Although Middle Eastern operations were of secondary importance, they were vital to both sides from the point of view of general strategy. The fortunes of war in the Middle East might have profoundly influenced the outcome of the war in Europe. The decision of the Ottoman government to side with the Central powers created a new front for Russia and affected the security of the British imperial life line—and in this sense constituted a distinct advantage to Germany.

From the German point of view, Turkey had to play an auxiliary role in order to divert some Russian and British energies from the main theater of war in Europe. Furthermore, Turkish advance in the East was to pave the way for the extension of German influence and, if successful, to affect the destiny of India. The German General Staff adopted the so-called Zimmermann Plan for India. The plan foresaw support for Indian nationalists and intense propaganda both among the Moslem and Hindu peoples of the peninsula.

In order to make full use of the Turkish alliance, Germany demanded that Turkey carry out several tasks without delay. These were to close the Straits to other powers; to cut the wartime route via the Suez Canal and Aden; to invade the Caucasus in order to immobilize an appreciable number of Russian troops; and to proclaim a holy war against the Entente countries.

To ensure the fulfillment of these aims Germany was represented in Turkey by a number of able diplomats.[1] She also secured far-reaching control of the Ottoman military machine. German officers assumed the following high functions in the Turkish army: General Liman von Sanders headed a mission to organize and train the army; General von Falkenhayn commanded the Turkish army in Palestine; and Field Marshal von der Goltz commanded the army in Mesopotamia. The German General Staff was represented by General von Lossow, and Admiral Humann, the naval attaché at the German embassy, acted as liaison officer between Berlin and the Ottoman navy.

Diplomatic and Military Maneuvers in Iran

Germany's diplomatic and military strategy in the Middle East was not limited to Turkey. She attempted to induce Iran and Afghanistan also to enter the war on her side.

In Iran Germany was represented by Prince von Reuss. Von Reuss maintained very cordial relations with the leaders of the Iranian Democratic Party. At the outbreak of the war, the latter were intensely anti-Russian and anti-British and leaned heavily

[1] During World War I: Baron von Wangenheim, Count Metternich, Herr von Kuehlmann, and Count von Bernstorff, successively. In October 1917 Emperor William II himself paid a visit to Constantinople.

toward an alliance with Germany. Their influence in the cabinet and in parliament was strong. Von Reuss's diplomacy bore fruit. In 1915 the prime minister of Iran, Mustaufi el-Mamalek, concluded a secret alliance with the Germans in return for certain political promises. These promises included a guarantee of Iran's independence and integrity, the supply of money, arms, and munitions, and the assurance of political asylum in Germany for the shah in the event that he should be compelled to flee his country. Von Reuss now proceeded to secure the co-operation of two other most important elements of strength in Iran: the Swedish-officered *gendarmerie* and the nomad tribes. The *gendarmerie* was the only independent and relatively efficient Iranian military formation. (The Iranian Cossack Brigade was Russian-officered and could not be regarded as a reliable weapon of the Iranian government.) The Swedish officers of the *gendarmerie* showed definitely pro-German proclivities and eventually decided to side openly with Germany. As to the tribes, which constituted roughly one-fifth of the Iranian population, they were armed and had an organization well suited to guerrilla warfare. In order to enlist the full co-operation of the nomad tribes and of the local governors, the German military attaché in Teheran, Count Kanitz, traveled extensively throughout the country, making lavish promises of German assistance. To aid him the German General Staff dispatched to Iran a number of military missions. The Klein mission operated in Kermanshah and the surrounding Kurd and Lur territory. The Zugmeyer mission extended its activities to Isfahan and Kerman. The Biach mission reached Yazd and Baluchistan, and former Consul Wassmus directed an uprising of the Qashqai, Bakhtiyari, and Tangistani tribes in southwestern Iran. These missions and their gendarme and tribal allies broke into many branches of the British-directed Imperial Bank of Iran, appropriated their funds, and captured a number of British citizens, including some consuls in the Iranian provincial towns.

The aim of all this German activity was to stir up anti-British and anti-Russian feelings among the people, and in this way to harmonize them with the pro-German attitude of the Teheran authorities. The Iranian government, though still persisting in outward neutrality, would thus be compelled, under the pressure of the aroused populace, to declare itself openly on the side of Germany. Such a declaration was to be accompanied—according to German plans—by a wholesale uprising of the people against the Russians and British. The resulting sabotage of the Anglo-Iranian Oil Company in Khuzistan would necessarily hinder the British war effort, inasmuch as the British navy drew heavily upon fuel supplies from that source.

By November 1915 the mood of the country was so pronouncedly anti-Entente that only a signal was needed to start the avalanche moving. The Russian and British ministers in Teheran were well informed of the state of affairs in Iran and to forestall a coup decided to act quickly. Strong warnings were issued to the Iranian government of the dire consequences of a precipitate pro-German action. Simultaneously, Russian troops, stationed in Kazvin (only thirty miles north of Teheran) moved toward the capital, threatening its occupation. Faced with such a contingency, the Iranian cabinet decided to transfer the seat of government to Isfahan in the center of the country, defying Allied pressure. Evacuation of the government offices began hastily. The German, Austrian, and Ottoman legations moved southward in a hurry, and established themselves temporarily at Qum. This evacuation, despite the necessity of abandoning the capital, actually was well suited to German plans because it meant the burning of bridges between Iran and the Entente powers. Yet the operation was not entirely successful, since at the last moment the young and weak-willed Shah Ahmed succumbed to strong Russo-British representations to remain in the capital. Faced with this turn of events, the cabinet decided to remain as well. As a result, only the outspokenly pro-German leaders of the Democratic Party left Teheran.

It was not exactly what the Germans wanted. Prince von Reuss did his best and promptly proceeded to create a rival Iranian government in Qum. It was, however, dangerous to remain there, because of the proximity of Russian troops. The latter did not occupy Teheran, but they were near enough to cause uneasiness. Eventually the separatist government moved to Kermanshah, where it was close to the Turkish border and where it could count on the protection of Ottoman forces in Mesopotamia. In Kermanshah the rival government was reorganized under the presidency of Nizam es-Saltaneh, the governor of Luristan. In December 1915 Nizam concluded a treaty of alliance with Germany promising to levy 40,000 troops in the area under his control. In return he was promised weapons and munitions, German instructors, a monthly subsidy, and a guarantee of his treasury. A German legation was formally accredited to Nizam's government, and a German military mission was dispatched to train

41

his forces.[2] Thenceforth, the political destinies of Nizam's government were linked with the fortunes of the Ottoman army in Mesopotamia. The Mesopotamian theater of war is treated in a separate section (pp. 59–60), but it may be stated here that Nizam's contribution to the Turkish-German war effort was altogether negligible.

Of all the German enterprises in Iran during the war the one conducted by Wassmuss was the most successful since he actually succeeded in provoking a rebellion of the southern tribes and in seriously threatening the British position there.[3] To Britain, German intrigue in Iran was very embarrassing. Some of the British troops in Mesopotamia had to be diverted to southern Iran to protect the oil fields, and such an extension of military commitments was most inconvenient. Southern Iran was a traditional British preserve, and it was there that the British authorities decided to make a bold move to stop the Germans and to restore peace and order.

Following an agreement with the Iranian government, a British military mission under Brigadier General Sir Percy Sykes was sent to the Persian Gulf port of Bandar Abbas in March 1916. The object of this mission was to organize an Iranian force and with it to restore normal conditions in the country. The force, named the South Persia Rifles, was promptly recruited, and it was reinforced by some troops from India. Before long Sykes was in a position to begin a number of forced marches into the interior. Within six months he secured control of Kerman, Yazd, Isfahan (where he joined with the Russian Cossacks sent from the north), Shiraz, and a large portion of Fars. He had to wage fierce battles with the German-influenced tribes, segments of the *gendarmerie,* and other pro-German elements. The cabinet in Teheran was of no help and vacillated between recognition of the South Persia Rifles and intrigue against it. By 1917, despite all the difficulties, Sykes managed to restore order and safety for the British in southern Iran. In 1917–1918 most of the German agents operating in this area fell into his hands. Even Wassmuss, despite all his ingenuity, was eventually captured.[4]

[2] A detailed description of German relations with Nizam's government is contained in Wipert von Blücher, *Zeitenwende in Iran* (Biberach an der Riss, 1949), pp. 27–127.

[3] A fascinating account of his intrigues may be found in Christopher Sykes, *Wassmuss, "the German Lawrence"* (London, 1936).

[4] For the activities of the German missions, see Sir Percy M. Sykes, *A History of Persia* (London, 1930), II, 442 ff.

The account of wartime Iran would be incomplete if we did not mention two further violations of neutrality by the belligerents. The northwestern province of Azerbaijan was invaded by Turkish and Russian troops early in the war. The province had to undergo all the vicissitudes of the war on the eastern Anatolian front and was also profoundly affected by Turkish operations in Transcaucasia toward the end of the war.

Eastern Iran also was not immune to the penetration of foreign troops. There Russian and British forces established what was known as the East Persian Cordon along the Afghan border. The reason for this operation lay in fear that some German or Turkish military detachments might traverse Iran and penetrate Afghanistan. This fear was not unfounded.

The German Expedition to Afghanistan

At the beginning of the war Enver Pasha persuaded the German General Staff that it would be of great advantage to the Central powers if Afghanistan entered the war on their side. According to the information available in Berlin, Afghanistan had a disciplined army of 20,000 regular troops, equipped with 350 field guns. The proximity of Afghanistan to India's most vulnerable spot—the Moslem provinces of the northwest—was a factor that Germany was eager to utilize to her own advantage. Accordingly it was decided to organize a German-Turkish mission that would proceed to Afghanistan and there induce the emir to take arms against the British Empire.

The mission in its ultimate composition was headed by Lieutenant Oskar Niedermayer and Herr von Hentig, legation secretary in the German Foreign Office. Von Hentig was the bearer of a personal letter from the Kaiser to Emir Habibullah. The Turkish part of the mission included Obaydullah Effendi, a deputy to the parliament, Kazim Bey, and a number of associates. The mission was accompanied by Kumar Mahendra Pratap and Barkatullah, Indian nationalist leaders resident in Berlin. Originally it was planned to send to Afghanistan a detachment of regular Turkish troops. Rauf Bey, former commander of the special Hamidiyeh Corps, was dispatched to Baghdad to make preparations. As a result of his quarrel with the German members of the mission, this project was abandoned.

The Niedermayer-Hentig mission had to traverse the territory of Iran. which was partly under Russian occupation, and to pass through

43

several towns where local British representatives wielded considerable influence. Furthermore, it had to pierce the East Persian Cordon
in order to reach the Afghan boundary. The mission's progress was
slow and cautious, but it succeeded, with a somewhat reduced personnel, in evading Russian or British capture and in August 1915
reached Afghanistan. Upon their arrival in Kabul, the members of
the mission were lodged as guests of Emir Habibullah. They had to
wait nearly two months for an audience with the ruler. When it was
accorded to them, the Germans put forward their offer of an alliance.
The Emir responded with cautious reserve and delayed his answer.
Afghanistan was officially neutral, but a pro-Turkish party under two
influential leaders, Nasrullah Khan and Inayatullah Khan, agitated in
favor of joining the Central powers. The mullahs, sensitive to the
caliph's call for a holy war, also pressed the Emir to join the Turkish-
German camp. The Emir's procrastination was dictated by his fear
of Britain and by his desire to determine which side was likely to win
the war. There is no doubt, however, that he personally favored the
Central powers. In January 1916 he went so far as to sign a draft
treaty of alliance with Germany. But before committing himself to
an open and definite break with Britain he insisted on the fulfillment
of two conditions by Germany: the dispatch of a strong force to
Afghanistan and a sizable subsidy in gold. To Niedermayer and Hentig it became clear that, unless these conditions were met, there was
no hope to expect more from the Emir. Consequently the mission took
its leave. Niedermayer, surmounting fantastic difficulties, managed to
cross Iran and reach the safety of Mesopotamia. Von Hentig went
through eastern Afghanistan, reached Sin-Kiang, and through China
and America returned to Germany.[5]

WAR AIMS AND POLITICAL STRATEGY OF TURKEY

The war aims of the Ottoman government could be stated as follows: (1) Turkification of the Ottoman Empire and its liberation from
Western tutelage; (2) reconquest of the irredentist areas of Egypt
and Cyprus (and possibly of Libya, Tunisia, and Algeria); (3) liberation and federation of the Turkish-inhabited areas of Russia (the
Caucasus and Turkestan); (4) re-establishment of the caliph's authority over all Islam. This was the program of the war party headed

[5] Details about the German expedition may be found in Oskar von Niedermayer,
Unter der Glutsonne Iran's (Dachau, 1925); Blücher, *op. cit.*, pp. 83–94; Sir
Percy M. Sykes, *A History of Afghanistan* (London, 1940), pp. 246 ff.

by Enver and Talaat and one which, on their insistence, was adopted by the cabinet as a whole.[6] Enver and his friends believed that these objectives could be attained in co-operation with Germany.

To fulfill this program, Turkey needed to combine military and political strategy. Furthermore, such a strategy was bound to affect not only Turkey's foreign relations, but also the domestic situation. The Ottoman Empire at the outbreak of the war was composed of a number of nationalities. Of the toal population of twenty-five million, the Turks constituted less than half, about ten million. The Arab subjects of the Empire were estimated at ten million also. In addition, there were about a million and a half Kurds, about two million Armenians, and about a million and a half people of miscellaneous races. Thus the Empire was far from being homogeneous, and the success of its policies depended to a great degree upon the loyalty of its subject peoples. Moreover, Turkey suffered from important limitations of sovereignty due to the existing system of capitulations and special rights accorded to foreign powers. For example, the Ottoman government was not allowed to raise the customs tariff above a level determined by international agreements; certain sources of public revenue were practically sequestered by foreign powers to assure the payment of the public debt; the Porte was forced to observe certain imposed rules with regard to the treatment of national and religious minorities; and Turkey's sovereignty over the Straits was limited.

Drifting into the war in the fall of 1914, Turkey was in a position to satisfy immediately at least the first point of her war program, that is, her liberation from foreign tutelage. On September 5, 1914, the Ottoman government formally repudiated the capitulations. The definite entry into the war in November put an end to foreign interference, at least for the duration of the hostilities.

The Problem of Loyalty: Arabs and Kurds

The loyalty problem proved to be much more complex. The Arabs were brethren in faith but had many grievances against the Ottoman administration. The Young Turks, following their revolution, had made a gesture of good will toward the Arabs. An association known as the Ottoman-Arab Fraternity (*El-Ikha el-Arabi el-Uthmani*) was created, and the propaganda of Ottomanism was

[6] For a detailed analysis of Turkish policies during World War I, see Ahmed Emin, *Turkey in the World War* (New Haven, Conn., 1930).

45

launched with a view to assuring common loyalty to the Empire on the basis of equality. But this proved to be a brief interlude only and was followed by utter disillusionment. Educated Arabs resented the Young Turk's policy of centralization and objected to the unequal representation in the Ottoman Chamber of Deputies, which had been created as a result of the 1908 revolution. Of the total of 245 representatives, 150 were Turks and only 60 were Arabs, despite the numerical parity or possible Arab majority in the Empire. The Arabs did not hide their resentment, whereupon the Turkish authorities suppressed the Ottoman-Arab Fraternity. This rupture was a signal for the Arabs to organize various nationalist associations. The Literary Club (*El-Muntada el-Adabi*), formed in 1909 in Constantinople, and the Ottoman Decentralization Party, established in 1912 in Cairo, carried on open propaganda for Arab home rule. Simultaneously the more radical Arab elements formed two secret societies. The first, *El-Qahtaniya*, created in 1909, was headed by Major Aziz Ali el-Masri and consisted principally of Arab officers in the Ottoman army. It operated in Constantinople and in five other centers throughout the Empire and advocated a dual Arab-Turkish monarchy. The second, *El-Fatat*, formed initially in Paris in 1911 among young educated Arabs, subsequently moved to Beirut and then to Damascus. It was El-Fatat which, in 1916, took Emir Faisal of Hejaz into membership and converted him to the cause of Arab liberation. The years 1912–1913 witnessed the creation of a powerful Committee of Reform in Beirut. The committee demanded Arab autonomy in the Ottoman Empire. Mention should also be made of an Arab congress in Paris in 1913, attended by twenty-four Arab nationalists, which formulated far-reaching demands for the emancipation of the Arabs.[7]

Thus when the war broke out, the politically conscious Arabs could hardly be regarded as a dependable element in the Empire. Yet despite these differences, a number of purely Arab formations were in the Ottoman army. Many officers, of higher and lower ranks, were also Arabs. Under these circumstances, the Ottoman government did not fear any mass defection on their part. The revolt of the Arabs in the Hejaz in 1916 was, therefore, a severe shock to the Turkish leadership. (See pp. 75–77.) With regard to the general problem of loyalty in the Ottoman Empire, it may be pointed out

[7] The most exhaustive treatment of the Arab national movement is contained in George Antonius, *The Arab Awakening* (London, 1938).

46

that the Hejaz revolt did not produce complete unanimity in the Arab world. Certain sections remained faithful to Turkey, such as Yemen, the Arabs of Libya, and the Rashids of central Arabia.

The Arabs of Syria and Mesopotamia, while favoring the revolt, were cowed into submission by the Turkish authorities. This was especially true of Syria, where at the beginning of the war Jemal Pasha (one of the triumvirate) assumed the duties of military governor. By dealing ruthlessly with the conspiring Arab nationalists in Beirut and in Damascus, he discouraged active anti-Turkish manifestations.

The Kurds were another Moslem minority in the Empire. A race of virile mountaineers, still in a seminomadic state of social organization, the Kurds were a perennial problem for the Ottoman and Iranian empires in whose borderlands they lived. They aspired toward greater freedom, and their history was marked by frequent uprisings against their overlords. If, owing to their primitive culture, they had no sense of nationality, they certainly could not be expected to have any loyalty to the vague idea of Ottomanism. Despite this the Kurds were altogether loyal to Turkey during the war. The secret of this "correct" behavior lay in the fact that the Turks skillfully channeled the Kurdish anarchistic tendencies into war against the Christians, and in particular against their close neighbors, the Armenians and the Assyrians. In this way the Kurdish minority appeased both its Islamic conscience and its predatory instincts. For the Ottoman Empire, therefore, the Kurds not only presented no problem during the war but proved relatively useful in the accomplishment of certain disagreeable tasks in the eastern provinces. Only after the end of the war were their autonomist tendencies revealed in a violent form.

The Problem of Loyalty: Armenians and Assyrians

Among the Christian minorities of the Empire, three were especially affected by the war, the Armenians, the Assyrians, and the Greeks. The Greeks were not a problem between 1914 and 1918. For a long time Greece herself was on the verge of joining the Central powers, and the Greek subjects of the Empire took care not to offend the patriotic susceptibilities of the Turks. Their drama belongs properly to the aftermath of the war, when the Empire lay prostrate, and it will be treated later within the general framework of the peace settlement.

47

The story of the Armenians was quite different. Victims of repeated massacres in the last three decades, the Armenians greeted
the entry of Turkey into the war with mixed feelings of fear and hope
—fear of possible Turkish reprisals, unchecked by any external pressure, and hope for the defeat of the Empire and the victory of the
Entente, in particular of Russia. The Russians had traditionally assumed the role of protector of the Armenians, said role being another weapon to speed up the disintegration of Turkey. The controversy over the disloyal behavior of the Armenians will probably
never be resolved. The Turks maintained that the Armenians showed
extreme disloyalty from the very beginning of the conflict. The
Armenians claimed that their behavior was quite correct. The truth
of the matter is that the wealthier and leading elements of the
Armenian community, fearful of dire consequences if there were
any show of disloyalty, insisted on full compliance with Turkish war
regulations and discouraged any anti-Turkish manifestations. But
the rank and file did not follow their leaders. Appeal to emotion was
stronger than appeal to reason, and emotionally the Armenian masses
were ready to greet the advancing Russian armies as liberators.

They were encouraged in this attitude by official pronouncements
of the Armenian Orthodox Church, which traditionally held great
sway over its communicants. In August 1914 the catholicos or head
of the Armenian Church residing in Echmiadzin, Russian Armenia,
proclaimed that the Russian tsar was the protector of all Armenians.
This proclamation appeared in the catholicos' official organ, *Ararat*,
and made it a sacred duty of all Armenians to give personal and
material support to the Russian armies. This appeal was followed in
November by an official Russian proclamation, exhorting the Armenians to rise against their Turkish "tyrants" and promising liberation.[8] Many Armenians responded to these appeals by deserting the
Turkish army, volunteering in the Russian army, and assisting the
Russian advance. There is no doubt that as a whole the Armenian
minority in the villages of Turkey was hostile to the Turks and that
their loyalty was highly doubtful.

The government's reaction was ruthless. In June 1915 it decided
to remove the Armenian population from the eastern war zone and
to deport it to the interior of Anatolia or to the northern desert
areas of Syria. This mass deportation was carried out in 1915 and

[8] Emin, *op. cit.*, p. 215. For the attitude of the Armenians, consult also
Maurice Larcher, *La Guerre Turque dans la Guerre Mondiale* (Paris, 1926).

1916 and has become known as the Armenian massacres. This term is not inappropriate. The deportations were characterized by unspeakable cruelties and wanton destruction of life and property. They resulted in an almost total uprooting of the Armenians of the eastern vilayets, who had lived there from time immemorial, and affected not only those suspected of disloyalty, but also women, children, and other innocent persons. The cruelty of this removal was matched only by the brutality of the cattlelike transportation facilities and the horrors of internment camps and forced settlements. Two million people are estimated to have been affected, of whom 600,000 lost their lives.[9]

Attempts to soften the Turkish attitude made by Pope Pius X, by the American ambassador in Constantinople, Henry Morgenthau, and even by German authorities were of no avail. Talaat Pasha, minister of the interior, who was chiefly responsible for the deportations, was determined to pursue his course unflinchingly, and he was fully supported by the cabinet. This policy "solved" the Armenian question in Turkey proper. It generated among all remaining Armenians an undying hatred for Turkey that even the transformation of the Turkish state in the early 1920's was unable to assuage. It accounts for many reprisals against the Turks (Russian or Ottoman) on occasions when the Armenians were in a position to get vengeance. Such occasions occurred with the arrival of Russian armies into eastern Turkish territory during the war and in 1918 in Baku. It also accounts for the willingness of the Armenians to compromise with or collaborate with Communist Russia every time her policies conflict with those of Turkey.[10]

[9] Simon Vratzian, *Armenia and the Armenian Question* (Boston, 1943), p. 27.

[10] The Armenian massacres undoubtedly constitute one of the blackest pages of Turkish history. Even granting the disloyalty of the Armenian people as a whole, which made it difficult to distinguish in practice between the actively disloyal and the outwardly correct in closely knit Armenian villages, no excuse can be found for the brutality with which the deportations were made. Nor can the matter be lightly dismissed, as does Prof. Ernest Jackh in *The Rising Crescent* (New York, 1944, p. 42), by stating that massacres are a time-honored device to settle political accounts in the East. It is in order, however, to keep the whole matter in proper perspective by pointing out that the Turks were not the only ones to commit mass atrocities during the First World War. First of all, the Armenians, when taking revenge, did not distinguish between guilty and innocent Moslems. Secondly, while the attention of the world was focused upon the tragic events in Turkey, Russia was similarly exterminating her Moslem subjects in Turkestan. Here is what Professor Toynbee says about it in *The Western Question in Greece and Turkey* (London, 1922):

49

Equally affected by wartime developments in the Middle East was the Assyrian minority. This group, united around its ancient Chaldean-Nestorian Church, was centered in two areas—the Lake Van region in Turkey and the Lake Urumia region in Iran. It was never so badly treated by the Turks as were the Armenians, but it was exposed to hostility and suspicion on the part of the Ottoman authorities. Encouraged by the Russian advance into eastern Anatolia in 1915, the Turkish Assyrians rose against the Turks and co-operated with the Russians. The Russian withdrawal in 1917–1918 left the Assyrians in a very exposed position; in order to avoid Turkish reprisals, about 20,000 of them fought their way to the British lines in northern Mesopotamia. The fate of those in Iran was even more dramatic. In 1918 when the Turks advanced into Iranian Azerbaijan, the Assyrians of Urumia were faced with a grave threat to their existence. Exposed to direct Turkish attacks, Kurdish depredations, and the general hostility of Iranians, the Assyrians kept their enemies at bay for a few months while feverishly seeking British protection. In the summer of 1918 the whole Assyrian population of the Urumian region was suddenly seized with panic and, led by Aga Petros, fled to the Kermanshah-Kazvin region, which was then under temporary British occupation. Only about half of the original population of 100,000 survived the hardships of the exodus. The British authorities gave them protection and subsequently moved them to Mesopotamia. There most of the Assyrians remained in refugee camps, though some were given auxiliary employment in the British army. Neither the Turkish nor the Iranian Assyrian people were allowed to return to their homes, even after the end of the war.[11]

Pan-Islamism and Pan-Turanism in Wartime

Ottoman political strategy in wartime could be summed up in two terms: Pan-Islamism and Pan-Turanism. It will be remembered that

"During the European war while people in England were raking up the Ottoman Turks' nomadic ancestry in order to account for their murder of 600,000 Armenians, 500,000 Turkish-speaking Central Asian nomads of the Kirghiz-Kazak Confederacy were being exterminated—also under superior orders—by that 'justest of mankind,' the Russian muzhik; men, women, children were shot down, or were put to death in a more horrible way by being robbed of their animals and equipment and then being driven forth in wintertime to perish in mountain and desert. A lucky few escaped across the Chinese frontier. These atrocities were courageously exposed and denounced by Mr. Kerensky in the Duma before the first Revolution, but who listened or cared" (p. 342)?

[11] As to the further fate of the Assyrians, see Chapter VII.

upon Turkey's entry into the war, the sultan in his capacity as caliph issued a call to a holy war or jihad addressed to all Mohammedans the world over. This proclamation, made on November 23, 1914, was signed by the highest religious dignitaries of the Empire, including the Sheikh el-Islam in Constantinople. The proclamation of a jihad was the culminating point of the policy of Pan-Islamism inaugurated earlier by Sultan Abdul Hamid II. The fact that Germany as a Christian power was on the side of Turkey did not deter the sultan from issuing the call. The German emperor, pursuing his traditional policy of courting Islam, had already (September 9, 1914) issued a proclamation that Moslems fighting in the Entente armies were not to be considered as belligerents, and when taken prisoner by the Germans, would be sent to Turkey, where they would be at the disposal of the caliph.

In Constantinople it was hoped that the proclamation of a jihad would evoke vigorous response both at home and abroad. At home, i.e., within the Empire, the jihad was to produce Arab loyalty. Abroad, the Turks expected an uprising of the Moslems in the colonial possessions of the Entente. These expectations proved largely futile. The Arabs did not gather in defense of "the faith and the throne," and a large segment among them, led by Sherif Hussein of Mecca, decided to pursue an independent course and chose the side of Turkey's enemies.[12] The significance of this step was tremendous and greatly outweighed the loyalty to Turkey shown by Imam Yehya of Yemen and by some nomad tribes of central Arabia.

Outside the Empire also, the call to a jihad failed to produce the expected results. In the African possessions of the Entente, the Senussis in Libya and the Mahdists in the Sudan responded. In August 1915 the Senussis rose against Italian rule. Aided by German subsidies and Turkish military instructors, they forced the Italians to vacate most of the Libyan hinterland and to limit their control to the coastal belt only. The Senussis also invaded the western extremities of Egypt and delivered a few attacks on some French posts on the Tunisian border. As to the Mahdists, there was considerable unrest among them, aggravated by the anti-British attitude of Ali Dinar, sultan of the Darfur province in western Sudan. In both cases the anti-Entente conduct of the Moslems was an isolated phenomenon and occasioned only minor military operations which could not influence the general course of the war in the Middle East.

[12] For an account of the military operations of the Arab Revolt, see p. 57.

In the Asiatic possessions of the Entente, the largest single group of people impressed by the proclamation was the Mohammedans of India, inhabiting the area now known as Pakistan, and numbering about seventy million souls. Yet, despite their reverence for the caliph, they did not undertake any overt military action against Great Britain. Some extremists did enter into a conspiracy and attempted to establish liaison with the Central powers, but these activities were not limited to the Moslems. A number of Hindu nationalists were included. Despite the failure of their efforts, the British bureaucracy in India was deeply concerned about the jihad and did its utmost to avoid any unnecessary provocation of the Moslem elements of the population.

This explains the political attitude of the British expeditionary force in Mesopotamia, of whose military exploits we shall speak later. The Indian-trained and Indian-oriented military and political leadership of the force was unwilling to seek Arab guerrilla support in this campaign because such support, it feared, might provoke dangerous complications in India. Indian Moslems greatly resented Britain's co-operation with Sherif Hussein of Mecca, whom they considered a traitor to the cause of Mohammedan solidarity. But at least the government of India was not responsible for these dealings with Hussein. (He was in contact with the Foreign Office through the Arab Bureau in Cairo.) If, however, the government of India were to employ Arab "traitors" in their war against the caliph in Mesopotamia, profound and violent repercussions in India might follow. This the government of India skillfully avoided, with the result that Moslem agitation never got out of hand.

The effects of the jihad, from the Turkish point of view, were deeply disappointing. In fact, Sherif Hussein's defection meant the failure of the Pan-Islamic strategy as such. In a crisis nationalism was a stronger force than was religion.

The use of Pan-Islamism as a weapon was not unanimously approved by the Turks themselves. Democratically minded leaders in the high echelons of the Union and Progress Party, such as Professor Zia Gök Alp, resented the reactionary and retarding influence of the Moslem religion upon the Ottoman Empire and wished to see a sweeping secularization of the country. They viewed with distaste any perpetuation of the hold of ecclesiastics upon Turkey as expressed by appeals to religious fanaticism. Zia Gök Alp and his friends were Turkish nationalists above everything. This meant that they rejected the vague (and in their eyes inadequate) concept of Ottomanism, which had been initially preached by the Young Turks, as well as the concept of Pan-Islamism. Ottomanism, argued Zia Gök Alp, did not prevent the Russians from disrupting the loyalty of the Balkan subjects of the Ottoman Empire by appeals to Pan-Slavism. This, according to Turkish nationalists, was one more proof that the only valid link on which a state could rely was the feeling of common blood, of belonging to a common nationality. Turkey's salvation thus lay in assuring the national consciousness of her Turkish subjects and in promoting the union of all peoples of Turkish race wherever they lived. This was the ideology of Pan-Turanism, an ideology born among the Turkic groups in Russia and now wholeheartedly adopted by Zia Gök Alp and his followers.

As to the policy of the government itself, it was eclectic. On the one hand, it did not wish to relinquish its Pan-Islamic course, still fondly hoping that it might prove useful in the prosecution of the war. On the other hand, it leaned more and more as time went on (especially after 1917) toward Pan-Turanism. That the two policies were mutually incompatible was conveniently ignored by Enver and his associates. The incompatibility was clear; it was illogical, for example, to appeal to the Iranians as Moslem coreligionists to fight on the side of Turkey (Pan-Islamism) and at the same time to threaten the disintegration of their state by appeals to Pan-Turkish unity (which would mean separation of Turkish-speaking Azerbaijan and its absorption by the Turkish Empire.) It was illogical to expect loyalty on a religious basis on the part of the Arabs and at the same time to preach a nationalist doctrine which in its logical conclusion must have provided for the independence of the Arabs as a nation.[18]

Apart from the confusion within Turkish ruling circles, there were also differences between Turkey and Germany on this account. These differences related to the content of the Central powers' propaganda in the Middle East and to the methods of carrying out their policy. With regard to the content, the German government initially approved the Pan-Islamic propaganda and even actively contributed to it. Emperor William II was represented by German agents as a friend of Islam, and rumors were circulated about his conversion to Mohammedanism. German missions in Iran and Afghanistan and

[18] On Pan-Turanism, see Emin, *op. cit.*, ch. xvi; T. Lothrop Stoddard, "Pan-Turanism," *American Political Science Review*, Feb. 1917, pp. 12–23; also Larcher, *op. cit.*, pp. 142 ff.

the propaganda literature prepared for use in India employed Pan-Islamic slogans. The failure of Pan-Islamic propaganda caused the German Foreign Office to believe that more stress should be laid on the nationalist struggle against British or French domination as such. On this basis, it was hoped, more response could be evoked among Iranians, Egyptians, or Indians. The Germans viewed with concern the Pan-Turanian propaganda emanating from Turkey. While such a policy might prove useful with regard to the Turkish groups inside Russia, at the same time it was bound to produce complications in sectors that were of immediate concern to Germany, namely, Iran and the Arab countries. In these sectors actual military operations were conducted; and their success depended upon the attitude of the populations toward the armies in the field.

The other point of difference was the method itself. The Turkish government insisted that problems of policy and propaganda in the Mohammedan East must be left largely to the discretion of Turkey and that the Turks must assume responsibility for them. For this reason German missions to Iran suffered all sorts of administrative chicanery in traveling through the Ottoman Empire and their entry into Iran on certain occasions was fatally delayed. The same reason accounted also for the inclusion of a Turkish staff under Obaydullah Effendi in the mission to Afghanistan headed by Niedermayer and Von Hentig. The German Foreign Office and the General Staff viewed these Turkish claims with apprehension, because the use of Turkish agents was not considered the best way to arouse confidence and friendship among the Arabs or the Iranians. Thus the failure to evoke popular enthusiasm for the Iranian separatist government of Nizam es-Saltaneh in Kermanshah was to a large extent due to the presence of Turkish battalions on Iranian soil. Iranians, because of their anti-Russian and anti-British attitudes, might become very friendly toward Germany, but hardly toward the traditional rival, Turkey.[14]

The growing inclination of the Turkish government toward Pan-Turanism, which became obvious after the Russian revolution in 1917, accentuated these differences between the allies. The Russian revolution opened before the Turks the prospect of fulfilling at least one of their major war aims, namely, the liberation and federation of the Turkish groups of Russia. Therefore, whatever strength

[14] A vivid description of these complications may be found in Blücher, *op. cit.,* pp. 72–73, 92–94.

54

Turkey could muster in the fourth year of the war was focused on the Caucasus. This attitude produced two consequences, both irritating to the German high command. First, it meant neglect of other theaters of war in the Middle East where Germany desired to hold up British advances. Secondly, active Turkish penetration in the Caucasus might deprive Germany of a rich prize in Caucasian foodstuffs and in raw materials such as manganese and oil. Hence, uncoordinated and precipitate Turkish action in this sector was greatly resented in Germany. In fact, it looked to Berlin in 1918 as if the Turks had abandoned the common war to fight their own private war for the sole benefit of Turkey.

THE MILITARY OPERATIONS IN THE MIDDLE EAST

In the first phase of the war Turkey took the initiative by invading the Caucasus. To attain their military ends the Turks did not hesitate to violate Iranian neutrality, and their troops entered Iranian Azerbaijan. Their first offensive brought them to the gates of Batum in Russia and of Tabriz in Iran. Simultaneously, the Turks began to recruit Moslem elements in the areas occupied by them, particularly the Ajars (Moslem Georgians) and the Azeris (Turkish-speaking inhabitants of Azerbaijan). Neither Batum nor Tabriz was, however, captured. In midwinter of 1914–1915, the Russians regained the initiative and succeeded in pushing the Turks back to the Russo-Turkish frontier. Throughout the war this front was mobile in a limited sense. The Russians actually gained the upper hand by penetrating into Turkish territory as far as Trebizond, Erzerum, Erzinjan, Mush, and Van. This military line continued roughly through Lake Urumia to Kermanshah and Hamadan in Iran. Enver's dreams about a quick success in the Caucasus and the liberation of its Mohammedan populations were not realized. From the German point of view, however, this operation fulfilled its purpose of containing a number of valuable Russian divisions. Events on this front took a very dramatic turn at the end of the war as a result of the Russian revolution. They will be reviewed in the section dealing with Transcaucasia.

The Dardanelles Expedition

In March 1915 the British navy tried to force the Dardanelles, but the attempt failed. It was followed by the landing on Gallipoli, on April 25, of an Allied expeditionary force composed of British,

Australian, New Zealand, and French troops. This force commanded by Sir Ian Hamilton was ordered to strike a blow at the heart of the Empire, Constantinople. The idea was Winston Churchill's, who was then first lord of the Admiralty in the British cabinet. This expedition, if successful, might have resulted in the elimination of Turkey from the war. But the attempt failed. The Turks, commanded by General Liman von Sanders, offered stubborn resistance and inflicted upon the Allies heavy casualties, estimated at 25,000 men. In January 1916 the Allies were forced to evacuate Gallipoli.

The Sinai Front

In February 1915 the Turkish high command made an attempt to cross the Suez Canal. The offensive, launched under the command of Jemal Pasha, failed because of superior British forces. The British, who had occupied Egypt since 1882, had organized a powerful army in the delta of the Nile. From this army later came the bulk of the troops for the Gallipoli expedition. Now its task was to defend Egypt and the Suez Canal and to put pressure on the Turkish concentrations in Palestine and Syria.

Throughout 1915 the front shifted back and forth in the coastal region of the Sinai peninsula. By 1916 a powerful British army known as the Egyptian expeditionary force, first under General Sir Archibald Murray and later under General Sir Edmund Allenby, launched an offensive against Palestine with the ultimate objective of conquering Syria.

The slow but steady advance of the British, accompanied by British victories in Mesopotamia, produced a temporary crisis in Constantinople. In January 1917 Grand Vizier Prince Said Halim resigned and was replaced by Talaat Pasha, who was determined to give a more energetic direction to affairs. With their German allies, the Turks decided to launch a decisive, quick offensive in one of the theaters of war in the Middle East, in order to destroy at least one British expeditionary force. This project known as *Yilderim* ("Lightning") was first planned for Mesopotamia, but because of pressing need along the Mediterranean coast it was applied to the Syro-Palestinian campaign. In May 1917 General von Falkenhayn arrived from Germany at the head of a mission of sixty-five officers and assumed command of the Turkish army in Palestine. A German brigade was sent as reinforcement. One of Von Falkenhayn's staff officers was Major Franz von Papen, later to become German am-

56

bassador to Turkey,[15] while one of his corps commanders was General Mustafa Kemal Pasha, who had already distinguished himself in the defense of Gallipoli. Despite heavy fighting, *Yilderim* failed. On December 9, 1917, General Allenby entered Jerusalem. The Turks were now definitely on the defensive, and nothing could stop their retreat. Even the relinquishment of high staff and command positions to the Germans did not save the situation. The final decisive battle on the Palestinian front took place at Mejiddo on September 18, 1918. It was followed by the occupation of Syria by British troops. Their progress was stopped by the conclusion of hostilities in October 1918.

The Arabian Front

At the outbreak of the war most of the Arabian peninsula, except Aden and the Persian Gulf states, was under Ottoman suzerainty. Turkish control was, however, only nominal over large portions of central Arabia. The Nejd and the Hasa in particular were virtually free, and their rulers conducted their domestic and foreign affairs independently of the will of the Ottoman government. The political status of the western part of Arabia—the Hejaz—was less clear. Turkish garrisons were stationed at some of the more important places in the Hejaz and also along the railway linking Syria with Medina. Politically the Hejaz was of doubtful loyalty because of the independent course followed by Sherif Hussein. Farther to the south there were Turkish troops in Yemen, whose ruler, Imam Yehya, was loyal to the Ottoman government.

The proclamation of the holy war, as we already know, did not produce the expected co-operation of the Arabs. Eventually two Arab princes of the peninsula allied themselves with the British: Ibn Saud of the Nejd and Sherif Hussein of the Hejaz. While Ibn Saud did not take an active part in the war against Turkey (India did not desire it), Hussein pledged the British army active military support. Hussein's decision was the result of an agreement with the British government to which we shall refer in a later section.[16]

On June 5, 1916, Hussein declared war against Turkey, a declaration which inaugurated what has since become known as the Arab Revolt. Warlike tribes were organized into a desert army whose

[15] Von Papen had been German military attaché in Washington for some time during the First World War. He was asked to leave the United States as a *persona non grata*, on account of his espionage activities.

[16] See below, pp. 75 ff.

main objective was to drive the Turks out of Arabia and to co-operate on the right flank with General Allenby's expeditionary force. The Arab army was commanded by Emir Faisal, third son of Sherif Hussein. Expert advice and leadership were provided by a number of British officers, chief among whom was Colonel T. E. Lawrence.[17]

The outbreak of the revolt threw German-Turkish plans into confusion. It occurred at a time when a German military mission, under Baron von Stotzingen, was proceeding through the Hejaz to Yemen in order to establish there a center of information and communications for the region around the southern Red Sea. Stotzingen and his men were surprised and cut off from contact with their headquarters. After the official proclamation of revolt in the suburb of Medina by Emirs Faisal and Ali on June 5, Arab forces attacked Turkish troops in Mecca and after three days of fierce battle compelled them to surrender. Next to be liberated was the Red Sea port and town of Jidda. By September 1916 the principal towns of the Hejaz, except Medina, were under Arab control. Arab forces were then divided into two parts: the first, under the command of Ali, Abdullah, and Zaid, remained in Hejazi territory and laid siege to Medina; the second, under Faisal, proceeded northward as an auxiliary force to General Allenby's main expedition. The exploits of the Arab force were spectacular and of great value to the success of the main operation.[18] Operating east of the Jordan River, the Arabs successively captured Wajh, Akaba, Maan, and Dara and proceeded toward their ultimate goal—Damascus. The advance of the Sherifian forces brought in their wake uprisings of Syrian and Transjordanian tribes against the Turks and caused many desertions from the Arab personnel of the Ottoman army. On October 1, 1918, British and Arab forces entered Damascus at the same time. Faisal entered at full gallop, heading a body of mounted Arab warriors. The ancient city of the Omayyads gave itself to a frenzy of enthusiasm in what was believed to be an hour of deliverance from centuries-long Turk-

[17] Among the British officers were Lt. Col. C. C. Wilson, who acted as British agent accredited to Sherif Hussein; Sir Reginald Wingate, who initially was commander-in-chief of operations in the Hejaz; Lt. Col. Alan Dawnay; Col. S. F. Newcombe, and Major P. C. Joyce. In addition, Col. E. Brémond headed a French military mission in Jidda. This mission lent to Arab forces a number of instructors, many of whom were Moroccan and Algerian officers.

[18] For an account of the Arab military operations, see T. E. Lawrence, *Revolt in the Desert* (London, 1927) and *Seven Pillars of Wisdom* (London, 1935).

ish rule. The remainder of Syria was liberated in two operations: a
British column fought its way along the coastal region through
Tyre, Sidon, Beirut, and Tripoli, and a combined British-Arab force
moving in a parallel direction successively captured Homs, Hama,
and Aleppo in Syria's hinterland. In the last days of the war, stiff
resistance was encountered at Aleppo, where the remnant of the
Seventh Turkish Army under General Mustafa Kemal Pasha attempted to bar the Allies' entry into Turkey proper. A few days
later the armistice put an end to the hostilities. According to British
estimates, the Arab Revolt was responsible for the containment of
about 65,000 Turkish troops.[19]

The Front in Mesopotamia

Allied operations against the Ottoman Empire would have been incomplete without an offensive in Mesopotamia. As early as November 6, 1914, British troops landed at Fao, the point where Shatt
el-Arab flows into the Persian Gulf. This was followed by the arrival
of a large expeditionary force from India. The specific objectives of
this operation were to protect the British-controlled oil wells and
refineries in southwestern Iran, to carry out a political countermove
against the call to a jihad, and to provide a manifestation of strength
to the Arab chieftains of the Persian Gulf coast (particularly those
of Mohammera and Kuwait). Thus, apart from its pure military significance in the eastern theater of war, the expedition had to perform
a definitely political task with regard to the Arab and Moslem world.
The weight attached to these considerations was pointed up by
the appointment of Sir Percy Cox, long-time British resident for the
Persian Gulf, as chief political officer to the expeditionary force. The
force, commanded in succession by Generals Delamain, Barrett, and
Maude, occupied Basra in November 1914 and undertook an offensive operation against Baghdad.[20] The ultimate aim was to effect a
junction with the Russian forces operating from the Caucasus, and
thus to close an iron ring around the eastern confines of the Ottoman Empire. The opposing Turkish army was under the command of

[19] According to Arnold J. Toynbee, *The Islamic World since the Peace Settlement* (*Survey of International Affairs, 1925*, vol. I; London, 1927), p. 283.

[20] For an account of this campaign, see Edmund Dane, *British Campaigns in
the Nearer East, 1914–1918* (London, 1917–1919); Sir Arnold T. Wilson, *Loyalties, Mesopotamia, 1914–17: A Personal and Historical Record* (London, 1930);
Edmund Chandler, *The Long Road to Baghdad* (London, 1919); C. V. Townshend, *My Campaign in Mesopotamia* (London, 1920).

an experienced German soldier, General von der Goltz Pasha, who aroused much spirit and effected great efficiency among his troops.

In contrast to Allenby's campaign in Palestine, the Mesopotamian expeditionary force had to rely entirely upon its own strength, since Arab irregulars were not accepted as allies. It was faced with an arduous task in a very unfavorable climate, and its lines of communication were extended, considering the distance from its Indian base. The force's operations were complicated by the fact that it also had to keep an eye on developments in the nearby territory of Iran. As we know from the preceding section, the possibility that Iran might take the side of the Central powers was never completely excluded. The German-sponsored rebellion of the tribes in oil-rich Khuzistan constituted a diversion which was apt to weaken the expeditionary force in Mesopotamia and which at one time had almost catastrophic consequences.

Because of these conditions the progress of the force was slow. On April 25, 1916, the British suffered a severe defeat when over 13,000 soldiers, under General Townshend, surrendered to the Turks after a protracted siege of five months at Kut el-Amara. The almost simultaneous death of Von der Goltz, however, deprived the Ottoman army of an able leader. He was replaced by the less-competent Halil Pasha, Enver's uncle. Baghdad fell to General Maude's forces on March 11, 1917, and a further British offensive was launched toward the north. During the following months a junction was effected with the Russian army advancing toward the Mesopotamian border from Iran. As a result of the Russian revolution, this army rapidly began to disintegrate, and little could be expected from it in the way of effective co-operation. Despite this disappointment, British forces proceeded steadily northward and by October 1918 reached the outskirts of Mosul. At the time of the armistice, Mosul was still in Turkish hands. Following the withdrawal of the Turkish troops, however, it was promptly occupied by the British, an action which was later to lead to a bitter international controversy.

Operations in Southwestern Arabia

Isolated from the major theaters of war was a Turkish garrison in Yemen. In 1915 the Turks and their Yemenite vassals invaded the territory of the Aden Protectorate. Occupying Sheikh Said, these forces advanced toward the outskirts of Aden, which they besieged but failed to capture. This Turkish operation presented a real threat to British control of this important coaling station and military base. There was also a possibility of losing to the Turks the small but strategically situated island of Perim at the southern entrance to the Red Sea. Perim was a cable station vital to the British network of communications. The Turkish-Yemenite operation was never coordinated with other major actions of the Central powers and was therefore unlikely to affect the general course of the war.

Operations in Transcaucasia

The Russian revolution and Soviet willingness to conclude a separate peace with the Central powers had many important consequences to Turko-German relations. The Turkish government sent Ibrahim Hakki Pasha and Zeki Pasha, ambassador and military attaché, respectively, in Berlin, to Brest-Litovsk as official delegates. The grand vizier, Talaat Pasha, eventually appeared in person to support Turkish claims. These claims included (1) the return of Kars, Ardahan, and Batum; (2) freedom of action in the Caucasus and in Iran; and (3) access to raw materials. Thus formulated, these claims represented a Pan-Turanian program. Germany supported these demands, but somewhat reluctantly since they were bound to complicate the future course of Soviet-German relations and since, as pointed out previously, they diverted Turkish attention from the prosecution of the war on other fronts in the Middle East. At any rate, Turkey's value to Germany as an ally had become questionable. It was felt in Berlin that the Turks had become more of a burden than an asset. The fact that Turkey kept the Straits closed to the Entente navies—originally a most important service from the German point of view—had lost much of its earlier significance. Now, because of Rumania's defeat and Russia's defection, the Entente no longer had any military interest in the Black Sea.

The outcome of German-Soviet negotiations was the Treaty of Brest-Litovsk of March 3, 1918, by which Russia ceded to Turkey the districts of Kars, Ardahan, and Batum. This cession had a nominal and historical value only. In reality, the Soviet government had lost control of the Caucasus as a result of the nationalist movement there. Three important ethnic groups in Transcaucasia—Armenians, Georgians, and Azerbaijanis—in December 1917 had created a Transcaucasian Seym (parliament), which proclaimed the inde-

61

pendence of the region. This coincided with the dissolution of Russian rule in Transcaucasia and the melting away of the Russian troops from the Turkish front. Not all the troops, however, deserted their positions; the Armenian and Georgian formations of the former tsarist army, for instance, remained on the front and did their utmost to stem the advance of the Turks. With its proclamation of independence, the Transcaucasian Seym assumed responsibility and command over these troops and added to them some freshly organized national formations composed of Armenians and Georgians. On December 5, 1917, the Seym managed to conclude an armistice, which was soon to be broken by a fresh Turkish advance. In this offensive the Turks not only enjoyed a superiority in numbers but also profited from inner dissensions within the enemy camp. These dissensions were due to the reluctance of the Azeris (Azerbaijanis) to co-operate with the Georgians and the Armenians. In fact, the Azeris, although members of the Transcaucasian Federation, welcomed the Turkish advance. Susceptible to Pan-Turanian ideology, they expected Turkey to protect their newly won independence from their traditional oppressor, Russia. Hence they refused outright to send troops to stop the Turkish invasion and to co-operate with other members of the Federation.

These weaknesses in the Federation led its leaders to sue for peace. Between March 1 and April 1, 1918, negotiations were conducted with the Turks in Trebizond, but they yielded nothing positive. After obtaining a legal title to Kars, Batum, and Ardahan (Georgian and Armenian areas) on March 3 at Brest-Litovsk, the Turks demanded formal recognition of this cession by the Transcaucasian Federation as a prerequisite to further negotiations. Failing to receive it, they resumed hostilities and, in a swift advance, occupied Batum on April 1 and Kars on April 12. Thereupon, the Seym renewed its plea for peace, this time on the basis of the Brest-Litovsk Treaty.[21]

The new conference, which opened in Batum on May 11, was accompanied by unceasing hostilities, especially between the Turkish and the Armenian formations. The Turks presented peace terms that were much harsher than those offered at Trebizond. They demanded important coastal regions of Georgia and impressive areas of Armenia. The latter, under these terms, was to be reduced to an

[21] For a more detailed account of Transcaucasian negotiations, see Larchea, *op. cit.*, pp. 140 ff., and Vratzian, *op. cit.*, pp. 32 ff.

area of 11,000 square miles around Erivan, the rest going either to Turkey or to what was expected to be the independent state of Azerbaijan. Apart from these territorial concessions the Turkish terms provided for virtual Turkish control of Transcaucasia politically, strategically, and economically. The harshness of Turkish terms so far as Georgian and Armenian territory was concerned and the friendly overtures to the Azeris deepened the dissensions within the Transcaucasian Federation and brought on the inevitable crisis. In order to salvage as much as they could from the disaster, the Georgians appealed to Germany for help. General von Lossow, German plenipotentiary at the Batum conference, was sympathetic toward the Georgian plea, as was the German government. On May 26, 1918, unable to continue collaboration, the Seym, at its meeting in Tiflis, proclaimed the dissolution of the Transcaucasian Federation. On the same day Georgia proclaimed her independence and placed herself under German protection, which concretely meant the guarantee of her borders against Turkish encroachments. Not displeased with this action, Azerbaijan promptly followed suit and proclaimed independence on May 26. Left alone Armenia did the same on May 28, 1918, although she would have preferred a continuation of Transcaucasian collaboration.

Faced with these developments the Turkish delegation now presented its peace terms to the three newly formed republics in the form of an ultimatum. This ultimatum affected Armenia chiefly, since Georgia enjoyed German protection, and Azerbaijan was being courted by the Turks. On June 4, 1918, the Treaty of Batum was concluded between Turkey, on the one hand, and the Georgians, Armenians and Azerbaijanis, on the other. Georgia kept Batum, but Armenia had to agree to considerable shrinkage in her territory. In addition, Armenia undertook to evacuate her troops which, as a result of wartime developments, were in Baku.

Thus Turkish plans regarding Transcaucasia were nearly fulfilled. The Turks, to be sure, had to renounce their designs on Georgia. The Georgians were soon encouraged by the arrival of a German division, under Colonel Kress von Kressenstein, which promptly occupied Batum and stood guard at other strategic points in the territory. A political and economic treaty with Germany, giving the latter virtual control over her resources, completed Georgia's dependence on Berlin. As to Armenia, the Turks had the satisfaction of seeing her territorially reduced and politically humiliated. A direct connection with Azerbaijan was established and the road seemed open for the fulfillment of the boldest Pan-Turanian dreams. These appeared to be close to realization because of the steps toward liberation being taken simultaneously by various Turkic groups in Russia. As a result of the March and November 1917 revolutions in Russia, the following Moslem groups attempted emancipation from Russian rule:

The Tatars of Crimea (proclaimed a republic, December 26, 1917)
The mountaineers of North Caucasus (formed the North-Caucasian Union, Sept. 20, 1917)
The Tatars of Kazan (proclaimed a republic in October 1917)
The Kirghiz of Orenburg (proclaimed independence on Dec. 20, 1917)
The Moslems of Turkestan (proclaimed independence in Kokand, December 1917)

To this should be added strong nationalist and emancipatory movements among the Bashkirs of Ufa, the Turkoman tribes of Transcaspia, and the khanates of Khiva and Bukhara.

To reach the heart of the Caucasus and to cross the Caspian Sea into Central Asia constituted the ultimate aim of the Pan-Turanians. The first step on this road was the conclusion of an alliance with the government of Azerbaijan in Ganja. This was done in the summer of 1918, and it resulted immediately in the recruitment of an auxiliary, all-Islam army, composed of Azeris, Ajars, and other Caucasian Moslems, to assist the main body of the Turkish army. This new force was put under the command of Enver's brother, Nuri Pasha, who had just arrived from Turkey and who was known for his Pan-Turanian ideas. The liberation of Baku, the most important center of the Azerbaijan Republic, was his first task as the new commander. Baku was the only city in Transcaucasia which remained under Russian control after the revolution. Its history had been stormy. Following the creation of the Transcaucasian Seym, Baku had become an integral part of the Transcaucasian Federation, a state of affairs which did not last long. In March 1918, the local Communist Party staged a successful coup and established a soviet under the leadership of one Stepan Shaumian, an Armenian friend of Lenin. The coup was not a mere palace revolution, and it deeply affected the Moslem masses of the city, on whom the Bolsheviks—many of them Armenians—committed shocking atrocities. It has been estimated that 10,000 Moslems perished during these few days of bloodshed. The fact that Baku was thus separated from the new republic of Azerbaijan meant that a mere political agreement between the republic and Turkey was not sufficient to assure possession of the city. It had to be conquered, and to that end the efforts of the Turkish and the All-Islam armies were directed.

Had it been only a question of capturing the city from the Bolsheviks, the problem would have been simple enough for the Turks. The Turkish forces were superior in numbers and organization, enjoyed the friendship of the population in the Azerbaijan countryside, and in case of fierce resistance could have besieged the city and starved it into submission. But, as it happened, it was not a matter of a military operation alone. There arose two complications, which were bound to make the Turkish task more difficult. The first was the German attitude. Germany viewed with definite disfavor unilateral Turkish action in this region and was ready to take her own action to frustrate Turkish plans. This had been proved earlier in Germany's sudden assumption of a protectorate over Georgia and in the occupation of Batum by the Kress division. Having succeeded in ousting the Turks from Batum, the Germans now attempted to gain control of Baku before the Turks could establish themselves there. With this purpose, the German government, in constant contact with Soviet leaders since Brest-Litovsk, concluded an agreement with Moscow, by which Soviet Russia authorized Germany to draw upon the oil resources of Baku and to organize its defense against the attack of any third party. In fulfillment of this agreement, which was later formulated as an addition to the Brest-Litovsk Treaty, a German military mission was dispatched to Baku via Astrakhan at the end of July 1918. The Soviet-German agreement provided that, in case of a Turkish approach to Baku, Germany would have to engage in hostilities against her own ally. This agreement bears witness to the extent of the deterioration in German-Turkish relations in the summer of 1918. Actually, an open clash between the two allies never came, because the German mission to Baku was not permitted to begin its real work. This was due to the fact that the Bolshevik soviet in Baku was overthrown by a rival group of Social Revolutionaries while the German mission was en route to the city (July 26). The so-called Centro-Caspian Dictatorship was subsequently established there. The new masters of the city were anti-German, and, when the German mission arrived by boat from Astrakhan on August 4, it was promptly arrested.

The sudden change of government in Baku presented the Turkish command with a new complication. The Social-Revolutionary dictators asked the British for aid, which was promptly extended to them. The British had viewed with great concern the Turko-German advance in the Caucasus as the result of the dissolution of the Russian army and were anxious to fill the gap created in the eastern front. The original British plan was to establish liaison with the three Transcaucasian republics and, exploiting their desire for independence, to assist them in the formation and training of their national armies. British representatives were sent to Tiflis to treat with the Transcaucasian nationalists, but their overtures found ready response only among the Armenians. The Georgians preferred, as we have seen, to seek German protection, which was readily available. The Azerbaijanis were pro-Turkish, and the city of Baku had been dominated since March 1918 by the Bolsheviks, who even in the face of the Turkish advance were not prepared to ask the British "imperialists" for help. After the overthrow of Bolshevik rule in the city, however, the British could gain access to it and thus take the first step toward the defense of Transcaucasia. Major General L. C. Dunsterville was dispatched with a brigade of troops through Iran and across the Caspian Sea and arrived in Baku in the middle of August. Despite his best efforts, his attempts to organize an efficient defense of the city failed, mainly because of the failure of the dictators to live up to their promises. Convinced that to remain in Baku under such circumstances would be suicidal, Dunsterville, after a few preliminary engagements with the Turks, evacuated his troops and went back to Iran.[22] The city was left to its own devices, and soon, on September 14, fell to the Turks and the All-Islam army. Bitter over the spring massacre of their coreligionists, the Moslems now vented their anger on the Armenian population of Baku. The loss of life ran into the thousands.

The conquest of Baku opened before the Turks very alluring Pan-Turanian vistas. One had only to cross the Caspian at its narrowest point to reach Qizil Su (Krasnovodsk) and to emerge in force onto the Turkoman Steppe, from which could be reached the vast expanse of Turkestan.

This possibility roused British fears, since such an advance of the Central powers, if successful, might bring them to Afghanistan and hence to the gates of India. There might then be an uprising in the

[22] L. C. Dunsterville, *The Adventures of Dunsterforce* (London, 1920).

Moslem provinces of the Indian Empire. It will be remembered that
to forestall such a move the British maintained during the war the
so-called East Persia Cordon, a line of troops along the Afghan
border, which at a certain point touched the line of tsarist Russian
troops. The melting away of the Russian troops in 1918 led the British to extend this cordon up to the border of Russia, and even into
Transcaspia when called to assist the Russian counterrevolutionary
center that had formed in Ashkhabad. This British action was later
developed into full-fledged military operations directed against the
Bolsheviks in Transcaspia.

As it happened, the Turks never crossed the Caspian. Within two
months after the conquest of Baku, the Ottoman government sued
for peace. The armistice of Mudros, October 30, 1918, put an end to
the hostilities between Turkey and the Entente powers. The armistice
with Germany followed on November 11.

WAR AIMS AND POLITICAL STRATEGY
OF THE ENTENTE

From a purely military standpoint, the Turkish belligerency was
an unpleasant fact for all the countries of the Entente, and all would
have preferred to see Turkey remain neutral. But there the unanimity
ended. To Russia, war against Turkey meant an opportunity to attain her traditional desire of controlling the Straits and, perhaps, of
dismembering the Ottoman Empire. As a long-range proposition,
there was no incompatibility between the basic ambitions of Russia and her struggle with Turkey. This was not the case with England. To the British, war with the Ottoman Empire was a paradox
and a diplomatic tragedy. It meant the end of their long-standing
policy of supporting Turkey and of the well-fixed axiom that Ottoman integrity and sovereignty must be preserved as a bulwark of
the British imperial life line. Now Great Britain was to lead the
Allies in defeating her traditional friend. To aggravate matters, this
defeat, as planned by the Entente, was to be not only military
but also political. It was to lead to the extinction of the Ottoman
Empire.

Russia was determined to obtain control of Constantinople and
of the Straits and to secure territorial gains in eastern Anatolia. Italy
had to be bribed into joining the war by specific promises of political and territorial concessions, some of them at the expense of
Turkey. Greece had to be cajoled onto the side of the Entente by a

variety of dubious maneuvers and promises, which included territorial gains on the Turkish Aegean coast. And finally, it was necessary for Britain and France to reach a harmonious settlement of their respective claims. Realizing that the Ottoman Empire was doomed, Britain was not averse to claiming major portions of it for herself and was willing similarly to accommodate France. Furthermore, wartime expediency compelled Britain to reach an understanding with two other groups—the Arabs and the Zionists. This resulted in a network of agreements, some of them contradicting others but all designed to dismember the Ottoman Empire.[23]

Secret Partition Agreements

The Constantinople agreement

On March 18, 1915, a secret agreement was concluded by Russia, on the one hand, and Great Britain and France, on the other, through an exchange of notes between St. Petersburg, Paris, and London. Russia was to annex "Constantinople, the western coast of the Bosphorus, the Sea of Marmara, and the Dardanelles; Southern Thrace as far as the Enos-Midia line; the coast of Asia Minor between the Bosphorus and the river Sakaria and a point on the Gulf of Ismid to be defined later; the islands in the Sea of Marmara and the Islands of Imbros and Tenedos."

In return, Russia recognized a number of claims made by Britain and France:

1) *Concerning Turkey*

    a) Constantinople was to become a free port for the Allies, and freedom of commercial navigation was assured in the Straits.

    b) Russia agreed to recognize the special rights of Britain and France in Asiatic Turkey through a separate agreement.

    c) The Moslem holy places were to be detached from Turkey and, together with Arabia, placed under independent Moslem rule.

2) *Concerning Iran*

    a) Russia agreed to the inclusion of the neutral zone, as provided by the Anglo-Russian agreement of 1907, in the British sphere of influence.

    b) However, to this agreement there were three reservations: first, that the districts adjoining the cities of Isfahan and Yazd should be included in the Russian sphere; second, that

[23] For relevant texts, see H. W. V. Temperley, ed., *A History of the Peace Conference of Paris* (London, 1924), VI, 1–22; also F. Seymour Cocks, ed., *The Secret Treaties and Understandings* (London, n.d.).

a portion of the eastern extremity of the neutral zone, which adjoins the Afghan territory, should be included in the Russian zone; and third, that Russia gain full freedom of action in her own zone of influence. (This last reservation meant virtual annexation of the zone in the long run.)

In addition to these territorial arrangements, Russia pledged assistance to the Allies in case they attacked the Dardanelles. Italy, upon her declaration of war, gave her consent to this Russo-Anglo-French agreement.

The Constantinople agreement formally marked the end of a century-old British policy. The capital of the once mighty Empire was to pass into the control of the Russians, who were to enjoy free access to warm waters, provided, of course, the war against Turkey was victorious.

The Treaty of London

On April 26, 1915, a secret treaty was signed in London by Britain, France, Russia, and Italy. This treaty was the price paid by the Allies for Italy's joining the Allied camp. Of the many territorial concessions promised the Italians, the following pertained to the Middle East:

1) Italy was given full sovereignty over the strategic Dodecanese Islands off the Turkish coast, under Italian occupation since 1912 (Art. 8).
2) All rights and privileges in Libya belonging to the sultan by virtue of the Treaty of Lausanne (1912) were transferred to Italy (Art. 10).
3) Article 9, the most important, stated:

> Generally speaking, France, Great Britain, and Russia recognize that Italy is interested in the Mediterranean, and that in the event of a total or partial partition of Turkey-in-Asia, she [Italy] ought to obtain a just share of the Mediterranean region adjacent to the province of Adalia, where Italy has already acquired rights and interests which formed the subject of an Italo-British convention. The zone which shall eventually be allotted to Italy shall be delimited, at the proper time, due account being taken of the existing interests of France and Great Britain.
>
> The interests of Italy shall also be taken into consideration in the event of the territorial integrity of the Turkish Empire being maintained and of alterations being made in the zones of interest of the Powers.
>
> If France, Great Britain and Russia occupy any territories in Turkey-in-Asia during the course of the War, the Mediterranean region bor-

dering on the province of Adalia within the limits indicated above shall be reserved to Italy, who shall be entitled to occupy it.[24]

As may be seen from this text, Italy's territorial claim in Anatolia was very vaguely described and could lend itself to varying interpretations. On the other hand, Italy took the precaution, as the second paragraph indicates, to safeguard her interests in the case of unforeseen changes. This passage was to serve later as legal justification for Italy's discontent with the peace settlement, insofar as it affected the Middle East.

Armed with these assurances, Italy declared war on Turkey on August 20, 1915.

The Sykes-Picot agreement

Having satisfied the main demands of Russia and Italy, the French and British governments proceeded in 1915 to adjust their own claims to the Asiatic portions of the Ottoman Empire. Sir Mark Sykes and Georges Picot were appointed to conduct negotiations. It must be pointed out that Britain had, in the meantime, entered into negotiations with Sherif Hussein of the Hejaz, with the object of securing his assistance in the war against Turkey; this assistance was to be made conditional upon British recognition of Arab national aspirations. The French government, aware of the possibility of an exclusive Arab-British deal and eager to secure for itself a portion of the Ottoman Empire, pressed for definite recognition of its claims. Such an understanding had been foreseen in the Constantinople agreement. Proceeding thus to define their rights, France and Britain desired to secure Russian approval, and for this purpose Sykes and Picot were sent to St. Petersburg in the early spring of 1916. There they presented their draft agreement and secured Russia's approval, at the price, however, of recognizing further Russian claims. This bargain was subsequently formalized on April 26, 1916, under the name of the Sazonov-Paléologue agreement.[25] It formed an integral part of the general settlement reached between Russia, France, and Great Britain usually referred to as the Sykes-Picot agreement. Officially the Sykes-Picot agreement was concluded on May 16, 1916, and contained the following provisions:

1) Russia was to obtain the provinces of Erzerum, Trebizond, Van, and Bitlis (known as Turkish Armenia), as well as territory in

[24] Temperley, op. cit., pp. 19, 20.

[25] Sazonov was Russian foreign minister and Paléologue French ambassador in Russia.

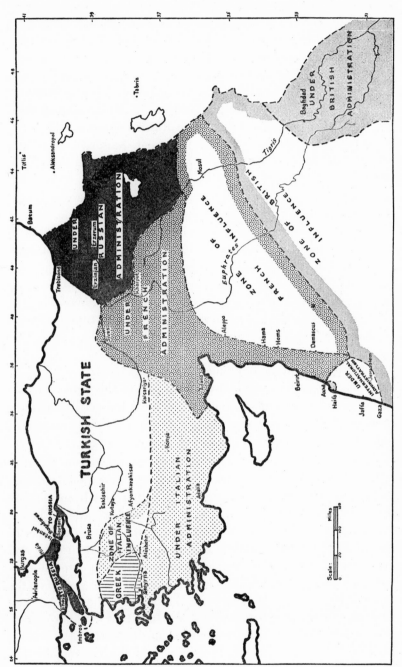

Map 2. The partitioning of Turkey according to the secret agreements of 1915–1917.

the northern part of Kurdistan, along the line from Mush, Sairt, Ibn Omar, and Amadiya, to the Iranian border. This represented an impressive area of 60,000 square miles between the Black Sea and the Mosul-Urumia region, containing rich deposits of copper, silver, and salt.

2) France was to obtain the coastal strip of Syria, the vilayet of Adana, and the territory bounded in the south by a line from Aintab and Mardin to the future Russian frontier, and in the north by a line from Ala Dagh through Kaisariya, Ak-Dagh, Jildiz-Dagh, and Zara to Egin-Kharput (the area commonly known as Cilicia).

3) Great Britain was to obtain southern Mesopotamia with Baghdad, as well as the ports of Haifa and Acre in Palestine.

4) The zone between the French and British territories was to form a confederation of Arab states or one independent Arab state. This zone was to be further divided into a French and a British sphere of influence. The French sphere was to include the Syrian hinterland and the Mosul province of Mesopotamia. The British sphere was to extend over the territory between Palestine and the Iranian border.

5) Alexandretta was proclaimed a free port.

6) Palestine was to be internationalized.

Since secrecy was deemed an essential part of this agreement, its terms were not communicated either to Italy or to Sherif Hussein.

The St. Jean de Maurienne agreement

Despite the original secrecy of the Sykes-Picot agreement, the Italian government knew about its terms by early 1917. Consequently, Italy pressed the other three powers for a precise definition of those Italian claims in Asia Minor that had been vaguely referred to as a "region adjacent to the province of Adalia" in the London Treaty of 1915. On April 17, 1917, the prime ministers of Great Britain, France, and Italy met at St. Jean de Maurienne and there drew up an agreement that gave Italy the right to annex a large tract of purely Turkish land in southwestern Anatolia (the vilayet and city of Smyrna, the sanjaks of Menteshe, Adalia, and Itchili, and the greater part of the vilayet of Konia). In addition to this, Italy obtained a sphere of influence north of Smyrna.

The St. Jean de Maurienne agreement was the last major inter-Allied understanding concerning the partitioning of Ottoman territory. It was subject to the approval of the Russians, who were absent from the conference. This approval was never given as a result of the revolutionary change of government in Russia.

The Clemenceau–Lloyd George agreement

Following the victorious campaign in Mesopotamia, the British found themselves in occupation of the Mosul area. Inasmuch as most of the fighting in the Middle East had been done by the British, the latter believed that some revision of the Sykes-Picot treaty was needed in order to compensate them. In December 1918, during Clemenceau's visit to London, the French and the British prime ministers reached an agreement by which France consented to the inclusion of the Mosul area (formerly in the French zone) in Britain's sphere of influence. In return, France was promised a share in the north-Mesopotamian oil deposits.

British-Arab Negotiations and Agreements

The existence of a strong nationalist movement among the Arabs of the Ottoman Empire has already been mentioned. This spirit of independence manifested itself through (1) nationalist agitation and conspiratorial activities among the educated Arabs in Syria, (2) assertions of independence by the chieftains of central and eastern Arabia, and (3) the independent course pursued by the Sherif of Mecca.

Aware of these manifestations, the British decided early in the war to use Arab nationalism to their own advantage. The immediate aim was to secure Arab military support in the war against Turkey. The long-range objective was to create an independent Arab state or confederation of states, which was to serve as a substitute for the Ottoman Empire. Such a confederation was envisaged as taking over the traditional role of a friendly Moslem power serving as a bulwark of defense for the British life line to India. This scheme had the virtue of solving a serious dilemma which had beset British foreign policy ever since England found herself compelled to cross swords with Turkey. The British had to decide which group of Arabs in the Ottoman Empire was representative enough to warrant the opening of negotiations. The Syrian intellectual nationalists were the most outspoken, and the most politically conscious, in a modern sense. They were, however, physically inaccessible, since Damascus and Beirut were deep within Turkish lines and under the firm control of the Turkish authorities. The only area relatively free from Turkish control was Arabia. Here the British concentrated their

73

efforts, which were twofold. There were agreements with Ibn Saud, ruler of the Nejd and its dependencies, and negotiations and agreement with Emir Hussein of Mecca.

Two things are worthy of note with regard to British action toward Ibn Saud. First, these negotiations were the responsibility of the government of India; consequently, they bore the imprint of the Indian school of diplomacy. Secondly, they were conducted for the short-range objective of securing the friendship or at least the neutrality of the ruler of the Nejd during the military operations in Mesopotamia. It will be remembered that the government of India was opposed to provoking a large-scale Arab uprising against the caliph, did not want active Arab participation in the campaign against Turkey, and gave little thought to the ultimate creation of an Arab kingdom to replace the Ottoman Empire. Indian policy was motivated by local considerations and in particular by the fear of complications with Indian Moslems if the policy of Britain was too hostile to the caliph.[26] The government of India sent the consul at Kuwait, Captain J. R. Shakespear, on a mission to Ibn Saud. The mission was successful. The visit of Sir Percy Cox, British resident in the Persian Gulf, followed, and the conclusion of a treaty of friendship came on December 26, 1915. This treaty was patterned after the treaties concluded earlier with the various chiefs of the Gulf states. The government of India recognized Ibn Saud as ruler of the Nejd and its dependencies, promised to defend him against aggression, and granted him an annual subsidy. In return, Ibn Saud pledged not to alienate any portion of his domain to foreign powers, to refrain from attacking the British-protected sheikhs along the Gulf coast, and to maintain friendly relations with Great Britain.

This treaty did not result in Ibn Saud's taking up arms against the Turks, but it did contribute to favorable developments in Arabia. Ibn Saud fought against the powerful pro-Turkish clan of the Rashids, did not respond to the Sultan's appeal for a jihad, and prevented the Turks from being supplied by sea via the Persian Gulf coast. He also refrained from attacking Sherif Hussein, with whom he might easily have picked a quarrel over some borderlands in central Arabia. His contribution to the British war effort was thus passive, but not negligible. A British mission under H. St. John Philby and Lord Belhaven added to the mutual good will.[27]

[26] See below, pp. 94, 431 ff.

[27] On British-Nejd negotiations, see H. St. John B. Philby, *Arabia* (London, 1930).

British negotiations with Emir Hussein of Mecca followed a separate course and resulted in very radical changes in the Arab situation in the Ottoman Empire. Hussein had spent many years in forced exile in Constantinople, had been appointed emir of Mecca in 1908, and by 1914 had established himself as a powerful influence in the Arab world. Having long hoped for the creation of an independent Arab kingdom and certainly not devoid of personal ambition, Hussein felt that World War I provided an excellent opportunity to realize his dreams. His unquestioned adherence to the holy war would have been of invaluable assistance to Turkey, but Hussein chose to temporize and gave the Porte various excuses of a practical nature for his delay. As early as February 1914, during a visit in Cairo, Hussein's second son, Emir Abdullah, sounded out the British on whether or not they were prepared to enter into an agreement with the Arabs. On this occasion Abdullah saw Lord Kitchener, then British high commissioner in Egypt, and intimated that the Arabs were ready for revolt if the British could give assurances of support. These suggestions first met with skepticism, but when the war began London and Cairo gave them more serious thought. Upon Kitchener's advice (he had become secretary of war in the meantime), Sir Reginald Wingate, governor general of the Sudan, and Sir Henry McMahon, high commissioner in Egypt, kept in touch with Sherif Hussein, and before long this evolved into full-scale negotiations.[28]

While these negotiations were underway, Hussein in the spring of 1915 sent his third son, Emir Faisal, to Damascus on a mission to reassure the Turkish authorities of his loyalty and also to sound out Arab public opinion in this important center of nationalist propaganda. It is noteworthy that Faisal was originally pro-Turkish and did not share his father's enthusiasm for a British alliance. His visit to Damascus completely changed his attitude. There he learned of the iron rule of Jemal Pasha and of the profound discontent of the Arab population. Moreover, he was initiated into Arab secret societies. Representatives of these societies were advocating Arab revolt and a British alliance, to be based on acceptance by the latter of a set of definite conditions. These conditions, known as the Damascus Protocol, were handed over to Faisal for transmission to his father. Subsequently they constituted the basis of Hussein's terri-

[28] A vivid account of these negotiations may be found in Antonius, *op. cit.*, chs. vii, viii, and ix, and in Ronald Storrs, *Orientations*, ch. viii.

torial demands in the course of his negotiations with Great Britain.

The agreement which emerged had the form of a series of letters, exchanged between the British high commissioner in Cairo, Sir Henry McMahon, and Sherif Hussein. Hussein promised to declare war on Turkey and to raise an Arab army which would assist the British in their military operations. Sir Henry McMahon, acting on the instructions of the British government, pledged England to support "the independence of the Arabs" in the large area bounded, in the north by the 37th parallel, in the east by the Iranian border down to the Persian Gulf, and in the south by the Arab Gulf states. As to the western boundary, Hussein demanded the Red Sea and the Mediterranean coast; McMahon while readily admitting the Red Sea boundary, excluded from his pledge the whole coastal belt of Syria "lying to the west of the districts of Damascus, Homs, Hama and Aleppo." This meant the exclusion of Lebanon and the Alawi country to the north but left considerable uncertainty about Palestine.

In addition to this basic recognition of Arab nationalist claims, Great Britain guaranteed the holy places against external aggression and promised advice and assistance in the establishment of new Arab governments. In return she secured the exclusive right of such advice and reserved for herself special administrative privileges in the vilayets of Baghdad and Basra. A corollary to this agreement granted Sherif Hussein substantial British subsidies in gold (amounting to £200,000 a month).[29]

On the strength of this agreement the Sherif gave the signal for the Arab Revolt on June 5, 1916. On November 2, 1916, Hussein proclaimed himself "King of the Arab Countries." This act proved to be too hasty and caused the British much embarrassment, especially in their relations with France. Eventually, a compromise formula was devised, according to which the Allies addressed Hussein as king of the Hejaz.

McMahon's pledge to Hussein preceded by six months the Sykes-Picot agreement. The latter was obviously incompatible with the former and, to put it bluntly, constituted a breach of the pledge to the Arabs. Its existence, therefore, was not disclosed to Sherif Hussein, except for some vague references to the need of harmonizing action with France, made during the visit which Sir Mark Sykes and Georges Picot paid to the Sherif in Jidda in May 1917.

[29] Toynbee, *op. cit.*, p. 283.

Not until December 1917 did Hussein learn the truth about the Sykes-Picot agreement. Upon seizing power in Russia, the Soviet government promptly published the secret wartime agreements found in the archives of the tsarist Foreign Ministry. These included the Sykes-Picot treaty. Turkish authorities communicated it through secret emissaries to Sherif Hussein and, pointing out British treachery, exhorted him to break with Britain and return "to the fold of the Caliph and of Islam." [30]

Profoundly disturbed, Hussein requested clarification from his British allies but obtained only vague replies, which could have been considered half-admissions and half-denials. Hoping for the best, the Arab ruler still decided to remain faithful to his ally.

Britain's Pledge to the Zionists

From the British point of view, the secret wartime agreements were dictated by the imperative necessity of gaining allies for the sake of winning the war. Russia, Italy, France, and the Arabs were such allies. It was also believed in Great Britain that an understanding with the Zionists would produce a new ally in the form of world Jewry. [31]

The Zionists, under the leadership of Dr. Chaim Weizmann, a lecturer in chemistry at Manchester University, were active in England during the war. Dr. Weizmann, who materially contributed to the British war effort by discovering a new method of producing acetone, attracted the attention of British officials to Zionist aspirations as early as 1914. Initially the outbreak of the war complicated the task of the Zionists. Zionism was an international movement, and the splitting of the world into two hostile camps was not conducive to the smoothness of organizational activity. Before the war, Zionist endeavors had been directed toward an understanding with the Ottoman Empire, as a controlling power in Palestine. The world headquarters of the Zionist Organization was situated in Berlin under the protective wing, so to speak, of the German government. Zionism had taken firm root in Russia, and the most ardent Zionists were Russian Jews. Russia's record of persecution, exclusion, and pogroms made these Zionist leaders intensely anti-Russian. Presented with an emotional and political choice between the cause of the Central

[30] A detailed story of the British-Arab diplomacy is contained in Antonius, *op. cit.*

[31] For a history of Zionism, see pp. 312–316.

powers and the cause of the Allies (including Russia), leading Zionists ardently hoped for Russia's defeat. Such a defeat at the hands of Germany would have meant a grave embarrassment if not actual disaster for the Allies. It followed, therefore, that Zionist political sympathies and the vital interests of the Allies were hardly compatible.

Inasmuch, however, as it was too risky for the future of the movement openly to join Germany, the Inner Actions Committee (the policy-making organ of the Zionist Organization) established a bureau in Copenhagan to stress their outward neutrality. Furthermore, aware of Dr. Weizmann's activity in Great Britain, the Actions Committee discouraged his intercourse with British statesmen.

These steps did not deflect Weizmann from his purpose. In order to secure freedom of action, he cut off his contacts with the Copenhagen bureau.[32] In his pro-Ally policy he was supported by two eminent European Zionists, Sokolow and Tschlenow, who arrived in London in November 1914. He was also in touch with American Zionists. The latter, upon the outbreak of war in Europe, held an extraordinary conference and reached a decision to conduct Zionist policy autonomously in view of the practical dissolution of the Berlin headquarters. A Provisional Executive Committee for General Zionist affairs, which was then established, included Justice of the United States Supreme Court Louis Dembitz Brandeis as chairman, Rabbi Stephen S. Wise as vice-chairman, and Jacob de Haas as secretary. Among its members were Nathan Strauss, Professor Felix Frankfurter, Judge Julian W. Mack, Eugene Meyer, and a number of other prominent American Jews.

The aim of Zionists in Great Britain and in the United States was to obtain a guarantee from the Allies that, in the event of Turkey's defeat, Palestine would be recognized as a Jewish commonwealth, unrestrictedly open to immigration. To this end, Weizmann secured the sympathy and actual collaboration of a number of public figures in Great Britain. Among them were C. P. Scott and Herbert Sidebotham of the *Manchester Guardian,* who helped in organizing the British Palestine Committee; such prominent British Jews as Sir Herbert Samuel and the Rothschilds; and, finally, Lord A. J. Balfour, Britain's foreign secretary. Weizmann's talks on the government level were well advanced by 1916. Early in 1917 Sir Mark Sykes was instructed to open formal negotiations on behalf of the Allies with Nahum Sokolow, acting for the International Zionist Organization.

[32] Chaim Weizmann, *Trial and Error* (Philadelphia, 1949).

The spring of 1917 brought two dramatic developments which proved to be decisive for the success of the Zionist cause. The first was the revolution in Russia; the second, America's entry into the war. The western Allies were intensely interested in keeping Russia in the war and in preventing a separate peace treaty with Germany. Prime Minister Lloyd George as well as Lord Balfour believed that, in view of the prominence of the Jews in the Russian revolutionary movement, it was essential to acquire their good will by responding favorably to Zionist aspirations.[33] It was also important to obtain full co-operation and maximum effort from Britain's new ally, the United States. Here, too, it was believed, the Jews could render inestimable service. Moreover, an Allied pronouncement in favor of Zionism might win over German Jewry to the Allied cause and, indirectly, help in producing internal disaffection in the Central powers. While, according to available evidence, these were the real reasons for Britain's decision to satisfy the Zionists, emotional motives guiding some statesmen and certain segments of the Allied public opinion should not be underestimated. Christian charity toward a persecuted race, the Old Testament heritage so important in shaping the historical consciousness of some Protestant groups, and democratic liberalism added the glow of virtue to purely practical calculations, or appealed to those for whom *Realpolitik* was not a sufficient inducement. In the United States where the Jewish population was fairly large, considerations of internal politics constituted an additional incentive to support Zionism.

In their negotiations with Great Britain, the Zionists insisted upon a British protectorate over Palestine as the best guarantee for the success of their program. This involved the repudiation of that part of the Sykes-Picot agreement which provided for the internationalization of the Holy Land. This amounted to another contradictory pledge. The British government was not averse to accepting this Zionist proposal.[34]

In May 1917 Britain's foreign secretary, Lord Balfour, paid a visit to the United States. There he talked to Justice Brandeis, both a leading Zionist and a close adviser of President Wilson. The British cabinet before committing itself desired to arrange for a formal endorsement by President Wilson of a pro-Zionist pronouncement. In the meantime American Zionists displayed energetic activity in a number of appeals. These appeals did not fall on deaf ears; they

[33] For Lloyd George's postwar testimony on this subject, see below, p. 82.
[34] J. M. N. Jeffries, *Palestine: The Reality* (London, 1939), pp. 141, 144.

79

could finally count on the support of eminent men in American official circles. William J. Bryan, Secretary of State; Robert Lansing; Newton D. Baker, Secretary of War; Josephus Daniels, Secretary of the Navy; Col. Edward House, and Norman Hapgood, all favored the Zionist aspirations. President Wilson not only supported Zionism but referred to himself as a Zionist in the course of his discussions with Brandeis, Frankfurter, and Wise.[35]

The Zionists' aim was to obtain from the President a public statement in support of Zionism. This Wilson was unwilling to make at that time, since the United States was not at war with Turkey. But following an official British inquiry addressed to Colonel House, Wilson instructed him, on October 16, 1917, to approve the pro-Zionist draft declaration proposed by the the British cabinet. Commenting on this memorable act, Dr. Weizmann stated in his memoirs: "This was one of the most important individual factors in breaking the deadlock created by the British Jewish anti-Zionists, and in deciding the British Government to issue its declaration." [36]

Weizmann and his colleagues in Great Britain encountered more difficulties than did their counterparts in the United States. Two influential groups of English Jews voiced explicit opposition to Zionism. (See Chapter IX.) In the British government Edwin Montagu, member of a prominent Jewish family and secretary of state for India, very actively opposed the issuance of any pro-Zionist declaration. His, however, was the voice of the minority. Lloyd George, Balfour, Milner, General Smuts, and Cecil all tended to favor the Zionist cause and believed in the justice and expediency of such a policy.

Dr. Weizmann's political activity was seconded in the military sector by Vladimir Zhabotinsky and Pincus Ruthenberg, who advocated the establishment of a Jewish Legion during World War I under Allied command. Their efforts bore fruit. A Zion Mule Corps was created as an auxiliary unit in Allenby's army. Composed of Jewish expellees from Syria and Palestine and including many European and American Zionists, it participated, under Colonel Patterson's command, in the Gallipoli and later Middle Eastern campaigns.

On November 2, 1917, following acceptance by the British cabinet of the major points of the draft submitted by the Zionists, Lord Balfour addressed the following letter to Lord Rothschild:

[35] Reuben Fink, *America and Palestine* (New York, 1945), p. 30.
[36] Weizmann, *op. cit.*, I, 208.

DEAR LORD ROTHSCHILD,

I have much pleasure in conveying to you, on behalf of His Majesty's Government, the following declaration of sympathy with Jewish Zionist aspirations which has been submitted to, and approved by, the Cabinet.

His Majesty's Government view with favour the establishment in Palestine of a national home for the Jewish people, and will use their best endeavours to facilitate the achievement of this object, it being clearly understood that nothing shall be done which may prejudice the civil and religious rights of existing non-Jewish communities in Palestine, or the rights and political status enjoyed by Jews in any other country.

I should be grateful if you would bring this declaration to the knowledge of the Zionist Federation.

Yours sincerely,
ARTHUR JAMES BALFOUR

The declaration was well timed because shortly afterward (in December 1917 and July 1918) Turkey and Germany tried to win Jewish favor by offering the German Zionists a chartered company in Palestine.[37] It was, however, too late to change general pro-Ally Zionist orientation.

Their task in Britain finished, the Zionists turned now to the other Allied governments to secure their approval of the Declaration. They were successful; France approved the Declaration on February 11, 1918, and Italy followed suit on February 23, 1918. Two days before the Mudros armistice President Wilson gave his open support of the Declaration in a letter addressed to Rabbi Stephen S. Wise on October 29, 1918.

Thus the destinies of Zionism became closely linked with the Allied cause. The Zionists obtained a status of unofficial allies. The Foreign Office went so far as to grant them the privilege of British diplomatic pouch. In return the Zionists were expected to render valuable assistance in the prosecution of the war. The extent to which they contributed to the Allied victory is, obviously, hard to determine, but it may be helpful to quote Britain's wartime prime minister, David Lloyd George, who made the following statement before the Palestine Royal Commission in 1936: "The Zionist leaders gave us a definite promise that, if the Allies committed themselves to giving facilities for the establishment of a national home for the Jews in Palestine, they would do their best to rally Jewish sentiment and support throughout the

[37] Royal Institute of International Affairs, *Great Britain and Palestine, 1915–1945* (London, 1946), p. 10.

world to the Allied cause. They kept their word." [38] Amplifying this statement in the House of Commons in 1937, Lloyd George declared that the Zionists "were helpful in America and in Russia, which at that moment was just walking out and leaving us alone." [39]

When the news of the Declaration reached King Hussein, he requested elucidation from the British authorities. In response, the British sent to Arabia Commander D. G. Hogarth of the Arab Bureau in Cairo. On January 4, 1918, Hogarth delivered to Hussein a message in which he assured him that Britain's determination to assist the return of Jews to Palestine went only "so far as is compatible with the freedom of the existing population," and made no mention of a Jewish state. Hussein accepted the message but "spoke with a smile of accounts which he would settle after the war." [40]

As soon as the major part of Palestine was occupied by General Allenby, that is, just before the end of the war, Dr. Weizmann decided to visit the Holy Land. In March 1918, accompanied by several Zionist leaders and by Major Ormsby-Gore, acting as a British liaison officer, Weizmann journeyed to Jerusalem, where in an impressive ceremony he laid the cornerstone of the Hebrew University on Mount Scopus. The presence of this Zionist commission provoked adverse comments both among the Palestinian Arabs and the British officers of Allenby's staff. This was a foreshadowing of the difficulties to come.

In summing up the First World War in the Middle East, it should be stressed that political and ideological factors were as important as were military ones and that, in their complexity, the former often overshadowed the latter. On the one hand were the ambitious war aims of the Young Turkish group ruling the Ottoman Empire and the resulting interplay of Pan-Turanism, Pan-Islamism, and German imperialist ambitions. On the other was the Entente, with its often conflicting war aims, contradictory pledges, and simultaneous support of the hardly compatible claims of Zionism and Arab nationalism. Politically the war was a milestone in British foreign policy, reversing as it did traditional axioms and creating new problems for Great Britain in the Middle East.

Militarily the war could be conceived as an attempt by Turkey and Germany to expand southward and eastward by bold but ill-prepared

[38] Quoted by Joseph Dunner, *The Republic of Israel* (New York, 1950), p. 32.
[39] Jeffries, *op. cit.*, p. 190. See also R.I.I.A., *Great Britain and Palestine*, p. 9.
[40] R.I.I.A., *Great Britain and Palestine, 1915–1945*, p. 148.

moves, which soon brought their offensives to a halt. The Entente's strategy consisted in one attempt to strike a decisive blow at the heart of Turkey—the Gallipoli campaign—which ended in failure and was never repeated. Instead, the Allies undertook a slow movement directed from the extremities of the Ottoman Empire toward its center. Such were the Palestinian and Mesopotamian campaigns and the Russian campaign in East Anatolia. Russia's campaign, successful in the beginning, ended in failure as a result of the revolution and permitted the Turks, at the very end of the war, to obtain spectacular success in the Caucasus. This success came too late to change the general military situation and lasted too short a time to affect political developments very much. Yet it was indicative of certain long-range potentialities of Turkish foreign policy if it ever turned to Pan-Turanism. It was the victory of British arms in the general background of the Allied victory in Europe which ultimately proved decisive in the Middle East.

On October 31, 1918, Turkish and British plenipotentiaries, the latter acting for the Entente, signed the armistice of Mudros, which formally ended hostilities in the Middle East. The armistice authorized Allied troops to enter the hitherto unoccupied parts of Turkey. An Allied Control Commission appeared in Constantinople, and British, French, and Italian troops occupied large portions of southern Anatolia. For Turkey, the armistice was concluded by the new government of Izzet Pasha, a nonparty man, which had replaced the Union and Progress Party cabinet earlier in October. On the day of the armistice Enver, Talaat, and certain other Young Turkish politicians fled from Turkey to Germany. The Ottoman Empire lay in ruins. The victorious Allies faced a stupendous task of political and economic reconstruction in the area.

CHAPTER III

The Peace Settlement

WHEN the statesmen of the Entente met in Paris in January 1919 to discuss the peace treaties, they faced two categories of problems in the Middle East. One pertained to the actual military occupation of the area. The other, no less important, referred to secret wartime agreements.

With regard to the military occupation, the whole region could be roughly divided into three parts: the Arab countries, Turkey proper, and Iran. At the end of the war Iran was, to all practical purposes, under British military control, but she presented no major problem at the Paris Peace Conference, since Iran, as a nonbelligerent, did not participate in the conference. Of the Arab countries, Mesopotamia, Syria, and Palestine were under British occupation. The British shared their responsibility with their Arab allies under Emir Faisal. The latter established himself in Damascus and exercised authority delegated to him by General Allenby. The area under Faisal's command was known officially as Occupied Enemy Territory Administration (O.E.T.A.) East. Beirut and the Syrian coastal area were under direct British supervision. As to Turkey proper, certain parts were occupied, as we know, by Allied forces. The British first moved into Cilicia and Adana but later relinquished control of these provinces to France. Italy landed troops in Adalia. Constantinople was under a combined Allied occupation. The British occupied the major portions of the Ottoman Empire because they had carried on the major part of the military operations there. This placed them in a strong bargaining position at the Peace Conference.

The second problem concerned the wartime agreements. As we

84

have seen in the preceding chapter, these conflicted. The major difficulty grew out of the incompatibility of these imperialist arrangements with the national aspirations of the native populations. When the conferees met in Paris, it soon became obvious that at least six different and mutually contradictory claims or attitudes had to be faced. These may be summed up as follows:

1) *Britain vs. France.* Britain was interested in a revision of the Sykes-Picot treaty, in order that her promises to the Arabs and her own interests in the area might be satisfied. France reacted negatively to all such suggestions, insisting on her "pound of flesh" and vigorously invoking the Sykes-Picot provisions and her traditional interests in Syria. The French government was opposed to any concessions other than the one which gave Mosul to the British, which as we know had been made before the calling of the Peace Conference.[1]

2) *Arab claims.* Emir Faisal appeared at the conference as a delegate of the kingdom of the Hejaz and chief spokesman of the Arab cause. At a hearing before the Council of Ten, he insisted on the Arab right to self-determination and on the fulfillment of Allied promises to the Arabs.[2] His formal appearance at the conference was preceded by a state visit to France and England. In France he learned of French intransigence concerning Syria, and in England he was strongly advised to come to terms with the French and with the Zionists. Subjected to various pressures and not experienced in the ways of diplomacy, Faisal stood adamant on the principle of Arab independence, but was induced to sign an agreement with Dr. Weizmann. In this agreement, dated January 3, 1919, he welcomed Jewish immigration to Palestine, but in the postscript made his benevolent attitude to Zionism dependent upon the fulfillment of wartime promises of independence by Great Britain.

3) *Zionist claims.* Although the Zionists did not represent an established state, they sent a delegation which was accorded a rather friendly reception in Paris. The Zionist delegation included, in addition to Dr. Weizmann, Professor Frankfurter and Jacob de

---

[1] See above, p. 73.

[2] On November 7, 1918, Great Britain and France had issued a common declaration to the Arabs, in which they proclaimed their objective to be "the complete and definite emancipation of the peoples so long oppressed by the Turks and the establishment of national Governments and Administrations deriving their authority from the initiative and free choice of the indigenous population." The full text is in Royal Institute of International Affairs, *Great Britain and Palestine, 1915–1945* (London, 1946), pp. 149–150.

Haas from the United States and Messrs. Sokolow, Ussischkin, Spiré, and a number of other representatives of European Zionism.

The major political problem for the Zionists was to obtain international confirmation of the Balfour Declaration and to secure its inclusion in the text of the peace treaties. The Zionists were opposed to the incorporation of Palestine into an Arab state. They were against the principle of national self-determination, which if applied to Palestine would make it an Arab state, and they also opposed the internationalization of Palestine. Inasmuch as they favored British control of the area, their interests coincided with those of Great Britain. The Zionist delegation presented a memorandum to the Peace Conference, which was followed by a hearing. Both were given sympathetic attention, and their work was crowned with success. International instruments, such as the Treaty of Sèvres and the mandates (which will be dealt with later in this book), included explicit recognition of Zionist aspirations.

4) *Greek claims.* Greece had belatedly entered the war on the side of the Allies, succumbing to Allied pressure and inducements. The man most instrumental in aligning Greece with the Entente was Eleutherios Venizelos, who enjoyed prestige and influence in Paris quite incommensurate with the strength and role of his small country. Allied inducements had included hints of compensation at the expense of Turkey, but they were never put into formal or explicit form comparable to the other secret agreements. Despite this fact, Venizelos claimed for his country the right to occupy Smyrna and the adjacent region in western Turkey. His arguments were ethnical and historical. He pointed to the large Greek population in Smyrna, which, he alleged, constituted a majority, and to the historical link between the western and eastern shores of the Aegean—a Hellenic sea—and their economic unity. In his pleas he was backed by Britain's prime minister, Lloyd George, and the British delegation. Britain's motives in supporting Venizelos were a mixture of pro-Christian, pro-Hellenic, and anti-Turkish emotions [3] added to the political calculation (1) that Greece was a strategic bastion in the eastern Mediterranean and hence it was proper to keep her happy and friendly; (2) that inasmuch as the Straits might pass under Russian control, it would be wise

[3] These anti-Turkish sentiments were characteristic of only one group of British statesmen and diplomats and were by no means universal. But this group was influential at the time of Lloyd George's premiership. (See Harold Nicolson, *Curzon: The Last Phase, 1919–1925: A Study in Post-War Diplomacy* (London, 1934), p. 94.

to hold a reserve line from Piraeus to Smyrna across the Aegean to bar, if necessary, further Russian expansion.[4] Britain's support resulted in authorization to Greece from the Supreme Allied Council to occupy Smyrna and the vicinity. Venizelos' diplomatic triumph was complete, and he could now indulge in ambitious dreams of reconstructing some kind of Hellenic empire—an heir to Byzantium—in Asia Minor. Greek troops landed in Smyrna on May 15, 1919, and gradually advanced into the interior.

5) *Armenian claims.* The newly created republic of Armenia, having passed through the vicissitudes of war and Turkish invasion, was anxious to obtain international recognition and an increase in territory. The Armenian delegation in Paris, led by Boghos Nubar Pasha, demanded the so-called Turkish Armenia, i.e., the six eastern vilayets of Turkey. This claim had some historical justification but little more than that. At the time the demand was made, most of the Armenians in those provinces had been uprooted; but even had they been living there, they would have been a minority of the population, the majority being decidedly Turkish.[5] The Armenian claims met with a mixed reception. Despite the friendliness generally shown the Armenians, there was an uneasy feeling at the Peace Conference that their claims were exaggerated.

6) *American attitudes.* The United States had not been a partner to the inter-Allied agreements; therefore, officially it was not bound by them. Moreover, American war aims as defined in the President's "Fourteen Points" of January 8, 1918, profoundly differed from the tenor of the secret treaties. Point One proclaimed the principle of "open covenants openly arrived at," which quite contradicted the secrecy of wartime deals. Point Twelve specifically dealt with Turkey:

The Turkish portions of the present Ottoman Empire should be assured a secure sovereignty, but the other nationalities which are now under Turkish rule should be assured an undoubted security of life and an absolutely unmolested opportunity of development, and the Dardanelles should be permanently opened as a free passage to the ships and commerce of all nations under international guarantees.[6]

The incompatibility of this American program with the policies

[4] *Ibid.,* p. 97.
[5] According to H. W. V. Temperley, ed., *A History of the Peace Conference of Paris* (London, 1924), VI, 82.
[6] For the full text of the Fourteen Points, see *ibid.,* I, 433.

of the other Allies was obvious. In Paris President Wilson refused even to consider the wartime agreements. The Allies, according to the President, had given their express approval of the Fourteen Points and hence had automatically annulled their secret agreements. They were bound to abide by the new principles of nonimperialism and national self-determination.

Had it been pushed to its logical conclusion, the President's program would have conflicted with practically every one of the secret agreements, with the exception, perhaps, of the British-Arab accord. It was incompatible with French, Italian, Greek, and Zionist plans. A device to compromise these conflicting interests and principles was found in the mandate system. The great powers were to be entrusted with mandates over some areas in the name of the League of Nations, whose covenant was being adopted in Paris. Even with the adoption of the mandate system, the question remained as to who should exercise the mandatory functions in specific areas. There were moments of tension during the conference, especially between the French delegation and the American President. In order to break the deadlock, Wilson proposed to send to the Middle East a joint Allied Commission whose task it would be to ascertain the desire of the populations "directly concerned." France refused to participate in this commission, and Britain, after brief hesitation, also decided to remain aloof from it. Notwithstanding this boycott and despite intense Zionist objections voiced by Professor Frankfurter, Wilson appointed a purely American commission composed of Dr. Henry C. King, President of Oberlin College, and Charles Crane, a prominent businessman and student of international affairs. Between May and July 1919 King and Crane made a six weeks' tour of Syria and Palestine, held hearings, and on August 28 presented their report.

In their tour of Arab centers King and Crane found an almost unanimous desire for full independence. The inhabitants of Syria, including the Palestinian Arabs, insisted on an independent and united Syrian state that would embrace not only the Syrian hinterland but also Lebanon and Palestine. Failing to achieve complete independence, the Syrians were prepared to accept the United States or Great Britain, their first and second choices, respectively, as their mandatory power. There was overwhelming opposition to France, except for a number of pro-French petitions from Lebanon. An equally overwhelming opposition to Zionism was expressed by Moslem and Christian Arabs alike.

During their visit in Aleppo, King and Crane interviewed a representative Arab delegation from Mesopotamia. The Mesopotamians also asked for independence and, in contrast to the Syrians, did not mention officially any preferences for a mandatory power. In fact, the delegation protested against Article 22 of the Covenant of the League of Nations, which had proclaimed the principle of mandates. The delegation insisted on a rather large Mesopotamia, which would include the frontier areas of Diarbekir, Deir ez-Zor, and Mosul on the northwest and Mohammera (an Iranian sheikhdom) on the southeast. It expressed preference for Abdullah or Zeid, sons of Hussein of the Hejaz, as their king, demanded complete independence for Syria, and objected to Hindu and Jewish immigration. It also stated that, upon the achievement of independence, it would welcome technical and economic assistance from America.[7]

On the basis of the foregoing investigation, King and Crane recommended an American mandate for Syria, or as a second alternative a British mandate, and a British mandate for Mesopotamia. The two commissioners favored constitutional Arab monarchies under the mandatory system and fully endorsed Faisal for the kingship of Syria. Furthermore, they voiced serious opposition to the establishment of a Jewish state in Palestine. They recommended "that only a greatly reduced Zionist programme be attempted by the Peace Conference, and even that only very gradually initiated," that Palestine become part of a united Syrian state, and that the holy places be internationalized.[8]

[7] Henry A. Foster, *The Making of Modern Iraq* (Norman, Okla., 1935), p. 90.

[8] The King-Crane report later elicited both favorable and unfavorable comments. Ray Stannard Baker in *Woodrow Wilson and World Settlement* (New York, 1922) says: "It was in many ways the most characteristic and interesting adventure in international politics ever undertaken by Americans, and it was the only commission appointed by the Paris Peace Conference which really carried out both the principle and the method of President Wilson, of inquiry into the real wishes of populations whose destinies were being decided. From the point of view of the old diplomacy it was truly a naïve enterprise; as unlike traditional European methods as shirt-sleeved Americans could make it" (II, 207).

Prof. Henry A. Foster in *The Making of Modern Iraq* makes the statement that "the King-Crane commission's first hand study would be a great satisfaction to the Americans, especially to Wilson, as well as to liberals everywhere. It was a procedure called for by the accepted principle of self-determination, and opposition to it by the British and the French indicated that they entertained fears as to the results" (p. 90).

Frank E. Manuel in *The Realities of American-Palestine Relations* (Washington, 1949) seems to sum up well the Zionist view when he accuses the King-Crane commission of bending to the influence of American Protestant missionaries

PEACE SETTLEMENT IN THE ARAB AREAS

The King-Crane report was not discussed by the Paris Peace Conference. The report was not rejected, but simply buried in the archives of the American delegation, and ignored by the conferees. It was not published until 1922, long after the peace settlement. This neglect of the report may be attributed to two facts: first, Wilson had left Paris for the United States in the midsummer of 1919 and in the pressure of more important business at home did not have the time or the desire to attend to what was, after all, only a secondary matter. In fact, beginning in July, the President had to fight strong domestic opposition to the League of Nations Covenant and to the whole Treaty of Versailles. This was, indeed, the basic issue; it affected the general problem of America's involvement in world affairs. And America's wishes and interests with regard to the Middle Eastern settlement depended upon solution of this fundamental question.

Secondly, the report was too blunt and too frank to please either France or Great Britain. In Wilson's absence the crusading spirit for self-determination ceased to be very conspicuous in the American delegation. The delegation had no desire to pick a quarrel with the British or the French over what seemed to be a minor issue. Wilson's absence, his domestic difficulties, and the resulting indifference in the American delegation left the field open for France, Great Britain, and the Zionists, all of whom were eager in greater or lesser degree to see the wartime agreements fulfilled. Britain, of course, had to choose between her pledges to the Arabs on the one hand and her promises to France and the Zionists on the other. Despite animosity toward and various differences with the French, the British were anxious to preserve French friendship and were unwilling to sacrifice the major interest of Anglo-French harmony to the minor interest of keeping Arab good will. Once this choice was made, there was no basic obstacle to satisfying the Zionists, who did not relax their efforts to secure a favorable solution.

Faisal's second appearance before the Allied Supreme Council in

in the Middle East (p. 239), all pro-Arab and anti-Zionist. "The final King-Crane Report," writes Dr. Manuel, "presented on August 28, 1919, was in the same spirit as the rather puerile telegrams" sent by King and Crane to President Wilson from Palestine, attesting to the bitter anti-Zionist feeling of the Arabs (p. 249). Dr. Manuel's view of the "puerility" of such objections finds another expression in his statement that "Wilson's Zionism had hit up against the wall of self-determination of peoples which meant the counting of heads" (p. 223).

the fall of 1919 did not make a great impression on anybody. But, because of uncertainty as to the ultimate degree of America's participation in world affairs, the European powers did not press for an immediate assignment of mandates. The matter was delayed until the spring of 1920. By that time the Covenant of the League of Nations had become a ratified instrument and could serve as a formal basis. By that time also the American Senate had definitely repudiated all Wilsonian arrangements and had caused the United States to withdraw from an active role in the peace settlement.

The San Remo Conference

On April 24, 1920, the Peace Conference met at San Remo. There the European statesmen signed an agreement on the mandates. France was given Syria, Great Britain was assigned a mandate for Iraq and Palestine. These were all class "A" mandates, which, as outlined in the Covenant, meant that the tutelage of the mandatory powers was only temporary and was to lead to ultimate independence of the areas in question. The mandate for Palestine (made formal by an agreement between Great Britain and the League of Nations only on September 23, 1922) incorporated the Balfour Declaration. The Wilsonian principle of self-determination was thus rejected. No American delegates were present. To be sure, the American ambassador in Rome, Robert Underwood Johnson (in private life a poet and author of the ballad "Oh to Be in Paris, Now That Pershing's There") did come to San Remo. He appeared, however, to be uninformed on the issues at stake and was severely handicapped by the failure of instructions from Washington to arrive in time. "For two days the representative of the United States sat in a hotel garden reading the newspapers while the British and French settled the most important matters affecting the Middle East." [9]

The San Remo conference solved another important problem as well, the division of oil resources in Mesopotamia. In December 1918, before the Peace Conference, Clemenceau and Lloyd George had agreed to the transfer of Mosul from the French to the British sphere of influence. In return, Britain had promised France a share in the Mosul oil deposits. Before the war a concession covering these deposits had been granted by the Ottoman government to the Turkish Petroleum Company. The company was 75 per cent British and 25

[9] Edgar A. Mowrer, *The Nightmare of American Foreign Policy* (New York, 1948), p. 51.

per cent German. On April 18, 1919, M. Berenger, on behalf of France, and Mr. Walter (later Lord) Long, on behalf of Great Britain, signed an agreement by which France was to receive the former German share and to permit the construction of a pipeline across the French mandated area from Mosul to the Mediterranean. This agreement could not, however, be regarded as final as long as the mandates were not officially assigned. The Berenger-Long agreement also contained clauses concerning the division of oil resources in other parts of the world, but those are beyond the scope of this discussion. At San Remo, on April 25, France and Great Britain confirmed that part of the Berenger-Long agreement which pertained to the Middle East. France was to receive a 25 per cent share in the Turkish Petroleum Company and to permit transport of oil by rail or pipeline from Mesopotamia and Iran through Syria.

The San Remo agreements concluded that phase of the Peace Conference which pertained to the postwar settlement of the Arab portions of the Ottoman Empire. The Treaty of Sèvres, concluded soon afterward with Turkey, was the first public document to state officially that Syria and Mesopotamia were provisionally recognized "as independent states subject to the rendering of administrative advice and assistance by a Mandatory until such time as they are able to stand alone."

This was the formal settlement. It had to be carried out in practice, and it was here that complications arose. The Arabs of Syria, Mesopotamia, and Palestine objected to the imposition of foreign control and believed the whole arrangement to be a betrayal of the Wilsonian principles. Their resentment was manifested violently in all three areas. In each, however, this resentment followed a different course.

Settlement in Syria

In Syria, it will be remembered, Emir Faisal acted as a military governor at Damascus during the interim period following the end of the war. His leadership of the Arab national movement was universally recognized in Syria. The Syrians viewed him as their future ruler and made this clear to the King-Crane commission. At the time that the commission was touring Syria, a national Syrian conference was in session in Damascus. It voiced demands for complete independence. The Syrians expected from Faisal a strong stand in Paris and put considerable pressure on him to be uncompromising. Faisal found himself in the very delicate position of being pressed in Europe for an understanding with the French and the Zionists and of being pulled in exactly the opposite direction back in Damascus. He might have realized that Syrian intransigence was unrealistic, yet he knew that to concede to Western pressure would be tantamount to losing his popularity and leadership among the Arabs. Therefore, upon returning from his second visit to the Peace Conference (in the fall of 1919) Faisal decided to identify himself with the nationalist party, irrespective of the more or less formal understandings reached in Paris with the French and the Zionists. Having taken this stand, he grew in popularity, and on March 1920 the Syrian National Congress which met in Damascus proclaimed him king of Syria. The Congress, it may be added, claimed to represent the whole of Greater Syria, i.e., it included Palestine and Transjordan.[10]

This bold course contrasted sharply with the reality of the military situation in Syria, which was definitely becoming disadvantageous to the Arabs. Back in November 1919, the British, in fulfillment of their wartime promises to the French, had begun to evacuate the coastal area of Syria. French forces, under General Gouraud, replaced them. For a few months a tense situation prevailed between Faisal's Arab forces in Damascus and Gouraud's administration in Beirut. A provisional *modus vivendi* was finally reached, by which the French tacitly recognized Faisal's rule in the hinterland and refrained from advancing beyond Baalbek. It is a matter of speculation whether or not greater restraint on Faisal's part would have permitted him to retain direct control of the Syrian hinterland under French suzerainty. But no restraint was shown. Faisal's acceptance of the Syrian crown in the spring of 1920 appeared to the French as a direct threat to their rights in Syria. A few armed clashes between the Arab and the French outposts in the border areas added to the deterioration of relations, and in July General Gouraud decided to undertake military action against Faisal. In a swift operation the French defeated the Arabs, who attempted to barricade the road to Damascus. On August 7, 1920, General Gouraud entered the Syrian capital and deposed the king. Faisal took refuge in British-controlled Palestine. France had become supreme in Syria.

Settlement in Mesopotamia

The situation in Mesopotamia also proved explosive. Mesopotamia, like Syria, had experienced a revival of nationalism, and a number of

[10] On this stage of Syria's history, consult Philippe David, *Un Gouvernement Arabe à Damas: Le Congrès Syrien* (Paris, 1923), p. 63.

prominent Iraqi families, such as the Gailanis, the Omaris, and the Suweidis, played an important part in the Arab national movement before and during the First World War.[11]

When the war came, many Iraqis actively supported the British in the hope of obtaining independence for their country. There were uprisings against the Turks at Nejef, Kerbela, Hilla, Kufa, and Tuweirij in 1915 and 1916. Some Iraqi officers in the Turkish army, such as Nuri es-Said, offered their services to the British and many of them eventually entered the Hejazi army to serve either on Faisal's staff or as field commanders. In fact, the number of Iraqis in the Sherifian service was considerable. The service was a school of active Arab nationalism, and it played an important role in Arab political awakening. The year 1919 was characterized by ferment and growth of anti-British feelings in Faisal's army. The revelation of secret war-time deals among the Allies, the promises to the Zionists, and above all, the possibility of losing Syria to the French combined to produce restiveness and political extremism among the Arab officers in Damascus. In Baghdad, this opposition was directed by a nationalist society of Iraqi Covenanters (El-Ahd el-Iraqiya) in which the Iraqi officers of Faisal's army often played a leading role. When, on March 8, 1920, the Syrian National Congress met in Damascus to offer the crown to Emir Faisal, the Iraqi Covenanters were instrumental in producing a resolution by which the rule of Iraq was offered to Faisal's elder brother, Emir Abdullah.

The high-pitched nationalism of Faisal's Iraqi officers coincided with the growth of discontent in Mesopotamia against British rule. Here British policy was not consistent. On the one hand, it was imperialistic. Political officers attached to the Mesopotamian expeditionary force, as members of the Indian Political Service, wanted Mesopotamia to be an extension of the British Empire in India and distrusted any manifestation of Arab nationalism. They viewed British Cairo policy in support of Hussein's ambitions as a dangerous playing with fire. They delayed the publication of Wilson's Fourteen Points for more than ten months. They regarded with dismay the influence of Faisal's Iraqi officers on popular attitudes in Mesopotamia. On the other hand, much against their will, they had to follow certain instructions from London, which reflected the liberal

---

[11] In particular, Abdur Rahman el-Gailani, naqib of Baghdad, and his son Sayid Mahmud el-Gailani; Rashid el-Omari of Mosul; Sayid Talib Pasha, son of the naqib of Basra; and Tewfik es-Suweidi.

American trend. Thus, for example, Arnold Wilson (acting civil commissioner during Cox's mission to Teheran) was instructed in 1918–1919 to organize a "plebiscite" in order to ascertain whether the people desired a single Iraqi state under British tutelage, and, if so, which among the leading Arabs could qualify to serve as ruler. Obviously, such questioning implied deference to popular will, whetted the nationalist appetites, and contrasted with the otherwise imperialist line followed by the British civil administration in Baghdad. The latter, in contrast to the British mission with Faisal, did not act in an advisory but in an outright administrative capacity. Its members brought their families to Mesopotamia and believed that they were to remain for good. Meanwhile the nationalist movement was gaining in strength. Encouraged by the example of an independent Arab government at Damascus, Faisal's Iraqi officers demanded the immediate establishment of a similar government at Baghdad. Even the traditional religious differences between the Shiis and the Sunnis were temporarily forgotten, and a mixed front of both sects came into being in 1919–1920.

The assignment of mandates at San Remo was the spark that started the conflagration. On May 3, 1920, two British officers were killed in one of Mesopotamia's provincial towns, and by the first of July the whole country was in the throes of rebellion. The British had over 130,000 troops in Mesopotamia, but even this number did not suffice to restore order. Reinforcements had to be sent, and not until October 1920 was the insurrection quelled. Britain's losses amounted to nearly 2,500 casualties and caused a further drain on her war-strained treasury. But Britain's will prevailed and, as in Syria, the people of Mesopotamia were compelled to accept a peace settlement imposed by outside forces. The return of Sir Percy Cox in October 1920 and the inauguration of a more cautious policy, by which former British executives became advisers to the hand-picked Iraqi government, did not change the realities of the situation.

Settlement in Palestine

Finally, a word must be added about the enforcement of the decisions of the big powers on Palestine. Palestine was subjected to a fervent nationalist propaganda emanating from Damascus. The people responded to it eagerly. The Palestinians desired Arab unity and, in particular, unity with Syria. The handing over of Syria to French military control meant that their desires were to be disregarded and that Arab lands were to be carved up and assigned to different rulers. Moreover, Palestine had to face Zionism. Under these circumstances, opposition to the Allied schemes became rampant, and in April 1920 anti-Jewish disturbances broke out in Jerusalem and Jaffa. A total of about fifty Jewish victims suffered its consequences. The outbreak gave a foretaste of a long series of riots that were to mark the stormy history of Palestine for the next thirty years. These disturbances did not, however, deflect Britain's determination to pursue her own policy. On April 24, the mandate for Palestine and Transjordan was assigned to Great Britain, and on July, 1, 1920, the military government gave way to a civil administration. Sir Herbert Samuel became the first British commissioner there. He set himself promptly to the task of implementing the Balfour Declaration, and in September set the first quota for Jewish immigration at 16,500.

Thus by superior force Great Britain and France succeeded in overcoming opposition and in enforcing the decisions of the Peace Conference upon the Arab countries. Of the two, Britain's task was more difficult. Apart from Egypt, she controlled three different areas —Iraq, Palestine, and Transjordan. She felt the need of formulating some long-range policy toward these areas, a policy which would be less costly and more subtle than military occupation and which, in the long run, would correspond to the vital requirements of British political strategy in the East.

Final Arrangements: Deals with the Hashimites

To devise a unified policy for the whole region, London created a Middle East Department in December 1920. It was placed under the Colonial Office, at that time headed by Winston Churchill. The colonial secretary convoked a general British conference on Middle Eastern affairs, which met in Cairo, March 12–24, 1921. It was presided over by Churchill himself, and attended by Sir Percy Cox and Sir Herbert Samuel, high commissioners for Iraq and Palestine, respectively, and by a galaxy of prominent British Arabists, such as Lawrence, Clayton, Cornwallis, Gertrude Bell, and others.

This Cairo conference made the following decisions. The kingship of Iraq was to be offered to the deposed king of Syria, Faisal. Abdullah, Faisal's elder brother, was to be offered the emirate of Transjordan. In order to appease Iraqi nationalism the mandate was to be replaced by a treaty of alliance, which would be concluded with Faisal upon his advent to the throne.

Simple as these decisions may appear, they required the consent of both Faisal and Abdullah. Faisal had been approached by the British government as early as December 1920, during his visit to London. To the initial offer of the Iraqi throne he reacted negatively because of Abdullah's right to Iraq.[12] Consequently Colonel Lawrence was entrusted with the task of persuading Abdullah to renounce his rights in favor of Faisal. Abdullah was at that time in Maan, east of Jordan, where he had arrived at the head of a body of Hejazi troops following Faisal's expulsion from Damascus. He was making plans for an armed incursion into Syria in order to avenge his brother and, if possible, to restore him to power. Despite his belligerent attitude, he raised no major objections to Faisal's candidacy for Iraq. Subsequently, Faisal was approached once again, and this time he accepted the offer. After the Cairo conference, Churchill went to Jerusalem, where he reached an agreement with Abdullah by which Britain would endeavor to obtain from France a liberalization of her policy in Syria in order that an Arab government under Emir Abdullah might be established in Damascus. Pending these negotiations, Abdullah was to administer, with British assistance and a subsidy, the area east of Jordan. As it happened, however, France was in no mood to change her policy in Syria and what was initially conceived as a temporary arrangement acquired all the features of permanency in the form of the emirate of Transjordan.

With the path thus cleared, all that remained was to bring Faisal to Mesopotamia and to have him accepted there as ruler. This was done and on July 11, 1921, the Council of State (an Arab body in Baghdad) declared him king of Iraq.

Thus, by 1921 the foundations for the new order in the Arab Middle East were laid. Despite the Wilsonian ideology of self-determination and despite American intervention in Paris, the new peace was imperialistic in character and corresponded in the main to the major wartime agreements. Yet for the Arabs it was not exactly a change from old to new masters. True enough, the new settlement did not fulfill the Arab political program as conceived in 1915. Nevertheless, it marked an important advance toward eventual emancipation. With the acceptance of the principle of mandates, the big powers had to pay at least lip service to self-determination and to

[12] See above, p. 94.

international responsibility. Furthermore, active and violent opposition to the new system, manifested in Syria, Iraq, and Palestine, revealed new, deeply stirred forces of nationalism which the West, in the long run, would no longer be able to disregard and with which, as in the case of Iraq, it would be obliged to compromise.

PEACE SETTLEMENT IN TURKEY

It was the intention of the victorious Allies to impose a new settlement upon Turkey without consulting her. Turkey was a defeated enemy. Her territory had been subject to wartime partition agreements. And, in contrast to the Arabs, there was no direct moral or political commitment to respect her territorial integrity. True enough, Point Twelve of Wilson's Fourteen Points had proclaimed that "the Turkish portions of the present Ottoman Empire should be assured a secure sovereignty," and in his speech on January 5, 1918, Lloyd George had stated, on behalf of Great Britain, that she was not fighting "to deprive Turkey of its capital or of the rich and renowned lands of Thrace, which are predominatly Turkish in race." [13] Both statesmen insisted upon freedom of navigation in the Straits under international control. But these pronouncements lacked precision and could hardly be construed as a guarantee that Anatolia, i.e., Turkey proper, would be left untouched. Early in the Peace Conference it became clear that the Armenians, then in favor of the Allies, would insist upon the inclusion of eastern portions of Anatolia in their newly proclaimed republic.

To study the problem of Armenia, President Wilson appointed a commission under Major-General James G. Harbord. The commission visited Asia Minor and in October 1919 recommended that there be a single mandatory power over Turkey and Transcaucasia, because of certain economic and ethnic considerations involved. Suggestions that the United States become a mandatory power over the Straits, Constantinople, Anatolia, and Armenia were repeatedly made by the British and other statesmen during the conference, but to no avail. President Wilson hesitated to assume any military responsibilities over the Turks with whom the United States had not been at war. The mandate idea was rejected.

Russia's absence from the conference tables (as well as her renunciation of secret agreements [14]) complicated the task of the Entente.

[13] Temperley, *op. cit.*, I, 190.

[14] Made by the Provisional government in April 1917 and repeated—with more gusto and publicity—by the Bolshevik government upon its advent to power.

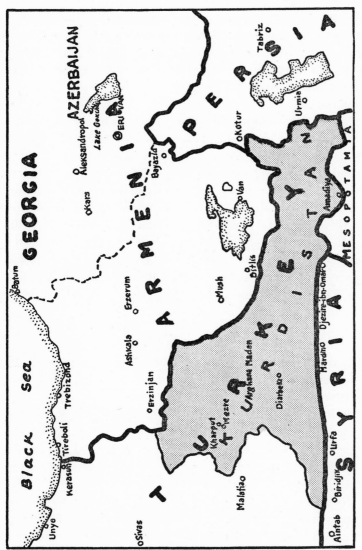

Map 3. Wilson's Armenian boundary. The heavy line denotes international boundaries; the broken line, the annulled boundary; and the shaded area, the plebiscite area.

Turkey, despite her defeat in the south at the hands of the British, was not encircled by an iron ring of victorious enemies. The Allies could assert their will in Constantinople, in the Straits, and in the Arab and south Anatolian portions of the Empire. But the center of Anatolia and its northeastern marches remained free from foreign pressure, and instead of hostile, land-grabbing tsarist Russia, Turkey faced there the revolutionary Soviets, which were hostile to the West and separated from Turkey proper by three weak Transcaucasian republics.

Under such circumstances, the Western powers might make more or less fantastic and elaborate plans as to how to implement the partition treaties, but they had to face the reality that their control of defeated Turkey was not complete. This discrepancy led to dramatic developments. On the one hand, the Allies arrived at various decisions concerning the disposal of Anatolia. These decisions, made partly in Paris and partly at San Remo in the course of 1919–1920, resulted in the Treaty of Sèvres, August 10, 1920, between the Allies and the Ottoman government.[15] But a number of political and military events occurred in Turkey, which threw Allied plans into confusion. These events rendered the Treaty of Sèvres a dead letter and resulted in a total revision of the peace settlement.

The Treaty of Sèvres

The Treaty of Sèvres was an embodiment of imperialism. Its main provisions were:

1) *Territorial clauses*
   a) *Arab lands.* Turkey was deprived of all the Arab portions of her Empire. The kingdom of Hejaz obtained recognition as an independent state. Turkey also renounced control of Syria, Palestine, and Mesopotamia, whose destinies were to be decided by the principal Allied powers.
   b) *Turkey in Europe.* Eastern Thrace was ceded to Greece up to the Chatalja line. Greece simultaneously received from the Allies Western Thrace (previously ceded to them by Bulgaria). She thus advanced her boundary to within twenty miles of the Turkish capital.
   c) *Smyrna and the Aegean islands.* The town and district of Smyrna were placed under Greek administration for a period of five years, after which the population was allowed

---

[15] The text is in *The Treaties of Peace, 1919–1923* (New York, 1924), II, 789 ff.

to request, by plebiscite, permanent incorporation into the kingdom of Greece. The islands of Imbros and Tenedos were ceded to Greece, and Greek sovereignty was recognized over a number of other Aegean islands. The Dodecanese Islands including the strategic Rhodes were ceded to Italy.

d) *Armenia.* Turkey recognized Armenia as an independent state, and consented to accept President Wilson's arbitration with regard to the boundary between the two states.

e) *Kurdistan.* Turkey agreed to grant the Kurdish area east of Euphrates local autonomy and to accept any scheme to this effect submitted by an international commission composed of the British, French, and Italian representatives. Turkey agreed also to accept modifications of her frontier with Iran in the Kurdish region. Moreover, Article 64 of the treaty stated:

> If within one year from the coming into force of the present Treaty the Kurdish peoples shall address themselves to the Council of the League of Nations in such a manner as to show that a majority of the population of these areas desires independence from Turkey, and if the Council then considers that these peoples are capable of such independence and recommends that it should be granted to them, Turkey hereby agrees to execute such a recommendation and to renounce all rights and title over these areas.
>
> The detailed provisions for such renunciation will form the subject of a separate agreement between the Principal Allied Powers and Turkey.
>
> If and when such renunciation takes place, no objection will be raised by the Principal Allied Powers to the voluntary adhesion to such an independent Kurdish State of the Kurds inhabiting that part of Kurdistan which has hitherto been included in the Mosul vilayet.

f) *The Straits and Constantinople.* Turkey agreed to international control of the Straits, and to demilitarization of adjacent zones.[16] Constantinople was to remain under Turkish sovereignty.

2) *Limitations of Turkish sovereignty*

a) *Limitation of armed forces.* The Turkish army was to be limited to 50,000 men. Compulsory military service was to

[16] For more details, see below, Chapter XV.

101

be abolished, and a limit was put on the armaments. The
army was to be subject to the advice of Allied or neutral
states. The navy was not to exceed a certain fixed maximum.
Allied commissions of control were authorized to supervise
the execution of these clauses.

b) *Financial clauses.* Turkey agreed to accept far-reaching
control by a financial commission representing Britain,
France, and Italy. This commission was to have wide powers
of control and supervision over the Ottoman public debt,
the Turkish state budget, currency, public loans and concessions, customs, and indirect taxes. With regard to the
last item, the commission's powers were to be executive in
character.

c) *The capitulations.* The capitulations were maintained in
force, and from the Turkish standpoint, new, humiliating provisions were added.

d) *The minorities.* Turkey accepted various clauses which
compelled her to respect the rights and privileges of national
and religious minorities, in particular of the Armenians,
Greeks, Assyro-Chaldeans, Kurds, and Christians in general.

Simultaneously with the Treaty of Sèvres a tripartite treaty was
concluded between Great Britain, France, and Italy. It provided
for the division of Turkish territory into French and Italian spheres
of influence. The French sphere corresponded exactly to the zone
assigned to France by the Sykes-Picot agreement. The Italian zone
covered the areas assigned to Italy in southwestern Anatolia according to two wartime agreements (London and St. Jean de Maurienne)
minus the region of Smyrna. It also extended somewhat beyond
these wartime limits in the northwestern sector. Turkey was not a
party to this agreement, hence was not legally bound by it. Politically,
however, the agreement affected her directly, since it represented an
attempt to fulfill the wartime partition schemes. It could, therefore,
not be divorced from the Sèvres Treaty and thus must be considered
as part of a larger whole.

The Treaty of Sèvres thoroughly humiliated Turkey and reduced
her to the status of a minor state whose territory was small and whose
sovereignty was subject to limitations amounting to a virtual protectorate. It is no wonder that resentment resulted. Some observers [17]
believe that, despite these humiliations, the war-weary Turks would

[17] Such as Temperley, *op. cit.,* VI, 45–46.

102

have accepted any dictated settlement had it not been for the last drop in the cup of bitterness, the Greek invasion.

The Greek Invasion and the War of Independence

The arrangement whereby Greece was authorized by the Supreme Allied Council to occupy Smyrna and the adjacent region [18] has already been mentioned. This operation, as was pointed out, was a part of the bargain between Greece and the Allies and was considered both as compensation for the wartime services rendered by Greece and as an additional safeguard of the maritime routes of Great Britain. It might be added here that, in addition to these considerations, it was believed in Paris that Greek contingents in Turkey would partially fill the gap created by the defection of Russia.

The Greek landing in Smyrna (May 15, 1919) acted as a powerful stimulant for Turkish action. The Turks might have surrendered to and endured Western dictation, but the thought of being invaded and occupied by the Greeks was revolting. The Turks traditionally considered the Greeks a subject race and simply could not stomach the reversal of roles. Strong resentment against Greece was manifested soon after the landing of Greek troops, i.e., long before the Treaty of Sèvres. The treaty, which formally recognized Greek territorial claims, added to the general disillusionment and intensified the revisionist action.

In this moment of crisis the Turkish nation was fortunate in finding a leader of exceptional ability and strength of will in the person of General Mustafa Kemal Pasha. Following the last stages of the Syrian campaign, Kemal found himself in Constantinople, bitter and critical both of the Allies and of the impotent Ottoman government. By an almost miraculous set of circumstances, he was appointed, in May 1919, inspector general of the Third Army in eastern Anatolia. He took a boat and on May 19 landed in Samsun, a date which is now a Turkish national holiday. Soon after he left the capital, the government, yielding to Allied suspicions, issued orders recalling him. It was, however, too late. Kemal appeared in eastern Anatolia determined to save the nation from foreign bondage. He refused to obey the recall orders and proceeded to assert his undisputable authority over what was left of the Turkish army in the region under his control. He then launched an intensive propaganda campaign appealing to the national pride of the Turks. Energetic and resource-

[18] See above, p. 87.

103

ful, Kemal succeeded in arousing the nation. Two national congresses were held under his leadership, in Erzerum and Sivas in July and September of 1919, respectively. The Erzerum congress resulted in the establishment of "the League for the Defense of Rights in East Anatolia," later to become a full-fledged political party. These congresses were followed by the convocation, on April 23, 1920, of the first Grand National Assembly in Ankara, at that time a small town in the arid part of Anatolia. Attended by many deputies to the Ottoman parliament and a number of other delegates, the Assembly challenged the authority of the sultan's government in Constantinople, declaring that the government was a virtual prisoner of the Allies and could not make binding decisions for Turkey. Earlier, on January 28, 1920, a group of nationalist deputies to the Ottoman parliament had drawn up in Constantinople a six-point program which was subsequently adopted as the National Pact by the Assembly at Ankara. Its six articles included:

1) Recognition of self-determination for the Arabs with a corresponding demand of freedom and unity for those parts of the Empire "which are inhabited by an Ottoman Moslem majority" (i.e., a Turkish or Kurdish majority).

2) Acceptance of a plebiscite for the three sanjaks of Batum, Kars, and Ardahan.

3) Acceptance of a plebiscite for Western Thrace.

4) A demand for the security of Constantinople as the seat of the caliphate and of the sultanate and, if this demand was recognized, consent to an international regime for the Straits.

5) Acceptance of international protection of minorities on condition that reciprocal protection be given to "Moslem minorities in neighboring countries."

6) Demand for complete political and economic independence, with an implicit rejection of the capitulations.[19]

These articles represented a formal political program. To implement it, Kemal had recourse to military action and to diplomacy. Militarily he was in a weak but not a desperate position. He had control over the forces of eastern Anatolia, which included the famous Ninth Army of the Caucasus. The latter had never been defeated; in fact, the armistice found it in the flush of victory after it had successfully reached the Caspian Sea. Its morale was high. These forces were reinforced by over 130,000 Turkish prisoners of

[19] The full text is in Temperley, *op. cit.*, VI, 605.

war, released by the Allies after the Treaty of Sèvres. By the force of his personality and his organizing genius, Kemal succeeded in welding these elements together into a new army, imbued with patriotic spirit and eager, despite nine years of wars, to fight for independence. He had to face five enemies: the Armenians in the east, the French in Cilicia, the Italians in Adalia, the Greeks in Smyrna, and the British in Constantinople. His first offensive operation took place in Cilicia. Early in 1920 his armies attacked the French and by spring had succeeded in ejecting them from the ethnic Turkish areas toward Aleppo. The French, faced with new responsibilities in Syria and desirous of putting an end to Faisal's influence, were content to conclude an armistice with Kemal on May 30, 1920, in Ankara. This permitted him to concentrate his forces on the Armenian front.

The situation in Armenia requires a brief explanation. It will be remembered that by the Treaty of Sèvres the Armenian Republic (originally founded in the former Russian province of Erivan) had enlarged its territory at the expense of Turkey. President Wilson, authorized by the treaty to fix the boundary, awarded Armenia in 1920 a large portion of Turkish territory, which included Trebizond, Erzerum, Mush, and Van. This new territory virtually covered the area which early in the war had been assigned to tsarist Russia in the secret treaties. Its population was predominantly Turkish, and Kemal was determined to wrest it from the rather nominal control of Armenia. Free from French pressure in Cilicia, the Turks under the command of General Kiazim Kara Bekir advanced against the Armenians, and in October 1920 captured Kars. Armenia was simultaneously attacked by the Bolsheviks,[20] who conquered Erivan and installed there a Communist government. By the Treaty of Alexandropol,[21] December 3, 1920, this government ceded to the Turks major portions of its western territory, which included the fortresses of Kars and Ardahan.

Thus, by the end of 1920 Kemal's nationalists had disposed of the French and Armenian danger in the east and could concentrate on the major task in western Anatolia—the expulsion of the Greeks. Before engaging in these decisive operations, Kemal settled three important problems of foreign policy. First, on March 13, 1921, he concluded an agreement with Italy whereby the latter agreed

[20] For further details, see below, p. 113.
[21] In Turkish "Gümrü," at present "Leninakan."

to evacuate Anatolia in return for extensive economic concessions. By June there were no more Italian troops on Turkish soil.

Secondly, on March 16 Kemal signed a treaty of friendship and collaboration with Soviet Russia. The treaty settled the vexatious boundary problem; Turkey agreed to cede Batum to Russia, in return for which Russia recognized Turkish possession of Kars and Ardahan, thus confirming the Treaty of Alexandropol.[22] Even more important was a pledge of political collaboration directed against the imperialist West. The treaty gave formal endorsement to the already existing military co-operation between the two countries. Following her victory over the White forces of General Denikin in April 1920, Soviet Russia had steadily supplied the Kemalists with weapons and munitions. The operations against Armenia, as we have seen, had been conducted simultaneously by the Turks and the Soviets. Moreover, the wiping out of the independent Armenian Republic permitted both parties to establish a land junction and greatly facilitated a further flow of supplies from Russia.

Thirdly, on October 20, 1921, Kemal made a deal with France. Known as the Franklin-Bouillon agreement after the French plenipotentiary who negotiated it in Ankara, this instrument provided for the final evacuation of Cilicia by the French in return for favorable economic concessions. This seemingly benevolent French behavior was not difficult to explain. Since French troops had already suffered defeat at the hands of the Turks, the agreement did not bring about a material change in the military situation. Moreover France, at that time, was not hesitant in embarrassing Great Britain. The two former allies were gradually falling apart, especially in their Middle Eastern policies, and France was profoundly irritated by what seemed to her the adventurous British support of the Greeks. Greek victory in western Anatolia would mean British ascendancy in the Aegean Sea and consequent British domination of the Turkish Straits. This went counter to French views. Under these circumstances, France was only too glad to reduce her inconvenient military commitments in Cilicia and thus render it easier for Kemal to continue his war against the Greek invaders.

Having thus secured Soviet assistance and neutralized French and Italian hostility, Kemal concentrated all his strength on the

[22] This was later confirmed once again by the Treaty of Kars, October 13, 1921, concluded between Turkey and the Soviet Transcaucasian Federation.

Greek war. His task was not easy. Thirteen months after their landing in Smyrna, the Greeks in June 1920 undertook an offensive into the interior of Anatolia. Before long they were in control of the Ismid region, and from there they pushed eastward. Taking advantage of Kemal's preoccupation with the Armenian front, the Greeks scored several victories, including the capture of Brusa. The winter provided a temporary lull in the operations, only to be followed by a renewed Greek offensive in March 1921. Taking Afyonkarahisar and Eskisehir, the Greeks captured Kutaia and drew dangerously close to Ankara. The bloody battle of the Sakaria River, August 24 to September 16, turned the tide in favor of the Turks. Still there was a long road ahead, and it was not until August 1922 that a decisive Turkish offensive was undertaken. Once started, the offensive was a dazzling success. Within two weeks the Turks drove the Greek army back to the Mediterranean Sea. On September 11 they took Smyrna, vented their vengeance on the Greek population, and compelled the Greek army to escape on the ships available in the harbor. Master of the major part of Anatolia, Kemal turned now toward Constantinople to achieve complete liberation of Turkish territory.

The Treaty of Lausanne

Alarmed by the Greek defeat and the Kemalist threat, Lloyd George on September 15 sent out an appeal to the Allies to defend the Straits. The response from France and Italy was negative. The next day a British contingent under General Harington landed at Chanak, on the Asiatic side of the Dardanelles. Kemalist forces approached, and for a brief tense period it looked as if Britain and Turkey were to be again at war. Both parties, however, manifested remarkable restraint. The Convention of Mudania, concluded on October 11 between Kemal and the Allies, put an end to this undeclared state of war. The convention provided for the return of Eastern Thrace and Adrianople to the Turks, while Kemal accepted a proposal for international control of the Straits. The road was paved for a comprehensive discussion of all peace problems. On November 20, 1922, a peace conference was opened at Lausanne. The two main protagonists, Lord Curzon and General Ismet Pasha, had many heated disputes over controversial issues. Ismet stubbornly insisted on the inclusion of Mosul in Turkey and on the abolition of capitulations, two points unacceptable to Curzon. For two months the conference was suspended, but in April it was resumed, and on July 24,

107

1923, the parties signed the Treaty of Lausanne.[23] The name covered the treaty itself as well as additional instruments such as the convention of the Straits, the Turco-Greek agreement about an exchange of populations, and various annexes and minor agreements. Its provisions included:

1) *Territorial clauses.* The integrity of ethnic Turkey was recognized, and the separation of Arab lands was confirmed. Turkey regained Eastern Thrace up to the Maritza River and the town of Karagach on its western bank. The islands of Imbros and Tenedos were restored to her, but other Aegean islands went to Greece. Italian possession of the Dodecanese and British possession of Cyprus were confirmed. No mention was made of Armenia, which meant an implicit recognition of the Turkish-Soviet treaties concerning the Transcaucasian border. Smyrna was restored to Turkey as an integral part of Anatolia. The boundary with Syria was to follow the line fixed by the Franklin-Bouillon agreement of October 20, 1921, which meant exclusion from Turkish territory of the sanjak of Alexandretta. The boundary with Iraq was left to future agreement between Great Britain as the mandatory power and Turkey. If such an agreement failed to materialize within a year, the parties promised to accept arbitration by the League of Nations. In the meantime, the *status quo* was to prevail; i.e., the Mosul area was to be under British-Iraqi jurisdiction. The problem of independence or autonomy for Kurdistan was not mentioned.

2) *Limitations of sovereignty.* In comparison with this aspect of the humiliating Treaty of Sèvres, the Treaty of Lausanne was a victory for Turkey. Capitulations were abolished, and in return Turkey agreed to accept neutral observers of her judicial system, with purely nominal powers. She was freed from foreign economic and financial control and from any Allied claim to reparations. No limit was placed on the size of her military and naval establishment, but she was to demilitarize a zone thirty kilometers wide along the Thracian border. Turkey accepted the standard treaties to protect minorities, such as were devised for certain European nations at the Paris Peace Conference. No specific mention was made either of Greeks or of the Armenians in this respect, and the antiquated millet system was implicitly abandoned.

3) *The Straits.* The one major limitation of Turkish sovereignty was on control of the Straits, which were to be internationalized.

[23] The text is in *The Treaties of Peace, 1919–1923,* II, 959 ff.

But even here Turkey notably improved her position. The new Straits convention provided for an international commission presided over by a Turkish citizen under the auspices of the League of Nations. A limited freedom of navigation through the Straits was proclaimed,[24] and four demilitarized zones on the European and Asiatic shores of the Bosphorous and the Dardanelles were established. Islands in the Sea of Marmara were also demilitarized. Turkey was allowed, however, a garrison of 12,000 troops in Constantinople as well as freedom of transit for her troops across the specified neutral zones.

4) *Exchange of populations.* A separate Greco-Turkish agreement provided for compulsory exchange of the Greek minority living in Turkey and the Turkish minority living in Greece. Greeks in Constantinople and Turks in Western Thrace were excluded from this transfer.[25]

The Treaty of Lausanne was a signal victory for the Turkish nationalists. By signing it, Kemal's government obtained formal international recognition and buried forever the remnants of Ottoman tradition. It fulfilled, in the main, the program outlined in the National Pact of Ankara. Turkey regained her independence and secured the unity of her ethnic territory. She threw off the shackles of foreign control in judicial, military, and economic matters. She emerged from this ordeal with her national pride restored, enjoying

---

[24] For more details, see Chapter XV.

[25] This agreement was greatly criticized during and after the conference for its inhumanitarian surgery, but it should be borne in mind that the bitterness engendered as a result of the Greek invasion of Anatolia made any other solution impracticable. Moreover, the exodus of thousands of Greek civilians in the wake of the Greek military evacuation of Smyrna was already an accomplished fact, which was followed and not created by the agreement. The exchange affected approximately 1,500,000 Greeks and 500,000 Turks. To Turkey it proved to be something of a blessing, since it eliminated from her territory a minority of questionable loyalty and vacated many professions and trades for younger Turkish intellectuals. There was, no doubt, an immediate economic loss resulting from the disappearance of a commercially skilled element of the population, but it was not a loss which, in the long run, could not be compensated by native forces. Furthermore, Turkey could fill certain depopulated areas with the Turkish deportees from Greece—an operation not without definite advantages. To Greece the forcible exchange was a tragic episode. The newly arrived refugees and deportees constituted about one-fifth of the total Greek population and proved to be both an economic burden and a chronic source of unrest in turbulent Greek politics during the interwar period. In human terms the suffering was incalculable, and the ruination of the once prosperous Greek colony of Asia Minor was complete. Such was the sad harvest reaped from Venizelos' adventure in 1919.

a new and progressive leadership, impoverished but confident in the future, and homogeneous in population. The Treaty of Lausanne was a difficult one to draft, but inasmuch as it was a freely negotiated and not an imposed treaty, it provided a sounder foundation for peace in the Middle East than had its ill-fated predecessor.

This feature of free negotiation was purchased at a heavy price of bloodshed and human suffering. But the peace settlement as it emerged in relation to Turkey was quite different from the settlement in the Arab portions of the defunct Ottoman Empire. In both cases the original intention of the European powers was to impose upon these areas an imperialistic peace which would subject them to semicolonial rule and which would conform to the wartime partition agreements. In both cases, however, there was a native revolt against these schemes. But whereas the Arabs, divided and ill-prepared, did not succeed, the Turks succeeded beyond all expectations. The West imposed its will, under the form of the mandatory system, upon the Arabs but saw its designs frustrated by the tough resolution of the Turks. In the long run, such a turn of events was to serve the real interests of the West. A healthy and strong Turkey in two decades was to become a bulwark protecting world peace against the destructive inroads of modern totalitarian states.

THE AFTERMATH OF WAR IN CAUCASIA AND CENTRAL ASIA

Although hostilities between the Entente and the Central powers ended in October–November 1918, turmoil on Russia's southern periphery continued for some time. There were two main causes for the unrest and the resulting prolongation of military operations: (1) The emancipatory movement of non-Russian nationalities of the Russian Empire; (2) Allied intervention against Bolshevism in Russia. Both causes were to complicate the peaceful conclusion of war.

The Russian revolution produced a pronounced weakness in the strength of the Empire, a weakness verging on complete disintegration. The subject nations of Russia, long aspiring to freedom, seized this opportunity to achieve independence. Georgia, Armenia, and Azerbaijan emerged as independent states in May 1918, and a similar movement toward emancipation developed at the same time in Central Asia. In Kokand a free government of Turkestan was

110

proclaimed in December 1917, the emirs of Khiva and Bukhara asserted their independence, and the Kirghiz population also manifested emancipatory tendencies. As pointed out earlier, several other Turkish-speaking groups in Russia also made attempts at emancipation, but we shall limit our observations to those groups which belong to the wider geographical area of the Middle East. Other movements, while important and indicative of the resentment of the Turkish-Tatar peoples against the Russian rule, were either geographically isolated or too remote from the Middle Eastern area of operations to be counted as factors in the dramatic developments which followed the armistice.

The exigencies of war with the Central powers had brought British troops to the soil of the Russian Empire. These troops came either to oppose directly Turko-German penetration eastward (such was the case in Baku) or to oppose it indirectly (by fighting the Bolsheviks). This indirect opposition requires some elucidation. In 1918 a general intervention by the Western powers into the affairs of Russia began. Its aim was to aid the anti-Communist elements in Russia to re-establish themselves in order to keep Russia in the war on the side of the Allies. Therefore any British expedition into Central Asia or the Caucasus could be interpreted in this light. But the Central Asiatic regions of the Russian Empire presented additional reasons for intervention. Upon its seizure of power, the Communist Soviet at Tashkent began to launch vigorous anti-British propaganda directed toward India and Britain's colonial empire. Having released from captivity about 200,000 German and Austro-Hungarian prisoners of war interned in Turkestan, the Tashkent Bolsheviks organized them into military formations to serve the new Communist government. The economic co-operation inaugurated between Soviet Russia and Germany after the Brest-Litovsk Treaty meant that the Tashkent Soviet, if allowed to act freely, would be in a position to supply Germany with millions of bales of cotton—a raw material needed badly by Berlin for the production of nitrate. Soviet co-operation with Germany, the presence of Communist-guided German and Austrian troops in Turkestan, the Communist propaganda emanating from Tashkent toward India, and the possibility of a junction between the German-Turkish elements in Transcaucasia and other anti-British forces in Turkestan produced considerable alarm in British quarters and were the main factors leading them to

111

undertake an expedition to Turkestan.[26] Actually two different British actions occurred. The first involved the sending of a small military mission, led by Colonel Sir George Macartney, by a roundabout route to Tashkent, in order to learn on the spot what the ultimate intentions of the Bolsheviks were. This mission was compelled to leave Tashkent after a brief stay in order to avoid being arrested by the local Soviet. Only one member, Lieutenant Colonel F. M. Bailey, remained in disguise in Turkestan, attempting to establish contact with anti-Soviet Moslem nationalists.[27] The second was the sending of a British force to Ashkhabad in Transcaspia in response to an appeal addressed to the British by a counterrevolutionary Russian government there. This force, under the command of General Sir Wilfrid Malleson, fought Bolshevik troops and their German and Austro-Hungarian mercenaries along the Transcaspian railway line between Ashkhabad and Tashkent. The furthest point reached by the British was the oasis of Merv.

When in October and November 1918, armistices had been concluded with the Central powers, the original anti-German objective behind the British expeditions into the Caucasus and Central Asia lost its significance. Thenceforward their continued presence in those regions was motivated by the anti-Soviet feeling of the British government and by protective measures in defense of India. The support of either Russian counterrevolutionary forces like those in Ashkhabad or of centers of anti-Soviet nationalist movements like those in the Caucasus or in Turkestan fitted well into this general policy. For this reason the Malleson force in Transcaspia was not withdrawn immediately following the armistice with the Central powers but remained there and fought with the Tashkent Communists until 1920. Similarly, following the armistice British troops reappeared in Baku and spread over other parts of Transcaucasia. They were accompanied by some French and Italian contingents. Their presence there, apart from assuring the evacuation of Turkish and German troops, was a guarantee against a possible Soviet thrust toward the area. The troops were instrumental in preserving the independence of Georgia, Armenia, and Azerbaijan. By the end of 1919 the British cabinet, and with it the governments of the other leading

[26] For a general summary of British Central Asian expeditions, see George Lenczowski, *Russia and the West in Iran, 1918–1948* (Ithaca, N.Y., 1949), pp. 31–41.

[27] A vivid account of his extraordinary adventures is contained in F. M. Bailey, *Mission to Tashkent* (London, 1946).

Entente powers, decided to put an end to their intervention in Russia. Orders were issued to the troops to evacuate the areas under their control. By the spring of 1920 British troops had withdrawn from the Caucasus and Transcaspia. The military vacuum thus created permitted the Soviet government to penetrate these areas. One by one centers of native resistance to communism fell. In Central Asia, Khiva was captured in June 1919, Ashkhabad in October of the same year, and Bukhara in September 1920. The rulers of Khiva and Bukhara fled to Afghanistan. In Transcaucasia, Azerbaijan experienced a Communist coup and Soviet invasion in April 1920. Armenia followed suit in November 1920, and Georgia in March 1921. All three countries were proclaimed Soviet Socialist republics. The attempt to free these non-Russian areas from Russian rule had failed, and the Soviet government succeeded in re-establishing its authority over the whole former area of the tsarist empire in Asia. This whole episode left a bitter legacy. On the part of the adjacent Moslem nations it resulted in a feeling of suspicion and hostility toward the new masters of Russia; with regard to England it created a constant worry over Soviet designs upon India and the British position in the Middle East; and on the part of Soviet Russia it produced a determination to wipe out the traces of independent nationalist thought among its subject Mohammedan races. Therefore, to some extent, the basic prewar pattern was reinstated—Russia vs. Britain and vs. native nationalism in the Middle East. This time, however, Russia was armed with the powerful weapon of Communist ideology, which in case of a Russian victory would mean not only imperialist bondage but also a radical change in the pattern of life of Middle Eastern peoples.

◄ PART TWO ►

THE NORTHERN BELT

CHAPTER IV

Turkey

E VEN before the replacement of the humiliating Treaty of Sèvres with the more honorable Treaty of Lausanne, profound changes took place in Turkey's internal politics. On November 1, 1922, barely three weeks after the armistice of Mudania, the Grand National Assembly proclaimed the abolition of the sultanate. A Kemalist leader, Refet Pasha, who later was to assume command in Thrace, appeared with Allied permission in Constantinople and promptly engineered a *coup d'état* to depose the sultan and his cabinet and to extend nationalist control over the capital. The sultan escaped aboard a British naval vessel. On November 18 the Assembly proclaimed the ex-sultan's cousin, Abdul Mejid, caliph with the clear understanding that his functions were to be limited to spiritual matters only. The Allies accepted these changes with good grace (in fact with a sigh of relief, since it ended the abnormal situation of having to treat with two Turkish governments at the same time). The negotiations that began soon afterward at Lausanne were conducted with the Ankara government, which represented Turkey *de facto* as well as *de jure*. At the time of the conference Kemal's fame was firmly established. He had been given by the Assembly the title of *Ghazi* ("Victorious"), as well as the rank of field marshal, after his victory at the decisive battle of the Sakaria River. His trusted friend and chief of staff, General Ismet Pasha, victor of the great battle of Inönü, ably headed the Turkish delegation.

ESTABLISHMENT OF THE REPUBLIC

From the constitutional point of view, the conference coincided with a period of transition. By the fall of 1923 basic decisions had

117

been made. On October 29, the Grand National Assembly proclaimed Turkey a republic, and elected Mustafa Kemal its first president. It soon transpired that, despite the clear limitation of the caliph's functions to the religious sphere, the very existence of this institution did not suit the reformist spirit of the new republic. On March 3, 1924, the last link with the past was severed. The Assembly formally abolished the caliphate. The caliph went quietly into retirement abroad, and a law was passed forever banning all members of the Osmanli dynasty from Turkish soil.

Soon afterward, on April 20, the Assembly adopted a constitution which, though it had a few peculiarities of its own, generally followed Western European patterns. It declared that the Grand National Assembly possessed "legislative authority and executive powers," the latter being exercised by the president of the republic and a council of ministers. The principle of responsibility to the parliament by the cabinet was established. Judicial authority was vested in the tribunals, which were proclaimed independent. The franchise was established on the basis of literacy. A four-year term was set for members of the Assembly, and the President was to be elected by the Assembly. Chapter V of the constitution was entitled "General Rights of Turkish Citizens" and laid stress on those civic freedoms and privileges which are characteristic of the heritage of the West. In particular it provided for individual liberty; the abolition of individual and group privileges; freedom of conscience, of thought, of speech, and of the press; the right to work; the right of private property and of association; freedom from arbitrary arrest; the prohibition of torture and forced labor; the sanctity of private residence; the inviolability of mail; compulsory and free primary education; and freedom from discrimination on account of religion and race.[1]

The letter of the constitution thus provided a legal framework for the new Turkish state. It was characteristic of new Turkish trends that the constitution followed a Western, democratic pattern, and not the Soviet model, in spite of the political alliance with new Russia. Yet it was not the letter but the spirit that actually counted. It is characteristic of the nations of the twentieth century to display fine-sounding constitutions, providing beautifully constructed demo-

[1] The full text of the constitution is contained in Helen M. Davis, ed., *Constitutions, Electoral Laws, Treaties of States in the Near and Middle East* (Durham, N.C., 1947), p. 341.

cratic machinery and containing impressive bills of rights, which in effect find no reflection in the real life of those nations. For this reason, the Turkish constitution, like any other similar instrument, could not accomplish a change in Turkey merely by being officially adopted. Nor could any rational person expect an immediate introduction of true Western democracy into a country which for centuries had known nothing but absolute rule.

Yet it is undeniable that Turkey, under Kemal, experienced a radical transformation, indeed a revolutionary change from the old order to the new. The most remarkable thing about the Turkish revolution is that it largely, though gradually, conformed to its professed ideals. It avoided the pitfalls of the Nazi and Soviet revolutions, which replaced the old order by a new absolutism. Despite all the temptations that the Fascist and Communist examples provided, and despite the temptation which possession of power in itself afforded, Kemal and his new Turkey represented a basically different trend than did the contemporary totalitarian machines. Instead of scorning and rejecting the Western heritage (which the totalitarians did with particular gusto), the new Turkish republic considered it an ideal worth struggling for.

In her search for a new, more prosperous, and more humane future, the new Turkey in the period between two world wars passed through a transitional stage which, in China, Sun Yat-sen termed "tutelage." This was a stage of re-education, sometimes employing forcible methods, under the guidance of a strong national leader. Once this re-education was accomplished, Turkey could hope to realize her democratic ideals.

It would be difficult to deny that, following the abolition of the sultanate and the caliphate, Kemal was a virtual dictator. This dictatorship was, however, tempered by at least three factors: (1) Kemal's basic Western liberal inclinations; (2) his benevolence and unselfishness; and (3) the sharing of power with the People's Party, the real source of his political strength, whose attitude he could not disregard.

The People's Party (*Halk Firkasi;* later renamed Republican People's Party, *Cümhüriyet Halk Partisi*) had grown out of the original Association for the Defense of Anatolia and Rumelia (created at the Erzerum and Sivas congresses) and was officially founded on September 9, 1923. It was dedicated to the wholesome regeneration of Turkey. It manifested a truly missionary zeal in the pursuance of its objective and took care not to repeat the errors previously committed by the Committee of Union and Progress. The People's Party professed a philosophy of nationalism and was willing to abide by the consequences of this profession. Thus, it demanded the right of self-determination for Turkey proper and in return recognized the same right for the Arabs. It rejected the idea of imperialism and argued that the expansion of the Ottoman Empire had brought more misfortunes than advantages to the Turkish nation. It condemned Pan-Islamism as a nefarious movement which not only retarded the modern secular development of Turkey but also entangled her in adventures and responsibilities that were of no concern to the people of Turkey. Pan-Islamism, it maintained, was also a chronic source of friction with foreign powers. Despite its emphasis on national ties, the party was also willing to abandon the concept of Pan-Turanism, which in practical terms meant denying support to irredentist tendencies among twenty million Turkish-speaking Mohammedans in the Soviet Union. Such a policy would facilitate good neighborly relations with the new Russia. In fact, of all the nationalist movements in the twentieth-century world, that of Turkey had the distinction of being sober-minded, restrained, and nonadventurous.

At the third congress in Ankara, the People's Party adopted "Six Principles of Kemalism," which expressed the fundamental political philosophy of the new Turkish republic. These principles were later (in 1937) formally incorporated into the constitution. They included (1) *Republicanism*, (2) *Nationalism*, based not on religion or race but on common citizenship and devotion to the national ideal; (3) *Populism*, meaning equality in law and repudiation of class privileges and of class war as well as of the abuses of capitalism; (4) *Etatisme*, meaning constructive intervention of the state in national economy; (5) *Secularism*, definite separation of church and state; and (6) *Revolutionism*, meaning the determination to depart radically from tradition and precedent if they did not serve national interests.

Kemalist Reforms

The National Pact of Ankara, the constitution, and the Six Principles provided the legal and ideological basis for the new life of the nation. Action was needed, and this action—vigorous and determined—came in a series of far-reaching reforms that radically transformed Turkey. Chronologically, the reforms in the new Turkish Republic may be divided into (1) those that occurred during the middle twenties and (2) those carried out in the middle thirties.

It seems more practical, however, for the purposes of this discussion, to group them according to their subject matter.

The major objective of Turkish reform was, in a general sense, to separate Turkey from the ancient Asiatic-Arabic sphere of culture and tradition and to transform her into a modern, Westernized nation.[2] The main attack was, therefore, directed against those institutions which were likely to perpetuate the old order. The abolition of the caliphate proved to be a good point of departure. It cleared the way not only to the establishment of a new kind of government, while freeing Turkey from an embarrassing complication in foreign relations, but also opened the way for a radical secularization of the Turkish body politic. One month after the abolition of the caliphate, in April 1924, the National Assembly abolished the authority of religious (Sharia) courts in civil matters and did away with the Ministry of Pious Foundations (Evkaf) and the priests' schools. The dervish orders were disbanded and their monasteries closed. Secret sects were banned. (The top religious position of Sheikh el-Islam had been abolished with the sultanate in 1922.) To deal with religious matters, two civilian bodies—the Board of Religious Affairs and the Board of Pious Foundations—were established.

Linked with religious reform and symbolical of the new spirit was the abolition of the fez and of the veil. Instructions concerning the dress to be worn by the clergy and public officials followed. In 1926 the European calendar replaced the old Islamic computation of the year.

The transfer of the national capital from Constantinople, the old seat of the caliphs, to the new city of Ankara provided another major move toward secularization. The new capital assumed a definitely modern exterior, and no mosques were constructed in its newer section. In 1935 Friday was replaced by Sunday as a weekly holiday. Finally, an amendment to the constitution, passed in 1928, deleted the article which stated that Islam was a state religion, and another amendment of 1937 proclaimed full freedom of conscience.

The record of laicization is impressive. It should be pointed out, however, that at no time did the Turkish republic fight religion as such. The Kemalist platform did not contain any doctrinaire material-

[2] A comprehensive account of Kemalist reforms may be found in August von Kral, *Kamâl Atatürk's Land: The Evolution of Modern Turkey* (London, 1938) and Donald E. Webster, *The Turkey of Atatürk: Social Progress in the Turkish Reformation* (Philadelphia, 1939). See also Arnold J. Toynbee, ed., *Survey of International Affairs, 1928* and Henry E. Allen, *The Turkish Transformation: A Study in Social and Religious Development* (Chicago, 1935).

istic principles. And although Kemal himself was indifferent to religion, some of his best friends, like Ismet and Fevzi Cakmak, were
deeply religious.

Many other reforms, although not directly concerning religion,
stemmed from the basic policy of secularization. Such were, for example, the judicial reforms, which were introduced in 1926. The
Turkish republic in a sweeping move discarded old Ottoman laws,
both religious and civil, abolished the millet system, and adopted
the Swiss civil code, the Italian penal code, and the German-type
commercial code as laws of the land. The new code of civil procedure
also followed the Swiss model. These laws established full equality of
citizens before the law, a very important aspect of which was the
emancipation of women. Polygamy was abolished, and women were
made eligible for public offices, professions, and positions of trust
in the economic and intellectual life of the country. In 1934 an amendment to the constitution gave women the right of suffrage, and soon
afterward a number of women deputies appeared in the Grand National Assembly.

Another reform linked to the general policy of secularization was
that of the alphabet. At the invitation of the Soviet government Turkey sent a delegation to a Turkological Congress which met in Baku
between February 26 and March 6, 1926. The Congress recommended
abandonment of the Arabic script as unscientific and detrimental to
the Turkic languages. Turkey adopted its recommendations in 1928.
The Latin alphabet was introduced, and the government sponsored
intensive studies looking toward the revival of the Turkish language
and its purification of foreign ingredients.

Following this reform, foreign-sounding geographical names in
Turkey gave way in 1930 to purely Turkish names. The Byzantine
Constantinople was replaced by the Turkish *Istanbul, Adrianople* by
Edirne, Smyrna by *Izmir,* and so on.

The development of a modern system of education was another
result of the policy of secularization. Public education was divorced
from church influences, and a constitutional provision concerning
free and compulsory tuition on the primary level was put into effect.
This was accompanied by a corresponding growth of secondary
schools and institutions of higher learning. Trade, agriculture, for-
estry, and commerce schools were built, and the government did not
hesitate to hire foreign teachers in order to assure high educational
standards. At the invitation of the government a Swiss professor, Dr.

Malche, presented a plan for the reform of university studies. A Medical Faculty, employing twenty foreign professors, was established in Istanbul and a School of Political and Social Sciences, which produced a number of able civil servants, diplomats, and statesmen, in Ankara. Athletics were encouraged, sports clubs flourished throughout the country, and Boy Scout organizations enjoyed popularity among teen-agers. In 1935 Russian specialists were invited to instruct Turkish athletes in the arts of gliding and parachuting.

The secret of Kemal's success may largely be attributed to the strict enforcement of educational reform. The new generation of village and high-school teachers constituted—with the People's Party members—a zealous cadre which spread Kemalist ideals and trained the minds of Turkish youth. Teachers became Kemal's most devoted propagandists, and—in contrast to many Western countries—were exceptionally well compensated for their services.

The old Ottoman state machinery also underwent a thorough overhauling. Badly needed reforms in the administrative system gave the new republic new efficiency. The country was divided into 62 *vilayets* (provinces), the latter subdivided into 430 *kazas* (districts), and these in turn parceled into a number of *nahiyes* (boroughs). General inspectorates, uniting some vilayets into larger districts, were created for certain special regions such as Kurdistan.

The Kemalist government successfully balanced the state budget, carried out a tax reform, and brought order into what had traditionally been a weak spot in Turkey, public finances. Throughout the 1920's a French financial expert was employed to advise on the financial recovery, and in 1933 Turkey successfully concluded a new agreement concerning the debts of the old Empire. The debt was reduced from 107,000,000 to 8,000,000 Turkish pounds.

Closely linked to the financial reform was the inauguration of general economic progress. Following its principle of *étatisme*, the government assumed direct control of several enterprises and engaged in a great deal of general over-all planning. Kemal acted on the basic premise that war-ravaged and foreign-exploited Turkey was poor in native capital, and that it was the state's responsibility to step in where private enterprise would not or could not operate. The government established state monopolies in such industries as tobacco, salt, liquors, matches, playing cards, arms, and munitions. It also acquired and established a number of factories in other fields. Without going to the extreme of compulsory nationalization, it gradually bought up most of the foreign-owned railways, co-ordinated their services, and embarked upon an ambitious program for their development. This program proved to be of tremendous importance in raising Turkey's economic and cultural life and served the purposes of national integration, industrialization, and defense.

The general economic policy of the new Turkey was that of autarchy and industrialization. This policy—a logical outcome of the principle of *étatisme*—required certain temporary sacrifices of the Turkish people, but in the long run assured them economic independence. The Soviet example played an important part in the formulation of this policy. While rejecting the extremist and doctrinaire aspects of the Soviet experiment, Kemalist Turkey willingly adopted the principle of economic planning. In the interwar period, a four-year plan for agriculture, a five-year plan for industry,[3] a three-year plan for mining, and a ten-year plan for the development of roads were formulated and carried out. To the extent that it served the national interest and did not endanger national independence or security, Turkey had recourse to the services of various foreign experts and construction firms. Soviet, German, Austrian, Hungarian, American, British, and other European experts were employed in the development of various economic enterprises.

The elimination of commercially skilled Armenian and Greek elements from many fields of economic endeavor caused some difficulties, especially as their services were often replaced by the bureaucratic machinery of new state-controlled enterprises. On the other hand, Turkey gained training in economic pursuits, and employed her own ethnic population. The former picture of Turkey split into a caste of "smart" aliens or minorities and another caste of "uncouth" Turks, either soldiers or peasants, was now replaced with a new one of the republic, unified by a homogeneous and soundly balanced Turkish society.

Of great importance in the economic development of the country were a number of government-controlled banks. The Central Bank issued notes and supervised over-all financial policies. The Sümer Bank financed new state-owned industries, the Eti Bank promoted mining, the Is Bank dealt with business transactions, and the older Agricultural Bank assisted farm production. The confidence generated abroad in the soundness of the new system was exemplified by a series of foreign loans granted Turkey during the interwar period.

[3] Initiated in 1934 and repeated in 1938 and 1946.

The state spared no effort to promote foreign trade by concluding barter agreements, organizing fairs and exhibitions,[4] and establishing chambers of commerce. Care was taken to balance foreign trade properly, and this was successfully achieved throughout the interwar period. Because of the prevailing *étatisme* in Turkey and of general autarchic trends in Europe, by 1939 80 to 90 per cent of Turkey's foreign trade was transacted on the basis of clearing agreements.

A further reform of family names broke still another link with the past. Family names are by no means a universal feature in Moslem countries, and their absence frequently contributed to confusion. In 1934 all Turks were ordered by law to choose legal surnames. At the same time old Ottoman titles and decorations were abolished. The Grand National Assembly gave the name *Atatürk* ("Father of the Turks") to Kemal, Ismet Pasha transformed himself into Ismet Inönü in commemoration of his victory over the Greeks, and other Turkish leaders were obliged to follow suit.

Turkey conducted a consistent demographic policy. Kemalist leaders were aware of the fact that their new state was deficient in manpower. Wars for twelve years had exacted a heavy toll of men. The Mesopotamian and Syrian campaigns during World War I were particularly costly, and if all the ambitious plans of the German High Command regarding the *Yilderim* had been put into effect, the loss of life to the Turks might have been even greater. In fact, if it had not been for large numbers of desertions [5] from the Turkish army in the last phases of the war, the biological survival of the nation might have been questioned. Both for economic and for military purposes it was essential to fill the gaps, and in 1934 the Grand Assembly passed an immigration law that encouraged Turks resident abroad to return and settle in Turkey. The new arrivals, who came mostly from the Balkans (Rumania and Bulgaria) but partly from Russia, were directed toward the western and central provinces of Anatolia. Some were settled in Eastern Thrace.

Finally, mention should be made of the social legislation. The latter kept pace with the growing industrialization of the country.

---

[4] Of which the Izmir fairs have gained international reputation.

[5] This, by the way, is no reflection on the military valor of the Turkish soldier, which is of the highest order. The testimony of T. E. Lawrence, General Wavell, and other authorities supports this statement. Mass desertions at the end of the war resulted primarily from the complete breakdown of many essential supplies and services, which in many cases made desertion the only practical way of survival.

A Central Labor Office in Ankara, with branches in provincial towns, administered the Labor Law, which was passed in 1936. Public health and social security matters were cared for by the Ministry of Hygiene and Social Welfare. Despite the cultivation of poppies there was never any widespread addiction to opium among the Turks (as was the case in Iran), and the state opium monopoly reduced the danger of an indiscriminate use of narcotics by the population.

Political Opposition and Kurdish Revolts

These reforms were severely criticized and bitterly resented by some groups in Turkey. *Etatisme* and its economic policies were opposed by business circles in Istanbul (preponderantly non-Turkish), who disliked high taxes and tariffs and the general autarchic tendency. It was, however, the secularization of public life that met with the strongest opposition, particularly among the backward Kurdish tribes in the east.

The first major Kurdish revolt occurred in February 1925. Led by Sheikh Said of Genj (west of Lake Van), the Kurds seized control in a number of southeastern vilayets, demanding the restoration of Islam to its old status as well as local autonomy. The government accused Said of intrigue with the Ottoman pretender, Prince Selim, and procaliphate circles, mobilized its army, and sternly suppressed the rebellion. Moreover, the government set up the so-called "independence courts," which dealt with cases of treason and sedition in a summary way. Kurdish revolts were repeated in 1929 and 1930, but never reached equally alarming proportions. The government succeeded in restoring order in both cases. A number of Kurds were deported to the interior or to Thrace. A general inspectorate for the area was established, and the eastern vilayets have become virtually inaccessible to foreign visitors.

Opposition to Kemal's rule was not limited to business and religious circles. The dynamic way in which Kemal forced Turkey to Westernize herself necessitated strong and uncompromising measures which did not harmonize with the professed democracy of the regime. Critics accused Kemal of being intoxicated with power, denounced the group of servile "desperadoes" with whom he surrounded himself, deplored drinking bouts in his residence in the Chankaya suburb of Ankara, and demanded curtailment of his authority. In 1926 Kemal decided to curb this opposition. In the summer his cabinet announced the discovery of a plot to assassinate him and proceeded to arrest considerable numbers of Young Turkish politicians, supporters of the deposed sultan, and also some dissidents from Kemal's own party. In the trial that ensued, eighteen of those arrested were sentenced to death. The dissidents from Kemal's party were treated more leniently, being generally banished for a period of ten years.[6]

Having thus smashed the opposition, Kemal and his party remained undisputed masters of the country. It was essentially a one-party system of government. The party's secretary-general traditionally combined his duties with those of the minister of interior. The democratic processes of free discussion and majority vote were visible more within the People's Party itself than in the official façade which was the Grand National Assembly. Most of the basic political decisions, including important legislation, were first debated in closed party sessions. Once a decision was made, the matter was sent to the Grand Assembly, where the same party members—now in their official capacity as deputies—made it law by formal vote.

There were a few temporary exceptions to this one-party system. In the early twenties there was an opposition group known as the Republican, later the Republican Progressive, Party. It was suppressed in 1925 on the order of an "independence court" in Ankara because of its alleged complicity with the Kurdish rebels. In 1930, with Kemal's permission and encouragement, another small opposition party was established. It was the Independent Republican Party, and its leadership was entrusted to Kemal's old friend, Fethi Okyar. Kemal wanted constructive criticism and hoped that a moderate opposition party would provide it. The experiment, however, proved disappointing, and the party was soon disbanded. In 1935 Kemal decided to allow the election of sixteen independent deputies from a number of vilayets. These included, among others, two Greeks, one Jew, and one Armenian. This small independent group thereafter became a permanent feature in the Grand National Assembly.

The government's policies were supported by a number of dailies and periodicals. These were under the general supervision of the Press Department in the Ministry of Interior and were serviced by the government-owned Anatolian News Agency. The semiofficial *Ulus* of Ankara usually reflected the official opinions of the government. Among other major newspapers were *Cümhüriyet*, *Tan*, and *Aksam*.

[6] The penalty of banishment was imposed on General Kazim Kara Bekir and Refet and Ali Fuat Pasha; on Hussein Reuf and Dr. Adnan Bey and his wife, Halide Edib, a well-known writer; and on a number of others.

The People's House in the capital published a weekly, *Ankara,* in French, seconded by a monthly, *La Turquie Kemaliste,* a Press Department publication. Both served to interpret Turkey to foreign observers. Official influence on the press, especially in matters of foreign policy, was considerable. It was possible for the government to inspire the publication of certain articles in outwardly independent journals in order to test the reaction of foreign powers. This device was frequently used during the periods of international crisis.

TURKISH FOREIGN POLICY

The transformation from the Ottoman Empire into a republic reduced Turkey from a major power to a small nation. This, however, was only an outward manifestation, since in reality the old Empire had been weak and disintegrating while the reborn Turkey of Kemal proved to be a relatively strong, closely knit, and homogeneous political organism. The new Turkey, however, was only a medium-sized country with a population of sixteen million bordering on giant Russia with her two hundred million people and exposed to the influence of the naval powers which dominated the Mediterranean. Thus, no matter how perfect Turkey's political and military machine was, her strength had obvious limitations. Perhaps the greatest merit of Kemal and his followers was their sober realization of these limitations and their moderate, realistic foreign policy, which corresponded to the strength of their country. There was nothing romantic or adventurous in Kemal's foreign policy—except, of course, during the initial period between his landing at Samsun and the Lausanne Treaty. During that brief period he and his patriotic friends achieved exactly the objectives that a sober mind would have deemed impossible of accomplishment. They—the nationalists—then challenged the authority of the victorious Entente and fought a successful war against several powerful enemies at once. But even if one considers this behavior romantic, one must realize that Kemal and his friends had little to lose except their lives. The Treaty of Sèvres had practically reduced Turkey to the status of a Western colony, and it would have been hard to conceive of any appreciably worse treatment for a defeated nation.

Victory over their enemies gave Kemal and his followers tremendous confidence in their own strength and ability and raised the morale throughout the entire nation. It would have been easy to adopt a dangerous and ambitious course of aggrandizement and

128

unrealistic imperialism. Yet this was not done. Since the signing of
the Treaty of Lausanne, Turkey has been essentially a *status quo*
power. The Turks have had as great a stake in the preservation of
peace as has had any other *status quo* country. There have, however,
been some differences between the Versailles powers, such as France
or Great Britain, and Turkey. These have been due largely to two
chief factors: First, Turkey could not shake off overnight the emotional load of resentment, especially against the British, which her revisionist war had generated. Secondly, the Treaty of Lausanne left
three matters unsettled, at least from Turkey's point of view—the
problem of Mosul (i.e., of the boundary with Iraq); the problem of
Alexandretta (i.e., of the boundary with Syria and the autonomy of
the sanjak); and the problem of the Straits. (Here, true enough, a
definite convention was signed, but it imposed irritating limitations on
Turkish sovereignty.) In these three matters only did Turkey favor
any revision of the peace settlement. These three problems, added to
the above-mentioned emotional bias against the "imperialist" Entente, led Turkey in the early twenties to seek the friendship of the
new proletarian state. Soviet Russia, because of her revolutionary program and her basic opposition to the Paris Peace Settlement and the
League of Nations, also favored revisionism. When in 1921 Bekir Sami
Bey, Kemal's foreign minister, went to Moscow to negotiate a treaty of
friendship, both parties considered themselves revisionist and anti-
Entente. After Lausanne, however, this was no longer true, since
Turkey became quite satisfied with her own peace settlement. Nevertheless, since Russia continued in her policy of opposition to the
status quo and since Turkey was still at odds on a few minor points
with Great Britain and France, countries whose relations with Soviet
Russia were strained, Turkey found it advantageous to continue her
collaboration with Russia despite differences in their respective political ideologies. Russia had an equally good reason to reciprocate,
because Turkey was anti-imperialist and anti-Entente. It was one
of the cardinal points of Soviet foreign policy of that period to
cultivate Turkey's good will and friendship, in order to show the
exploited nations of Asia that Moscow was their only and true friend.
Furthermore, Turkish friendship carried with it the promise of an
advantageous accommodation in the Straits, in case of war with the
capitalist West—a consideration which no Russian government could
disregard.

At the Lausanne conference the Soviet delegation (permitted to participate on a limited basis) staunchly supported Turkey on the question of the Straits, but the Entente's will prevailed to the chagrin of both delegations.

The Mosul Controversy

The case of Mosul indirectly contributed to the cementing of Turko-Soviet friendship. According to the Treaty of Lausanne, Mosul was to remain under the temporary occupation of Great Britain, pending the conclusion of a definitive agreement. If no agreement was reached within a year, the matter was then to be referred to the Council of the League of Nations. Great Britain brought the Mosul controversy to the League in 1924. An international commission, headed by the Estonian General Laidoner, was appointed to investigate the matter. Following the receipt of its report, the Council, on December 16, 1925, awarded Mosul to Iraq on the condition that the British mandate over that state should continue for twenty-five years.[7] Disappointed, Turkey questioned the legality of the award, contending that the Council's function was that of conciliation and not of arbitration. The following day, December 17, the Turkish foreign minister rushed to Paris and there concluded a new treaty of friendship and nonaggression with the Soviet plenipotentiaries. The treaty, amounting to a virtual political alliance, was to last for ten years, at which time it could be renewed. It marked the apogee of cordiality in Soviet-Turkish relations. Although the friendship was maintained and as late as 1934 Russia granted Turkey an industrial credit and expert assistance for the execution of the Turkish five-year plan of industrialization, a gradual cooling off in the relations could be observed. Soviet Russia could not wholeheartedly approve the stern measures taken by Kemal against Communist propaganda in Turkey, nor could she be too enthusiastic about the gradual reconciliation between Turkey and the West, as evidenced by a series of treaties.

The most important act of reconciliation occurred with Great Britain. As pointed out earlier, resentment had accumulated against the British. British support of the Greeks in 1919, the championing of national minorities, British occupation of Constantinople after the war and the resulting arbitrary arrests and deportations, the British pro-Arab attitude and support of the Kurds, together with the Mosul

[7] For a detailed account of the conflict, see Leon Crutiansky, *La Question de Mossoul* (Paris, 1927). For a general background, consult Harry C. Luke, *Mosul and Its Minorities* (London, 1925).

problem, accounted for this resentment. The Kurdistan problem
seemed particularly irritating. A number of British intelligence officers in the Iraqi mandatory administration entertained the idea that
an independent Kurdish state under British influence might be carved
out of the territories of Iraq, Turkey, and possibly Iran. This idea
originated long before the Lausanne Treaty, and the support of
Kurdish aspirations was used as a weapon against the recalcitrant
Turkish nationalists. The provision about Kurdish autonomy in the
Treaty of Sèvres, the Kurdish rebellion of 1925 (which coincided with
the Mosul controversy), and finally British insistence on retention of
the Kurdish-inhabited province of Mosul appeared to the Turks as
evidences of a sinister plot to undermine Turkish political and territorial integrity.[8]

Much wisdom and moderation were required to put aside these
suspicions and to make a friendly advance toward their former
enemies. On June 5, 1926, Turkey concluded a treaty with Great
Britain definitely settling the Mosul question. Turkey agreed to relinquish her claims to Mosul in return for the promise that 10 per cent
of Mosul's oil production should be available for her use. To Turkey's
satisfaction, no mention was made of Kurdish autonomy or independence. Moreover, the British accepted the Turkish decision not to
allow the Assyrian expellees of World War I to return to their homes
in Turkey. The treaty resulted in definite improvement in Anglo-
Turkish relations. In 1929 part of the British Mediterranean fleet paid
a courtesy visit to Istanbul, and former enmity gave place to a steadily
growing friendship.

Turkey and the Balkans

Political settlement with Britain was followed by a reconciliation
with Britain's traditional protégée, Greece. Here again in a truly
statesmanlike fashion, emotion was overcome by sober wisdom.
Following the Greek adventure in Asia Minor and the drastic exchange of populations, no real political ground for continued enmity
remained. The two countries shared an equal interest in preserving
the peace and in preventing Bulgaria from embarking upon a revisionist drive in Thrace. Reconciliation took the form of a Greek-

[8] These fears seemed exaggerated. It is true that field agents of the British
intelligence (Major Soane and his group) often supported the scheme of Kurdish
independence, but other and prominent specialists on the Middle East, including
Sir Percy Cox, opposed it, and the latter's views ultimately prevailed. See Philip P.
Graves, *Briton and Turk* (London, 1941), pp. 221–222.

Turkish treaty concluded on October 30, 1930, in Ankara. It settled the property claims of the exchanged populations and many other controversial questions. The two parties reaffirmed their attachment to the territorial *status quo* and accepted the principle of naval equality in the eastern Mediterranean.

Turkey's entry into the League of Nations on July 18, 1932, confirmed her peaceful intentions and her rapprochement to the *status quo* camp in Europe.

The treaty with Greece marked the beginning of an active Turkish policy in the Balkans, an area of traditional interest. Turkey dreaded Italy's revisionism. Mussolini's indiscreet remarks concerning the Mediterranean as "mare nostrum" and his undisguised ambitions in the Near East, together with the Italian possession of the strategic Dodecanese Islands just off the Turkish coast, filled Turkish leaders with grave anxiety. The Turks, to whom the Balkans were the first line of defense in case of Italian expansionism, were vitally interested in the stability of the peninsula and in the political solidarity of those southeastern European nations. They greeted with enthusiasm and actively encouraged the trend toward unity manifested by the Balkan states. On February 9, 1934, Turkey became a party to the Balkan Entente Pact which united Greece, Yugoslavia, Rumania, and herself in a mutual guarantee of peace, independence, and territorial integrity and which established consultative machinery among its signatories. An ideal settlement would have been to create a Balkan federation which would include Bulgaria as well. Despite various overtures to join the Entente, Bulgaria remained sulkily apart, ardently revisionist, and a hotbed of Macedonian terroristic intrigue. The Bulgars insisted on access to the Mediterranean and on the return of southern Dobruja, and refused to commit themselves to accept existing boundaries. The openly expressed determination of the Entente to preserve the *status quo* put a practical check on Bulgarian revisionism. It also served as a timely reminder to the major European revisionists that they could not count on dissension among the Entente members.

Turkey's fears of Italy were not unfounded. In a major speech on March 18, 1934, Mussolini announced his African and Asian ambitions. In the fall of 1935 Italy invaded Abyssinia. Turkey faithfully supported League action against the aggressors. Undeterred by sanctions, Italy completed this conquest by spring, and thus made a serious alteration in the Middle-Eastern–African structure. This trend was accentuated by Hitler's unilateral violations of the peace treaty, such as the rearmament of Germany announced in March 1935, and the remilitarization of the Rhineland a year later. The European totalitarians were obviously on the move, and diplomatic revisionism had given place to military action.

Attached to peaceful reform and reconstruction, Turkey could not but view with apprehension these imperialistic manifestations. She was, therefore, irresistibly drawn toward closer co-operation with France and Great Britain, two pillars of the European *status quo*. The trend toward rapprochement was reciprocal, since these two countries also needed Turkey's co-operation. Aware of this, Turkey was in a position to bargain and thus to settle the two remaining questions that prevented complete harmony between her and the West—the problems of the Straits and of Alexandretta.

The Straits question was settled to Turkey's satisfaction by the Agreement of Montreux on July 20, 1936.[9] Turkey's main request— the remilitarization of the Straits—was accepted by the Lausanne Treaty signatories, with the exception of Italy, who boycotted the conference. By this act Turkey regained military control of this strategic waterway and strengthened her position in the Mediterranean–Black Sea region.

Sanjak of Alexandretta

The problem of Alexandretta proved more complicated because of the involvement of a third party, Syria, in this Franco-Turkish dispute. The Franklin-Bouillon agreement of 1921 [10] provided for a special administrative regime of the sanjak of Alexandretta, which had an estimated 40 per cent Turkish population. For a number of years the matter remained unchanged, the Turks hoping that one day a revision might be reached with France. The conclusion of the Franco-Syrian Treaty of September, 1936, by which Syria was promised independence [11] including Alexandretta, made the question more acute and provoked Turkish protests. Turkey brought the matter to the League of Nations Council. The Council, having first secured French and Turkish acceptance, drew up in May 1937 a special statute calling for demilitarization, autonomy, and special guarantees for the Turkish population of the sanjak. Despite these arrangements, unrest and disorders prevailed in the district. They led, in December of that year, to the denouncement by Turkey of the Turko-Syrian

[9] See Chapter XV.   [10] See above, p. 106.   [11] See below, p. 271.

133

treaty of friendship of 1926 and to a campaign of recrimination with France. On July 3, 1938, following the dispatch of a military mission to Ankara, France and Turkey reached an agreement whereby the sanjak was proclaimed a Franco-Turkish condominium. It was to be policed by French and Turkish troops pending a general election which would determine the sanjak's future status. On July 5 Turkish troops entered the disputed area, and in September the population went to the polls in the midst of feverish pro-Turkish and pro-Arab agitation. The election gave the Turks a majority of 22 out of 40 seats in the Assembly, which promptly, on September 2, proclaimed autonomy under the name of the Republic of Hatay. The republic hoisted Turkish flags and sent a delegation to Ankara asking for union with the mother country. French troops were still in the territory, in a rather awkward position, and their unwarlike appearance contrasted sharply with the spick-and-span Turkish regiments sent into the sanjak with the obvious aim of impressing the populace. For all practical purposes, Turkey was supreme in the sanjak, and this fact only awaited official bilateral confirmation.

Alliance with France and Britain, 1939

Such a confirmation came on June 23, 1939, when France and Turkey concluded a nonaggression pact, preliminary to a full-fledged alliance, toward which they were driven by the onward march of the Axis powers. France consented to the annexation by Turkey of the Republic of Hatay and granted her credits for the purchase of armaments. By this act the last remaining grievance against the West was eliminated, and the road was paved for closer co-operation.

Reconciliation with France found a parallel development in the strengthening of Anglo-Turkish bonds. Ever since Mussolini's Ethiopian adventure, the two countries had been drawing closer together. During his short-lived reign, Edward VIII visited Istanbul while cruising in the Mediterranean on his yacht. The Turkish fleet paid a courtesy visit to the British naval base of Valetta at Malta, and Ismet Inönü, Kemal's closest associate and foremost statesman, attended the coronation of George VI. On May 27, 1938, Britain and Turkey concluded three credit agreements, and a year later (May 12, 1939) both countries issued a "declaration of mutual guarantee" which was soon followed by the above-mentioned Franco-Turkish pact.

In the summer months of 1939 Great Britain and France sought to establish a common front with Russia, in view of the German threats

134

to world peace. Turkey followed these developments with close attention, interested as she was in the strengthening of the peace front. The conclusion of the Nazi-Soviet pact of August 23, 1939, gave Turkish leaders a severe shock. Since Atatürk's death and Ismet Inönü's election to the presidency (November 10, 1938), they had been determined to cultivate the great Kemalist heritage, to preserve peace, and to avoid dangerous entanglements. Their disappointment was keen when they learned that their formidable Soviet neighbor, hitherto friendly and since 1934 openly espousing the *status quo* and collective security, had joined hands with the Nazi proponents of armed revision. It meant, moreover, that their friendship with France and Great Britain, instead of being approved, would now be criticized in Moscow. After the Nazi-Soviet pact, Turkish-Soviet relations became strained. The German attack on Poland on September 1 and the Soviet invasion of Poland's eastern provinces on September 17 added considerably to the tension. War had become a reality, and a false step by Turkish diplomacy might easily prove disastrous to the cause of national survival.

Moscow Negotiations, 1939

In late September the Turkish foreign minister, Sükrü Saracoglu, left for Moscow for the purpose of concluding a new pact with Russia.[12] Conversations toward such a pact had been going on for some time between the Soviet ambassador at Ankara, Terentieff, and the Turkish government. Both parties, however, sought different objectives. Turkey desired a pact that would reaffirm Soviet support of the *status quo* in the Black Sea region, and by the same token confirm Soviet respect of Turkish independence and territorial integrity, and that would clear the way for a proposed Turkish alliance with Great Britain and France. Russia's objectives were quite different. Having moved closer to Germany, she now resented the prospect of a British-French-Turkish alliance. Germany at that time was primarily interested in keeping Britain and France from building a chain of encircling alliances in the Balkans and the Near East. She viewed with concern the guarantee that London and Paris in April 1939 had given to Greece and Rumania to defend their integrity

[12] David J. Dallin, *Soviet Russia's Foreign Policy, 1939–1942* (New Haven, Conn., 1942), p. 111. An exhaustive documentary treatment of the Soviet-Turkish negotiations is contained in Harry N. Howard, *Germany, the Soviet Union, and Turkey during World War II* (Department of State Bull.; Washington, 1948), pp. 63 ff.

135

and she sought to neutralize the Balkan states and Turkey. Turkey held a key position, since Franco-British aid to Rumania would have to pass through the Straits. To keep Turkey from co-operating with the West thus became one of the major objectives of German foreign policy at the beginning of the war.

German persuasion alone, however, would not be sufficient to sway Turkey's decision. Germany needed the aid of Russia, who as a close and powerful neighbor was in a much stronger position to press for a change in Turkish policy. Captured wartime documents show that the German ambassador in Moscow, Count von der Schulenburg, one of the main architects of the Soviet-Nazi Pact, was in constant contact with the Kremlin during Saracoglu's visit to Moscow and pressed Foreign Commissar Molotov to heed German desiderata. Soviet leaders were willing to follow his advice. Having chosen neutrality in the German-Western war, Russia was ready to aid Germany in neutralizing the Black Sea region, and thus to bar the opening of a second front in the Balkans. Such a front would bring hostilities close to the Soviet border, a situation Russia wanted to avoid. Moreover, the presence of a Franco-British fleet in the Black Sea—a possible result of an alliance with Turkey—might create serious security problems for "collaborationist" Russia. Thus, both to appease Germany and to keep the conflict away from her borders, Russia desired Turkish neutrality.

Considering the basic divergence in objectives, it is no wonder that Saracoglu's mission to Moscow failed. It was an extraordinary visit in the annals of diplomacy, because the foreign minister remained away from home for almost a month at a time of great international crisis. His trip coincided with the visit that the German foreign minister, Joachim von Ribbentrop, paid to the Soviet Union. The Nazi minister, who had come to discuss the division of eastern Europe into the German and Soviet spheres, was given priority in Moscow, and Saracoglu was kept waiting for weeks between conferences.

Stalin and Molotov submitted to him two proposals: (1) to close the Straits to British and French warships, and (2) to conclude a mutual assistance pact with the Soviet Union, which would draw Turkey away from her contemplated alliance with Britain and France.

Saracoglu flatly refused the first demand inasmuch as it would mean a unilateral violation of the Montreux Straits Convention and would cause hostilities with the West. As to the second proposal, lengthy negotiations ensued, during which the Turkish minister constantly

136

consulted London and Paris. By that time Turkish-British-French conversations for a definitive alliance were far advanced, and most of the major points of the agreement settled. In order to reconcile her Western friendships with Soviet objections, Turkey was willing to formulate her proposed alliance with Britain and France in such a way that it would explicitly exclude any common anti-Soviet action. This concession was made with the approval of the British and the French, who fully understood Turkey's difficult position. Such an arrangement might prove satisfactory to Russia, and at one time during the Moscow negotiations the Soviet leaders seemed to be ready to conclude a pact on that basis. But German pressure prevailed, and Moscow insisted that, in her treaty of alliance with the West, Turkey must promise to refrain from engaging in war with Germany. This, of course, was unacceptable to Saracoglu, as it would render the Turko-British-French alliance meaningless. Germany preferred to see no Russo-Turkish pact at all than a pact which would result in safeguards to Russia only, and not to herself. Anxious to oblige the Nazis, the Soviet leaders finally informed the Turkish foreign minister that they were not interested in the pact.

The net result of Saracoglu's visit to Moscow was that he learned, much to his uneasiness, of a rather pronounced degree of Nazi-Soviet co-operation and of consequent Soviet opposition to Turkish links with the West. The trip impressed upon Turkish leaders the need for great caution in their international relations but did not deflect them from the basic course of co-operation with the West.

Saracoglu left Moscow on October 17, and before he reached Ankara Prime Minister Refik Saydam on October 19 signed the Treaty of Alliance with Great Britain and France. The treaty was not quite an equal arrangement. On the one hand, Great Britain and France promised Turkey aid and assistance in case of aggression by a European power. On the other, Turkey pledged help to her partners only if the war extended to the Mediterranean area. Turkey's aid and co-operation with the other two signatories was explicit in case the latter had to fulfill their guarantees to Greece and Rumania. No signatory was allowed to sign a separate armistice or peace treaty with enemy powers. Protocol no. 2, added to and forming an integral part of the treaty, stated: "The obligations undertaken by Turkey in virtue of the above-mentioned Treaty cannot compel that country to take action having as its effect, or involving as its consequence, entry into armed conflict with the U.S.S.R."

137

The treaty was to be valid for fifteen years and was accompanied by a financial agreement, according to which Britain and France granted Turkey a credit of £25,000,000 for the purchase of war materials, a loan of £15,000,000 in gold, and an additional credit of £3,500,000 to liquidate British and French "frozen" commercial assets.

Moscow was highly critical of the treaty when it was officially announced, and Molotov in his speech of October 31 made vocal his disapproval of Turkey's action.[13]

Turkey and World War II, 1939–1941

During the Second World War Turkey's foreign policy was motivated by desire to avoid attack or occupation by the totalitarian powers. The Turks were anxious to avoid German bombing and they believed that Germany would prefer to conciliate rather than crush them. Distrust and fear of Russia were always present in Turkish minds, and they were dominant in Turkey's foreign policy.

Until spring of 1940 her only major move was to close the Straits (in 1939) to foreign warships, in line with Arts. 20 and 21 of the Montreux Convention. The defeat of France and the last-minute intervention of Italy posed a problem for the Turkish government. War had, indeed, extended into the Mediterranean, and, if the Tripartite Treaty of Alliance was to be literally observed, Turkey was bound to take action against Italy. With the surrender of France on June 26, 1940, however, it became clear that conditions had changed so radically that it would be unrealistic to expect Turkey to rush headlong into the conflict. This was precisely the stand taken by Prime Minister Saydam when in June he told the Grand Assembly that Turkey would remain nonbelligerent.

Throughout 1940 Turkey feared a German move eastward, and she was active, as Britain's partner, in promoting greater unity among the Balkan states. The main obstacle was, as usual, Bulgarian revisionism, and to overcome this Turkey advised Rumania to reach some compromise over the controversial territorial issues. Her advice fell on deaf ears, and both Rumania and Bulgaria gradually slipped into the German orbit.

Mussolini's invasion of Greece in October 1940 brought Fascist aggression close to Turkey's door. The Greek crisis prompted Britain's foreign secretary, Anthony Eden, to pay a hurried visit to Ankara in

[13] Dallin, *op. cit.*, p. 111.

February 1941 in order to review the war situation with Turkish leaders and to obtain their approval for the use of British troops in defense of Greece. Such a step meant a diversion of some forces that might be needed later to aid Turkey. Hence the British felt it necessary to consult Ankara. This visit was preceded by Anglo-Turkish staff talks, which took place in the autumn of 1940.

The first half of 1941 witnessed smashing German victories in Yugoslavia and Greece, the conquest of Crete, and the dispatch of a German force to Libya. The situation was further aggravated by an anti-British rebellion in Iraq and Axis infiltration into Vichy-held Syria. The German army was also in occupation of Rumania and Bulgaria. All Greek islands in the Aegean, even those close to the Turkish coast, were in German hands. By June 1941 Turkey was almost surrounded by countries dominated by German military might or political influence. The sole exception was her frontier with Russia, but the latter's enigmatic policy was far from reassuring.

Turkish-German Relations

The physical approach of German power to Turkey's frontiers brought Turkish-German relations to a showdown. In the course of their relations with each other there had been friendship and there were still some romantic memories of a common struggle in the days of World War I. While many Turks resented Germany's intention to make Turkey another "Egypt," i.e., a virtual protectorate, many others, especially among the military, had a warm feeling for the martial and efficient Teutonic nation. Despite political controversies during World War I, there had been surprisingly little mutual recrimination after defeat in 1918. Whatever emotional hostility remained in both nations was directed against the victorious Versailles powers who, as viewed from Berlin and Ankara, imposed humiliating peace terms upon the vanquished. Under these circumstances it was not difficult for the Weimar republic to regain the friendship and confidence of the Turks. The employment of numerous German professors, experts, and construction firms by the Kemalist administration eloquently testified to the speedy revival of the old bonds of friendship.

Hitler's advent to power did not per se alienate Turkey from Germany. After all, the Turks were not prone to shed tears over the ill treatment of a national minority by another country. Moreover, some dynamic features of the new regime in Berlin filled them with a

139

certain amount of admiration. As for the lack of parliamentary democracy under Hitler's rule, few worried about that in Turkey. Economically, co-operation with Germany was promising, and the barter agreements which Dr. Hjalmar Schacht skillfully negotiated in Ankara in the 1930's increased the volume of Turkish foreign trade, relieved the pressure of depression, and permitted Turkey to sell some goods to Germany at prices 20 to 40 per cent higher than those of the world market. By 1939 up to 90 per cent of Turkey's foreign trade was transacted through clearing agreements, and Germany received about one-half of all Turkish exports.

The basically revisionist character of Nazi foreign policy did not quite comport with the Turkish devotion to the *status quo,* but, so long as Germany kept her hands off southeastern Europe, Turkey had no particular cause for alarm. The cooling of Turko-German relations came gradually as a result of the formation of the Rome-Berlin Axis. Turkish fears of Italian expansionism have already been discussed.[14] Implicit German support of Italian claims underlined the difference between German and Turkish objectives. By her participation in the Nyon conference of 1937, on the policing of the Mediterranean during the Spanish Civil War, Turkey stressed her interest in preserving the *status quo* and the principle of collective security, both features unpleasant to Germany. The Munich agreement of 1938 gave Turkey new concern since it illustrated the close collaboration between the European dictators. Mussolini's attack on Albania on April 7, 1939, precipitated Turkish negotiations with Britain and France and definitely marked a point of separation from the Axis camp. Eager to prevent Turkey from joining the Western powers, in late April 1939 Hitler sent as ambassador to Ankara, the ex-chancellor of the Reich, Franz von Papen. It was hoped in Berlin that Von Papen, a former staff officer in Falkenhayn's army in Syria and a man possessing much diplomatic skill and good Turkish contacts, would be able to influence Turkey's policies. This was not the case, however, as the conclusion of the Turkish-French-British alliance subsequently proved. But Von Papen did not relent in his efforts to improve Turkish-German relations. Generally speaking, his diplomacy in Ankara passed through three distinct stages. During the first (1939–1940), he attempted to keep Turkey neutral and to dissuade her from an Anglo-French alliance. During the second (1941–1943), he exerted pressure to bring about closer economic, political,

[14] See above, p. 132.

140

and military ties between Berlin and Ankara. During the third (1944), he again reverted to an effort to keep the Turks neutral.

While the Turks needed no urging to stay neutral, it was more difficult to get them to co-operate with the Axis. In the spring of 1941 Germany's position was so strong after her Balkan victories that Turkey reluctantly agreed to begin negotiations on a bilateral treaty. Von Papen sought to secure Ankara's permission to unlimited transit of German war materials and passage of a disguised contingent of troops through Turkish territory toward Iraq, Syria, and Iran. In return he was authorized to promise rectification of the Turkish border in Thrace, a few Greek islands in the Aegean, and a guarantee of Turkish security and the safety of the Straits.[15]

On June 18, 1941, Von Papen succeeded in concluding a ten-year treaty of nonaggression with Turkey. The Turks accepted it as a safeguard against German aggression but took care to insert a clause which stated that previous commitments of the signatories would not be affected by the treaty. German motivation was clear; they desired to neutralize Turkey and isolate Russia prior to their invasion of that country scheduled for June 22.

The rapid advance of the Reichswehr in Russia emboldened Germany in her relations with Turkey. Berlin began to exert pressure on Ankara for closer collaboration. Germany was interested in Turkish raw materials, especially in chrome, which was essential for the production of high-grade steel. Turkey, however, had a chrome agreement with Great Britain, which she refused to violate.

What ensued could be called a "chrome war" between Germany and the Western Allies, with Turkey as a reluctant battleground. Economically, the efforts of the two protagonists to outbid each other netted Turkey tremendous gains, since the prices paid to her were far above the world market price. Politically, however, the whole process was most embarrassing and dangerous.

On October 9, 1941, partly succumbing to German pressure, Turkey concluded with the Reich a trade pact to last until March 31, 1943. It provided for the sale of 90,000 tons of chrome ore to Germany in 1943–1944 (i.e., after the expiration of the Anglo-Turkish chrome agreement). In return, Germany promised to deliver war equipment worth 100,000,000 Turkish pounds, of which 18,000,000 pounds' worth would be shipped before the end of 1942.

[15] *La Politique Allemande, 1941–1943: Documents Secrets du Ministère des Affaires Etrangères d'Allemagne* (Paris, 1946).

Throughout 1941 and 1942 Von Papen pressed Turkey to become "more and more friendly" toward Germany and to grant the Reichswehr transit facilities to the Arab countries and the Suez Canal. In addition to the inducements mentioned in connection with the Turkish-German pact of June 18, 1941, Germany used two other devices to win Turkey's support. The first was the revelation of the far-reaching Soviet ambitions to secure military control of the Straits, which Molotov had repeatedly stressed to the German government during the period of Nazi-Soviet collaboration. Considering these Soviet claims, Turkey had, according to Berlin, nothing to gain and much to lose from an Allied victory. The second device was an attempt to revive and encourage Pan-Turanian tendencies in Turkey. The advance of the German army into the southern, Moslem-inhabited regions of the Soviet Empire (the Crimea and the Caucasus) gave Germany a trump card of major importance in her relations with Turkey. The German Foreign Office wanted to give these Turkish-speaking areas autonomy and invited some Turks to aid in the administration as expert advisers. Germany showed a disposition to negotiate with Turkey about the future status of the areas in question. By conceding to Turkey the right to organize the liberated Turko-Tatar areas of the Soviet Union into a federation, Von Papen and an influential group in the German Foreign Office hoped to secure Turkish collaboration during the war.

Although these inducements profoundly impressed Turkish Pan-Turanians and attracted the attention of some military leaders including Marshal Cakmak, the official Turkish attitude was noncommittal. In an important conversation with Von Papen on August 27, 1942, Prime Minister Saracoglu stated that as a Turk he "passionately [desired] the annihilation of Russia," and that such an exploit, about to be accomplished by the Führer, did not occur more than once in a century. He believed that Germany had a major mission to carry out in liberating the Turkish peoples of Russia. As prime minister of Turkey, however, he must take care not to give the Russians the slightest pretext to annihilate, by way of reprisals, the Turko-Mongol minorities. For this reason it was necessary for him to maintain absolute neutrality.[16]

Turkey was unwilling to compromise her neutral position by embracing Pan-Turanism. Moreover, it was doubtful whether any tangible arrangement could result from these talks because of the

[16] *Ibid.* pp. 89 ff.

opposition of Alfred Rosenberg's German Ministry for the East to any schemes of Turko-Tatar autonomy. Rosenberg and his clique of power-grasping Nazis did not share the view of the Foreign Ministry on this situation. Selfishly looking for governorships of the occupied areas and anticipating a speedy conquest of the Caucasus, they went so far as to dispatch to Turkey a man who loudly advertised himself as the "Gauleiter of Tiflis," much to the mortification of the German ambassador.[17] In September 1942 Ribbentrop abruptly instructed Von Papen to discontinue the Pan-Turanian conversations in view of the stubborn Turkish neutrality.

This attitude could not be shaken by Von Papen's personal skill, or by his lavish use of money to foster German propaganda,[18] or even by the great advantage of having access, during the critical period, to the secret documents of the British embassy.[19] The maximum advantage Germany could obtain was to conclude two new trade agreements with Turkey: the first on June 2, 1942, followed by a Turkish promise in September to ship her 45,000 tons of chrome, representing half of Turkey's annual production, and the second on April 21, 1943, for the exchange of $30,000,000 worth of goods in the next year.

From the time of the Battle of Stalingrad and the Anglo-American landing in North Africa in the fall of 1942, Germany's military position steadily deteriorated, and so did her diplomatic position. On April 20, 1944, Turkey stopped further shipments of chrome to Germany. On June 15 she put an end to the secret passage of minor German naval craft through the Straits, and on August 2, 1944, she broke diplomatic relations with the Reich.

Turkey and the Western Allies

Turkish attitudes were obviously influenced by the changing fortunes of the war and also by skillful Allied diplomacy. The entry of the United States into the war profoundly affected Turkish political thought. Even before this happened, Turkey had been granted, on

---

[17] L. C. Moyzisch, *Operation Cicero* (New York, 1950), p. 5.

[18] In December 1942 Ribbentrop reportedly sent Von Papen five million Reichsmarks in gold to support pro-German elements in Turkey (*La Politique Allemande*, p. 115).

[19] Between October 1943 and April 1944 the valet of the British ambassador, Sir Hughe Knatchbull-Hugessen, regularly opened the ambassador's safe, photographed the documents, and supplied them to the German secret service agent, L. C. Moyzisch. He was paid £5,000 for a roll of films. Details of this fascinating story are contained in Moyzisch, *op. cit.*, and in the article by Robert W. Kempner, "The Highest Paid Spy in History," *Saturday Evening Post*, Jan. 28, 1950.

December 3, 1941, American lend-lease assistance. This proved to be valuable because of the wartime collapse of foreign trade and the fact that, throughout the war, Turkey was obliged to maintain an army of two million men, thus diverted from their productive occupations.

During the war Turkey maintained close contact with the British, who played a major part in supplying her with military equipment. In December 1942 the British cabinet decided "in principle" to try to bring Turkey into the war on the Allied side. In early February 1943 Prime Minister Churchill and President Inönü, accompanied by high military advisers, met in Adana to look into the problem of Turkish belligerency. Both parties agreed that before Turkey made any move she must be properly equipped militarily. The Adana meeting was consequently followed by visits to Ankara of top British commanders in the Middle East. [20] These men counted on Turkey's entry into the war by the fall of 1943. The result of these talks was an infiltration of Turkey by Royal Air Force personnel, incognito.[21] But, faced with the threat of German reprisal bombing of Istanbul, the Turkish government refused to abandon its position of non-belligerency. Yet Turkey was not absolutely neutral. In September 1943 she gave evidence of this by aiding, first to supply and then to evacuate, those British troops who, following Italy's collapse, had taken over some of the Dodecanese Islands and who were later forced to give them up to the Germans. The evacuation could be attributed to German air superiority, and it served as a reminder to the Turks to proceed with caution.

Although the Turkish position found sympathetic understanding in London and in Washington, at the Moscow and Teheran conferences in October and November 1943, the United States, Russia, and Great Britain agreed that Turkish belligerency should be secured by the end of 1943. What followed constituted another chapter in the "diplomacy of pressure." On his way from the Moscow conference, British Foreign Secretary Anthony Eden met Turkish Foreign Minister Numan Menemencioglu in Cairo and pressed him for a declaration of war. In December, again in Cairo, President Roosevelt and Prime Minister Churchill, fresh from their meeting in Teheran, reiterated this demand to President Inönü, requesting as a first step Allied use of Turkish air bases. The Turks agreed "in principle" but made their

[20] Sir Sholto Douglas, Sir Henry Maitland Wilson, and Sir John Cunningham, representing the R.A.F., the Army, and the Navy, respectively.

[21] Moyzisch, *op. cit.,* p. 56.

144

agreement conditional upon further supply of arms from the West. A British military and air delegation that arrived in Ankara in late January 1944 left empty-handed. The Allies did not conceal their disappointment.

Beginning with the spring of 1944, however, Turkey, as has been pointed out, made several moves to sever economic and political relations with Germany, and this trend was culminated by the declaration of war on the Reich on February 23, 1945. This last act did not evoke much enthusiasm in Ankara, inasmuch as the Turks did not like to imitate Mussolini by entering the war at the eleventh hour.[22] The decision was made largely in order to gain admittance to the United Nations Conference at San Francisco.

Turkish-Soviet Relations

Turkey's relations with Russia were strained. On the one hand, Turkey feared Soviet revisionism in the Straits, and these fears, as we have seen, were skillfully fanned by Von Papen. On the other, Russia resented, first, Turkey's alliance with the Western powers, and then after the Nazi invasion, Turkey's neutrality. After France's collapse in 1940 the German government published a White Book, which revealed that at the time of the Russo-Finnish war in 1939–1940, France had planned, with Turkish approval, to use Turkish bases to bombard Baku in the event of war with Russia.[23] Although vigorous denials were subsequently made by Ankara, this revelation was not conducive to the lessening of tension.

After the German invasion Russia desired Turkey's entry into the war on the Allied side. On September 2, 1943, a Soviet propaganda mouthpiece, *The War and the Working Class*, accused Turkey of prolonging the war by protecting Germany's flank in the Balkans. It was clear that the old friendship was rapidly giving way to open hostility. The increase of Pan-Turanian sentiment in Turkey added another element of friction. In fact, the Turkish government became so alarmed lest the Soviets might be provoked to action that in mid-

[22] Sir Hughe Knatchbull-Hugessen, *Diplomat in Peace and War* (London, 1949), p. 196. The book contains four chapters on Turkey between 1939 and 1944.

[23] This was the so-called "Gamelin Plan," to attack Russia through the Caucasus. It was presented at the request of French Premier Edouard Daladier, and based on recommendations of General Maxime Weygand, commander-in-chief in Syria. Réné Massigli, French ambassador in Ankara, allegedly informed his government that Turkey would co-operate in the execution of these plans. For details, see Dallin, *op. cit.*, pp. 166 ff.

145

May 1944 it publicly dissociated itself from Pan-Turanism. This took the form of arresting a number of Pan-Turanian leaders and of issuing dramatic official declarations about the alleged discovery of a plot against the government, hatched by the "Gray Wolf Society." On May 18 martial law was imposed, and Radio Ankara, in feigned indignation, called the group of plotters a "pro-German one, based on racialism and Fascist principles." On May 13, at a public celebration of National Youth Day, President Inönü intimated that the plot might have been abetted by "foreigners," and paid tribute to the Soviets who "were our [only] friends" during the War of Independence. In June the Pan-Turanian leaders, mostly school teachers but with a sprinkling of bigger names, were court-martialed.

Following this episode, anti-German articles critical of fascism and racialism appeared more frequently in the Turkish press. The Grand Assembly revoked the recently imposed Varlik-Vergisi law which, by instituting a capital levy, proved to be a particular nuisance to the Jews and other national minorities. It was obvious that Turkey was taking pains to ensure her place in the camp of the Allies.

On January 12, 1945, Turkey agreed to open the Straits for the flow of supplies to Russia and on January 29 severed relations with Japan. These steps did not assuage Russian hostility. On March 21 the Soviet government denounced the Soviet-Turkish pact of friendship and nonaggression, which had originally been concluded in 1925 and which had repeatedly been renewed. Turkish-Soviet relations entered in a new and dangerous phase.

From June 1945 on, it was public knowledge that Russia insisted upon four conditions as terms for the renewal of the nonaggression treaty. They included (1) the return to Russia of Kars and Ardahan, (2) the granting of military bases in the Bosphorus and the Dardanelles, (3) a revision of the Montreux Straits Convention, and (4) a revision of the Thracian boundary in favor of Communist-dominated Bulgaria.[24] The nature of these demands became clear when, on December 20, three important Soviet newspapers published an article written by two Georgian scholars who demanded that Turkey restore to the Georgian SSR a Black Sea coastal region situated southwest of Batum, 180 miles long and 75 miles wide. The region included the districts of Artvin, Ardahan, Oltü, Tortum, Ispir, Bayburt, Gümüsane, Giresun, and the important port of Trebizond.

Throughout 1946 Soviet pressure for the revision of the Montreux

[24] Howard, *op. cit.*

Convention continued. Russia demanded that the Straits should come under the control of Turkey as well as other Black Sea powers and that defense of the Straits should be jointly organized by Turkey and and Russia.[25] These demands were steadily rejected by Ankara to the growing impatience of Moscow.

Uneasiness in Turkey at this time was reflected by the extension of martial law, despite the end of the war. From Moscow came a mounting barrage of anti-Turkish propaganda, intensified by the publication in the summer of 1946 of German Foreign Office documents concerning Nazi relations with Turkey. In December the Turkish government announced the arrest of over seventy members of the Turkish Socialist Workers' and Peasants' Party and the Turkish Socialist Party for Communist subversive activities. The two groups were banned and their six press organs suppressed.

By the spring of 1947 Turkish-Soviet relations had reached an all-time low, and Turkey seriously feared armed intervention. On March 12, 1947, President Truman delivered his famous message to Congress in which he proposed assistance to Turkey and Greece, in view of the grave Soviet threats to their security. While this American action introduced a new factor of stability into the Near East which could not be ignored by the Soviets, it did not improve the strained relations between Moscow and Ankara. Later in the year the Russians lodged an official protest against the activities of the Turkish repatriation mission in Germany, Greece, and Italy. The mission had offered Turkish citizenship and other inducements to Moslem displaced persons (mostly fugitives from Russia) if they emigrated to Turkey. In December 5,000 university students in Ankara demonstrated against five reputedly pro-Communist professors, demanding their dismissal. The attitude in the country became increasingly anti-Soviet. It was highlighted on April 27, 1950, when an official communiqué declared that Turkey had "finally and conclusively" rejected Soviet demands for joint control of the Turkish Straits.

Turkish-American Friendship

Much of this growing defiance of Soviet pressure must be ascribed to the rapprochement between Turkey and the United States. American diplomacy initially endeavored to accommodate Russia when the latter brought up the question of the Montreux Convention. At the Big Three Conference of Potsdam, July 5, 1945, the American

[25] For details of the Straits problem, see Chapter XV.

147

delegation, with the British, endorsed what they believed to be legitimate Soviet demands concerning maritime traffic to and from the Black Sea. On November 2, 1945, the United States went so far as to set forth its own formal proposals, very favorable to Russia and, in fact, somewhat reminiscent of the privileged status that tsarist Russia had enjoyed under the Treaty of Unkiar Iskelessi (See Chapter XV). But the United States, with Britain, steadfastly refused to accept Soviet contentions concerning the administration and the defense of the Straits by the Black Sea powers. In a note of August 19, 1946, addressed to Moscow, the American government made it clear that it would oppose any virtual monopoly of power by Russia in the strategic waterway.

The "Truman Doctrine" of opposition to Soviet imperialism, previously referred to, was proclaimed when Soviet pressure on Turkey and Greece was at its highest. In Greece Soviet-sponsored guerrillas endeavored to overthrow the legitimate Athens government; their success would have gravely impaired Turkish security. The British, who had hitherto been mainly responsible for the bolstering of Greek defense and for the supply of war equipment to Turkey, declared that they were no longer in a position to continue these responsibilities. In a bold decision the American government assumed the burden, declaring that the preservation of Greek and Turkish independence was vital to the security of the United States. This was the first major commitment of the United States in the Middle East of a semimilitary nature, and Congress, not quite ready to face the realities, spent a number of weeks debating the necessary appropriations. By mid-May 1947 Congress approved the expenditure of $400,000,000, to be spent on economic and military aid, of which $100,000,000 was assigned to Turkey. Turkey greeted this action with relief and gratitude. President Truman's message marked the beginning of an era of growing American interest in the welfare and security of Turkey and set in motion a number of measures to aid and reassure that country. On May 2, 1947, elements of the United States Mediterranean fleet visited Istanbul, giving rise to enthusiastic pro-American demonstrations. In June an American military mission arrived in Ankara to become a permanent addition to the diplomatic representation. In the same month Turkey signed a contract with two American firms for construction and modernization of airfields.[26] The Turkish chief

[26] Westinghouse Electric and J. G. White. Previously, in October 1946, a contract had been signed with the Radio Corporation of America for the installation of modern radio equipment aboard 31 ships of the Turkish merchant marine.

148

of staff paid an official visit to the United States in the fall of the same year. American experts were hired to advise on railway, sea transport, telegraph, and telephone organization. In the spring of 1948 Turkey received from the United States a number of naval vessels, including long-range submarines, and a contingent of attack bombers, granted under the Turkish assistance act. Simultaneously, arrangements were made for the training of Turkish naval crews in America.

The adoption by Congress of the European Recovery Program contributed to the strengthening of the ties between the two countries, Turkey being included among the sixteen recipients of American aid. A permanent mission of the European Co-operation Administration (ECA) was added to the growing number of private and official American institutions in Ankara.

The year 1949 brought, in the midst of the mounting East-West crisis, further manifestations of co-operation between Washington and Ankara. Aware of the increased American interest in the defense of Europe, Turkey made skillful diplomatic efforts to lay stress on her European character from the strategic and the political points of view. In February the Turkish government suggested the conclusion of a Mediterranean defense pact, and in August, much to her gratification, Turkey was admitted to the Council of Europe, a deliberative body recently created at Strasbourg.

The negotiation and conclusion by the United States of the North Atlantic Treaty on April 4, 1949, aroused in Turkey keen interest and a desire to be included in the alliance, alongside Greece. The North Atlantic partners were not yet ready to extend their formal commitments so far. However, largely to assuage Turkish fears, Dean Acheson, the American secretary of state, declared on March 23, 1949, that the United States' continuous interest in the security of the nations of the Middle East, particularly Greece, Turkey, and Iran, had in no way been lessened by the negotiations on the North Atlantic Treaty.

On December 27, 1949, the United States and Turkey concluded a cultural pact providing for the use of $5,000,000 worth of lend-lease surplus property for student exchange. In May 1950 the Department of State informed the public that in three years under the Truman Doctrine and the Marshall Plan Greece and Turkey together had received a total of $700,000,000 in military and of $764,000,000 in economic assistance. Scarcely a month later it was announced that

149

the European Co-operation Administration had allocated to Turkey $275,000 to carry out a major maritime rehabilitation project and that a nine-man group of American shipping experts was to advise Ankara on the execution of this plan.

The outbreak of the Korean war in June 1950 found Turkey eager to show her devotion to the principles of world peace. On July 25 she offered the United Nations a brigade of 4,500 fully equipped troops, which without much delay were shipped to Korea. There they participated in some of the fiercest battles of the war, displaying great military valor and gaining universal praise from the military experts. These troops suffered heavy casualties in the dramatic retreat of midwinter 1950–1951 caused by the sudden Chinese Communist intervention, but their morale remained unimpaired. The American press paid glowing tributes to the gallantry of the Mehmetciks.

Following the official Turkish application on August 1, 1950, for membership in the North Atlantic Treaty Organization, much sympathetic thought was given on both sides of the Atlantic to this request.[27]

TURKEY'S NEW DEMOCRACY

The steadily growing friendship with America was strengthened by notable domestic developments in Turkey. Since the termination of the war, progressive liberalization in Turkish political life could be noticed. The one-party system virtually ended when, in January 1947, a newly created Democratic Party held its first national congress in Ankara. Six months later press dispatches announced the inauguration of another organization, the Turkish Conservative Party (*Türk Muhafazakar Partisi*), headed by Rifat Atilhan, which proclaimed its support of religious instruction. The ending of martial law early in 1948 marked a gradual relaxation of strict government controls and made life easier for the opposition.

This new trend found its dramatic (and to many observers unexpected) expression in May 1950 when freely conducted national elections resulted in complete victory for the new Democratic Party.[28]

[27] On September 20, 1951, the North Atlantic Council at its meeting at Ottawa formally extended to Turkey (and Greece) an invitation to join the alliance. Soon afterward Ambassador W. A. Harriman and Gen. Omar N. Bradley, chairman of the U.S. Joint Chiefs of Staff, visited Ankara to explore with Turkish leaders the practical aspects of Turkey's inclusion in NATO.

[28] The Democratic Party secured 387 seats out of a total of 487 in the Assembly. The People's Party gained 63 seats.

This was followed by the election of Celal Bayar, founder of the Democratic Party, to the presidency of the republic. The new president entrusted the formation of a new cabinet to fifty-one-year-old Adnan Menderes. Fuat Köprülü became foreign minister. The Democratic Party program laid greater emphasis on free enterprise in the nation's economic life but otherwise differed little from the People's Party platform. The Democrats owed their resounding victory primarily to the popular desire for a change of administration. The People's Party government had been in office ever since 1922 and, like any human institution, had developed burdensome bureaucratic characteristics. The immediate cause could be found in the high cost of living, resulting partly from the economic inefficiency of state-owned enterprises and partly from the impact of the uncertain international situation upon the domestic life of the nation. The important fact was that the Turkish people wanted a change and they obtained it in an orderly and peaceful manner. With regard to Turkey's international position, no division of opinion was registered. Bayar, the president-elect, declared on the day of electoral victory: "It is important for this country's security and even for the cause of world peace that friend and foe alike should know that any change whatsoever in the Government is not going to change our foreign policy."

The new government's action upheld the statement. The new regime relaxed the stress on secularism, emphasized so greatly during the preceding period.[29] On July 7, 1950, the twenty-seven-year-old ban on religious radio programs was lifted. Radio Ankara began brief broadcasts of readings from the Koran.

Although the Turks, and their foreign friends, had good reasons to rejoice at Turkey's smooth transition from tutelage to democracy, they soon found that democracy could not be speedily implanted without much work and tribulation. Such questions as the choice between a two-party or a multiparty system, the immutability or flexibility of Kemalist principles, and the role of religion in the state had to be considered in terms of their relevance to an orderly development of democratic processes. With regard to the number of parties, there was a definite trend toward a two-party system, al-

[29] The first sign of change came as early as 1947, when the People's Party government decided to permit religious instruction in schools. It was, however, largely a political move, designed to offset the successes which the opposition Democratic Party scored with the peasantry by appealing to their religious emotions.

151

though attempts were made to introduce other parties. While such parties as the Socialist, Peasant, Democratic Islamic, or National Uplift could be considered as minor and ephemeral, this was not true of the Nation (*Millet*) Party, which rallied to its standard important conservative and proreligious elements. But precisely because the *Millet* Party stood for principles opposed to the basic tenets of the Republic, in particular to secularism, it incurred accusations of sedition, and its very existence posed the problem of limits to free speech and assembly in the new democracy.

The party's fourth Congress held in Ankara in June 1953 could be regarded as a major anti-Kemalist manifestation. Alarmed at the reactionary course the party was following, the government took energetic steps to put an end to its activities. After search and closure of the party's headquarters, the government suspended the party's press organ *Millet* and indicted fifteen of its members for advocating return to the turban and veil, polygamy, teaching in the Arabic alphabet, and restoration of the monarchy, i.e., in general terms, propaganda in favor of a theocratic state. On January 27, 1954, a court in Ankara ordered dissolution of the party, but the verdict was subsequently voided by Turkey's highest tribunal, the Court of Cassation. Moreover, the party promptly reconstituted itself as a Republican Nation Party, thus, at least through its title, indicating abandonment of royalist schemes. In the May 1954 elections the party, campaigning under its new name, won five seats to the Grand National Assembly on the basis of 480,249 votes cast in its favor.[30]

Although this figure was far from impressive, it could not be taken as fully indicative of the party's position in the country. This was due to two factors. In the first place, the Republican People's Party (R.P.P.), one of the two major parties in the country, managed to secure only 31 seats out of a total of 541, and yet its strength —as represented by 3,193,471 votes—was much greater than the negligible number of seats acquired would indicate. If this was true of the R.P.P., there was no reason to apply a different yardstick to the Republican Nation Party. In the second place, the 1950's witnessed a widespread revival of religious fraternities such as *Ticani, Badi al-Zaman, Bektasi, Naksibendi,* and *Kadiriya* and of pro-Islamic political organizations such as the Democratic Islamic

[30] *Cahiers de l'Orient Contemporain*, 1954, 1. (Henceforth referred to as *Cahiers.*)

Party, the National Uplift Party, and a militant association known as *Büyük Doğu*. All these groups professed an extreme pro-Islamic philosophy and, at times, practiced terrorism and vandalism, the latter directed at statues of Kemal Atatürk. Their aggressiveness received considerable publicity when in the fall of 1952 some members of *Büyük Doğu* and the Islamic Democratic Party assaulted and seriously wounded Ahmet Emin Yalman, editor of the respected *Vatan* and one of the foremost figures of Turkish journalism, for his allegedly "anti-Islamic" attitudes. Thus, it was certain that the poor showing of the *Millet* at the elections did not truly portray the strength of traditionalist and proreligious feelings in the country.

But how strong was the religious reaction, and why did it reveal itself under the Democratic administration? As for the first question, any answer must be tentative inasmuch as Turkey has not yet developed all the modern methods of gauging public opinion used in the more advanced West. It seems fairly certain that, qualitatively, the religious reaction represented a hard core of irreconcilables who were thoroughly dedicated and determined to wage an intense struggle to achieve their objectives. Quantitatively, however, they were definitely in a minority inasmuch as both major parties, the Democratic and the People's Republican, favored secularism. Moreover, most of the younger and of the educated elements opposed return to Islam as a guiding principle of the state.

With reference to the second question, the revival of religious reaction was due partly to the relaxation of government controls in conformity with the new spirit of democracy and partly to the policy and tactics of the Democratic Party itself. This party, in order to win the contest with the old party of Atatürk, tried to woo to itself all those elements in Turkish society which for one reason or another had grievances against the dictatorial controls of the Kemal-İnönü era. Thus the Democrats appealed to businessmen, intellectuals, and urban consumers who had grown restive under the regime of *étatisme*, lack of civil liberties, and inflation, respectively. But the Democrats' greatest untapped source was the conservative countryside, to which the People's Party, urban-minded and reformist, had never paid adequate attention. To gain popularity in the rural and provincial communities, Democrats did not hesitate to entice voters by moderate (and never too explicit) promises of greater tolerance toward religion, especially in the school and in radio programs. Furthermore, the party allowed the gradual formation among its members of a pro-Islamic wing.[31] These tactics were responsible for the confusion created in the minds of many concerning the party's true intentions. In reality, the Democratic leaders were as dedicated to the Kemalist principles as were the People's Republicans. But because of tactical concessions made in the heat of the campaign, they later had to face a strong Islamic movement, which, if unchecked, was likely to shake the foundations of the Republic.

To cope with these dangerous trends the Democrats resorted partly to legislation and partly to police action and judicial proceedings within the framework of such laws as existed. On July 25, 1951, the Grand National Assembly adopted a law protecting the memory of Atatürk. The Democrats also banned, through appropriate judicial channels, certain anticonstitutional groups and, as mentioned above, took steps against the *Millet* Party, which appeared as the most serious challenger of the existing system.

In the initial stages this policy met with full approval from the People's Republicans. Their leader, former President Inönü, declared on January 21, 1953: "We cannot but give our support to the government for the measures it has taken with a view to protecting the structure of the country against all reactionary movements." In another speech delivered shortly afterward, he added: "It is good that the government . . . has decided to defend the reforms of the Republic. The duty of the government is to prevent the religion from being used for political purposes and the duty of the opposition is to help the government in this task." [32]

But repression (however clothed in judicial vestments) immediately posed the problem of where the line between licit and illicit political activity should be drawn. It also created the danger that, once used, it might be applied to other political foes as well. In fact, this was precisely what happened. The Democrats did not withstand the temptation of curbing the opposition as a whole. The sharp edge of this policy pointed against their most formidable rivals, the People's Republicans. The method used was the passage

[31] A typical manifestation of the pro-Islamic tendency within the Democratic Party was a petition presented at a local party conference held in Konya in March 1951. The petition asked for the substitution of the fez for the European hat, the reintroduction of veils, the abandonment of Latin script in favor of Arabic, the suppression of statues, the banning of the civil code, and the re-establishment of religious law and polygamy.

[32] *Cahiers,* 1953, 1.

of a series of legislative acts by the Democrat-dominated Grand National Assembly. These acts included a law depriving the People's Republican Party of its "People's Houses" (August 8, 1951); an amendment to the penal code making offensive criticism of cabinet members a punishable crime (June 1, 1953); a law placing a ban on the political activities of professors (July 21, 1953); a law confiscating certain properties of the Republican People's Party (December 12, 1953); a press law instituting penalties for articles offending official persons (March 7, 1954); and two laws directed against the privilege of tenure of officials, professors, and judges (fall, 1954). The People's Republicans naturally opposed this legislation, and, when on July 23, 1953, the Democrats introduced a bill forbidding the use of religion for political purposes, they voted against it, despite their earlier approval of the Democrats' secularist policy. The bill in question, together with the ban on political activities of professors just mentioned, had been presented by the Democrats as "laws of national safety," an ominous-sounding title.

Bolstered by this kind of legislation and the mental climate it engendered, the Democrats scored a resounding victory at the polls on May 2, 1954, gaining 503 seats out of a total of 541. Increasingly intolerant of criticism, they did not hesitate to put on trial the dean of Turkish journalism, Husein Cahit Yalçin, and a number of other newspapermen, who, in due course, received jail sentences. By August 1955 the rift between the Democrats and their Republican opponents became so intense that the latter refused to run in the municipal and provincial elections. Soon after this decision the R.P.P.'s secretary general, American-trained Dr. Kasim Gülek, was placed under arrest and indicted.

While thus trying to silence the opposition, the Democrats suffered dissension within their own ranks. Both the rightist wing in the party and the liberal elements began to oppose the leading group headed by Premier Menderes. The latter did not hesitate to deal harshly with those whose extreme pro-Islamic stand brought them close to the outlawed traditionalists.[33] In one case expulsion from the party was followed by indictment and punishment. The

[33] Early in 1953 the party expelled a few deputies for belonging to an illegal "Nationalist Association," a proreligious group. At the party congress held in February 1953 Premier Menderes strongly attacked religious trends within the party, stating that the "Democratic Party is not a boarding-house or a hotel" which will harbor people disagreeing with the party's ideas and convictions. "The Democratic Party," he said, "favors manifestations of all

liberal critics were aggrieved by the premier's economic policies and his repressive political measures. In mid-October 1955 nine deputies, including two former ministers, were expelled from the party for revolting against Menderes' leadership. Shortly afterward ten more deputies, in a gesture of solidarity, severed their party links to act henceforth as independents. A few days later their example was followed by sixty delegates, who walked out of the party's annual conference. These defections led, in December, to the creation of a new party named *Hurriyet* (Freedom). Headed by Fevzi Lutfu Karaosmanoglu, a deputy from Manisa, and Ibrahim Oktem, a deputy from Bursa, the party rallied around itself twenty-nine deputies, thus becoming the third most important force in the Assembly.

In the conduct of national affairs the Democratic cabinet focused its attention on economic development, which, largely due to American assistance, took a bold swing upward. It will be recalled that the Democrats, in contrast to their predecessors, tried to de-emphasize *étatisme*. In conformity with this objective they passed two laws designed to promote free enterprise. The first, of January 18, 1954, encouraged investments by foreign capital. The second, of March 7, 1954, reversed a long tradition by virtually inviting foreign oil enterprises to start prospecting and production under attractive terms. Speaking at the opening of the tenth session of the Grand National Assembly in November 1954, President Celal Bayar proudly pointed out that in the last few years agricultural production had increased by 200 per cent; that Turkey then had six to seven times as many tractors as she had in 1950; that industrial production had registered a 100 per cent increase, and that the power output had been raised from 800,000,000 K.W.H. to 3,000,000,000 in four years. Similarly impressive advances had been made in the road network, which increased from 2,630 kilometers in 1950 to 22,000 in 1954; in bridge construction (an increase from 289 to 1,189 units); and in the merchant marine, which by reaching a level of 700,000 tons had doubled its previous tonnage.[34]

Yet this spectacular development was not without its drawbacks,

---

sorts of respect toward Islam in Turkey, but opposes the Sharia because" its reintroduction would produce "confusion of religion with politics and with mundane affairs" (*Oriente Moderno,* Feb. 1953).

[34] *Cahiers,* 1954, 2.

the principal of which was undoubtedly the inflationary spiral, which gravely affected Turkey's economic stability while exposing millions of people to suffering and shortages. In their zeal to develop and modernize, the Democrats seemed to disregard certain persistent laws of economics as well as the capacity of their underdeveloped country to assimilate the new wealth and technology. Consequently, by the end of 1954 they found themselves in need of a new "injection" of funds to meet their foreign and domestic commitments. Rather naturally, they turned toward the United States for help, asking for a $300,000,000 loan, in addition to all the regular grants currently received from Washington under the headings of Mutual Security or Technical Assistance. But for the first time since the proclamation of the Truman Doctrine, they met with a refusal. Official Washington was critical of the overextension of their economy and resented their disregard of the recommendations made by American experts assisting in Turkish development plans. Linked to the criticism and the resentment was undoubtedly a feeling of uneasiness in American circles over the turn the internal politics of Turkey were taking. This uneasiness had, to be sure, never become a matter of public record, but the West had given too much publicity to the happy growth of Turkish democracy to accept with complete equanimity developments not consonant with the professed ideal.

TURKEY'S INTERNATIONAL POSITION IN THE 1950'S

Turkey's Democratic government continued the foreign policy of its predecessors in its entirety. Based on recognition of Soviet imperialism as danger Number One, this policy aimed at consolidation of political links with the West and improvement of Turkey's military and strategic position. In conformity with these objectives the Turks sought not only to cultivate their friendship with the United States and Britain but also to improve relations with their immediate neighbors in the Balkans and the Middle East. Marshal Tito's defection from the Soviet camp and his veering toward the West enabled the Turks to work for an entente of free Balkan states as an additional barrier to Soviet expansionism. Negotiations aiming at this objective resulted, first, in the signing on February 28, 1953, of a pact of collaboration between Turkey, Yugoslavia, and Greece. This was not a mean achievement, considering the ideological di-

157

vergencies and the distrust existing among the states in question. With mutual confidence thus restored, the three countries took a further step by concluding a formal treaty of alliance on August 9, 1954.

Unfortunately, this new spirit of friendship was not destined to last long. Barely had the new treaty been signed when Greece raised the question of Cyprus. This strategic island in the eastern Mediterranean is a crown colony of the British Empire, but its inhabitants are predominantly Greek with a sizable Turkish minority. During 1954 the Cypriote Greeks began to urge union with Greece, but their demands met with strong opposition on the part of both the island Turks and the Ankara government. The latter objected, on strategic grounds, to any change in the status of Cyprus. Following the evacuation of British troops from the Suez Canal Zone (see p. 427), Cyprus was to become the principal British (and therefore Western) base in the Middle East. A surrender of this valuable stronghold to the vagaries of Greek politics and administration would entail considerable weakening of the West's strategic position. The Turks were most anxious to have in their hinterland a strong Allied base, from which, in case of emergency, aid and supplies could be rushed. Needless to say, the British, as masters of the island, fully shared their views. Though fully aware of the Turkish and British stand on the matter, the Athens government not only lent its support to the Cypriotes' demands but went so far as to submit the question to the United Nations. Real political solutions, however, are rarely reached through the United Nations. As with Iran, Indonesia, Palestine, and Korea, so now with Cyprus, local events tended to determine the decision.

Although rebuffed twice in the United Nations, which refused to place the dispute on its agenda,[35] the Greeks did not relent in their campaign for union. Before long Cyprus became the scene of widespread terrorism, directed mainly against the British but involving Turkish victims as well. A British-Greek-Turkish conference convoked in London early in September 1955 emphasized, instead of reducing, the existing divergencies. It was immediately followed, on September 6, by bloody rioting in Istanbul, in the course of which angry mobs attacked and burned most of the Greek (and some Armenian) establishments in the city, killing and wounding a good many of their owners and employees.

[35] On December 17, 1954, and September 23, 1955.

158

With Yugoslavia turning back toward neutralism [36] and the Cyprus issue dividing Greece and Turkey, the usefulness of the Balkan Pact became highly questionable. By the end of 1955 relations between Athens and Ankara had reached their lowest point in the thirty-five years following the Peace Settlement.

Greater success was Turkey's in her relations with the states in the Middle East. Anxious to secure her right flank by closer ties with Asian countries threatened by Soviet expansion, Turkey spearheaded the action to bring about an alliance of the Northern Tier states. As a first step a mutual assistance pact was concluded with Pakistan on April 2, 1954. Subsequently a treaty was signed with Iraq (February 24, 1955). This became the basis for a regional alliance, to be known as the Baghdad Pact. In the course of the year Britain, Pakistan, and Iran formally adhered to the pact, thereby establishing the Middle East Treaty Organization (METO), with a permanent secretariat in Baghdad.[37] Premier Menderes, with Iraq's Nuri es-Said, can be regarded as the principal architect of this new alliance. By inducing Iraq and, especially, long-hesitant Iran to join the alliance, Menderes successfully forged a chain stretching from the Bosphorus to the highlands of Kashmir and uniting four Moslem states along the Soviet periphery in a common policy of defense. But the success was not total. The inclusion of Iraq in METO provoked a major split in the Arab League and precipitated Egypt's estrangement from the West. From the standpoint of Turkish and Western defense needs, this was an unfortunate development in view of the strategic importance of Egypt and the facilities she can offer in the event of war. Despite this setback, Turkish policy must be adjudged both bold and consistent. The effectiveness of the METO will ultimately be determined by the willingness and ability of the United States and Britain to come to the aid of the four Moslem members in case of aggression. Nevertheless, by establishing a permanent organization the signatories have laid a foundation for such assistance and military planning can go ahead. This, no doubt, adds to Turkey's security.

By the middle 1950's Turkey had done her utmost to strengthen

[36] In 1954–1955 President Tito of Yugoslavia made conciliatory gestures toward Moscow, and in May 1955 Premier Bulganin and Communist Party Secretary Khrushchev visited Belgrade. In December 1955 Tito visited Egypt in an attempt to establish closer relations with the neutralist bloc in the Middle East.

[37] For further details, see the section "The Baghdad Pact," pp. 260–265.

herself militarily and to secure the assistance of friendly major powers. Her foreign policy continues to be distinguished by cool realism and wisdom. In domestic affairs, however, she faces new and difficult trials. Her experience between 1950 and 1955 proves once again that democracy cannot be established at a moment's notice and that more than a single magnanimous gesture is needed to implant it as a working system. Yet while the issue of democracy is still awaiting solution, it cannot be denied that Turkey has made great strides toward modernization and Westernization and that in this respect she is as unique in the Middle East as is Japan in the Far East. To her credit it may be said that, while she decisively rejected the burdensome imperialism of the Ottoman Empire, she remained united in her desire for peace and national independence. The moral fiber of the Turks has rendered them immune to the inroads of foreign ideologies, and their martial virility has warned potential aggressors that an attack on Turkey would be a costly affair and a dangerous gamble.

Commanding as she does the land and maritime gateways to two continents, Turkey continues to occupy a key strategic position. And despite her current internal problems, she still stands out in the Middle East as a land of strength and stability. That this is so is due in large measure to the statesmanlike qualities of her leaders, who, whatever their deficiencies, have never hesitated to put the welfare of the nation above their own.

CHAPTER V

Iran

AT THE end of World War I Iran found herself in an unusual
position. Russia, convulsed from a revolution and civil war,
relaxed her traditional pressure. The new Soviet government had to
fight for its life against foreign intervention. In contrast, Britain's
strength appeared increased. British troops were in occupation of
most of the Middle East. They were stationed throughout Iranian
territory, using it freely as a transit ground for their expeditions to
the Caucasus and Transcaspia. Britain was to be Iran's neighbor not
only in India but also in Iraq. There was a strong temptation in
British official circles to round out their possessions by including Iran
in the British-influenced protective zone adjacent to India and the
Persian Gulf. Consequently, considering Iran as her own preserve,
Great Britain influenced the Allies to refuse to seat the Iranian
delegation when it appeared at the Peace Conference in Paris.[1] Instead, Britain's foreign secretary, Lord Curzon, instructed Sir Percy
Cox in Teheran to negotiate a treaty that would assure Britain political
ascendancy in Iran. The treaty was signed on August 9, 1919, in
London. Its provisions included British assistance to Iran through
military and financial missions, which would have extensive powers

[1] The official reason for the refusal was that Iran, being neutral in the war, was
not entitled to participation in the conference. This was, however, a flimsy excuse,
considering that Zionists and other nongovernmental delegations were accorded
full hearings. The Iranian delegation, true enough, had little to contribute to a
realistic solution of Middle Eastern problems, having come to present extravagant
territorial claims which included Transcaspia, Merv, and Khiva up to the Oxus
River, several districts in the Caucasus, including Nakhichevan, and the Kurdish
area of Mesopotamia as far as the Euphrates.

in the reorganization of the Iranian army and treasury, and a loan of £2,000,000 to Iran.

The treaty amounted to a virtual protectorate and produced widespread resentment among Iran's democrats and nationalists. Curzon, an old imperialist of the nineteenth-century Indian school, greatly underestimated the strength of postwar Asiatic nationalism and hoped that it would be possible to extend Britain's influence without committing his country to direct colonial administration and responsibility. Events proved him wrong. The Iranian Majlis (parliament) refused to ratify the treaty, and the two British missions—the military under General W. E. R. Dickson and the financial under Armitage Smith—were eventually compelled to leave Teheran after a period of inactivity. Nothing could be done about the treaty unless force was used. Britain was not prepared to go that far. In fact, according to the traditional British doctrine, Iran was never treated as an area of direct colonial expansion but simply as a buffer state between India and Russia. Moreover, Britain was demobilizing, and the taxpayers were loath to assume more commitments in the Middle East. At the end of 1919 British troops commenced to evacuate the Asiatic borderlands of Russia, leaving the counterrevolutionary forces to their own devices. The British military establishment in Iran was reduced in 1920, and between January and April of 1921 it was withdrawn entirely. Under such circumstances, Britain could hardly expect Iran to ratify the abortive treaty.

In contrast to Anglo-Iranian relations, Iran's postwar dealings with Soviet Russia augured well. In 1918 the revolutionary government in Moscow voluntarily renounced all the privileges and concessions that tsarist Russia had secured in Iran. In its proclamation "To the toiling Moslems of Russia and the East," the Soviet government declared itself a staunch friend and ally of the exploited peoples of Asia and at the Conference of the Peoples of the East, held in Baku in September 1920, it launched a great anti-imperialist propaganda offensive. In 1920 negotiations for the conclusion of a treaty of friendship began in Moscow between Iranian and Soviet representatives. The new Russian regime was eager to secure collaboration with her southern neighbors—Turkey, Iran, and Afghanistan. Treaty arrangements with these countries would put an end to Soviet diplomatic isolation and would constitute a victory over the Western imperialists in Asia and the Middle East.

Unfortunately, these initial friendly moves were marred by an

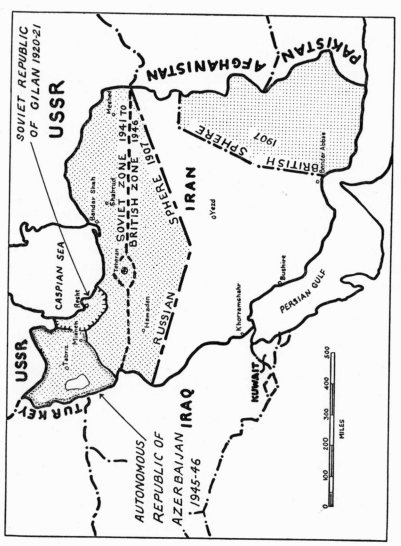

Map 4. Iran.

episode which caused many people to question the sincerity of Soviet protestations. Pursuing the remnants of Denikin's White Russian forces, the Soviet fleet and expeditionary force under Commissar Raskolnikov landed in the Iranian Caspian port of Enzeli (Pahlevi) on May 18, 1920, compelling a small British garrison to withdraw. The Red army troops soon occupied most of the area between the Caspian coast and the Elburz Mountains, joined hands with the local rebel, Kuchik Khan, and helped him proclaim in Resht the Soviet Republic of Gilan. Iran vigorously protested. Moscow explained that Raskolnikov's expedition was the work of the newly established Soviet republic of Azerbaijan, over whose actions it had no control, and later insisted on retaining the Red army there so long as the British kept their troops in Iran. These two explanations failed to convince the Iranians. Despite these difficulties negotiations proceeded, and on February 26, 1921, Iran and Soviet Russia concluded a treaty of friendship. The treaty was a pleasant contrast to the abortive British treaty inasmuch as it reiterated previous Soviet renunciation of old Russian concessions and properties and, in many ways, gave expression to Soviet friendship toward the people of Iran. An annex to the treaty provided for common exploitation of the Caspian fisheries. This was about the only remnant of the old subservient attitude toward Russia. Article 6 of the treaty reserved for Soviet Russia the right to send troops into Iranian territory should the latter become a base for anti-Soviet aggression.[2]

The conclusion of the Soviet-Iranian treaty marked the end of what may be called a period of postwar settlement in Iran. Soviet troops were withdrawn from Gilan nine months later (October 1921), and Kuchik Khan's regime collapsed following an Iranian military expedition into that area. The British treaty was officially rejected

[2] From the Iranian point of view, this was an unfortunate clause in the treaty. The Soviets insisted on its inclusion on the ground that Iran, even against her will, might be occupied by Western imperialists and hence one day serve as a base for counterrevolutionary White forces. No documented evidence has so far been revealed to explain why Iran agreed to this clause, but it is probable that Iran was eager to effect the evacuation of Soviet troops in Gilan and at the same time to oppose any extension of British influence by speedily concluding the treaty. In the official communication appended to the treaty, the Soviet envoy in Teheran made it clear, however, that Article 6 was intended "to apply only to cases in which preparations have been made for a considerable armed attack upon Russia," and that it was "in no sense intended to apply to verbal or written attacks directed against the Soviet Government." (The relevant texts are included in George Lenczowski, *Russia and the West in Iran, 1918–1948* [Ithaca, N.Y., 1949], p. 318.)

by the Iranian government. After seven years of war, tribal rebellion, insurrection, and general chaos, Iran had at last regained her independence. One is tempted to describe it as "independence by default," since it was largely due to domestic developments in Russia and to Britain's reluctance to commit herself to further imperial action. Basically, Iran was still a very weak country, whose continued existence as a sovereign nation depended upon two factors: (1) the attitude of her neighbors, and (2) the strength of her own political leadership.

REZA KHAN AND HIS REFORMS

Five days before the signing of the Soviet-Iranian Treaty, Iran experienced a coup staged by Reza Khan and Sayid Zia ed-Din Taba-Tabai. Reza commanded the Iranian Cossack Division, and Zia, a man in his early thirties, was a radical writer and reformer. Reza's force, the Cossack Division, was at that time the only efficient unit of the Iranian army. It had been created in 1878 as a brigade and followed the Russian pattern of organization. Russian officers traditionally held key positions in this unit, and during the period of Russian political ascendancy the brigade served as an additional safeguard to Russian interests in Iran. After the Soviet revolution this formation continued to be officered by Russian Whites under Colonel Starosselsky, who rendered meritorious service to Iran, taking Resht from the Red army in 1920. Reza Khan had been first a trooper and then an officer under Starosselsky's command.[3] Ambitious, he was determined to exploit Russia's temporary weakness after the revolution in order to get rid of the Russian officers in the division. His views coincided with those of the British, who, following their treaty with Iran in 1919, hoped for control of the Iranian army. Aided by the British commander in northwestern Iran, Reza took advantage of the momentary setback suffered by the division at Enzeli in August 1920 and engineered the dismissal of all Russian officers.[4] Their positions were filled by British officers commanded by Colonel Smyth,

[3] As a noncommissioned officer, he had at one time been in charge of a small detachment guarding the German legation in Teheran, and in this capacity he maintained friendly relations with the more important native servants such as the chief butler. After the war when he once visited the legation as the shah, he was served food by some of his former friends who were still in the legation's employment. *Tempora mutantur!* (See Wipert von Blücher, *Zeitenwende in Iran* [Biberach an der Riss, 1949], p. 165.)

[4] This action was formally confirmed by the Iranian government under Premier Sepahdar.

165

who remained with the division until 1921. Reza himself assumed command of the division. British officers gave him technical advice during his march on Teheran, and hence he has often been considered by his adversaries as a British creation. The accusation was not quite just, because Reza, while ready to avail himself of British aid at a certain moment of his career, was essentially a nationalist opposed to any foreign interference in the affairs of Iran.

His rise to power was rapid. As a result of the coup of February 1921, he became the Iranian commander-in-chief and minister of war. Zia ed-Din assumed the premiership and in his zeal for radical reforms adopted harsh measures against many wealthy conservatives. Three months later Reza forced Zia to resign and flee the country; thereafter he exercised paramount influence in government. He became prime minister in 1923 and soon afterward forced the weak-willed shah, Ahmed, to depart for an "extended trip to Europe." For some time he toyed with the idea of republicanism and encouraged agitation to this end. Widespread clerical opposition to these schemes, however, made him change his mind to the extent that any mention of a republic was formally prohibited by law. On October 31, 1925, the Majlis deposed the absentee shah and on December 13 proclaimed Reza Shah-in-Shah of Iran. Thus, the century-and-a-quarter-old Kajar dynasty came to an end, and the new Pahlevi dynasty came into power.

Reza Khan's chief ambition was to emulate his Turkish counterpart, Mustafa Kemal. He wanted to emancipate Iran from foreign influence and to strengthen her by adopting Western reforms and technology. To achieve these ends he needed first to strengthen his own position and the power of the central government.

The army became the object of his particular attention. Only a well-organized, well-paid, and disciplined military force could assure him success. His first job was to restore order in the country. In a series of successful expeditions—and he often had recourse to ruthless means—Reza defeated the pro-Communist rebel Kuchik Khan, put an end to provincial rebellions in Khorasan and Azerbaijan, and subdued unruly nomad tribes including the powerful Kurdish tribes of the north. He also ended the semiautonomous status of Sheikh Khazal of Mohammera, who had wielded control over the oil-rich area of the southwest. By the time of his coronation in the spring of 1926, Reza's royal dictatorship was undisputed and the Majlis was just an appendage filled with the Shah's nominees.

Reza turned next toward internal reforms.[5] These played a double role by marking at once the steps of internal progress and of external emancipation. Aware that the political dependence of the Kajar rulers often resulted directly from an empty treasury, Reza Shah decided to tackle this problem first. As early as 1922 he invited an American expert, Dr. Arthur Chester Millspaugh, to reorganize Iran's public finances. Millspaugh stayed in Iran until 1927, and through his skillful administration provided the government with a steady income. This success permitted the Shah to proceed with a technical project of major significance—the construction of the great Trans-Iranian Railway, which would link Teheran with both the Caspian Sea and the Persian Gulf. The Shah believed, and rightly, that much would depend upon the development of communications in the country. The maintenance of effective government control over outlying regions, the security of the country, and its economic prosperity would all be enhanced if roads and transportation were in good condition. The Trans-Iranian Railway was begun in 1927, to be completed in 1939. The remarkable feature about it was that the whole scheme was financed entirely by the government of Iran itself from special taxes placed on tea and sugar. The technical side of the construction was entrusted to a number of foreign engineering firms, with no preponderance given to any one nation.

In addition to this, the Shah ordered the construction of many important highways and promoted the establishment of air communications. Between 1927 and 1932 the German Junkers airline provided a passenger and mail service between the capital and a number of provincial towns, and in 1928 the Shah granted a concession to the Imperial Airways, a British firm, to fly over the Iranian coast between Iraq and India. In 1931 Iran took over from the British management the Iranian network of the Indo-European Telegraph Company.

Reza's plans for reform were not restricted to technological advances only. He wanted to modernize the country in the social and educational fields as well. In 1927 he introduced the French judicial system, thus challenging the competence of the religious courts in civil matters. A year later he formally abolished the capitulations. Another law in 1931 forbade foreigners to own agricultural land. The trend toward secularization was clearly discernible, but never did it assume

[5] For a review of Iranian reforms, consult L. P. Elwell-Sutton, *Modern Iran* (London, 1941), chs. v–vii; William S. Haas, *Iran* (New York, 1946), pp. 137 ff.; and E. E. Groseclose, *Introduction to Iran* (London, 1947).

proportions similar to those in Turkey. Reza Shah wanted no sharing of authority with any independent group in Iran, and he considered the influence of backward Shia clergy as detrimental to the Westernization of the country. But he proceeded cautiously. The failure of prorepublican agitation in 1924 and the defeat of his reforming neighbor, King Amanullah of Afghanistan, at the hands of the mullahs in 1929 taught him that what was possible in half-Europeanized Turkey was not yet possible in Iran. Furthermore, the Iranian constitution [6] expressly stated that "the official religion of Iran is Islam, and the true sect is the Jafariya. The Shah of Iran must profess and propagate this faith." It also forbade the Majlis to pass legislation contrary to the principles of Islam and provided for consultation of the theologians in the legislative process; furthermore, such consultation was to be binding. The Shah did not feel that he could openly challenge these provisions. As a result, instead of launching a frontal attack, he used various devious ways, evading and ignoring the Shia hierarchy rather than curbing them directly.

In fact, everything that pertained to the establishment of a modern educational system or the emancipation of women was bound to reduce the influence of the clergy. And in these fields a good deal was done in the interwar period. Officially, compulsory primary education was decreed; and though it never worked perfectly in practice, because of the shortage of teachers and funds, impressive advances were made in spreading the network of schools. Since the beginning of the century Iran had possessed some institutions of higher learning, but in 1934 a university of six faculties was established in Teheran and provided with spacious modern buildings. It had also a theological faculty, but since 1930 compulsory religious education has been eliminated from the primary and secondary schools. The school curricula stressed patriotism and civic-mindedness. As a reaction to external influence, a law of 1932 forbade foreign primary schools in the country. It eventually affected all schools sponsored by foreign missionaries, and Teheran College, an American Presbyterian secondary school, had to close its doors. Sports were encouraged, and a number of modern stadia were erected in the principal towns. The government made participation in Boy Scout and Girl Guide organizations compulsory for teen-agers mainly to imbue the young generation with the spirit of nationalism. These activities obviously kept the youth of the country from religious pursuits and contemplation.

[6] Supplementary Constitutional Law of October 8, 1907.

Quite a blow, though indirectly, was delivered to religious influence by the prohibition of oriental dress in 1928. The fez and the turban were replaced first by the so-called Pahlevi hat (a kind of French kepi, which was compulsory for all males) and later by a regular European hat.

The Shah also promoted various measures to emancipate women. Under his influence the Majlis passed legislation curbing the exaggerated divorce privileges hitherto possessed by husbands and made women eligible for public offices, though not to representative political functions. Through instructions given to army officers and government officials, the Shah encouraged the adoption of Western dress for women, and in 1935 his wife and daughters made a public appearance in European costumes. From that time veils were forbidden. This reform caused some riots, but enforcement was strict and all had to comply with the law.

The Shah also ordered the revision of the language, with a view to purifying it from Arabic influences. This became one of the specific tasks of the Iranian Academy of Literature, founded in 1935. In contrast to Turkey, however, no reform of the alphabet was attempted despite the fact that the Arabic script does not meet the requirements of the Persian language. In March 1935 the state was officially named Iran to replace the Hellenistic name of Persia.

Hygiene also became a subject of official solicitude, and in the twenties and thirties an impressive number of modern hospitals were built. To cope with labor questions in the nascent Iranian industry, a factory act was passed in 1938. The daily and periodical press was expected to propagandize these reforms and it fulfilled its task. The press was discouraged from criticizing the government, and the number of dailies in Teheran was restricted to four. In 1940 the first government-owned broadcasting station was inaugurated in the capital. Its programs were primarily educational.

Economic Developments

With social reform went economic development under governmental control and inspiration. Iran did not officially adopt the principle of *étatisme* as did Turkey, but government intervention in economic life was practiced on a large scale. After the resignation of Dr. A. C. Millspaugh, the Shah entrusted Dr. Lindenblatt, a German economist, with the organization of the National Bank of Iran in 1928. The bank was given the privilege of issuing banknotes, a privilege that had been withdrawn from the British-controlled Imperial Bank of Iran. The government made an impressive effort to establish many new industries in Iran (usually with German assistance) and to promote foreign trade. In 1931, largely as a protective measure against Soviet trade tactics, the government established the so-called foreign trade monopoly, which left transactions to free enterprise but subjected them to strict governmental controls. The Shah himself took an active part in the process of industrialization by investing his personal funds in a number of enterprises and constructions. Using either public or private capital, he spurred the construction of modern buildings; he himself owned some impressive hotels in some of Iran's showier places.

Iran's great wealth lies in her oil deposits, but at no time has Iran exploited her own resources. These operations she left to foreign firms. This circumstance contributed to several international controversies, and for this reason oil will be reviewed in a subsequent section (see pp. 175, 192 ff.).

Reza Shah's reforms certainly stirred Iran from lethargy, and, if the Shah had been permitted to continue them for another decade, much benefit might have accrued to Iran. But his work was interrupted by the Second World War. Of his two aims—emancipation from foreign influence and Westernization—Reza Shah succeeded in the first but did not quite accomplish the second. His task was more difficult than was Kemal Atatürk's because his was a more backward country and because his education and personality were different from Kemal's. Reza Shah had never been in Europe, and his concepts of modernization were sometimes naïve. Moreover, he was a despotic and greedy individual, apt to neglect his subjects in order to satisfy his personal ambitions, possessing no real concept of the rule of law, and lacking the unselfishness that rendered Kemal a true statesman and father of his nation.

IRAN'S FOREIGN POLICY

As a small nation that had almost miraculously retained her threatened sovereignty in 1919, Iran was essentially a *status quo* power, unwilling and unable to pursue active expansionist policies. But at times Iranian political leadership manifested a disturbing lack of political realism. Such was the case when, at the Paris Peace Conference, Iran attempted to present far-reaching claims to the

Kurdish areas of northern Iraq and to formerly Iranian, but for many decades Russian, territories in the Caucasus and Central Asia. This was true also of Iran's claims to the British-protected Bahrein Islands, situated in the Persian Gulf and inhabited by the Arabs. While the claims to Iraqi and Russian territory were quickly forgotten, the claim to the islands was often revived for demagogic purposes by groups seeking popularity in Iran.

Iran's foreign policies can be classified under two major headings: (1) those relating to the other countries of the Middle East, and (2) those relating to the great powers.

With regard to the Middle East, Iran sought peace and friendship with her neighbors. This is noteworthy because there had long been enmity between Iran and Turkey, on the one hand, and between Iran and Afghanistan, on the other. On April 22, 1926, with the encouragement of the Soviet Union, Iran, Turkey, and Afghanistan concluded a treaty of friendship. Despite this, the vexatious Kurdish problem stood in the way of a complete reconciliation between Ankara and Teheran. The Kurdish uprising that occurred during June and July 1930 accentuated these difficulties. The basic desire for good neighborly relations brought a settlement of outstanding frontier problems in 1932. In the same year King Faisal of Iraq paid a state visit to Iran, and in 1934 Turkish-Iranian friendship was confirmed by Reza Shah's visit to Ankara. In 1937 Iran, Turkey, Iraq, and Afghanistan concluded the Saadabad pact, which established an Eastern Entente. The pact provided for nonaggression, consultation, and mutual co-operation in stamping out subversive activities among the signatory states. It was viewed with thinly disguised hostility by Russia, who believed it to be another type of *cordon sanitaire*.

Little can be said about Iran's relations with Arab countries other than Iraq. Countries like Syria, Lebanon, or Palestine were still under mandates and did not have policies of their own. Egypt and the states of the Arabian peninsula were geographically removed, without points of contact except for occasional pilgrim traffic to Saudi Arabia. Generally, Iran stood aloof from the problems of the Arab countries and did not share their agitation over Palestine. As with most of the Middle Eastern states, Iran's main problems centered in her relationships with the big powers and not with her oriental neighbors.

171

Irano-Soviet Relations

Traditionally these powers were Russia and Great Britain. After the conclusion of the 1921 treaty, Iran's relations with the Soviet Union could be described as correct but not cordial. Cordiality was precluded because of several factors. The unfortunate episode in Gilan, previously referred to, imbued the Iranians with considerable distrust, despite friendly protestations from the Soviet Union. Furthermore, rebellions that broke out later in Iranian Azerbaijan and in Khorasan occurred dangerously close to the Soviet border, and Reza Shah had good grounds on which to suspect the sponsorship or connivance of Soviet authorities. On the other hand, his ruthless determination to stamp out communism drove the Iranian Communist Party underground. This fact irked Moscow, despite the official doctrinal stand that classified Reza's regime as an antifeudal semibourgeois revolution, and, hence, a positive step forward, according to Marxist dialectics. In addition, economic problems considerably marred the felicity of Irano-Soviet relations.

The question of northern oil concessions was one of these problems. Freed by the treaty of 1921 from subjection to tsarist Russia, Iran repeatedly attempted to grant concessions to British and American corporations. A special clause in the Irano-Soviet treaty forbade Iran to grant to foreigners those concessions which had been renounced by Soviet Russia. Moscow therefore protested vigorously against any new deals between Iraq and the Western capitalists. It was open to question whether or not Russia was right from a legal standpoint, since, as the interested British party claimed, the disputed concessions did not belong to Russian but to Georgian subjects at the time of the treaty. It was not, however, the legal argument that prevailed in the last analysis, but rather political considerations. Fearful lest it completely alienate Russia, the Iranian government canceled all arrangements with British and American corporations in 1924. The question was not reopened until 1937, when Iran granted to the Amiranian Oil Company, a subsidiary of the Seaboard Oil Company of Delaware, a concession extending to the northern provinces. No Soviet protests were recorded this time, but the concession never became operative because the company renounced its rights in 1938, owing to general world conditions.

Irano-Soviet trade constituted another bone of contention. Petrovsky, Soviet ambassador in Teheran, once gave the following fitting description of Russo-Iranian relations: "What counts in Persia is North Persia only and the latter is fully dependent on Russia. All North Persian products that must be exported can find their only market in Russia. If we Russians stop buying them, Persia is bankrupt in one month. This is Russia's strength which has no equivalent on the British side." [7] Petrovsky's statement was not inaccurate, and Russia more than once made use of this economic weapon in her dealings with Iran. In 1926 a dispute over fishery rights in the Caspian moved Russia to place an embargo on imports from Iran (with the exception of cotton), and Iran's northern provinces suffered severely as a result. Sporadically Soviet commercial representatives in Iran would grant import permits to Iranian traders as a means of influencing people and decisions or as compensation for services rendered. In 1927 the boycott was lifted at the price of a new fishery agreement, which favored Soviet interests. Motivated by political considerations, Russia did not hesitate to dump her products, such as sugar and oil, on the Iranian market to the detriment of Iran's trade with other countries. During the 1920's, Iran was constantly harassed by these spasmodic crises in her trade with Russia. Iran was also in a weak position because her system of free enterprise could not withstand the pressures applied by the Soviet monopolistic trade organization. Largely to circumvent these inconveniences, Reza Shah in 1931 decided to establish a foreign trade monopoly and, with the advent of Hitler to power, gradually began to reorient Iranian trade toward Germany.

Although the Iranian Communist Party was weak, decimated, and intimidated, Soviet Russia never ceased to keep a vigilant eye on the affairs of Iran. Soviet trade officials, spies, GPU, and Comintern agents roamed freely throughout the country, which in many ways was ideally suited to such undercover activities. As long, however, as Reza Shah was in power, there was no likelihood of a revolution, despite growing dissatisfaction with his despotic methods. If Iran were to fall prey to communism, it would be only as a result of external aggression, and this, in the interwar period, Russia was unwilling to undertake.

Irano-British Relations

Iran's relations with Britain during this time passed through various phases ranging from outward correctness to open quarreling.

[7] Blücher, *op. cit.*, p. 187.

Even when their relations were not too friendly, Iran was closer to Britain than to any other power. This was due partly to Britain's presence in India and in Iraq and to her supremacy in the Persian Gulf. Primarily, however, it was the result of the operations of the Anglo-Iranian Oil Company in the province of Khuzistan. The presence of this large company with one of the world's biggest refineries on the island of Abadan necessitated the development of a network of services directly or indirectly connected with the basic oil interest. The British Residency for the Persian Gulf in Bushire, a number of consulates staffed by Indian Political Service officers, branches of the Imperial Bank of Iran, official and unofficial agents working among the tribes—all contributed to the fact that for Britishers, civil or military, Iran was familiar ground. In Iran the British had a twofold diplomatic system: on the one hand, through their embassy in Teheran, they dealt with the Iranian government and, on the other, through local consuls and agents, with the provincial potentates and powerful nomad tribes of Qashqais, Bakhtiyaris, Lurs, and Kurds. Even the power of Reza Shah did not affect to any great degree this traditional pattern.

In 1927 a quarrel broke out between the two countries over the oil-rich Bahrein Islands. Iran claimed sovereignty over Bahrein on historical grounds, but Britain refused to consider the problem. By 1928 Britain and Iran were at odds over a number of issues. Britain resented Iran's unilateral denunciation of capitulations and asked for some *quid pro quo* to protect her subjects. Iran refused to grant Britain the right to fly over her coast to India, in the meantime concluding air agreements with Germany and the Soviet Union. Reza Shah was determined to curb the power of Sheikh Khazal of Mohammera, an old-time British protegé whose domains extended over the oil-rich Khuzistan. Britain claimed payment of debts by Iran in connection with the wartime formation of the South-Persia Rifles. Iran for some time refused to recognize the British-controlled government of Iraq. And, finally, there was a controversy over the customs tariff.

All these problems were successfully solved by the conclusion on May 16, 1928, of an Anglo-Iranian treaty which restored normal relations. The treaty gave certain safeguards to British nationals resident in Iran in lieu of the old capitulations. It also cleared the path to an agreement between Iran and the Imperial Airways (concluded in December 1928), which gave the latter the right to fly over the

Iranian coastal area on the Persian Gulf. In 1932 a new crisis broke out, this time of major proportions. Desirous of obtaining a higher share in the profits of the Anglo-Iranian Oil Company and accusing the British of dishonest accounting practices, Reza Shah unilaterally canceled the company's concession. Britain protested, sent warships to the Persian Gulf, and brought the matter to the Council of the League of Nations. The latter's consideration of the case was, however, dropped when it was learned in 1933 that the government of Iran and the company had concluded a mutually satisfactory agreement. The new concession was to be valid for sixty years and provided for a considerable increase in royalties to Iran, as well as for the gradual "Iranization" of the company's personnel. It was greeted in Iran as a major diplomatic victory, which, indeed, it was. From that time on relations between Iran and Britain were on the whole friendly, but there was a visible waning of British influence.

To sum up Irano-Soviet-British relations, it may safely be asserted that, under Reza's energetic rule, Iran succeeded in emancipating herself from the domination of her two powerful neighbors. This emancipation was political and to a large extent economic as well.

Irano-German Relations

The process of emancipation was accompanied by growing friendship between Iran and Germany. Reviving her pet theory of the "Third Power," Iran turned toward the Reich when it became obvious that the latter had recuperated from wartime defeat. From 1928 on, Iran availed herself more and more of the economic and technical services of Germany. This trend took on a definite upward swing when Hitler came to power. To Iran's desire for a powerful friend, the Third Reich reciprocated by displaying special interest in the affairs of the Middle East in general and of Iran in particular. Germany began to supply Iran with ever-growing numbers of experts and goods. Iranian communications, industry, building, hospitals, and agriculture owed a great deal to German assistance. Trade between the two countries grew by leaps and bounds. A clearing agreement negotiated by Dr. Hjalmar Schacht during his visit in Teheran in 1935 laid solid foundations for trade between the two states. Iranian dignitaries paid state visits to Berlin, and the Reich was not slow in sending men like Baldur von Schirach, a Nazi youth leader, to Iran on good-will tours. By 1939 Germany accounted for 41 per cent of the total foreign trade of Iran, and the number of Germans resident in Iran as technicians, traders, or "tourists" had risen to 2,000. Nazi propaganda scored notable successes by emphasizing the common Aryan background of the two peoples, as well as their struggle for equality and independence under the leadership of "enlightened" rulers. Reza Shah did not hesitate to praise the authoritarian regime in Germany as the best safeguard against communism.[8]

The general outcome of these policies was, on the one hand, the enhancement of Germany's position in Iran to the detriment of Soviet and British influence and, on the other hand, the strengthening of Iranian nationalism. The latter began to manifest overconfidence rather than sober political thinking.

Iran and World War II

Upon the outbreak of the war in 1939, Iran proclaimed her neutrality. Iranian ruling circles were mostly pro-German, and trade with Germany, carried on via Russia, increased. The German invasion of Russia in June 1941 presented the West with the problem of supplying the Russian allies. There were four possible routes: through Murmansk, through Vladivostok, through the Turkish Straits, and over the Iranian highlands. Neither the Murmansk nor the Vladivostok routes could handle really large supplies. Turkey closed the Straits. To force their opening would have necessitated war with her, an alternative the Allies refused to consider in view of the fact that Turkey was a nonbelligerent ally of the West. Thus Iran remained the only practical transit route to Russia, through which, given proper organization, bulky supplies could be shipped. But there were many German technicians in Iran who, on orders from Berlin, could sabotage Allied transportation arrangements should Iran open her territory. Consequently, Soviet Russia and Great Britain twice (June and August 1941) asked Iran to expel the Germans. Iran refused, whereupon on August 25 British and Soviet forces entered the country and soon occupied it. Iranian military resistance was negligible. Russia and Britain divided the country into two zones of occupation: Russia obtained control of the five northern provinces of Azerbaijan, Gilan, Mazanderan, Gorgan, and Khorasan, and Great Britain got the rest of the country. Teheran became a neutral enclave. Under Soviet and British pressure Reza Shah abdicated in favor of his twenty-year-old son, Mohammed Reza, and left the

[8] *Ibid.*, p. 331.

country aboard a British vessel for South Africa. There he died in 1944. A new pro-Ally cabinet came into power. On January 29, 1942, it concluded a Tripartite Treaty of Alliance with Great Britain and the Soviet Union. The treaty stated that the presence of foreign troops on Iranian territory did not constitute a military occupation, gave the Allies transit and communications facilities in Iran, reaffirmed Iranian independence, and provided for the withdrawal of the Allied troops within six months after the end of the war with the Axis. Toward the end of 1942, 30,000 noncombatant American troops moved in and took charge of lend-lease supplies to Russia.

To Iran, these swift events were a severe shock, revealing as they did the country's weaknesses and the error of counting on Germany for protection. Iranian foreign policy had to be completely re-oriented. Everything receded into the background before the major task of regaining full independence. This was not an easy task to accomplish. Iran had to change overnight from neutrality to alliance, revamp the enemy occupation into friendly co-operation, gain the recognition and gratitude of the Allies, obtain a seat at the future peace conference, and secure the evacuation of the Allied armies. The last of these objectives seemed especially difficult inasmuch as the Soviet Union showed signs of considering her occupation as more than a temporary expedient.

As to internal affairs, foreign occupation and Reza's abdication brought in their wake an interruption of the reforms, an upsetting of normal economic life, and pronounced inflation and unrest. The loudly advertised democracy, which was supposed to follow Reza's dictatorship, had little chance to flourish. Because of the presence of foreign troops, most of the old internal problems were now linked to Iran's foreign relations. There was a visible recrudescence of ex-tremist movements. On the one hand, the hitherto restrained Shia clergy reasserted their influence. This was accompanied by a return of the nomad tribes to militant autonomy. On the other hand, the radical leftist elements emerged in the shape of the Communist-dominated *Tudeh* ("Masses") Party, thus complicating the nation's turbulent politics.

The policy of the occupying powers was of the utmost importance. Russia's interest in Iran was traditional, and published Nazi-Soviet documents reveal that in the fall of 1940 the Soviet Union seriously contemplated including Iran and Iraq in her sphere of influence.[9]

[9] "Nazi-Soviet Relations 1939–1941," *Documents from the Archives of the German Foreign Office* (Department of State, Pub. 3023; Washington, 1948), p. 257.

Less than a year later Soviet troops were in actual occupation of Iran's richest provinces, Iran's anti-Soviet ruler had been deposed, and the country was open to intrigue and infiltration. Russia did not waste a good opportunity. Soviet wartime policy in Iran was both revolutionary and imperialistic—revolutionary in the sense that Soviet organs did everything possible to upset Iran's stability and to create conditions for a violent change and imperialistic because Russia gave plentiful evidence of desiring permanent extension of her power over Iran. Russia carried on her revolutionary tactics through a variety of means. She supported the Communist Tudeh Party, whose leaders owed liberation from Reza's jails to the Red army, stirred up labor trouble, supported a number of pro-Soviet newspapers, bribed politicians and intellectuals, and operated a huge propaganda machine. Soviet imperialism was evidenced by intrigue among and support of national minorities, such as the Armenians and the Kurds, propaganda favoring separation for Turkish-speaking Iranian Azerbaijan, arbitrary censorship on all the in- and out-going news in Iran, economic pressure and exploitation, and intimidation of Iranian officials, police, and army. In the fall of 1944, Soviet Assistant Commissar for Foreign Affairs Kavtaradze arrived in Teheran and demanded an oil concession to cover the northern provinces. When Prime Minister Mohammed Saed refused it, a veritable storm broke out. Soviet-supported newspapers vociferously asked for the granting of the concession, accusing the government of pro-Fascist tendencies; big rallies of the Tudeh Party, protected by Soviet tanks, were held in Teheran and other cities and passed pro-Soviet resolutions; and, at a press conference in Teheran, Kavtaradze publicly censured Saed for his stubbornness. The situation became so tense that Saed was forced to resign and was replaced by a more conciliatory successor. At the same time, on the motion of a deputy, Dr. Mohammed Mossadegh, the Majlis passed a law forbidding the government, under severe penalties, to grant or even negotiate oil concessions without parliamentary approval. Having failed in his mission, Kavtaradze left for Moscow. This was a setback for the Soviets, but only a temporary one as later events were to prove.

To Iran, all these pressures were highly embarrassing, but little could be done to counteract them. In the British zone, the government had relative freedom of action and could, at least, keep the native Communist activities under control. The Soviet zone, however, was completely at the mercy of Soviet authorities. The only

178

effective resistance to Soviet schemes had to come from the big powers, i.e., Great Britain or the United States.

The main burden of resistance fell to Great Britain. British authorities in Iran were fully aware of the uneasy Irano-Soviet situation and did their best to offset Soviet propaganda and pressure. The British, realistically enough, tried to oppose Soviet encroachment by using, with moderation, somewhat similar weapons. Thus to counteract Tudeh activity, they supported a nationalist party *Eredaye Melli* ("National Will") formed by former Premier Zia ed-Din, who had returned from prolonged exile in Palestine. To the activities of official Soviet propaganda, they opposed their own propaganda emanating from the embassy's Public Relations Bureau and the British Council. They handled skillfully an impressive number of anti-Soviet dailies and periodicals and co-operated, instead of obstructing, in the solution of Iran's economic problems.

In this cold war of propaganda and political intrigue Britain was handicapped by the moderation if not the actual timidity of her tactics. Eager to maintain unity with her Soviet ally, Great Britain acted under inhibitions alien to the Soviet mind. For this reason she was usually on the defensive. She hesitated to use the same offensive language, a normal feature of Soviet propaganda, and in the over-all balance sheet of psychological warfare she appeared to be losing ground. This was not so much the result of lack of attempts at persuasion but rather of Iranian respect for and fear of strength. And strength was manifested primarily by the Soviet Union.

What was, under such circumstances, the attitude of the United States? The most important fact about American policy was that it was not at all co-ordinated with that of the British. Co-ordination existed only in the economic sphere and in the purely technical sphere of speeding up the supplies to Russia. Both Britain and the United States assisted Iran through their wartime regional agency, the Middle East Supply Center. Otherwise, their ways parted, not because there was any basic discrepancy in principles but because the United States appeared to be quite indifferent to and aloof from the political problems of Iran.

The United States extended both technical and economic assistance. Early in 1943, at the request of the Iranian government, Dr. A. C. Millspaugh arrived for the second time to administer Iran's public finances. He was granted wide executive powers by the Majlis and was authorized to hire sixty American aides. An American military mission was invited to advise on the administration of the army, and another mission, headed by Colonel Norman Schwarzkopf of Lindbergh kidnaping fame, was entrusted with the reorganization of the *gendarmerie* (rural police). American experts were active also in the departments of agriculture, municipal police, health, and others. Unfortunately a quarrel developed between Dr. Millspaugh and some powerful members of the government, and early in 1945 Dr. Millspaugh resigned in the midst of a recriminatory campaign in the press.[10] Iran benefited also from American economic assistance. In 1942 lend lease was extended to her, and Americans assumed their share of responsibility in the previously mentioned Middle East Supply Center.

Politically, Americans showed good will and friendliness toward the Iranians. This good will was symbolized by the release on December 1, 1943, during the Teheran Conference of President Roosevelt, Prime Minister Churchill, and Premier Stalin, of a communiqué complimentary to Iran. This communiqué was Roosevelt's idea. It acknowledged Iran's services in "the transportation of supplies from overseas to the Soviet Union," promised her economic assistance both during and after the war, and, invoking the Atlantic Charter, reiterated the Big Three's "desire for the maintenance of the independence, sovereignty and territorial integrity of Iran." The communiqué was greeted with joy by the Iranians who were eager to hear good tidings concerning their eventual return to full independence, but it was not a legal commitment on the part of the United States. In that period of blooming friendship with Russia, the United States was neither ready nor willing to give any far-reaching political guarantees to Russia's small neighbors. Washington apparently believed that an optimistic joint statement from the Big Three would be sufficient. In pursuing such a policy, the American government indicated that (1) it valued wartime unity with the Soviet Union above other considerations and (2) that it was either unaware of or indifferent to Soviet pressure on Iran. The official American attitude was correct, but not much more. At the time of Kavtaradze's visit, it became known, for example, that some British and American corporations were seeking oil concessions in southeastern Iran. Premier Saed's refusal to grant concessions extended to those powers as well. This elicited a statement from the American ambassador,

[10] His own account of his mission may be found in A. C. Millspaugh, *Americans in Persia* (Washington, 1946).

Leland B. Morris, that the United States respected Iran's sovereign right to refuse concessions. When Dr. Millspaugh was dismissed by the Iranian government, the American embassy officially washed its hands of what was described as a controversy between Iran and a private American citizen. This was no doubt an honorable, but a purely negative, policy. The United States did nothing to deliberately oppose Soviet schemes in Iran and it left the burden of counteraction on the British. The Iranians, who, after Germany's ouster, had looked toward America as a friendly Third Power (and who for this reason had invited many American experts), were disappointed. By the same token the Soviet authorities, encountering no common Anglo-American front, were greatly emboldened.

The Azerbaijan Crisis

As soon as the Japanese surrender was signed on September 2, 1945, serious antigovernment disturbances broke out in the Soviet-controlled province of Azerbaijan. Attempts by the Iranian government to quell them proved unavailing, nor did the Western powers show any firmness toward Russia when the case of Iran was discussed at the September meeting of foreign ministers in London. Encouraged by these manifestations of indecision, the Soviet Union made a daring bid for the control of Iran. On December 12, 1945, former Tudeh members, acting under the new name of Democrats and aided by thousands of Soviet agents who crossed the border, deposed the Iranian governor at Tabriz, and proclaimed the Autonomous Republic of Azerbaijan. The Red army gave them full protection, intimidated local Iranian officials, and prevented the central government troops, sent by Teheran, from reaching the province. The autonomous Azerbaijan government under the veteran Comintern agent Jaafar Pishevari openly thanked the Red army for assistance and proceeded to carry out revolutionary changes in the economic and social structure of the province. Soon afterward an independent Kurdish republic was set up under Soviet auspices in Mahabad. Its leaders, supplied with Soviet uniforms and weapons, concluded an alliance with the Tabriz rebels.[11]

Unable to do anything at home, Iran appealed to the newly formed United Nations, accusing Russia of aggressive interference. The Soviet delegate in the Security Council denied the accusation but

[11] For a detailed treatment of this episode, see Archie Roosevelt, Jr., "The Kurdish Republic of Mahabad," *Middle East Journal,* July 1947.

averred that the Red army had, indeed, stopped the Iranian army from marching to Azerbaijan in order, as he put it, "to avoid bloodshed." Iran's case was strengthened when on March 2, 1946, the Soviet Union failed to live up to its pledge in the Tripartite Treaty of 1942 to remove her troops six months after the end of the war. This was a second count in Iran's complaint. The Security Council did not manifest any particular energy in the handling of the dispute and limited its debates to procedural questions. In the meantime (February and March 1946) Iranian Premier Qavam es-Saltaneh went to Moscow in an attempt to negotiate a solution. Communist agitation in Teheran reached disturbing proportions and prevented the Majlis from assembling. Unable to prolong its sessions, the parliament disbanded leaving the prime minister to face Soviet pressure alone. Acting under duress, Qavam made three important concessions to Russia. First, on April 4 he concluded an agreement establishing a joint Soviet-Iranian company for the exploitation of oil in the north. The agreement was to be valid for twenty-five years and was to be renewable. Russia and Iran were to have 51 and 49 per cent of the stock, respectively. The agreement, moreover, acknowledged Soviet interest in the welfare of Azerbaijan. Secondly, Qavam instructed the Iranian delegate in the United Nations, Hussein Ala, to withdraw Iran's complaint from the Council's agenda. Despite formal Soviet concurrence and Secretary General Trygve Lie's support of these requests, the Security Council decided, nevertheless, to continue consideration of the matter. Thirdly, on August 2, Qavam offered three portfolios in his cabinet to the Communists. This was Russia's price to evacuate her troops from Iran. The Red army left Iran's territory on May 9, 1946, more than two months after the stipulated deadline.[12]

Iran's position was difficult. She had to buy her freedom by alienating her northern oil resources to Russia, by permitting Communist infiltration into her government, and by leaving unsolved the Azerbaijan issue, in which Russia expressly reserved continuous interest.

Despite this high ransom, it was a matter of surprise to many that Russia agreed to withdraw her troops. While the truth can only be guessed at, so long as Soviet archives remain closed to the outside world, a few hypothetical explanations may be attempted. One is that

[12] American troops left Iran by December 31, 1945, and the British evacuated their forces by March 2, 1946, the latter thus honoring the Tripartite Treaty.

Russia desired the ratification of the oil agreement by the Majlis, and the Majlis could not be elected so long as the Red army remained in northern Iran. Another is that Russia feared the effects of adverse publicity upon the still influential pro-Soviet "liberals" in the Western world. A third explanation is that, just as she did twenty-five years earlier during the Gilan episode, Moscow decided to turn from a direct to an indirect method of conquering Asia, once the direct method proved too embarrassing. Finally, rather stiff resistance by Secretary of States James Byrnes at Lake Success and the encouragement given Iran by the American ambassador, George V. Allen, may have been influential. In fact, this last factor may have been decisive.

The withdrawal of Soviet troops removed a major intimidating factor in Soviet-Iranian relations. The problem arose as to how long, if at all, Iran would have to honor the servitudes imposed upon her under duress. The premier seemed hesitant and willing to fulfill his part of the bargain, but he met with stiff opposition in the southern part of the country, a traditionally British preserve. There, in the summer of 1946, a confederation of tribes was formed, which demanded immediate dismissal of the Tudeh ministers from the cabinet and a suppression of Communist agitation. The latter was particularly intense in the Anglo-Iranian oil fields. The riots provoked by the Tudeh in Abadan induced Great Britain to send troops into the neighboring port of Basra in Iraq in order to safeguard her interests there. Threats of forming a separate southern state were heard, also demands from certain Arab chieftains that parts of Arab-inhabited Khuzistan should be joined to Iraq. Under these pressures, Premier Qavam reoriented his policy. First he dismissed the Tudeh ministers. Then, after a few months of inconclusive negotiations with the Azerbaijan separatists, he ordered government troops into Azerbaijan, encountering only weak and spasmodic resistance. After a full year of separate existence, the rebel regime collapsed as soon as the army reached Tabriz, December 15, 1946.

On October 22, 1947, the newly elected Majlis refused by almost unanimous vote [13] to ratify the Irano-Soviet oil agreement. What followed can be described as a state of continuous tension between Russia and Iran. Russia protested against the Majlis' decision and, in a series of diplomatic notes, accused Iran of all sorts of misbehavior. Soviet broadcasts intensified their hostile propaganda, the recurrent theme of which was that by favoring Western "imperial-

[13] With the exception of two Communist deputies.

183

ists" Iran was permitting her territory to be used as a base of aggression against the Soviet Union.

POSTWAR PROBLEMS AND ANXIETIES

The rejection of the oil concession closed a definite chapter in Iran's history. The last tangible consequence of the war period was eliminated, and the country was again free to seek its own salvation. Internally, however, the situation was far from reassuring. The removal of the dictator did not automatically solve any major problems, and the new democracy had a difficult task to prove its superiority over the old paternalistic rule. In fact, the new system resembled more an oligarchy of a thousand wealthy families than a democracy in the Western sense. The Majlis was representative, with a few exceptions, of the rich landowning and merchant class, and as such it reflected conservative and essentially *status quo* trends. What the country needed was sweeping reform, but parliament could hardly be expected to serve as an instrument of any radical changes. Under such circumstances, there was a marked revival of disturbing political extremism both on the left and on the right. Step by step the Tudeh rose to the surface after the initial shock of Communist defeat in Azerbaijan. On the other hand, utterly obscurantist clerical circles whipped up religious fanaticism among the ignorant masses. This movement found its leader and prophet in the person of Mullah Kashani, who may be considered an Iranian counterpart of the Egyptian Sheikh Banna, himself an exponent of the oriental version of Ku Klux Klanism and of Know-Nothing philosophies. This movement was reinforced by the extreme nationalism of a bloc of Majlis deputies under the leadership of Dr. Mohammed Mossadegh.

One ray of hope in this rather gloomy picture came from the youthful shah, Mohammed Reza Pahlevi, who seemed fully aware of both the internal and external dangers menacing Iran and seriously desired the improvement of economic and social conditions. His was not an easy task, however. If he pursued the truly democratic policy of following the parliament's wishes, his dreams of reform would be reduced to naught. If he attempted to act on his own, he could easily be accused of dictatorial ambitions. As it was, the Shah chose the middle road, conforming to the duties of a constitutional monarch, but at the same time, trying to strengthen his own position. Pursuing this line, he brought about an important constitutional change. In 1948, the Constituent Assembly, called specifically for this purpose, established a senate which had initially been authorized by the constitution of 1906 but which had never been set up. The advantage of this measure was that, out of sixty senators, the Shah was entitled to appoint thirty and thus to gain more voice in parliamentary decisions. The Shah favored also a literacy test for elections. This outwardly undemocratic move was really quite progressive, since such a test would assure greater influence to the more independent urban electorate and would reduce the power of great landowners, whose elections to the Majlis were assured by the masses of illiterate and economically dependent peasantry. The project, however, was defeated in the parliament.

The economic system loudly cried for radical reforms. The withdrawal of foreign troops produced unemployment and a general deflationary trend. Business suffered severely, and by 1949 Iran experienced an alarming number of bankruptcies. The hard winters of 1948 and 1949 caused catastrophic crop failures, especially in the rich provinces of Azerbaijan and Mazanderan. The cereal and fruit crops were especially affected. The results were a sudden reduction in fruit exports, the slaughtering of cattle by the peasants, and actual famine. Government income from taxes fell to an alarming low. This was made worse by the fact that many unscrupulous land magnates were considerably in arrears. In 1951 the treasury found itself in such a state that the payment of the salaries of public officials had to be delayed for a two-month period.

Such circumstances naturally caused unrest, and extremists found it relatively easy to gain adherents. In April 1948 Iranian authorities had to resort to mass arrests of Tudeh members in the northern provinces. Political assassinations multiplied,[14] and the government was more than once obliged to proclaim martial law in large areas of the country. A Kurdish rebellion in September 1950 added to the general sense of insecurity.

These conditions provided ideal grounds for Soviet intrigue. Ever since the rejection of the oil agreement an uneasy tenseness had prevailed in Russo-Iranian relations. Soviet diplomacy alternated between intimidation and blandishments, and Russia used both direct and indirect methods to bring pressure upon Iran. The nonratification of the oil agreement brought forth energetic Soviet notes, accusing Iran of breaking her word and of general hostility toward Rus-

[14] On November 4, 1949, Court Minister and former Premier Hazhir was assassinated by a member of a religious sect.

185

sia. In the spring of 1948, in another series of notes, the Soviet Union severely blamed Iran for the activities of American military and *gendarmerie* missions, who were charged with trying to convert Iran into a Western bloc state for anti-Soviet operations. The growing rapprochement between Iran and the United States (which will be discussed later) was greatly resented by Russia. Soviet-Iranian relations deteriorated steadily. A clandestine radio of "free Azerbaijan," situated just across the border in Soviet territory, broadcast vituperative propaganda against Iran, promising freedom and justice to the Azerbaijanis and Kurds if they rose against the oppressive rule of the government. The Soviet press published a number of intimidating articles with frequent references to Article 6 of the unfortunate 1921 treaty, which, it will be remembered, permitted Russia under specific circumstances to enter Iranian territory. At the same time Soviet authorities obstructed the appointment of an Iranian director to the jointly operated Caspian fisheries and applied a virtual economic boycott of Iranian export products.

By the spring of 1949 Soviet-Iranian relations reached a crisis. On February 4, 1949, a Tudeh follower [15] made an attempt on the life of the Shah, wounding him slightly. The following day the Tudeh party was officially outlawed. Soon afterward arrests were made among its members, to be followed, on March 2, by the trial of fourteen prominent Communist leaders, including Dr. Morteza Yazdi, ex-minister of health; Hussein Jowdat, a Tudeh youth leader; and Nur ed-Din Kianuri, leader of a Tudeh workers' union. On February 27 martial law was proclaimed following the discovery of an alleged country-wide plot to overthrow the government. In March and April official Iranian sources announced three clashes on the Soviet-Iranian border in which Soviet armored divisions made deep forays into Iran. This resulted in the kidnaping of a number of Iranian soldiers. In April Soviet Ambassador Sadchikov left Iran for Moscow, and his departure was followed by the closing of Soviet consulates in Tabriz, Rezayeh, Maku, and Ardebil. Simultaneously, Russia ordered Iran to close her consulate in Baku. Russia also deported some 150 Iranian nationals resident in the USSR—a time-honored Soviet device for introducing her agents into Iran.

Iran reacted to this campaign in two ways. First, she attempted to retaliate in kind by reviving an old claim for gold and currency,

[15] According to the official version, he also had some links with a fanatical Islamic group.

which the Soviet Union had owed Iran since 1942.[16] She also demanded prompt payment of $10,000,000 in customs charges and more than $1,000,000 in railway charges, which Russia had failed to pay Iran. Furthermore, the government made an effort to put an end to foreign infiltration by expelling some satellite nationals [17] and threatening the expulsion of two Armenian archbishops reputed to be Soviet agents. A decree of July 27, 1949, amplified these measures by declaring that all leaders of non-Moslem religious groups must be subjects of Iran and "concerned with religious matters only."

Second, the Iranian government questioned the validity of the Soviet-Iranian Treaty of 1921. According to some press reports, Iran denounced the treaty in a note to the Soviet Union, but this was not officially confirmed. Anyway, Iranian official circles argued that the United Nations Charter invalidated the controversial Article 6 of the Treaty,[18] and it was rumored that Iran might bring the question of Soviet pressure before the Security Council. This did not materialize. Instead, Iran's ambassador in Washington, Hussein Ala, handed over to Secretary of State Dean Acheson a detailed memorandum which contained pertinent documentation and appealed for United States support. On March 23, 1949, Secretary Acheson made a public statement in which he declared that Soviet charges that Iran was being transformed into an American military base were "altogether false and demonstrably untrue." He added that American interest in the security of the Middle East, "particularly in Greece, Turkey and Iran," had in no way been reduced by the negotiation of the North Atlantic Treaty.

Growth of Friendship with the United States

This significant declaration climaxed a lengthy period of growing friendship between Iran and the United States. In resisting Soviet pressure Iran frequently looked toward the United States, whose military and economic power filled the Iranian leaders with hopeful expectancy. The Truman Doctrine speech of March 12, 1947, proclaiming the policy of containment of communism and the pledge of assistance to Greece and Turkey, was greeted in Iran as evidence of American interest in the security of the Middle East. On October

[16] In 1942, 11.5 tons of gold, $9,000,000 in American currency, and $11,000,000 in Iranian currency, were deposited by Iran in the Soviet Union. These deposits were not returned by Russia until 1955.

[17] Czechoslovak engineers. [18] See above, p. 164.

6, 1947, the two countries concluded an agreement extending the life of the American advisory military mission to the Iranian army. It included a clause preventing military experts from other states from advising the Iranian army without the consent of the United States. This was followed, on July 29, 1948, by a grant of $10,000,000 in American credits for the purchase of surplus military equipment and of $16,000,000 for repair and shipping costs. The first shipment of these arms arrived in Iran in March 1949 a few days after Secretary Acheson's declaration.

American aid was not limited to the military realm and did not exhaust itself in mere official activity. In 1947 the engineering firm of Morrison-Knudsen from Boise, Idaho, made thorough surveys of Iranian economic conditions. These served as the basis for a subsequent seven-year plan of development. The plan was approved by the Majlis on February 15, 1949. It provided for an expenditure of $650,000,000 and was one of the boldest and most comprehensive ventures ever attempted to improve social, educational, economic, and technical conditions in Asia. Iran invited an American consortium, Overseas Consultants, Inc. (O.C.I.), to prepare detailed blueprints and to act in an advisory capacity. The first O.C.I. team arrived in Iran in January 1949 and was soon enlarged by a number of experts and technicians. Paying $600,000 to the O.C.I. per year, Iran hopefully counted on American loans, although basically the plan was to be financed from the royalties paid by the Anglo-Iranian Oil Company.

It seemed, therefore, a good omen when, on October 6, 1949, the United States Congress adopted the Mutual Defense Assistance Act, which in the framework of a general billion-dollar appropriation contained a special fund of $27,640,000 for military aid to Iran, the Philippines, and Korea. It was estimated that from this sum Iran would receive about $10,000,000.[19] This, however, was too small an amount to cope with Iranian military and economic needs. Iran hoped for a $250,000,000 loan from the International Bank of Reconstruction and Development and for a grant or loan of the same size directly from the United States.

In the meantime, as previously mentioned, Soviet-Iranian relations were deteriorating, and Iran felt an urgent need of some reas-

---

[19] A formal agreement to this effect was signed with Iran on May 23, 1950. Iran was the thirteenth—and last—of the series of states with which such agreements were concluded.

suring decisions. In order to seek such increased military and economic aid, Shah Mohammed Reza made a trip to the United States. Arriving on November 16, 1949, he paid a state visit to official Washington, addressed the United Nations at Lake Success, and made a six-week good-will tour through the country. Outwardly it was a success. The press gave him excellent coverage, and the youthful Shah favorably impressed the American public with his charm and modesty. Columbia University inaugurated an Iranian Study Center, and arrangements were made for the rebroadcasting of the Voice of America programs through the Teheran radio. Prior to his departure on December 30, the Shah and the President issued a joint statement in which Truman, recalling the Three Power Declaration of Teheran on December 1, 1943, confirmed American interest in and "desire for the maintenance of the independence and territorial integrity of Iran," promised support for International Bank loans for Iran, expressed readiness "to facilitate Iranian economic development through the provisions under Point 4," and offered on the basis of the existing congressional authorization "certain military assistance essential to enable Iran . . . to develop effective measures for its self-defense." [20] This statement, however, did not contain any definite military commitment, nor did it mention any concrete loan. From the military and economic point of view, the visit was a failure, and the Iranians did not conceal their disappointment. The Shah, who had arrived in the United States in the President's plane "Independence," refused to accept the offer of an official plane for his return trip and went, instead, on board a Dutch air liner.

The reasons for American reticence are not hard to discover. The year 1949 was the year of Chiang Kai-shek's collapse in China, and the fall of the graft-ridden Kuomintang despite extensive American aid shocked American public opinion. A firm conviction was forming in Washington that while aid to Western Europe was put to good use, financial aid to the corrupt governments of Asia was just "money poured down the rat-hole." [21] This meant that unless Iran adopted measures of reform and purged her government of undesirable elements, she could not expect much from the United States. This was,

[20] The text is in the *New York Times*, Dec. 31, 1949.

[21] In the fall of 1949 and the spring of 1950, conferences of American envoys to the Middle East countries were held in Istanbul and Cairo, respectively. The reports of the participants on the internal situations in their respective countries were far from reassuring, and the reports on Iran were said to be particularly gloomy.

in fact, what the American ambassador, John Wiley (1948–1949), conveyed to Iranian leaders.

Attempt at Reform

Obviously impressed by the Chinese debacle and by American admonishments, the Shah returned to Iran firmly determined to purge his administration and to institute the much-needed reforms. The year 1950 was to be the year of administrative, social, and economic reform to prove to the West that Iran was worthy of its aid. In February the Shah transferred his royal estates to the Imperial Organization for Social Welfare, to be parceled out on convenient terms to the poor peasants. Soon afterward the government shook up the administration of the vulnerable province of Azerbaijan. Five governors, nine prefects, six chiefs of police, and seven high grain-office officials were suspended. These measures, taken in conjunction with the previously mentioned steps to strengthen the Shah's constitutional authority, testified to the young ruler's earnest desire to pull his country out of the morass and imbue it with a new spirit.

Meanwhile Soviet pressure was renewed.[22] Determined to form a cabinet that would fully support him in his reformist plans, the Shah in June 1950 appointed General Ali Razmara prime minister, and this appointment of an honest and energetic man met with warm approval in the West. Razmara's task was to clamp down on corruption, carry out the reforms under the seven-year plan, and prove by his actions that Iran was following a new path. His appointment coincided with that of Henry F. Grady as United States ambassador to Iran. Mr. Grady had gained renown as the official "watchdog" of American aid to Greece and was viewed by many as an "operating" ambassador, who would supervise the hoped-for economic aid to Iran. In fact, he brought with him three State Department economists, whose presence was an encouraging sign of active American interest.

To deserve further American aid, the Shah and his new prime minister vigorously pushed the work of reform. A plan for regional councils, prepared by Razmara, provided for increased provincial self-government and for a curb on centralistic bureaucracy. In the early fall a new purge in the administration resulted in the dismissal

[22] In May 1950 a widespread Soviet spy network in Iran was revealed by an escaped Soviet employee, and soon afterward the Soviet Union formally complained that the oil surveys made for the government by American experts close to the Soviet border resulted in the taking of aerial photographs of Soviet territory and thereby created an "abnormal situation" in Soviet-Iranian relations.

of 400 officials, and soon afterward, in the midst of an uproar in the Majlis, the Imperial Anticorruption Commission presented a list of 500 names of high officials unfit to hold public office. These measures were popular with the masses, but they met with strong criticism in influential political circles and threatened to bring on a cabinet crisis. Yet both the Shah and General Razmara pursued their course with determination.

Under these circumstances, the announcement in September (officially confirmed on October 10) of a mere $25,000,000 loan from the Export-Import Bank of Washington came as a severe shock to the Iranians. For reasons not yet fully explained, the quest for more substantial loans was refused both by the World Bank and by the American government. The United States was apparently not prepared to go beyond this sum and beyond the token appropriation of a half-million dollars made additionally under the Point Four Program.[23]

Iranians were disappointed and angered. In several interviews with American correspondents, the Shah made public his deep disappointment and wondered why the United States had given generous help to former Axis countries, while refusing more extensive aid to an ally, Iran. There was an angry anti-American outburst on October 4 in the Majlis when one of the deputies asked why Iran "bothered" with the United States. The deputy questioned the expensive activities of Overseas Consultants, Inc., and asked whether or not the United States had paid Iran for the use of her railway during wartime. Growth of a pronouncedly anti-American feeling was strongly felt throughout the country. In mid-November the generally pro-Western Razmara canceled the relaying facilities of the Voice of America and the BBC and allowed the publication of Soviet Tass dispatches in the Iranian press. Ambassador Grady's position became embarrassing inasmuch as, despite his reputation as a "watchdog," he had nothing to watch over, and in November he went to Washington for consultation. The seven-year plan suffered a severe setback due to the lack of expected funds, a setback intensified by a quarrel between Overseas Consultants and the Iranian directorate under M. Nakhai. The American experts prepared to depart and their contract was not extended.[24]

[23] On October 19, 1950, the United States and Iran announced that a fund of $500,000 was made available to the Joint Iranian-American Commission for Rural Improvement. The commission set up its headquarters in Isfahan.

[24] The last of them left in January 1951.

Russia was not slow to take advantage of this situation, and instead of intimidation, she adopted a policy of part blandishments. On November 4 she concluded with Iran a $20,000,000 trade agreement, implementing the treaty of 1940, and thus considerably eased Iran's economic position. She also offered to negotiate such outstanding questions as the afore-mentioned boundary dispute, the return of Iranian gold, and the release of Soviet-held Iranian border guards. All these inducements alternated, as usual, with threats. On December 20 General Razmara told the press of alerting Iranian border garrisons, because of danger to the territorial integrity of the state. Soviet-Iranian negotiations were, nevertheless, proceeding, and in mid-December it was revealed that ten important Tudeh leaders, previously sentenced, had been released from prison by some Iranian officers in what was described as a "kidnaping" operation.

The Oil Crisis

The failure to obtain financial aid from the United States spurred the Majlis to press for a radical revision of the Anglo-Iranian oil concession, to increase the royalties to the state. Negotiations had already dragged on for some time. Iran argued that she was victimized by the high corporation taxes paid by the company to the British government and by the low rate of royalties. Iran pointed also to more favorable deals that Saudi Arabia and some Latin-American countries had obtained with American oil corporations. The Anglo-Iranian Company was prepared to make certain concessions, but they were regarded as insufficient by the government. In the winter of 1950–1951 Dr. Mossadegh's National Front in the Majlis began clamoring for the nationalization of the oil industry. Razmara opposed this as impractical and in doing so flirted with danger. His was not a popular attitude, but so long as he remained in power and was openly supported by the Shah, his wise counsel prevailed. The prime minister became a special target of the fanatical Islamic brotherhood *Fadayan Islam* ("Crusaders of Islam"), which preached liberation of Iran from foreign influences and advocated immediate nationalization of the oil industry. On March 7, 1951, a member of this brotherhood shot and killed Razmara while the general was attending a religious service in one of the mosques.

The consequences were momentous. On March 15 the Majlis unanimously passed a law nationalizing Iran's oil industry. The Senate confirmed it on March 20, the day henceforth regarded as the official date of nationalization. To British protests, Iran replied firmly that the matter was entirely within her domestic jurisdiction. Early in April Communist-led riots broke out in the Anglo-Iranian fields in Khuzistan. The workers went on strike, and a number of employees, including two Britons, were killed. Speaking to Parliament, Foreign Minister Herbert Morrison stated that his government would take action to protect British lives and property, and the press reported movements of the British navy in the Persian Gulf.

In the meantime, important cabinet changes took place in Iran. After Razmara's death, the Shah called Hussein Ala, a moderate pro-Western statesman and former ambassador to Washington, to assume the premiership. Ala endeavored to soften the effects of nationalization by making it clear that Iran did not want to deprive the West of oil supplies. At the same time it was thought that some compromise might be worked out whereby the company would become Iranian property but the technical side of production and distribution would be left to competent foreign technicians. But this was not what the extreme nationalists wanted. Their mounting pressure led to Ala's resignation on April 27. On April 28 the Shah reluctantly entrusted Mossadegh with the formation of a new cabinet. On the same day the Majlis, and on April 30 the Senate, voted immediate nationalization of the oil industry retroactive to March 20. The Shah, who does not have the right of veto, was obliged to sign these laws on May 2. The prime minister was known to oppose all foreign aid including assistance by the United States military mission to the Iranian army. But despite their outward victory, the nationalist extremists were in a predicament, because the Communists took advantage of the inflamed situation resulting from the nationalists' use of demagoguery and mob action. The Khuzistan disturbances continued, and the Anglo-Iranian Oil Company was compelled to shut down its industrial plant. Production stopped, and so did company payments to the government. Martial law was proclaimed in Khuzistan, and armored army units were dispatched to restore order. On May Day, the day following Mossadegh's appointment to the premiership, the Tudeh, still officially outlawed, organized a mass rally in the parliament square in Teheran. A crowd estimated at 30,000 carried anti-Western and pro-Soviet placards displaying anti-imperialist slogans. Even Mossadegh, father of the nationalization law, was not spared some posters depicting him as a puppet riding in the turret of an American tank.

Informed opinion held that Iran was not able to assume management of a complex industrial enterprise like the Anglo-Iranian, without gravely impairing the output. Moreover, the Anglo-Iranian's activities included marketing operations, and these were served by a fleet of company tankers, which could easily be withdrawn to prevent seizure. It was certain that any sudden transfer, such as contemplated by the law of May 2, would cause serious disruption in the company's activities and would further endanger the already precarious situation of the Iranian treasury. Little could be elicited on this subject from the new prime minister who, when queried by foreign observers, limited himself to impassioned but vague outbursts against foreign imperialism and exploitation. Mossadegh definitely rejected, however, the British government's pleas for negotiations and the company's request for arbitration, which had been provided for by the concession agreement.

Events in Iran caused well-understood concern in the United States. With Razmara's death a blow was dealt to the hopes of substantial reform, and the political curve in Iranian affairs assumed a disquietingly downward trend. Iranian oil was essential to the success of the European Recovery Program. Furthermore, the ability of the Communists so rapidly to assume quasi-leadership of the nationalist landslide constituted an additional cause for concern. The situation was not eased by the fact that the Soviet press openly accused the United States of engineering Razmara's death, allegedly to aid American oil corporations to dislodge the Anglo-Iranian. The American State Department officially proclaimed its neutrality in the conflict between Iran and Great Britain, but it took lively interest in the developments. In April Assistant Secretary of State George McGhee and the British ambassador in Washington, Sir Oliver Franks, held a series of conferences to review the Iranian crisis. The American government considered the nationalization step as irrevocable but hoped for an amicable settlement between the two parties.

Contrary, however, to the early expectations, the Anglo-Iranian oil crisis developed into a long-drawn affair which passed through the following main phases during the summer and the fall of 1951:

1) After considerable prodding from the British embassy the Iranian government agreed to receive in mid-June a mission composed of a few directors of the Anglo-Iranian Oil Company. In the

course of negotiations Iran demanded that the A.I.O.C. turn over at once to the government all revenue derived from the sale of Iranian oil as of March 20, after deducting expenses and 25 per cent to guarantee the company's probable claims. This proved unacceptable to the company. The latter's counterproposals were rejected by Iran and the talks broke down.

2) On May 26 the British government brought the matter to the International Court of Justice at The Hague. On July 5 the Court, without pronouncing itself on the basic issue of its competence, issued a temporary decision enjoining both parties to preserve the *status quo* pending a final solution, so as to assure an uninterrupted flow of oil. Challenging the Court's competence in what she claimed to be a domestic affair, Iran gave notice of withdrawal as one of the signatories of the Court convention.

3) Four days later President Truman in a personal message appealed to Premier Mossadegh to reopen negotiations with the British and, with Mossadegh's consent, dispatched W. Averell Harriman as his personal representative to Teheran to bring about the renewal of talks.

4) After a visit in Teheran (mid-July), followed by a visit in London, Harriman succeeded in persuading both parties to reopen negotiations. This time, however, it was a British government (and not a company) mission which arrived in Teheran to negotiate. It was headed by Sir Richard R. Stokes, lord privy seal, and had two other cabinet ministers as members.

5) In their talks with the Iranians (August 6–22), the British declared themselves ready to accept the principle of nationalization provided adequate compensation was devised and provided Iran chartered a British company to take charge of the technical aspects of production. The Iranians insisted on freedom to hire British technicans individually and not as an organized unit. This proposal was accepted by the British mission on the condition that a British general manager be appointed in a supervisory executive capacity. The Iranian government rejected this suggestion, as a result of which the negotiations broke down and the British withdrew their offer.

6) On September 27 Iranian soldiers took over the Abadan refinery and locked out British technicians. Two days earlier the Iranian government canceled the residence permits of all the British employees of the company effective October 4. On October 3 the British government duly evacuated the remaining 300 members of the

company's personnel. The National Iranian Oil Company took full charge of the oil fields and the Abadan refinery.

7) Simultaneously (September 29), Britain brought the matter to the attention of the UN Security Council, urging that body to condemn Iran for a breach of international obligations. After considerable diplomatic activity and unofficial exchanges of views, Britain agreed to soften the proposed resolution to a request by the Council that both parties renew their negotiations. Premier Mossadegh, who arrived in New York to plead Iran's case, argued that the Council was not competent to deal with this matter and threatened withdrawal from further UN deliberations. Iran's plea of noncompetence was supported by the Soviet delegation, while the American delegation argued in favor of the Council's competence. Failing to reach any decision on the merits of the case, on October 19 the Council ultimately decided to ask the World Court for an advisory opinion as to the Council's competence.

8) Following this inconclusive debate, Dr. Mossadegh paid a visit to President Truman, who was reported to have urged Iran's premier to reopen his talks with the British and to follow a more realistic course of action. The ensuing four-week negotiations with Assistant Secretary of State George McGhee (conducted by Mossadegh from a sickbed in Washington's Walter Reed Hospital) ended in a deadlock, and on November 19 the Iranian premier left for Iran. Passing through Cairo he was given a rousing welcome by the Egyptians. A few weeks later it became known that the World Bank had presented certain suggestions toward the solution of the controversy. Despite the obvious loss to Iran resulting from the stoppage of oil production, the crisis did not show any signs of abatement in December 1951.

Throughout the crisis Russia seemed to play a waiting game. Her press voiced support of Iran's struggle against foreign imperialism and her representatives in the UN Security Council backed Iran on certain procedural issues, but the official attitude was that of nonintervention. By contrast, Iranian Communists eagerly seized the opportunity to advance their cause in the face of the deteriorating relations between Iran and the West. On May 8, 1951, the emboldened Tudeh Party addressed an open letter to the prime minister in which it formulated seven demands. These were:

1) Expulsion of the United States military mission to Iran.
2) Legalization of the Tudeh Party.
3) Recognition of Communist China.

196

4) Rejection of foreign arms aid.

5) Release of political prisoners.

6) An end to martial law in the southern oil fields.

7) Nationalization of the Bahrein oil fields where the American-owned Bahrein Petroleum Company was producing 10,000,000 barrels of oil a year.

In the following months the Tudeh organized a number of monster rallies and demonstrations which frequently ended in armed clashes with police or with the nationalist supporters of Mossadegh. Internal security showed disquieting signs of deterioration, and cases of prominent editors or politicians seeking refuge in the sanctuary of the Majlis multiplied. By the fall of 1951 Iran was in turmoil. Alternately threatened and cajoled by Russia, in open quarrel with Britain, and at odds with the United States, the government was far from secure, increasingly resorting to demagoguery in order to maintain its popularity. The *New York Times* gave a sober appraisal of the situation in two editorials entitled, "Recklessness in Iran" and "Emotion versus Common Sense." It required, indeed, a great deal of common sense among Iran's leaders to turn their country away from self-destruction toward sound progress and self-development. Unfortunately, Dr. Mossadegh's method of appeal to mob hysteria precluded a rational approach to the vital issues facing his people.

In the months following the expulsion of British personnel from the oil fields and the refinery, several attempts were made to solve the Anglo-Iranian oil dispute. Between December 1951 and March 1952 representatives of the World Bank visited Iran in order to advance their suggestions, but no agreement resulted. Further endeavors of the British and American governments, made either singly or jointly in the fall of 1952, in January 1953, and in the summer of 1953, also proved to be of no avail. Premier Mossadegh refused to discuss the oil problem in terms other than those provided by the nationalization law, the latter enjoining operation of the industry by Iran herself. Nor were proceedings under the auspices of international agencies any more fruitful. The Security Council's debate having proved inconclusive, attention shifted to the International Court of Justice, whose competence in the case was challenged by Iran. Ultimately, on July 22, 1953, the Court pronounced itself incompetent to deal with the dispute.

Iran's view was thus vindicated, but her victory lacked positive elements. Her oil still had to be extracted, refined, and marketed, and this could not be done so long as the dispute remained unsettled. Marketing and transportation presented two of the main difficulties. The Anglo-Iranian Oil Company announced that it would sue any buyers of Iranian oil for unlawful acquisition of its property. For this reason, as well as out of a feeling of solidarity with an expropriated concessionaire, no major world oil corporation would agree to purchase oil from Iran. By the same token, tanker tonnage, most of which was controlled by these companies, was denied to Iran. Mossadegh tried to break this virtual blockade by resorting to transactions with certain independent corporations in Italy and Japan. But these minor deals in the two years following nationalization accounted for less than one day's sales of the A.I.O.C. when the latter was in operation. From the economic point of view the results were extremely disappointing. Moreover, A.I.O.C. promptly contested these deals in the courts of Aden, Italy, and Japan, demanding the impounding of the oil cargoes in question. Although these legal actions were successful only in Aden, the Italian and Japanese courts recognizing the validity of the contracts, the judicial proceedings added new complications and delays which harmed Iranian interests.

Stoppage of the flow of oil from Iran caused considerable inconvenience to its regular consumers, particularly to Britain, who was obliged to draw upon her none too abundant reserves of hard currency to purchase "dollar oil" from other areas. Similarly, certain markets east and south of Suez suffered temporary shortages. But contrary to Iranian expectations, the world at large quickly readjusted itself to the new situation, Iran being promptly replaced as producer by Saudi Arabia, Iraq, and particularly Kuwait, all of whom considerably increased their output to fill the gap. On its part, the A.I.O.C. began the construction of a new giant refinery in politically safe Aden, and other major corporations stepped up their development programs, substantially increasing the refining capacity of Europe and the British Isles. Consequently, the only real loser was Iran.

The oil dispute affected the totality of Irano-British relations. Taking the side of the company, the British government canceled the convertibility facilities hitherto granted to the Iranian sterling balances in London and placed a ban on the exportation of certain goods to Iran. Iran retaliated by closing foreign cultural institutions in the provinces, expelling certain British missionaries, curtailing the privileges enjoyed by the British Bank of Iran,[25] and in January 1952 ordering the closure of all British consulates outside Teheran. Finally, after a rather extravagant ultimatum demanding settlement of the oil question on his terms, Premier Mossadegh in October 1952 broke off diplomatic relations with Great Britain.

The worsening of British-Iranian relations had a deleterious effect on Teheran's ties with the United States. The Iranians acted in the belief that because of their strategic importance the United States would save them from economic collapse and subsequent slipping into the Soviet orbit. They therefore expected America either to buy their oil or to grant them financial assistance. Official Washington was unwilling to do either, partly out of consideration of its British ally and partly out of fear that countenancing Iranian nationalization would jeopardize the network of concessions and investments in other parts of the world. Yet, not prepared to write off the strategic importance of Iran, the American government continued to lend Iran limited aid under the technical assistance program. Such a policy, though not devoid of risks, had the advantage of preserving ties with Iran while not encouraging Dr. Mossadegh in his intransigent attitudes. Iranian extremists were, of course, very intolerant of anybody who did not side with them; hence American-Iranian relations suffered considerable strain, which in some instances was expressed by insults and attacks on Americans living in the country.

Meanwhile an internal crisis was gradually ripening within Iran. In the early stages of the oil dispute Dr. Mossadegh found support among extreme nationalists (mostly members of the Iran Party), religious fanatics grouped around Ayatollah Abol Ghassem Kashani, students, some bazaar merchants, Socialists, and Communists. Though ill-assorted, this coalition worked effectively so long as it aimed at relatively simple and negative objectives, such as the expulsion of the British and the silencing of opposition. Members of the latter, by the way, were so intimidated by mob action or threat of assassination that free and sober discussion of vital national issues became virtually impossible.

As for Dr. Mossadegh, who was hailed by his friends as a heroic

[25] Previously the Imperial Bank of Iran, later renamed the British Bank of Iran and the Middle East, and finally emerging as the British Bank of the Middle East.

fighter for democracy, he exulted in the atmosphere of popular hysteria and mob terror and, with the passage of time, adopted markedly antidemocratic methods of political action. Thus, in the spring of 1952, seeing that elections to the Majlis were not likely to result in a solid progovernment majority, he interrupted the electoral proceedings and convoked a truncated Majlis composed of eighty-odd deputies instead of the full strength of 136. By the some token he insisted, soon afterward, on personal control of the Ministry of Defense, hitherto a preserve of the Crown. Failing to convince the Shah, who was anxious to maintain his prerogatives in regard to the army, Mossadegh resigned on July 16, 1952, whereupon the Shah asked Qavam es-Saltaneh to form a cabinet. Qavam immediately declared that he was determined to solve the oil controversy, restore the economic balance, and put an end to the demagoguery and religious fanaticism which were harmful to the vital interests of the nation. His declarations were met by an outburst of criticism from all the elements of the pro-Mossadegh coalition, which rallied around Mullah Kashani and resorted to rioting to defy the new premier. Abandoned by the Shah and the Majlis (both thoroughly intimidated by mob action), Qavam tendered his resignation and, fearing for his life, went into hiding.

His place was taken by Mossadegh, whose return to power on July 22 coincided with the pronouncement by the World Court of its incompetence in the oil dispute. Thus reinforced, Mossadegh asked and obtained from the Majlis the right to rule by decree during the ensuing six months. At the same time the Shah conceded to him control of the army. Soon afterward, the Majlis declared the Senate session terminated, thus to all practical purposes legislating the upper chamber out of existence. Needless to say, the Senate, composed of more conservative elements, lacked enthusiasm for Mossadegh's policies.

Armed with full powers, the premier effected a purge in the army and in certain government departments to assure loyalty to his policies on the part of officers, civil servants, and diplomats. He also issued, on August 13, 1952, a land-reform decree which enjoined landowners to turn over to their tenants 20 per cent of their land revenue, half of which was to go to individual peasants and another half to village councils for communal improvements. The decree was motivated in part by the premier's desire to effect reforms, but it was largely due to his determination to steal the headlines from the Shah's program to distribute the imperial estates to needy peasants. Ultimately, under Mossadegh's prodding, the Shah agreed to transfer the administration of the imperial estates to the government, thus conceding another point to the ambitious premier.

But the stark reality of an oilless (and cashless) economy had to be faced. Fed for a year and a half on patriotic slogans, the populace could not live forever in a frenzy of enthusiasm while basic goods became scarce and the gap between prices and incomes increased. The heterogeneous coalition behind Mossadegh was bound to fall apart when confronted with positive tasks in a hopeless economic situation. Starting in January 1953, the coalition began to disintegrate. The immediate cause of dissension was Mossadegh's request for a year's extension of his powers. Both Mullah Kashani and Hussein Makki, a leading member of the National Front and the "hero of Abadan," opposed this request. Although the premier obtained his powers, the rift began to widen until, by early summer of 1953, Dr. Mossadegh found himself isolated from the majority of his former political friends. In fact, the original National Front of eight deputies lost most of its initial members. The latter were replaced by a larger but much less cohesive group in the Majlis. The premier remained surrounded by a hard core of Iran Party diehards, who now had a vested interest in preventing any settlement with Britain. By summer the Majlis had shaken off its former docility, and its debates were becoming so acrimonious as to embarrass the government. In mid-July twenty-seven National Front members resigned their seats in protest against the mounting criticism of the opposition. This step deprived the Majlis of a quorum, thus removing it as a decision-making body capable of curbing Mossadegh's excesses.

Meanwhile the Shah, thwarted in his attempts to restrain the premier, left the capital on what was officially termed a long vacation in a Caspian Sea resort. This made Mossadegh the virtual ruler of the country. The premier's next step was to call for a formal dissolution of the Majlis, to be approved by a popular referendum. Although the proposed measure was clearly unconstitutional, plans for a referendum went ahead. Between August 3 and 10 the balloting took place, resulting in 99.93 per cent approval of Mossadegh's policy. Approval had been ensured by the setting up of separate voting booths for those who approved and those who opposed the contemplated decree.

This was the apogee of Mossadegh's power. From then on the decline was swift. On August 12 the premier announced the dissolution of parliament. Three days later a colonel of the Imperial Guard delivered to him a letter of dismissal from the Shah. General Fazlollah Zahedi was appointed in his place. Mossadegh defied the order, ordered the messenger arrested, and had the detachment accompanying him disarmed. Appraised of the news, the Shah and the Queen fled Iran in the Shah's airplane, first to Baghdad and later to Rome. The sovereign's flight touched off major riots in Teheran, during which Communists and extreme nationalists vied with each other in denouncing the monarchy and destroying the statues of the Shah and his father. Prominent in these antiroyalist demonstrations was Hussein Fatemi, foreign minister and Mossadegh's most trusted associate. But after two days the tide of popular opinion took a sharp turn in the opposite direction. Saner elements of the population, obviously perturbed at the revolutionary chaos, spontaneously turned against the antiroyalists, while at the same time certain anti-Mossadegh units in the army defied the premier. This disaffection within the army resulted from secret preparatory activity of certain officers under the over-all direction of General Zahedi, who had been in hiding to avoid arrest by Mossadegh. How well organized this group was and how much planning it had done before it acted on August 18 and 19 have not yet been fully revealed. When the group struck, General Zahedi was still in hiding, and the actual leadership, if there was any, of the military operations was not his. A tank battle raged in Teheran for many hours, ending in victory for the royalist forces. On August 19 General Zahedi emerged from concealment and took over the reins of government. The following day Mossadegh surrendered to him, while the security forces began to arrest and pursue the former premier's associates.[26] A few days later the Shah returned in triumph to Teheran. The Mossadegh era had come to an end.

Return to Normalcy

One of the first acts of General Zahedi was to appeal to the United States for financial aid. The American response came forthwith:

---

[26] Following a trial before a military court, Dr. Mossadegh was sentenced to a three-year prison term. His foreign minister, Hussein Fatemi, received a death sentence, which was promptly carried out. Other Mossadegh collaborators were sentenced to varying prison terms.

President Eisenhower, who only two months earlier had refused a similar request from Mossadegh,[27] now promptly decided to give Iran a $45,000,000 emergency grant-in-aid in addition to $23,400,000 earmarked under the United States technical assistance program. Such aid, however, could only be a palliative, pending the basic improvement of Iran's finances, which hinged on settlement of the oil dispute. By mid-October, Herbert Hoover, Jr., a newly appointed oil adviser to the United States Department of State, arrived in Teheran to pave the way for the reopening of oil negotiations. The resumption by General Zahedi of diplomatic relations with Britain added another factor conducive to an early settlement of the dispute.

The new Iranian regime sincerely wished to reach a satisfactory solution, but it could not disregard public opinion, which was unalterably opposed to the return of the British. Even the staunchest diehards in the A.I.O.C. realized that a return to the *status quo ante* was impossible. Consequently, as a result of exploratory talks that took place in mid-winter of 1953–1954 in Washington and London, an international consortium of eight companies [28] was formed in April 1954 to resume Iranian oil operations. On August 5, 1954, the consortium's delegation, headed by H. W. Page of Standard Oil of New Jersey, signed an agreement with Iran which provided for the extraction, refining, and marketing of Iranian oil by the consortium, the profits from these operations to be divided on a 50-50 basis in accordance with the pattern prevailing in the Middle East and other oil-bearing areas. The consortium was to act on behalf of the

[27] On the ground that it would be unfair to American taxpayers to extend loans or grants to Iran, the latter being in a position to utilize her oil resources.

[28] These companies and their respective shares in the consortium's stock were as follows:

British-Dutch group	Anglo-Iranian Oil Co. (British Petroleum Co.)	40%	54%
	Royal Dutch-Shell	14%	
French group	Compagnie Francaise des Petroles	6%	6%
American group	Standard Oil Co. of New Jersey	8%	
	Standard Oil Co. of California	8%	
	Socony-Vacuum Oil Co. (Socony Mobil Oil Co.)	8%	40%
	Texas Oil Co.	8%	
	Gulf Oil Co.	8%	

In 1955 each of the American companies agreed to cede one-eighth of its holdings (together 5 per cent of the total) to American independent companies, of whom nine subsequently acquired shares in the consortium. The latter's official name is Iranian Oil Participants, Ltd.

National Iranian Oil Company through two operating companies incorporated in Holland. Over a ten-year period Iran was to pay damages to the A.I.O.C. for the nationalization of its properties, but the A.I.O.C. also recognized certain indebtednesses to Iran, as a result of which the amount of compensation was to be moderate. Moreover, the operating companies were to have international management, with Iranian representation on their boards. Soon representatives of these companies arrived in Iran and proceeded to reactivate the oil industry. On its part, the United States, acting in response to Iranian requests, made available to Iran two additional sums above the $45,000,000 initially granted in order to save the new government from financial troubles pending the resumption of regular oil revenues.

While thus normalizing his relations with Britain and the United States, Premier Zahedi did not neglect the Soviet sector either. For reasons not yet fully clear but perhaps as a part of her peace campaign, the Soviet Union offered to settle with Iran the outstanding financial and boundary questions. Free of illusions as to the nature of Soviet objectives, Zahedi nevertheless followed up the Soviet proffer and in the ensuing negotiations reached an agreement whereby Russia was to return to Iran the eleven tons of gold she had owed since the war and the frontier was delimited in certain disputed districts. Considerable time elapsed between the agreement and the implementation of its financial clauses. In fact, the delay was so long as to make many observers skeptical concerning Russia's will to abide by her promise. On June 1, 1955, however, Moscow finally did return the gold, and its gesture was interpreted as a move designed to counter any possible military alignment of Iran with the Western powers.

In internal affairs General Zahedi concentrated on the restoration of order and security, which had reached a disquietingly low point under his predecessor. Zahedi's major achievement in this respect was discovery in the fall of 1954 of a major Communist espionage network in the Iranian army, a network which involved some six hundred officers, including a good number of colonels. This sensational discovery prevented the Communist plotters from overthrowing the government and assassinating the Shah, as they had planned to do within a few days, and allowed the Iranian police rather effectively to destroy the Tudeh organization in the country. Among the more constructive accomplishments were General Zahedi's revival of the dormant Seven-Year Plan Organization and the appointment of an outstanding Iranian financier, Abol Hassan Ebtehaj, to its directorship.

Having performed these vital services in the foreign and domestic field, Zahedi resigned in the spring of 1955, leaving the way open for a more reform-minded minister. He was replaced by Hussein Ala, a venerable statesman who, as court minister, had advised the Shah for many years. Ala's appointment was indicative of the Shah's desire to assume more direct influence in the government and gradually to transform himself from a monarch who reigns to a monarch who rules. The new premier promised a concerted drive on corruption, but within a few days of his appointment he had to leave Iran for medical treatment in Europe. During his absence Iran's basic instability once again became evident when, for reasons not yet fully explained, the government, prodded by the Shia hierarchy, applied repressive measures to the Bahai sect. These measures included the dismantling of the fine Bahai temple in the center of Teheran and resulted in instances of mob violence against peaceful Bahai communities in the provinces.

Upon his return from abroad Premier Ala found a major international problem awaiting solution. It was the question of whether or not Iran should join the Baghdad Pact, recently concluded by Turkey, Iraq, Pakistan, and Britain and designed to serve as a regional alliance of a defensive nature. The decision was not easy to make inasmuch as Russia, in the course of the year, had twice warned Iran not to contemplate such a step, invoking the treaty of 1927 as the basis of her objections.[29] Reinforcing Russia's protests was the legacy of "Mossadeghism," i.e., suspicion and dislike of the West. However, the Shah and certain other political men realized the importance of being formally included in the Western defense system and thus benefiting from such military guarantees and economic aid as this participation was likely to provide. More specifically, adherence to this pact might mean an opportunity to modernize and strengthen Iran's army largely at Western expense. These hesitations were definitely removed after the visit of President Celal

---

[29] This was the "Treaty of Guarantee and Neutrality" concluded on October 1, 1927. It provided for the maintenance in force of the earlier treaty of February 26, 1921, stipulated nonaggression, and, in Art. 3, contained a mutual pledge not to participate in alliances or political agreements which might be directed against the security of either signatory. The text is in *Oriente Moderno,* March 1928.

Bayar of Turkey to the Shah in September 1955. On October 11 Premier Ala announced his government's resolve to sign the Baghdad Pact, and within a week this decision was ratified by both houses of parliament. Shortly afterward Ala attended the first meeting of the Middle East Treaty Organization, which was held in Baghdad.

By joining the alliance, the Shah and his government have made a bold move toward definition of Iran's position in the East-West conflict, thus creating for the first time since the war a basis for far-reaching Western commitments in favor of her defense and the strengthening of her army. With steadily increasing oil revenues and a greater feeling of security Iran is finally in position to look toward the future with considerable confidence. Her internal affairs will in the long run, be of primary importance, and the way the new revenues are spent is likely to affect her destiny in the years to come.

⊣ CHAPTER VI ⊢

Afghanistan

AFGHANISTAN was established as a separate and independent
state in 1747 by Ahmed Shah, an Afghan general of the Iranian
king, Nadir Shah. Ahmed Shah, a member of the Sadozai branch of
the Durrani tribe, united under his rule not only Afghanistan as we
know it today, but also Baluchistan, Kashmir, and Punjab. His capital was at Kandahar. Under his successors the capital was moved
to Kabul and the frontiers of the state shrank. Indian provinces were
lost and eventually became absorbed by the expanding British Empire. In 1809 the latter entered into the first agreements with Afghanistan in order to enlist her support against possible French or Iranian
invasions of India.

Britain's interest in Afghanistan was based on strategic considerations. The main physical feature of Afghanistan is the Hindu Kush
range, which passes from the northeast to the southwest through the
whole length of the country. Hindu Kush is the watershed of two
river systems, the Indus and the Oxus (Amu Daria), and the only natural frontier of India in the northwest. Britain had a vital interest in
preventing any hostile power from dominating this great barrier.
Ever since Napoleon planned a joint invasion of India with the Russians, British eyes have been on the Hindu Kush. The British had to
choose between occupying the Hindu Kush and annexing Afghanistan to India or attempting to dominate the area indirectly by treating
it as a satellite and a buffer state. For seventy years (1809–1879)
British policy vacillated between these two alternatives. In contrast
to the situation in neighboring Iran, in Afghanistan it was Britain
who was on the offensive, while Russia either stood apart or, at most,

tried to use the Iranians as her spearhead. Britain's overbearing policy led to two Afghan wars, the first in 1839–1842 and the second in 1878–1879. Both were caused by the pro-Russian policies of the Afghan rulers who were unwilling to subject themselves to British direction. During the first war the British conquered Kabul and captured Dost Mohammed, the Great Emir and founder of the Barakzai dynasty (another branch of the dominant Durrani tribe). Then, having restored him to power, they secured his neutrality in the conflict between British and Russian interests.

In the second war the British occupied a larger part of the country, ousted the pro-Russian Emir Shir Ali, and in 1879 concluded the Treaty of Gandamak with his successor, Yakub. Yakub agreed to cede Khyber Pass to Britain and to accept British control of his foreign relations in return for an annual subsidy of £60,000. An anti-British outbreak, however, complicated these arrangements and resulted in Yakub's abdication a few months later. On July 20, 1880, a final settlement was reached with Yakub's successor, Abdur Rahman (1880–1901): Britain transferred to him the control of the country and evacuated her troops, but retained the direction of Afghan foreign relations and pledged assistance against external aggression. This agreement was confirmed on March 21, 1905, with Emir Habibullah (1901–1919), to whom Britain extended, in addition, a yearly subsidy of £160,000. Thus, for four decades (1880–1920) Britain chose to exercise indirect control only. Afghanistan was free from British troops and enjoyed full internal independence, but her "friendly" ruler, subsidized by the government of India, was forbidden to have dealings with other powers than Britain.

BOUNDARY DISPUTES

Inasmuch as Britain pledged to assist Afghanistan against external aggression, it was important to know where Afghan boundaries lay. There was considerable doubt on this point, a doubt rendered more acute by the Russian advance in Central Asia in the 1870's and 1880's. By annexing Merv in 1884 Russia came dangerously close to Afghanistan, and by conquering the Panjdeh oasis she actually invaded Afghan territory. Britain's reaction to these moves was so strong that for a while there was talk of war, but in 1885 the two powers compromised and settled the major portion of the northern Afghan boundary. This agreement was supplemented in 1895 by exact delimitation of the Pamir boundary in the easternmost tip of

Afghanistan. Two years earlier, in 1893, Britain and Afghanistan settled the Afghan-Indian boundary by the so-called Durand agreement.

The settlement of the boundaries was a positive achievement inasmuch as it removed an immediate cause of friction between the states directly concerned. But the boundaries thus established were bad and impractical. The major part of the northern boundary ran along the unprotected Oxus River or through a flat steppe, and therefore could not possibly be considered as a strategic frontier. Moreover, it split a single ethnic area in two, leaving on both sides the non-Afghan tribes of Turkomans, Uzbeks, and Tajiks, on whom Afghanistan's hold had always been tenuous. As to the southern boundary, it was better in the strategic sense, running as it did through the crests of mountains, but, unfortunately, it also divided a single ethnic area, leaving on the Indian side a few million of purely Afghan tribes. The mountainous character of this borderland made effective control over them so much the more difficult.

Britain's control of Afghan foreign relations was resented by Russia. She accepted it, however, in the Anglo-Russian agreement of 1907, declaring that Afghanistan was outside her sphere of influence. During the First World War Afghanistan remained neutral, but, as we know, Emir Habibullah violated the nonintercourse pledge by receiving and parleying with the German mission under Niedermayer and Von Hentig. Mindful, however, of the proximity and power of British India, he did not dare to conclude an alliance with the Central powers.

EMANCIPATION FROM BRITISH TUTELAGE

On February 20, 1919, Habibullah was killed by an assassin. Next day his brother, Nasrullah Khan, leader of the anti-British conservative party, was proclaimed emir by the mullahs and the tribes. This choice was challenged by Habibullah's younger son, Amanullah, then governor of Kabul, who with the aid of the army, overthrew Nasrullah and ascended the throne on February 27. One of his first steps was to sentence Nasrullah to death for alleged complicity in the murder of his father. This action aroused considerable anger in religious circles. Partly to silence domestic opposition and partly to profit from Britain's postwar weariness, Amanullah, in early May, proclaimed a Jihad against the British and ordered his army to invade India.

209

The Third Afghan War, as it was called, caused Britain consider-able embarrassment. It came at the time of grave internal disturb-ances in the Punjab. An Indian nationalist, Obaydullah, known for his contacts with Berlin and Moscow, proclaimed himself head of the Provisional Government of India. In Peshawar, there was actually an attempted uprising. Native militiamen in the British service de-serted their ranks and in some cases joined the enemy, while all along the Afghan border, the warlike Pathan tribes rallied around Aman-ullah. The British were ill-prepared to cope with this aggression in view of their postwar demobilization, but eventually they managed to gather 140,000 troops on the northwest frontier. This army, aided by air action over Kabul and Jelalabad, succeeded by the end of May in forcing the Afghans to retreat to their territory. Amanullah sued for an armistice, and it was granted to him. The British, who by that time were in a position to enter and occupy Afghanistan, re-frained from doing so. It was not their intention to cause a complete disintegration of the Afghan state, which they desired to preserve as a buffer between India and Russia. Besides, this brief war had already cost the Indian treasury £16,000,000, and a military occupa-tion would add heavy new burdens.

For these reasons, the British were glad to conclude with the Emir, on August 8, 1919, the Treaty of Rawalpindi. Despite her victory, Britain retreated from her hitherto privileged position by recognizing the complete independence of Afghanistan in internal and external affairs. This step was in keeping with the spirit of the times, but its political wisdom was debatable inasmuch as it rewarded the ag-gressor. Thereafter, Amanullah was able to claim victory over the British in obvious disregard of the military realities. This release from British control promptly set in motion a chain of events which Britain traditionally had tried to avoid. In the course of 1919, an Afghan mission went to Moscow and a Soviet mission was received in Kabul. Obaydullah, Mahendra Pratap, Barkatullah, and other Indian revo-lutionaries, who were in touch with the Soviet-sponsored Pan-Hindu Revolutionary Committee at Tashkent, established a forward base on Afghan territory, and Amanullah rejected a British request for their expulsion. He further invited the Turkish general, Jemal Pasha, known for his hatred of Britain, to reorganize the Afghan army. Jemal's presence in Kabul encouraged anti-British attitudes and activities. The Afghans felt so self-confident as to demand that Brit-ain modify the Treaty of Sèvres in favor of Turkey.

210

On February 28, 1921, Afghanistan and Soviet Russia concluded a treaty of friendship which provided for the exchange of diplomatic representatives and the opening of Soviet consulates in Herat, Maimena, Mazar-i-Sherif, Kandahar, and Ghazni; an annual subsidy of one million gold rubles and a supply of munitions to Afghanistan; the transfer of Panjdeh to Afghanistan; and the construction of the Kushk-Herat-Kandahar-Kabul telegraph line. This treaty was one of a series negotiated simultaneously by Russia with her southern neighbors, whose confidence and friendship she was seeking. It was a rebuff to the British, who at that time did not even possess a legation in Kabul, and it reaffirmed Afghan independence. While this treaty was being negotiated, an Afghan diplomatic mission made a tour of European capitals seeking recognition, inviting foreign technicians, and trying to establish commercial relations. This emancipation from traditional tutelage greatly irked Britain and when, during their visit in London, Afghan delegates insisted on conducting negotiations with the Foreign Office instead of the India Office, they were brusquely dismissed by the irate Lord Curzon, Britain's foreign secretary.

Amanullah's exuberance in his newly won ability to play Russia against Britain somewhat subsided when he learned of the Soviet conquest of Bukhara and of the rough treatment that the peoples of Central Asia had received from the Bolsheviks. More amenable to negotiations, he received a British mission in Kabul and on November 22, 1921, concluded a new treaty, which reaffirmed Afghan independence and the existing boundaries, provided for the exchange of diplomatic representatives and the establishment of British consulates, gave Afghanistan transit and customs facilities in India, and pledged mutual co-operation in maintaining tribal peace in frontier areas. On Britain's insistence, Amanullah agreed not to allow the establishment of Soviet consulates in Ghazni and Kandahar, two towns situated in dangerous proximity to the Indian border. On the other hand, in deference to Amanullah's wish, the treaty was concluded in the name of the British government and not on behalf of India,[1] and Britain agreed to address him as "His Majesty."

Afghan-Soviet Relations

On the whole, Amanullah leaned more heavily toward Russia than toward Britain. On March 1 and June 22, 1921, he concluded treaties

[1] However, an Indian civil servant, Sir Henry Dobbs, negotiated it.

of friendship with Turkey and Iran, respectively, and subsequently opened wide the gates to an influx of Turkish officers, teachers, and other experts. It will be recalled that at that time Turkey was actively co-operating with the Soviets and her relations with Britain were not good.

Amanullah displayed his pro-Soviet leanings in other instances as well. Thus he permitted the establishment of a branch of the Soviet State Trading Company (*Vneshtorg*), seriously considered a concession for a Soviet state bank, accepted the services of Russian experts in road surveys and construction, employed thirty Soviet instructors in the Afghan air force, and consented to the training of Afghan pilots in Tashkent. In 1926 he concluded with Russia a pact of neutrality and nonaggression, which was followed in 1927 by an agreement to establish an air line between Tashkent and Kabul. He also opened negotiations for a trade agreement.

Amanullah did not blindly give his body and soul to the Russians. On a few occasions his and their policies diverged. His ambition to pose as a defender of Islam and a champion of national self-determination fitted ill with the pattern of Soviet conquest of the neighboring khanates of Bukhara and Khiva. The emir of Bukhara, fleeing certain death at the hands of the Bolsheviks, took refuge in Afghan territory. Amanullah not only did not object to this but actually took an active interest in the Basmachi rebellion, which in 1922 seriously undermined Soviet power in Central Asia. Indeed, Amanullah went so far as to contemplate the creation of a Central Asian Confederacy under his own leadership. To this end he concentrated substantial forces along the northern border and established liaison with the Pan-Turanian leader, Enver Pasha. The Soviets demanded a declaration of neutrality and withdrawal of troops from the border regions. Amanullah complied, and Enver's death soon put an end to whatever plans these leaders had had regarding Central Asia. The Basmachi movement continued down to 1931.

In 1925 a quarrel broke out between the Afghan and Soviet governments over an island in the Oxus River. Finding that the matter was of minor importance, the Soviet government conceded the right of Afghanistan and withdrew its troops. With characteristic conceit, Amanullah's government claimed a major diplomatic victory. The fact of the matter was that, by making this truly negligible concession, Russia secured a diplomatic success which soon afterward paved the way for the above-mentioned neutrality pact and air agreement.

There is no doubt that, while maintaining the appearance of utmost correctness, Russia was consistently pursuing a slow but certain policy of penetration. She was, in the first place, taking full advantage of Amanullah's anti-British frame of mind to proffer various forms of collaboration, which the unstable ruler, believing himself very shrewd, accepted as a counterbalance to British influence. In the second place, Russia very skillfully exploited the fact that the northern part of Afghanistan was inhabited by Turkish-speaking minorities divided from their Soviet-governed brethren by an ill-protected and rather artificial boundary. And while the Soviets, in their own crude way, were paying a great deal of attention to their Central Asian possessions, the Kabul government, separated as it was from the Oxus by the powerful barrier of Hindu Kush, took slender interest in the development of Afghan Turkestan.

The Soviets, therefore, had a fertile field for propaganda. In the early twenties this propaganda had to overcome some difficulties that arose as a result of the rough handling of Afghan and Indian merchants in Bukhara and Tashkent by the Bolsheviks. The news of this treatment spread and did not help Soviet prestige, but later Russia agreed to compensate Afghan traders for their losses. While propaganda about Communist principles probably made little headway with the primitive Turkomans, Tajiks, and Uzbeks on the Afghan side of the border (and the Soviets did not stress Marxism too heavily), the road and railroad building, the telegraph connections, and the increased trade opportunities offered by the Soviets did not fail to cause favorable comment. The extension of Soviet railways to Kushk and Termez on the Afghan border helped stimulate mutual trade while serving Soviet strategic purposes. The essence of Soviet propaganda consisted in encouraging the growth of local autonomous or separatist movements, which could be used as a lever of pressure on the Afghan government in case of need. At the same time, Soviet economic penetration was bound to make Afghanistan's northern provinces more and more dependent on Russia both as a market and as a source of merchandise. This situation resembled that prevailing in northern Iran, and in both cases the mountain ranges separating the capital of the country from its northern provinces inexorably drove the latter into the arms of the Russians.

Afghan-British Relations

While Amanullah was no doubt aware of this situation, he did not consider it alarming enough to adopt countermeasures or to ally himself with Britain. On the contrary, his eyes were directed toward the turbulent borderland in the south, inhabited by native Pathan tribes. We have already mentioned that this tribal area was rather artificially divided by the Durand Line, which constituted the Afghan-Indian border. Another peculiarity was that the Pathan tribal area was not included within the administrative boundary of the government of India. British control over the area was exercised by a few scattered military outposts and political officers, and as such it was very slender. British policy with regard to the North-West Frontier Province oscillated between strictly limited commitments of the so-called "close border" policy and the more ambitious "forward movement." [2] In any case, there was always a considerable belt of mountainous territory between the last British outposts and the Afghan border, which was a virtual no man's land. Britain's reluctance to occupy this region and to subject it to the regular administration was based on the same premises that caused her to refrain from annexing Afghanistan proper. The effort and expense involved in the direct policing of these unhospitable and rugged lands would be disproportionate to the results obtained. This being the case, the rulers of Kabul claimed the right to oppose any manifestation of British control in the region. Yet some measure of control was needed, at least to protect the neighboring settled communities to the south from nomad raiding. In addition, the Afghan emirs wanted to extend their own influence over these tribes. This policy had both aggressive and defensive motivations. By favoring and subsidizing the tribes, the Afghan rulers could use them as a weapon against the British if necessary. Also as these tribes from across the border could be a major nuisance to Afghanistan herself and as their attitude could weigh heavily in domestic developments and dynastic rivalries in Kabul, it was of vital importance to Afghan rulers to cultivate their friendship.

Amanullah's conceit, coupled with his anti-British complex, led him to pursue a "pinprick" policy toward Britain through the instrumentality of these tribes, and, as a result, much of his own and British energy was devoted to this troublesome area.

REFORMS AND REBELLIONS

While trying to balance Soviet and British influences, Amanullah was also striving to Westernize his backward country. In principle,

[2] For a thorough discussion of the tribal problem, see Sir Kerr Fraser-Tytler, *Afghanistan: A Study of Political Developments in Central Asia* (London, 1950).

this was a commendable ambition, and, if successful, it could act as a deterrent to subversive doctrines or movements. But Amanullah had little understanding of Western civilization and attached undue importance to outward appearances. In an attempt to emulate Mustafa Kemal of Turkey, he promulgated, on April 9, 1923, a Fundamental Law, following which he issued a number of reform edicts aiming at the modernization of the country in every conceivable field.

To implement these reforms, Amanullah turned to foreign technicians and advisers of a number of nationalities. He gave preference to the Germans because, like Reza Shah in Iran, he sought the friendship of a "disinterested third power." This reliance on German technical aid proved to be an enduring factor in the interwar period. Even after his fall, the Germans continued to grow in numbers, providing teachers, military instructors, technicians, artisans, bank employees, nurses, doctors, and scientists. In 1924 a German school for teachers was established in Kabul. The Germans constructed paper and textile factories, built electrical plants, and flooded the Afghan market with electrical appliances and other goods. Colonel Christenn assumed the command of the Afghan Military Academy. In the thirties, with the advent of Hitler, this German penetration became more intensive, just as it did all over the Middle East. In 1935 a German scientific expedition explored the Hindu Kush, and in 1936 the Lufthansa established an air service between Berlin and Kabul.

Amanullah's reforms, especially those in the educational field, encountered considerable opposition among conservative circles. He had a forewarning of trouble when in March 1924 the Lame Mullah raised a rebellion in Khost in protest against the allegedly antireligious provisions of the new civil code. For ten months the Mullah defied the authorities, and it cost the government much effort and money to restore order.

Instead of slowing down his reforms, Amanullah went ahead and in December 1927 embarked, with a large retinue, on a seven-month tour of Europe. Studiously avoiding New Delhi—another manifestation of his anti-Indian complex—he went straight to Bombay and from there proceeded to Italy, Germany, France, and England. He was received everywhere with the honors due a member of royalty, and negotiated, wherever he could, new pacts and agreements with an eye to enhancing Afghanistan's prestige and economic prosperity. On his return route, he paid a fortnight's visit to Moscow, during which the Russians undertook to supply him with thirteen airplanes and a quantity of munitions. He concluded his tour by a visit to Turkey and Iran, where his reformatory zeal experienced another upward surge. Upon his return, the King renewed his efforts to modernize the country. In a series of public speeches he outlined his program of reform, making frequent references to secular education and a new status for women. He thereby deepened the chasm between himself and the clergy, whose disapproval was becoming more and more pronounced.

Internal Crisis

On November 14, 1928, a tribal rebellion broke out. Encouraged by the mullahs and led by their conservative chieftains, the tribes rose one after another and within two months reduced the government to impotence. In the ensuing chaos, a Tajik highway robber nicknamed Bacha-i-Sakao ("water-carrier's son") gathered a body of tribal warriors and outlaws and on January 17, 1929, took the capital by storm. Three days earlier Amanullah had abdicated in favor of his elder brother, Inayatullah, and had fled to Kandahar. There he tried to organize resistance, but, failing to evoke popular response, he crossed the Indian border and went into exile in Europe.

In the critical days of the rebellion, the Soviet and Turkish ambassadors advised him strongly to fight to the bitter end and, should he be successful, to press his reforms. The Soviets proffered more than advice. Shortly before Amanullah's overthrow, his ambassador to Moscow, Ghulam Nabi, organized a military force on Soviet territory and, equipped and supplied by the Russians, led it into Afghanistan to rescue the King. He arrived too late, however, to change the course of events. The people of the north, who were very hostile to Amanullah, failed to rally to his banners, and after a few weeks Ghulam Nabi crossed back into Soviet territory. For several months the fate of Afghanistan hung in the balance. The destruction of the regime, however inadequate it had been, left a dangerous vacuum very tempting to foreign penetration. But neither Russia nor Britain were prepared at this juncture to divert their energies toward the conquest of Afghanistan.

Ascending the throne, Bacha-i-Sakao, or Habibullah Ghazi as he called himself, began a reign of terror. Foreign legations and many foreign residents were evacuated. Bacha-i-Sakao issued a proclamation canceling all Amanullah's reforms, thereby hoping to secure the approval of the clergy. But the mullahs were equally opposed to the usurper. Within a few months, the country was seething with restlessness, and the conditions were ripe for a counterrevolt. The opposition found a leader in the person of Mohammed Nadir Khan, a member of the Barakzai branch of the Durranis and Afghan ambassador to France. Nadir and his three brothers returned to Afghanistan in March 1929 and began recruiting a force of their own in the south. They did not limit their activities to Afghan territory but extended them to the no man's land south of the border. In fact, their army, in its final shape, was mainly composed of the Waziri and Mahsud tribes of India. With this tribal army Nadir and his brothers defeated Bacha's forces and entered Kabul. On October 16, 1929, Nadir Khan was proclaimed king of Afghanistan.

Nadir's accession provoked an angry outburst in the Soviet press, which accused Britain of using him as her instrument. The Red Shirt rebellion which broke out in the next year in Waziristan was interpreted by the British as partly resulting from Soviet machinations among the border tribes. The rebellion, coinciding with the anti-British crusade preached by the Fakir of Ipi, caused Britain considerable embarrassment at a time when she was anxious to restore normal relations with Afghanistan. Although the British disclaimed any responsibility for or connivance in Nadir's *coup d'état*, they greeted it with a feeling of great relief. In the hands of his irresponsible bandit predecessor, the strategic barrier of Hindu Kush was exposed to all sorts of dangers which could only result in great impairment to the security of India. Nadir Shah was a soldier [3] and a statesman of experience and maturity, acquainted with the West and thoroughly realistic.

Nadir Shah

Despite the fact that he had gathered his army in British territory, Nadir Shah was not and never intended to be a British puppet. In fact, in the early twenties he had been a strong supporter of an aggressive tribal policy on the northwest frontier of India. With the assumption of royal power, however, he abandoned this adventurous course, partly because he genuinely desired good neighborly

[3] In 1919, during the Third Afghan War, Nadir Khan was a general in command of an army.

217

relations and partly because he believed in the pacification of tribes on both sides of the border as a prerequisite to an orderly government in Afghanistan.

His internal task was stupendous. The bandit's rule left complete anarchy in Afghanistan. The country was politically divided, and Nadir Shah's own tribal supporters looted the royal palace and the city upon entering the capital. Within four years Nadir did an impressive job of consolidation and reconstruction. In February 1932 he promulgated a new constitution which established a two-chamber assembly, the upper chamber of which was to consist of appointed notables. The constitution resembled the earlier Amanullah constitution but was devoid of the provisions irksome to the conservatives. Although the issuance of these new Fundamental Rules caused little change in the essentially autocratic and patriarchal political system, it symbolized Nadir's domestic policy as a whole. This policy was patterned where feasible on Western standards, but it was cautious, with no radical departures from the deeply ingrained habits of this Mohammedan country. There was nothing spectacular in Nadir's rule, except perhaps for two brusque executions, one of the captured Bacha-i-Sakao and another of Ghulam Nabi, who, upon his return from Russia, began to organize intrigues against the new king. As usual, the real authority in the country was divided between the ruler and the tribal chiefs. The latter were occasionally called for consultation in a Great Assembly (*Loe Jirga*), which was actually much more important than the bicameral legislature.

Nadir's four brothers filled the key positions in the government: Mohammed Hashim Khan was prime minister, a post he held for seventeen years from 1929 to 1946; Shah Wali Khan was minister in Paris and his special function was to keep an eye on the exiled Amanullah and his intrigues abroad; Mahmud Shah Khan was commander-in-chief of the Afghan army; and Aziz Khan was minister in Berlin, where he died of an assassin's bullet in the early 1930's. The posts of court minister, foreign minister, and minister of education were also held by the King's relatives.

Nadir's foreign policy was a traditional one, aiming at the preservation of balance between Britain and Russia, but it was more impartial than that of Amanullah. No more use was made of the services of Russian experts, but British experts were not invited either. The Germans and the nationals of other countries, France, Switzerland, Poland, and Czechoslovakia, were favored, and an impressive number of Turks were employed as military, medical, and educational advisers. These foreigners were engaged only as operating experts and not as key executives.

In 1930 a serious border incident threatened to disturb Afghan-Soviet relations. It was barely half a year after Nadir's assumption of power, and the northern provinces were not yet fully subjected to his control. A Basmachi leader from Ferghana and one of Enver's associates, Ibrahim Beg, took advantage of this state of affairs to establish a base in Afghan Turkestan from which he conducted guerrilla warfare against the Soviet authorities. The latter retaliated in June by sending a sizable force across the Oxus, forty miles deep into Afghan territory. This violation of Afghan territorial integrity spurred the Kabul government to action. In the fall of the same year a regular Afghan force crossed the Hindu Kush and after a brief fight drove Ibrahim Beg into Soviet territory. To avoid further possible misunderstandings with Moscow, Nadir Shah removed to the south the Bukharan and other Soviet refugees who had hitherto lived in Afghan Turkestan.

Nadir Shah's able rule was cut short by his assassination, in November 1933, by one of his personal enemies, yet the foundations he had laid were so solid that his twenty-year-old son, Mohammed Zahir Shah, succeeded to the throne without incident. Under the guidance of his paternal uncles, the new ruler continued his father's cautious and realistic policies. In 1937 Afghanistan joined with Iran, Iraq, and Turkey in the Saadabad pact. In the course of the next year Afghan-British relations were exposed to temporary tension as a result of the Shami Pir rebellion. Shami Pir, in an attempt to restore Amanullah, rallied a tribal force on the Indian side of the border and invaded Afghanistan. He was defeated by the government troops, and the British did their best to curb the rebellion on their side of the border. No ill feelings between Britain and Afghanistan resulted from this episode.

THE SECOND WORLD WAR AND AFTER

During the Second World War Afghanistan remained neutral. This neutrality was exposed to a severe strain when, in 1941, following their occupation of Iran, Britain and Russia asked Afghanistan to surrender all the Axis nationals resident in her territory. A *Loe Jirga* of tribal chieftains was called and, after a heated debate, it endorsed the government's willingness to comply with the Allied request. This realistic decision spared Afghanistan the treatment which Iran had incurred by rejecting similar Allied demands.

The war brought a serious dislocation to Afghan economy because Russia, hitherto the principal supplier of manufactured goods, was unable to export. This made Afghanistan largely dependent upon imports from India, which, in turn, resulted in increased political dependence on Britain. But the British very tactfully refrained from exploiting their superiority. By 1944 Afghan fears of British supremacy had receded to such a degree that an agreement was reached between the two governments for the training of Afghan army officers in India. Two hundred officers were sent to British training centers, and negotiations were opened for the delivery of British surplus arms after the war.[4] This change of attitude was also reflected in the increased willingness of Afghans to engage British experts in such fields as education, radio, and textiles. The British Council [5] began to function in Kabul, and British schoolmasters were invited to organize the fourth foreign secondary school in the capital, the other three being French, German, and American. This growing confidence found expression in the mutual raising of their diplomatic missions to the rank of embassies in 1948.

Although Afghanistan suffered some economic inconveniences during the war, she was at the same time able to build up a considerable dollar balance as a result of the export of Persian lambskins (karakul) to the United States. In fact, for a number of years, but especially in wartime, Afghanistan enjoyed a monopoly in this field, her only competitor, Russia, having seriously dislocated production as a result of forced collectivization and an ensuing slaughtering of sheep by reluctant peasants. Thus, right after the war Afghanistan was able to plan certain public works urgently needed to raise the standard of living of her population. This was fortunate because there was a growing demand for reform, stimulated by increased contact with Westerners and by knowledge of Soviet achievements in Central Asia. The British had not been the only ones to disseminate their culture during the war; Soviet authorities had organized visits of Afghan intellectuals to Tashkent and did not miss an opportunity to impress them with the "superiority" of their system.

[4] For accounts of the recent period, see Sir Giles Squire, "Recent Progress in Afghanistan," *Royal Central Asian Journal*, Jan. 1950; Prince Peter of Greece, "Post-War Developments in Afghanistan," *R.C.A.J.*, July–Oct. 1947; and M. Philips Price, "A Visit to Afghanistan," *R.C.A.J.*, April 1949.

[5] An organization dedicated to the spread of British culture abroad.

Under these circumstances, the resignation of the conservative prime minister, Hashim Khan, and his replacement in 1946 by a younger brother, Mahmud Shah Khan, was welcomed as a sign of a more liberal trend. One of the first acts of the new prime minister was to grant amnesty to political prisoners. This was followed by such acts as the inauguration of the first university in Kabul (1946) and the enlargement of the network of schools. Even some girls' schools were started, despite the grumbling of the mullahs. To cope with this dangerous clerical opposition, the government rather shrewdly opened a state college for future mullahs, hoping thereby to imbue the new generation of clergy with more liberal ideas. All these moves were, however, gradual and cautious, and despite reform Afghanistan remained one of the most backward Moslem countries, with no unveiled women to be seen in the streets and with the majority of people wearing oriental garb.[6]

Economic Needs

Economic problems towered above everything else. Despite the dollar balance accumulated in wartime, the country remained essentially poor, two-thirds of its population leading a pastoral life in rather barren hilly areas. It was clear that if Afghanistan wished to achieve greater material progress she needed to develop other exports than karakul and fruit. Karakul exports had suffered a serious setback after the war as a result of competition from South-West Africa and the Soviet Union.[7]

Under these circumstances, Afghanistan hopefully turned toward the United States. The latter had three characteristics which attracted the Afghans: it had technical know-how, it was wealthy, and it was politically disinterested. In 1946 Afghanistan engaged the Morrison-Knudsen Corporation of Boise, Idaho, to carry out various technical projects such as the construction of roads, bridges, dams, electrical plants, and irrigation canals. Of these, a road linking Kabul with Kandahar and regulation of the Helmand River were the most noteworthy projects. The latter, incidentally, gave rise to a quarrel with Iran, in whose territory the Helmand empties; Iran feared that the damming of the river would divert much-needed waters from

[6] For a description of present social conditions in Afghanistan, see Arthur V. Huffman, "The Administrative and Social Structure of Afghan Life," *R.C.A.J.*, Jan. 1951.

[7] In this connection, see Peter G. Franck, "Problems of Economic Development in Afghanistan," *Middle East Journal*, July and Oct. 1949.

the Iranian Seistan oasis. An American oil firm, Inland Exploration Company, prospected in the country, but so far the results have been modest. Negotiations were inaugurated with Trans World Airways to establish regular air communications and connections between Kabul and the outer world. In 1948 Afghan and American legations were elevated to embassies (diplomatic relations between the two countries had been established in 1943). Also in 1948 the Afghan minister of economics, Abdul Mejid Khan, visited the United States seeking a loan and technical assistance. His visit was successful. In 1949 the Export-Import Bank of the United States granted Afghanistan a $21,000,000 loan for development purposes. The Afghan government also requested the World Bank to lend financial aid, and there was some likelihood that this American-influenced institution would favor its application. Although Afghanistan did not declare war on the Axis, she was admitted to the United Nations in 1946. Thereafter the United Nations took active interest in Afghanistan's development, and in 1950 a mission of economic experts was sent from Lake Success to Kabul to investigate Afghan needs under the technical assistance program.

Afghan-Soviet relations during and after the war were generally correct. A few outstanding boundary problems, such as the ownership of certain islands on the Oxus and the water rights in the Kushk oasis, were settled amicably by an Afghan-Soviet boundary commission on September 29, 1948. The Oxus boundary was fixed as the *thalweg* of the river. Trade between both countries was gradually revived, Russia exporting sugar, cotton goods, and petroleum and purchasing Afghan wool. But no Soviet trade agencies were permitted to operate in Afghanistan and no Afghan traders were allowed to enter Soviet territory. The exchange of goods was made at fixed points of the frontier, with not much opportunity for political penetration. In 1950 both countries concluded a trade agreement, one of a series which Russia was then negotiating with her southern neighbors. The Afghan government, fully aware of the technical and agricultural progress made in Soviet Central Asia, began to pay more attention than before to the development of Afghan Turkestan. Fears that improved conditions in Russia would contrast with the poverty and backwardness of Afghanistan were well founded, but the danger was somewhat lessened by the fact that Afghan Turkestan—the area most exposed to Soviet infiltration—was underpopulated and the land question there was never acute. In fact, the government was interested in transferring some of the nomadic Afghans from the south to farm the uncultivated lands in the north. Moreover, in contrast to many other Moslem countries, Afghanistan did not suffer from great differences in wealth. The country was generally poor, but very few beggars were in evidence. True enough, Russia did not renounce her revolutionary schemes and continued to send her agents across the border partly to operate in Afghanistan and partly to reach Pakistan and India. The effects of Communist propaganda on the Afghans were not very spectacular,[8] but it would be unwise to disregard the fact that Uzbeks, Tajiks, and Turkomans lived on both sides of the border and that those under Soviet rule were being drawn into a major social and economic experiment while their southern brethren continued a rather lethargic existence under the primitive conditions of slow-moving eastern society. The movement of refugees continued to be mostly in a southward direction, and their tales of oppression, secret police surveillance, and ruthlessness undid much of the Soviet propaganda. With all this, it was clear that should Russia choose to invade Afghanistan, she could do it with relative ease. The Afghan army was obviously not in a position to oppose a great power, and its role was limited to internal policing. Likewise, the Hindu Kush was no longer a formidable obstacle to a modern army as it had been in the past, and it would take only a matter of days for the Soviet troops to emerge on the frontier of Pakistan and Kashmir.

The end of British rule in India in August 1947 posed new and perplexing problems to the "Guardians of the Hindu Kush." The long-feared might of Britain was replaced by two native and relatively weak countries. To Afghanistan, this meant a lessening of her external security, and she automatically became more exposed to Soviet pressure. To make matters worse, Afghan-Pakistan relations suffered serious aggravation from the very beginning. When Pakistan was about to be created, the Kabul government demanded a plebiscite in the North-West Frontier Province to determine the future allegiance of several million Pathans residing in the area. This was refused by Pakistani leaders. As a result, the no man's land south of the Durand Line was inherited by Pakistan. Afghanistan then began

---

[8] According to the Afghan foreign minister, one of the captured Soviet agents, when interrogated by Afghan police, bitterly complained: "The Afghans are so stupid, they do not even understand what I am driving at." (See *R.C.A.J.*, Jan. 1950, p. 15.)

to advocate the creation of an independent state of Pakhtunistan. A number of frontier incidents occurred and feeling ran high on both sides of the border between 1947 and 1949.

By 1950, however, this conflict showed signs of temporary abatement, owing to some extent to restraining British influence on both governments. Despite Pakistan's emancipation, British intelligence officers continued to be employed in the North-West Frontier Province, and Pakistan's political agent in Quetta was a Britisher. The creation of an independent Moslem state south of Afghanistan deprived Afghan extremists and such borderland troublemakers as the Fakir of Ipi of the time-tested anti-infidel slogans. On the other hand, Pakistan, as a dominion, continued her association with the British Commonwealth. Britain, therefore, had a continuing interest in the political destinies of the Hindu Kush.

With reference to the East-West conflict, it should be pointed out that Russia was never greatly interested in Afghanistan per se. She always treated this remote country as an alternate invasion route to the subcontinent of India. In 1950–1951 she seemed to be bent on enveloping India from the east, through China and Burma. This perhaps explains why there was a lull on the Afghan front.

Afghanistan's Foreign Relations in the 1950's

In early September 1953 Mahmud Shah Khan resigned as prime minister after seven years in office. His replacement by General Mohammed Daud Khan, hitherto minister of defense and interior, brought no appreciable change in the character of the Afghan government, which remained essentially paternalistic. It appeared, however, that the new premier was inclined to press with greater vigor than his predecessor the Pakhtunistan issue between his country and Pakistan. On December 28, 1953, he asked Britain to agree to a revision of the Treaty of Kabul of 1921, in which the Durand Line had been confirmed as the boundary between Afghanistan and British India. Legally, it was an unusual procedure, inasmuch as on August 15, 1947, Britain had been succeeded by Pakistan as a sovereign power south of Afghanistan. Politically, however, it meant a reassertion by the Kabul government of its interest in the disputed border area. Although somewhat pushed into the background during the last years of Mahmud Khan's ministry, the Pakhtunistan issue continued to impede normalization of the Afghan-Pakistani relationship. The Afghans held to their basic view that the Pathans, seven million strong (in reality they probably did not exceed two and a half million), had a right to sovereign existence as a state of Pakhtunistan, which would embrace the territory between the southern Afghan boundary and the Indus River.

How far south this territory should extend was a moot question. If literally interpreted, the expression "between Afghanistan and the Indus" would mean the major part of Pakistan and would include Pakistan's capital, Karachi, as well as Baluchistan, a province bordering on Iran and the Indian Ocean. Such a claim would have some slight historical justification inasmuch as the short-lived empire of Afghanistan's founder, Ahmed Shah Durrani, did indeed extend that far south. The Afghans, to be sure, never defined the extent of their territorial claims (acting as agent for the would-be Pakhtunistan), but their official pronouncements and pamphlets contained wistful references to the historical past as well as to the necessity of obtaining access to the sea for their landlocked country. In promoting the Pakhtunistan scheme, the Afghans stressed two points: that they themselves did not covet the area in question but wanted to see it an independent state and that there should be a plebiscite to determine the wishes of the Pathans. It is noteworthy, however, that, although a substantial number of the latter inhabited Afghan territory, the Kabul government did not envisage a plebiscite on their side of the border. The issue was further confounded by the tendency of Afghan propaganda to identify two-thirds of Afghanistan's population as Pathans (or Pakhtuns), thus removing any distinction, historical or social, between them and the population of the contested area. On its part, Pakistan rejected any idea of a plebiscite in its territory.

The simmering Pakhtunistan issue came to a head late in March 1955, when the government of Pakistan announced its plan to abolish the traditional political divisions within the country and to unite all of Western Pakistan into a single province by May 31. Afghan reaction to this measure was prompt and negative. Broadcasting from Radio Kabul on March 29, Prime Minister Mohammed Daud Khan denounced Pakistan's decision as a hostile move, warning Karachi of the "grave consequences" likely to ensue if Pakistan persisted in its plan. The next day a mob estimated at 15,000 persons attacked and plundered the Pakistani embassy in Kabul, destroying public and private property and defiling Pakistan's flag. Similar attacks occurred shortly afterward against Pakistani consulates in

Jalalabad and Kandahar. Afghan police did not try to prevent these demonstrations; rather, according to some reports, they actually helped the assailants. The news of these outrages provoked widespread indignation in Pakistan, which, in turn, expressed itself in an assault on the Afghan consulate in Peshawar on April 1. Pakistan demanded official apology and "honorable amends," recalled its diplomatic and consular representatives from Afghanistan, and closed the border to commercial traffic between the two countries. Tempers rose on both sides, and a month later report of a "general mobilization" in Afghanistan was circulated in Karachi.

In the meantime Egypt and Saudi Arabia had offered to mediate the dispute, and by mid-May their offer was accepted by both sides. Subsequently a Saudi prince, Emir Musaid ibn Abdur Rahman, and an Egyptian envoy arrived in Kabul to end the conflict between the two Moslem powers. Soon Turkey and Iraq, both recent signatories of the Baghdad Pact, lent their good offices also, as a result of which Kabul in the early summer of 1955 witnessed intense diplomatic activity in which the political backgrounds of the mediators (neutralist and pro-Western, respectively) added new complications to the already difficult controversy. It should be pointed out, however, that the mediators' task was technically limited to the dispute over the insult to the flag and damage to property, inasmuch as Pakistan had accepted mediation only on condition that the issue of Pakhtunistan be kept out of the discussions.

Although these attempts at mediation virtually broke down in June (despite the vaguely optimistic communique of the Saudi mediator), the dispute was concluded by early autumn. In a ceremony in Kabul on September 13 Afghanistan's foreign minister, Sardar Naim Khan, hoisted Pakistan's flag on the embassy's building, thus satisfying Pakistani honor. In return, Pakistan lifted the ban on the movement of goods across the border. This ban, incidentally, had caused landlocked Afghanistan considerable inconvenience, exposing it to major shortages of gasoline, cement, and textiles. It proved once again how vulnerable Afghanistan was in this respect and how effectively Pakistan could use its control of access routes to Afghanistan as an instrument of pressure.

It is not surprising, therefore, that, with the basic issue of Pakhtunistan still unsolved, Afghanistan did not cease its agitation for independence for and a plebiscite in the border area. On November 19 Pakistan's prime minister, Chaudry Mohammed Ali, publicly denounced the Afghan campaign of infiltration, sabotage, and propaganda in the land of the Pathans. His declaration coincided with the five-day-long session of the *Loe Jirga,* which met in Kabul on November 15 to consider vital national issues. According to established tradition, this grand assembly of Afghan chieftains meets very seldom and only on occasions when issues of exceptional importance, such as war, peace, or some basic reorientation in foreign policy, are involved. Its last previous meeting had been in 1940, when it was called to decide the question of Afghanistan's position in the war.

The present session of the *Loe Jirga* was obviously connected with the dispute with Pakistan. Opening the session, Premier Daud Khan declared that the "balance of power between Pakistan and Afghanistan has been destroyed by Pakistan's military alliance with the United States." [9] He then placed two questions before the assembly: (1) Should Afghanistan continue to demand a plebiscite in the disputed Pathan area? (2) Should Afghanistan take steps to restore the balance of power between itself and Pakistan? On November 20 the five hundred members of the *Loe Jirga* passed three resolutions, the first fully supporting Daud's demand for a plebiscite, the second authorizing the government to "find ways and means of returning to the balance of power that was upset by Pakistan's decision to accept arms aid from the United States," [10] and the third refusing to recognize Pakhtunistan as part of Pakistan. The intent of these deliberations was clear: inasmuch as the Afghans had not renounced their ambitions in the borderland and yet had found that Pakistan, due to its ties with America, would have the means to frustrate their plans, they were to turn to Russia for support and assistance.

From the time of this momentous decision events began to move swiftly on the Afghan scene. Exactly a month after the *Loe Jirga's* session, on December 15, two principal leaders of the Soviet Union, Premier Nikolai A. Bulganin and Communist Party Secretary Nikita S. Khrushchev, arrived in Kabul on a state visit, thus concluding their extended tour of Asian countries. Unprecedented in the annals of Russian-Afghan relations, this visit was in tune with the new Soviet policy of exploiting such psychological and political differences as existed between the West and Asian nations and of wooing the latter by promises of aid in their development. During their

[9] *New York Times,* Nov. 16, 1955.   [10] *Ibid.,* Nov. 22, 1955.

stay in the Afghan capital the Soviet leaders publicly expressed their support of Afghan views regarding Pakhtunistan and pledged economic and technical assistance to the Kabul government. No official mention was made of arms supplies, but it would not be surprising if these were on the agenda of the Soviet-Afghan conversations. In fact, there had been earlier indications that Afghanistan might import arms either from Russia or from her satellites: a year before an Afghan military mission had visited Czechoslovakia, presumably in search of weapons, and on November 1, 1955, the Afghan ambassador in Cairo had declared that if Afghanistan did not receive arms from the West it would be obliged to seek them in the Soviet Union. The Soviet visit ended with the signing of three documents. The first contained a Soviet pledge to extend a credit of $100,000,000 to Afghanistan, to be implemented by a separate agreement. The second contained a joint Soviet-Afghan statement expressing support for the principles of peaceful coexistence and self-determination, with specific reference to the decisions of the Bandung conference, and for world peace and the admission of Communist China to the United Nations. The third was a protocol extending the 1931 Soviet-Afghan treaty of neutrality and nonaggression for the next ten years, with automatic renewal every year afterward and the possibility of termination by either party on six months' notice.

These agreements marked an important step in the new Soviet diplomacy in Asia. Soviet rapprochement with Kabul had actually begun in the early 1950's when Russia offered to build oil storage tanks and a network of roads in Afghanistan. By the summer of 1954 Afghanistan had accepted loans totaling $8,000,000 from the Soviet Union for two grain silos in Pul-i-Khumri and Kabul; mills; a hospital in Jalalabad; oil storage tanks in Kabul, Herat, Mazar-i-Sharif, and Kilif; an oil pipeline between Mazar-i-Sharif and Termez (the latter in Soviet territory); roads; and municipal utilities in Kabul. The pipeline bringing Soviet oil to Afghan territory was especially significant because, while catering to a major need of Afghan economy, it made Afghanistan dependent on the Soviet Union. In addition to funds, Russia had also provided experts, and by 1955 it was estimated that three hundred Soviet and Czechoslovak technicians were employed in Afghanistan. Soviet cultural missions and exchanges of scholarships inevitably followed those economic activities. Moreover, in 1954 Afghanistan had secured a $5,000,000 loan from Czechoslovakia for the purpose of erecting a cement and a glass factory and a tannery. By the time of the Bulganin-Khrushchev visit it was estimated that Afghanistan had received a total of $14,-000,000 in credit from the Soviet bloc.

Meanwhile the United States was also assisting Afghanistan in its development plans. Between 1947 and 1955 the United States had granted the Kabul government about $9,000,000 under the technical assistance program. Financed by these funds were projects in public administration, agriculture, forestry, education, health, and sanitation. In addition, the Morrison-Knudsen Company mentioned earlier had undertaken to carry out major works to develop irrigation, power facilities, and flood control, mostly in the Helmand Valley. These contracts amounting to approximately $40,000,000 were to be financed by two loans, of $21,000,000 and $18,500,000, granted in 1950 and 1954, respectively, by the Export-Import Bank of Washington at 4.5 per cent. Certain additional sums, exceeding $2,500,000, have also been made available by the United States for the purchase of wheat.

Thus, American loans and grants to Afghanistan prior to the Soviet leaders' visit compared favorably with the amount of aid received from Russia. The sudden announcement, however, as a result of this visit, of the $100,000,000 loan by Moscow definitely upset the existing balance and posed new and perplexing problems for American diplomacy. In the first place, did Afghan acceptance of Soviet aid imply a political and possibly military tie which might be dangerous to America's allies in this part of the world? At a press conference held in Kabul after the Russians' departure Premier Daud Khan denied that the agreements with Russia meant the abandonment of Afghan neutrality and he refused to condemn the Baghdad Pact.

Assuming that this statement truly portrays the current Afghan attitude, the next question is whether Afghanistan can avoid slipping into the Soviet orbit in view of the opportunities for infiltration afforded by the multifarious Soviet activities in its territory. Moreover, if by accepting Soviet offers Afghanistan hopes to force the West to increase its economic grants, it is following a policy which can hardly evoke a sympathetic response in Washington. Trying to outbid Russia in indiscriminate giving of technical aid and goods would be a psychologically dangerous policy, which would encourage rather than discourage cynicism among the nations as yet uncommitted in the East-West conflict.

Last but not least among the questions raised by Afghanistan's acceptance of Russian aid is that of loyalty to allies, in this particular case Pakistan, which in 1955 joined the Baghdad Pact. Although anxious to bring about a reconciliation between Kabul and Karachi, the United States was not in a position to question Pakistan's sovereign right to the territory up to the Durand Line. It is understood that the American government favors some arrangement easing Afghan commercial traffic through Pakistani territory, preferably a free port in Karachi. The United States is reportedly prepared to help in financing such a project. In line with this policy President Eisenhower bypassed the problem of Pakhtunistan when replying by letter to a message on this subject received from King Mohammed Zahir Shah of Afghanistan in the fall of 1955.

As for Afghanistan, it was not the first country in the Middle East to respond favorably to Soviet offers of aid and possibly arms supplies. Egypt had set the pattern some three months earlier, but in contrast to Afghanistan Egypt did not have a common boundary with Russia. By accepting Soviet offers and quarreling with Pakistan over what to sober minds would appear to be a secondary issue, the Afghan leaders were gambling with the independence of their country.

-| PART THREE |-

THE FERTILE CRESCENT

CHAPTER VII

Iraq

O N AUGUST 23, 1921, Faisal ascended the throne of Iraq. The decision to offer him the crown had been made earlier in the year, as you will recall, at a British Middle East conference. A 96 per cent endorsement from the people of Iraq was obtained by means of a referendum. This referendum was described by Gertrude Bell, secretary of Sir Percy Cox, as "politics running on wheels greased with extremely well-melted grease." [1]

King Faisal's coronation marked the opening of a new period in Iraq's history. Internally, the new kingdom was confronted with the task of welding the heterogeneous peoples of Mesopotamia into a single nation, raising them from the backward condition inherited from the Ottoman Empire to a higher level, and establishing order and security. Externally, Iraq's problems revolved around her relationships with Britain. Both external and internal problems were closely intertwined.

THE IRAQI GOVERNMENT

Purely administrative problems are outside the scope of this study; hence little will be said about them here. [2] What really mattered from the political point of view was the general trend toward

[1] Lady Florence Bell, ed., *The Letters of Gertrude Bell* (New York, 1927), II, 533 ff. Yet not everything was perfectly smooth: to prevent opposition, British authorities arrested and deported to Ceylon Sayid Talib Pasha, who aspired to the crown of Iraq.

[2] A thorough treatment of administrative and constitutional evolution in Iraq may be found in P. W. Ireland, *Iraq: A Study in Political Development* (London, 1937).

emancipation from British control. Under Colonel Wilson's rule, the administration of Iraq was exercised mainly by the British, but even before Faisal's ascent it was partly transferred to the Iraqis themselves. In the transitional period of 1920 the *naqib* (chief of nobility) of Baghdad headed the administration of the state. With Faisal's arrival, a regular cabinet was formed, but the British continued to retain key functions via advisers to the various ministries, the advisers holding more permanent and better-paying positions than their nominal Iraqi superiors. Moreover, such important positions as inspector general of police and directors of health, customs and excise, agriculture, public works, irrigation, and telegraphs were all British subjects. As for the provincial administration, the former British political officers were transformed into advisers (later administrative inspectors) to the Iraqi officials, but their real power remained largely undiminished. These British district advisers played a very important role in perpetuating British control over the country, irrespective of formal Anglo-Iraqi arrangements, especially in the tribal areas. The tribes constituted about one-sixth of the Iraqi population and traditionally presented a dilemma to any settled government. In the early days of their occupation the British introduced into the tribal areas the so-called Sandeman system, developed and tested in India. According to this system, control over the tribes was exercised through their hereditary chieftains. In other words, the government, instead of establishing direct control over the people, would use the local chief as its agent by recognizing his authority, by sometimes subsidizing him, and by protecting his "dynastic" interests. This system had the virtue of not destroying the age-old tribal society and of assuring a large measure of order and peace without much direct interference. The drawback of the system was that it tended to perpetuate "feudal" relationships among a large segment of the people and that it made difficult any constructive policy aiming at progress and modernization of the nation as a whole. Politically, the system meant that the tribal sheikhs were often friendlier to the British than the town dwellers and that in case of crisis the British could always, to some extent, manipulate this tribal reserve force. With the gradual transfer of administrative functions to the Iraqis, this problem was inherited by the Iraqi government itself. Like every new nationalist government, it tried to establish its uncontested supremacy over the whole area of Iraq and inevitably ran up against tribal opposition. In some cases the tribes resorted to violence. Thus, after Iraq obtained her full independence, the Middle Euphrates tribes rose, in 1935, in a large-scale rebellion, which had to be curbed by the army after severe fighting. Even in 1950, two decades after Iraq's formal emancipation, the tribal problem was far from solved.

Minority Problems

The question of tribal relationships was closely related to the question of minorities. These groups constituted slightly over 20 per cent of the Iraqi population. The largest single minority was the Kurds living in the northern parts of the country, around Mosul, Kirkuk, Suleimaniya, and Rowanduz.[3] These warlike mountaineers, partly settled and partly nomadic, were a chronic source of difficulties for Iraq. Scattered throughout Iraq, Turkey, Syria, Iran, and the Soviet Union, the Kurds, whose total numbers were estimated at about four and one-half million, were too backward and immature to create their own sovereign state and yet too independent to agree to unrestricted foreign domination. At the time of the "referendum" in 1921, the Kurds for the most part abstained from voting as a token of their disapproval of being ruled by an Arab government. Throughout the interwar period the Kurds remained a turbulent minority, occasionally resorting to uprisings when their patience with government tyranny or corruption was exhausted. Rebellions on a larger scale occurred in 1922–1924, 1930–1931, and 1932, under the leadership of Sheikh Mahmud of Suleimaniya, and it cost the government much effort to suppress them. Although a basically internal matter affecting Iraq's security, these uprisings, like so many other domestic problems of Iraq, had their international facets as well. Because the Kurds were distributed over five countries, whatever happened in one of them was bound to affect the Kurds situated in the others. The fact that the Kurds lived in more or less compact groups in the frontier districts made it easier for them to escape across the borders to neighboring states whenever it appeared necessary for them to do so. This, in turn, was bound to provoke international quarrels between the nations involved, and between Iraq and Iran in particular, the

[3] For background information on Kurdistan, see Col. W. G. Elphinston, "The Kurdish Question," *International Affairs*, Jan. 1946, and by the same author, "Kurds and the Kurdish Question," *R.C.A.J.*, Jan. 1948; also W. L. Westerman, "Kurdish Independence and Russian Expansion," *Foreign Affairs*, July 1946. For a pro-Soviet view of the Kurdish problem, consult Lucien Rambout, *Les Kurdes et le Droit* (Paris, 1947).

governments accusing one another of harboring the troublemakers, even of assisting their rebellions.

The Kurdish problem was also linked with the policies of the big powers, in particular with those of Great Britain and the Soviet Union. After the First World War, the British toyed with the idea of a British-protected Kurdish state,[4] which would enable them to push their influence northward into the strategic area bordering on the Caucasus. Moreover, the support of Kurdish aspirations could be used as a lever of pressure on recalcitrant Kemalist Turkey, on Iran, and especially on Iraq, in which the percentage of Kurds was higher than in any other country. The scheme of a Kurdish puppet state was, however, abandoned, because Britain realized that the matter was too explosive, that it was likely to upset the balance and stability of the Middle East, and that its promotion would eventually benefit the Soviets more than anyone else. This view coincided with the definite British policy of influencing Iraq by winning over Arab public opinion through various political concessions. Choosing to follow a definitely pro-Arab policy, Britain found it difficult to promote at the same time schemes that would reduce the Arab-ruled area, and for this reason she changed her stand on the Kurdish question. This, however, did not mean that friendship with the Kurds was thrown overboard. On the contrary, it continued to be cultivated, especially on the local level, by various British political agents, both in Iraq and in Iran. This served two purposes at once: first, to keep the Kurdish question as a tactical reserve in case of difficulties with Baghdad or Teheran and, secondly, to ward off foreign penetration, whether Soviet or German. Yet, in pursuance of their basically pro-Arab policy, the British air force helped the Iraqi army suppress the Kurdish revolt of 1932.

Apart from the Kurdish, there were Turkish, Iranian, Turkoman, and Assyrian national minorities—usually settled in definite geographical areas—and a number of other minorities, such as the Jews and various religious sects, scattered all over the country or centered in towns. Of all these groups, the Assyrians posed one of the most difficult problems.[5] In contrast to other minorities, they were mostly newcomers, having fled to Iraq from Turkey or Iran under very try-

[4] See above, p. 131, and the relevant footnote; also the statement by Dr. G. M. Lees in R.C.A.J., Jan. 1948, p. 50.

[5] For background information on the Assyrians, see W. A. Wigram, The Assyrians and Their Neighbours (London, 1929); R. S. Stafford, The Tragedy of the Assyrians (London, 1935).

ing circumstances during the First World War. Living first on British charity and later settling temporarily in a few score villages in northern Iraq, the Assyrians were protected by the British mandatory authorities, who recruited among them men for guard duty on Royal Air Force air fields and installations. As Nestorian Christians, the Assyrians enjoyed the support of the Anglican Church and had the confidence of official British circles. This dependence upon foreign protection, coupled with their state of destitution and their martial qualities, produced intergroup difficulties with the Arabs of Iraq, who always considered them as unwelcome intruders. Tension increased when the Assyrian patriarch and secular leader, Mar Shimun, asked for restoration of the millet system, which would give greater autonomy to his coreligionists. Matters came to a head when, in 1933, a desperate group of Assyrians crossed from Iraq into Syria in search of some more promising haven, only to find that the French mandatory authorities were determined to prevent their infiltration, by force, if necessary. Discouraged, the Assyrians tried to return to Iraq, but met with opposition at the Iraqi frontier posts. In the ensuing skirmish the Assyrians killed a few Iraqi soldiers and then crossed the border. The uproar which this incident created led the Iraqi government to organize a punitive expedition, which burned some twenty Assyrian villages, massacring their inhabitants. No Arab voice was raised in protest against this ruthlessness, and the commander of the expedition, Colonel Bekr Sidki, earned a reputation as a national "hero," young King Ghazi (Faisal's successor) promptly promoting him to a higher rank. The "Assyrian Massacres" caused the League of Nations to investigate the position of this unfortunate minority, and at one time it was proposed to settle all the Assyrians in Brazil, but this never materialized.

Religious Tensions

Another internal problem was the animosity between the two main Moslem sects of Iraq, the Shiis and the Sunnis. The former were slightly larger in numbers, but more backward owing to their reluctance to accept secular education. As a result, they had fewer properly trained individuals who could fill responsible government positions. The successive Iraqi cabinets contained, as a rule, a Sunni majority, sometimes including only one Shia minister to keep up the appearance of proportional representation. The Shiis were rather cool to King Faisal as an "imported" Sunni prince. Their geographical concentration in the south of Iraq added to the existing difficulties. The Shiis, through their clergy, had many links with Iran, a predominantly Shia country. Indeed, many leading mujtahids or ulemas were of Iranian nationality—a fact partly due to Reza Shah's anti-clerical course, which resulted in a number of migrations to Iraq. These Iranian clerical dignitaries, preoccupied with religious matters and often fanatical, owed no loyalty whatsoever to the concept of Iraqi statehood and often obstructed the normal functioning of the Iraqi administration. The Shia hierarchy was not only anti-Sunni, but also anti-British, and frequently used passive resistance to counter many common Anglo-Iraqi projects. In 1922 King Faisal was so annoyed by their pre-electoral activity that he ordered forty Iranian ulemas to be deported back to Iran. All in all, the Shiis, who were centered around their holy places of Nejef and Kerbela, constituted a powerful force that no Iraqi government could afford to ignore.

Iraq's Internal Politics

Iraq had been one of the most remote and least-developed corners of the Ottoman Empire, and she was much less advanced than her sister Arab nations bordering on the Mediterranean. A simple transfer from the Ottoman to the British Empire and then to native control could not quickly change these basic factors. Illiteracy was widespread. Iraq's educational facilities, though growing, were poor and inadequate. Baghdad did not have a single real institution of higher learning. Foreign schools, even if they carried the imposing title of "colleges" (as was the case with the American Presbyterian institutions in the Near East) were on the level of secondary schools at the very best. The Iraqi upper class was educated either in Turkey or in the West or not educated at all. The so-called intelligentsia group was infinitesimally small. Regular political parties could hardly be expected to exist, yet in the interwar period Iraq witnessed the appearance and disappearance of a number of political parties. For example, there were three nationalist parties: *Hizb el-Watani* (National Party), *Hizb el-Nahdha* (Renaissance Party), and *Hizb el-Hurr* (Independence Party) in the twenties; the *Ikha el-Watani* (Brethren), the *Ahali* (People's Group), and the Society for National Reform in the thirties. But none of these groups could be compared to traditional political parties in the West. Personalities played a much more important role in Iraqi politics than programs. It was

238

the attitude of leading families or tribal chieftains, of prominent army officers and religious leaders, that really counted. The family of the *naqib* of Baghdad, Sayid Abdur Rahman el-Gailani, wielded great influence in the capital; the same was true of the powerful Omari family of Mosul. In the south it was Sayid Talib Pasha, son of the *naqib* of Basra, who was not only one of the leading nationalists but also an aspirant to the crown. Prominent leaders among the Shia laity—Sayid Mohammed es-Sadr from Baghdad and Jafar abu Timman from Khadimain—also carried great weight in internal politics. Among the officers from the Sherifian service, Nuri es-Said, Jafar el-Askari, Yasin el-Hashimi, and a number of others emerged as influential leaders upon Faisal's ascent. Faisal tended to surround himself with his former brothers-in-arms from the Hejaz campaign, but he was careful not to antagonize others by too open favoritism. There was, for that matter, definite animosity between the Sherifian veterans and former officers from the Turkish service.

As to the King himself, his popularity and strength was rather hard to gauge. A native of the Bedouin kingdom of the Hejaz, a descendant of the Prophet, commander of the Sherifian army in the desert campaign, and a short-lived ruler of Syria, Faisal had some appeal as an all-Arab leader but no deep personal links with Iraq. On the contrary, he had strong bonds with the British, to whom he owed his crown. This identification with Britain was a serious hindrance to his popularity with some Iraqi nationalists, yet no one could classify this brave soldier as a bribed collaborator. On July 10, 1924, Iraq's Constituent Assembly adopted an Organic Law (constitution) which gave the country all the external trappings of parliamentary democracy, but this act had little influence upon the actual course of Iraqi politics. In fact, Faisal emerged as a benevolent despot who did not feel too embarrassed by formal constitutional limitations. By contrast, he had to and did accommodate himself to those real centers of power in Iraq—the Shia divines, the leading families, the army officers, and the tribes. His was not an easy role because he had to act as a middleman between the British mandatory authorities and the more vocal Iraqi nationalists. There is no doubt that he himself aspired toward greater emancipation for Iraq, but at the same time he was realistic enough to know his country's limitations and Britain's strength.

239

IRAQ'S GRADUAL EMANCIPATION

This brief account of King Faisal's position leads us to the external relations of Iraq in the interwar period. The pattern of these relations was relatively simple: Iraq aspired to more freedom and independence, while Britain, having invested blood and money in this area and aware of its strategic and economic value, was anxious to preserve her supremacy. Conscious of the eruptive potentialities of Iraqi nationalism, as evidenced in the 1920 uprising, Britain acted cautiously, compromising wherever possible. The transfer of Iraq affairs from the India to the Colonial Office in 1921 permitted the British government to plan and execute a more consistent policy, better co-ordinated with its policies toward other Arab countries in the Middle East.

Treaties with Britain

Faced with strong nationalist agitation, the British government did not ask the League of Nations for the formal assignment of a mandate but, instead, decided to exercise its control by means of a treaty with Iraq. Such a treaty was concluded on October 10, 1922. Together with four important subsidiary agreements, it confirmed British control of Iraq by giving Britain the right: (1) to appoint advisers to the Iraqi government, (2) to assist the Iraqi army, (3) to protect foreigners, (4) to advise Iraq on fiscal matters, and (5) to advise Iraq on matters of foreign relations. The treaty also provided for an open door policy to be implemented by Great Britain, foresaw British financial assistance to Iraq, and guaranteed the non-alienation of Iraqi territory by Britain. It was to operate for twenty years, but by a protocol signed in 1923, its period was reduced to four years. In its really vital provisions, the treaty did not much differ from the draft mandate that had come up for consideration before the Council of the League of Nations in September 1921, but had never been formally adopted. As for Britain's responsibility to the League of Nations, it was based on the decision of the Allied Supreme Council in San Remo on April 25, 1920, assigning Iraq to Britain as a mandate and on Article 22 of the Covenant of the League, which dealt with the mandatory system.

To the British, the treaty of 1922 was just another form of control, but properly sugar-coated for the Iraqi taste. In fact, H. A. L. Fisher, the British delegate at Geneva, had made it clear during the session of the Council in November 1921 that his government considered it advantageous to exercise the mandate by means of a treaty. This, however, was not the Iraqi view. Iraqis viewed the treaty as a definite rejection of the mandatory status and as the first step toward full independence. Much as the treaty was preferred to a mandate, many nationalists agitated against its terms. The Constituent Assembly which met in 1924 was in considerable doubt as to whether or not to ratify it. Fortunately for the British, the Assembly contained forty representatives from the tribes, who favored ratification. This fact, together with strong British pressure on other members, led the Assembly to ratify the treaty on March 27, 1924.

From 1924 to 1930, Iraq's demands for a greater measure of freedom grew more vocal.[6] The Anglo-Iraqi treaties of January 13, 1926, and December 14, 1927, marked further steps in the modest relaxation of British control, especially in financial and military sectors. The latter treaty, moreover, contained a British promise to support Iraq's candidacy to the League of Nations in 1932.

The treaty of 1927 did not satisfy Iraqi nationalists. There was, indeed, little change in the political realities, and the British high commissioners of the Indian school, men such as Sir Henry Dobbs, acted with virtually undiminished authority. With the arrival in 1927 of Sir Gilbert Clayton, an Arabic expert formerly associated with the Hejazi Force and a personal friend of Faisal, the atmosphere changed. Negotiations looking to a more satisfactory settlement were opened and, after Clayton's sudden death, were concluded by his successor, Sir Francis Humphrys.

On June 30, 1930, the high commissioner and Nuri es-Said Pasha, foreign minister, signed a new Anglo-Iraqi treaty, the final one of the series.[7] This treaty provided for a twenty-five-year alliance between Great Britain and Iraq; confirmed Britain's intention to support Iraq's admission to the League of Nations in 1932; and proclaimed Iraq's full independence and the termination of British mandatory responsibilities on the date of Iraq's entry into the League. In it or in the annexes were the following major provisions:

[6] In contrast with Iraqi aspirations for independence were the doubts of the Council of the League of Nations as to Iraq's fitness for self-government. These were manifested in 1925 when Mosul was assigned to Iraq on condition that the British mandate be continued for another twenty-five years. (For details of the Mosul controversy, see p. 130.)

[7] The full text may be found in Helen M. Davis, ed., *Constitutions, Electoral Laws, Treaties of States in the Near and Middle East* (Durham, N.C., 1947), p. 143.

1) *Foreign policy.* Both parties agreed to "full and frank consultation in all matters of foreign policy which might affect their common interests," and each undertook not to adopt a policy "which is inconsistent with the alliance or might create difficulties for the other party."

2) *Defense.* In case of war, Britain undertook to defend Iraq. Iraq's role would "consist in furnishing to His Britannic Majesty on Iraq territory all facilities and assistance . . . including the use of railways, rivers, ports, aerodromes and means of communication."

3) *Bases and right of transit.* Iraq was to lease to Britain sites for air bases in the vicinity of Basra and west of the Euphrates; and Britain was empowered to maintain forces in these localities. She was also authorized to maintain forces in other areas of Iraq (Hinaidi and Mosul) during the transitional period, which was not to exceed five years. Moreover, she was granted the right of transit for her troops across Iraqi territory.

4) *Immunities.* British forces in Iraq were to enjoy immunity from local jurisdiction and taxation.

5) *Training of Iraqi army.* In case Iraq decided to invite in foreign military instructors, to train her own officers abroad, or to buy arms and equipment in foreign countries, Britain would have an exclusive right to provide such services, and armaments and equipment were "not to differ in type from those of the forces of His Britannic Majesty."

6) *Diplomatic representation.* The British high commissioner was to be replaced by an ambassador, who would enjoy a permanent position of seniority among foreign diplomatic representatives.

This treaty was of great importance because it set the pattern for other treaties with Arab countries. Britain's treaty with Egypt in 1936 and France's treaties with Syria and Lebanon in the same year followed the Iraqi treaty in their major provisions.

Release from Foreign Control

On October 3, 1932, Iraq was admitted to the League of Nations following favorable but somewhat hesitant reports from the Permanent Mandates Commission. Prior to admitting Iraq, the League asked her to give guarantees for the protection of minorities, including the Kurds; the rights of foreigners; respect for human rights, and the recognition of debts and treaties concluded by the mandatory power. In compliance with these conditions, Iraq on May 30, 1932, issued a declaration containing the required guarantees.

During the ensuing period of independence, Anglo-Iraqi relations deteriorated steadily, but Britain continued to maintain her predominant position. The deterioration was due not only to the greater freedom acquired by Iraq but also to the premature death in 1933 of King Faisal, Britain's trusted friend. His successor, the twenty-one-year-old King Ghazi, was an inexperienced and somewhat irresponsible youth whose interests lay more in automobile and motorcycle racing than in affairs of state. The country relapsed into a state of political instability characterized by constant shifts in the cabinet and a recurrence of tribal and minority unrest. Soon after Faisal's death, the government dealt severely with the Assyrian minority, and this tragedy, previously referred to, bore eloquent testimony to the dubious maturity of a new state whose national ambitions could seek an easy outlet in minority persecution.

The Organic Law of 1924, which established a pseudo-democracy for the upper stratum of elderly politicians, was obviously not likely to solve Iraq's social and economic problems. Iraq, like many other agricultural countries, suffered from the effects of worldwide depression in the early 1930's. The production of oil by the Iraq Petroleum Company began only in 1930, and some time was needed before Iraq could count on a steady and substantial income from that source.

The Coup of 1936

Iraq's ruling oligarchy was divided during this period into two main groups: those who favored the British alliance, and those who opposed it. The first group was headed by former officers of the Hejazi Force, such as General Nuri es-Said, General Jafar el-Askari, and Jamil el-Madfai. The second, more numerous, included such notables as Yasin el-Hashimi (whose brother, General Taha el-Hashimi, was a nonpolitical chief of staff of the army), Hikmat Suleiman (very pro-Turkish, brother of the prewar Young Turk General Mahmud Shevket Pasha), Rashid Ali el-Gailani, and Kamil Chadirchi. This anti-British group had formed in 1930 the *Ikha el-Watani* (Brotherhood) Party and had opposed the signing of the Anglo-Iraqi treaty. This group dominated Iraqi politics between King Faisal's death and 1936, although it had to co-operate with some pro-British politicians.[8]

Ikha's inefficient and conservative rule provoked widespread discontent among the populace, which was especially noticeable among

[8] See Majid Khadduri, "The Coup d'Etat of 1936: A Study in Iraqi Politics," *Middle East Journal*, July 1948.

younger groups of Iraqi intelligentsia. Iraq's lack of progress and governmental instability were contrasted with the spectacular achievements of the new Turkish regime and the solidity of the Kemalist government. In 1931 some educated young men in Baghdad formed the *Ahali* (People's) Group, which began to preach "populism," a mixture of socialism and democracy, advocating radical reform in the country. As long as the group was limited to young intellectuals, its influence upon Iraqi politics was negligible, despite the fact that it published a rather popular newspaper. Ahali acquired much greater significance when, as a result of a split in the ranks of the leading Ikha group, it secured the co-operation of Hikmat Suleiman and of a few other experienced leaders. It then became possible for Ahali to aspire to political power. Simultaneously, considerable ferment could be noticed in the army. A number of officers believed that the Western-imposed division of the Arab world into separate states was highly artificial and that no radical solution for Arab ills could be found unless these states were united into some Pan-Arab federation. They blamed the politicians in power for perpetuating this division for the sake of their selfish ambitions. These officers believed that the army was the only organized group capable of accomplishing the desired change and initiating the necessary reforms. The leader of this military group was General Bekr Sidki, a divisional commander and the "hero" of the before-mentioned Assyrian punitive expedition. Hikmat Suleiman, Bekr's personal friend, helped to establish liaison between the *Ahali* group and the army. On Bekr's initiative, it was decided to organize a conspiracy and to overthrow the existing cabinet of Yasin el-Hashimi. On October 29, 1936, Bekr Sidki executed the *coup d'état;* helped by another divisional commander, General Abdul-Latif Nuri, and by the chief of the Iraqi air force, Mohammed Ali Jawad, he and his "National Reform Force" marched on Baghdad, demanding the immediate resignation of the Yasin cabinet and the appointment of Hikmat Suleiman as head of the government. Terrified by an air raid on the capital executed by Jawad's air force (actually only four light bombs were dropped), Yasin and his cabinet resigned, and King Ghazi, adopting a policy of nonresistance, asked Hikmat Suleiman to form the government. Jafar el-Askari, popular minister of defense in Yasin's cabinet, was the only casualty of the coup, having been treacherously murdered on Bekr's orders while attempting personal negotiation. It was characteristic of the

Iraqi situation that when Yasin's cabinet gathered for its last emergency meeting in the royal palace, British Ambassador Sir Archibald Clark-Kerr (later Lord Inverchapel) attended it.

The new regime was to be based on co-operation between the progressive Ahali group and the army, but it soon became clear that the aims of these two groups were hardly compatible. The newly created progovernment party, called the Society for National Reform, was a façade behind which serious conflicts were in the making. Bekr Sidki, who reserved for himself the position of chief of staff, established a virtual military dictatorship, while Hikmat was forced to abandon his Ahali friends and to follow Bekr's line. Both men were under the spell of the Kemalist experiment, and both tried to imitate it in Iraq, with doubtful success. The only positive result of Bekr's rule was the rapprochement with Turkey which was expressed by the conclusion, on July 9, 1937, of the Saadabad pact. This pact, signed by Iraq, Turkey, Iran, and Afghanistan, provided for some co-operation among its signatories. Bekr's lack of political acumen, combined with the arrogant behavior of his close associates, caused him to lose popularity rapidly. His Kurdish background, the exiling of some influential leaders,[9] and the murder of Jafar el-Askari, who had been the real founder of the Iraqi army were against him. On August 11, 1937, while on their way to watch Turkish military maneuvers, Bekr and Jawad were assassinated in Mosul by their rivals in the army.

As for the British attitude during these events, it was largely noncommittal. Violent changes in Iraq's government made without Britain's previous knowledge and approval were not likely to cause enthusiasm in London, but inasmuch as Bekr Sidki had not been primarily motivated by anti-British feelings, Britain made no overt attempt to get rid of him. His pro-Turkish policy even elicited some faint praise in the British press, the year 1937 being one of gradual Turko-British rapprochement as a result of the dangerous European situation. Britain's readiness to come to terms with this new power in Iraq was expressed by a loan of one million pounds granted to Bekr's government in July 1937, barely one month before his assassination. No regrets, however, were heard in London when the dictator disappeared from the scene, and British diplomacy made a quick readjustment to the new situation. A moderate statesman,

[9] Namely, Yasin el-Hashimi, Rashid Ali el-Gailani, and Nuri es-Said. They sought refuge in Syria and Egypt.

Jamil Madfai, assumed the premiership. The old pattern of personal rivalries and intrigue was restored, with this difference, that the army, having once tasted power, constantly interfered with political developments. It was an army clique which in 1938 removed Jamil Madfai and replaced him with another friend of Britain, Nuri es-Said. And it was still another clique which in March 1939 attempted to oust Nuri as too pro-British.

On April 4, 1939, King Ghazi met his death in an automobile accident near Baghdad. The resulting disorders and the assassination of Mr. Monckton, British consul in Mosul, by an angry mob bore testimony to the anti-British temper of the populace, which was inclined to ascribe any Iraqi misfortune to British machinations. German and Italian propaganda made their substantial contributions to this state of mind, the German minister in Baghdad, Dr. Fritz Grobba, doing much to promote pro-Axis feelings in the country. Ghazi, whose death brought a feeling of relief to London, was succeeded by his infant son Faisal II. A regency was established under the King's maternal uncle, Prince Abdul Ilah, a man acceptable to the British. At this time of growing world crisis, Britain could reasonably expect Iraq to remain faithful to her treaty pledges.

IRAQ DURING WORLD WAR II

In September 1939, in compliance with the treaty of alliance, the Iraqi government, headed by Nuri es-Said, severed diplomatic relations with Germany. The first two years of the war were rather uneventful. In March 1940, Nuri was replaced by Rashid Ali el-Gailani, a man hostile to the British. This, with Britain's initial reverses at the hands of Germany, gave rise to neutral trends in Iraqi political circles. As a leading British periodical described it, Arab neutrality was based on the following argument: "If Britain wins we shall be safe anyway. If the Nazis are going to win, our only hope is to do nothing to offend them now." Thus, as the paper pointed out, "So long as the issue is undecided, the Axis has the benefit of the doubt." [10] Iraq's cautious course was well illustrated by the government's policy of ignoring the declaration of war on Britain and France by Italy. Italian Minister Gabrielli was allowed to stay in Baghdad and to spread Axis propaganda for nearly a year after Italy's entry into the war, and no amount of British pleading caused the Iraqis to change their minds.

[10] *The Economist,* Jan. 11, 1941.

Iraq's position toward Britain was thus governed by Britain's strength vis-à-vis the Axis. The serious defeats suffered by the British in the spring of 1941 in the Balkans, with the Italo-German offensive in Libya, were immediately reflected in the growth of anti-British sentiment in Iraq. This sentiment was heightened by the fact that Baghdad had become a center of pro-Axis intrigue. The exiled mufti of Jerusalem, Haj Amin el-Husseini, and a number of extremist Syrian politicians established themselves there, adding considerably to the nationalist fervor.

As a result of the interplay of Iraqi politics, Rashid Ali lost his office to General Taha el-Hashimi in January 1941. Determined to return to power, Rashid, in conspiracy with a group of four colonels known as the "Golden Square," [11] executed a *coup d'état* on April 3, ousting Taha and assuming the premiership. Regent Abdul Ilah, Nuri es-Said, and a majority of the cabinet members escaped to Transjordan. Despite Rashid Ali's assurances that he would honor the Anglo-Iraqi treaty, Britain was determined to restore the legitimate government to power. Sir Kinahan Cornwallis, an expert on Arab affairs of long experience, arrived in Baghdad as the new ambassador to bolster up British diplomatic action, and toward the end of April a British-Indian military contingent landed in Basra in accordance with the treaty provisions. The arrival of the second contingent, however, provoked Iraqi opposition, and fighting began on May 1. Iraqi artillery surrounded the British air base at Habbaniya, while other forces kept watch on the compound of the British embassy in Baghdad where the British colony found refuge.

Rashid Ali and his associates hoped to secure Axis military assistance. Consequently Defense Minister Sayid Naji Shawkat was dispatched to Ankara to establish liaison with German Ambassador von Papen. The results were disappointing. Germany, busy in Greece and getting ready for the invasion of Russia, was not prepared to divert any substantial amount of aid to Iraq. Moreover, she could not secure transit of arms and troops through Turkey despite pressure on Ankara. The only open channel was Vichy-controlled Syria. Syria's high commissioner, General Dentz, did grant the Germans the use of the Aleppo-Mosul railway for transport of munitions and of the airfields for transit and refueling purposes, but the Nazis were unable to organize a large-scale air operation on such short

[11] These were Colonels Saleh ed-Din, Kamil Shahib, Fahmi Said, and Mahmud Salman.

247

notice. Eventually, a number of German planes, reportedly not more than twenty-three, landed in Iraq, and for some time Mosul was under German control.

Meanwhile Britain rushed additional troops from Palestine, reinforced by the motorized regiment of Emir Abdullah's Arab Legion from Transjordan. These forces relieved the hard-pressed British garrison at Habbaniya, fought a successful battle at Falluja, and in co-operation with the Basra-based troops entered Baghdad at the end of May. The rebellion was crushed. Rashid Ali, whose short-lived rule was highlighted by the establishment, on May 16, of diplomatic relations with Russia, escaped to Iran. His associates and the mufti also fled abroad, by way of Teheran or Aleppo, and eventually a number of them found their way to Berlin, where they resided until the end of the war.

Under a Pro-Ally Government

The collapse of Rashid Ali's regime enabled the regent and the exiled ministers to return to Iraq. Jamil el-Madfai was installed as premier, to be followed, in October 1941, by Nuri es-Said, who remained in this post until 1944. The country was now governed by the pro-Ally group, and no major political difficulties were experienced during the next four years.[12] Large numbers of British troops poured into Iraq, to be known first as the British Tenth Army, later as the "Paiforce" (Persia and Iraq Force).[13] A Polish army, which had been formed in Russia and transferred to the Middle East, was assigned to guard the northern approaches of Iraq in 1942–1943 against a possible German break-through in the Caucasus. In 1942 Iraq became a recipient of lend-lease aid from the United States, and an American military mission arrived in Basra to aid in forwarding war supplies to the Soviet Union. On January 16, 1943, Iraq declared war on Germany, Italy, and Japan, and on the 22nd she signed the United Nations Declaration, the first Arab country to become eligible to attend the future San Francisco conference.

In this latter part of the war, Iraq's energies, so far as foreign relations were concerned, were focused on collaboration with other Arab

[12] Three of the rebellious commanders were subsequently tried and sentenced to death by Iraqi military courts. Rashid Ali was sentenced to death *in absentia*. After the war he was granted asylum in Saudi Arabia.

[13] For an account of its activities, see *Paiforce: The Official Story of the Persia and Iraq Command, 1941–1946* (London, 1948).

states in the creation of the Arab League. Nuri es-Said was very active in promoting the new league and in advocating, simultaneously, the "Greater Syria" plan, which would result in the unification of Syria, Iraq, and Transjordan under a common Hashimite crown.[14] The Iraqis manifested also a growing interest in the United States as expressed by the regent's visit to Washington in May 1945 at President Truman's invitation. Afterward Iraqi and American legations were elevated to the rank of embassies. A by-product of the wartime Soviet-British alliance was the reopening in 1942 of the Soviet legation in Baghdad.

Internally, most of the country except the Kurdish area was quiet. A Kurdish political organization, *Komala,* organized in Iran in 1943, spread its activities to the Kurdish centers of Iraq, keeping the nationalist spirit alive. Encouraged by Soviet sponsorship of Iranian-Kurdish independence, the Barzani tribe of Iraq, led by Mullah Mustafa, rose in rebellion in 1943 and succeeded in defying the government until the fall of 1945, when it was forced to flee to Iran. There the Barzanis joined hands with the leaders of the short-lived Kurdish republic at Mahabad. Following its collapse, they escaped northward, seeking refuge in the territory of the Soviet Union.

This Kurdish episode once again illustrated how closely internal and external developments in the Middle East were interwoven. The presence of a sizable group of Iraqi Kurds (including several well-trained Iraqi army officers) in Russia added another potential complication to the already tangled Kurdish problem.

AFTER WORLD WAR II

Upon Prime Minister Nuri's resignation in 1944, the reins of government were taken over by Hamdi el-Pachachi (1944–1946), whose policies did not basically differ from those of his predecessor. Both prime ministers stayed in power longer than any preceding or subsequent Iraqi government. Following Pachachi's term of office, Iraq fell back into the familiar merry-go-round of quickly changing cabinets whose life did not exceed an average of nine months. In 1946, in a move paralleling similar Egyptian action, Prime Minister Tewfik es-Suweidi asked Great Britain for a revision of the treaty of 1930. Iraq's aim, as could be expected, was to remove from the treaty those remnants of British control which were irksome to her national

[14] For more details, see Chapters VIII and XVI.

pride. Although Iraq, like the rest of the Middle East, experienced a postwar wave of resurgent nationalism, she did not have in 1946–1947 such violent anti-British manifestations as those in Egypt.[15] This calm could be attributed partly to the less sophisticated character of Iraqi political circles, as contrasted to the Egyptian, and partly to the nearness of the Soviet Union, whose action in Azerbaijan in 1945–1946 made the more sedate Iraqi politicians think twice before they embarked upon adventurous policies. To this we may add that, in contrast to Egyptian King Farouk, long resentful at the personal humiliations inflicted by the British, Iraq's regent, Abdul Ilah, owed much to Britain and as a Hashimite favored British-Arab understanding.

The revelation of widespread Communist activities (largely stemming from the Soviet legation in Baghdad) and the subsequent arrest and trial in January 1947 of a number of leading Communists stressed once again the reality of the Soviet danger. This undoubtedly strengthened the hand of the regent when in August 1947 he visited London in pursuance of his policy of friendship with Britain. In deference to Iraqi sensibilities, British troops were evacuated from Iraq soon afterward, in October 1947. Only Royal Air Force units remained on the treaty-provided air bases of Habbaniya and Shaiba. Subsequent negotiations for treaty revision were conducted by Foreign Minister Saleh Jabr, who brought them to a successful conclusion on January 16, 1948, by signing a new treaty with Mr. Bevin at Portsmouth. The new treaty, which in many ways resembled the old one, gave Britain the right to send troops to Iraq in the event of war or imminence of war. In return, Britain surrendered her right to occupy two air bases in Iraq but could continue to land aircraft there. The treaty also provided for the training and equipping of the Iraqi army by Great Britain.

There was every likelihood that the new instrument, though with some grumbling, would be accepted by the parliament. Events, however, took a totally unexpected course owing to the sudden emergence of the Palestinian problem. It was Saleh Jabr's misfortune that

[15] This led Col. V. H. Dowson, a British agent long resident in Iraq, to assert with confidence in 1946: "Official classes are now very *friendly with the British,*" and to add, no doubt with an eye to Egyptian developments: "Schoolboy government, such as they have in another country, where the students of the schools and colleges dictate the cabinet's policy, is only in its infancy; and ministers have shown admirable firmness in suppressing its manifestations" (*R.C.A.J.*, July–Oct. 1946, pp. 254 ff.).

he had to negotiate with Britain just after the United Nations General Assembly had passed a resolution recommending the partition of Palestine. Public opinion in Iraq, as in other Arab countries, became highly inflamed, and, when the news of the treaty reached Baghdad, anti-British and anti-American riots occurred. Obviously frightened by these outbursts, Regent Abdul Ilah announced, on January 21, that the new treaty did not "realize the national aims of Iraq" and therefore could not be ratified. Upon Saleh Jabr's return from London, he and his cabinet resigned, and on the next day, January 28, the unfortunate prime minister fled by plane to Transjordan to escape the danger of assassination. Mohammed es-Sadr, former president of the Senate, formed a new cabinet.

The Palestinian war, in which Iraqi troops participated alongside Emir Abdullah's Arab Legion, had an upsetting effect on Iraq. The initial sober realism of 1946–1947 gave way to ill-tempered nationalist manifestations, both official and unofficial. On Iraq's demand, the advisory British mission to the Iraqi army was withdrawn on May 16, 1948. The United States Information Office was stoned by an angry mob. Hurried legislation was passed making active Zionism a crime punishable by death. The centuries-old Jewish community in Iraq was exposed to hostility and abuse, and even anti-Zionist protestations of loyalty by Chief Rabbi Sassoon Khadduri proved of little avail. An Iraqi court sentenced to death one of the most prominent Jewish merchants, Ades, for supplying arms to Israel, and the sentence was publicly carried out before an excited multitude. Simultaneously the Jewish minority was subjected to vigorous Zionist propaganda, urging it to emigrate to Israel, a new state badly in need of manpower for both defense and economic reasons. This progaganda probably did more to induce the Jews of Iraq to abandon their homes and business establishments than any actual chicanery at the hands of Iraqis. The Iraqi government was reluctant to allow mass emigration inasmuch as it did not desire any strengthening of Israel. Some Iraqi leaders, moreover, were inclined to hold the Jews as virtual hostages to be used as a lever of pressure should Israel mistreat her own Arab minority. Militating against these considerations was the attractive prospect of "cleansing" the country of an unpopular minority group which would not only leave to aspiring Iraqi competitors its solid position in the world of trade but would also, in the process of hurried leaving, liquidate its properties at a nominal value. Ultimately the latter considerations apparently prevailed,

251

and on March 3, 1950, the Chamber of Deputies passed an emergency bill permitting the Jews to renounce their nationality and emigrate, and soon afterward the government gave permission to an American company, Near East Transport, Inc., to fly more than 50,000 Jews to Israel. Iraq's vindictive spirit went so far as to refuse clearance for the planes if they were to fly directly to Palestine. As a result, flights had to be made first to Cyprus. It was only in 1951 that Iraq agreed to relax these cumbersome regulations. By June 1951, 160,000 Jews had emigrated from Iraq to Israel.

The Palestinian war had an upsetting effect on Iraq's finances also. By cutting the flow of oil through the pipeline linking Kirkuk with Israeli-held Haifa, Iraq deprived herself of about £1,000,000 a year in revenue. (She was, incidentally, the only Arab state to make such a substantial economic sacrifice in the "cold war" with Israel, and this in spite of the accusations of submission to imperialism made by Egypt and other critics in the Arab world.)

Internal Iraqi politics gradually resumed their normal course after the treaty crisis of 1948 with perhaps this difference, that the successive governments have become more sensitive to public opinion as expressed by student demonstrations and mob violence.[16]

Domestic Politics in the 1950's

In the early years of the 1950's Iraq's political forces were divided into two major groups: the ruling conservative group deriving its strength primarily from landowning elements, more particularly the sheikhs of the Middle Euphrates, and the nationalist and socialist opposition relying, by and large, on support in the cities. The conservative group tended to rally around the person of Nuri es-Said, who emerged, as time went on, not only as an undisputed leader of the *status quo* forces, but also as the "strong man of Iraq," chief supporter and servant of the Hashimite dynasty, bold spokesman for closer ties with Britain and the West, and an all-Arab statesman of high repute. Endowed with energy and personal charm, Nuri succeeded in organizing not only a devoted following among the traditionalist rank and file but also in subordinating to his leadership an impressive number of conservative elder statesmen. Such

---

[16] That not everything was perfect in Iraq's public life was evidenced by an abortive coup staged in February 1950 by Ali Khalid, chief of police. The coup miscarried, and Khalid was promptly put under arrest by the government.

former premiers as Jamil el-Madfai, Arshad el-Umari, Ali Jowdat, or Tewfik es-Suweidi, though they might have worked at cross-purposes under less skillful guidance, tended to co-operate with each other and with Nuri as a fairly harmonious team.

The only major defection from this "club" was that of the prominent Shia leader Saleh el-Jabr, who in June of 1951 formed his Socialist Party of the Nation (*Umma*). But while not at all negligible, Saleh Jabr's opposition could be termed "loyal" in contrast to that of some other groups, and his party really did not differ radically from Nuri's party. It agreed with the latter on foreign policy while professing a more progressive attitude in domestic matters. In social composition Saleh Jabr's party was not dissimilar to Nuri's. Its principal strength lay in Shia districts, but it should be pointed out that the *Umma* was not an exclusively Shia party, nor was Nuri's following recruited among the Sunnis only. In fact, Nuri's Union Constitutional Party—as his organization was known—enjoyed strong support among the Shias to the extent of dominating such Shia districts as Diwaniya, Hillah, and Amara. The adjective "Socialist" in the name of the *Umma* Party should not be interpreted too literally. There was a tendency in the Middle East to equate progress with socialism, and the latter term was definitely in vogue. Actually, in its attitude to private property and free enterprise the *Umma* Party was almost as conservative as Nuri's group.

As for the Union Constitutional Party, it would be incorrect to regard it as a mere alliance of old reactionaries. To Nuri's credit it should be pointed out that he surrounded himself with a rather impressive team of competent specialists and administrators in the prime of life. Such men as Dr. Mohammed Fadhil el-Jamali, Iraq's foremost diplomat and foreign affairs minister; Dr. Dhia Jafar, frequent minister of finance; Dr. Nadim Pachachi, interchangeably in charge of national economy and development; and Khalil Kenna, secretary general of the Union Constitutional Party and for a period minister of education, were individuals of high caliber whose talents were essential to the orderly conduct of Nuri's government. Because of this trusted team of associates it was Nuri's government which by and large ruled the country in the 1950's irrespective of whether or not Nuri headed the cabinet himself.

Apart from Saleh Jabr's *Umma* Party, opposition forces rallied to the standards of either the Independence (*Istiqlal*) Party or the

253

National-Democratic Party. The Independence Party, led by Mohammed Mehdi Kubbah, Faiq Samarrai, and Siddiq Shanshal, stood
for complete emancipation from and severance of links with Britain.
It was an outspokenly nationalist group, advocating abrogation of
the Anglo-Iraqi Treaty of 1930 and a policy of neutralism in the
East-West conflict. In full agreement with this foreign program was
the National-Democratic Party, which in addition advocated socialism as a solution for domestic problems. Led by Kamil Chadirchi
and Mohammed Hadid, the party had a strong appeal for students and intelligentsia while also scoring successes among the urban proletariat. Its organ, *Sawt al-Ahali,* time and again suspended
by the government, steadily campaigned for the restoration of democratic processes in Iraq, for social justice, and for emancipation
from Britain in both the political and the economic fields. A virtual
successor to the *Ahali* group of the 1930's, the National-Democratic
Party was viewed with particular dislike and suspicion by the Nuri
group. The latter, in fact, did not hesitate to accuse it of tolerance
toward and infiltration by Communists.

In 1951 the ranks of the opposition were swelled by the formation
of a group known as the United Popular Front. In contrast to the
Istiqlal and the Socialists, the new group never assumed the proportions of a mass organization. Yet it is noteworthy that its central committee included such prominent figures as General Taha el-Hashimi
and Muzahim el-Pachachi, both former premiers of moderate political views. Soon after its formation the Popular Front (*El-Jabha esh-
Shaabiya*) decided to co-operate with Chadirchi's Socialists and
went on record as favoring neutrality in world politics, revision of
the Anglo-Iraqi treaty, and nationalization of oil.

For some time the oil problem provided a focusing point of political activity. The nationalization of the oil industry in neighboring
Iran produced understandable repercussions in Iraq, where on
March 24, 1951, eighteen deputies in the parliament demanded that
a similar measure be applied to the Iraq Petroleum Company and
its affiliated groups in the country. Although the opposition was not
unanimous as to whether or not the oil industry should be nationalized, it strongly campaigned for the obtainment of more favorable
terms for Iraq in the negotiations conducted by the government
with the company in the course of 1951. The signing of a revised
concession agreement on February 3, 1952, and its subsequent ratification by the Nuri-dominated parliament on February 14 and 17

254

served as a new excuse for the opposition to brand the government as unpatriotic and subservient to "imperialist" interests. Attempts to sabotage the new agreement by a general strike and street demonstrations failed owing to the skill and determination of Nuri Pasha to save his country from the political and economic dangers which had beset Iran under Mossadegh's regime.

Having weathered the oil storm, Nuri resigned as premier, to be replaced by an "independent," Mustafa el-Umari, on July 11, 1952. The period of Nuri's temporary absence from the cabinet was marked by intensified activity on the part of the opposition. Influenced and encouraged by the successful revolution in Egypt (which occurred within two weeks after Nuri's resignation), on October 28 the *Istiqlal,* the National-Democrats, and the United Popular Front presented notes to Regent Abdul Ilah demanding universal direct suffrage, a purge of the administration, a limitation on land ownership, disarmament of the tribes, lowering of prices on consumers' goods, revision of the constitution in order to limit royal prerogatives, abrogation of the 1930 treaty with Britain, and rejection of Western-sponsored regional defense plans. A similar note was presented to the regent by Saleh Jabr in the name of his *Umma* Party.

The regent's reply was considered unsatisfactory, and the opposition redoubled its efforts to obtain reforms and threatened to boycott the forthcoming elections unless the electoral law were amended to provide for one-degree instead of two-degree voting. A student strike at the Pharmacy School in Baghdad on November 22 became a town-wide riot which severely shook the government. Anarchy threatened as security forces failed to prevent mob attacks on the headquarters of Nuri's party and of the Development Board, as well as on the United States Information office and the premises of the *Iraq Times.* The riot was symptomatic of the political situation in Iraq where urban intelligentsia and the poor were in a rebellious mood toward both the government and foreign influences. The extreme turn the demonstrations took could be attributed partly to skillful infiltration by Communists and partly to inability of the police and the opposition parties to control the mob once it was in motion.

Faced with an untenable situation, Umari and his cabinet resigned on the first day of the demonstrations. On November 23 the regent asked General Nur el-Din Mahmud, army chief of staff, to form the cabinet. Mahmud's first acts were to proclaim martial law and close the schools. Arrests of leaders of the *Istiqlal* and the National-Democrats followed. After having applied these repressive measures, General Mahmud the next day broadcast his cabinet's decision to implement a number of the reforms demanded by the public. Among the latter were the reduction of certain taxes, free higher education, reorganization of the army and purging of the administration, preparation of a law on social security, and, most important perhaps, adoption of universal direct suffrage. The policy was obviously designed to "steal the thunder" from the opposition without upsetting the bases of Iraqi society. Thus, while on the one hand the premier banned publication of twenty-eight newspapers including the organs of all political parties, on the other he made good his promise of direct suffrage by promulgating a new electoral law on December 16.

Legislative elections held under the new law on January 17, 1953, resulted in a victory for the progovernment forces,[17] but despite interference and intimidation charged against the government by the opposition the latter did succeed in electing twenty-one deputies, to whom could be added certain independents dissatisfied with the existing regime.

Having restored public order and normalcy to the country, General Mahmud resigned (apparently his talents were limited to matters of basic security), and a new cabinet, headed by Jamil el-Madfai, with Nuri as minister of defense, came into being. Despite the presence of another man in the driver's seat, it was still Nuri's regime. No wonder then that it was Nuri and not Madfai who was later singled out by Saleh Jabr as the man responsible for the "dictatorship" prevailing in Iraq. Thus, while the authority of the ruling group was reasserted, the basic problem of reform awaited solution. Nuri's opinion, shared by his more conservative associates, was that the country needed development—technical and economic —rather than reform. With reference to the land, Nuri opposed either limitation of property holdings or division of large estates, favoring instead reclamation and irrigation schemes which would more or less automatically tend to solve certain pressing economic

[17] Nuri Said's Constitutional Union Party obtained 67 seats, Popular Front 11, *Umma* Socialists 8, *Istiqlal* 1, independents (many of them favoring Nuri) 48, of a total of 135 seats.

problems. To use an allegory, the veteran statesman did not believe so much in a different cutting of the cake as in an increase in the size of the cake. Consequently he attached special importance to the newly created Development Board, and as time went on tended to appoint his younger and more capable associates to direct it.

Yet even within the ruling group voices were heard indicating that the way the "cake" was cut was not a matter of indifference. These voices emanated partly from a liberal wing of Nuri's party and partly from circles close to the Court, whose dynastic interests were not always identical with those of the wealthy sheikhs. The coming of age and subsequent ascension to the throne of eighteen-year-old King Faisal II on May 2, 1953, provided an opportunity for these moderate partisans of change to suggest a change in the prevailing pattern. Although it would be hard to assess the degree of popularity of the Hashimite dynasty in Iraq—no poll being conceivable and individual opinions varying from deep attachment to profound dislike—the ascension of the young ruler undoubtedly did evoke a friendly response from great numbers of people. His youth, his position as the orphan son of a popular and nationalistic father, and his personal charm gained him many well-wishers, who looked, not without sentiment, to this young heir of the once-glorious Abbassid capital.

If there had been any doubt as to the restlessness of the discontented elements in Iraq, it was quickly dispelled by the June riots of political prisoners in Baghdad. Another outbreak of prisoners early in September, this time in Kut, seems to have broken the Madfai cabinet. A rather prolonged cabinet crisis during the first two weeks of September was terminated by the appointment, on September 17, of one of Iraq's most outstanding statesmen, Mohammed Fadhil el-Jamali as premier. Jamali was a good friend of Nuri and belonged to the ruling group, but, in addition, he enjoyed a special position of trust with the Court (to the extent of being dubbed the regent's righthand man) as well as a reputation as a moderate and enlightened liberal. He seemed an almost ideal leader for a peaceful transition from a somewhat petrified traditionalism to a new, more socially conscious era. Most of his associates in the new cabinet were rather young and well educated. They included, significantly enough, two members of the United Popular Front, one of whom was placed in charge of economy and social affairs. His finance

257

minister, Abdul Karim el-Uzri, had fairly advanced ideas about progressive taxation, which he tried to embody in proposed new legislation.

Although Jamali's cabinet, a cabinet of "loyal liberals," started under good auspices, it soon faced mounting difficulties in a number of sectors. In December a major strike broke out among oil workers in Basra. The resulting violence—again attributed to Communist infiltration—led to a proclamation of martial law and to stern reprisals by the government. The *Istiqlal* and Socialist papers launched new attacks on the government, while the cabinet suffered its first internal dissension, the resignation of the two Popular Front ministers in protest against martial law. Even the abolition of the latter in January 1954 did not restore harmony between the premier and the Popular Front. As time went on, Jamali became a target not only for leftist and nationalist opposition but also for old-time pro-Nuri deputies in the parliament. Too conservative for the opposition, he was deemed too progressive for the old guard, who took strong exception to some agrarian and taxation projects of his cabinet. Under these circumstances, Jamali, a veteran expert in foreign affairs, had little time to concentrate on inter-Arab relations, which as the result of dramatic shifts in Egypt and Syria were entering a new and decisive phase. On January 11, 1954, Jamali presented to the Arab League's Political Committee a plan for Arab federation to be achieved by successive stages, thus reviving the Fertile Crescent plan. It was tabled by the League Committee, and subsequent events at home prevented him from pursuing the matter any further.

Toward the end of March the Tigris overflowed in one of the worst floods in the history of Iraq, threatening Baghdad with death and destruction. All the energies of the Jamali cabinet centered on protecting the capital, which was indeed saved by the efforts and devotion of both the government and the people. After emerging from this hour of trial and tribulation, the Jamali cabinet encountered renewed hostility from the pro-Nuri majority in parliament. The problem went to the King (and his still influential uncle, Abdul Ilah, now a crown prince): Should the premier be supported and the parliament dissolved in order to produce a new legislature more in step with Jamali's program? Or should the premier be dismissed owing to the mounting opposition in parliament? Ultimately a middle-of-the road decision was made: parliament would be dissolved, and the premier would resign.

On April 29 Arshad el-Umari formed a new "nonpartisan" cabinet, the task of which was to conduct elections to the new legislature. The elections, which took place on June 9, gave the following results: Constitutional Union Party 56; *Umma* Socialist 14; National Front 12; United Popular Front 0; Independents 51; unidentified 2 out of a total of 135 seats in the Chamber of Deputies. The two most noteworthy features of the election were the diminution of Nuri's strength (a loss of eleven seats) and the appearance of twelve National Front deputies, all representing radical socialist or nationalist tendencies. With the fourteen *Umma* deputies they constituted an outspoken bloc of twenty-six members opposed to Nuri's leadership. The latter was in London at the time, but one of his associates, Dr. Dhia Jafar, accused the National Front of Communist proclivities. This statement can be taken as representing the view of Nuri and his conservative group. Following the inauguration of the new parliament, Premier Umari resigned, and Nuri, back from London, was offered the premiership. Dissatisfied as he was with the election results, Nuri accepted on the condition that the new parliament promptly be dissolved and that his own line of policy (as expressed in a memorandum to the King) be adopted. Complying with his wishes, the King decreed the dissolution of the parliament on August 3 and the following day appointed Nuri prime minister. New elections, this time supervised by Nuri and his associates, were promptly scheduled for September 12. The intervening two weeks witnessed the suppression of eighteen political newspapers, the passing of stringent decrees designed to curb communism and Communist-infiltrated trade unions, search and closure by police of the National-Democratic Party headquarters, and a decision by the Union Constitutional Party to dissolve itself, thus paving the way for a nonparty system.

As could be expected, the September elections resulted in an overwhelming victory for the Nuri forces. The Popular Front (a complete loser in June) now secured two seats, and the *Istiqlal* two also, but these seats were secured more as a result of a "gentleman's agreement" between the ruling group and the individual deputies elected than as the result of a genuine electoral struggle. In fact, the *Istiqlal* soon disavowed the two members claiming to represent it. Between September 16 and 19 new stringent press and assembly decrees were passed, to be followed, a few days later, by the dissolution of all political parties.

259

Thus, by the fall of 1954 Iraq had returned in her internal affairs to where she stood before the "liberal" experiment of the Jamali period: the conservatives were back in power and Nuri's sway over national affairs was not only reconfirmed but further entrenched. Opposition was dispersed and driven underground, and renewed emphasis was placed on development rather than on reform. Outwardly, the country returned to normalcy, and this imposed stability distinguished it from a number of other Arab states, seething as they were with unrest and excitement.

The Baghdad Pact

Having removed the internal obstacles, Nuri es-Said was in a position to concentrate on the major foreign policy issues awaiting solution. A few years had already been spent in a search for a formula which would strengthen the Free World's defenses against Russian imperialism and yet be palatable to the peoples of the Middle East. In 1953, however, the original Western plan to form a Middle East Defense Organization had had to be abandoned reluctantly, mainly owing to Egypt's opposition. Other ways were explored, and the new formula, as devised by Washington and London, was to concentrate on the so-called Northern Tier, i.e., the chain of countries between Turkey and Pakistan, which, more conscious of the Soviet danger, were expected to enter into bilateral or multilateral military assistance agreements. With the major lines of strategy thus outlined, the initiative was promptly seized by Turkey, who first of all concluded a military assistance pact with security-minded Pakistan (April 2, 1954) and then with dynamic diplomacy followed it up with similar agreements between herself, Iraq, and Iran. Other Arab countries were further possibilities. Although not a direct participant in negotiations, the United States gave evidence of backing up these defense plans by continuing its aid to Turkey, concluding a mutual assistance treaty with Pakistan (May 19, 1954), and simultaneously offering military aid (but not a pact) to Iraq.

Iraq had to make two basic decisions: (1) whether or not to become a party in the Northern Tier defense pacts and (2) how to shape her relationship with Britain, to whom she was linked by the treaty of 1930. A decision to join in Western-sponsored military pacts would strengthen Iraq against the only real danger that might possibly threaten her—the danger of Soviet aggression and Communist subversion. This strengthening would come about through political guarantees, military assistance, and arms supplies. The latter especially would bolster up a regime which had to place much reliance on its army and police. The disadvantages of this course would be in estranging the Egyptian-led majority of the Arab League and in antagonizing sizable segments of domestic public opinion, already restive over internal issues. With regard to the second basic decision—concerning the Anglo-Iraqi treaty—public opinion in Iraq strongly favored abrogation or at least radical revision. It might be unsafe for any, even the strongest, government to flout the feelings of the majority on this question. The treaty was due to expire in 1957, and pressure not to renew it would undoubtedly mount as the termination date approached. The government could, of course, do nothing and allow the treaty to lapse in due time. But the disadvantage of such a course was that relations with Britain would deteriorate and the government in its purely passive role would get no credit from the populace.

Nuri Said had little if any hesitation regarding the course to follow. An old political realist, he was determined to join the Western-sponsored security system and at the same time he wanted to take the opportunity to rid Iraq of the unequal treaty with Britain. The reasoning behind this resolve was as follows: Iraq does not want to sever links with Britain, but she does not wish to continue them on an unequal basis (i.e., with Britain possessing air bases and special privileges in Iraq). To terminate the Anglo-Iraqi treaty and thus force the British to evacuate Iraq before the date of expiry would be a major national achievement. At the same time Iraq should not reject the security which the British alliance offered, but she should transfer it from the narrow field of bilateral relations with Britain to the broader field of a regional pact in which Britain would participate not as a sole partner but as one of a number of powers.

Considerable opposition to these plans, especially on the part of the Cairo-Riyadh axis, could be anticipated. As soon as Nuri was installed in office, he was visited by Major Saleh Salem, a member of the Egyptian military junta in charge of inter-Arab affairs,[18] who did his best, at a conference in Sarsank in mid-August, to dissuade Nuri from pursuing this policy. According to some reports, Salem went so far as to promise that Egypt would not object to a Syro-Iraqi union provided Iraq stayed out of the "foreign pacts." Nuri,

[18] His official position was that of minister of national guidance and Sudan affairs.

however, remained unshaken and made neither promises nor commitments. Following this attempt at direct intervention, Egypt concentrated her efforts on the Arab League, trying to influence Iraq through League resolutions.

In the meantime Iraq and Turkey made further moves toward closer collaboration. Between January 6 and 14, 1955, Turkish Premier Adnan Menderes visited Baghdad, and on January 13 he and Nuri Said announced that a mutual assistance pact would soon be signed. The announcement provoked an outburst of criticism in Egypt, where Premier Colonel Gamal Abdul Nasser promptly called for a conference of Arab premiers in Cairo to discuss the League's relations with the West. Boycotted by Nuri, the conference convened on January 22. In the course of discussions the Egyptian premier insisted on a resolution which would not only declare any military pacts concluded by League members outside the League as inconsistent with the League's charter and the inter-Arab security pact but would also condemn Iraq for her expressed desire to sign a pact with Turkey. The assembled premiers were not ready, however, to go that far and proposed instead that a commission of four (composed of the premiers of Syria, Lebanon, and Jordan and Major Salem of Egypt) be sent to Baghdad to mediate. The brief visit of this commission to the Iraqi capital (January 31–February 2) proved fruitless, and the conference ended without producing a resolution or even a final communiqué.

On February 24, 1955, the Turkish-Iraqi Pact was signed in Baghdad by the President of Turkey and the King of Iraq, who were with their premiers and foreign ministers. Strictly speaking, the pact did not provide for an alliance. But it stipulated co-operation to assure the contracting parties' security and defense, noninterference in internal affairs, the possibility of the future adhesion of other states interested in the security of the Middle East provided they are recognized by both parties, and the creation of a permanent ministerial council to implement the pact if and when at least four parties became signatories to it. The signing of the pact was followed by an exchange of interpretive letters between the Turkish and the Iraqi premiers, in which it was stated that both countries would work together toward the implementation of the United Nations resolutions concerning Palestine.[19] In a political sense this represented the price Turkey had to pay for wooing away one of the Arab states

[19] The text is in the *Middle East Journal*, Spring, 1955, p. 177.

from the rest—the recognition that henceforth she would stand closer to the Arabs than to Israel on vital issues affecting the latter's security and territorial integrity. On February 26 the Turkish and the Iraqi parliaments ratified the pact by overwhelming majorities.

During subsequent months Egypt and Saudi Arabia displayed feverish activity to isolate Iraq from other members of the League, to prevent others from joining the Turkish-Iraqi Pact, and to promote a new, tripartite security pact, which would link Cairo with Riyadh and Damascus and thus constitute a counterweight to the Northern Tier alliances. Their efforts were partly successful (see Chapter XI below), but they failed to intimidate Iraq. On the contrary, their aggressiveness (which went so far as to support a "Free Iraq" radio station located in Egypt and broadcasting propaganda injurious to Nuri and his government) strengthened Iraq's resolve to follow an independent policy.

In Baghdad on March 30, 1955, Britain and Iraq initialed an agreement whereby (1) Britain adhered to the Turkish-Iraqi Pact of February 24; (2) both parties agreed to abrogate the Anglo-Iraqi Treaty of Alliance of June 30, 1930; and (3) Britain undertook to supply military aid and in case of aggression recognized by both parties as endangering Iraq's security promised, at Iraq's request, to come to the latter's assistance. On April 4 this new agreement was signed in Baghdad by both parties. It did not require ratification by the Iraqi parliament, being treated as an annex to the Turkish-Iraqi Pact, which, in Article 5, foresaw such future adhesions.[20]

Britain's adherence was of momentous significance inasmuch as it introduced the first major power into a pact hitherto linking medium or small states only. While strengthening the pact in a military sense, this step implied also a possibility of further extension of British influence in this region. The failure of the United States (a tacitly sponsoring power) to join the pact was due partly to America's reluctance to burn the bridges in her relations with Egypt and partly to the protests of Israel, who attacked the pact as hostile to herself. From the Iraqi point of view this American hesitation had unfortunate effects inasmuch as it exposed the pact to further criticism that in reality it was nothing but a British instrument and that, instead of linking Iraq's security with the West in general (thus avoiding domination by any single power), it allowed Britain to

[20] The text is in *Cahiers*, 1955, 1.

"leave by the door but come back by the window." These objections were likely to be especially well founded in the case of Iran, should she be invited to join the pact. They were not likely, however, to deter Pakistan, already a signatory of a collaboration treaty with Turkey (see p. 159 above). Indeed, Pakistan did declare her adherence to the pact on June 30, thus completing the foursome required for the establishment of a permanent pact organization.

Adherence by Iran became the next problem on the agenda. For various reasons including those mentioned above Iran was reluctant to commit herself to the Western bloc, and as the fall of 1955 approached it looked as if the Baghdad Pact (as it has come to be known) would have to do without that geographical link between Pakistan and the rest of the signatories. But following the visit of Premier Menderes of Turkey to Teheran in early fall, Iran reversed herself and in October joined the pact.

Thus the Northern Tier defense scheme became a reality, and the pact powers could proceed, without further impediments, to set up a permanent organization. The latter came into being at the first meeting of the pact powers, which was held in Baghdad November 20–22, 1955. Presided over by Nuri Pasha, the meeting was attended by the premiers of the pact's Middle Eastern signatories and the foreign secretary of Britain. It resulted in the establishment of a permanent secretariat with headquarters in Baghdad and in the selection of an Iraqi, Awni Khalidi, as its first secretary general. To Nuri Said the event was a crowning of his long-range efforts and a vindication of his foreign policy. Though estranged from Egypt and Saudi Arabia, Iraq had found her place among those Islamic nations for whom the menace of Soviet imperialism and atheism overshadowed such potential dangers or inconveniences as might result from closer ties to the West.

With foreign policy thus attended to, the major problem for the government is now internal. Despite the support Nuri has received on the pact from a surprisingly large number of political figures, his policy is not favored by the masses, the students, and the intelligentsia outside the bureaucracy. The elements that demand reform and purge at home are, by and large, opposed to Nuri's course in foreign affairs. No amount of persuasion seems to win converts among the people, whose minds are made up and whose negative attitudes are principally due to their frustration over domestic developments. Consequently, the key to stability will, in the long run, be found in the government's ability—and willingness—to effect much-needed reforms. No other way can be devised to discharge the political tension which, despite the overt restoration of order, continues to exist in Iraq.

CHAPTER VIII

Syria and Lebanon

GENERAL Gouraud's seizure of Damascus on July 24, 1920, put an end to Faisal's rule over the Syrian hinterland, and France extended her authority over the whole area assigned to her at the San Remo Conference. The Act of Mandate was signed in London on July 24, 1922, thus formalizing the relationship between France and the Levant under the auspices of the League of Nations.

FRANCE AND THE LEVANT

The mandate of Syria-Lebanon corresponded roughly to the wartime Sykes-Picot agreement. In this way the peace settlement confirmed the wartime arrangements. The reason why France and not some other country was awarded the countries of Levant must be sought in the long historical association between France and these countries. This association began as early as the crusades. It will be remembered that in 1535 Francis I obtained from the sultan the first capitulations, which resulted in the establishment of French trading outposts and consulates in Syria. Henry IV, Richelieu, and Louis XIV continued this relationship. Colbert actively promoted trade with the Levant in the epoch of mercantilism. By the Treaty of 1740 France obtained the renewal of the capitulations. As we know from a preceding chapter, the treaty contained special references to the Levant and to the holy places in Palestine, favoring French interests there and virtually designating France as a protector of Latin Christianity in the area. By an agreement with the sultan in 1802, Napoleon confirmed the capitulatory privileges. France's interest in the Levant has been considerable ever since. She was sympathetic toward Mohammed Ali, who, as has been mentioned earlier, extended his rule to Syria in the 1830's. Definite ties of friendship developed between France and the Maronite Christians of Lebanon. In 1842–1845 and again in 1860 France intervened in favor of Lebanon, forcing the Sublime Porte to recognize Lebanon's autonomy. French educational and religious institutions, such as the Jesuit University of Beirut, were established in the Levant, and this in turn contributed to a considerable extension of French cultural influence. It is significant that when nationalistically minded Arab intellectuals decided to hold their congress in 1913, they chose Paris as a meeting place, and the majority of its members came from Syria and Lebanon. Thus, when the partitioning of the Ottoman Empire became a reality, France considered herself as the rightful trustee of the Levant.

Her disappointment was great when she perceived that postwar Arab nationalism was not compatible with her concept of her cultural mission in the Levant. The Syrians made it clear to the King-Crane commission that they did not want any foreign tutelage, but if it was going to be imposed upon them anyway, they would favor an American or British mandate to a French one. France saw Emir Faisal ruling in Damascus at the head of a fiercely nationalistic desert army, and Faisal was susceptible to British rather than to French influences. If France was to assert her rule over Syria, the continuance of Faisal's rule in the hinterland was unthinkable. General Gouraud's action in expelling him from Damascus was, therefore, the logical sequel to the partitioning decisions and the subsequent peace settlement.

Having established her undisputed military mastery over Syria, France then faced the problem of finding the best way to perpetuate her rule. The answer seemed clear: it was the old maxim, *divide et impera.* Barely six weeks after Faisal's removal, on September 1, 1920, General Gouraud decreed the division of the mandated territory into four distinct units: Great Lebanon, the state of Damascus (including the Jebel Druze district), the state of Aleppo (including Alexandretta), and the territory of Lattakia (or Alawi territory).[1]

France was represented in the Levant by a high commissioner under whom the French governors of the component units functioned. The basic tendency to maintain the division of the Levant persisted

[1] A detailed study of territorial divisions and changes may be found in A. H. Hourani, *Syria and Lebanon, A Political Essay* (London, 1946). Consult also Raymond O'Zoux, *Les Etats du Levant sous Mandat Français* (Paris, 1931) and J. Achkar, *Evolution Politique de la Syrie et du Liban, de la Palestine et de l'Iraq* (Paris, 1935).

267

throughout the French mandatory regime despite some territorial and administrative reshufflings. In 1922 Jebel Druze was accorded the status of a separate state, and in 1924 the French created an autonomous sanjak of Alexandretta (partly to satisfy Turkish susceptibilities and partly to conform to their basic policy of division). On January 1, 1925, however, the states of Aleppo and Damascus became unified under the title of the state of Syria. French policy in the Levant tended to follow the pattern of administration in the French colonies. It was centralized rule par excellence, with little or no regard for local autonomy. French administrators in Syria-Lebanon were not exactly of the highest caliber. (In contrast to the British, a colonial career did not attract many brilliant young Frenchmen.)

Lebanon after World War I

Of the four main divisions in the mandated territory, French policy appeared relatively successful in two, namely, in Lebanon and Lattakia. Lebanon, inhabited by a mixed population and containing a slight Christian majority, enjoyed her separate status and looked toward France for protection. In 1925, the Lebanese Representative Council drafted a constitution which, promulgated by the high commissioner, became law in May 1926. It gave Lebanon Western-patterned parliamentary institutions with a president, a cabinet, and two-chamber (later one-chamber) parliament. Article 30 mentioned specifically the republic's dependent relationship to France, in conformity with the League of Nations mandate. The constitution was amended in 1927 and in 1929.

The year 1931 and the first months of 1932 were difficult for Lebanon. The country suffered an acute economic crisis, which was reflected in unemployment, strikes, and general unrest. Public finances were subjected to particular strain, and the native Lebanese authorities did little to alleviate the situation. On May 9, 1932, French High Commissioner Ponsot suspended the constitution, appointed a caretaker government, and took energetic steps to restore order in the Lebanese treasury. This crisis led the French to change their minds about the propriety of Western-modeled democratic institutions for a retarded country like Lebanon. The result was the decision to transform Lebanon from a parliamentary republic into a semiauthoritarian corporative state. On January 2, 1934, a new high commissioner, Count de Martel, promulgated a new Lebanese constitution which assured representation to the professions, limited the authority of the parliament, reinforced the executive power, and provided proper safeguards for public finances against irresponsible spending.

Gradually a tradition was established whereby the president of the republic was to be a Maronite Christian and the prime minister a Sunni Moslem, thus assuring a balance between the two prominent sections of the population. The constitution did not provide for any state religion, so freedom of worship became a reality. Some traces of the former Turkish millet system could be found in the arrangement which gave the corporate religious communities the right to regulate some matters relating to the personal status of their members. Lebanon's political forces were divided between the religious leaders, of whom the Maronite patriarch was the most influential, and the political parties. Of these, the most important were the Unionist group, headed by Emile Eddé, which was known for its insistence upon full Lebanese independence, and the Constitutionalist group, under Bishara el-Khuri, which favored closer relationships with other Arab countries. Otherwise the differences between these groups were not very profound.

Like Lebanon, the territory of Lattakia had a relatively peaceful existence. The Alawis constituted a separate Islamic sect which was anxious to reserve its identity and which feared domination by the Sunnis of Syria. The French made full use of these fears, encouraging particularism and considerably aiding the territory in its material progress.

Syria after World War I

Conditions in Syria and in the Jebel Druze [2] were far from satisfactory. French rule in these states was resented because of its centralization and because of its separation from Syria of districts which were regarded as Syrian by Sunni Arab nationalists.[3] Within five years considerable tension developed. This gave rise, by the end of 1925, to an insurrection which broke out in the Druze mountains and which soon spread to Damascus and other parts of Syria.[4] In order

[2] For conditions in the Druze district, see Narcisse Bouron, *Les Druzes* (Paris, 1930).

[3] The nationalist case is ably presented in Edmond Rabbath, *Unité Syrienne et Devenir Arabe* (Paris, 1937). See also Elizabeth P. MacCallum, *The Nationalist Crusade in Syria* (New York, 1928).

[4] This insurrection was supported by a variety of political groups such as the People's Party of Syria, the Future of Islam of Konya, the Inter-Islamic Committee of Berlin, and the Third International of Moscow. Professor Faris Bey el-Khuri

to quell the rebellion, the French sent reinforcements to Lebanon, armed Circassian and Armenian auxiliaries to fight the insurgent Arabs; under the orders of General Sarrail, the high commissioner, they bombarded Damascus in the spring of 1926. Soon afterward Suweida, the capital of Jebel Druze, was captured by French troops. By the end of 1926 the insurrection had been crushed. A new high commissioner, Henri de Jouvenel, entrusted to Ahmed Nami Bey the formation of a government in Damascus, which, it was hoped, would follow French guidance.

At the same time French policy tended to follow the constitutional pattern developed in Lebanon. In 1928 the French high commissioner directed the convocation of a Syrian Constituent Assembly. Elections to the Assembly resulted in the emergence of a powerful National Bloc (*Kutla*) founded by Ibrahim Hananu. Among its leaders were men such as Hashim el-Atassi, Jamil Mardam Bey, Saadullah el-Jabri, and Faris el-Khuri. Within the bloc operated another group known as *Istiqlal,* which advocated complete independence of Syria. Headed by Shukri el-Quwatli, this group included Emir Adil Arslan and a Lebanese nationalist, Riyadh es-Sulh. The bloc did not secure a majority of seats, but being more determined and disciplined than other groups it played a role out of proportion to its numbers and soon began to dominate Syrian politics. Its members were elected to the most important positions in the Assembly.

The Assembly drew up a constitution which, in some important respects, was unacceptable to the French authorities. The points objected to in particular were a provision for a united Syria (which would mean the obliteration of the separate status of Lebanon and of other areas under French mandate as well as of Palestine and Trans-jordan) and provisions concerning Syrian armed forces and foreign relations, which made no mention of the mandatory relationship to France. For this reason, a new high commissioner, M. Ponsot, first suspended the Assembly and then after several unsuccessful attempts at negotiation dissolved it altogether. In May 1930 he issued a constitution for Syria by his own decree. This new document embodied virtually all the articles of the old one except those to which France objected. Article 116 specifically confirmed France's responsibilities under the mandate of the League of Nations. Jebel Druze and Lat-

---

was an intellectual leader of the insurrection. In the Jebel Druze, the insurgents were led by the leading family of Sultan el-Atrash. In Damascus the leadership was assumed by Dr. Shahbandar.

takia remained outside Syria. Special articles provided for the establishment of the so-called Common Interests (to Syria, Lebanon, and other areas) to be administered largely by French officials.

The new constitution was accepted by the people of Syria without violent opposition, and in 1932 elections to the single Chamber took place. They resulted in a victory for the "moderates," i.e., those who were willing to co-operate with the French. Nevertheless, the extreme nationalists succeeded in obtaining around 25 per cent of the seats. The Chamber elected Mohammed Ali el-Abid president of the republic, and he in turn appointed a moderate, Haqqi el-Azem prime minister. The new cabinet included, however, a number of nationalists. The latter soon emerged as the most influential group in the Chamber of Deputies, demanding a Franco-Syrian treaty to replace the mandatory regime. Their stand was strengthened by developments in British-controlled Iraq where a treaty had just been substituted for the mandate.

Treaties with France

The negotiations which ensued lasted for nearly four years. They were first conducted in Syria by High Commissioner Ponsot but, owing to the intransigence of the Kutla group, ended in failure. Eventually they were transferred to France. A Syrian delegation composed of six members with representatives of both moderates and nationalists went to Paris and there, on September 9, 1936, concluded a treaty. This document, which was signed by Vienot, French undersecretary of foreign affairs, and Hashim Bey el-Atassi, chief Syrian delegate, was composed of a main treaty, a military convention, and annexes and was to be valid for twenty-five years. The main provisions were as follows: Syria was to become independent within three years and was to be sponsored by France for membership in the League of Nations; France and Syria entered into a military alliance; France obtained the right to maintain two air bases; French land forces were permitted to stay in the Alawi and Druze districts for five years; these districts, however, were to be incorporated into Syria; French military instructors were to advise the Syrian army, and France was to supply it with armaments and military equipment; in case of war Syria's duty was to co-operate with France on her own soil by protecting and maintaining aerodromes and by furnishing communications and transit assistance as well as water.

In the annexed letters, Syria agreed to recruit technical advisers and experts in France, to establish a special judicial system for the protection of foreigners, and to accord the French ambassador the right of precedence over other diplomatic representatives. All these provisions followed the pattern of the Anglo-Iraqi treaty of 1930, but there were some differences. These consisted in the following provisions: (1) despite Syria's sovereignty over Lattakia and Jebel Druze, the administrative autonomy of these areas was expressly provided for; (2) a special regime was established for foreign schools, charitable institutions, and archeological missions; (3) a promise was made to negotiate a university convention; (4) Syria promised to respect the acquired physical and legal rights of Frenchmen; (5) a monetary agreement was concluded; (6) a financial agreement was attached to the treaty.

It was relatively easy for the French to conclude a similar treaty with Lebanon. The treaty was signed by Count de Martel and Emile Eddé on November 13, 1936, following negotiations conducted in Beirut. The Lebanese treaty was a virtual duplicate of the Syrian one except for provisions which referred to territorial and minority questions peculiar to Lebanon and for the fact that no limit was put upon the time, type, or number of French forces to be stationed in Lebanese territory.

In the late fall, elections took place in Syria. They resulted in an overwhelming victory for the National Bloc, which secured a majority in the eighty-six-member Chamber.[5] The Chamber elected Faris el-Khuri as its president, and, upon accepting Mohammed Ali el-Abid's resignation from the presidency of the republic, elected Hashim el-Atassi to this post. Jamil Mardam Bey became prime minister. The first important act of the new parliament was to ratify the Franco-Syrian treaty. The next was to incorporate Jebel Druze and Lattakia into the Syrian republic. Gradually the French high commissioner began transferring his functions to the Syrian government.[6] The Syrians were full of hopes, and this optimism was highlighted by the return of some prominent exiled leaders to whom amnesty had been granted.

In Lebanon political developments took a parallel course, although the Sunni Arabs did not share the Maronites' joy over the conclusion of the treaty. To them the treaty meant abandonment of hope for a

[5] Out of this number sixteen represented religious minorities and seven the Bedouin tribes.

[6] See John Morgan Jones, *La Fin du Mandat Français en Syrie et au Liban* (Paris, 1938).

reunion with Syria. In January 1937 the constitution of 1926 was restored. The new electoral law adopted in 1937 provided for a Chamber whose members were to be elected in the ratio of two-thirds on a sectarian basis to one-third by nominations. The elections in the fall of 1937 were organized in accordance with this provision. No radical change could be observed in Lebanese politics, which continued to be marked by personal rivalries and sectarian issues.

The early optimism of the Syrian and Lebanese nationalists was soon dissipated. First, France delayed and eventually refused to ratify the treaties. This was due partly to political changes in France (the Blum Popular Front administration gave place to a right-of-center coalition) and partly to a feeling of national insecurity. Faced with the resurgence of German and Italian militarism, France was reluctant to liquidate her Syro-Lebanese base in the eastern Mediterranean. Secondly, Syria ran into difficulty almost immediately in her quest for unity. The opposition came from Turkey, and the quarrel centered on the sanjak of Alexandretta.

The Sanjak of Alexandretta

Ever since the peace settlement, Turkey had watched anxiously over the sanjak, which was inhabited by a mixed Turkish-Arab-Kurdish population. In fact, Alexandretta remained the only Turkish *terra irredenta,* Turkey being otherwise quite satisfied with her existing boundaries. When Turkey concluded the Franklin-Bouillon agreement in 1921 she made sure that the special status of Alexandretta would be recognized by France and that the sanjak would be granted adequate autonomy. With the conclusion of the Franco-Syrian treaty, which provided for a unified Syria, Turkey felt that the future of Alexandretta was jeopardized, and she immediately raised objections. The Turkish argument ran as follows: when concluding the Franklin-Bouillon agreement, Turkey had not considered France as a mandatory power over Syria; Turkey had never regarded the sanjak as a part of Syria; Turkey had entrusted the care of the Turks in Alexandretta to France alone, and for this reason she was bound to object to the transfer of responsibilities to Syria; the only legitimate solution was for France to conclude with the sanjak a separate treaty similar to those concluded with Syria and Lebanon.

France did not accept this Turkish thesis in its entirety but was willing to compromise. Consequently, in December 1936, the matter was brought to the Council of the League of Nations. On January

27, 1937, the Council recommended that the sanjak be granted full autonomy in its internal affairs. Its foreign relations were to be entrusted to Syria, and it was to be linked to Syria by a fiscal and monetary union. Turkish was proclaimed an official language. The Council reserved for itself the right to approve those foreign policy acts of Syria which would affect the status of the sanjak. A Council delegate of French nationality was to reside in the sanjak with the right of temporary veto. France and Turkey were to enforce, if necessary, the Council's decisions; and a statute and fundamental law for the sanjak were to be drafted and submitted for the Council's approval. On May 29, 1937, the Council adopted the statute on the basis of which the new regime was to begin on November 29. Simultaneously, France and Turkey concluded a treaty guaranteeing the integrity of the sanjak. Thus the first dent in the unity of Syria was made: the sanjak was virtually separated from the new republic and its predominantly Turkish character was recognized.[7]

In Syria, both the public and the government protested vigorously against these decisions, and the Syrian parliament refused to accept the new statute for Alexandretta. France was severely criticized for abandoning her new Syrian ally and for appeasing Turkey. The National Bloc suffered a decline in popularity for not having struggled for the sanjak with greater determination.

The Syrians viewed the 1937 arrangements as temporary and as leading inevitably, should France persist in her pro-Turkish policy, to the final incorporation of the sanjak in the Turkish state. In this they were right. Menaced by Germany and Italy, France was determined to seek allies in the Mediterranean. She believed the Turks to be more valuable and reliable than the Syrians. The same reasons which led France to suspend the ratification of her treaties with Syria and Lebanon caused her to choose the Turkish side in the sanjak controversy. By 1938 it became obvious that Turkey would regard a satisfactory solution in the sanjak as the price for linking her fate with that of France. On July 3, 1938, France and Turkey concluded an agreement in Antioch for the joint garrisoning of the sanjak by French and Turkish troops. The next day a Franco-Turkish treaty of friendship was signed at Ankara. And on July 5 impressive formations of crack Turkish troops entered the sanjak. Electoral lists, drawn up under joint Franco-Turkish supervision, showed a Turkish

---

[7] For a discussion of this problem from a French point of view, see Paul du Véou, *Le Désastre d'Alexandrette, 1934–1938* (Paris, 1938).

majority of 63 per cent, which meant that the Turks would be entitled to a majority of seats in the sanjak's Assembly.

The elections held in September 1938 resulted, as could be foreseen, in the establishment of a Turkish-dominated Assembly. Its president, as well as the president and prime minister of the sanjak, which had become the republic of Hatay, were all Turks. Intensive agitation followed for the joining of Hatay with Turkey. The republic of Hatay, which was a virtual French-Turkish condominium, lasted less than a year. On June 23, 1939, in Paris, France and Turkey concluded a treaty of mutual assistance, and on the same day, by an agreement signed at Ankara, France ceded to Turkey the sanjak of Alexandretta.

SYRIA AND LEBANON DURING WORLD WAR II

France's refusal to ratify the treaty of 1936 had a bad effect upon Syrian political life. Splits occurred in the dominant National Bloc, and a vocal opposition, known as the Constitutionalist Party, was formed around Dr. Abdur Rahman Shahbandar, who had returned from exile. Cabinet crises followed each other in rapid succession, leading to a virtual stalemate in government activities. On July 7, 1939, the president of the republic resigned, and on July 10 the new French high commissioner, Gabriel Pueaux, suspended the constitution, dissolved the Chamber, and appointed a nonpolitical Council of Directors to govern the country under his authority. This was followed by decrees restoring separate regimes for the Druze and Lattakia districts and introducing a special administration for the northeast province of Jezira. Thus, on the eve of the Second World War France re-established direct rule over Syria in the hope of strengthening her eastern Mediterranean bulwark. The French administration also curbed various pro-Nazi and extremist organizations, including the Communist Party.

Similar measures were undertaken in Lebanon soon after the outbreak of the war. There the high commissioner also suspended the constitution and dissolved the Chamber. The president of Lebanon, however, remained in office, but the normal cabinet was replaced by a single secretary of state who governed through civil servants under French supervision.

Toward the French, who were facing a threat to their survival, Syrian and Lebanese political circles expressed, at least outwardly, their loyalty, stressing also their attachment to the camp of democ-

275

racy. In reality, however, Arab public opinion was hostile to France and to the Allies in general. Resentment at what was believed to be a betrayal of the Arabs after World War I, appeasement of Turkey in the Alexandretta issue, the nonratification of the Syrian and Lebanese treaties, and the excitement over the Zionist question in Palestine—all contributed to a definitely anti-Ally trend in the Levant. As one observer has aptly phrased it, "From the point of view of the exploited nations of the East, there was nothing to choose between the oppression exercised in the name of democracy and that exercised in the name of Fascism." [8]

During the first months of the war France assembled in Syria a large force, known as the Army of the Levant, under the command of General Weygand. It was expected that, if war were to extend to the eastern Mediterranean, this army would have a major role to play. France's defeat in June 1940 put an end to these plans. Syria and Lebanon found themselves under Vichy control and most members of the French civil and military administration refused to adhere to General de Gaulle's Free French Committee.

The attitude of French officialdom could be explained in part by the traditional anti-British feeling of the French in Syria. Britain had been blamed for setting a dangerous precedent by her treaty with Iraq in 1930, which greatly emboldened Syrian nationalists. Some Frenchmen had never succeeded in shaking the suspicion that, back in the 1920's, Britain would have been only too glad to see Faisal prevail and to substitute her control of Syria for French control. Moreover, the French knew of Britain's annoyance at the fact that Syria and Lebanon had become centers of intrigue for Arab refugees from Palestine, who conducted anti-British guerrilla operations from this safe shelter.

The Vichy authorities hoped to prevent the British from seizing the French Levant, but at the same time they were compelled to open their gates to Axis influence. In August 1940 the Italian and German Armistice Commissions arrived in Beirut, and before long signs of Axis infiltration began to multiply. Herr von Hentig, chief of the Near East Department of the German Foreign Office, arrived in Syria, and German propaganda, usually successful with the Arabs, was stepped up considerably. The real crisis occurred in May 1941 when General Dentz, Vichy high commissioner, permitted German aircraft to land and refuel on Syrian airfields when in transit to Iraq

[8] Hourani, op. cit., p. 230.

to aid Rashid Ali's rebellion. The pretense of Vichy neutrality could no longer be maintained, and Great Britain decided to act.

British Intervention in the Levant

On June 8, 1941, British troops, commanded by General Sir Henry Maitland Wilson, invaded Syria from Palestine, Transjordan, and Iraq. Free French elements accompanied them. Vichy forces offered resistance, but after a month of fighting General Dentz sued for peace. On July 14, an armistice was signed. Syria and Lebanon were included in the area under the British Middle East Command and subjected to occupation by the British Ninth Army. To unify Levant's economy with the rest of the Middle East, the British included it in the sterling bloc in September.

The question of Franco-Syrian-Lebanese relationships remained to be solved. On the day of the invasion, the French commander, General Catroux, issued a proclamation in which he stated that Free France intended to put an end to the mandatory regime, to proclaim Syria and Lebanon free and independent, and to negotiate a treaty which would define their mutual relations. Catroux's declaration was endorsed in a separate statement issued in Cairo on the same day by Ambassador Sir Miles Lampson in the name of Great Britain. On June 24 General de Gaulle appointed General Catroux "Delegate General and Plenipotentiary of Free France in the Levant"—a title replacing the former title of high commissioner—and instructed him to negotiate treaties with Syria and Lebanon at the earliest possible date.

In making these promises, the Free French no doubt pursued a policy advocated by the British. The dramatic changes in Syria gave the British an opportunity to restore to some degree their good standing with the Arabs, a standing which had undergone severe strain as a result of the Palestinian controversy. It soon became clear that British and French interpretations of the June 8, 1941, pledges varied. General de Gaulle conducted a policy of procrastination, trying to postpone the moment of Syrian and Lebanese liberation and insisting upon the privileged position of France even after the treaties were concluded. In contrast, Great Britain interpreted these pledges literally, and while not denying France a privileged position in the Levant, she pressed for a speedy transfer of essential controls and services to the Syrians and Lebanese. Attempts were made to reconcile these attitudes: on August 15, 1941, Oliver Lyttelton, British

277

minister of state for the Middle East, and General de Gaulle exchanged letters in which they reaffirmed that "Great Britain has no interest in Syria or Lebanon, except to win the war" and that once independence of the Levant states has been achieved, "France should have the predominant position in Syria and Lebanon over any other European Power." [9] On September 9, 1941, similar declarations were made by Prime Minister Churchill in the House of Commons. But they could not dispel the basic divergence in French and British policies. Nor was the tension alleviated by the appointment of Major-General Sir Edward Spears, a staunch representative of imperial traditions, as head of the British mission to the Levant. The French resented his interference in Syrian politics and suspected him of sinister plots with the Arabs against France's position in the Levant.

EMANCIPATION OF SYRIA AND LEBANON

In the meantime General Catroux undertook the rather ungrateful task—from the French point of view—of reaching an agreement with Syria and Lebanon that would lead toward their emancipation. On September 28, 1941, he proclaimed the independence of Syria, stating in particular that (1) she would "enjoy from now onwards the rights and prerogatives of an independent and sovereign state"; (2) she would have the power to appoint diplomatic representatives abroad; (3) she would have the right to organize her national forces; (4) she would be obliged to accord France and her Allies necessary aid and facilities during the war; and (5) the foregoing stipulations should be replaced as soon as possible by a final settlement "in the form of a Franco-Syrian Treaty which will definitely guarantee the independence of the country." [10]

This act was followed by the proclamation of Lebanese independence on November 26, 1941. Its terms were similar to those of the Syrian proclamation. To implement these documents, General Catroux asked Sheikh Taj ed-Din to assume the presidency of Syria and requested Alfred Naccache, president of Lebanon, to remain in that post.

Soon afterward Great Britain extended *de jure* recognition to both republics, and in February 1942 General Spears was appointed first British minister to Syria and Lebanon. Other recognitions followed, but the Arab states were guarded and slow in acknowledging Syrian and Lebanese independence. As for the United States, it reserved

[9] Quoted by Hourani, *op. cit.*, p. 245.   [10] *Ibid.*, pp. 249–250.

its judgment until the formal termination of the mandate, which it believed should come about by the conclusion and ratification of bilateral treaties between the two states and France. In 1942 George Wadsworth was appointed American consul general and diplomatic agent to both Levantine governments.

Despite this formal emancipation France was neither willing nor ready to transfer major functions of government to the new republics. The question of the constitutionality of both regimes remained in abeyance, both Presidents Taj ed-Din and Naccache owing their offices to General Catroux's appointment and not to the freely expressed will of their peoples. Moreover, General de Gaulle objected in the name of Free France to the holding of elections in both countries.

In consequence, the mood of expectation gradually gave way to one of hostility. Public opinion did not spare Britain either, believing that she countenanced France's behavior. In Syria the National Bloc experienced a revival, this time under the leadership of Shukri el-Quwatli, and there was a marked tendency toward left-wing extremism as expressed by the growth of Socialist and Communist movements.

Under the pressure of public opinion, the Free French authorities in March 1943 decided to re-establish the suspended constitutions in both Syria and Lebanon. Elections held in the summer of that year resulted in the establishment of nationalistically minded parliaments in Damascus and Beirut. In Syria the National Bloc regained its dominant position and its new leader, Shukri el-Quwatli, was elected to the presidency of the republic. Faris el-Khuri, Saadullah el-Jabri, Jamil Mardam Bey, old leaders of the bloc, once again took the reins of power by assuming key legislative and executive positions.

In Lebanon events followed a parallel course. The pro-French leaders were dismissed from their posts and replaced by nationalists, some of whom, as for example the new prime minister, Riyadh es-Sulh, had long-standing ties with Syrian nationalist leaders. The Lebanese Chamber, composed of thirty Christians and twenty-five Moslems, elected Bishara el-Khuri president of the republic.

The advent to power of the nationalists in both countries foreshadowed a more determined struggle for complete emancipation from French tutelage. This tutelage was expressed in a number of legislative and administrative restrictions placed upon both republics by France. In particular, the French delegate general still retained the right to issue decrees which restricted both parliaments in the free exercise of legislative power, and he could still invoke those provisions of the Syrian and Lebanese constitutions which, with reference to the League of Nations mandate, made France responsible for the maintenance of order and security and for the defense and conduct of foreign relations of both countries. Moreover, the delegate general administered directly the Common Interests, in particular the customs, maintained control over local levies known as the *Troupes Spéciales* and over the state security police, and exercised authority over nomad tribes and press censorship. He also was in a position to exert influence, through French technical advisers, in the Syrian and Lebanese administrations. Moreover, French intelligence officers, known as agents of the *Services Spéciaux,* were still much in evidence in both states.

The nationalist governments of Syria and Lebanon objected to all these prerogatives and demanded their abolition. De Gaulle's Free French Committee retorted that France's responsibilities could not be terminated without the approval of the League of Nations or of its successor. It also argued that the special prerogatives enjoyed by France could be relinquished only as a result of treaties which would safeguard French interests in the Levant.

Nationalist reaction to this refusal was stronger than the Free French had expected. On November 8, 1943, the Lebanese parliament adopted a resolution to drop from the constitution all those articles that referred to France as a mandatory power. Two days later the new French delegate general, Helleu, placed the president of the republic and the majority of his cabinet under arrest, suspended the constitution, and appointed Emile Eddé as head of the state and of the government. The Lebanese replied with a general strike and anti-French riots. The British did not hide their disapproval of the precipitate French action, feeling that such action was likely to endanger order and security in the area under British military command. Faced with nationalist outbreaks and with simultaneous British pressure, General de Gaulle promptly recalled Helleu, sending General Catroux to smooth out the differences. Lebanese leaders were released and reinstated in their functions.

On January 24, 1944, a similar crisis occurred in Syria, though in less violent form. On that day the president of the republic and the members of parliament took an oath of allegiance to the constitution, expressly leaving out Article 116, which referred to French

280

mandatory responsibilities. This action did not, however, have the same revolutionary character as the earlier Lebanese defiance, because, instead of preceding, it followed an agreement, reached on December 22, 1943, with the French Committee of National Liberation. The agreement, which extended to both Syria and Lebanon, provided for the definitive transfer of powers from the delegate general to the governments concerned. The nationalists had triumphed.

In the course of 1944, all the functions of the delegate general were transferred to the Syrian and Lebanese governments with the exception of the *Troupes Spéciales*. French delay in placing them under Syro-Lebanese command caused resentment. Mutual irritation was increased by French insistence upon the conclusion of treaties which would bind Syria and Lebanon to France and which, according to the French view, were necessary to relieve France of her mandatory responsibilities. France insisted in particular: (1) on safeguards for French cultural establishments in the Levant; (2) on the recognition of her economic rights; and (3) on the recognition of her strategic interests in the area (she asked for air and naval bases and the right to organize and command Syrian and Lebanese armies).

The Twilight of French Influence

Negotiations concerning these treaty arrangements were scheduled to begin on May 19, 1945. Four days earlier, however, fresh French reinforcements disembarked in Beirut. The Lebanese protested vigorously against their arrival. The ensuing strikes and riots which broke out in Beirut soon spread all over Lebanon and Syria. French citizens were assaulted, and both governments broke off their negotiations with the French delegate general, General Beynet. For a few days the political situation in the Levant remained in suspense. Nothing less than the sovereignty of both states was at stake. So long as the French could maintain military control over the whole region, the independence of Syria and Lebanon would remain illusory—and both parties realized this fact perfectly well.

In this moment of tension direct British intervention again tipped the scales in favor of the two republics. At the end of May Prime Minister Winston Churchill asked General de Gaulle, in a form resembling an ultimatum, to order his troops to cease fire and withdraw to their barracks. Threatened with imminent British action, De

281

Gaulle complied with this demand. Peace was restored, but treaty negotiations with France were not renewed. Encouraged by British support, Syria and Lebanon on June 21, 1945, issued a joint declaration dismissing all French citizens from their services and announcing the transfer of the *Troupes Spéciales* to their national control. On July 7 France gave her formal consent to this transfer. It had been accomplished in forty-five days.

In the meantime the independent international status of both republics was given explicit recognition by a number of diplomatic acts. In July 1944 the Soviet Union, and in September of the same year the United States, granted the Levant states full and unconditional recognition in which no mention was made of the special position of France. Both republics participated as independent states in the negotiations leading toward the creation of the Arab League, and both signed the League pact on March 22, 1945, as founding members. In conformity with the Yalta decisions, Syria and Lebanon declared war on Germany and Japan on March 1, 1945, signed the United Nations declaration in April, and by these acts gained admission to the United Nations conference at San Francisco. From that time on, sovereign status was accorded both republics without question by the outside world or even by France. The only question that remained to be settled was the withdrawal of foreign troops from the republics' territories. On December 13, 1945, the British and French governments issued a joint statement promising gradual evacuation of their forces from the Levant. This statement elicited protests in Beirut and Damascus, where the nationalist governments were anxious to see a speedy departure of foreign troops. On February 4, 1946, Syria and Lebanon brought the matter to the attention of the United Nations Security Council. After a brief debate the American delegation moved that the Council express its confidence that foreign troops would be evacuated as soon as practicable and that negotiations to that end would be undertaken without delay. Despite seven affirmative votes, this proposal was not adopted because of a Soviet veto. Russia voted against it on the ground that it was too vague. Thereupon France and Great Britain declared that despite the veto they would abide by the resolution. At the end of April they informed the Council that they had agreed to withdraw their troops from Syria without delay and from Lebanon by gradual stages. Withdrawal from Syria was carried out in the same month, and by December 31, 1946, the last foreign soldiers had departed from Lebanon. Thus both republics achieved complete political emancipation.

THE REPUBLIC OF LEBANON

Lebanon's postwar history can be reviewed under two headings: (1) internal politics and (2) her relations with the big powers and the states of the Middle East.

Internally the young republic continued her traditional political pattern.[11] The presidency of the republic remained in the hands of a Christian, and the position of prime minister was reserved for a Moslem. Bishara el-Khuri and Riyadh es-Sulh continued in their respective positions despite various political shifts and changes in the cabinet's membership. In the spring of 1947 the first elections since the achievement of independence took place in Lebanon in the midst of a political campaign marked by extremist tendencies and occasional violence. The return from exile of Anton Saadeh, who assumed the leadership of the Syrian National Party, and of Fawzi el-Kawukji, a revolutionary of Palestinian fame who spent the war years in Germany, added to the political unrest of the country. There was a simultaneous revival of the semi-Fascist organization *Phalanges Libanaises* and of the Communist Party. The severance of ties with France, a quarrel over the customs administration with Syria, and unemployment resulting from the withdrawal of foreign troops, all resulted in serious economic difficulties and social unrest. The elections, which gave a substantial majority to the government's supporters (the Constitutionalist Party), aroused a storm of protest from the opposition because of alleged irregularities. In September 1947 opposition groups meeting in Tripoli demanded the dissolution of the Chamber and called for new elections. No action was taken on this demand because in 1948 the attention of the people was diverted to the Palestine issue. Beginning with the fall of 1948, the government took sterner measures against those extremist groups which threatened order and security. Strict surveillance, including temporary arrests and short-term jail sentences, was applied to Mustafa el-Aris, a trade unionist chief and leader of the outlawed Communist Party. On July 7, 1949, the government arrested Anton Saadeh with a number of his associates, accusing them of a plot against the government. On the next day Saadeh was executed by

[11] For a discussion of postwar politics, see G. E. Kirk, "Independent Syria and Lebanon," *R.C.A.J.*, July–Oct. 1948.

order of a military court. Ten days later Lebanese police locked and sealed the headquarters of the *Phalanges Libanaises,* which was accused of subversive activities. While this action was being taken against the extremists, the government made a move toward stricter control of public opinion by suppressing all newspapers with a circulation of less than 1,500, as well as sixty-two political newspapers which failed to post a security bond.

Despite the outward stability of the regime (President Khuri was sworn into office in September 1949 for another term of six years, and Riyadh es-Sulh remained prime minister), there were undercurrents of unrest and violence, as exemplified by the unsuccessful attempt upon Riyadh es-Sulh's life in March 1950 by a member of the outlawed Syrian Nationalist Party. In April 1951 the second elections in the independent republic were held under the supervision of a caretaker cabinet headed by Hussein el-Oweini. The general consensus was that this time the government had refrained from interference and the elections were termed honest by official circles and the opposition alike. The Constitutionalist Party maintained its majority in the Chamber, with the Progressive Socialist Party of Kamal Jumblat (a Druze leader), the National Bloc Party (Mediterranean Culture Group) of Raymond Eddé, the *Phalanges* of Pierre Gemayel, and a group of independents led by Camille Shamoun forming the opposition. No basic departure, however, could be noticed from the essentially sectarian character of Lebanese politics, and proportional representation according to religious sects was maintained in the Chamber.

Relations with the West

In international affairs, Lebanon was anxious to cultivate good relations with the powers of the West, particularly with the United States. American cultural institutions, especially the American University in Beirut, provided a significant link between the two countries, a link strengthened by increasing economic exchanges. American air lines and an oil company extended their business operations to Lebanon, the latter making Sidon (Saida) a terminal of the Trans-Arabian Pipe Line (Tapline) which carries oil from the fields of Saudi Arabia. Monetary and financial issues beclouded Lebanon's relations with France, but not to the breaking point. Lebanon's pro-Western orientation was also evidenced by the earlier-mentioned curbs on Communist activities and by her refusal to recognize some of the Soviet satellite regimes in eastern Europe. Nevertheless, Lebanon maintained diplomatic relations with the Soviet Union. The latter apparently took full advantage of this situation by converting her legation in Beirut into the reputedly greatest Soviet propaganda center in the Middle East.

Lebanon's delegate in the United Nations, Dr. Charles Malik, repeatedly went on record as favoring Western concepts of human rights and Western policies. In July 1950 Lebanon endorsed the United Nations Korean resolutions which branded the North Korean Communists as aggressors, and she seemed generally anxious to cultivate Western friendship. The Palestinian controversy revealed once again, however, the Arab character of the republic. Lebanon strongly objected to the partitioning of Palestine and subsequently sent some forces against Israel. The pro-Israel policy of the United States provoked anti-American demonstrations, especially among students, but they were less violent in character than those in Syria, Iraq, or Egypt. In June 1951 Dr. Malik made a speech in Beirut foreshadowing Lebanon's practical reconciliation with the existence of Israel and even admitting that Israel, with other Arab states, would have a role to play in the defense of the Middle East against external aggression.[12]

Relations with the Middle East

Lebanon's relations with her Arab neighbors continued to be conditioned by two factors: (1) her essentially Arab character as a nation and (2) the preponderance of the Christian element in her population. While the first factor pushed Lebanon into co-operation with the Arab states through the instrumentality of the Arab League and otherwise, the second acted as a brake on the pro-Arab tendencies and dictated to the little republic a cautious course that would permit her to maintain her independence and individuality. It was this second facet of Lebanese policy which led her consistently to oppose the Greater Syria scheme advocated by King Abdullah of Transjordan, as well as to insist on the retention of full sovereignty by the members of the Arab League. This same factor made it imperative for Lebanon always to keep the door open for an understanding with the West as a time-tested guarantee against complete submergence in her Moslem environment.

[12] New York Times, June 13, 1951.

The Coup of 1952 and Its Aftermath

Although Lebanon was an island of tolerance in comparison with her sister countries, her democracy suffered from two deficiencies: one was the strictly sectarian basis of her political processes; another was the narrowness of her political structure. To an impartial observer Lebanon's politics appeared like a never-ending game of musical chairs in which the principal actors were always the same, with temporary absences from the scene of this or that individual due to the normal hazards of the political profession. The people at large were expected either to mind their business in the lopsided economy of this little state or simply to conform to the wishes and ideas of their feudal lords, party chieftains, and ecclesiastical leaders (the latter abounded in this sect-ridden country). Those who found that their native land was too crowded and poor could emigrate to the more promising lands of South or North America, provided the latter were liberal enough in their immigration policies. This, in a broad generalization, was the state of affairs prevailing until the summer of 1952.

In June of that fateful year in the annals of Arab history, a new organization dedicated to radical reform came into prominence. Called the Socialist and National Front, it demanded an end of sectarian representation, a purge in the administration, and eradication of abuses in the government. Although the Front could boast of no more than eight deputies in the seventy-seven-man parliament, it had considerable appeal to the masses. Moreover, it was headed by a few reformist leaders whose reputations had not suffered in the all-pervading atmosphere of corruption. Among these leaders were Kamal Jumblat, a Druze chief and head of the Progressive Socialist Party, Camille Shamoun, former minister to Britain, Emile Bustani, a self-made millionaire businessman known for his outspokenness, Ghassan Tweini, the Harvard-educated youngest member of parliament, and certain others, representing, on the whole, the anti-feudal and antisectarian trends.

The Egyptian revolution of July 23 had a stimulating influence on the attitudes and activities of the Front. By the end of July three other groups raised their voices against the government. These were the *Phalanges* of Pierre Gemayel, the National Committee of Mohammed Khalid, and the National Congress of Mohammed Idris, who demanded the formation of an extra-parliamentary cabinet, dissolution of the chamber, and speedy institution of reforms. On August 17 the Socialist and National Front held a mass rally at Deir el-Kamar, which was attended by an estimated fifty thousand people. The orators, who included Kamal Jumblat, Camille Shamoun, and Hamid Franjiyeh, called for immediate reform, threatened rebellion, and demanded the resignation of the President. In fact, it was President Bishara el-Khuri rather than the premier, Sami es-Solh, against whom criticism was directed. On August 20 Solh accepted the Front's demands and published a program of reforms, which embraced revision of the electoral law, dismissal of incompetent officials, sale of state lands, and creation of an economic council. His program was, however, unacceptable to certain cabinet members, who, considering Solh as a Kerensky of Lebanese revolution, presented their resignations. On September 9 the premier appeared before the parliament, where he delivered a scathing attack on the prevailing administration of the country, choosing certain members of the President's family as his particular target. His denunciations included presidential interference with the activities of the Ministry of the Interior, prevention of the passage of measures against gambling, tolerance of and conniving with smuggling to Israel and traffic in narcotics, attempts to influence judicial processes, and usurpation of the powers of the prime minister. Having delivered this indictment, Sami es-Solh resigned. Press censorship, dominated by the President, forbade publication of Solh's attack.

Nevertheless, events began to move rapidly in Lebanon. On September 11 the Socialist and National Front called for a general strike to force the President to resign. Pierre Gemayel, head of the *Phalanges,* and his political allies seconded this appeal. Popular response was overwhelming, and on September 15 and 16 all trade and activity in Beirut, Tripoli, Saida, Zahle, and Baalbeck came to a standstill. The press declared that the strike was a virtual plebiscite in favor of the opposition. The President, in a futile gesture, appealed to General Shehab, army chief of staff, to restore order, but, meeting with a refusal, he resigned on September 18. His last constitutional act was to appoint that same general as prime minister.

Thus the opposition carried the day in a bloodless revolution which has since become known as the *Inkilab* ("overturn"). The immediate problem was to fill the vacancy created by Khuri's resignation. Had the opposition been a truly revolutionary and cohesive group, it would have suspended the constitution and established a

287

regime of its own. But this was not the case. Although Jumblat, Shamoun, and their colleagues were united in common enmity to the Khuri regime, they lacked organization and determination to act ruthlessly if necessary. Consequently, instead of dispersing the existing Khuri-packed parliament, the Deir el-Kamar leaders chose to act through it. On September 23, in deference to the mood of the times, parliament, by a vote of 74 out of a total of 76, elected Camille Shamoun to the presidency. Thus the *Inkilab* proved to be not only a bloodless but also a "constitutional" revolution. Such an outcome had its distinct disadvantages, at least from the reformist point of view, inasmuch as it set the new President against an essentially conservative, old-regime parliament, while giving the latter a chance to recoup its strength in the days to come. This was proved soon after Shamoun's election when an attempt to form a truly reform-minded cabinet failed. Eventually a compromise formula was devised: a strictly nonpolitical cabinet headed by a diplomat, Emir Khalid Shehab, and comprising only three other members recruited from the upper bureaucracy was formed. This cabinet received from the parliament full power to legislate by decree for the succeeding six months.

Among the more notable decrees passed by the government during those months was a revision of the electoral law which reduced the number of deputies from 77 to 44 and granted the right to vote to women who held a primary education certificate. This law did not abolish the traditional sectarian representation and, at the most, gave the President of the Republic a somewhat greater chance to influence the deputies. Otherwise the "reforms" of the new cabinet revolved chiefly around the "reclassification" of civil servants and similar personnel matters. It was not a very impressive record, and soon signs of discontent and disappointment with the new regime began to appear. By the spring of 1953 relations between President Shamoun and his erstwhile associate, Jumblat, deteriorated to such a point that the Socialist and National Front was hardly a working coalition. Having risen to the highest office in the state, the President soon gave evidence of accommodating himself to the traditional pattern of Lebanese politics and in all his acts tended to tone down the original and rather radical ideals of the *Inkilab*. By contrast, the much more idealistic Jumblat insisted on the implementation of the revolutionary program, paying little heed to its practical aspects and such considerations as tactical alliances. In May most of the original members of the Front voted against the newly formed cabinet of Saeb Salam, thus returning to the opposition. The new prime minister, to be sure, spoke of the need to achieve the aims of "the September revolution," but this sounded more like lip service to virtue than sincere intention to effect radical changes in Lebanon's political and economic structure.

The basic question of whether the locus of power had shifted from the first "forty families" of Lebanon to the less-privileged strata had to await the answer of the popular ballot under the new electoral law. The electoral campaign abounded in bitterness, violence, and even assassinations. The violence of conflict was in no small measure due to the reduction of the seats in the legislature, which made the competition among the 116 candidates much more acute. In the midst of the campaign Jumblat accused the President of conspiring against his party's candidates as a result of pressure by concessionary companies, oil corporations, "Intelligence Service," and promoters of Middle East defense schemes. He also revealed a bribe offer by a representative of a foreign power if he would abstain from political activity, but he failed to substantiate his allegation.

The new parliament elected in July 1953 reflected some change in Lebanon's political scene, but the difference was not radical enough to warrant a statement that the locus of power had shifted sociologically. Of a total of forty-four deputies, twenty-three were members of the previous parliament, and the remaining twenty-one could not be regarded as representing new social strata. In a few cases traditional feudal holds on certain districts were broken, and the monopolies of certain leading families, such as the Asads in southern Lebanon, were successfully challenged by their adversaries. But there was no indication that the winners would espouse a social philosophy much different from that of their predecessors.

The political shift, if any, was indicative of the growing power of the new President, who, notwithstanding the regularity of electoral procedures, could appreciably influence the elections in keeping with the tradition of his office. The "forty families" continued to be amply represented in the new parliament, while the Progressive Socialist Party managed to secure, after a fierce struggle, just one seat—for its leader. Frustrated, Jumblat expressed his disappointment in a major parliamentary speech on October 1, 1953:

Since the events of September 1952, 3000 new officials have been appointed and an additional twelve million pounds spent. . . . The budget which one submits to us is almost entirely designed to support from nine to ten thousand officials. . . . It's not this way that one runs a State. . . . One could almost say that the State does not exist. Those in authority say that the financial situation is "healthy." The same was being said under the old regime. Well, there are many today who do not satisfy their hunger, industry is wobbly, and most of the taxpayers don't pay their taxes.

It is absurd to continue to import to an excess and to export nothing or almost nothing, as we do now. We cannot live indefinitely on invisible receipts, on the smuggling of gold and hashish. . . . What matters at this hour is to mete out justice to those who have betrayed the September revolution and the people.[13]

Cabinet changes were rarely due to deep policy divergencies. The trivial matter of who should represent Lebanon in Paris was sufficient to produce a crisis in the summer of 1955, resulting in the resignation of the foreign minister. On the other hand, attempts made by a few deputies to abolish the traditional system of sectarian representation made no headway whatever. The system was even vigorously defended by such prominent figures as Hamid Franjiyeh and Sami es-Solh. The balance between numerous denominations was precariously maintained, and under the outward surface of harmony strong undercurrents of hostility between Christians and Moslems were discernible. Moslems criticized a system in which Christians, on the basis of their alleged (and slight) numerical superiority, filled not only the highest office of the state but also a disproportionately large number of civil service positions. Consequently, they insisted on a general census which, they were confident, would prove their numerical preponderance over the Christians. Christians, on their part, did not enjoy debating these matters in public but, when compelled by circumstances, argued that they contributed 80 per cent of the tax revenue and that a census would be welcome provided it included the Lebanese living overseas. The latter argument was based on the important role these predominantly Christian emigrants continue to play in the life of the country. Whatever the faults of the religiously mixed ruling class, it seriously tried to calm and de-emphasize the exaggerated sectarian zeal of the rank and file. In line with this policy, the courts sentenced to prison terms two writers found guilty of inciting religious strife.[14]

[13] Quoted in *Cahiers*, 1953, 2.
[14] Mustafa Khalidi was sentenced for writing *Moslem Lebanon Today* and Georges Shakar for his *Révolution et Contrainte*. Both judgments were delivered in 1954.

Foreign Policy Problems in the 1950's

In matters of foreign policy no appreciable change occurred after the 1952 coup. Lebanon continued her basically pro-Western orientation by accepting American technical assistance, maintaining trade and cultural relations with Western countries, and serving as a home for many Western schools and missions, including a French and an American university. But this pro-Western orientation was tempered by the realization that the rest of the Arab world was in a sulky mood toward the West and that it favored neutralism. When the Baghdad Pact began to loom as a major problem in the Middle East in 1954–1955, Lebanon was exposed to many pressures and embarrassments. She would have welcomed the military and economic assistance from the West which would follow joining the pact. And she would not have minded obtaining reassurance from Iraq and other pact powers against possible absorption by Syria. But with the Arab League on record as strongly condemning the pact, Lebanon could not afford to estrange the League without incurring grave internal and external risks. A tourist and investment boycott by Saudi Arabia and Egypt might cause her serious losses. By the same token, the traditional though unwritten entente with Egypt was too precious to be gambled away. Consequently, Lebanon tried to steer a neutral course between Cairo and Baghdad, exchanging state visits with the leaders of both blocs but refusing to join either the Baghdad Pact or the new alliance promoted by Egypt and Saudi Arabia. In keeping with this spirit of caution President Shamoun emerged as a principal advocate of reconciliation among the Arab states. His intense diplomatic activity and his calls for the preservation of Arab unity were the more remarkable in view of the fact that his country was less Arab in character than others in the League. Yet this solicitude was understandable in the light of Lebanon's smallness and vulnerability.

Relations with Israel were officially hostile (as befitted a member of the Arab League), but they lacked the bellicosity which characterized relations between Israel and Egypt or Syria. When in 1955 some Israelis were ambushed in northern Palestine by Arab assailants presumably coming from Lebanon, Lebanese authorities promptly transferred an Arab refugee camp from the frontier area to the center of the country, at the same time adopting stern measures to prevent illegal crossing of boundaries. This action conformed with the position of Lebanon, which was militarily too weak to face

291

possible Israeli reprisals and yet too dependent on the good will of sister Arab nations to ignore their pressure for a strong stand against Israel should such a border incident develop into a major issue.

Although on this particular occasion Lebanon succeeded in extricating herself from an embarrassing situation, it was inevitable that she should be pressed to adopt a clear policy in the Palestinian conflict. Narrowed to its essentials, the question was whether Lebanon was ready to assume her share of responsibility in the military agreements being negotiated during 1955 among Israel's neighbors. The Israeli raid on Syria in mid-December 1955 (see p. 362) brought this matter from the realm of mere speculation to that of actual negotiation. By the close of 1955 Syria took definite steps to link Lebanon to herself militarily, with Egypt acting as the whip in this transaction. Lebanon could no longer postpone her decision. She might, true enough, refuse the offer by abandoning her position of neutrality in the inter-Arab conflict and by joining the Baghdad Pact. But unless she did so it was hard to see how she could avoid a military agreement with Syria (and indirectly with Egypt) without exposing herself to complete isolation in Arab affairs.

THE REPUBLIC OF SYRIA

Syria's politics after the war were full of violence and abrupt changes. More than three years after Syria's emancipation the power of government rested in the hands of the National Bloc leaders, Shukri el-Quwatli, Jamil Mardam Bey, Saadullah el-Jabri, and others, who had spent the greater part of their lives struggling for independence. Having won freedom for their country, this rather elderly generation proved to be ill-fitted for the postwar task of construction and reform. Critics maintained that the National Bloc leaders were interested only in reaping personal rewards for their victory and in perpetuating their rule. The first elections in independent Syria, in July 1947, were carried out with less corruption than in Lebanon. Yet they, too, elicited vigorous protests against government interference. In 1947 the progovernment majority passed a constitutional amendment allowing the re-election of the president for a second term. In April 1948 the Chamber availed itself of this right, re-electing Shukri el-Quwatli to the presidency of the republic.

Devoted to the principles of republicanism, the National Bloc leaders (whose political philosophy has been likened to that of late-eighteenth-century liberals) realized that their own position of power could not be divorced from Syria's sovereignty and separateness as a nation. They therefore opposed plans for the unification of the Arab world that would result in the submergence of Syria in a larger —and presumably monarchical—entity. In particular they opposed the Greater Syria scheme advocated by the Hashimite Kingdoms of Transjordan and Iraq and favored by King Abdullah of Transjordan, who made no secret of his ambition to rule the vast area comprising Syria proper, Lebanon, Iraq, Transjordan, and Palestine. King Abdullah, however, was not the only one who strongly favored this scheme. The Greater Syria plan was also advocated by Anton Saadeh's Syrian National Party, which drew its membership from the young radical elements of both republics. It was also backed by the Constitutionalist group of Aleppo men, which in 1948 assumed the name of People's Party, attracting considerable numbers of moderate politicians and extending its activities to all parts of Syria. These groups, however, did not favor Abdullah for their prospective king.

It is possible that the Quwatli regime might have continued in power for an indefinite period if it had not been for the problem of Palestine. The bungling of the Palestine war in 1948 by the Quwatli-Mardam Bey government resulted in discontent and general disaffection. It vividly exposed the regime's weaknesses, causing chaos and disorder, which, in December 1948, assumed the form of antigovernment riots verging on a spontaneous mob revolution. Prime Minister Jamil Mardam Bey was forced to resign. Law and order were eventually restored by the chief of staff of the army, Colonel Husni Zaim, who toured the country and, combining force with persuasion, succeeded in saving Syria from disintegration. The failure of the Syrian government in the Palestinian war strengthened the case of the pro-unionists, who claimed that greater unity among the Arabs and closer collaboration with Iraq and Transjordan might have averted military disaster. Faced with widespread criticism, the Quwatli group tried to shift the blame for the Palestinian failure to the army. This was the spark which set off a great explosion.

The Husni Zaim Coup

On March 30, 1949, Colonel Husni Zaim executed a bloodless *coup d'état*.[15] Placing President Quwatli and Prime Minister Khalid el-Azem under arrest, Zaim dissolved the parliament and assumed dicta-

---

[15] For an analysis of violent political changes in Syria, see Alford Carleton, "The Syrian Coups d'Etat of 1949," *Middle East Journal*, Jan. 1950.

torial powers. His coup expressed the reaction of the Syrian people against the ineptitude of the Quwatli regime. There was a widespread desire for change, and Zaim's action met with general approval, eliciting manifestations of joy and hopeful expectation. Zaim drew his main support from two discontented yet different groups. One was the army and the other the younger reformist circles desiring a radical change. The latter were drawn from such diverse camps as the Hama branch of Saadeh's National Syrian Party (pro-unionist, semi-Fascist, and believing in the leadership principle) and the People's Party (pro-unionist, moderately conservative but believing in democratic principles).

Supported by these groups, Zaim inaugurated a "New Order" based upon Turkish patterns. (He himself was reputed to be a great admirer of Kemal Atatürk.) His reforms included the extension of suffrage to literate women, the virtual separation of church and state, curbs on the clergy, the introduction of a civil code largely based upon European models, and the inauguration of extensive public works. Ideological and practical considerations pushed him toward the co-operation with Iraq and Jordan advocated by pro-unionists. There was also a compelling need to accept their military aid at the time of the armistice negotiations with Israel. Such aid was likely to strengthen Syria's position and guarantee her protection against the threat of an Israeli invasion. Furthermore, if Zaim's pledges of reform were not to remain an empty word, they had to be backed up by some quick steps toward economic recovery—and this was possible only with friendly foreign co-operation. Iraq and Jordan were Syria's two principal customers, accounting for over 60 per cent of her exports, principally grain. Therefore, expansion of trade with them would be a basic factor in Syria's economic recovery. Soon after he assumed power, Zaim entered into negotiations with the Hashimite states. A desire for rapid economic progress led him to resume talks with the Trans-Arabian Pipe Line Company, which, if allowed transit to its Mediterranean terminal in Sidon, would supply ready cash for the war-depleted Syrian treasury. It should be pointed out that negotiations with Tapline had been interrupted by the Quwatli government as a reprisal against United States support of Israel. Zaim was no more pro-Israeli than his predecessor, but in order to obtain both private and public aid from the United States he was willing to abandon Quwatli's stubborn and impractical resistance.

Zaim was anxious to secure formal diplomatic recognition of his regime. This quest for recognition, coupled with the desire for immediate economic help from abroad, led him to change his policy rather suddenly and turn toward Egypt and Saudi Arabia as partners and friends. Barely three weeks after the coup Zaim accepted an invitation from King Farouk to visit Cairo. Received with great cordiality in the capital of the weathiest of the Arab states, Zaim quickly secured Egyptian recognition and far-reaching promises of financial and military aid. Saudi Arabia promptly followed suit, Ibn Saud readily pledging substantial loans from his gold-filled treasury. In view of these facts, Lebanon did not delay recognition.

Zaim's diplomatic victory was bought at a price. The price was his renunciation of the Greater Syria schemes and his rejection of any closer political union with Iraq. Having to choose between the promise of slow economic recovery through political co-operation with the Hashimite kingdoms and quick political and financial benefits through Egyptian and Saudi Arabian aid, Zaim decided to choose the latter. Moreover, such a solution appealed to him on purely personal grounds. A Greater Syria scheme, if implemented, would put an end to Zaim's career as head of an independent state and would make him no more than a caretaker during the transitional phase. In Cairo his ambition was fanned, and he was encouraged to make his position permanent. In addition to Egyptian and Saudi Arabian blessing, he could be reasonably sure of American and French support. Although the American legation in Damascus maintained strict neutrality toward domestic Syrian developments, it was no secret that American policy gave high priority to cordial relations between the United States and Saudi Arabia on account of the American oil investments in the latter country. Ibn Saud stubbornly resisted the Greater Syria scheme which would increase the strength of his rivals, the Hashimites, and favored the *status quo* with Syria as an independent state. American policy, therefore, also favored the preservation of an independent Syria. Thus Zaim's newly revealed ambition to establish himself permanently did not run counter to American aims; in fact, the United States may have welcomed the beginning of a really reformist, antifeudal movement in Damascus. Zaim's energetic anti-Communist pronouncements added to his popularity with the State Department. As for France, she had traditionally resented the Greater Syria scheme, believing it to be British-inspired. Blaming Britain for her wartime political defeat in the Levant, France was ready to back any anti-British solution in Damascus. Although unable

to offer military and political support, France was still in a position
to offer financial aid to Zaim, a consideration he could not disregard.

This about-face in Zaim's foreign policy had immediate domestic
repercussions. Abandoning closer union with Iraq and Jordan, Zaim
had to part with the pro-unionist elements who had initially supported him and to rely more heavily upon the army. This policy
alienated from him large numbers of the aspiring younger generation
of Syrian politicians. Zaim's ban on all political parties in the summer
of 1949 and his failure to form a party of his own produced a dangerous political vacuum, testifying to his lack of skill in handling domestic politics.

Gradually the initial enthusiasm over his advent to power wore
off, and the people began to become aware of his mistakes. These
included some moves interpreted as pro-French and, as such, subject to severe criticism; certain measures toward self-aggrandizement,
such as the assumption of the title of marshal amid pompous ceremonies; his move into luxurious quarters; his assumption of the title
of head of the state following a dubious referendum; the extradition
to Lebanon of fugitive leader Anton Saadeh after the latter had
been granted the right of asylum (Saadeh was subsequently sentenced to death in Lebanon); and delay in economic reforms. It
was, however, his loss of the army's support which ultimately tipped
the scales against him. Zaim relied chiefly on Kurdish and Circassian
units, employing them in the interior while leaving the purely Arab
formations on the Palestinian border. This produced resentment and
resulted in an anti-Zaim conspiracy.

The Hinnawi and the Shishakli Coups

On August 14, 1949, Zaim and his prime minister, Muhsin el-
Barazi, were captured and summarily executed in a coup engineered
by Colonel Sami Hinnawi. In a statement released shortly afterward,
Hinnawi declared that this action had been taken by the army in
fulfillment of the aims of the first coup, which had been betrayed by
Zaim and his government. Hinnawi then asked former President of
the Republic Hashim Bey Atassi to form a civilian caretaker government pending the formation of a Constituent Assembly. The task
of the Assembly was to adopt a new constitution in place of the one
which had been suspended by Zaim. Although the Hinnawi coup
was the work of the army alone, it gave a new chance to the People's

Party. Frustrated by Zaim, it now came into prominence. In the November 1949 elections to the Constituent Assembly (in which women were permitted to vote for the first time), the People's Party secured 42 of the total of 114 seats, becoming the largest single party in the Assembly. Its leader, Rushdi el-Kikhya, was elected president of the Assembly. Quwatli's National Bloc Party boycotted the elections. Hashim el-Atassi was made temporary president of the republic.

Reversing Zaim's policy of friendship with Egypt and Saudi Arabia, Colonel Hinnawi reopened negotiations with Iraq and Jordan for a closer political union. In this he was supported by the People's Party, which consistently favored the Greater Syria scheme. When the Assembly met for the first time on December 12, it gave the problem of union with Iraq high priority as a basic constitutional question. The leading clique in the army did not, however, favor this solution. To forestall a move for the union of Syria and Iraq, the army, led by Lieutenant-Colonel Adib el-Shishakli, deposed Hinnawi in the third coup of the year. In the name of the army, Shishakli proclaimed his opposition to the Greater Syria scheme but disavowed any intention of ruling the country himself. Despite these assurances the army watched political developments very carefully, however, and it intervened actively each time the government appeared about to take an action of which it did not approve. Thus, shortly after Shishakli's coup, in late December 1949, the army vetoed the appointment of Nazem el-Qudsi, deputy leader of the People's Party, to the office of prime minister. Instead, President Hashim el-Atassi was obliged to ask Khalid el-Azem, an independent, to form a cabinet. In Azem's cabinet, the People's Party lost all three of the key portfolios of Foreign Affairs, Defense, and Interior, which were given to men whom the army trusted.

The army's chief civilian spokesman in the succeeding cabinets was Akram Hourani, head of the Department of Defense. Hourani attempted to counter the influence of the People's Party by founding a new group named the Arab Socialist Party and by organizing a forty-five-man Republican Bloc in the Assembly.

The new regime's policy toward the big powers tended to be neutral and almost isolationist. It was certainly not pro-French.[16]

---

[16] Syria definitely broke her economic ties with France. On January 31, 1948, she left the "franc bloc," thus differing from Lebanon, which reached an agreement with France on this issue. In February 1949 France and Syria signed a

Nor was it pro-British, if we realize Britain's interest in the achievement of the Greater Syria scheme. Indirectly, it suited the United States, inasmuch as the Shishakli-Azem government renewed friendly ties with Egypt and Saudi Arabia. (Ibn Saud went so far as to grant Syria a substantial loan in January 1950 in an apparent effort to bolster up its anti-Hashimite regime.) But the cordial relations with the United States which characterized the Zaim regime were definitely abandoned. Instead, Syria followed a tortuous path, vacillating between negotiation concerning limited technical assistance and loud denunciations of Washington because of its pro-Israeli policy. In Syria, as in other Arab countries, there was a feeling of frustration and disenchantment regarding America. This caused some prominent members of El-Azem's government to declare themselves publicly in favor of pro-Soviet policy. The recurrent theme of these statements was that the Arabs would rather become "Sovietized" than "Judaized" and that it was proper to collaborate with the Soviet Union as "an enemy of our enemy," i.e., of the United States, in the same way that the Arabs had collaborated with Nazi Germany as the enemy of Britain.[17]

As early as February 1950 Khalid el-Azem made it clear that Syria would not seek an American loan and that she proposed to "go it alone" in her development schemes. To the best of their ability, Syrian authorities obstructed American-sponsored United Nations aid to Palestine Arab refugees and adopted a hostile attitude toward the Clapp mission. The United States legation's protests against the anti-American tenor of Syrian editorials in 1950 provoked an even stronger press campaign against what was termed American interference with the freedom of the press. Repeated pronouncements of American public figures about Israel as the "principal stronghold of democracy and American ideology"[18] in the Middle East had the effect of keeping Syrian anger alive. Incidents such as the tearing

---

monetary agreement providing for the latter's final separation from the franc bloc and repayment by France of the Syrian currency cover.

[17] Statements to this effect were made in the spring of 1950 by three members of Khalid el-Azem's cabinet: Maaruf Dawalibi, minister of national economy (in April); Mustafa Sebai, Moslem Brotherhood leader and minister of education (April 29); and Akram Hourani, minister of defense (May 22). Dawalibi opened negotiations for an extensive trade agreement with Russia but subsequently was dropped from the cabinet.

[18] These were the words used by Vice-President Alben W. Barkley, in a speech made on May 26, 1951, in Chicago.

down of the American flag and the exploding of a bomb in the garden of the United States legation, as well as official plans for a discriminatory tax rate upon American goods, testified to the depth of Syrian hostility. Syrian newspapers vigorously attacked President Truman's message of May 24, 1951, promising aid to the Middle East on the ground that it placed Israel on the same level with the Arab states. Syrian journalists boycotted a press reception organized soon afterward by the United States Information Services. On June 7, 1951, Prime Minister Khalid el-Azem publicly rejected American technical aid under the Point Four program.

So far, however, Syria's bitterness toward the United States has not resulted in an understanding with Russia. Syria's reply to the United Nations' appeal for aid to the republic of Korea was to declare her support of all resolutions aimed against aggression, thus both approving the action taken in Korea and implicitly registering regret that different standards were applied in Palestine.[19]

Shishakli's Dictatorship

Adib Shishakli's rule lasted a little over four years. Between December 1949 and December 1951 the colonel allowed a civilian government to function, contenting himself with the role of power behind the scenes; between December 1951 and February 1954 he exercised direct rule.

The first phase was characterized by an uneasy co-operation between the People's Party—the dominant group in Syria's politics after President Quwatli's overthrow in 1949—and the army. Cabinets created during those two years usually represented coalitions of Populists, Independents, and certain other elements, with the premiership being rotated between Independents and Populists. Work on the constitution, suddenly interrupted by the coup of December 1949, was resumed, and the constitution was adopted in September 1950.[20] It contained strong Pan-Arab accents, but made no explicit references to union with Iraq. The co-operation between Shishakli and the Populists was severely tested early in November 1951 by the differences that arose with regard to Syria's attitude toward Middle East defense plans and certain internal

[19] This declaration was made on July 8, 1950. For details concerning the attitude of Arab states during the Korean crisis, see *Middle Eastern Affairs*, Aug.–Sept. 1950, pp. 247 ff.

[20] See Majid Khadduri, "Constitutional Development in Syria," *Middle East Journal*, Spring, 1951.

jurisdictional questions. Behind these divergencies was the basic question of Syria's possible union with Iraq, a matter which was far from buried. The only element capable of keeping peace between Shishakli and his civilian opponents was Syria's president, venerable Hashim el-Atassi. A civilian and a strong believer in constitutional government, he leaned toward the Populists, thus frustrating Shishakli's designs and putting a brake on his influence.

Unable to co-operate with Shishakli, Premier Hassan Hakim (an Independent of pro-Western tendencies) resigned on November 10, 1951. The prolonged cabinet crisis that ensued was resolved only eighteen days later, when a Populist known for his anti-Zionist and pro-Soviet utterances, Maaruf Dawalibi, formed a cabinet basically unchanged; i.e., it was composed of Populists and Independents. Obviously discontented with the prolonged Populist hold on cabinet offices, Shishakli decided to end the pretense of noninterference and on the night of November 28–29 executed a new coup in the course of which he placed under arrest the prime minister, his cabinet members, and certain other leaders. In the declarations that followed, Shishakli delivered a scathing attack on the Populists, accusing them of "destructive work" and of trying to achieve a federation which would restore "the throne" and destroy Syrian independence. He also declared that the immediate cause of the coup was the Populist determination to appoint a civilian to the Ministry of Defense and detach the gendarmerie from the army. On December 2 Shishakli dissolved the Chamber. On the same day President Atassi resigned, leaving the door open for Shishakli to assume the highest office himself. The latter decided, however, to remain in his position as chief of staff, while entrusting his associate, Colonel Fawzi Salu (later promoted to general) with the functions of "chief of state," prime minister, and minister of defense.

The coup ushered in the second phase of Shishakli's rule, a phase of undisguised dictatorship. During this period a number of typically dictatorial measures were applied, such as the banning of political parties and of the Moslem Brotherhood; the launching of the "Arab Liberation Movement," designed to substitute for the old parties "patriotic" work for the state and the "Arab nation" (August 1952); "consolidation" of the press, i.e., forcible reduction in the number of papers; glorification of the army; a ban on the political activities of civil servants; the removal of tenure and the dismissal of a number of university professors; [21] and a ban on student strikes and unauthorized demonstrations. Decree 151 of March 3, 1952, made it mandatory for any foreign company operating in Syria to be represented in the country by a Syrian citizen or a Syrian company. Another decree forbade direct communications between Syrians (including the Syrian University, the Arab Academy, and the Directorate of Antiquities) and foreign cultural institutions. Decree 189 forbade the acquisition of real estate by foreigners, while still another regulation imposed a number of restrictions on the admission of foreigners to Syria. Not all of these measures, however, were of a repressive type. Among the more positive ones could be mentioned a decree of October 23, 1952, on agrarian reform, which provided for the distribution of domanial estates, and a decree abolishing honorary titles and titles of nobility.

Following the rather well-worn patterns of military dictatorships Shishakli emphasized order, security, and patriotism. The first anniversary of his second coup was celebrated with military parades and oratory. In a speech Shishakli called Damascus the "capital of present Arabism and the heart of the Arab nation, where rests Saladin, hero-liberator of Palestine." His servile press spoke of Syria as a "giant in an armor of steel and iron" [22] and recalled Omayyad conquests. But references to the "Arab nation" were no more than lip service to the popular cause of Pan-Arabism, for in reality the dictator and his clique clung tenaciously to the separateness of Syria as the only solution apt to guarantee the preservation of their high positions and honors. Repeated emphasis on discipline and "Arabism" could not conceal the growing political isolation of Shishakli and his army friends. Barely a year after the second coup the government announced the discovery of a plot among some "subaltern officers," who, it claimed, as former members of certain political parties, had succumbed to subversive ideas. Actually, higher ranks were involved as well, and on December 30, 1952, a number of colonels and majors were cashiered.[23] These army dismissals were

[21] This measure was applied to such prominent professors and former members of parliament as Munir Ajlani, Abdul Wahab Haumad, and Rizkallah Antaki, as well as to Mustafa Sibai, professor of sacred law and leader of the Moslem Brotherhood.

[22] Al-Yawm, Dec. 5, 1952.

[23] The list included the names of Col. Mustafa Safa (reputedly of Populist tendencies) and Lt. Col. Adnan Malki (with Socialist connections).

301

soon followed by the escape abroad of several of the principal Socialist leaders: Akram Hourani, Michel Aflaq, and Salah el-Bitar, all three accused of conspiracy against the regime. Hourani's escape was noteworthy because earlier he had not been opposed to collaboration with Shishakli.

Despite this growing political estrangement Shishakli made several moves toward the formal legalization of his regime. Late in June 1953 he published a constitutional draft and followed it promptly on July 10 by a plebiscite, which resulted in overwhelming approval of the constitution and the election of himself (the only candidate) to the presidency of the Republic. The new constitution established a presidential system (in contrast to the parliamentary one existing until then) which markedly increased the power of the chief executive.

In the meantime, however, the opposition was gaining ground. A "national congress" of former political parties which met in Homs on July 4 called the regime "tyrannical." The Moslem Brotherhood and the ulema of Damascus, Aleppo, and Hama also raised their voices in protest against the new constitution. Despite these warnings Shishakli went ahead with his plans. On July 30 a newly passed electoral law decreased the number of seats from 108 to 82 (a device often used by power-seeking rulers to obtain greater influence upon fewer deputies), and on September 12 a presidential decree allowed the formation of political parties—with strings attached. In the subsequent electoral campaign only two parties presented candidates: Shishakli's own Liberation Movement and the Syrian National-Social Party.[24] As could be expected, the elections resulted in a victory for Shishakli's Movement, with one deputy being elected on behalf of the S.N.S.P. and a number of deputies remaining independent.

On October 24 the newly elected parliament met and chose Maamun Kuzbari as speaker. Simultaneously Shishakli made gestures of reconciliation toward the opposition: between July and October he released some politicians (such as Dawalibi) from prison and guaranteed safe return to the exiled Socialist leaders. This was accompanied by another measure designed to win popular applause and whip up nationalist feelings: on October 8, 1953, a

[24] Known also, especially in Lebanon, as P.P.S. (*Parti Populaire Syrien*), a party founded by the late Anton Saadeh. It is not to be confused with the People's (or Populist) Party.

new press decree forbade newspapers to accept advertisements from foreign companies and institutions without prior official authorization. Yet even this popularity seeking was not of much avail. In December a wave of student demonstrations and lawyer strikes profoundly rocked the country as it spread from Aleppo to other centers. In January 1954 Shishakli had to resort to repression once again: he placed under arrest eleven leaders of the old regime, including former President Hashim el-Atassi, and followed this with a proclamation of martial law in several provinces. To add to his difficulties, two hundred Druze chiefs, meeting in the security of Lebanese territory, passed resolutions against the regime. A few days later a leading Druze, Sultan Pasha el-Atrash, fled from Suwaida to Jordan.

Ultimately it was the army that decided Shishakli's fate. On February 25 troops under Colonel Mustafa Hamdun mutinied in Aleppo, and the rebellion soon spread to other cities. Seeing the futility of resistance, Shishakli resigned and immediately left Syria, first for Lebanon and later for Saudi Arabia and France. After a brief interim period during which Speaker Maamun Kuzbari assumed the duties of the presidency, the old president, Hashim el-Atassi, was reinstated. On March 1 a new cabinet came into being. Although headed by a Nationalist prime minister (Sabri el-Assali), it was dominated by the Populists, who reserved for themselves the key ministries of defense (Maaruf Dawalibi), foreign affairs (Faidi el-Atassi), and interior (Ali Buzu, secretary general of the party). Simultaneously the last legally elected speaker, Nazem el-Qudsi, convoked the pre-Shishakli parliament, which had been dissolved in December 1951. Not invited to attend were those deputies who had served in Shishakli's parliament. The new regime promptly reestablished the constitution of September 1950 and reinstated the army officers who had been dismissed by the dictator between 1951 and 1954.

Return to Constitutional Life

With the passing of the dictator Syria resumed her constitutional life, and the assumption of power by the Populist-led coalition reflected rather accurately the actual political configuration in the country. A complete return to the conditions antedating the period of dictatorship was unthinkable. The National Party, which had dominated Syrian politics before Zaim's coup, lost too much of its popularity as a result of the "bungling" of the Palestinian War to gain full reinstatement. The Nationalists' loss was the Populists' gain, and, had it not been for army intervention between 1949 and 1954, the Populists would have assumed control of Syria and, perhaps, brought about a union with Iraq.

It would be unwise, however, to write off army intervention as a mere accident stemming from the ambitions of restless officers. The undeniable fact is that the dictators enjoyed initial success and that this was due to a favorable response by the people. The traditional parties, whether the National or the Populist, did not suffice as channels of expression for those elements in Syrian society which chafed under existing economic and social inequalities. They sought to find a satisfactory solution either by supporting the dictators or by joining the more radical groups, whether leftist or rightist. This explains why, even under the repressive conditions of Shishakli's regime, such groups as the Moslem Brotherhood, the Arab Socialist Renaissance Party,[25] the Syrian National-Social Party, and the Communists gained considerable ground. The restitution of the constitution lifted the lid on the activities of these groups, and their true strength was revealed.

This strength was tested in September 1954 at the time of the first postdictatorship elections. The elections were preceded by the formation in June of a "neutral" cabinet under Said Ghazzi, an Independent, chosen to assure impartiality. Prior to disbanding parliament adopted a new electoral law raising the number of seats to 142. This measure helped to register more accurately the moods prevailing in the country. The results of the balloting were as follows: Independents 64; Populists 34; Nationalists 12; Socialists 16; S.N.S.P. 2; National Liberation Movement 2; Socialist Co-operative Party 2; Tribes 9; Communists 1. Of the organized parties, the Populists scored the greatest success, but they did not gain a stable majority in the new legislature. The Socialists' sixteen members was a spectacular achievement in view of their newness and their negligible representation in the past. Damascus proved to be quite a mixed city politically, with no single group able to claim ascendancy.

[25] This party was a result of the fusion of Akram Hourani's Socialist Party and Michel Aflaq's Arab Renaissance Party. The new organization inherited from the latter its Pan-Arabism, spreading from Syria into Jordan, Iraq (where it met with reprisals), and Lebanon (where it was purely nominal and generally unknown to the public, due to the rallying of Socialist elements around the person of Kamal Jumblat).

Socialists were strong in Hama, Akram Hourani's native town; and Populists asserted themselves in their traditional strongholds of Aleppo, Homs, and the Jezira province. A Populist, Nazem el-Qudsi, was re-elected speaker, and, inasmuch as the elections had confirmed the Populists' lead, a cabinet largely staffed by Populists was formed in October, with Independent Faris el-Khuri as prime minister.

Intermingling of Foreign and Domestic Problems

The Populists' hold on the government was soon exposed to a severe strain by the Baghdad Pact. Though originally designed to group the Northern Tier states (see pp. 260–265), this pact was never intended to be exclusive, and both Iraq and Turkey attempted to draw into it other Arab states. The presence of the Populists at the helm in Syria seemed to favor their hopes. With a few exceptions the Populists were not averse to collaboration with the West. They had, moreover, a traditionally friendly attitude toward both Iraq and Turkey. The removal of Shishakli—whom Iraq had refused to recognize until late in 1952—seemed to have eliminated a major bloc barring a closer entente between Syria and her pro-Western neighbors. Nevertheless, the Populists proceeded cautiously, mindful of the hazards that lay ahead. The experience of being overthrown twice within four years for desiring union with Iraq could not be ignored. Neither could the general mood of the populace, hostile as it was to any dealings with the West. The masses, as is often the case, were motivated more by emotion than by reason. Hence no matter how beneficial a link with the West might be, popular opinion was decidedly against it. It would be easy for any demagogue—and these were not lacking—to whip up a cry against "imperialism" threatening Syria by extension of the Hashimite rule of Iraq, against the Turks (have not they snatched Alexandretta from the Syrians?), or against the West in general on account of its responsibility in setting up the state of Israel. By contrast, Egypt's support of the Arab League evoked sympathetic response, and the League, despite its failure in the Palestinian War, was still regarded as the best hope for Arab unity and strength. To advocate action ignoring these feelings was, to say the least, a risky undertaking. This explains why the Populist ministers behaved noncommittally at the December 1954 conference of the Arab League, when collaboration with the West was made subject to rather exacting conditions. This also explains why Prime Minister Faris el-Khuri and Foreign Minister Faidi el-Atassi refused, at the subsequent conference of Arab premiers, to take a clear stand for or against Iraq.

A few days earlier Turkish Premier Adnan Menderes had stopped for a few hours in Damascus on his return trip from Baghdad. But even this brief visit embarrassed the Populists and prompted self-defensive explanations. In a public statement Faidi el-Atassi argued that there was nothing wrong in trying to improve relations with Turkey. "If one has an enemy such as Israel, one prefers to have one enemy only," he declared. On his part, discussing the projected Baghdad Pact, Faris el-Khuri defended its political legitimacy by saying: "Besides, the intended pact is directed against the state of Israel." [26]

These cautious remarks were not sufficient to avert popular wrath. The Populists' refusal to take a clear stand against Iraq brought about a government crisis which resulted in their elimination from power. The crisis was precipitated by the resignation from the cabinet of two Nationalist ministers. On February 12, Sabri el-Assali formed a new cabinet composed of Nationalists, Democratic Bloc members,[27] one Socialist, and one member of the Liberation Movement. Khalid el-Azem, leader of the Democratic Bloc, took charge of foreign affairs. The change thus accomplished was equivalent to a radical reorientation of Syria's policy, particularly in foreign affairs. In order to secure a workable majority in the Chamber the Nationalists, a minority group of barely twelve deputies, had to ally themselves with their erstwhile enemies, the Socialists, and with certain other elements with whom they had relatively little in common. Opposition to the Baghdad Pact provided the only real unifying link among these heterogeneous elements. It was claimed that Saudi Arabian and Egyptian influence was largely responsible for the formation of this coalition.

Shortly after the formation of his cabinet Sabri el-Assali made a policy statement in which he declared:

Our government follows in its foreign policy the recommendation adopted at the conference of Arab ministers of foreign affairs which was held in Cairo last December, namely, that the policy of Arab states is

[26] *Cahiers*, 1955, 1.
[27] The Democratic Bloc accounted for some nineteen deputies originally elected as Independents.

based on the [Arab] pact of defense and economic co-operation.[28] It views, however, with reserve, the recommendation enjoining collaboration with Western powers subject to specific conditions. . . . Our government agrees with the recommendation of the conference of chiefs of Arab governments which was recently held in Cairo, the recommendation which enjoins us not to accept alliances and not to adhere to the Turkish-Iraqi Pact.[29]

Syria's opposition to the Baghdad Pact was thus clear. In the dramatic contest between the pro-Iraqi and pro-Egyptian forces, the latter have carried the field for the third time in the last five years.[30] But how far would the new government go in espousing the Egyptian policy? Pressures and inducements from the Cairo-Riyadh axis began to mount steadily. Syria was urged to sign a tripartite treaty which would link herself, Egypt, and Saudi Arabia in defense and economic co-operation. She was also wooed by Saudi Arabia with the promise of a loan.

Although personal convictions—and tangible interests—led some members of the Assali cabinet to advocate a complete alignment with Cairo and Riyadh, the cabinet as a whole hesitated to commit itself to a policy fraught with many dangers. These dangers were both internal and external. Internally, the position of the Populists, still strong, especially in the north, could not be disregarded. As soon as they were pushed into opposition, the Populists began to claim that Assali's cabinet managed to survive only at the price of major concessions to the leftist elements. Rather than see Syria go Communist the Populists might separate the north from the rest of the country. The suggestion was also advanced that a "Free Syrian Government" might be created somewhere on the territory of Iraq and, to save Syria from communism, might invite the Iraqi army to intervene. Such a procedure would involve a possible external danger to the sovereignty and territorial integrity of Syria. It might be noted here that Turkey did not hide her disappointment over the turn of events in Damascus. A series of notes and speeches accusing Syria of anti-Turkish policy were delivered by the Turks, while border incidents began to multiply. Some relief was felt in Damascus when Molotov, in late March, reassured the Syrian envoy

[28] For details of the pact, see p. 512.   [29] *Cahiers*, 1955, 1.

[30] Zaim's about-face after his visit to Cairo was the first Egyptian victory, and Shishakli's coup of 1949, the second.

that Russia "would not stand with crossed arms" if Turkey resorted to force in her dealings with Syria. But this was not adequate compensation for the feeling of growing isolation from immediate neighbors: Turkey, Iraq, Jordan, Israel, and Lebanon.

All these fears explain why Syria, despite overt protestations of loyalty to the Egyptian-led Arab League and a verbal promise to conclude a pact with Cairo and Riyadh, was delaying her signature in obvious procrastination.

In the spring of 1955 the depth of Syria's political division became obvious in connection with dramatic developments in the army. On April 22 Lieutenant-Colonel Adnan Malki, chief of the Third Bureau of the Syrian army staff, was assassinated by a sergeant who happened to be a member of the Syrian National-Social Party. What followed could be called a mass persecution of the S.N.S.P. Army officers with links to the party were purged, the immunity of its deputy to parliament was lifted, and a trial involving charges of treason and conspiracy was instituted. The proceedings were definitely political despite the outward forms of legality observed by the authorities. One of the official statements called Malki's assassination "the first act of a plot to suppress the Chief-of-Staff and the officers hostile to certain foreign projects." By "foreign projects" were meant both the Baghdad Pact and the Syro-Iraqi federation.

The purge and trial of the S.N.S.P. revealed a number of interesting—and disquieting—aspects of the Syrian situation. These could be listed as follows: (1) Despite Shishakli's eclipse, the army had regained its influence on Syria's government and had again become an important factor in the country's politics. (2) Aware of this, various political parties were trying to infiltrate the military establishment. (3) The two groups which were competing most vigorously for the officers' loyalties were the Arab Socialist Renaissance (Baath) Party and the S.N.S.P. (4) The ideological struggle between these two parties could be summed up as a contest between, on the one hand, leftist, pro-Egyptian, and partly pro-Soviet orientation and, on the other, rightist, pro-Western, and profederation tendencies. (5) Colonel Malki was a foremost leader of the Socialist wing in the army. (6) The legal proceedings notwithstanding, it was doubtful whether Malki's assassination was an act of premeditated conspiracy. Certain evidence pointed to personal motives, and the connection of the assassin with S.N.S.P. might have been purely coincidental. Yet the removal of Malki from the scene was undoubtedly a major blow to Socialist influence in the army. (7) Because Assali's Nationalist government had made common cause (at least tactically) with the Socialists, it tried to exploit to the maximum the indignation caused by the murder of a popular and youthful officer and to capitalize upon the frenzy of nationalism which this act evoked. (8) The purge and prosecution of S.N.S.P. thus served two purposes: to stop a dangerous political rival from influencing the army and to gain acclaim by making the pro-Western S.N.S.P. a scapegoat of popular wrath. (9) Indirectly, the prosecution was an attempt on the part of the Nationalists and Socialists to discredit anybody who dared to advocate closer links with the West or with Turkey and Iraq. This implied a warning to their most formidable rivals, the Populists. (10) The proceedings against S.N.S.P. revealed another recurring aspect of Syrian politics, namely, the readiness of the ostensibly democratic government to subordinate law to its political interests. Premier Assali wanted to introduce martial law in the country, which would have permitted him to set up special tribunals designed to apply swift procedures. This proposal was vetoed by President Atassi and it met with significant opposition within the cabinet. Consequently, when the matter was put up to the parliament, the premier managed only to secure some modification of penal procedures.

To sum up, by the early summer of 1955 it seemed that the Nationalist-Socialist coalition could maintain itself in power only by constantly whipping up popular resentments against real or imaginary foreign dangers. It was a fairly dangerous situation in which the Nationalists believed that they could hold power without conceding on essential points to the Socialists, while the latter treated the Nationalists as a convenient front and a vehicle to be used to spread their influence and secure a firmer foothold in the army. Sooner or later both partners would have to face a showdown because of the incompatibility of their objectives. The summer months brought the expected crisis and the occasion for it was supplied by the presidential elections.

President Atassi's five-year term was due to expire on September 5, 1955, and it soon became known that former President Shukri el-Quwatli (an old-time Nationalist, then resident in Egypt), Foreign Minister Khalid el-Azem, and one of the Populist leaders would contest for the vacancy. The Nationalists were ready, naturally

309

enough, to campaign for Quwatli (the "campaigning" meaning political persuasion of the deputies in parliament, who elect the
president). But at the outset the Socialists announced their opposition to Quwatli, a man too symbolical of the "ancien regime" to
be palatable to the radically minded youths flocking to Socialist
standards. It was, therefore, on the issue of the presidency that
the Nationalist and the Socialist roads parted. The Socialists decided
to throw their support to Khalid el-Azem, who also enjoyed the
friendship of Egypt and Saudi Arabia—not altogether a negligible
factor. Under the circumstances there was no hope of reconstituting
the coalition, and no single candidate could be sure of a majority
in the chamber. The only solution was a possible withdrawal of one
of the candidates, and this was, indeed, what happened. In a rather
bold maneuver the Populists decided at the last minute not to present a candidate of their own; instead they threw their support to
Quwatli. As a result, on August 18 the latter was elected to the
presidency by ninety-one votes. Forty-one deputies voted for Khalid
el-Azem, who, upon learning of his defeat, promptly resigned his
cabinet position.

Despite minor demonstrations by some young army officers
against the president-elect, Quwatli was installed without obstruc-
tion. As he owed his election to the solid bloc of the Populists and
their Independent allies, Quwatli was politically indebted to both,
a debt exceeding his obligation to the rather small number of
Nationalists. On September 13 he asked Said Ghazzi, a former premier, to form a cabinet. In the new government the Populists regained their former pre-eminence, with their party secretary, Ali
Buzu, again becoming minister of the interior. Some posts were
given to Independents. The Nationalists remained outside the cabinet and soon declared themselves in opposition.

Thus the presidential elections resulted in a political configuration
similar to that prevailing after Shishakli's demise. This time, however, the Populists were wiser: they had learned the inflammable
nature of the issue of "foreign pacts." In order to continue in office,
they would have to tread very cautiously on the slippery ground of
inter-Arab relations and, in all probability, disguise some of their
true feelings by catering to the masses. On the other hand, Quwatli's
moderate friendship with the Egyptians could not be overlooked
either. No surprise was registered, therefore, when, on October 20,
1955, the new government acceded to the Egyptian demand to

sign a mutual defense pact,[31] but the pact did not include Saudi
Arabia as a third partner. The official Syrian formula was to promote "bilaterality" and to shun exclusive multilateral agreements
such as that initially suggested by Egypt. This formula left the door
open for economic negotiations with Saudi Arabia or, if need be,
a military pact with Iraq. Thus the Syrian government responded
to the popular demand for a closer military link with Egypt without
burning the bridges of understanding with Iraq. The Populists sincerely hoped that this formula would work and consequently did
not hesitate to conclude, on November 9, 1955, an economic pact
with Saudi Arabia, whereby the latter granted Syria the long-
expected $10,000,000 loan.[32]

When it came to the next step which would have balanced the
Syrian position—the conclusion of a pact with Iraq—difficulties
arose. A combination of latent factors and an immediate cause contributed to the problem. The immediate cause was an Israeli attack,
on December 11, 1955, on the Syrian outposts east of Lake Tiberias.
Fifty-six Syrian lives were lost. Syria's complaint to the U.N. Security Council and her demand that Israel be expelled from the United
Nations, important as it was, was overshadowed by the emotional
wave which flooded the country. The pent-up resentments against
Zionism and imperialism found new expression in the mass demonstrations that accompanied the burials of victims of Israeli aggression. Under those circumstances, to suggest rapprochement with
pro-Western Iraq was too dangerous for anyone with political aspirations in Syria. A move of this sort would have to wait until
"the dust settled," and early in 1956 there was little indication that
the dust would settle in the near future.

[31] The text is in the *Middle East Journal,* Winter, 1956.
[32] The text is in the *Bulletin de la Presse Syrienne,* no. 770, 1955.

CHAPTER IX

Israel

THE hope of one day returning to the Promised Land has never died among the Jews. Religious Zionism has been cultivated in various centers of the Diaspora (Dispersion) throughout history, and in the nineteenth century a number of Jews came to Palestine to settle in Jerusalem, Safed, and Tiberias. Many of these were the so-called *Halukah* (charity) Jews, supported by funds from abroad. This yearning to return to Zion was especially strong among the Russian and east European Jews, who suffered manifold disabilities and frequent persecutions. The intensification of anti-Semitism in Russia in the last two decades of the nineteenth century gave rise to the creation, in Odessa, of the organization *Hovevei Zion*[1] and the establishment in 1882 of the first Zionist colonies in Palestine. These were Rishon le Zion in Judea, Zichron Jacob in Samaria, and Rosh Pina in Galilee. In the 1880's other settlements followed. They were peopled mostly by Jews from Russia, Rumania, Galicia, and Lithuania. Wealthy Jewish financiers in the West, such as Baron Edmond de Rothschild, contributed generously to aid the pioneers. A Jewish Colonization Association (ICA), founded by Baron Maurice de Hirsch, undertook the task of buying land in Palestine and provided the settlers with necessary implements and capital.

THE ZIONIST MOVEMENT

In 1896 Dr. Theodor Herzl, a native of Budapest and Paris correspondent of the *Neue Freie Presse* of Vienna, gave Zionism a defi-

[1] With Leon Pinsker and Asher Ginsberg (Ahad Ha'am) as leaders. At the same time Eliezer Ben Yehuda preached the revival of the Hebrew tongue.

nitely political turn. At the age of thirty-six he wrote in his book *Judenstaat* ("The Jewish State") as follows: "Our national character is too historically famous and in spite of every degradation, too fine to make its annihilation desirable." "The distinctive nationality of the Jews neither can, will, nor must be destroyed." "The Jewish question . . . is a national question which can be solved only by making it a political world-question to be discussed and settled by the civilized nations of the world in council." [2]

In 1897 Herzl founded *Die Welt,* a weekly, which became an official mouthpiece for Zionism. In the same year, on his initiative, the first Zionist Congress assembled at Basle, Switzerland. The Congress adopted a resolution favoring "a home in Palestine" for the Jewish people and created the World Zionist Organization, which elected Herzl to its presidency. From that time on Herzl strove to obtain from the Ottoman government permission to create a Jewish charter company for the settlement of Palestine. Inasmuch as this was the period of German-Turkish friendship, he appealed to Kaiser William II to aid him in this quest and suggested that such a company be formed under a German protectorate.

In 1903 mass pogroms of the Jews occurred in Kishinev and Gomel in Russia; these rendered the Jewish question more acute than ever. Herzl negotiated with the British government and obtained from it the offer of Uganda as a territory for settlement. But this offer was rejected in 1904 by the Russian Zionist majority of the Seventh Congress of the World Zionist Organization. The Congress refused to consider any alternatives to Palestine.

In 1904 Herzl died, but Zionism continued to attract ever larger numbers of adherents. It soon grew into a powerful movement, ably financed by the Jewish National Fund (*Keren Kayemeth*), which was organized to acquire land in Palestine, and by the Palestine Foundation Fund (*Keren Hayesod*). It developed leftist (*Poale Zion*), rightist (*Mizrahi*), and center (General Zionists) political factions, and soon spread throughout the Western Hemisphere. In the United States the Zionist Organization recruited members largely among eastern European Jews, who at that time, because of Russian persecutions, were coming to America in large numbers. Other Jewish communities in the United States—the Sephardi (Spanish) and the German, which were more prosperous and better assimilated—were

[2] Theodor Herzl, *The Jewish State* (New York, Scopus Publishing Co., 1943), pp. 38, 24, 20.

either indifferent or hostile to Zionism. Yet even among them Zionism found converts.

Zionism was and is a national movement, and as such it has encountered opposition among the Jews themselves. This opposition has been dictated by several considerations. Ultra-Orthodox Jews objected to the political aspects of the movement, believing that the return to Zion must be brought about by divine intervention and not by temporal agencies. Such views were cultivated by *Agudath Israel*.

The Socialists (and later the Communists) considered Zionism as a reactionary bourgeois movement. The rabbis of the reformed synagogues and their adherents opposed Zionism on the basis of its nationalist character. Believing that Judaism denotes religion and not nationality, they represented assimilationist tendencies. In Great Britain two Jewish organizations, the Board of Deputies of British Jews [3] and the Anglo-Jewish Association, opposed Zionism on this ground. Their opposition grew more vocal during World War I, when it became known that Dr. Chaim Weizmann was trying to secure an official British declaration in favor of Zionism. On May 24, 1917, Montefiore and Alexander, presidents, respectively, of the Anglo-Jewish Association and of the Board of Deputies, published an open protest against the Zionist program in *The Times*. In it they stated that political Zionism was incompatible with the religious basis of Jewry and that it introduced the concept of

a secular Jewish nationality, recruited on some loose and obscure principle of race and of ethnographic peculiarity. But this would not be Jewish in any spiritual sense, and its establishment in Palestine would be a denial of all the ideals and hopes by which the survival of Jewish life in that country commends itself to the Jewish conscience and to Jewish sympathy. On these grounds the Conjoint Committee of the Board of Deputies and the Anglo-Jewish Association deprecates most earnestly the national proposals of the Zionists.[4]

Similar protests were voiced in the United States by the American Jewish Committee, headed during World War I by Jacob H. Schiff, Louis Marshall, and Mayer Sulzberger. Schiff declared on one occasion:

I believe that I am not far wrong if I say that from fifty to seventy per cent of the so-called Jewish Nationalists are either atheists or agnostics and that

[3] In 1917, however, a split occurred in the Board, its president being anti-Zionist while the majority were on the side of Zionism.

[4] Quoted by J. M. N. Jeffries, *Palestine: The Reality* (London, 1939), p. 147.

the great majority of the Jewish Nationalist leaders have absolutely no interest in the Jewish religion.[5]

Mayer Sulzberger, former president of the Court of Common Pleas in Pennsylvania, opposed Zionism on the ground that it constituted a denial of democracy:

Democracy, he said, means that those who live in a country shall select their rulers and shall preserve their powers. Given these principles a Convention of Zionists looking to the government of people who are in Palestine would be in contravention of the plainest principle of democracy. It can have no practical meaning unless its intent is to overslaugh the people who are in Palestine and to deprive them of the right of self-government by substituting the will of persons outside, who may or may not ever see Palestine.[6]

The Zionists insisted on the national—and to some extent racial— definition of Jewry. Dr. Weizmann in a reply to Alexander and Montefiore stated positively:

It is strictly a question of fact that the Jews are a nationality. An overwhelming majority of them has always had the conviction that they were a nationality, which has been shared by non-Jews in all countries.[7]

Following a similar line of thought, Justice Brandeis formulated a definition that contained such concepts as "blood":

The meaning of the word Jewish in the term Jewish Problem must be accepted as coextensive with the disabilities which it is our problem to remove. It is the non-Jews who create the disabilities and in so doing give definition to the term Jew. These disabilities extend substantially to all of Jewish *blood*. [They] do not end with a renunciation of faith, however sincere. They do not end with the elimination, however complete, of external Jewish mannerisms. The disabilities do not end ordinarily until the Jewish *blood* has been so thoroughly diluted by repeated intermarriages as to result in practically obliterating the Jew.[8]

These quotations from leading Zionist and anti-Zionist authorities illustrate the profound split over the problem of Palestine among the Jewish people themselves. As H. M. Kallen has stated, it was a struggle between "assimilationist individualism and self-respecting

---

[5] *Ibid.* p. 153.   [6] *Ibid.*   [7] *Ibid.*, p. 149.

[8] Italics mine. Quoted from *Brandeis on Zionism, A Collection of Addresses and Statements by Louis D. Brandeis,* with a Foreword by Mr. Justice Felix Frankfurter (Washington, D.C., 1942), p. 14. H. M. Kallen, who in his *Zionism and World Politics* (New York, 1921) seems to espouse the Zionist cause, terms the Jews "members of the race" (p. 53). Dr. Weizmann similarly refers to the Jews as "an old race" in *International Affairs,* Sept.–Oct. 1936, p. 673.

nationalism." This struggle was difficult for the Zionists, especially for Dr. Weizmann, in England, where many prominent Jewish families, members of the British aristocracy, held influential positions in business and public life [9] and refused to compromise their British status by identifying themselves with Jewish nationalism. Yet eventually the Zionists emerged victorious. In the Balfour Declaration they obtained a formal acknowledgement of their importance as spokesmen for the Jewish world.[10] The Declaration set the stage for a new period in Jewish history—the building of a national home in Palestine. In this new period the Zionists were to transform themselves from mere missionaries into state builders. They applied themselves to the new task with zeal and vigor.

THE BRITISH MANDATE AND THE JEWISH AGENCY

The opening of the Peace Conference brought to Paris strong Zionist delegations, both from Great Britain and from the United States. Their activities and their success have already been recounted. On April 25, 1920, the Allied Supreme Council allocated the mandate over Palestine to Great Britain, and on July 22, 1922, Great Britain was formally confirmed as mandatory power by the Council of the League of Nations. The mandate expressly provided for a Jewish national home in Palestine, incorporating into its text, almost verbatim, the Balfour Declaration. The mandatory power was to be responsible for the development of self-governing institutions. Article 4 dealt with the recognition of a Jewish Agency to co-operate with the mandatory power in establishing a Jewish national home. It added that "the Zionist organization . . . shall be recognized as such agency." Article 6 imposed upon the mandatory power the duty of facilitating Jewish immigration and land settlement "while ensuring that the rights and position of other sections of the population are not prejudiced." Article 18 contained a clause forbidding discrimination between members of the League of Nations, and Article 25 made possible the exemption of Transjordan, as part of the mandate, from the provisions of the Balfour Declaration.[11]

[9] Such as Lord Melchett of the Imperial Chemical Industries; Sir Philip Sassoon, Lloyd George's private secretary; Sir Herbert Louis Samuel, home secretary, and other members of the Samuel family; Edwin Montagu, secretary of state for India; Marquess of Reading, lord chief justice and later viceroy of India; and the Rothschilds. Some of the above-mentioned were later converted to Zionism.   [10] See above, p. 80.

[11] The full text of the mandate for Palestine may be found in Royal Institute of International Affairs, *Great Britain and Palestine* (London, 1946), p. 151.

With the assignment of the mandate at San Remo in 1920, the British military government gave way to a civil administration. Sir Herbert Samuel, member of a prominent British-Jewish family but not a Zionist, was appointed first high commissioner of Palestine. The Jewish population of the Holy Land, at the time of the armistice, numbered 55,000 souls. (See Appendix VI.) The new civil administration opened the gates for immigration into Palestine and this immediately brought Arab protests. In 1921 anti-Jewish disturbances broke out. They provoked Winston Churchill, at that time colonial secretary, into writing the so-called Churchill Memorandum (June 3, 1922), in which he reaffirmed Britain's desire to create a Jewish national home in Palestine; reassured the Arabs that the Balfour Declaration did not contemplate that Palestine as a whole was to be converted into a Jewish national state; and proclaimed that Britain would facilitate Jewish immigration to the extent dictated by the economic absorptive capacity of the country. This statement met with the formal approval of the Zionist Organization but elicited protests from Arab spokesmen. From that time on, the government of Palestine issued yearly immigration quotas, and the number of Jews in the land steadily increased.

It is proper, perhaps, at this point briefly to describe the organization of both Jewish and Arab communities. Article 4 of the mandate provided for a Jewish Agency, which would co-operate with the mandatory administration in the establishment of a national homeland. Originally the Jewish Agency was composed of Zionists only, but in 1929 it was enlarged to comprise non-Zionist Jews as well. The president of the World Zionist Organization remained, however, president of the Jewish Agency. This Agency was the official spokesman of world Jewry with regard to Jewish settlement in Palestine. As such, it co-operated with the mandatory power in many fields including education, health, and agriculture. It was granted by Great Britain official right to select candidates for immigration, and as a result only those who had received the Agency's "certificates" could apply for visas to Palestine at the British consulates. The Agency also controlled the policies of the Jewish National Fund (*Keren Kayemeth*) and of the Palestine Foundation Fund (*Keren Hayesod*). During most of the time that the mandate was in force, Dr. Weizmann was president of the Agency by virtue of his leadership in the Zionist Organization. The Agency had a standing executive committee in

Palestine, headed by David Ben Gurion. Its Foreign Department was administered by Moshe Shertok.

The Jewish Community

Apart from the Jewish Agency, which represented world Jewry, the Jews of Palestine had their own communal organization composed of an elected Assembly and a General Council (*Vaad Leumi*). It enjoyed certain rights of self-government. The Jewish community was composed of a number of political parties. These parties were divided into three major groups: (1) parties belonging to the Zionist Organization, (2) the Revisionist group which did not belong to the above organization, and (3) the non-Zionist group.

The first or Zionist group was divided again into the following parties:

a) Mapai (*Miflagath Poalei Eretz Israel*), a Socialist Labor party, with the most members and the most power, headed by David Ben Gurion;

b) Hashomer Hatzair, a left-wing Socialist party, next largest and favoring a binational Arab-Jewish state;

c) Poalei Zion, a small left-wing group;

d) The General Zionists, representing the professional and middle class strata; divided in turn into "A" and "B" factions. The "A" faction following Dr. Weizmann's leadership was more progressive and tended to co-operate with the Socialists; and the "B" group was more conservative;

e) Mizrahi, an orthodox religious party within the Zionist organization; with rightist tendencies and favoring religious education;

f) Aliya Hadasha (New Immigrants Party), formed in 1942 from the German, Austrian, and Czech immigrants; critical of the existing Zionist leadership;

g) Ihud (Union), an intellectual group headed by Dr. Magnes, president of the Hebrew University of Jerusalem, favoring a binational state in Palestine and largely resigned to Arab supremacy.

The second group was composed of those Zionists who had seceded from the Zionist Organization in 1935 and who had formed the New Zionist Organization, under the leadership of the extremist Vladimir Zhabotinsky. This group, also called Revisionist, violently opposed any policy of moderation and demanded the creation of a Jewish state over the whole of Palestine and Transjordan.

The third group, composed of non-Zionist Jews, organized itself into *Agudath Israel,* a strictly religious and nonpolitical body. In 1920 Agudath claimed to represent 20 per cent of the Jewish inhabitants in Palestine. It differed profoundly from Mizrahi.

The Jewish community possessed also a number of other social and economic organizations, chief among which was *Histadruth* or the Jewish Federation of Labor. Histadruth was more than a mere trade union organization. It controlled many industries and agricultural co-operatives, hospitals, schools, marketing organizations, and a workers' bank. It was divided politically into the same groups as was the community as a whole. Numbering nearly 130,000 members, Histadruth was the most powerful socially minded, nongovernmental Jewish organization in Palestine.

The Jewish community displayed a marked tendency toward collectivism despite the fact that the financing of the Zionist settlement in Palestine was done mainly by contributions from wealthy Jewish capitalists abroad. One manifestation of such a tendency was the development of nearly 1,200 co-operative societies in Palestine connected with many branches of agriculture and industry. These included producers' and consumers' co-operatives; banking, credit, and insurance co-operatives; and similar societies for marketing, transport, irrigation, and land purchasing. Chief among them was *Tnuva,* a big organization for the distribution of the products of Jewish farms.

The early Zionists envisaged the regeneration of the Jewish nation through contact with nature and the soil. The Jew had to cast off the crippling memories of eastern European ghettos and acquire new mental and physical vigor through work on the land.[12] Palestine was also to develop specialized industries and to play the role of a small Belgium of the Middle East, supplying the surrounding Arab lands with the products of her skilled labor. Agriculture, however, was to be the main objective because of its regenerative value.

Much stress, therefore, was laid on the development of Jewish agrarian communities. These were, for the most part, collective settlements, among which three basic types predominated: the *Kvutza,* the *Kibbutz,* and the *Moshav Ovdim.* They differed in their degree of collectivism and of readiness to accept new members. The Kvutza was the oldest type of collective farm, it had a strictly closed

[12] He was to transform himself from a nonproductive middleman, from a *Luftmensch* (as Walter Preuss described him), into a solid farmer and producer.

membership and was communistic in its economic and social principles. The Moshav Ovdim represented the loosest form of collectivism and contained elements of individual free enterprise.[13] All these settlements bore a definite imprint of the social radicalism prevailing among most of their original founders, i.e., the Russian Jews who emigrated to Palestine in the late nineteenth and early twentieth centuries. The co-operative and semicentralized nature of Jewish agriculture permitted a lot of planning and led to monoculture trends as exemplified by the impressive development of citrus fruit. Much of the citrus produce of the Jewish agricultural settlements was earmarked for export, while other foodstuffs had to be imported. Scientific experimental stations including the famous one at Rehovoth (Dr. Weizmann's residence and laboratory), and excellent agricultural schools (such as Mikveh Israel near Tel-Aviv) contributed to the high level of Zionist agriculture.

Despite this impressive effort to return to the land, only a minority gained a livelihood from agricultural pursuits. In the interwar period only 23.8 per cent of the Jewish population resided in rural areas, and, according to the Jewish Agency, only 13.2 per cent of Jewish wage earners were engaged in agriculture in 1943. In fact, the trend was toward greater concentration in urban occupations.[14]

The Arab Community

The Arab community presented an altogether different picture. Politically the Arabs were far from being as efficiently organized as were the Jews. There was no Arab equivalent of the Jewish Agency, nor was there anything resembling the Jewish community organization, *Vaad Leumi*. The Arabs possessed their Supreme Moslem Council, whose charter was approved by the government. Originally all its members were elected, but later some were appointed by the British high commissioner. The Council controlled the Moslem religious courts and charitable endowments or the *waqfs*. Its president was the grand mufti of Jerusalem, Haj Amin el-Husseini. Arab political activity was channeled through the Arab Executive, elected by the Palestine Arab Congress. This, in turn, gave way to the Arab Higher Committee, created in 1936 as a result of the union of five out of six Arab political parties.[15] Considerable fluidity characterized

13 See H. F. Infield, *Cooperative Living in Palestine* (New York, 1944).
14 R.I.I.A., *Great Britain and Palestine*, p. 37.
15 These were: (1) The Palestine Arab Party (Jamal Husseini), (2) The National Defense Party (Raghib Bey Nashashibi), (3) The Reform Party (Dr.

Arab politics, but two major political groups could be discerned: the first was led by the mufti, who dominated the Arab Higher Committee; the second was led by Raghib Bey Nashashibi, who resented the mufti's influence and who leaned toward a compromise with the British. It is noteworthy that the Moslem and Christian [16] Arabs managed, to a large extent, to forget the differences handed down from the Ottoman period and to unite in the face of the Zionist challenge.

The Arab community was backward in some respects. Nearly 73 per cent of the population lived in rural areas, and this number included around 65,000 nomads. Arab agricultural methods were primitive. Only 25 per cent of Moslem children attended schools in contrast to 100 per cent of Jewish youth. The Arabs did not get outside financial aid, as did the Zionists, and obviously could not boast of the modern schools, hospitals, and other institutions of the well-organized Jewish community.

British Attitudes

Standing between and above these two communities was the British mandatory government. Palestine was under the jurisdiction of the British Colonial Office, but service in the Holy Land was never considered very desirable in the British colonial hierarchy. Consequently the human resources of the British in Palestine were not so good as those, for example, in the Sudan, Egypt, or India. British colonial officials, who had long dealt with eastern subject races, were somewhat at a loss facing the well-educated European and often sophisticated Zionist community. In the latter, the eastern European Jew predominated—an element hitherto little known to the British. Moreover, the average Jewish intellectual, especially after the great influx of central European Jews in the middle 1930's, was more highly educated, and perhaps more intelligent, than his British counterpart in the Palestinian administration. There had been little in England's colonial experience to guide British civil servants in such situations, and inevitable tensions arose. Many a British official who initially was not prejudiced against the Jews became anti-Semitic after a tour of duty in Palestine. This was certainly true of many army officers.

Khalidi), (4) The National Bloc (Abdul Latif Bey Saleh of Nablus), (5) Congress Executive of Nationalist Youth (Yakub Ghussein), and (6) The Istiqlal (Independence) Party (Auni Bey Abdul Hadi).

[16] The latter were estimated at 87,000 in 1945.

Apart from these psychological difficulties, political attitudes prevented real British-Zionist friendship. It was obvious that after the Churchill Memorandum of 1922 the British government treated the Balfour Declaration as a political liability that stood in the way of a coherent policy toward the Arabs. British statesmen realized what political dynamite Zionist immigration was in the Arab world. This policy found its reflection in the mandatory administration, especially on the lower operating echelons, where pro-Arab attitudes prevailed.

In the meantime, with Jewish immigration steadily increasing, Arab opposition was becoming more and more intense. The Arabs demanded self-determination and insisted, from the early 1920's, upon the establishment of a democratic, parliamentary form of government. Added to this were two other demands—to stop Jewish immigration and to forbid land sales by Arabs to Jews. From the beginning, the Arabs adopted a policy of nonco-operation with the mandatory regime. In conformity with this policy they rejected an early British suggestion to create an Arab Agency equivalent to the Jewish.

The political history of Palestine after the inception of the mandate was stormy. The Wailing Wall incidents in 1929 gave rise to violent disturbances, during which the intransigent attitude of the Arabs became manifest. Anti-Jewish riots occurred again in 1933. Hitler's rise in Germany and the resulting Jewish exodus brought a new wave of immigration into Palestine, which alone accounted for over 60,000 new arrivals in 1935. This caused renewed Arab unrest. Matters came to a head in 1937, when the Arabs began a wholesale campaign of terror, commonly referred to as the Arab Rebellion. The Rebellion lasted through 1939, nearly until the outbreak of World War II.

British official reaction to these manifestations of Arab nationalism was unvarying. After each new crisis a commission was sent to Palestine to investigate, and each time it returned with a more or less voluminous report.[17] Until 1937 these reports tended generally to be unfavorable to Zionist aspirations. They advocated restricting immigration, invoked the principle of absorptive capacity, and stressed that the Jews had no rightful claim to share in the government of the country. In 1935 the high commissioner made public a plan for a partly elected and partly nominated legislative assembly, which would give the Arabs a majority. These proposals proved un-

[17] In particular, the Shaw Commission in 1929; the Hope-Simpson Commission in 1930; the Royal (Peel) Commission in 1936; the Partition Commission in 1938.

acceptable either to the Zionists or to the Arabs; moreover, they drew criticism from the Permanent Mandates Commission of the League of Nations. In 1937 the Royal Commission, having abandoned hope for a reconciliation between the Jews and Arabs, came forward with a proposal of partition. Palestine was to be divided into an Arab state, a Jewish state, and a neutral enclave around Jerusalem and Bethlehem that would remain under British administration. The Arab Higher Committee virtually rejected the scheme. The Zionist Congress which met at Zurich, August 3–17, 1937, instructed the Executive to enter into negotiations with Great Britain "with a view to ascertaining the precise terms of His Majesty's Government for the proposed establishment of a Jewish State." [18]

In 1938 the British government dispatched to Palestine a technical partition commission, whose task it was to prepare a blueprint for partition, on the basis of the Royal Commission's recommendations. This new commission was at the same time authorized to make its own suggestions. Its report, in which it proposed a detailed scheme of partition, was promptly rejected by the government. Instead, Great Britain convened early in 1939 a round-table conference attended by Zionist and Arab representatives from Palestine and by delegates from the existing Arab states.

The London Conference and the White Paper, 1939

The composition of the conference introduced an element of novelty into Palestinian politics. Hitherto the British had tried to settle the controversy by consultation with Arab leaders from Palestine. Now, however, yielding to the growing insistence of surrounding Arab countries, they decided to invite representatives of Iraq, Egypt, Saudi Arabia, Yemen, and Transjordan. A difficulty arose in connection with the Palestinian Arab representation. In 1937, as a result of the Arab Rebellion, the government of Palestine had arrested and deported to the Seychelles five leading members of the Arab Higher Committee.[19] Moreover, the government had deprived the mufti, Haj Amin el-Husseini, of his office as president of the Supreme Moslem Council and chairman of the General *Waqf* Committee, and issued warrants for his arrest as well as that of his relative, Jamal el-Husseini, president of the Arab Party. Both the mufti and Jamal

[18] R.I.I.A., *Great Britain and Palestine*, p. 106.
[19] Ahmed Hilmi Pasha; Fuad Saba; Yakub Ghussein; Dr. Hussein Fakhri el-Khalidi, Mayor of Jerusalem; and Haj Rashid Ibrahim.

escaped, and took shelter under the protective wing of the French mandatory administration in Lebanon and Syria, respectively. The mufti continued to direct the activities of Arab guerrillas in Palestine. Led by Rahim Haj Ibrahim and Aref Abdul Razzik, the guerrillas waged a campaign of terror and intimidation, not only against the British and the Jews, but also against the moderate Arab elements headed by the Nashashibi family. It was very difficult for Great Britain to secure spokesmen for the Palestinian Arabs who could act with a degree of moderation and at the same time get support from the Arab masses. After much wrangling it was eventually decided that Palestine would be represented by six delegates, who would act on behalf of all Palestinian Arab parties. These included both moderates, such as Raghib Bey Nashashibi, and some former members of the Arab Higher Committee, released from the Seychelles. The latter were permitted to consult with the exiled mufti, who, though absent and outlawed, still wielded great influence.

The Jewish delegation comprised not only Zionists and members and nonmembers of the Jewish Agency, but also other prominent Jewish leaders from Great Britain, the United States, and the European continent. It was headed by Dr. Chaim Weizmann.

The conference met in London in February and March 1939. The Arabs and the Jews held separate meetings because of the refusal of Palestinian Arabs to sit with the Jewish delegation. The conference produced no agreement; each party adhered stubbornly to its own formula. The Arabs reiterated their demand for independence and insisted on the stoppage of Jewish immigration. The Jews made an eloquent plea for implementation of the Balfour Declaration in "this blackest hour of Jewish history" and stressed the need of continued uninterrupted immigration. British compromise proposals were rejected by both parties. The conference disbanded without producing any agreement.

On May 17, 1939, the British government issued a White Paper, which laid down new principles concerning Palestine. Reversing its former policy, the government proposed the creation, within ten years, of an independent Palestinian state to be linked with Britain by a special treaty. The most important provisions concerned immigration and land transfers. On both points Britain virtually gave way to Arab demands: Jewish immigration was to be limited to 75,000 for the next five years, after which it was to cease altogether; and Palestine was to be divided into three zones—the first, in which land transfers from Arabs to Jews were to be allowed; the second, in which they were to be restricted; and the third, in which they were to be forbidden.

These proposals were rejected by Arab spokesmen because they did not go far enough, but basically the Arabs had scored a considerable victory. The Zionists were profoundly shocked and promptly denounced the White Paper as a betrayal of promises and appeasement of the Arabs. The Permanent Mandates Commission of the League of Nations also voiced its criticism, declaring an incompatibility existed between the Paper and the terms of the mandate.

Britain's defense was to explain that she was not bound by the principle of economic absorptive capacity but instead had to take into account the political absorptive capacity of the Arab world as a whole. The truth of the matter was that in 1938 and 1939 Nazi and Italian propaganda among the Arabs assumed alarming intensity and took full advantage of increased Jewish immigration to blame Britain and place her in a very embarrassing position. The tenseness of the international situation in the months preceding the outbreak of the war led Britain to adopt a conciliatory policy toward the Arab world, situated as it was astride the vulnerable part of the English imperial life line.

The tragedy of the Zionists stemmed from the fact that, as Jews, they had a great stake in curbing German imperialism and in desiring ultimate Nazi defeat. Any policy aimed at the strengthening of the Western camp—and such was the policy of courting Arab favor—should have been welcomed and supported by them. But this was incompatible with the basic Zionist aim of converting Palestine into a Jewish state with the immediate objective of rescuing Jewish victims of Nazi tyranny in Europe.

The Wartime Truce

The outbreak of the Second World War in September 1939 found the two protagonists unreconciled and the British more determined than ever to enforce their new policy on Palestine and to prevent the outbreak of an Arab rebellion in the Middle East.

As for the Zionists, they expressed through Dr. Weizmann their readiness to stand by Great Britain and the democracies. This was coupled with repeated demands that independent Jewish military units be created as part of the Allied armies. The British responded to the latter request by allowing voluntary enlistment in the British auxiliary formations in the Middle East, by creating a Palestine Pioneer Corps, and by raising six battalions of the Palestine Companies of the Buffs. Great Britain took care, however, to open these formations to both the Jews and the Arabs, apparently unwilling to sponsor purely Jewish formations. Not until the fall of 1944 did Britain accede to Jewish demands by forming a Jewish brigade, which eventually took part in the final stages of the Allied campaign in Italy.

The war brought to Palestine an artificial truce, largely due to the presence of numerous Allied divisions, making continuance of the Arab guerrilla warfare suicidal. Arab response to the call for volunteers was not very enthusiastic. The Arabs lacked the incentive possessed by the Jews. Moreover, they could never forget the mufti, who visited Germany at the beginning of the war and joined hands with the Nazi leaders against "British imperialism." [20] Nevertheless British policy, though termed "appeasement" by the Zionists, was successful in restraining the Arab peoples from a concerted revolt against Britain in her hour of need. In Palestine it brought about a cessation of rebellion.

NEED FOR A NEW POLICY FOR ZIONISM

The truce lasted until 1943. In that year Palestine witnessed a new upsurge of terrorism. This time, however, the roles had changed, since it was the Jews who attacked. Their primary target was the British administration. Two factors contributed to this state of affairs. First, there was an unusual increase in illegal Jewish immigration from Nazi-occupied Europe. The unfortunate victims of Nazi persecution were arriving in Palestine on overcrowded, leaky ships, and the British authorities either forbade their entry or interned the immigrants in camps on Cyprus and in other overseas possessions. Tragic events occurred, including the sinking of an immigrant ship, the *Struma*, off the Turkish coast (the British had refused to permit it to dock in Palestine). The more extremist Jewish elements lost their patience and resorted to violence in the hope of compelling Britain to ease the immigration laws.

Secondly, increased pressure for a pro-Zionist solution began to be exerted by American Zionists. On May 11, 1942, the American Zionist Organization meeting in New York, adopted the so-called

[20] For an account of the mufti's activities, see Rosalind W. Graves, "The Grand Mufti of Jerusalem," *Current History*, Nov. 1946.

Biltmore Program, presented to it by David Ben Gurion, head of the Jewish Agency's executive committee. The Biltmore Program called for (1) the establishment of a Jewish state, which would embrace the whole of Palestine; (2) the creation of a Jewish army; and (3) the repudiation of the White Paper of 1939 and unlimited immigration into Palestine, which would be controlled not by the British but by the Jewish Agency.

This program went much farther than did the Balfour Declaration, and so elicited protests from more moderate Jewish groups in the West. It received endorsement, however, from the Small Committee of the General Council of the Zionist Organization in Jerusalem on November 10, 1942, and thus became official policy of world Zionism. By stepping up their demands, the Zionists gave expression to their growing conviction that a policy of moderation did not pay, that Britain could no longer be relied upon, and that it was expedient to seek the support of the United States. Allied victories at El-Alamein and in North Africa removed the danger of enemy action in the Middle East, and this encouraged the Zionists in their policy of disregarding Arab nationalism.

Hand in hand with the Biltmore Program went intensive Zionist activity among the leading politicians in the United States. Yielding to Zionist pleas, many state legislatures passed pro-Zionist resolutions, and in February 1944 a resolution was introduced before both Houses of Congress. The resolution called for the opening of Palestine to unrestricted Jewish immigration and for the ultimate reconstruction of Palestine "as a free and democratic Jewish commonwealth." It also requested official American intervention (good offices) to secure these goals. Had the resolution passed, it would have committed the United States to definite political action on behalf of the Zionists. At the last moment, the vote upon it was postponed because of the objections of General Marshall, then chief of staff, who, on the basis of reports from the Middle East, believed that such a resolution would harm the Allied war effort. Despite this temporary setback, it was clear that the Zionists were firmly resolved to achieve their aims in Palestine and that they found powerful allies in official Washington. In fact, after a visit of Zionist leaders a few days later, President Franklin D. Roosevelt made public a statement favoring Zionist aspirations.

Irritated by immigration restrictions and inspired by American Zionist successes, the Palestinian Zionists displayed remarkable dynamism in their struggle against Great Britain. Officially the Jewish Agency agreed to observe a truce with the Arabs for the duration of the war. But this official attitude was not shared by the extremist wing of the New Zionist Organization (Revisionists). And it was this extremist wing that set the general political tone in Palestine. The war gave the Jews a unique opportunity to equip themselves with arms, partly stolen from the Allied forces. In fact, there was considerable illegal traffic in military equipment. The Jewish community possessed three underground military forces. The first was *Haganah*, a large defense force, created initially to protect Jewish settlements against Arab attacks, to which belonged most of the able-bodied members of the Jewish community. Haganah was illegal, but the British tolerated it because its aims were defensive. Zhabotinsky's Revisionists had their smaller but more effective force called *Irgun Zvai Leumi*. Irgun used decidedly terrorist tactics, but for some time it considered itself bound by the truce. The third force was the so-called Stern Gang, a splinter group of the Irgun led by a Polish Jew, Abraham Stern. This group never accepted the truce and indulged freely in terrorism. In 1942–1943 both Irgun and the Stern Gang embarked upon a determined policy to compel the British to accede to the Biltmore Program by terrorist tactics. Terrorist activity was particularly bad in 1944. The high commissioner for Palestine, Sir Harold MacMichael, barely escaped with his life while traveling on the Jerusalem-Jaffa road. On November 2 two members of the Stern Gang assassinated Lord Moyne, British minister of state for the Middle East, in Cairo. Dozens of attacks by Irgun and the Stern groups on British police stations and on civil and military officials contributed to the steady deterioration of security in the Holy Land. These acts of terror were condemned by the official Zionist bodies and by the chief rabbis of Palestine. The New Zionist Organization even went so far as to repudiate its own offspring, the Irgun, for breaking party discipline. But it was clear that the terrorists would not have succeeded if it had not been for the support that they received in Jewish settlements or in Jewish sectors of larger towns. Their dramatic struggle eventually focused the attention of the world upon Palestine, and although it did not evoke enthusiasm in the West, it did compel Great Britain and indirectly the United States to crystallize their policies toward Zionism.

In the meantime the plight of European Jewry had become more desperate, because of the extension of Soviet dominion over eastern and central Europe. The Jews constituted a big proportion of displaced persons in the western sectors of Germany. They comprised three basic categories: (1) those victims of the Nazi persecution who had survived the ordeal and had been released from the German concentration camps by the Allies; (2) those Polish Jews who had been deported to the Soviet Union in 1939–1940 and who were after the war permitted to leave the USSR (having aquainted themselves at first hand with the realities of a Communist state, they did not want to remain in Soviet-dominated Poland, despite the policy of non-discrimination loudly proclaimed by the new regime); (3) those Jews from eastern Europe who found that the Communist pattern of politics and economy in the Soviet satellite countries did not leave much room for the trader, middleman, or independent businessman —occupations predominantly filled by Jews in that part of the continent.

The press in Western countries either misunderstood or was unwilling to face the realities of the situation in eastern Europe in 1945 and 1946. It was thought that the Jews were emigrating because of acute anti-Semitism, which lingered even after Hitler's downfall. There was anti-Semitism in that area, but two reservations should be made. First, anti-Semitism was not a new phenomenon in eastern Europe. It had existed before the war and it had been expressed in anti-Jewish legislation. But it had never caused a mass exodus of Jews;[21] such an exodus was without doubt a result of Soviet occupation of the area in question. Secondly, some new acute manifestations of anti-Semitism were partly attributable to the role individual Jewish Communists played in the establishment of the puppet regimes in eastern Europe.[22] Thus, while a minority of Communist-oriented Jews benefited by the radical change in this area, the Jews as a whole were simply squeezed out of their professions and trades as a result of Sovietization in the satellite states. They lost all hope for the future.[23] The teeming camps of displaced persons in Western Germany

[21] Actually, in 1938 and 1939 there was a trend toward re-emigration of Jews to their eastern European countries of origin, from both Germany and Palestine.

[22] Such as Jakub Berman, secretary general of the Council of Ministers in Poland; Rudolph Slansky, secretary general of the Communist Party of Czechoslovakia; Ana Pauker, foreign minister of Rumania; Mathias Rakosi, premier of Hungary.

[23] According to the statement made on January 2, 1946, by Lt. Gen. Sir Frederick E. Morgan, chief of the United Nations Relief and Rehabilitation Administration in Germany, thousands of Polish Jews were infiltrating into the American occupation zone in accordance with a "well-organized, positive plan to

confronted the West with a major political and humanitarian problem and added considerably to the pressure that the Zionist organization was exercising for a favorable solution in Palestine.

The Anglo-American Committee of Inquiry

The stage for the next act in the Palestinian drama was set on August 31, 1945, when President Truman addressed an appeal to the British prime minister, Clement Attlee, asking for immediate admission of 100,000 Jewish refugees to Palestine. In reply the British government proposed the creation of an Anglo-American Committee of Inquiry to study the matter, thus shifting part of the burden of responsibility to the United States. The American government accepted this suggestion, and as a result both governments appointed a committee, composed of nonofficial citizens of the two countries.[24]

The joint committee held hearings in Washington and in London, visited the displaced persons camps in Germany and Austria, and made a tour of Palestine. It pursued generally an open-minded approach to the subject under its investigation, but its composition was

---

get out of Europe." This migration, he said, was sponsored by an unknown secret Jewish organization. His revelations were based on a U.S. Third Army intelligence report on the organization, by Zionist groups, of an underground route in Europe, which made it possible for the Jews to enter the American zone in Germany at the rate of 2,000 a week. These statements were partly confirmed by the U.S. commander in Europe, Gen. Joseph T. McNarney, in the latter's report to the President on January 29, 1946. Moreover, officials at the State Department commented that at least some of the statements made by General Morgan concerning the exodus of Jews from Poland conformed with information in the possession of the U.S. government, and added that "a number of official and semi-official indications have been provided by the Warsaw government that it is encouraging the migration of part of its Jewish population." After issuing his statement, General Morgan was promptly suspended from his post by Herbert H. Lehman, director general of the UNRRA, on the ground of being guilty of racial bias. After an explanatory letter, however, in which he denied any anti-Semitic attitudes on his part, General Morgan was reinstated. (See *Washington Post,* Jan. 3, 4, 8, 31, 1946.)

24 The American members of the committee were Judge Joseph C. Hutcheson, Jr., of Houston, Texas, Bartley C. Crum of San Francisco, Dr. James G. Mc-Donald, former League of Nations commissioner for German refugees, Frank W. Buxton, editor of the *Boston Herald,* Dr. Frank Aydelotte, director, Institute for Advanced Study, Princeton, and William Phillips, former U.S. ambassador to Italy. The British group was composed of Sir John Singleton, judge, King's Bench, London, Lord Robert Morrison, a Labour peer, Richard H. S. Crossman, Labour M.P., Maj. Reginald Manningham-Buller, Conservative M.P., Wilfrid Crick, adviser to Midland Bank, and Sir Frederick Leggett, a labor conciliator.

responsible for a diversity of opinions. Three members, James G. Mc-Donald and Bartley C. Crum of the American group and Richard Crossman, M.P., of the British group, strongly favored the Zionist cause.[25] Crum in particular resented the advice given the committee by officials of the State Department and of the Foreign Office. This advice, which was well received by many members of the British delegation, was to the effect that no political solution in the Middle East should disregard the Soviet factor[26] and that Britain and the United States should stand united in the face of the Soviet threat.[27]

Having completed its task, on April 20, 1946, the committee presented a unanimous report with three major recommendations: (1) that "the Government of Palestine be continued as at present under mandate pending the execution of a trusteeship agreement under the United Nations"; (2) "that 100,000 certificates be authorized immediately for the admission into Palestine of the Jews who have been the victims of Nazi and Fascist persecution," and (3) that the land transfer limitations be rescinded.[28]

The United States and Great Britain neither accepted nor rejected these recommendations. Instead the two governments appointed a new Anglo-American Commission, composed of higher officials, to devise ways to implement the committee's recommendations. As could be expected, the official approach to the Palestine problem was more conservative. The resulting Grady-Morrison plan revived the old British project of a federalized Jewish-Arab Palestine and made further Jewish immigration dependent upon common Jewish-Arab consent.

[25] Two of them subsequently gave personal accounts of their mission: Bartley C. Crum in *Behind the Silken Curtain* (New York, 1947) and Richard Crossman in *Palestine Mission* (London, 1947).

[26] Gist of the statement made by Loy Henderson, head of the Office of Near Eastern and African Affairs, Department of State (Crum, *op. cit.*, pp. 7–8).

[27] *Ibid.*, p. 35. The author adds: "Naturally, I found my American colleagues [on the committee] much less preoccupied with anxieties over our national security," and ventures his own opinion that "there might be points at which British imperial and Russian nationalistic interests did not coincide, but surely the United States and Russia had few points at which their basic interests were in conflict." On his part, Crossman described Crum, with whom he was on excellent terms, as follows: "Indeed, he was the only American with us who had a political career in front of him, which could be made or marred by the attitude he adopted toward the Jewish question" (Crossman, *op. cit.*, p. 22).

[28] The full text of the report is in the *New York Times,* May 1, 1946.

331

The Zionists were profoundly disappointed by these developments. They had expected that the British Labour Party, which had repeatedly issued pro-Zionist statements, would favor their cause. But once in power British Labourites suddenly abandoned their old proclamations and reverted to traditional diplomacy. Ernest Bevin, Socialist foreign secretary, followed his Conservative predecessors in their policy of not antagonizing the Arab world.[29] News of the mufti's escape from Germany to the Middle East—probably with the connivance of some Western powers—added to Jewish bitterness. In October 1946 President Truman renewed his appeal for immediate admission of 100,000 Jews. Under these circumstances, the chances for a negotiated settlement of the Palestinian question became slimmer than ever.[30] Moreover, a definite swing developed in the World Zionist Organization in favor of an intransigent policy toward Great Britain. In December 1946, at a World Zionist Congress in Basle, American Zionist leaders, backed by the Revisionists, assailed Dr. Weizmann for his policy of "appeasing" Britain and asserted that British rule in Palestine was "illegal." Dr. Abba Hillel Silver, president of the Zionist Organization in America, declared that "we have the right to resist this rule and I pledge the support of American Jewry to this resistance." [31] Dr. Weizmann's retort, "I'm not impressed about speeches on resistance made in New York when resistance is supposed to take place in Palestine," elicited the cry "demagogue" from Dr. Emmanuel Neuman of the United States. American Zionist leadership carried the day, insisting on a Jewish state in all Palestine and promising more effective measures to bring this about.

Palestine before the United Nations

Britain's position was slowly becoming untenable. Subjected to official American pressure, at odds with the Zionists and with the Arabs, and facing growing disorders in its mandated territory, the British government decided to take the question of Palestine before the United Nations. On April 2, 1947, Britain requested the calling of a special session of the General Assembly to consider the problem. The General Assembly, which met between April 28 and May 15, set

[29] The text of Bevin's speech at a Labour Party conference at Bournemouth containing significant passages about Palestine may be found in the *New York Times*, June 13, 1946.

[30] Bevin subsequently deplored the fact that the Palestinian issue had been made "the subject of local elections" in the United States (*New York Times*, Feb. 26, 1947). [31] *New York Times*, Dec. 11, 1946.

up a United Nations Special Committee on Palestine (UNSCOP). The committee, composed of eleven states [32] under the presidency of a Swedish delegate, visited Palestine and presented a report to the regular fall session of the General Assembly.

The report recommended the establishment of an independent and economically unified Palestine at an early date, pending which the area would have to pass through a transitional stage under United Nations supervision. Here the unanimity ended, and the report was divided into a majority and a minority plan. The majority plan, endorsed by Canada, Czechoslovakia, Guatemala, the Netherlands, Peru, Sweden, and Uruguay, provided for the partitioning of Palestine into an Arab state, a Jewish state, and the internationalized city of Jerusalem. The minority plan, favored by India, Iran, and Yugoslavia, advocated a federated state of Palestine composed of two states, Jewish and Arab, each enjoying local autonomy. Immigration into the Jewish state would be permitted for three years up to its absorptive capacity, which would be determined by three Arab, three Jewish, and three United Nations representatives. The Arab states favored the minority plan, because it satisfied their basic desiderata, namely, a single independent state with an Arab majority and a limitation of Jewish immigration. The Zionists, somewhat reluctantly, accepted the majority plan. It did not satisfy the extremists, but at least it gave promise for a completely independent Jewish state.

PARTITION FOR PALESTINE

Both plans were thoroughly debated by a special Ad Hoc Committee of the General Assembly at its fall session in 1947. Arab and Jewish representatives were heard again. As the session drew to its close, it became obvious that the Zionists were determined to obtain a decision favoring the majority plan. The political atmosphere at Lake Success grew tense, and speculation was rife as to whether or not the Zionists would be able to obtain the necessary two-thirds majority, depending to a great extent on the attitude of the numerous South American and Caribbean republics.[33] On November 29, 1947—a date memorable in Jewish history—the General Assembly

[32] Australia, Canada, Czechoslovakia, Guatemala, India, Iran, the Netherlands, Peru, Sweden, Uruguay, and Yugoslavia. No major powers were included.

[33] For the political activity to secure Latin-American support, see Kermit Roosevelt, "The Partition of Palestine: A Lesson in Pressure Politics," *Middle East Journal*, Jan. 1948.

voted to recommend the partition of Palestine, with an economic union as proposed by the majority report.

The Arab state was to include the central and eastern part of Palestine, from the valley of Esdraelon down to Beersheba, western Galilee, and a strip of land along the Mediterranean coast from Gaza southward and along the Egyptian border to the Red Sea. Jaffa would constitute an enclave in the Jewish state, which was to extend over eastern Galilee and the valley of Esdraelon, a coastal area from Haifa to south of Jaffa, and a major part of the Negeb. Jerusalem and Bethlehem with the adjoining territory were to stay outside of both states and be subject to an administration responsible to the Trusteeship Council. The Assembly also took note of Britain's decision to terminate the mandate by August 1, 1948; provided for the establishment of the two states within two months after British withdrawal; established a five-nation UN Palestine Commission to implement the resolution; and called upon the Security Council to assist in its implementation of the plan, instructing it to interpret as a threat to peace any attempt to change the partition plan by force.

Thirty-three states voted for this motion, thirteen voted against, and ten abstained. Among the big powers who favored partition were the United States, the Soviet Union, and France. Great Britain and China abstained from voting, and so did Argentina, Chile, Colombia, El Salvador, Ethiopia, Honduras, Mexico, and Yugoslavia. The negative votes included the Arab states of Egypt, Iraq, Lebanon, Saudi Arabia, Syria, and Yemen and also Afghanistan, Cuba, Greece, India, Iran, Pakistan, and Turkey.

Acting in accordance with the Charter and following regular democratic procedures, the majority of civilized mankind gave its verdict on the future status of the Holy Land. Procedurally there was no flaw in the decision. Its political implications, however, were obvious. Practically the whole of ex-colonial Asia and the Near East opposed the solution, a fact which was vitally to affect Asia's affairs. To the Arabs and other Asiatics, the United Nations decision meant that once again the outside world—predominantly Western and far removed from the scene—had imposed its will upon Eastern peoples. This, in their view, was not compatible with repeated progressive-liberal protestations of respect for Asia's nationalism and self-determination.

The Arabs felt particularly resentful toward the United States, since they believed that it was this country whose presence or influ-

Map 5. Palestine. Light shading shows area allotted to Israel by
the United Nations; dark area, that occupied by Israel.

ence helped to rally enough votes for the partition. They also reproached Americans for "betraying" many promises made both by President Roosevelt and President Truman to the effect that no basic decision on Palestine would ever be taken without the agreement of both parties directly concerned.[34]

The Arab states challenged the resolution's binding validity from a legal point of view. They argued that, according to the UN Charter, the Assembly did not possess the right of binding decision but only of recommendation. Consequently they assumed an attitude of nonco-operation. More forthrightly the Arab Higher Committee of Palestine on February 6, 1948, stated that "any attempt by the Jews or any other power or group of powers to establish a Jewish state in Arab territory is an act of oppression which will be resisted in self-defense by force." [35]

The Arab-Jewish War

Deeds were soon to confirm these words. In the neighboring Arab states volunteers were recruited for the defense of Palestine, and after January 1948 armed detachments of Arabs began entering Palestine and attacking Jewish settlements. By February 1 these clashes had resulted in over 2,500 casualties, and the toll mounted as the days went by. Faced with this violence, Great Britain on January 1 declared that since the Jews and the Arabs could not agree on a solution, she would not aid the United Nations in the implementation of the partition plan, would terminate her mandate by May 15, 1948, and would oppose an earlier entry of the UN Palestine commission into the country.[36]

[34] See below, p. 443.

[35] Larry L. Leonard, "The United Nations and Palestine," International Conciliation, Oct. 1949, p. 650.

[36] For a highly critical analysis of British policy, see The British Record on Partition as Revealed by British Military Intelligence and Other Official Sources, A Memorandum Submitted to the Special Session of the General Assembly of the United Nations, April, 1948, published by The Nation Associates as a supplement to The Nation (New York), May 8, 1948. The latter periodical as well as the group sponsoring it—The Nation Associates—have distinguished themselves by their vigorous support of the Zionist cause. Apart from the above-mentioned document, The Nation Associates in June 1948 submitted to President Truman a memorandum "pointing out—to use The Nation's words—how his Palestine policy has been undermined by the State Department working in close co-operation with the Middle Eastern oil companies." The basis of the memorandum was a report, allegedly written in Cairo in December 1947, by James Terry Duce, vice-president of the Arabian American Oil Company, to

The Arab opposition also affected American policy. On March 19 the United States declared in the Security Council that, since partition proved unworkable, Palestine ought to be subjected to a temporary UN trusteeship. This change of policy met with outspoken criticism from the Zionists. Another special session of the General Assembly, which sat between April 16 and May 15, 1948, discussed this new American proposal but failed to produce majority support for it. The Soviet Union, in particular, insisted on the implementation of the November partition resolution. Eventually the Assembly recommended the appointment of a United Nations mediator and of a United Nations commissioner for Jerusalem.

On May 14, 1948, the British officially terminated their mandate over Palestine, withdrawing their last forces from the country. On the same day the National Council at a session in Tel-Aviv proclaimed the Jewish state of Israel. A few hours later President Truman extended *de facto* recognition to this new state on behalf of the United States.

Soon afterward Arab armies from Syria, Lebanon, Transjordan, Iraq, and Egypt entered Palestine. Arab and Jewish forces were obviously unequal. On one side were the regular armies of established Arab states, of which Egypt alone had nearly twenty million inhabitants. Among these armies, the Arab Legion of Transjordan proved to be the most effective. Commanded by Brigadier John Bagot Glubb Pasha, it employed forty British officers in key positions and played a disproportionately important role if we consider the small size and population of Transjordan. Next in effectiveness was the Iraqi force, which had to cross a long stretch of the Syrian desert to reach Palestine. The Egyptian army made a very poor showing, caused to no small degree by corruption and abuses in its rear. The regular armies of Syria and Lebanon were supplemented by a voluntary force, the Arab Liberation Army, commanded by Fawzi el-Kawukji who had been in the service of Nazi Germany during World War II. The Palestine Arabs formed the so-called Army of Judea, under the command of Abdul Kader el-Husseini, nephew of the grand mufti. Behind these Arab armies stood the Arab League, professedly united and determined to destroy Israel.

Opposing them was the army of Israel commanded by Yaakov

W. F. Moore, president of the company. A summary of this report may be found in *The Nation* of June 26, 1948, under the title "Blood and Oil, Aramco's Secret Report on Palestine," pp. 705 ff.

Dori, with Colonel Yigal Yadin, a thirty-one-year-old native of Jerusalem, as its chief of operations. The backbone of the Israeli army was the old self-defense organization, *Haganah*. The latter was divided into the *Palmah*, an elite force sponsored by the leftist Mapam Socialist Labor Party; *Hish*, a regular field force; and *Mishmar*, a home guard of elderly people. The Palmah insisted on retaining its special character and tended to act independently of the main force. The Israeli army numbered at its peak about 75,000 members. It had women's auxiliary services, which helped greatly by releasing men for front-line duties.

The two former terrorist organizations—*Irgun* [37] and the Stern Gang [38]—continued to operate apart from the army, and on a few occasions clashed with the armed forces over matters of policy. Israel's forces were handicapped somewhat by lack of over-all unity. Their morale, however, was very high and their equipment adequate. Arms and munitions, even airplanes, were purchased abroad, chiefly in Czechoslovakia, and considerable quantities were smuggled out of western Europe and the United States.[39] Jewish volunteers from the United States and from other countries, some of them with a good military education, strengthened Israeli forces.

International Repercussions

The creation of Israel and the resulting Arab-Jewish war had far-reaching international repercussions. On May 20, 1948, the Security Council appointed Count Folke Bernadotte, president of the Swedish

[37] Irgun was commanded by Menachem Begin. Peter H. Bergson, head of the Hebrew Committee of National Liberation in the United States, acted as Begin's chief aide for fund-collecting purposes.

[38] The Stern Gang leaders were Nathan Friedman-Yellin and Matitiahu Shmuelovitz.

[39] According to the provisions of the UN-imposed truce, an embargo was placed on all shipments of arms to the belligerent parties. Both sides adhered to this prohibition only half-heartedly and both were ready to violate it whenever they were able to do so. In this illegal contest Israel was in a stronger position than the Arab states because she had ample dollar funds to pay for the weapons supplied by the Soviet satellites. The latter were quite willing to evade the embargo, provided they were paid in dollars. This contrasted with the attitude of Britain who, by faithfully observing the embargo injunction, made it hard for the Arab states, particularly Egypt, to replenish their stocks of arms and munitions, most of which were of the British type. It may be added that treaties concluded in 1930, 1936, and 1946, respectively, between Great Britain, on the one hand, and Iraq, Egypt, and Transjordan, on the other, contained a provision that the military equipment of these Arab states should follow British patterns.

Red Cross, as UN mediator for Palestine. Bernadotte's work and the Council's action with regard to the conflict constitute a complicated chapter in United Nations history, and it would be tedious to reproduce all the details. Suffice it to say that under UN auspices Israel and the Arabs concluded two truces, two breathing spells in the war. On September 16 Bernadotte recommended to the UN General Assembly a change in the proposed partition boundaries, which amounted to assigning the Negeb to the Arab state. The following day he was assassinated in Jerusalem by Jewish terrorists. Dr. Ralph Bunche, an American, took over his duties, and, aided by the Conciliation Commission, initiated armistice discussions between the belligerents on the island of Rhodes. Between January and July 1949 a series of armistices were concluded by Israel, on the one hand, and Egypt, Lebanon, Transjordan, and Syria, on the other. Basically the armistice agreements maintained the territorial disposition resulting from the war operations. This meant that about three-quarters of Palestine came under the authority of Israel. The war extended Israel's *de facto* boundaries, which now included the northern, western, and southern parts of Palestine. The Arabs retained the central-eastern part adjoining Transjordan, but with a respectably wide Jewish corridor between Tel-Aviv and Jerusalem, and the so-called Gaza strip along the Mediterranean. The central-eastern part was occupied by Transjordan's Arab Legion, the Gaza strip by the Egyptians. No peace treaties were negotiated.

The Jewish-Arab war profoundly altered the strategic and political situation in the Middle East. Points of major significance are as follows:

1) Israel emerged victorious from the conflict. Except for the Arab Legion, most of the Arab forces suffered heavy defeats and proved unequal to the task.

2) Israel owed her victory to her higher morale, better equipment, and superior organization. Israel represented Western efficiency. The Arabs were defeated largely because of the poor morale of troops, bad leadership, and, above everything, political dissensions among the participating states.[40]

[40] The Arabs, not without certain justification, laid some of the blame for their poor success on the UN-sponsored truces. "Nearly every Arab, in every Arab country," observes *The Economist* (March 5, 1949), "believed and still believes that, had it not been for the first truce imposed upon them by UNO, Britain and other outsiders, they would have won the war. There is no doubt that certain Jewish areas were at this junction extremely hard pressed. Certainly,

3) The Arab League proved to be an inadequate instrument of determined political action. Rivalry between Egypt and the Hashimite kingdoms of Transjordan and Iraq prevented co-operation. It also made impossible the creation of an Arab state in Palestine. Egypt sponsored the so-called all-Palestinian Arab government, which was proclaimed on September 20, 1948, in Gaza under the mufti's leadership. Transjordan refused to recognize its authority and eventually (December 1, 1948) annexed the east-central part of Palestine.

4) Israel owed a great deal to assistance extended from abroad and to the solidarity of Jewish people the world over. Israel's intelligence services, both in Palestine and abroad, including that in England, proved definitely superior to those of the Arabs.[41]

5) The war abounded in cruelties and violations of international law. Jewish settlements were better defended than were Arab villages. "Scores of Arab villages, deemed uninhabitable, had been razed [by the Jews] as insurance against their owner's return." [42] The Jews massacred all the Arab civilian population in the village of Deir Yasin in April 1948.

6) The war drove nearly one million Arabs out of their homes. This flight was partly due to the fear of Jewish reprisals and partly to the urgings of Arab political leaders to evacuate probable battle areas. The refugees fled to the surrounding Arab countries or to the Arab-occupied parts of Palestine. In the spring of 1949 the number of Arab displaced persons eligible for relief was officially estimated at 940,000.[43] At the beginning of the war there were 1,320,000 Arabs

---

had the truce not been declared on June 11th, the Arabs would have killed more Jews than they did, which would from their point of view have been so much gain." Furthermore, as the periodical rightly points out, "Arab soldiers are not temperamentally suited to living in truce conditions. Some of them were short of pay packets, others of comforts, many found the Palestinians—particularly around Gaza—a disappointing, thieving lot. By July, therefore [at the time when the first truce came to an end], they were fighting with little heart and less skill."

[41] According to Kenneth W. Bilby, *New Star in the Near East* (New York, 1950), "Even the activities of the British Foreign Office in respect to the Arab world were reported in detail to the government at Tel-Aviv" (p. 70).

[42] *Ibid.*, p. 3.

[43] The exact number of Arab refugees is still a matter of controversey, estimates varying from well over 1,000,000 on the one hand to a little over 500,000 on the other (the latter from official Israeli sources). According to the first report of the secretary-general on United Nations Relief for Palestine Refugees, issued on November 4, 1949, the number of destitute Arabs eligible for aid was 940,000, distributed as follows: Lebanon, 127,800; Syria, 78,200; Transjordan, 94,000; Arab Palestine, 357,400; Israel, 37,600; Gaza strip, 245,000; total 940,000.

and 640,000 Jews in Palestine. The establishment of Israel resulted in the displacement of nearly 70 per cent of the Arab population, which the Israeli government refused to readmit.[44]

THE INTERNAL SITUATION IN ISRAEL

Israel is an almost unique phenomenon in the annals of history. Other nations, to be sure, have been created as a result of successive waves of immigration. But Israel did not follow the usual pattern. In the Jewish community in Palestine, emphasis was laid from the very beginning on the total social transformation of the incoming settlers, on their de-urbanization and on their productivity. The immigrants, except the oriental Jews, were imbued with a pioneering spirit that made such a transformation possible. Although nothing has changed ideologically since the creation of the state, the new mass immigration has posed entirely new problems. First of all, the rate of immigration assumed tremendous proportions. In the first thirty-three months of Israel's existence 500,000 immigrants entered.

Of the above number the refugees who have actually left their homes are estimated at between 600,000 and 700,000; the remaining are those who have not moved, but who as a result of the hostilities have become destitute or homeless. (See S. G. Thicknesse, *Arab Refugees, A Survey of Resettlement Possibilities* [London, 1949]; "The Palestine Refugees," *R.C.A.J.*, Jan. 1950; and W. de St. Aubin, "Peace and Refugees in the Middle East," *Middle East Journal*, July 1949.)

[44] It may be interesting at this juncture to quote George Antonius, who in his *Arab Awakening*, written ten years before the creation of Israel, forcefully presented the Arab case in the Palestinian controversy. Said he: "The treatment meted out to Jews in Germany and other European countries is a disgrace to its authors and to modern civilization; but posterity will not exonerate any country that fails to bear its proper share of the sacrifices needed to alleviate Jewish suffering and distress. To place the brunt of the burden upon Arab Palestine is a miserable evasion of the duty that lies upon the whole of the civilized world. It is also morally outrageous. No code of morals can justify the persecution of one people in an attempt to relieve the persecution of another. The cure for the eviction of Jews from Germany is not to be sought in the eviction of the Arabs from their homeland. . . . The logic of facts is inexorable. It shows that no room can be made in Palestine for a second nation except by dislodging or exterminating the nation in possession" (pp. 411–412). Reprinted by permission of the publisher, G. P. Putnam's Sons.

In stark contrast to these words stands the following statement of the pro-Zionist writer, Dr. Joseph Dunner, in the Preface to his *The Republic of Israel:* "There is no doubt that the emergence of the first Jewish Commonwealth in nineteen hundred years has changed the course of Jewish and world history. That a people, bitterly abused, oppressed and pogromized, could rise again, must give courage and hope to all who believe in the forward march of the human race. It is proof of what the human spirit and dedication to a noble purpose can do in spite of heavily weighted odds" (p. ix).

In February 1951 Israel's population was officially estimated at 1,400,000, of which 170,000 were Arabs. Nearly 110,000 immigrants lived in temporary camps, i.e., 10 per cent of the total Jewish population was without permanent lodgings or work. Speedy integration of these new arrivals proved a major social and economic problem for the budding state and made orderly planning difficult. But the government adopted the policy of unrestricted immigration as one of its cardinal principles. The new immigrants did not display the same pioneering spirit as did those who had come in the early days of the mandate. Having survived Nazi persecution in Europe or escaped reprisals in the Arab countries of the East, these new settlers sought above everything security, which they conceived primarily in terms of the restoration of their old social and economic status. They tended, therefore, to settle in compact neighborhoods and to persist in their old occupations no matter how unproductive the latter might have been or proved to be in the new environment. This difference between them and the earlier settlers was deepened by their inferior economic status and accentuated by a certain bureaucratic formalism in the new state.[45]

Economic Problems

Economically Israel faced equally challenging problems. Even during the mandatory period the Jewish *Yishuv* had a deficit economy, but the deficit became worse after the establishment of statehood. That Israel avoided and avoids bankruptcy is due primarily to the voluntary contributions of American Jewry. The targets of the 1949 and 1950 fund drives in the United States known as the United Jewish Appeal were $250,000,000 a year, most of which was to help Israel. These were large sums compared to the Israeli state budget, which in 1949–1950 amounted only to $285,000,000. In October 1949 Prime Minister Ben Gurion stated that Israel's deficit was £I (Israel pounds) 7,000,000 ($20,000,000) a month.

In April 1949 Israel adopted a four-year plan—a bold program for the development of new industries and agriculture and the rehabilitation of the immigrants. But the speed of immigration continued to transcend economic absorptive capacity, and there were press reports of demonstrations by immigrants, who demanded "bread and work." Israel's economic position was not made easier by the

[45] For an analysis of Israel's internal situation, see Edwin Samuel, "The Government of Israel and Its Problems," *Middle East Journal*, Jan. 1949.

economic boycott of the surrounding Arab states and Iraq's ban on the flow of Kirkuk oil through the pipeline to the refinery at Haifa. Some lessening of deficit spending was brought about by the conclusion of trade agreements with a number of European countries. But the main appeal had to be made to American Jews.

In October 1950 American Jewry pledged Israel $1,000,000,000 over the next three years for the resettlement of 600,000 Jews. This was followed by flotation in the United States of an Israeli bond issue totaling $500,000,000. Headed by Henry Morgenthau, Jr., former American Secretary of the Treasury, the issue showed promise of success. In the spring of 1951 Prime Minister Ben Gurion toured Jewish centers in the United States to make a final appeal in behalf of the great fund drive.

Political Problems

Politically Israel represented, as could be expected, Western parliamentary democracy. In January 1949, elections based on universal suffrage resulted in the establishment of a one-chamber parliament (Knesset) of 120 members. The political parties which had been in existence under the mandate continued with slight modifications in their names or composition. The Moderate Socialists of David Ben Gurion (*Mapai*) emerged as the dominant party, with the Left-Wing Socialists (*Mapam*), Orthodox Jews, and Revisionists (*Herut*) as the three other most important groups. The Communist Party, allowed to act freely, polled 15,287 votes and secured four seats. In February 1949 the Knesset voted by 50 to 38 to acquire a constitution "by evolution over an unspecified period of years."

From the beginning, Israel had a coalition cabinet of four parties: Mapai, holding a majority of the portfolios, Mapam, Orthodox, and General Zionist. The Revisionists were excluded from the executive branch, and at one time legal proceedings were initiated against some of their leaders. In 1948–1949 there was even some doubt, in view of their terrorist record and their independent course, whether or not they could be integrated in the new state. Experience has shown, however, that these fears were exaggerated. Nevertheless, they continued to represent the most chauvinistic and expansionist tendency in Israel. If one excepts the Communist Party, which can be regarded as an instrument of an alien power, the only other group which found integration difficult was the United Religious Front. These stubborn orthodox elements, who were given three portfolios in Ben Gurion's cabinet, challenged the Socialist-espoused principle of the separation of church and state. Their refusal to acknowledge the secularization of Israel's public life brought about a serious cabinet crisis in the fall of 1950. The orthodox leaders demanded a ban on nonkosher meat imports and on transportation on Sabbath days and insisted on religious education for youth. The November 1950 municipal and rural elections brought moderate gains to parties of the right (General Zionists and the Revisionists) but the Socialist parties still commanded a strong position. *Histadruth* (the General Confederation of Labor) continued to occupy the key position in Israeli politics.

The second elections, held in July 1951, did not change the basic pattern of Israel's internal politics. The most significant development was perhaps the strengthening of the General Zionists (Dr. Weizmann's party), who more than doubled their representation. This could be largely ascribed to the influx of many new immigrants of a more conservative type, especially from Soviet-dominated Europe, but also from the Arab countries, who were not likely to support the traditional Socialist trends in Israel.[46]

The Arab Minority

The position and future of the Arab minority in Israel were not clear. Officially the Arabs were permitted to enjoy civic freedom and rights as citizens of the new state. Unofficially, according to some sources,[47] discrimination was practiced against them in many ways. Israel established a Ministry for Minorities, later renamed the Ministry of Police, under Sephardi Minister Behor Shitrit, and it may be assumed that internal security overrode other considerations. On May 3, 1950, Israeli forces with mortars and automatic weapons drove 12,000 Arabs from two villages near Hebron in order to clear the area for cultivation by Jewish settlers. Whether the Arabs were citizens of Israel or infiltrees from Jordan, the method employed was not consonant with Israel's professed democratic procedures. In

[46] The composition of the Knesset in January 1949 and August 1951 follows (the first figure following a party name is the number of seats in 1949, the second the seats in 1951): Mapai, 46, 45; Mapam, 19, 15; United Religious Front, 16, 0; Poale Mizrahi, 0, 8; Agudath Israel, 0, 2; Herut (formerly Irgun), 14, 8; General Zionists, 7, 20; Progressive, 5, 4; Sephardim, 4, 2; Communist, 4, 5; Arab parties, 2, 5; Fighter, 1, 0; WIZO, 1, 0; Yemenites, 1, 1.
[47] Norman Bentwich in his review of Dunner's *The Republic of Israel*, in *Middle Eastern Affairs*, Jan. 1951.

September of the same year Egypt accused Israel of expelling 6,000 Arab nomads across the border into Egyptian territory, and the accusation was confirmed, with a slight reduction in numbers, by Major General William E. Riley, chief of staff of the Palestine Truce Commission, in his report to the United Nations Security Council.

ISRAEL'S FOREIGN POLICY

"The Arab-Jewish struggle . . . has unsettled and poisoned the Middle East for three decades. . . ." This statement by a high Israeli official seems to penetrate to the root of the matter.[48] Israel's existence has posed one of the most baffling problems in the annals of modern diplomacy. The international relations of Israel may be divided—for the purpose of orderly presentation—into two main sectors: relations with the Middle East and with the great powers.

Middle East Relations

In her Middle Eastern diplomacy, Israel's relations with Turkey and Iran should be treated separately from her relations with the Arab world. Turkey, although she voted against partition, never manifested hostility toward Israel. In fact, she was the first in the Middle East to extend diplomatic recognition to the new Jewish state. Religious considerations could not mar this generally friendly relationship, inasmuch as Turkey had become a secularized state. Being more Westernized and prosperous than most of her oriental neighbors, Turkey even had some affinities with Israel. The main difference lay in the fact that Turkey, insisting on her European rather than her Middle Eastern orientation, definitely chose the side of the free world in the East-West struggle, while Israel was cautious not to identify herself with either political bloc.

Iran was more sensitive to the bonds of Islamic solidarity than was Turkey. For this reason her attitude toward Israel was much more reserved. During his visit in the United States in late 1949, the Shah was asked point-blank by a reporter whether or not Iran had recognized Israel and whether he "wished Israel well." In reply, he stated that Iran, as a Moslem country, could not act without due regard to the feelings of other Moslem countries and reserved her decisions

[48] "Israel in the Pattern of Middle East Politics," by Iaacov Shimoni, director of the Asia Division of the Israel Ministry of Foreign Affairs, *Middle East Journal,* July 1950, p. 286.

until proper consultation had occurred.[49] After some lapse of time, Iran did grant Israel *de facto* recognition.

The most vital problem for Israel centers in her relations with the Arab states. These relations, despite the armistices of 1949, have been consistently bad. The Arab countries have never reconciled themselves to the existence of the Jewish state in their midst. They were humiliated in the war of 1948 and have not recovered from the moral and political consequences of their defeat. To preach hostility toward Israel and to promote a "second round" which would result in her complete obliteration was and is the most popular line of behavior for Arab statesmen and politicians. The Arab emotional upset over Israel has become so great that it dwarfs other considerations and ideas and distorts Arab thinking on many an international and domestic problem.

This hatred of Israel is intensified by Arab fear, in part genuine and in part artificially fanned, of alleged Israeli expansionism. Although Israel's official policy has been one of maintaining the postwar *status quo*, one can point to a few facts which lend credence to Arab contentions. The first is that the extremist Revisionist bloc (Herut, former Irgun) remains very much alive in Israeli politics, and as a determined and dynamic body it is apt to wield an influence out of proportion to its real numbers. This bloc, which secured fourteen seats in Israel's first election, has a great appeal to American Jewry. Thus, for example, Menachem Begin, its leader and former head of the terrorist Irgun, visited the United States on what was believed to be a successful fund-raising trip. In New York he was received with high honors, not only by the Jewish community but also by the mayor, and he was the hero of the day in a city-sponsored motorcade through the garment district.[50]

Furthermore, even the official Israeli attitude was not entirely reassuring. During the war in 1948 Israel enlarged her territory over what was originally projected in the UN partition plan and refused to withdraw to the assigned boundaries. Israel's contention was that by invading Israel on May 15, 1948, the Arabs had invalidated the partition resolution and therefore the Arab states had no legal claims under it.[51] Israel (with the kingdom of Jordan) stubbornly rejected all proposals and official United Nations resolutions

[49] *New York Times*, Nov. 18, 1949.
[50] See pictures of his enthusiastic reception in the *New York Times*, Nov. 27, 1948.   [51] Shimoni, *op. cit.*, p. 283 n. 5.

for the internationalization of Jerusalem. In fact, Prime Minister Ben Gurion challenged United Nations authority to the extent of moving Israel's capital from Tel-Aviv to the Jewish-held part of Jerusalem in late 1949.[52]

Israeli leaders had placed great stock in the authority of the United Nations at the time of the partition, but they tended to disregard the United Nations in such matters as the truces, the boundaries, and Jerusalem if UN action collided with their vital interests. This deepened Arab fears. Moreover, the Arabs showed anxiety over the prospects of Israeli economic domination of the Middle East, an anxiety nurtured by fear of the financial and banking power of world Jewry. Finally, mention should be made of Arab suspicion that the Socialist Israeli regime might set a dangerous pattern for left-wing trends in the Arab lands, upset their traditional social structures, and act as a stimulant to numerous minorities in the Arab world.

The tragic problem of Arab refugees added a seemingly inexhaustible source of constant irritation. In fact, this problem hung like a sword of Damocles over the shaky Arab governments, placing them in a most embarrassing and dangerous position. On the one hand, they insisted on the right of the refugees to return to their homes. This legalistic attitude led them to refuse to study any long-range constructive resettlement projects.[53] And they were obviously unable to back up their legal claims by force, thus revealing their impotence. On the other hand, their social and economic structures were profoundly disturbed by the presence of refugee multitudes, and their public funds were strained in granting them relief. The policies of the Arab states toward the refugees were not uniform. Jordan, for example, granted all refugees citizenship. Egypt went to the other extreme of forbidding the refugees the right to work and thus condemning them to idleness, a situation full of explosive potentialities. The fact that the United Nations was not able to devote

[52] The initial plan of the Israeli government had been to move all government offices to Jerusalem and to proclaim it the capital, in defiance of UN resolutions internationalizing the city. Because, however, of possible diplomatic objections to such a move on the part of various member states of the United Nations, the Israeli government decided to transfer only certain departments to Jerusalem, while leaving others in Tel-Aviv. The prime minister and the foreign minister continued to carry on their functions in Tel-Aviv.

[53] Such as those prepared by the Clapp mission which toured the Middle East in 1949. See *Final Report of the U.N. Economic Survey Mission for the Middle East*, U.N. Conciliation Commission for Palestine, Document AAC. 25/6, Dec. 28, 1949.

347

more than about $50,000,000 a year—a pittance—to refugee relief, when at the same time the International Refugee Organization was amply provided with funds to deal with European displaced persons, added to Arab bitterness.

In the summer of 1949 the United Nations Conciliation Committee for Palestine arranged for negotiations with the Israeli and Arab delegations in Lausanne to settle all the outstanding problems including that of the refugees. But by the end of the year the conference wound up in deadlock, because of completely irreconcilable Jewish and Arab attitudes. Israel maintained that the readmission of all the refugees was utterly unrealistic and out of question and that any decision in this regard could be taken only as a part of the over-all political settlement, which would transform the existing armistice agreements into formal peace treaties. The Arab delegations stood firmly on the principle that the first prerequisite of any peace settlement was the readmission of all the refugees.

Nothing was achieved, and the state of hostility between the Arabs and Israel continued. This hostility had another tragic consequence, namely, the uprooting of many old and frequently prosperous Jewish communities in Arab countries. Reprisals against the Jews of Yemen led them to emigrate en masse to Israel, causing no little trouble for the new progressive state in having to absorb a backward, oriental, and almost alien mass of refugees. No contrast could be greater than between a lice-infested, Arabic-speaking, brown-skinned, and superstitious Yemenite coolie and a London-bred and Oxford-educated English Jew, and the latter predominated in the higher echelons of the Israeli Foreign Office. The Jews of Aden, French North Africa, and Libya were also persecuted, and they flocked to Israel. The greatest tragedy was, perhaps, that of the 160,000-strong Jewish community in Iraq. Prosperous and settled in the land even before the coming of the Arabs, these Jews now found life in Iraq unbearable. By the spring of 1951 they had availed themselves of the Iraqi law which permitted them to opt for Israeli citizenship and emigrate.

The only Arab state with which Israel reached a relatively successful *modus vivendi* was Jordan. This was primarily due to the coincidence that they agreed on a few main points, while Jordan quarreled with other Arab states. Thus, for example, the disposition of the Arab-held parts of Palestine ceased to be a Jewish-Arab problem and became an inter-Arab problem, the other Arab states resenting

Jordan's unilateral annexation of this area. Jerusalem was another sector where Israel's and Jordan's policies coincided. Jordan's interest in a free transit route to the Mediterranean led her to enter into negotiations with Israel for a five-year pact. In the spring of 1950, however, because of the pressure of other Arab states, Jordan decided to break off the talks. Despite all the internecine rivalries, Arab solidarity was not quite extinguished. The economic boycott of Israel, proclaimed by the Arab League and reaffirmed as recently as 1950, emphasized again, however imperfect it was in practice, that the Arab ocean had not reconciled itself to the volcanic eruption of the Jewish island in its midst.

Israel and the Big Powers

The friendship of Israel and the United States is an important feature of Israeli relations with the big powers. American influence was largely responsible for the UN partition resolution, and the United States was the first among the big powers to recognize the new Jewish state. Israel expected and obtained economic aid from the United States. During Dr. Weizmann's visit in Washington in May 1948 he was promised a $100,000,000 loan. The promise was fulfilled when the Export-Import Bank announced in January 1949 that this credit had been made available to Israel. No Arab country had ever received direct financial aid from the United States of the same magnitude. In January 1949 the American government granted Israel full *de jure* recognition and appointed a well-known pro-Zionist, Dr. James G. McDonald, as first United States ambassador in Tel-Aviv. Israel invited American specialists such as Dr. Walter C. Lowdermilk to advise her on irrigation and other technical matters. She also concluded contracts with the Ford and Kaiser-Frazer corporations, which resulted in the establishment of motorcar assembly plants in the new state. In 1950 the two countries signed a Point Four agreement that extended to Israel further American assistance.

On the part of the United States this pro-Israeli policy was not achieved without hesitations and sudden shifts. It will be recalled that at one time the United States was prepared to abandon the partition resolution in favor of a trusteeship arrangement. Another shift occurred when Secretary of State Marshall announced official American endorsement of the Bernadotte plan in the fall of 1948. Furthermore, repeated messages were sent by Presidents Roosevelt and Truman to various Arab states and rulers, tending to reassure them that the

United States would not support any solution in Palestine contrary to Arab wishes. These twists in American policy were to a large extent due to the division of responsibility between the White House and the Department of State. While the latter was concerned with the Middle East as a whole, the former tended to treat the Zionist problem in isolation from the rest of the area and as a factor of domestic politics; hence, the inconsistencies. The White House prevailed on all important occasions, and despite its tortuous ways American diplomacy could generally be described as pro-Israeli.

Israeli-British relations are in glaring contrast. Nothing could better illustrate the strange ways of human emotions than the transformation of the Jewish-British friendship of World War I into the outright hatred of Britain at the end and after World War II. Britain's policy, after as during the mandate period, continued to be pro-Arab. Even after the termination of the mandate the British, who occupied Haifa until June 30, 1948, refused to admit Jewish immigrants in that harbor. Britain endorsed the Bernadotte plan because it slightly favored the Arabs and also because by granting the Negeb to the future Arab state it promised British-protected Jordan access to the Mediterranean. Britain resumed her shipments of arms to the Arab states as soon as the conclusion of the Arab-Israeli armistice agreements eliminated United Nations rulings on this matter. And to stress her lack of enthusiasm for Israel, Great Britain abstained from voting on both occasions when Israel's application for membership in the United Nations was being decided.

Despite this political coolness, Israel was linked to Great Britain by more economic bonds than she was to any other country (if we except American charity). The British held sizable Israeli sterling balances in London; they controlled Palestine Potash Ltd., a big concern extracting salts from the Dead Sea; they owned the refinery at Haifa; and they imported considerable quantities of Israel's citrus crops. Notwithstanding the political difficulties, this great nation of traders gradually came to terms with Israel on economic lines, thus normalizing mutual relations.

Israel's relations with the Soviet Union are full of ambiguities. The original Leninist doctrine taught hostility toward Zionism as a nationalist-bourgeois movement. In the interwar period, Soviet agents in the Middle East supported Arab nationalism as opposed to Western imperialism and preached that Zionism was an instrument of British imperial policy. Soviet espousal of the partition resolution came, therefore, as a surprise to many who were acquainted with the basic Communist line. Yet it was logical as a step toward the elimination of Great Britain from this strategic area on the Mediterranean coast. Moreover, it could be explained as an expression of Russia's desire to confuse and unsettle the Middle East, so that she may eventually profit from the new ferment. Be that as it may, the fact remains that, despite her support of the partition resolution, Russia was not regarded by the Arabs as the chief villain of the drama, that role being reserved for the United States. Russia's tactics in the Middle East were tortuous, but one could discern in them a reversion to the old pro-Arab trend to the extent that it served to embarrass the West. It would not be surprising if one day the world should discover that Soviet encouragement was behind some of the popular anti-Zionist demonstrations in the Middle East. One should not forget, however, that basically Soviet policy was dedicated to the social and political revolution in the Middle East, and that all Soviet moves, either pro-Arab or pro-Jewish, had to be treated as tactics subordinated to this major objective.[54]

The Soviet Union extended full diplomatic recognition to Israel a few days after the United States and sent an envoy to Tel-Aviv. Israel sent a minister to Moscow, Mrs. Golda Myerson, a prominent leader in the dominant Mapai party, who later was recalled to become a member of Ben Gurion's cabinet. Relations between the two countries were highlighted by the conclusion in August 1949 of an agreement whereby all former Russian Orthodox properties (including churches, convents, and hospices) in Jerusalem and elsewhere in Israel were taken over by the Soviet government and the Soviet-controlled Orthodox Church. This arrangement placed Soviet representatives in a strategic position in the heart of Jerusalem and delivered into their hands the hitherto anti-Communist Orthodox organization in Palestine. Russia promptly appointed a member of the Soviet Orthodox hierarchy archbishop of Jerusalem. Israel also concluded a number of trade treaties with the Soviet European satellites, thus linking to some extent her economy to that of the postwar Soviet empire.

Israel's policies toward Russia cannot be adequately understood unless they are related to the larger problem of the East-West con-

---

[54] For a typically Marxist approach to the Palestinian problem, see A. B. Magil, *Israel in Crisis* (New York, 1950). The book reveals the party line followed in 1950.

flict. In this conflict Israel has pursued a policy of neutrality, loath to commit herself to either bloc.[55] Israeli and Soviet policies were alike in that both countries extended recognition to the Communist government of China.[56] They were also alike in their opposition to the UN General Assembly's resolution in 1950 rescinding the ban on full diplomatic relations with Franco Spain. But following the Communist invasion of South Korea in June 1950, Israel declared herself opposed to any aggression and pledged her support of United Nations action. Her contribution to the allied war effort has consisted in sending some medical supplies to Korea.

A member of the United Nations since May 11, 1949, Israel has obtained diplomatic recognition from the majority of member states and has thus legally entrenched her position. The Anglo-American-French agreement of May 25, 1950, providing for the sale of arms to the Middle East for defensive purposes only added another guarantee of Israel's security. But her political future remained uncertain in view of the unabated hostility of the Arabs. It was, moreover, doubtful to what extent the strategic interest of the West could be reconciled with Israel's existence. The West, and the United States in particular, was interested in strengthening the Middle East by promoting greater technical and governmental efficiency in these underdeveloped areas, by building up their military power, and by encouraging greater political unity. But greater unity and an improved military position for the Arabs meant a greater danger to Israel, and Israeli officials did not hide their fear of Arab unification schemes. Israel argued that a transformation of the Arab states into progressive societies dedicated to the welfare of the common man would result in automatic abandonment of vindictive attitudes.[57] But this was mere speculation. It presupposed that progress would eliminate nationalism. Israel herself seemed to be a living refutation of this thesis; she was progressive but also nationalist.

[55] This neutrality or (later) "independence" of the Israeli foreign policy was stressed in careful statements by Israel's official spokesmen. (For an authoritative statement, see "Israel's Foreign Policy and International Relations," by Walter Eytan, director-general of the Israeli Foreign Office, *Middle Eastern Affairs*, May 1951.)

[56] It should be pointed out, in all fairness, that Great Britain and a number of other non-Communist countries have also recognized Mao's government.

[57] See Shimoni, *op. cit.*, p. 285.

INTERNAL TRENDS IN THE 1950'S

Israel's cabinets in the 1950's represented coalitions of the dominant Socialist *Mapai* Party with the General Zionists and—to a lesser extent—religious elements. For the major part of this period the premiership remained in the hands of David Ben Gurion, who emerged not only as the practically undisputed leader of Israel but also as the living symbol of those dynamic values and the assertive spirit that characterized modern political Zionism.[58] In 1953 Ben Gurion retired from active leadership to live in a kibbutz in the Negeb, leaving the reins of government to his close lieutenant Moshe Sharett. But the darkening of the international skies in 1955 brought him back to power, first as defense minister and later, in November, as premier. Throughout these years Israel's politics were characterized by the struggle of the dominant left-of-center group to preserve the unity of the new nation on an essentially Western foundation of society. This proved to be an arduous task because of certain serious obstacles, foremost of which was the gradual orientalization of Israel's population. What originally began as a fairly homogeneous Ashkenazi community from eastern Europe had been transformed by the mid-1950's into a culturally heterogeneous group in which oriental Jews constituted over 50 per cent of the population. Moreover, because of their higher birth rate, their numerical preponderance was likely to increase as time went on.

Against the background of this orientalization—with all its social and economic implications—stood the centrifugal tendency of certain elements which had never fully accepted the philosophy and program of the leading political group in the country. First among these was the orthodox religious bloc, which aimed at revival of a Jewish theocratic state. Measures advocated by this bloc included compulsory religious education, a ban on imports of nonkosher food, opposition to military service by women, compulsory jurisdiction of rabbinical courts, and general supremacy of the *Torah* over lay legislation. These views obviously clashed with the attitude of the dominant Socialist elements who, with their Marxist anteced-

---

[58] Dr. Chaim Weizmann, first president of Israel, had died on November 9, 1952. Soon afterward Dr. Albert Einstein, an American citizen, was offered the presidency by Premier Ben Gurion, but he refused it. On December 8 Itzhak Ben-Zvi was elected president.

ents,[59] had an essentially secularist and, not infrequently, atheistic approach to social problems. Another centrifugal force was represented by *Herut*. An heir to the Revisionist organization and to the terrorist groups of wartime, this party continued as spokesman for extreme nationalist elements that advocated expansion southward and eastward. Not only the Egyptian-held Gaza strip and Jordan's west-bank area but also the lands east of the Jordan River were objects of their territorial ambitions.[60]

Moreover, despite their outward adaptation to the existing parliamentary system in Israel, these extremist elements did not entirely forget their defiant attitude toward law in the mandate days, often resorting to acts and tactics hardly in keeping with the spirit of democracy. As a result there was an undercurrent of violence in Israel's politics, expressed by such manifestations as a mob attack on the Knesset during the latter's debate on German reparations; a call for a campaign of "civil disobedience" issued by the *Herut* leader, Menachem Begin, followed by a sabotage plot in Haifa (credited to some *Herut* members) in connection with the same question; and bomb explosions in the Soviet Legation and in the home of Israel Rokach, a General Zionist who was formerly minister of interior.

Communism could not be disregarded as a problem either. The knowledge now available on Communist tactics indicates that the party seldom relies on overt activities only and that it tends to employ, with increasing success, the method of infiltration into other organizations. In the Middle East in general, the line drawn between the Communists and the Socialists has never been as clear as in some more advanced countries of the West. In Israel this phenomenon found its reflection in the existence of the Left-Wing Socialist Party, the *Mapam*, which rather consistently showed pro-Soviet leanings. To be sure, this did not automatically mean that the party as a whole was a Communist-front organization. Yet its pro-

[59] On May 25, 1953, four General Zionist members of the cabinet "resigned in protest against the Mapai (Socialist) party's insistence that on May Day and other labor holidays, schools in working class districts should have the right to fly the red flag, symbol of socialism, alongside the flag of Israel and to sing the Internationale in addition to the Israeli anthem" (quoted from the *Middle East Journal*, Summer, 1953).

[60] For *Herut*'s program and territorial demands, see J. B. Schechtman, "Revisionism," in *Struggle for Tomorrow*, ed. by B. J. Vlavianos and F. Gross (New York, 1954), and James G. McDonald, *My Mission in Israel* (New York, 1951), p. 145.

nounced leftist tendency in conjunction with its pro-Soviet orientation left it open to accusations of dangerous closeness to communism. On February 21, 1952, two prominent members of the *Mapam,* Mrs. Hanna Landau, deputy speaker of the Knesset, and David Livshitz resigned from it on the ground that it "had become indistinguishable from the Communists." [61]

Elections to the third Knesset, which took place in July 1955, revealed that the centrifugal or even extremist trends were in the ascendant. The period of bourgeois moderation, characteristic of the 1951 elections, seemed to be over, and this time the political center lost rather heavily to the forces of the far right and the far left. The most spectacular change, perhaps, was the virtual doubling of *Herut* representation from 8 to 15. Otherwise leftist groups (*Mapam, Ahdut Avoda,* Communists, and Progressives) registered gains at the expense of the center, and there was a slight increase in the strength of religious parties. Despite the orientalization of the population, political affiliations tended to follow the already-existing pattern, and no successful attempt was made to build parties corresponding to the ethnic origins of the population. Such minor representation as the Yemenites and the Sephardim had had in the previous Knesset disappeared altogether in the new legislature.

The effects of this new shift in political configuration were soon felt in the composition of the cabinet. General Zionists, who were the most Western-minded members of the dominant coalition and who lost one-third of their seats in the Knesset, were removed from the government and their places were filled by the left-wing parties. The new cabinet formed on November 2, 1955, by Ben Gurion represented an alliance of *Mapai* (9 portfolios), *Mapam* (2), *Hapoel Hamizrachi* (2), *Ahdut Avoda* (2), and Progressives (1). The assignment of two ministries to *Hapoel Hamizrachi,* an orthodox labor party, could be interpreted as a device to appease the religious groups in the country while preserving the essentially leftist character of the new coalition.[62]

Economic questions claimed, as usual, a high priority in government activities. The budget continued to show a steady deficit, which was balanced by grants from the United States, contributions

[61] *Middle East Journal,* Spring, 1952.

[62] Concerning the co-operation between Socialists and "theocratic fundamentalists," see a lengthy analysis by Henry Hurwitz in "Israel, What Now?" *Menorah Journal,* vol. XLII, nos. 1 and 2, 1954.

from Jewish organizations abroad, and the floating of an Israeli bond issue in America. Between 1948 and 1955 Israel received $367,000,000 from the United States government under the form of loans, grants-in-aid, and technical assistance. This compared favorably with the total of $163,000,000 granted to all the Arab states during the same period.[63] Although the big wave of immigration had come to an end, immigrants, encouraged by the Israeli government and the World Zionist Organization, continued to flock to the country. This posed a never-ending financial problem, as it was estimated that the settling of immigrants required about $3,000 a person. Moreover, because of their oriental origin most of the new arrivals lacked the necessary skills to perform productive work in agriculture or industry, thus increasing the difficulties of absorption. The lack of adequate water resources prevented full development of contemplated irrigation schemes, while no progress was made on the utilization of the water of the Jordan River owing to the opposition of the neighboring Arab states.[64] At the same time the continuous boycott of Israel by the Arab League separated Israel's industries from their natural outlets. Stringent controls of imports

[63] Actually, the period for the Arab states should read July 1, 1945, to June 30, 1955. Between her creation as a state and the end of 1955 Israel received an estimated total of $2,000,000,000 from external sources. This was composed of the following sums (in round figures): direct United States government aid—$367,000,000 (grants-in-aid, $226,000,000; Export-Import Bank loan, $135,000,000; technical assistance, $6,000,000); Israel bond sales in U.S., $227,000,000; United Jewish Appeal, $360,000,000; West German reparations, $160,000,000; other contributions (gifts, capital investments, etc.) from all external sources, $886,000,000.

These figures were compiled from the following sources: testimony of Arthur Z. Gardiner of the U.S. Department of State before the House Committee on Foreign Affairs on May 10, 1954 (New York Times, June 14, 1954); H. H. Howard, "The Development of United States Policy in the Near East, South Asia and Africa during 1954," Department of State Bulletin, Feb. 28, 1955; New York Times, Feb. 6, 1956; Eliezer Livneh, "Israel's Two Thousand Million Dollars—Where Have They Gone?" Jewish Observer and Middle East Review, Nov. 19, 1954; and Operations Report, International Cooperation Administration, Nov. 16, 1955.

[64] On October 14, 1953, Eric Johnston, prominent leader of the American film industry, left for the Middle East on behalf of President Eisenhower on a mission to secure Arab and Israeli collaboration on the development of the Jordan River with a view to benefiting all the riparian states. His proposals met with a cool reception in Arab capitals, and such negotiations as were conducted in the course of his subsequent visits to the Middle East showed little progress.

and currency had to be maintained, and rationing of foodstuffs was not uncommon.

Despite all these difficulties, Israel was putting to good use the generous aid it received from abroad. Every year marked new developments in collective farming, construction, mining, and industry. Noteworthy in this connection was the agreement signed on September 10, 1952, with the Western German Republic whereby the latter agreed to pay Israel, in the course of fourteen years, $822,-000,000 in goods as reparations for the damages inflicted upon European Jewry by the Nazi regime.[65] Money thus obtained was earmarked, in large part, to finance Israel's development projects. In September 1955 an exploration party struck oil in Huleikat (Helez) in the Negeb, having completed a well abandoned years earlier by the Iraq Petroleum Company. This important discovery would open new vistas of economic self-sufficiency if the oil proved to exist in commercial quantities.

The Arab minority continued to suffer from a number of practical disabilities. It was restricted in its freedom of movement as many Arab-populated areas of Israel were subject to the authority of Israeli military commanders. Its economic opportunities were limited because such funds as Israel could obtain from abroad and such planned effort as she made to develop the country were destined to benefit Jewish and not Arab inhabitants. Except for local municipal and village offices, positions in the state administration were, to all practical purposes, denied to Arabs.

The most grievous disability resulted from an important piece of legislation known as the Land Acquisition Law of March 10, 1953. This law authorized the state to seize the property which "(1) On

[65] From the legal point of view this agreement was without precedent, inasmuch as it involved payments to a new state in compensation for deeds committed before the establishment of that state toward persons who might or might not have become its citizens. Politically, the agreement temporarily strained the good relations prevailing between the Bonn Republic and the Arab states. The latter accused Bonn of strengthening Israel and thus working against the Arabs. The West German government replied that shipments to Israel under the agreement would not include strategic goods. A joint Arab mission which visited West Germany failed to persuade the Bonn government to abandon the agreement. For some time Arab states contemplated an economic boycott of West Germany in reprisal, but eventually they desisted from doing so on the ground that, in their view, Germany was not a free agent in this transaction, having been prodded into it by the United States.

April 1, 1952, was not in the possession of its owners; (2) Was used or earmarked within the period from May 4, 1948, to April 1, 1952, for purposes of essential development, settlement or security; (3) Is still required for one of these purposes." Owners of such property were given the right to indemnity, which was to be based on the value of the property on January 1, 1950, with an increase of 3 per cent for each year thereafter, to be paid in Israeli currency at the current rate of exchange.[66] Although primarily affecting the refugees living outside Israel's territory, the law was likely to hurt considerable numbers of Arabs in Israel because of the displacements that had occurred during or after the war of 1948. Even if some of these displacements were voluntary, in a purely technical sense, in most cases they were caused by fear such as had motivated the mass flight of refugees to the safety of the neighboring Arab states in 1948. The law did not differentiate between voluntary or involuntary absence from one's land, merely stating that it covered property "not in the possession of its owners" on a certain date. Official Israeli sources denied that the law was discriminatory, claiming instead that it applied to all absentee landowners irrespective of nationality. Such assertions, however, could not disguise the fact that Arabs were subjected to legal harassment and ill-compensated deprivation of property and that by and large they were treated as second-class citizens.[67]

ISRAEL'S FOREIGN RELATIONS IN THE 1950'S

No improvement occurred in Israel's relations with the Arab states. In general, they deteriorated. Technically at war with Israel, the Arab states not only continued their economic boycott of the new state but intensified it by drawing up additional stringent regulations and establishing regional boycott offices. Foreign commercial and industrial firms were given a choice of either continuing their business with Israel or with the Arab countries under penalty of being blacklisted. Airlines could not include Israel in routes passing through Arab territories, and merchant ships were enjoined not to call on Israeli ports during voyages that led them through Arab waters. Egypt exploited her special position in the Suez Canal and the Gulf of Aqaba to prevent Israel-bound vessels from reaching

[66] The text is in the *Middle East Journal*, Summer, 1953.
[67] For a competent treatment of the problem, see Don Peretz, "The Arab Minority in Israel," *Middle East Journal*, Spring, 1953.

their destination. Egypt dominated the Gulf of Aqaba because the only navigable passage at the entrance of the Gulf was located in her territorial waters and was effectively covered by her shore batteries. This tended to immobilize the new Israeli harbor, Elath, situated at the head of the Gulf.

A peace settlement seemed far away. Israel did not cease protesting that she desired peace and that she was prepared to sign a peace treaty to replace the existing armistice agreements. The Arab states made any talk of peace conditional upon Israel's compliance with three resolutions of the United Nations, namely, those enjoining the internationalization of Jerusalem, the readmission of Arab refugees to their homes, and the rectification of boundaries so as to conform to the original partition resolution of November 1947.[68] Inasmuch as Israel steadily rejected these conditions as a prerequisite to a peace treaty, and the Arabs were adamant in insisting upon them, the likelihood of the two parties coming together was as remote as ever. In fact, one might legitimately suspect that behind this complete inflexibility on both sides was a basic reluctance to consider a peace settlement. While on many counts peace might be welcome to Israel, it also presented potential disadvantages, foremost among which was freezing of the existing modest and inconvenient boundaries—an idea repugnant to a good many Israelis long conditioned to think in terms of Palestine as a whole as their rightful possession. Also Israel could count on continued high-level generosity on the part of American Zionists so long as she was threatened with a war of revenge and so long as an aura of crisis surrounded her position in the Middle East. Any improvement in international relations might adversely affect the readiness of the

[68] The Palestine partition resolution of November 29, 1947, provided for the internationalization of Jerusalem. On December 9, 1949, the General Assembly again adopted a resolution that Jerusalem should be administered under a separate international regime. The General Assembly resolution of December 11, 1948, provided "that refugees wishing to return to their homes and live at peace with their neighbors should be permitted to do so at the earliest practicable date, and that compensation should be paid for property of those choosing not to return and for loss or damage to property which under principles of international law or in equity should be made good by Governments or authorities concerned." Concerning the boundaries, the Arab states and Israel on May 12, 1949, signed agreements with the United Nations Conciliation Commission to consider the partition plan of 1947 "as a starting-point and framework for the discussion of territorial questions" (L. L. Leonard, "The United Nations and Palestine," *International Conciliation,* Oct. 1949, p. 737).

American Zionist community to make heavy cash outlays for the upkeep of Israel. As for the Arabs, the bitterness engendered by their defeat in Palestine was so great and so widespread among the masses that it was unsafe for any Arab government, however strong, to go on record as favoring peace or negotiations with Israel.

Against this background of mutual inflexibility, the border situation was going from bad to worse. Violations of the armistice boundaries were frequent and were being committed by both sides. Their nature, however, differed according to who was involved. In the first place there were frequent exchanges of fire between the military outposts and clashes between border patrols, which unwittingly or knowingly crossed into alien territory. Such incidents ran into the hundreds within a single year and could be considered almost a routine matter for the Mixed Armistice Commissions which watched over the truce along the borders. Marauding Bedouin bands, traditionally accustomed to disregard boundary lines, occasionally caused minor disturbances. But so far as the Arabs were concerned, violations were usually committed by individual infiltrators, mostly refugees or farmers who crossed the boundary to rejoin their relatives or to revisit their farmlands located on the other side of the border.[69] The Israelis were determined to stop these infiltrations by a policy of retaliation, the chief advocate of which was Premier Ben Gurion himself.[70] Consequently the border violations committed by the Israelis had the character of well-organized military raids against Arab communities of the neighboring countries. Among a number of such raids, four assumed the proportions of major military operations and as a result attracted considerable attention and publicity abroad. These were the raids carried out against the Arab villages of Kibya and Nahhalin in Jordan, the Egyptian headquarters in the Gaza strip, and a Syrian village east of the Sea of Galilee. The Kibya attack was executed on October 14, 1953, by 250 to 300 "well-trained Israeli soldiers" according to the head of the Palestine Truce Supervisory Organization, Major-General Vagn Bennike. Fifty-three Arab villagers, regardless of age and sex, were killed

[69] In this mass of infiltrators there were some who, because of their total destitution, were intent on robbery or revenge and who, accordingly, were guilty of killings and assaults. Israel claimed an impressive number of such crimes had been perpetrated, especially in border settlements.

[70] See article by Harry Gilroy, "Policy of Retaliation Is Defended by Israel: Officials Say Reprisals Are Their Only Answer to Aggression," *New York Times*, Dec. 18, 1955.

and their houses destroyed. The pattern resembled the Deir Yasin massacre in 1948; it was an indiscriminate killing of civilians with the obvious purpose of sowing terror among the borderland Arab population. On October 15 the Mixed Armistice Commission and on November 24 the U.N. Security Council strongly condemned Israel for the attack. The Council actually approved by a vote of 9 to 0 a motion of censure presented jointly by the United States, Britain, and France. The Kibya raid coincided with another serious border incident, namely, an attempt by the Israelis to drain the Huleh swamps and construct a hydroelectric plant in the demilitarized zone between Israel and Syria. Inasmuch as this operation involved diversion of Jordan water to Israel, Syria lodged a protest before the United Nations. General Vagn Bennike, in his capacity as chief of the Truce team in Palestine, issued an order enjoining Israel to cease work on the Huleh canal. Despite this Israel went ahead with her project, which, in turn, brought about a rather strong reaction on the part of the United States. On October 20, 1953, Secretary of State John Foster Dulles suspended aid to Israel, earmarked under the Foreign Operations Administration, until such time as Israel complied with Bennike's order.[71] This determined action seemed to be more persuasive than the rather ineffectual United Nations resolutions, and on October 28 Israel declared that she would stop the Huleh operations. On the same day President Eisenhower declared that aid to Israel would be resumed.

The Kibya and the Huleh incidents caused considerable excitement in the Arab countries. On January 9, 1954, King Saud of Saudi Arabia declared in an interview that, if necessary, the Arabs should sacrifice up to ten million men in order to eradicate the menace of Israel, this "cancer" on their body, as he termed it. It was, no doubt, in line with this general impetuousness, that on March 17, 1954, an unknown party of assailants, presumably Arab, killed eleven Israelis riding in a bus at Scorpion Pass, near Beersheba. Israel promptly accused Jordan of the deed, but the Mixed Armistice Commission, lacking evidence, refused to condemn the Jordanian government for this action. In reply, Israel proclaimed a boycott of the Commission.

If the murder in question was an act of Arab revenge for Kibya, the subsequent Israeli retaliation again surpassed in scope the Arab

[71] U.S. aid under the technical assistance program was not to be affected by this decision.

action. Eleven days after the killings in Scorpion Pass two companies of the Israeli army attacked the village of Nahhalin in Jordanian
territory. This time the toll was nine Jordanians killed and nineteen
wounded. The village mosque was sacked. The Mixed Armistice
Commission, still boycotted by Israel, condemned the latter for the
attack.

Following these tragedies on the Israeli-Jordanian border, the
center of difficulty shifted to the Israeli-Egyptian border area. The
artificial line separating the refugee-populated Gaza strip and the
El-Auja enclave from the Negeb was a constant source of irritation
between the two parties, but until February 28, 1955, no major
military engagements were recorded. On that day, however, an Israeli force estimated at half a battalion attacked and destroyed the
Gaza garrison headquarters of the Egyptian army, killing 38 and
wounding 31 Egyptians. Procedure in the United Nations was the
same as before: first the Mixed Armistice Commission and then, on
March 29, the Security Council censured Israel for the attack. Again
the Council's resolution was based on a motion presented by the major Western powers.

The fourth major raid executed by Israel occurred on December
11, 1955, in the Syrian territory east of Lake Tiberias. A strong
Israeli detachment attacked Syrian border outposts and a village,
killing forty-nine persons. This time there was no pretense of spon-
taneity (such as was claimed in the Kibya raid), and the Israeli government openly admitted that the raid was in retaliation for sniping
by Syrian border outposts against Israeli fishermen sailing close to
the eastern shore of the lake. The Security Council issued the most
strongly worded condemnation of Israel's action yet recorded. The
British government went so far as to voice its "indignation" over
the raid. American public opinion, to the extent to which it was
informed of the affair, was also shocked. Even in Israel a few newspapers expressed doubts as to the wisdom of such actions.[72] There
seemed to be general agreement that Israel's retaliatory deed was
out of all proportion to the Syrian provocation.

These strong military measures posed the question as to whether
Israel used them only as retaliation for border infiltrations or
whether, perhaps, they were a device to force the Arab states to
come to terms in a general peace settlement. If the latter was the

[72] See Harry Gilroy, "Israelis Divided by Raid on Syria," New York Times,
Dec. 15, 1955.

purpose, the results did not follow expectations. Instead of becoming more pliable, Arab attitudes stiffened, and, because of the clearly demonstrated military superiority of Israel, Arab governments began to take serious steps to redress the balance of armaments. Egypt's new military rulers claimed that their original objective had been internal reform, but this had had to give place to considerations of national security after the Gaza attack. Consequently, they turned to the Soviet bloc in search of arms and before the end of 1955 consummated a deal with Czechoslovakia.[73]

Egypt's move provoked an immediate reaction in Israel, where the possibility of a preventive war was seriously discussed. The Israeli government advanced the doctrine of "balance of armaments" as a guiding principle in the maintenance of peace in the region. In the name of this doctrine Israel appealed to Washington to allow her to purchase arms in the United States. This request, strongly supported by Zionist groups in America, did not elicit an immediate reply from the Department of State, the latter having to consider many aspects of the case. Israel's raid in the Lake Tiberias area tended to slow down rather than to accelerate Washington's decision.

The bitterness of the Israeli-Egyptian conflict and the resultant race in armaments could not be divorced from the general problem of regional security in the Middle East and of the over-all position of Israel vis-à-vis the major powers. Israel viewed with undisguised suspicion any attempt by the United States and Britain to forge closer links with the Arabs by drawing them into a regional defense alliance. She also expressed nervousness about any withdrawal of Western military control in the area. Thus, in 1954 when Britain and Egypt concluded their agreement concerning the Suez Canal, Israel voiced her misgivings about the removal of British troops in the Canal Zone. Also when the United States first offered arms to Iraq in order to build up a Northern Tier alliance, and later when it gave its blessing to the projected Baghdad Pact, Israel and her sympathizers launched a vigorous campaign to counter the policy of "arming the Arabs." [74] Israel had little sympathy with United States' attempts to erect a barrier against Soviet penetration in the

---

[73] See p. 429 below.
[74] See *Security and the Middle East: The Problem and Its Solution*, proposals submitted to the President of the United States by a group of citizens and distributed by the Nation Associates, April 1954.

Middle East, and, paradoxically, she shared with Egypt and Saudi Arabia a decidedly negative attitude toward the Middle East Treaty Organization.

Despite this divergence in views on regional security, Israel seemed to be veering toward the United States. This was partly due to the continuous aid Israel was receiving from the United States, coupled with the conviction that, if hostilities broke out, only the latter could be counted upon as a friend in need, and partly to the notable deterioration in Soviet-Israeli relations. This deterioration was first noted in the winter of 1952–1953 when two groups of Jews within the Soviet orbit became victims of Communist justice. The arrest and sentencing of a group of Jewish doctors in Russia for an alleged plot against the security of state resembled the familiar scapegoat techniques of Nazi Germany too much to remain unnoticed in Israel. The trials (followed by death sentences) of Rudolph Slansky, secretary-general of the Czechoslovak Communist Party, and his associates, most of them Jews, had strong discriminatory undertones leading many observers to wonder whether they were not indicative of a concerted anti-Semitic drive in the Soviet bloc. These trials provoked lively comment in Israel, which reached its culmination when a bomb planted by unknown assailants exploded in the Soviet Legation in Tel-Aviv on February 9, 1953. Three days later the Soviet Union broke off diplomatic relations with Israel and did not resume them until July 15, 1953. Following this significant episode certain Soviet satellites, such as Rumania, resorted to mass persecution of Zionists, while Russia herself began to give increasing evidence of courting Arab favor, first by supporting the Arabs in Security Council debates dealing with Israel's retaliatory raids and later by offering certain Arab states arms and technical assistance at a time when Arab-Israeli relations had reached a low point. This new Soviet attitude found full expression in a speech delivered on December 29, 1955, by Communist Party Secretary Nikita S. Khrushchev, who stated that "from the first day of its existence, the State of Israel has been taking a hostile, threatening position toward its neighbors. Imperialists are behind Israel, trying to exploit it against the Arabs for their own benefit." [75]

Because of this shift in Soviet tactics, it was hard for Israel to maintain her original policy of neutrality; by the inexorable force of circumstances she was driven closer to the United States. In the

[75] *New York Times,* Dec. 31, 1955.

meantime the latter had somewhat modified its policy toward Israel. Consequently, American response to Israeli advances was not as cordial as it had been in the first years of Israel's existence. The immediate cause of this modification was undoubtedly the victory of the Republican Party at the polls in the fall of 1952. In contrast to the Democratic administration, which seemed to have leaned definitely toward Israel, President Eisenhower's administration endeavored to introduce what was officially termed "a policy of impartial friendship in the Middle East." [76] Although this new approach was far from hostile to Israel, which continued to enjoy many benefits and even priorities, it was, nevertheless, marked by a few changes. Among them could be mentioned, a visit paid by Secretary of State Dulles to the Arab capitals and Israel in the summer of 1953. Inasmuch as it was the first such visit of an American secretary of state in the area, it underlined the latter's importance and flattered the Arabs' self-esteem. Upon his return Secretary Dulles presented a realistic report in which he recommended "that the United States should seek to allay the deep resentment against it that has resulted from the creation of Israel" and recognized the existence of Arab fears "that the United States will back the new State of Israel in aggressive expansion." [77] Furthermore, all of the sensational raids executed by Israel against Jordanian, Egyptian, and Syrian territory and the Huleh dispute occurred while the Republicans were in office, and each evoked fairly strong condemnation by official Washington. While it is open to speculation whether the American reaction would have been any different under a Democratic administration, the undeniable fact is that these raids hurt the cause of Israel in informed American opinion. When Israel, in defiance of United Nation resolutions, moved her Foreign Ministry to Jerusalem in July 1953, thus completing the process of making the latter capital of the state, the United States, along with major Western powers, refused to move its embassy from Tel-Aviv, expressing its disapproval of Israeli action. Also for the first time since the creation of Israel, the United States government voiced its doubts as to the nature of Israel as the nucleus of a worldwide community and ten-

[76] Harry N. Howard, *United States Policy in the Near East, South Asia, and Africa—1954* (Department of State Publication 5801, 1955).

[77] Harry N. Howard, *The Development of United States Policy in the Near East, South Asia, and Africa during 1953* (Department of State Publication 5432, April 1954).

dered some advice to Israeli leaders. This happened on two occasions, when Assistant Secretary of State Henry A. Byroade made
public statements on Arab-Israeli relations. Speaking on April 9,
1954, in Dayton, Ohio, Byroade declared:

To the Israelis I say that you should come to truly look upon yourselves
as a Middle Eastern state and see your own future in that context rather
than as headquarters, or nucleus so to speak, of worldwide groupings
of peoples of a particular religious faith who must have special rights
within and obligations to the Israeli state. You should drop the attitude
of the conqueror and the conviction that force and a policy of retaliatory killings is the only policy that your neighbors will understand. You
should make your deeds correspond to your frequent utterances of the
desire for peace.[78]

In another speech delivered to the American Council for Judaism
on May 1, 1954, in Philadelphia, Byroade urged Israel to adopt a
policy of restricted immigration inasmuch as the Arabs, fearful of
Israel's possible expansion, were entitled to know "the magnitude
of this new State." [79]

[78] This paragraph had its counterpart in a speech which Byroade addressed
directly to the Arabs: "To the Arabs I say you should accept this state of
Israel as an accomplished fact. I say further that you are deliberately attempting to maintain a state of affairs delicately suspended between peace and
war, while at present desiring neither. This is a most dangerous policy and
one which world opinion will increasingly condemn if you continue to resist
any move to obtain at least a less dangerous *modus vivendi* with your neighbor" (*ibid.*).

[79] *Ibid.* The American Council for Judaism was formed in 1943 under the
presidency of Lessing J. Rosenwald as "a group of those Jews who completely
dissociate themselves and their Judaism from the national-political philosophy
of Zionism; and who stand on the principle that they are individual American
citizens who regard the United States of America as their single and only
homeland; who have and want no other national attachments; and who believe . . . that the officers of [the United States] Government should serve
the best interests of *all* Americans and America's acknowledged responsibility
of leadership in the free world" (quotation from a statement by Clarence L.
Coleman, president of the American Council for Judaism since 1955, *Council
News*, vol. 9, no. 11, Nov. 1955). A more complete statement of A.C.J.'s
objectives can be found in "Resolutions Adopted by Eleventh Annual Conference," *Council News*, vol. 9, no. 4, April 1955. Commenting on Byroade's
speech, Rabbi Dr. Elmer Berger, executive vice-president of the Council,
declared: "Mr. Byroade's clarification is welcomed as a declaration of historic
importance by American Jews who understand the history of this problem.
In the face of a half-century of Zionist agitation designed to convince the
governments of the world that the Jews are a nation, an American government has given a ringing, unequivocal declaration that Judaism is a religion
and that Jews owe no obligations to, and possess no rights in, the political

366

These statements caused considerable resentment both in Israel and among American Zionists, and Israel's government lodged a formal protest against Byroade's second speech as an unwarranted interference with Israel's sovereign right to formulate her immigration policies. Soon afterward the *Jerusalem Post* called for removal from the chairmanship of the Israeli-Jordanian Mixed Armistice Commission of Commander Elmo H. Hutchison, U.S.N., who was believed by Israelis to be partial to the Arab cause. Coming at a time of excitement over the contemplated American arming of the Arabs, these protests and appeals marked a low point in American-Israeli relations. In an attempt to break the deadlock created by Arab-Israeli hostility, Secretary Dulles came forward, on August 26, 1955, with a new plan to settle the Palestinian dispute. The plan proposed: (1) "resettlement and, to such an extent as may be feasible, repatriation" of the 900,000 Arab refugees whose "sufferings are drawn out almost beyond the point of endurance"; (2) "an international loan to enable Israel to pay the compensation" "due from Israel to the refugees," with "substantial participation by the United States in such a loan"; (3) "adjustments needed to convert armistice lines of danger into boundary lines of safety" inasmuch as "the existing lines separating Israel and the Arab states . . . were not designed to be permanent frontiers"; (4) "formal treaty arrangements," in which the United States would join as soon as the adjustments had been made, "to prevent or thwart any effort by either side to alter by force the boundaries." [80]

It is reported that in the winter of 1955–1956 Secretary Dulles endeavored to induce the political leaders of both major parties in the United States to keep the Arab-Israeli issue out of the forthcoming electoral campaign. Owing to the intensification of the Soviet menace to the Middle East, he wanted to promote a truly bipartisan policy which would be based on the national interest rather than on considerations of partisan advantage.

As could be expected, Arab and Israeli reactions to these American initiatives differed considerably. The Arabs viewed with suspicion any suggestion of resettlement of the refugees and definitely

---

entity which Zionism calls a 'Jewish' state" (*ibid.*). The Council represents a minority of American Jews. In the words of retiring President Rosenwald, "We should, by now, realize that although our growth should be steady, it is also likely to be slow" (*ibid.*).

[80] The text is in the *New York Times*, Aug. 27, 1955.

took exception to the granting of further loans to Israel, even if these were earmarked as compensation for the refugees. They saw no reason why, if money was to come from outside, Israel, a hostile state, should be made a dispensing agency. The American suggestion to "adjust" the frontiers was too vague and too timid to satisfy their basic quest for a substantial territorial revision. There was, incidentally, a certain change in emphasis in Arab demands. Up to this time repatriation of the refugees had always received top priority as a prerequisite to a peace settlement; in the fall of 1955 the territorial issue began to loom as perhaps the most decisive of all. As early as March 20, 1955, Major Saleh Salem, then Egyptian minister of national guidance, had stated that if the Negeb were returned to the Arabs so as to enable them to restore the land bridge between the Arab lands to the east and to the west, a major obstacle to peace might be removed. Although this was not an official policy statement either of the Egyptian government or of any other Arab state, it could, nevertheless, be taken as an indication of the new attitudes that were taking shape. As for Israel's reaction to Dulles' proposals of August 26, it was, by and large, positive, but her leaders immediately made the reservation that, so far as any change of boundaries was concerned, there could be only minor technical readjustments which would remove obvious inconveniences but involve no major territorial changes. With regard to Dulles' plea for keeping the Palestinian issue out of domestic politics, it would have been highly improper for Israel to take a stand on it; hence no direct comment was heard from Tel-Aviv. But Israel's sympathizers in the United States did not conceal their disapproval of this proposal.[81]

At this juncture it might be appropriate to ask what the attitude of Britain was toward these new developments in the Palestinian controversy. Beginning with the settlement of the Sudan and the Suez issues with Egypt in 1953–1954, British policy began gradually to veer toward satisfying Arab views on the matter. And inasmuch as the territorial issue began to take precedence over other points in the dispute, Britain gave her attention to the solution of that issue in the fall of 1955. Speaking at the Lord Mayor's Banquet in London on November 9, 1955, Prime Minister Sir Anthony Eden suggested that "if there could be an accepted arrangement between them about their boundaries, we—Her Majesty's Government and,

[81] See a letter by Messrs. Moron and Pollock to the editor New York Times, Jan. 4, 1956.

I believe, the United States Government and perhaps other powers too—would be prepared to give a formal guarantee to both sides." In elucidation of the word "arrangement" he explained that he meant "some compromise" between the Arabs and the Israelis concerning the territorial settlement. He concluded his statement by offering to mediate in the conflict.[82]

Eden's statement evoked favorable response among the Arabs, some of whom hailed it as the first acceptable basis for discussion. Israel reacted negatively, suspecting British appeasement of the Arabs at the price of a major territorial concession by Israel. The State Department's reaction was cautious and noncommittal. While praising Sir Anthony's initiative for peace, American officials pointed out the difference in the British and American approaches to the problem, especially the contrast between the American formula for territorial "adjustments" and the British formula of a "compromise."

To sum up these observations about Israel's position vis-à-vis the major powers, it might be said that by the mid-1950's her relations with Russia had notably deteriorated, owing to the new Soviet tactic of wooing the Arabs, and that a definite cooling off could be noted in her relations with Britain. Under the circumstances Israel was compelled more than ever before to look to the United States for economic aid and political friendship. In the meantime the American government had had a second look at the Arab-Israeli problem, and its response to Israel had lost some of its earlier cordiality. Israel's previous appeal to the American public as a haven for Jewish refugees from Europe and as a "bastion of democracy" in the Middle East had worn off somewhat because of the new reality of nearly one million Arab refugees and because of Israel's retaliatory raids against her Arab neighbors. The traditional "biblical" appeal to Bible-conscious Americans was still powerful, and so were domestic political considerations, but both of these tended to decrease in importance as the new awareness of Soviet danger in the Middle East began to permeate the thinking of the American public. Yet it would be unrealistic to dismiss all the factors that were working for closer ties between Israel and the United States. Despite certain deviations from the previous pattern of American-Israeli relations, the United States could probably still be regarded as Israel's most reliable friend.[83]

[82] The text is in the *New York Times*, Nov. 10, 1955.

[83] In this sense, see a significant editorial, "Israel is Here to Stay," *Life*, March 19, 1956.

CHAPTER X

Jordan

IN THE days of the Ottoman Empire the area east of the Jordan river was a rather neglected subdivision of the vilayet of Syria. The Damascus-Medina railroad passed through it, and its only other noteworthy feature was the Greco-Roman ruins at Amman (Philadelphia), Jerash, and Petra. In its western mountainous region Transjordan supported a settled population of a quarter of a million. Its eastern parts merged into the great flat desert which divides Iraq from Syria and the Hejaz. During the First World War Transjordan was a battleground between Faisal's Arab army and the Turks. In the course of the operations the Hejaz railway was severely damaged.

Between November 1918 and July 1920, Transjordan formed an integral part of the short-lived Arab kingdom of Syria, but its southern boundaries were ill defined. While Amman and Kerak in the north were under the Damascus government, the southern town of Maan and the port of Akaba on the Red Sea owed allegiance to King Hussein of the Hejaz. The problem of frontiers was, however, not important at that time inasmuch as King Hussein considered himself a ruler of all Arab lands, with patriarchal authority extending over his son Faisal in Damascus. After the collapse of Faisal's government in Syria, i.e., from July 1920 to March 1921, there was no native government in Transjordan. The area was under the direct supervision of the British authorities as part of the mandate of Palestine assigned to Britain at the San Remo conference.

It will be recalled from our earlier account of the peace settlement that in February 1921 King Hussein's second son, Emir Abdullah, arrived in Transjordan from the south. His intention was to invade French-held Syria with the aim of restoring Faisal to power, but he was persuaded by the then secretary for the colonies, Winston Churchill, to accept instead the emirate of Transjordan. On April 1, 1921 Abdullah was established as emir at Amman, with a monthly subsidy of £5,000 from the British government. Born in 1882, Abdullah had always been active in politics.[1] Before the war he represented the Hejaz as a deputy in the Ottoman parliament and was one of its vice-presidents. Later he acted as his father's foreign minister. He was always somewhat overshadowed by his warrior-brother Faisal despite the latter's younger age. His reputation suffered a severe setback as a result of the rout inflicted on him by Ibn Saud at the battle of Turaba in 1919. This did not prevent his being chosen, a year later at the Syrian Congress at Damascus, king of Iraq. Before this decision could be enforced, however, Faisal was overthrown by the French and subsequently offered the crown of Iraq by the British. Abdullah's plans were thus frustrated and he had to content himself with the rule of Transjordan. His emirate was a highly artificial unit, and its existence was threatened by Ibn Saud, who coveted large portions of Abdullah's territory. Not until the conclusion of the Treaty of Jidda in 1927 did Ibn Saud acquiesce in the retention of Maan and Akaba by Transjordan, and even then only on a *status quo* basis without repudiating his legal claim.

As a part of the mandate for Palestine Transjordan had been specifically exempted from those provisions that pertained to the establishment of a Jewish national home. Hence its interwar history lacked the controversy and sensationalism characteristic of Palestine. By the same token, no European states save Britain had any dealings with Transjordan, as a consequence of which its politics were devoid of big-power rivalry or high-level intrigue. Britain's interest in this largely barren stretch of land was dictated by three considerations: (1) it constituted a link in the British-controlled land route between the Mediterranean and the Persian Gulf; (2) its ruler was a Hashimi prince and Britain's policy was to cultivate Hashimite friendship; and (3) it was an Arab area and, no matter how unimportant, Britain did not wish to see it subjected to the influence of another power.

Government and Military Forces

The government of Transjordan was organized along the lines tested by time in similar British semicolonies. There was, in the first

[1] For details of his political career, see *Memoirs of King Abdullah of Transjordan* (New York, 1950).

place, Emir Abdullah's native Arab government. Many of its civil and military servants had been formerly employed by Faisal in Damascus; they were glad, therefore, to find a new home and work when the Syrian kingdom collapsed. On April 16, 1928, an Organic Law for Transjordan was promulgated by the British authorities with Abdullah's consent. It vested "the powers of legislation and administration" in the emir, who was to be assisted by an Executive and a Legislative Council. The law-making authority of the emir and of the Legislative Council was limited by Transjordan's treaty obligations. The Legislative Council was based on indirect suffrage and guaranteed proportional representation to the religious and national minorities as well as to the Bedouins.

Above this native structure stood the mandatory government for Palestine and Transjordan, represented in Amman by a permanent resident.[2] The resident supervised the Arab administration and assisted it through a body of British advisers and executives who were attached to various government departments. On February 20, 1928, an Anglo-Transjordanian agreement was signed in Jerusalem. It confirmed Britain's supreme authority in the area in virtue of the mandate and gave the British resident special prerogatives in regard to Transjordan's legislation, foreign relations, fiscal matters, and the protection of foreigners and minorities. By an amendment of 1934 the emir obtained the right to appoint consular representatives abroad.

From its very creation Transjordan was subsidized by the British government. These subsidies, which on the average amounted to £100,000 per year in the 1920's, steadily increased until in the 1940's they began to exceed the sum of £2,000,000. They were dictated by economic and political considerations. Economically Transjordan was poor, mostly agricultural or pastoral and with an adverse trade balance. It was included in the Palestinian customs area and it had a reputation as a smugglers' paradise. Its extended and ill-guarded desert borders with Syria, Saudi Arabia, and Iraq made illicit traffic tempting and easy.

The emirate's most outstanding feature was its army, known as the Arab Legion. Established in 1921 as a small body of 1,000 men, this picturesque desert force gradually grew in numbers and prestige. The Legion was organized by Captain F. G. Peake, who had com-

---

[2] Lt.-Col. (later Sir Henry) Cox occupied this post for most of the interwar period.

manded the Egyptian Camel Corps during the war. One of those Englishmen who delight in making the desert their home, Peake in his seventeen years of command raised the Legion to a high level of efficiency, fought the Bedouin raiders, repulsed the incursions of the Wahhabi *Ikhwan* and did his best to assure order and security. For his meritorious service the emir awarded him the title of pasha. In 1939 he was replaced by Major John Bagot Glubb, an officer with wide experience in the Arab countries. The Legion was composed of volunteers only and its ranks were open to any able-bodied man of Arab nationality. It had not only Transjordanians, but also Iraqis, Hejazis, Palestinians, Syrians, and others in its midst. It was thus the nucleus of a Pan-Arab army, should such ever be created, and served as a valuable instrument of British policy.[3]

Apart from the Legion there existed in the emirate a formation known as the Transjordan Frontier Force, which had been created after the Anglo-Transjordanian treaty of 1928. Its sole function was to defend the frontiers, and because such defense was, under the terms of the treaty, a specific British responsibility, the Transjordan Frontier Force was a British imperial formation under the command of the high commissioner for Palestine.

During the Second World War both formations were increased and modernized, and both were used outside the frontiers of Transjordan. The creation, in 1940, of a Desert Mechanized Regiment in the Arab Legion made the latter one of the most effective Arab armies in existence. The Mechanized Regiment played an active role in crushing the Rashid Ali rebellion in Iraq in 1941 and soon afterward took part in the Syrian campaign. It was the increase in the size and quality of the Arab Legion that made British subsidies to Transjordan so much higher during and after World War II. Possession of the Legion, a force out of proportion to Transjordan's size and poverty, enabled Abdullah to play a major role in the postwar developments in Palestine and in the Arab world at large. In fact, during the Arab-Israeli war in 1948 the Arab Legion, commanded by Glubb [4] and employing forty British officers, was the only Arab army which gave a good account of itself and which prevented Israel from overrunning the whole of Palestine.

[3] A first-hand account of the Legion's activities is contained in Brigadier John Bagot Glubb, *The Story of the Arab Legion* (London, 1948). See also C. S. Jarvis, *Arab Command* (London, 1942).
[4] He held the double rank of brigadier and pasha.

The Interwar Period and the Second World War

The interwar history of Transjordan was relatively uneventful.[5] Internal problems consisted mainly in preserving security so as to protect trade and the settled population from the depredations of the nomads. The Transjordan sector of the Hejaz Railway was repaired and put back into operation. But owing to the controversy between the Hejaz and the mandatory powers over the legal status of the railway, its Syrian and Hejazi sectors were not restored. As a result the Transjordan sector could not play its natural role as a transit link in the pilgrim traffic and, isolated as it was within the emirate's territory, it operated at a loss.

Transjordan's minorities—about 6,000 Circassians and small groups of Shishans, Druzes, Turkomans, and Bahais, as well as 30,000 Christian Arabs—did not present any major difficulty and did not lessen its essentially homogeneous character. Its total population, estimated at 340,000 in 1944, was predominantly Arab and Sunni Moslem. Under general British supervision the emir's government, presided over by Tewfik Pasha Abul Huda for most of the interwar period, enjoyed stability and tranquillity. Amendments adopted in 1938 to the Organic Law and in 1941 to the agreement with Britain changed little of the basic political and administrative pattern of British control.

The Second World War never extended to Transjordan territory; hence it affected the emirate only indirectly. The most noteworthy event was the above-mentioned participation of the Arab Legion in the Iraqi and Syrian campaigns. For a while Amman became a place of refuge for some Iraqi statesmen who fled Baghdad during the Rashid Ali coup. Another development worth noticing was the construction, between 1938 and 1941, of the Haifa-Baghdad road, of which 340 kilometers out of a total of 1,080 passed through Transjordan. This was the long-contemplated and finally realized British imperial highway which carried great military traffic during the war, thus stressing once again Transjordan's strategic value to Great Britain.

With regard to Transjordan's international position between 1921 and 1945, little can be said because the country was weak and ut-

---

[5] A thorough analysis of the country's economic conditions may be found in A. Konikoff, *Transjordan, An Economic Survey* (Jerusalem, 1946). On the period in question, see also Baha Uddin Toukan, *A Short History of Trans-Jordan* (London, 1945).

374

terly dependent upon Britain. Ever since Ibn Saud's conquest of the
Hejaz there had been, as we know, a latent hostility between him and
Emir Abdullah, and while in the 1920's it was Abdullah who feared
the Wahhabi expansion to the north, in the later period the roles
were reversed. Abdullah's frustrated ambition led him to embrace
the Greater Syria project as early as the middle twenties.[6] The plan
had, however, little chance of fulfillment short of a British decision
to dislodge the French from Syria, a decision unlikely to occur in the
interwar period despite Anglo-French rivalry. As to British control
of Transjordan, it was complete and undisturbed by manifestations
of nationalism such as had led to concessions to Egypt and Iraq. Politically, Transjordan and the ambitious Abdullah were Britain's reserve force with certain potentialities for the future. But bent as she
was upon the preservation of the *status quo,* she was not anxious to
make use of these potentialities in the interwar period. Britain's cultivation of Abdullah's good will was not devoid of certain aspects of
opera bouffé. Thus the Emir was made an honorary commodore of
the Royal Air Force and was consistently flattered in many small but
ceremonious ways. In an exchange of notes in 1943–1944 Britain
made an implicit promise to grant Transjordan independence after
the war. Consequently, when the former mandates came up for discussion in the United Nations in early 1946, the British delegate declared that Transjordan would not be proposed as a trust territory
because Britain intended to recognize her independence. Soon afterward, on March 22, 1946, in London, Britain and Transjordan signed
a treaty of alliance largely patterned after the Anglo-Iraqi treaty of
1930. Britain recognized Transjordan as an independent state, agreed
to exchange diplomatic representatives, pledged subsidies to the Arab
Legion, and undertook to defend the emirate against external agres-
sion. In return she secured the right to maintain troops in its territory, to use its communication facilities, and to train Abdullah's
armed forces. Both countries agreed to a "full and frank consultation
. . . in all matters of foreign policy which may affect their common
interests."[7]

Jordan's Postwar Position

On April 25, 1946, Emir Abdullah assumed the title of king. Politically educated circles in Transjordan were not too pleased with

[6] See Chapter XVI.

[7] Helen M. Davis, ed., *Constitutions, Electoral Laws, Treaties of States in the Near and Middle East* (Durham, N.C., 1947), p. 333.

the terms of the treaty and demanded its revision. Inasmuch as Britain was conducting simultaneous negotiations with Egypt and Iraq for treaty revision, she agreed to review her arrangements with Transjordan as well. As a result a new Anglo-Transjordanian treaty was signed in Amman on March 15, 1948. It differed from the preceding one in that it reduced Britain's military prerogatives in the emirate. Nevertheless, Britain retained the right to possess two air bases in Transjordan (at Amman and at Mafraq). Moreover, to deal with Transjordan's external security an Anglo-Transjordanian Joint Defense Board was to be set up.

In the course of the Palestinian war of 1948 King Abdullah's Arab Legion occupied the central and eastern part of Palestine (Judea, Samaria, and the northern portion of the Negeb) but was not able to prevent the establishment of an Israeli corridor to Jerusalem. In Jerusalem itself Abdullah's forces occupied the old city. The political and military drama attending the partition of Palestine gave King Abdullah an opportunity to assert himself in the politics of the Middle East. Ambitious to extend his domains and able to do it on account of the strength of his Legion, Abdullah emerged from the obscurity of the interwar period as a new and important force in the Arab world. In 1947 he traveled to Ankara, where he called for a Turko-Arab bloc which would also include Iran, Afghanistan, North Africa, and Pakistan. This visit, as well as his trips to Baghdad and Riyadh, and a state visit (on board a British warship) in Spain in 1949 were indicative of his increasing ambition and stature. His Greater Syria scheme received more attention and publicity than ever before and, in view of the unstable character of Syrian politics, it appeared capable of realization.

Abdullah's Palestinian policy placed him at odds with the rest of the Arab League. His ambition to dominate Arab Palestine as an opening phase of the Greater Syria plan clashed, first, with the ambitions of the mufti of Jerusalem (then commuting between Cairo and the Levant), secondly, with Egyptian and Saudi Arabian sensibilities. Disregarding the League's wishes, he unilaterally annexed the Arab part of Palestine on December 1, 1948. By this act he almost incurred expulsion from the League and temporarily strained his good relations with the brotherly Hashimite kingdom of Iraq. To make this decision irrevocable Abdullah on April 26, 1949, adopted a new name for his country, namely, the Hashimite Kingdom of Jordan. His

376

unification decisions were approved by Jordan's new bicameral legislature [8] on April 24, 1950. The unification of the lands west and east
of the Jordan River more than doubled the kingdom's population. It
resulted, moreover, in the inclusion of some Palestinian Arabs in the
Jordanian cabinet. A Palestinian notable, Ruhi Bey Abdul Hadi,
became Abdullah's foreign minister in May 1949. In addition, Jordan
had to shelter and feed about 400,000 Arab refugees from other parts
of Palestine to whom it generously offered Jordanian citizenship.

Generally speaking, Jordan's postwar position was somewhat para-
doxical. On the one hand, there was Abdullah's growing stature and
increased influence in the Arab world. On the other, his kingdom was
more than ever dependent upon Britain's aid. An increase in the
British subsidy to the Arab Legion to the sum of £3,500,000 in 1949
bore eloquent testimony to this state of affairs. Because it believed
that Abdullah was an outright British puppet, the Soviet Union
vetoed Jordan's admission to the United Nations in August 1947 and
has continued its opposition ever since. In 1951 sixty-nine-year-old
King Abdullah stood in the midst of the Arab world as a potential
unifier of the Fertile Crescent. How realistic his dreams were it is
hard to say. As a Bedouin ruler he was accustomed to changes and
fluctuations in Arab politics and he knew from history that his
nomad ancestors were capable of building great empires. In the
person of Ibn Saud he had a living example of a chieftain who by
his dogged will succeeded in unifying a major part of southern Arabia. Abdullah did not possess the martial qualities of the great Wahhabi ruler, but he possessed political skill and enjoyed the support of
a great power.

His assassination on July 20, 1951, put an end to a man who, whatever his shortcomings, had bold visions of the future and consistently
strove to achieve them. He was killed at the Omar Mosque in Jerusalem during the Friday prayers by a young adherent of Haj Amin
el-Husseini's militant group known as the Sanctified Struggle (Jihad Muqaddas). The kingdom of Jordan, deprived of his leadership, faced a somber future. Crown Prince Talal at the time of
Abdullah's death was in Switzerland undergoing treatment for a
nervous breakdown, and for a few weeks it was uncertain whether
he would be able to rule the country. It was reported, moreover, that

[8] Established as a result of the newly won independence by the constitution
of March 1, 1947.

in contrast to his late father, Talal disliked the British and resented Jordan's dependence upon British aid. Eventually, on September 5, he was proclaimed king of Jordan, thus putting an end to the doubts concerning the succession. As to his foreign policy, Talal seemed anxious to part with certain features of his father's diplomacy. Thus he buried—at least outwardly—the Fertile Crescent scheme by allowing his premier, Tewfik Pasha Abul Huda, to deny, on September 18, 1951, any attempt on Jordan's part to effect union with Iraq. Furthermore, soon after his accession, he hastened to pay an extended visit to Riyadh (November 10–18), thus stressing, at the very outset of his reign, a desire for friendship with the rival house of Saud.

The first weeks of Talal's rule coincided with the crisis in Anglo-Egyptian relations caused by the unilateral abrogation of the 1936 treaty by Egypt (see p. 416). According to some reports Cairo made a proposal to Amman to follow the Egyptian example, denounce the Anglo-Jordanian treaty, and expel British civil and military advisers. In return Egypt was to supply her own officers for Jordan's Arab Legion and to pay the Jordanian government sums equivalent to current British subsidies. Whatever the degree of accuracy of these reports, the fact is that Talal did not avail himself of the Egyptian aid. Whether this was a reflection of his genuine loyalty to the British alliance, of disappointment in the efficacy of the Egyptian action, or of lack of trust in the alleged promises of Cairo remained a matter of speculation.

With regard to King Abdullah's tragic death, it was not clear whether the murder was the spontaneous act of a fanatic or the manifestation of some wider conspiracy among political enemies. Jordanian authorities maintained that the latter was the case. A trial before the Amman military court of a number of persons accused of complicity in the late King's assassination ended on September 3 by the sentencing to death of six men, four of whom were hanged the next day. Among the latter was Dr. Musa Abdullah el-Husseini, a cousin of Jerusalem's exiled grand mufti. Of the remaining two, who were sentenced *in absentia*, one was Colonel Abdullah el-Tel, former Jordanian governor of Jerusalem, who sometime before had deserted King Abdullah and found shelter in Egypt.

Whatever the future plans and alignments of Jordan's new ruler, it was certain that by the sudden changes in Amman British policy had suffered a serious blow. Likewise, Abdullah's death meant the removal of a stabilizing influence in the Middle East. For despite his revisionist Greater Syria policy, Abdullah was the first Arab ruler to accept the existence of American-supported Israel as a fact and to draw from it realistic conclusions.

Internal Developments since Abdullah's Death

King Talal's reign was not destined to last long. Suffering from a nervous disease, he absented himself from Jordan for lengthy periods in order to undergo treatment in European clinics. After mid-May 1952 the country was ruled by a Crown Council in the King's absence. Eventually despairing of improvement in Talal's mental capacity, the bicameral parliament on August 11, 1952, deposed him and proclaimed his son, Hussein, king of Jordan. As a minor, the new ruler was permitted to continue his studies in Sandhurst while his duties in Jordan were assumed by a Regency Council. His younger brother, Emir Mohammed (twelve years old) was proclaimed crown prince.

On coming of age (i.e., reaching his eighteenth year) Hussein was enthroned in Amman on May 2, 1953, the day on which his second cousin, Faisal II, ascended the throne of Iraq. This simultaneous accession of two young Hashimites in Amman and Baghdad meant the shelving for the foreseeable future of schemes of union of Jordan and Iraq inasmuch as it was unlikely that either of the two kings would willingly give up his throne for the sake of a merger.

Although important in an essentially authoritarian country, these matters of royal incumbency were overshadowed by more profound social and political changes that Jordan had been undergoing ever since its annexation of central Palestine. Demographic statistics bore eloquent testimony in this respect. The original population of Transjordan was estimated at 400,000. Since the creation of Jordan this number had been increased by 400,000 west-bank-of-the-Jordan residents, by 100,000 refugees from Israel who were able to support themselves, and by 472,000 Palestinians who were completely destitute and, classified as refugees, had to rely on international assistance. This total of 1,372,000 was more than three times the original population. But the resources of the country were not multiplied by three; they were not even doubled. Moreover, the Transjordan of the years before 1948 enjoyed free access to the Mediterranean through British-controlled Palestine, with attendant economic advantages. The new kingdom of Jordan was, by contrast, an almost landlocked country. Its only port on the Red Sea, Aqaba, required major investments to make it capable of handling increased trans-oceanic traffic; it lacked, moreover, adequate road or rail connection with the interior.

Politically, the addition of the Palestinian population had a two-fold effect on the kingdom. On the one hand, the destitute refugees provided a permanently discontented and frustrated element, which not only hated Israel, America, and Britain for having caused its misfortunes and sufferings but also envied and criticized the Jordanian government itself. On the other, the west-bank residents were, on the whole, better educated and more sophisticated than the original Transjordanians and they viewed with resentment the latter's political supremacy in the kingdom. Consequently, Jordan witnessed the rapid growth of articulate opposition to its government. This opposition was divided into a number of groups, some of which rallied around prominent personalities while others sought inspiration in ideologies. Subhi Abu Ghanima, a long-standing opponent of King Abdullah and his system, directed a clamorous group of critics from his place of exile in Damascus. The same was true of the exiled mufti of Jerusalem, Haj Amin el-Husseini, whose Jordanian followers operated openly under the leadership of Kamal Arakat, former *Futuwwah* chief, and Mustafa Bushnaq. From his place of exile in Cairo Colonel Abdullah el-Tel did his best to maintain contact with certain elements in the Arab Legion. Among those who operated in Jordan was Suleiman Pasha Nabulsi, a former cabinet minister and ambassador to London, who, having broken with the ruling group in the early 1950's, emerged as a leading personality in the so-called National Front and the National-Socialist Party, both leftist organizations violently opposed to the government.

To this list of opposition leaders and groups might be added a few inter-Arab parties whose ideologies called for a revolutionary change in Jordan's system. Such were the Jordanian branch of the Moslem Brotherhood, directed by Mohammed Abdur Rahman Khalifa, and the Arab Renaissance Party (*Baath*), whose socialism appealed to students and young people. The latter's leaders, Abdallah Rimawi and Abdallah Nawas, commanded a particularly strong following in Ramallah and Jerusalem, respectively, both west-bank centers. Nor could one ignore the existence of the outlawed Communist Party, which, under the direction of Fuad Nasser, was especially active—and successful—among the numerous Palestinian refugees.

As time went on, these opposition groups gained in importance, while the Palestinian elements, whether loyal or opposed to the government, increased their influence upon politics and administration. Both phenomena were reflected in the electoral struggles and the debates of the parliaments elected after 1948. To understand the elections after that date, it may be useful to have a look at the first election, held in 1947 before the unification of the east and the west banks. At that time Transjordan had 100,000 voters, who, according to the newly adopted constitution, were to elect twenty deputies to the Lower House. The election passed without any major disturbance, the candidates campaigning either as independents or as members of the only party—*El-Nahda* (Revival), which was a government creation. Consequently, with the exception of Nabulsi, who was elected as an independent, all other deputies could be regarded as supporters of the government. This idyllic picture underwent a radical change soon after the merger of the territories. The west bank was accorded twenty seats in the Chamber, whose total was increased to forty. The number of voters rose to 304,000, of whom 157,000 were Palestinians. The first postmerger election, held in April 1950, returned a parliament so strongly filled with critics of the regime as to make the government's position very embarrassing.

It was this opposition-dominated parliament which in May 1951 rejected the government-submitted budget, thus actually passing a vote of nonconfidence, a novelty in Jordan's political history. Inasmuch as the constitution did not provide for a responsible cabinet, this step was pronounced unconstitutional and, within a few days, the King dissolved the Chamber. A third election, held in August 1951, gave the government a slight majority, but the opposition counted as many as 18 members of a total of 40. It could, moreover, get the support of some progovernment members on certain issues. This new parliament at once began to press for a revision of the constitution, which would transform the hitherto nonresponsible government into a responsible one. Its efforts were successful, and on January 2, 1952, a new constitution was promulgated. Article 53 provided that a two-thirds majority against the government on a vote of confidence must result in dismissal of the cabinet. Having secured recognition of the new parliamentary principle, the opposition now began to agitate for an amendment of Article 53 so that the two-thirds vote necessary to overthrow the cabinet would be replaced by a simple majority. No decision was reached immediately.

Young King Hussein had ascended the throne, and it seemed as if the new ruler might effect a measure of political reconciliation. His first step was to remove from the premiership Tewfik Pasha Abul Huda, the "grand old man" of Jordanian politics and one of the figures most objectionable to the opposition. His position was entrusted to Fawzi el-Mulki, who chose a liberal leader, Anwar el-Khatib, as minister of economy, reconstruction, and development. In November 1953 the old opponent of the regime, Subhi Abu Ghanima, returned, at the King's invitation to his homeland. In January 1954 sufficient voting strength was mustered in the parliament to amend Article 53. New vistas were opened to parliamentary democracy in Jordan.

However, this was the climax of the opposition's success. Frightened by the increasingly violent criticisms both within and without parliament, the government launched a counteroffensive aiming at the restoration of its authority and the curbing of criticism. On January 17, 1954, it dissolved all political parties and provided for the licensing of new ones. In the spring the staunchest champion of traditionalism, Abul Huda, resumed the premiership, and early in June he presented a ministerial declaration to the parliament asking for a vote of confidence. Anticipating violent opposition and an adverse vote, he had parliament dissolved on June 22. This was followed by the suspension of such political parties as were then in existence and of numerous newspapers. On August 18 defense regulations giving special powers to the cabinet were enacted. With the ground thus prepared, the government called for new elections in October, this time resolved to keep the opposition from gaining ascendancy. As might have been expected, the elections abounded in violence. Suleiman el-Hadidi, chief of the *Baath* Party, and Suleiman Nabulsi were arrested. Abdur Rahman Shukair, leader of the National Front, and Mohammed Khalifa, head of the Brotherhood, escaped to Damascus. Opposition leaders charged intimidation and terror. But after four years of experimentation with unchecked parliamentarism, the government finally secured a friendly Chamber which in its opening session gave the premier a 35-to-3 vote of confidence. Two National Front candidates campaigning as independents, were elected. Those were Abdul Qader es-Saleh and Rashad Massawadah, whom government sources promptly identified as extreme leftists.

These dramatic political changes were occurring against an extremely difficult economic background. One of the standing complaints of the opposition was the earmarking of most of the budget for internal security and nonproductive administrative purposes. The aggravating fact was that Jordan was not viable as an economic unit and for its survival as a state had to rely on continuous foreign, mostly British, aid. In 1954 its budget of over £16,500,000 provided for over £8,000,000 for military expenditures, while at the same time the British subsidy was slightly over £8,500,000. In 1954 and 1955, however, Britain made an effort to increase her economic assistance, which had been negligible up to that time. In December 1955 the British subsidy to Jordan was divided into £3,000,000 for economic aid and £7,750,000 for military aid, the latter mostly for the Arab Legion, with a small amount for the Jordanian National Guard. As for the United States, its first aid to Jordan was only through its technical assistance program, which in 1954 amounted to no more than $1,400,000. In June of 1954, following repeated Jordanian requests, the United States concluded with Jordan an economic aid agreement—the first negotiated with any Arab government—which provided for $8,000,000 in aid to be taken out of a $47,000,000 fund provided by Congress for the Arab states. The Jordanians went ahead with their economic planning. In November 1954 the Jordan Development Board announced a Five-Year Plan of works which were to cost $200,000,000 and embrace 274 projects.

International Position in the 1950's

These figures clearly indicate how heavily Jordan was dependent on Great Britain. If we consider the subsidies and the fairly large number of British experts employed in Jordan, we might easily conclude that Jordan was completely subject to Britain's will. Such a judgment would not be wholly warranted by the political realities in Jordan. As one author has aptly remarked, before the Palestinian war there was a king in Jordan without a people and there was a

383

foreign power. After 1948 the missing element, the people, appeared in the form of the politically conscious mass of Palestinians.[9]

The passing of the old patriarchal king and his replacement, first by a mentally unstable individual and then by a youth just out of school, removed the traditional props and motive forces of the Jordanian state which had existed under Abdullah. Jordanian governments, especially since 1951, have been exposed to new and powerful pressures. One of these was the pressure from below of the impoverished or destitute masses. This accounted for a good deal of political radicalism and extremism. Added to it was the increasing violence on the frontier with Israel. Israeli attacks and killings at Kibya (October 1953) and Nahhalin (March 1954) so stirred emotions that no "moderate" dared advocate a compromise with the Zionist neighbor. The speeches from the throne and the ministerial declarations since Abdullah's death invariably repeat the formula of "no peace, no negotiations with the Jews." In fact, at least one cabinet crisis in those years—Premier Mulki's resignation in May 1954—was generally ascribed to his objection to alleged British prodding to start negotiations with Israel. Somewhat earlier the economy minister in Mulki's cabinet, Anwar el-Khatib, contrasting the $1,400,000 of Point Four aid to Jordan with the $52,000,000 contribution by the United States to Israel, declared as follows:

If the United States is not prepared to supplement technical assistance with cash help for economic projects, there is no necessity to keep Point Four in Jordan. . . . On the other hand, Israel is fighting with American aid. It takes dollars to buy American ammunition like that found after the Israeli raids on Nahhalin and Kibya. America is feeding her creation, Israel, and making no effort to restrain that creation from frontier attacks.[10]

The Palestine question was the source of general nationalist resentment, which intensified popular resentments caused by economic and social factors. Linked with the nationalist pressure was a third kind of pressure, one stemming from the intensified political activity of the Cairo-Riyadh axis.

All these pressures came to bear upon the Jordanian government in 1955, and at one particular moment the country was very close to a revolution. The background was provided by the Turkish-Iraqi

[9] For the developments of this period, consult Esmond Wright, "Abdallah's Jordan," *Middle East Journal*, Autumn, 1951.

[10] *New York Times*, April 2, 1954.

negotiations to conclude a regional defense pact, which Arab countries would be invited to join. It was generally assumed that Jordan, as a Hashimite and British-influenced country, would follow Iraq's example and become a signatory. Rather unexpectedly, however, Premier Tewfik Abul Huda and Foreign Minister Walid Salah did not take Iraq's side during the Arab League meeting in January 1955; instead they leaned toward Egypt and Saudi Arabia, both vigorous opponents of the pact.[11] Although Abul Huda's cabinet resigned shortly afterward, the new government of Said el-Mufti did nothing for over six months to revive the question.

This rather unnatural calm was disturbed in the fall by the flight of Walid Salah, who, declaring that his life was in danger because of his opposition to imperialism, sought refuge in Damascus and later in Cairo. Then early in December Amman was subjected to new pressure as the result of a visit paid to it by General Sir Gerald Templer, chief of the British Imperial General Staff, who was reported urging Jordan's immediate adherence to the Baghdad alliance. His visit coincided with that of Egyptian Colonel Anwar es-Sadat. The latter naturally represented the opposite point of view and skillfully ingratiated himself with the people during his tour of Amman and Jerusalem. By that time it was well known that the common people in the Arab states were very hostile to the Baghdad Pact. Toward the middle of December when the Jordanian cabinet was about to reach a decision in this matter, its four west-bank ministers resigned, no doubt aware of the mood of their fellow Palestinians. This precipitated a crisis which was resolved on December 15 when thirty-six-year-old Hazzah el-Majali, former interior minister and a staunch advocate of the Iraqi alliance, formed a new cabinet. The new premier promptly declared that negotiations with Britain to bring Jordan into the Baghdad Pact would be resumed "in proper time." He also revealed that the preceding government had "approved in principle" Jordan's adherence to the pact but that there were still differences between Britain and Jordan.[12]

His declarations touched off major riots in Amman and other towns. Angry mobs attacked many foreign and international institutions, such as the American consulate and the United Nations Relief and Works Agency headquarters. Shouting defiance of the

[11] For further details on inter-Arab rivalries, see the section on the Baghdad Pact (pp. 260–265) and p. 507.
[12] *New York Times*, Dec. 18, 1955.

new government, they protested against "foreign pacts," imperialism, Israel, and the British hold on the Arab Legion. It appeared
that the opposition parties, whether legal or outlawed, all joined
in the strongest condemnation of any further link with the West.
Responding to their call, government officials went on strike, thus
creating a new and dangerous precedent. On December 19 Majali
resigned. On the same day, yielding to public pressure, King Hussein dissolved the parliament, promising to hold new elections in
April. On December 20 a sixty-seven-year-old former premier, Ibrahim Hashim, formed a caretaker cabinet which included two other
former premiers, Fawzi el-Mulki and Samir er-Rifai. Following a
new wave of demonstrations, he promptly pledged not to adhere to
any pacts. In the meantime it was revealed that Britain had offered
to increase her annual subsidy to Jordan in return for joining the
pact, a revelation not likely to clear the already surcharged atmosphere. The outgoing premier, Majali, accused Saudi Arabia of a
campaign of bribery, the aim of which was to weaken Jordan's government. A few days later a newly created National Committee,
representing a coalition of leftist and nationalist groups and parties,
met in Amman to map strategy for the forthcoming elections to the
new parliament. Its agenda included a demand that Egypt, Saudi
Arabia, and Syria jointly offer Jordan a subsidy to replace the British grants and thus free Jordan from Britain's dominance. Prominent
among the Committee's organizers was Suleiman Nabulsi, who op-
timistically declared that, given free elections, the opposition would
obtain 70 per cent of the vote.

The ten days following Christmas witnessed a gradual return to
calm and order. Misled perhaps by this recession in the clamor, the
government on January 4, 1956, made public its decision to approve
the finding of the Supreme Court that the dissolution of parliament
decreed in December had been illegal and that the old Chamber
would be reconvened. In reply, the opposition parties called a protest meeting for January 6, but the government promptly forbade it.
The ban inspired new rioting, which broke out with particular intensity on January 7. This time the demonstrators not only attacked
Western consulates and institutions but also marched on the royal
palace in an attempt to storm it. There was widespread looting in
town, a feature not conspicuous during the December riots. Moreover, excited crowds in a number of Jordanian towns, especially on
the left bank, clamored for annexation of their territory by Syria,

while a similar demonstration in favor of Saudi Arabia was reported in the southern town of Maan. Communist elements rather than the accepted opposition leaders were said to be in the forefront of these activities, and there were rumors about some defections from the Arab Legion, partly caused by the earlier resignation of General Ahmed Sidki el-Gindi, deputy chief of staff.

The gravity of the situation brought about the fall of Hashim's caretaker cabinet and its replacement on January 9 by one of Samir Rifai. The new premier immediately proclaimed martial law, placing a virtual blackout on the flow of news and travel from and to Jordan. At the same time, however, he bowed to public opinion by reiterating his predecessor's promise that Jordan would reject the Baghdad Pact. Soon afterward he lodged formal protests with Egypt and Saudi Arabia against their inflammatory broadcasts and incitement to disobedience in Jordan. These, in fact, were believed by many observers to be the principal cause of the upheaval, Saudi subsidies to anti-Hashimite elements being particularly potent. Jordanian protests, however, seemed to have little effect on the Cairo-Riyadh axis, which was determined to pursue its policy of opposition to the Western influence in Amman. By mid-January Egypt, Saudi Arabia, and Syria came forward with the long-expected offer to replace the British annual subsidy by one of their own. By that time, however, the government had regained its hold on the country. With self-confidence restored, it not only shelved the subsidy proposals but also, on January 18, reconvened the dissolved parliament, thus notifying the foreign and domestic opposition that no further interference with the existing system would be tolerated.

On March 1, 1956, King Hussein in a surprise move abruptly dismissed the commander of the Arab Legion, Lieutenant-General John Bagot Glubb (with two senior British officers), and ordered his expulsion from the country forthwith. Simultaneously he appointed a senior Arab officer of the Legion, General Radi Ennab, to the position vacated by Glubb. This decision gained the King tremendous popularity, which was expressed in joyful manifestations lasting several days in Jordan, and made him overnight a hero in the Arab world at large. It did not, however, result in repudiation of the alliance with Britain, both the King and his ministers stating that they not only wanted to continue the treaty relationship but also hoped to maintain the services of a number of British officers in the Legion.

387

In Britain, Glubb's dismissal provoked great consternation, and *The Times,* in an editorial, called it the most "sinister" event in the Middle East since the Egyptian-Czechoslovak arms deal. Despite this the British government did not revoke its subsidies to Jordan, contenting itself with the recall of fifteen senior British officers of the Legion.[13]

In mid-March when Egypt, Saudi Arabia, and Syria met in Cairo to concert their policies and renewed their offer of a subsidy in place of the British one, they met with Jordan's refusal. In fact, within forty-eight hours of the issuance of the "Arab Big Three's" declaration (March 12, 1956) Hussein hastened to meet his cousin Faisal of Iraq in a desert border station, thus reaffirming his desire not to sever the bonds of solidarity with the other Hashimite kingdom.

The riots fomented in 1955–1956 by the concerted action of internal and foreign opponents to the Jordanian dynasty and government had shaken the very foundations of the country. Not viable economically, Jordan was obliged to rely on foreign aid from one source or another. But whereas for more than a third of a century it had been taken for granted that Britain's monopoly of influence in Jordan was secure and unchallenged, the events of the winter of 1955–1956 proved that this was not true. The stormy upheaval failed by a narrow margin to upset the Hashimite dynasty and its followers. To a dispassionate outsider this popular rebellion might have appeared to be courting suicide, along much the same pattern as that set by Dr. Mossadegh in Iran in 1951. But even the prospect of catastrophe did not deter the populace and its leaders from challenging the existing system. This, no doubt, indicated that a point of near despair had been reached by sizable segments of Arab public opinion both in Jordan and abroad over the burning domestic and international issues. Apart from these rebellious moods, the calculated policy of other Arab states cannot be ignored either. Acceptance of the tripartite Arab subsidy would have freed Jordan from Britain's dominance but would automatically have subjected it to the influence of Cairo, Riyadh, and Damascus. This might easily lead to the complete disintegration of Jordan as an independent state, with Syria and Saudi Arabia emerging as likely successors to its territory. In the case of Syria, a country devoid of major natural

13 For General Glubb's account of his dismissal, see a series of articles by him in the *New York Times,* March 12–16, 1956.

resources, it would mean adding to its already heavy economic burdens a million semidestitute people. In the case of Saudi Arabia, there would be an influx of restless human elements which would increase the ferment already beginning to appear in this patriarchal society. Consequently, although the Cairo-Riyadh policy seems to be coolly calculated, one may wonder whether the would-be successors to the Jordanian state really want to assume the added responsibilities.

⊣ PART FOUR ⊢

WEST AND EAST OF THE

RED SEA

CHAPTER XI

Egypt

SITUATED at the junction of Africa and Asia, Egypt has always held a strategic position which, added to the fertility of her land, has attracted the great state builders and conquerors of the past. Egypt's strategic significance was immensely increased with the construction in 1869 of the Suez Canal. Although the canal was the property of a private, predominantly French company, strategically it fell under the control of Great Britain, who fully realized its importance to the imperial life line. Arabi Pasha's antiforeign riots gave the British an opportunity, in 1882, to occupy the delta of the Nile and to establish their rule in this still nominally Ottoman province. It was not long before Britain extended her dominion to the Sudan, although this operation encountered considerable opposition. The dervish rising of Mahdi Mohammed Ahmed in 1882, the extermination of General Gordon's British garrison in Khartoum in 1884, France's expedition to Fashoda in 1896, and Kitchener's victory at Omdurman in 1898 were steps in a process which ended January 19, 1899, in the establishment of the Anglo-Egyptian condominium over the Sudan.

DOMINANCE OF BRITAIN

Thus in the last two decades of the nineteenth century Britain became the controlling power of the whole Nile valley. Her interests in Egypt were represented by one of the ablest empire builders of modern history, Lord Cromer. Cromer gave Egypt a sound fiscal administration and an improved irrigation system and helped her assume a leading commercial position among the countries of the Middle East.

His successors, Sir Eldon Gorst (1907–1911) and Lord Kitchener (1911–1914), continued, under the nominal authority of the khedive, to exercise uncontested power in Egypt.

By the beginning of World War I Britain was so firmly entrenched that it was a mere formality for her to proclaim, on December 18, 1914, that Egypt was a British protectorate. Khedive (Viceroy) Abbas Hilmi, then on a visit in Constantinople, was deposed *in absentia* and replaced by Hussein, another member of the Mohammed Ali dynasty. With the British blessing Hussein assumed the title of sultan. Upon his death in 1917, he was succeeded by Fuad I, who, like his predecessor, enjoyed British confidence. Throughout the war Egypt was governed by Prime Minister Rushdi Pasha, who in all important matters followed British advice. As the war progressed, Egypt became a great British military base, from which attacks were launched toward Gallipoli and Palestine. Cairo became a center of Britain's Arab diplomacy. Ever since the conclusion of the Anglo-French Entente in 1904 Britain's predominant position in Egypt had been taken for granted by the Allies, so that there was no need to include Egypt in the secret treaties of World War I. As a result, Britain's relations with Egypt during that period were devoid of the political angles of international diplomacy and were largely concerned with administrative problems.

The Rise of Nationalism

This uncomplicated relationship changed abruptly with the end of the First World War. Egypt experienced a rise of nationalism. Several factors accounted for it: the presence of large British, Australian, and New Zealand forces and the inevitable incidents deriving from it wounded Egyptian national pride; the large-scale spending of foreign armies produced inflation and profiteering from which fixed-income groups suffered severely; British recruitment of Egyptians for labor battalions depleted Egypt's labor force and resulted in a neglect of agriculture and in severe breakdowns in food production; and last, but not least, Wilson's Fourteen Points and the Anglo-French Declaration of November 8, 1918, promising independence to the Arab countries helped to arouse a keen desire for complete freedom from foreign tutelage.

In 1918–1919 Egypt witnessed intense nationalist agitation, which erupted into anti-British riots. The nationalists were led by a militant orator, Saad Zaghlul Pasha, of fellaheen origin, who had been minister of education under Cromer. In November 1918, two days after the armistice, Saad Zaghlul, accompanied by Ali Shaarawi Pasha and Abdul Aziz Fahmi Bey, called on the British high commissioner, Sir Reginald Wingate, demanding full independence for their country. This self-styled "Delegation of Egypt" (*Wafd el-Masri*), supported by thousands of telegrams and signatures, met with no success. Early in 1919 Saad Zaghlul founded a new party, the *Wafd*, which soon became the main vehicle of Egyptian nationalism.

Facing tremendous agitation in the country, the British decided to strike at the very nerve center and in March 1919 deported Zaghlul, with three other prominent Wafdists,[1] to Malta. It was of no avail. Instead of calming the atmosphere, it provoked a spontaneous uprising, commonly referred to as the Egyptian revolution, in which students, workers, and other classes acting in concert paralyzed the life of the country. On March 17 Cairo became practically isolated, and the new British high commissioner, Lord Allenby, had to rush troops from Syria to curb the insurrection.

The uprising brought home to the British the fact that Egyptian nationalism could no longer be disposed of by military measures and that some compromise was necessary to preserve their supremacy in the delta of the Nile. They released Zaghlul from confinement and allowed him to proceed to Paris, where he laid his claims before the Peace Conference. From Paris he proceeded to London to plead Egypt's case.

In the meantime the British cabinet decided to send Lord Milner to Egypt to investigate and to advise on a proper solution. Milner's mission (December 1919 to March 1920) resulted in a report recommending the replacement of the existing protectorate by a treaty of alliance which would give Great Britain the right to defend Egypt, control the Suez Canal, and guide Egypt's foreign relations. Subsequent negotiations between London and Cairo ended in a deadlock. In 1921 there was a renewed wave of nationalist riots, whereupon Zaghlul and other leaders were again deported, this time to Aden, Gibraltar, and the Seychelles.

Unable to reach a bilateral agreement, the British government decided to proceed alone, and on February 28, 1922, in a statement issued by the high commissioner, it put an end to the protectorate and proclaimed Egypt's independence. The proclamation contained

[1] Hamid el-Bassel, Ismail Sidki, and Mohammed Mahmud.

395

four points "absolutely reserved to the discretion of His Majesty's Government," namely, (1) the security of the communications of the British Empire in Egypt; (2) the defense of Egypt against all foreign aggression or interference, direct or indirect; (3) the protection of foreign interests in Egypt and the protection of minorities; and (4) the Sudan.[2] This declaration was satisfactory to Sultan Fuad, who on March 15 hastened to assume the title of king (*malik*), but it was rejected by the nationalists, who considered it a totally inadequate substitute for true independence.

There was no real change in the pattern of political control in Egypt, except for the abolition of martial law, which had been in force since November 2, 1914. King Fuad, by a royal rescript of April 19, 1923, promulgated a constitution which followed Western patterns but reserved considerable rights to the crown. Following an act of amnesty, Zaghlul and his associates returned from their forced exile and plunged headlong into the political campaign preliminary to the first constitutional elections. The elections, held in January 1924, gave Zaghlul's Wafd Party an overwhelming victory. Commanding 188 seats as against 27 for the opposition, Zaghlul was made prime minister and without delay began to press for a revision of the unilateral declaration of independence. Zaghlul's hope that Britain's Labour Party cabinet headed by Ramsay MacDonald would be more responsive to Egypt's aspirations proved to be vain. Talks initiated in London between the British and the Egyptian prime ministers broke down mainly on account of the Sudan, control of which the British were unwilling to give up. As usual, the breakdown of negotiations provoked disorders in Egypt, this time resulting in frequent assaults upon British civil and military personnel.

On November 19, 1924, Sir Lee Stack, *sirdar* (commander-in-chief) of the Egyptian army and governor-general of the Sudan, was killed by a Wafdist fanatic. British reaction was unusually strong. High Commissioner Lord Allenby presented a curt ultimatum to the Egyptian government demanding punishment of the assassins, an apology, an indemnity of a half-million Egyptian pounds ($1,500,-000), a prohibition of political demonstrations, and withdrawal of Egyptian troops from the Sudan. Moreover, he demanded the reten-

[2] See Royal Institute of International Affairs, ed., *Great Britain and Egypt, 1914–1936* (London, 1936). The full text is in Helen M. Davis, ed., *Constitutions, Electoral Laws, Treaties of States in the Near and Middle East* (Durham, N.C., 1947), p. 55.

tion by Egypt of British advisers in the ministries of Finance, Justice, and the European department of the Ministry of Interior. He also informed Egypt that the area to be irrigated in the Gezira district of the Sudan would be extended. This meant that vital Nile water would be channeled to British Sudanese plantations at the expense of Egypt. To back up these demands Allenby ordered the seizure by British troops of the Alexandria customs. It was the Sudan irrigation proposal that irked Zaghlul most and rather than accept it he resigned on November 24, 1924. His successor, Ziwar Pasha, who formed a non-Wafd cabinet, accepted the ultimatum, whereupon the British evacuated the customs and, somewhat later, reversed their decision concerning Gezira irrigation. The results of these dramatic events were twofold: (1) Britain intensified her hold on Egypt by continuing to control, through her advisers, vital departments in the Egyptian government (especially internal security); (2) Egypt's influence was practically eliminated from the Sudan by the withdrawal of her troops and officials.

Egypt between 1924 and 1936

The Stack murder closed a definite chapter in Anglo-Egyptian relations. The following period (1924–1936) was characterized by two simultaneous processes: one was the prolonged and frequently interrupted negotiations with Britain for a bilateral treaty which would give ampler recognition to Egypt's national aspirations; the other was the accentuation of internal political struggle between the Palace and the Wafd.[3] Anglo-Egyptian negotiations (Chamberlain-Sarwat, 1927–1928; Henderson-Mahmud, 1929; Henderson-Nahas, 1930) were inconclusive. In May 1930 they were suspended, not to be renewed until 1935. The Sudan and British troops in Egypt were the two main obstacles toward an agreement. In the meantime the unilateral declaration of February 28, 1922, remained as a basis of relations between the two countries.

Failure to satisfy nationalist demands usually produced, in the early twenties, mob demonstrations and anti-British violence. It was, therefore, noteworthy that similar failures in the decade between 1925 and 1935 did not provoke major outbursts. The explana-

[3] On this period, consult Anthony M. Galatoli, *Egypt in Midpassage* (Cairo, 1950); Amine Youssef Bey, *Independent Egypt* (London, 1940); and P. A. Gargour, *Etapes de l'Indépendance Egyptienne* (Paris, 1942). For an anti-British account, see Conrad Oehlich, *Englands Hand in Ägypten* (Berlin, 1940).

tion must be sought in Egypt's internal politics. These were characterized by two important factors. First, Saad Zaghlul Pasha passed from the political scene. Following the second elections in 1926, which again returned a strong Wafd majority, Zaghlul was a natural candidate for the premiership but he was prevented from assuming office by a British veto. The Chamber then elected him to its presidency. In this somewhat obscure position Zaghlul remained for one year, but in 1927 death cut short his political career. Thus the most formidable adversary of British rule in Egypt, a man deified by the Egyptian populace, passed away, and the Wafd lost its most inspiring leader. He was succeeded by Mustafa Nahas Pasha.

The second feature of internal politics was the determination of the king to curb the influence of the Wafd and to assert his own authority. Assisted by another center of power, the divines of the famous Moslem El-Azhar University, King Fuad succeeded in rallying around the Palace a number of aspiring politicians, who for various reasons did not accept Nahas Pasha's leadership and sought to satisfy their ambitions independently of the Wafd. Acting on their own or with the King's or Britain's blessing, these men launched a number of political parties, some quite ephemeral, some durable. In 1922 Mohammed Mahmud Pasha founded, with Adly Yeghen Pasha, the Liberal Constitutional Party, which was supported by aristocratic and intellectual circles but had little popular support.[4] In 1925 Yehya Ibrahim Pasha established the Unionist (*Ittihad*) Party, which was identified with the Palace. The party evoked very little response in the country and was notoriously unsuccessful in many subsequent elections.[5] Five years later Ismail Sidki Pasha formed the People's (*Shaab*) Party, an organization with a rather misleading name inasmuch as it had little, if any, mass following. More significant was the split that occurred in 1932 in the ranks of the Wafd. It resulted in the establishment of a new party called *Saadist* (or *Saadi Wafd*) by two former Wafd leaders: Ahmed Maher and Nokrashi Pasha. This secession was the only move in party politics likely to harm the Wafd, but even this did not have much effect on the Wafd's predominance. Except for the old National (*Watani*) Party, an insignificant and irreconcilable group of the deposed Khedive Abbas

[4] Other prominent members were Ahmed Gaffar Bey, Mahmud Abdul Razek Pasha, Gaffar Wali Pasha, and Heikal Pasha.

[5] Other prominent members were Hilmi Issa Pasha, Sayid Abu Ali Pasha, and Ahmed Ali Pasha.

398

Hilmi, all these parties were more moderate than the Wafd: they were willing to support the King and ready for a realistic accommodation with Great Britain.

The pattern of Egyptian politics was roughly as follows: in a series of national elections (1923, 1925, and 1929) the Wafd emerged overwhelmingly victorious, but, except for two brief periods after Zaghlul's death (in 1928 and 1930) when Nahas Pasha headed the government, cabinets were formed by non-Wafdist premiers acceptable to the King and, indirectly, to the British. The paradox of Egyptian politics was that no Palace-supported party could ever win the elections in a free ballot because of Wafd popularity, yet the monarchy had a definite mass appeal.

The fact that hostile Wafd majorities perennially faced anti-Wafd cabinets was so frustrating to the Palace that, in 1930, King Fuad decided to curb Wafd supremacy by all the means at his disposal. To this end he appointed a "strong man," Ismail Sidki Pasha, as prime minister, dissolved the parliament, revoked the 1923 constitution, and on October 22, 1930, promulgated a new constitution and a new electoral law introducing a two-grade, indirect voting system. Thus armed with new legislative weapons and assisted by his new Shaab Party, Sidki in 1931 obtained a victory in the Wafd-boycotted elections, establishing under royal authority a virtual dictatorship for the next four years. This was the most peaceful period in Anglo-Egyptian relations. Sidki's government concentrated on economic issues in order to combat the depression. There was no political history to record.

The Anglo-Egyptian Treaty

The relative internal and external peace which Egypt experienced between 1930 and 1935 came to an end with the outbreak of the Italo-Ethiopian war in September 1935. A year earlier Sidki had resigned on account of ill health, and the departure of this energetic statesman from active political leadership again brought to the fore the problem of the relations between the Palace and the increasingly restive Wafd. Under strong nationalistic pressure the ailing King Fuad first suspended the authoritarian constitution of 1930 and then on December 12, 1935, notwithstanding British advice to the contrary, restored the constitution of 1923. This coincided with the creation of the so-called National Front, the result of a temporary reconciliation between the King and the Wafd. Four months later King Fuad died.

He was succeeded by Farouk I, a sixteen-year-old youth who had to interrupt his secondary education in Switzerland to assume the crown.

The passing of the moderate Fuad-Sidki diumvirate and the restoration of the old constitution gave the Wafd a new opportunity to reassert itself in Egyptian politics. In May 1936 the Wafd won a resounding victory at the polls, whereupon Nahas Pasha promptly formed an all-Wafd cabinet. One of the first steps of the new government was to ask Great Britain for the renewal of negotiations to replace the *status quo* by a treaty. The British government responded favorably because it was anxious to reach a settlement with Egypt in view of the growing Italian menace in the eastern Mediterranean and the Red Sea basin. The realization of this menace and the object lesson Mussolini had given to underdeveloped countries by his treatment of Ethiopia also made the Egyptians more conciliatory. Repeated British offers during the preceding negotiations to defend Egypt against external aggression assumed a new significance in the light of Fascist dynamism. Egyptian moderates who privately conceded that a humanitarian British tutelage was better than outright Fascist control saw their position strengthened. After considerable interparty bickering it was decided that in the forthcoming negotiations Egypt should be represented by a thirteen-man delegation composed of seven Wafd members and six representatives of other political parties. Nahas Pasha headed the team. Britain was represented by the high commissioner, Sir Miles Lampson, accompanied by high-ranking diplomatic and military experts.

On August 26, 1936, the Anglo-Egyptian treaty was signed in London. It contained the following main provisions:

1) Egypt and Britain entered into an alliance, with Britain pledging to defend Egypt against aggression and Egypt placing her communication facilities at Britain's disposal in case of war;

2) Recognizing Britain's vital interest in the Suez Canal, Egypt consented to a British garrison of 10,000 men and 400 pilots in the Canal Zone, where barracks were to be constructed at Egypt's expense. British troops were to evacuate the rest of Egyptian territory, but Britain was allowed to retain her naval base at Alexandria for eight more years;

3) British personnel in the Egyptian army and police were to be withdrawn. Instead a British military mission was to advise the Egyptian army to the exclusion of other foreigners, and Egyptian officers could not be trained abroad in other countries than Britain. Egypt

regained full freedom to increase her armed forces; [6]

4) Unrestricted immigration of Egyptians into the Sudan was to be permitted and Egyptian troops were to return to the Sudan;

5) Britain was to support Egypt in her plea for the abolition of capitulations;

6) Britain promised to support Egypt's candidacy for membership in the League of Nations;

7) The British high commissioner was to be replaced by an ambassador, the latter receiving permanent diplomatic seniority rights;

8) The treaty was to be of indefinite duration, but at the end of twenty years negotiations toward its revision were allowed. It was, however, agreed that "any revision of this treaty [would] provide for the continuation of the alliance between the High Contracting Parties." [7]

If we compare these provisions with the Four Reserved Points of 1922, we see that both parties gave way in important matters. Britain retained practically undiminished her right to guard the security of imperial communications but had to compromise on the issue of defense and made a complete concession with regard to the protection of foreigners and minorities. The basic problem of the Sudan remained unsolved, Britain's consent to readmit Egyptians into the condominium being only a restoration of the situation that had existed before the ultimatum of 1924.

On December 22, 1936, the treaty was ratified by the Egyptian parliament despite some adverse criticism. To the Egyptians the treaty meant the inauguration of independence inasmuch as it replaced the unilateral British fiat of 1922. On May 8, 1937, the Montreux conference of powers who enjoyed capitulatory privileges in Egypt resulted in an agreement to abolish the capitulations but to maintain the Mixed Courts in Cairo and Alexandria for the next twelve years. On May 26 Egypt was admitted to the League of Nations.

The treaty of 1936 marked an apogee in the history of the Wafd, whose leader, Nahas Pasha, looked forward to a long period of undisputed power in Egypt. This self-assuredness brought him, however, into conflict with the young King who, like his late father, became wary of the Wafd's hold on the people. Thus the old pattern was revived, the King, backed by the rector of El-Azhar, Sheikh El-Maraghi, by the Liberal Constitutional Party, and by the Saadists, opposing the Wafd. In 1937 Farouk dismissed Nahas Pasha and

[6] Previously objected to by the British.
[7] The full text is in Davis, *op. cit.*, pp. 56 ff.

appointed in his place Mohammed Mahmud Pasha, a Liberal Constitutionalist. This was a repetition of the Sidki experiment of 1930–1934. Premier Mahmud Pasha again played the role of a "strong man," heading a non-Wafdist cabinet in the face of Wafdist parliamentary opposition.

As in 1931, the Palace was again determined to put an end to the abnormal situation of constant hostility between the parliament and the executive by changing the political complexion of the parliament. Mahmud Pasha suppressed the Fascist Green Shirts (Young Egypt—*Misr el-Fatat*) and the Wafdist Blue Shirts, Nazi-patterned youth groups, and made preparatory moves toward national elections with the ultimate aim of ousting the Wafd from power. His task was made easier by the fact that until the conclusion of the treaty with Britain the Wafd had thrived on Anglo-Egyptian antagonism, but now this basis of popular appeal was removed. In February 1938 the King dissolved the Wafd-dominated parliament, and in the elections held in April Mahmud Pasha's progovernment coalition won a spectacular victory. The Wafd suffered an eclipse which was to keep it from power for the next four years.

Egypt during World War II [8]

Egyptian foreign and domestic politics, as we have seen, were closely interwoven. They followed, moreover, an uncomplicated pattern: on the one hand, Egypt struggled for emancipation from Britain's rule without intervention by any major outside power; on the other, Britain, with Palace connivance, strove to break the Wafd monopoly of popular appeal by encouraging splinter parties and personal rivalries in the name of the time-honored principle of "divide and rule."

With the coming of the Second World War this basic pattern continued, but it underwent some modifications—owing to the appearance of an external factor. With Britain's position in the Middle East seriously threatened by Italy and Germany, Egypt could reorient her policy of gradual emancipation and co-operation with Britain into one of open defiance and collaboration with the Axis powers. Or she could remain passive and noncommittal waiting for "the dust to settle" and then make up to the winners. Both Axis powers had been diplomatically active in Cairo a year or two preceding the out-

[8] For a superficial, but chronologically detailed account of this period, see Jean Lugol, *Egypt and World War II* (Cairo, 1945).

break of the war. A number of German staff officers, diplomats, and Nazi dignitaries (including Dr. Goebbels) paid visits to Egypt. Italy had the support of 60,000 Italian residents of Egypt, possessed influential commercial and banking establishments, and did not spare funds and efforts to create friendly feelings. German and Italian broadcasts in Arabic from Zeesen and Bari, respectively, were quite popular with Egyptian audiences. The Egyptians, to be sure, could have no particular stake in a complete victory of the Axis, but a relative weakening of Great Britain, together with self-insurance in case of her total defeat, appealed to many Egyptians as worth striving for. For many an Egyptian statesman, therefore, this was a problem of accurate appraisal, a problem not devoid of an element of gambling. The policy of obvious co-operation with the British, while commendable during the war itself in view of the presence of large British forces in the country, might boomerang in case of Axis success. On the other hand, nonco-operation, depending upon its degree, might prove dangerous during the war and, in case of British victory, might ruin a political career after the war.

These considerations led to a division of opinion among the leading Egyptians when the war began. The British requested and obtained the proclamation of martial law in September 1939, the institution of censorship, the rupture of diplomatic relations with Germany, the internment or expulsion of German nationals, and use of Egyptian communication facilities according to the treaty of 1936. Egypt became the principal British, and later Allied, base in the Middle East. Over half a million Allied troops, including British, Indian, Australian, New Zealand, South African, Polish, Czechoslovak, Greek, Yugoslav, and American soldiers, found themselves in the course of war on Egyptian territory. Cairo was a real hub of Allied diplomatic and economic activity. The Anglo-American Middle East Supply Center was located here, and there was hardly an Allied statesman of prominence who did not, at one time or another, visit Cairo to attend a diplomatic conference, to inspect troops, or to stop enroute to some distant place. In Cairo the British established the important wartime office of minister of state for the Middle East, occupied in succession by Captain Oliver Lyttelton, Mr. Richard Casey, and Lord Moyne. American administrators of the lend lease and other regional agencies operating in the Middle East were likewise stationed in Cairo. And last, but not least, President Franklin D. Roosevelt, Prime Minister Winston Churchill, Generalissimo Chiang

403

Kai-shek, and Turkish President Ismet Inönü held their famous conference in the city in the late fall of 1943.[9]

At the time of the outbreak of the war the Egyptian government was headed by Ali Maher Pasha, an Independent working in close affiliation with the Saadists and Liberal Constitutionalists. He followed a policy of limited co-operation with Britain, which, as time progressed, changed into gradual hostility. The failure of the Western Allies to prevent the collapse of Poland, the defeatist period of the "phony war," 1939–1940, the German successes in the west in the spring of 1940, and the Dunkerque evacuation seemed to prove that Britain's might was on the wane. The Italian minister in Cairo, Count Mazzolini, did his best during that period to foster this impression among the Egyptians, stressing that in case of an Italo-British conflict Italy would have no iniquitous designs on Egypt. When Italy declared war on the Allies in June 1940, Britain asked Ali Maher to declare war on Italy. Ali Maher resisted and, as a result of British pressure on King Farouk, was forced to resign. From his retirement he continued to agitate against the British, which eventually led to his arrest and forcible confinement to his country residence in 1942. Ali Maher's successors did not declare war on Italy either but agreed to break off diplomatic relations. There was no question of the mass internment of Italian nationals, their large number making it impracticable, but selected individuals, usually pointed out by British security agencies, were interned. In August 1940 Italian troops in their first major offensive entered Egyptian territory. But Rome made it clear that this move was directed against Great Britain only; hence the Egyptian government did not consider it a *casus belli* and persevered in its refusal to declare war. Similarly, Egypt refused to be drawn into belligerency when General Erwin Rommel's German Afrika Korps crossed the Egyptian border in April 1941. But this passive resistance was the extent of Egypt's efforts to interfere with Allied conduct of the war. There were individual attempts to co-operate actively with the Axis. Such, for example, was the unsuccessful attempt of the ex-chief of staff, General Aziz el-Masri, to join forces with the Iraqi rebel, Rashid Ali el-Gailani, in May 1941. Such also was the betrayal by some Egyptian

[9] To this may be added a series of conferences President Roosevelt held with the following Middle Eastern and African rulers: King Farouk, King Ibn Saud, Emperor Haile Selassie, and President Shukri el-Quwatli of Syria, on board the U.S.S. *Quincy* on the Great Bitter Lake in Egypt, in mid-February 1945, following the Yalta conference.

staff officers of British defense plans concerning Siwa oasis. But generally the Egyptians were in no mood to act recklessly. The presence of large Allied contingents was, of course, a powerful deterrent against any active hostility. Moreover, the British seemed to possess effective mastery of internal security. A British subject, General Russell Pasha, was commandant of the Egyptian police, and Colonel Fitzpatrick Bey, his deputy. A Britisher was chief prosecutor in the Mixed Courts, and another Britisher headed the censorship division. British officials held strategic positions in border passport control and similar security agencies. There was little likelihood of the situation getting out of hand.

The British were anxious not to antagonize these political forces in Egypt that had influence over the masses. Any mob demonstrations or rioting, should it occur, would be a major embarrassment to Britain, whose strength had to be spared for the war effort. The British realized that the Wafd, despite its somewhat forced eclipse in 1938, still remained the most powerful single factor in Egyptian politics and that it was able to do serious harm to their position in Egypt, should it so choose. The fact that the non-Wafdist government did, after all, co-operate with Britain might have supplied the Wafd with new ammunition and might have turned it from its pro-treaty stand into traditional anti-British demagoguery. Moreover, the British were fully aware of Nahas Pasha's anger at being kept out of office for an unduly long period. They also knew of the thirst of Wafdist politicians for lucrative government jobs. All these considerations led the British government to decide that the safest way to keep Nahas and the Wafd out of mischief was to put them back into power. This meant, of course, a reversal of British policy. It required also persuading King Farouk, Nahas' personal enemy, to sign the act of appointment. Farouk refused and had to be coerced. On February 4, 1942, British armored units surrounded the Royal Abdin Palace in Cairo, whereupon British Ambassador Sir Miles Lampson (later Lord Killearn) accompanied by the commander-in-chief of the British forces in Egypt called on the King and gave him the choice of either signing Nahas' nomination or being deported from the country. Farouk complied, and Nahas assumed the premiership. The return to power of the Wafd necessarily resulted in increased corruption (the Wafd is a party with a well-organized patronage system) and in greater governmental inefficiency. Speculation, hoarding, and similar practices showed an upward trend—the British had been fully aware that this would happen. Yet, politically, it was a shrewd move and spared them many inconveniences.

In his new role Nahas was quite co-operative, as evidenced by his willingness to confine anti-British Ali Maher Pasha to domestic arrest (the decision was not quite disinterested). He helped Britain to recruit local labor for various works in the rear bases and co-operated in tracking down spies, saboteurs, and fifth columnists. The premier's prestige suffered considerably when, some time after his appointment, he quarreled with one of his close and most able associates, a Coptic Christian, Makram Ebeid Pasha. Ebeid resigned from the cabinet and soon afterward published a documented Black Book in which he mercilessly exposed the corrupt practices of the Wafd. A number of Wafdists seceded with him, founding the new *Kutla* (Bloc) Party. Wafd fortunes were at a low ebb, but the British continued to support Nahas to avoid ministerial crises at the time of the greatest military decisions in North Africa. By the fall of 1944 the Axis danger to the Middle East was successfully removed as a result of El-Alamein and North African victories. Consequently the British felt that they could withdraw their support from Nahas, leaving Egyptian politics to resume their natural course. As soon as this became known (October 1944), Farouk dismissed Nahas and reinstated the Saadists in power. At the elections of January 1945, which were boycotted by the Wafd, a coalition of the Saadist and Kutla parties secured a substantial majority in the parliament.

The war was drawing to an end, Britain's prestige was high, and in the person of the new premier, Dr. Ahmed Maher Pasha, the British had a friendly and realistic statesman anxious to secure a place for Egypt in the postwar community of nations. The Big Three communiqué issued at the Yalta Conference made a declaration of war on the Axis a prerequisite to attendance at the projected United Nations conference at San Francisco. The Egyptian government decided to declare war, and on February 24, 1945, Ahmed Maher appeared in parliament to make a public statement to this effect. Unfortunately he was assassinated by a fanatical student nationalist while reading the royal decree. He was succeeded by Nokrashi Pasha, another Saadist leader, who continued in office until 1946.

NATIONALISM AND INTERNAL TURBULENCE

With the end of the war a new era opened in Egyptian politics. Ahmed Maher's murder was indicative of a new trend toward extremism. The Second World War caused disturbances in the Egyptian social and economic structure similar to the First, and its effects on the political psychology of the Egyptians were analogous. It also provoked a wave of antiforeign nationalism, which tended to assume violent forms as soon as the British began to withdraw their large military contingents. Despite these general similarities between the two postwar situations, there were noteworthy differences. Whereas after World War I the Wafd became the spokesman for Egyptian nationalism, after World War II this role was taken over by other, more extreme groups. This extremism was manifested on both the left and the right wings of the political scale. On the left was the Communist Party, which, as a result of Soviet world influence, gained greatly in prestige. Soviet victories during the war and the establishment of a Soviet legation in Cairo in 1942 aroused interest in communism among students and young intellectuals in particular. Financed by Henri Curiel, a bookseller and the son of a well-known Sephardi-Jewish millionaire, the Communist Party, though illegal, penetrated into many editorial offices, government bureaus, organizations, and political parties including the Wafd. In the labor sector the Communists concentrated on three textile industrial centers: Mahalla el-Kubra, midway between Cairo and Alexandria; Shubra el-Khayma, on the outskirts of Cairo; and Filature Nationale in Alexandria. There they exploited legitimate labor grievances to foster their aims through strikes and disturbances. They assumed leadership in the Workers' Congress, a body created in 1946, as well as in the Egyptian representation to the leftist World Federation of Trade Unions.[10] Although the party membership probably did not exceed 5,000, the party's influence, especially on the younger intelligentsia, was out of proportion to its actual numbers.

On the right wing of the political scale stood the powerful Moslem Brotherhood (*El-Ikhwan el-Muslimin*).[11] Organized in 1929 in Ismailia by Sheikh Hassan el-Banna, the pro-Islamic and anti-Western Brotherhood gained a large following at the end of the Second World War, extending its influence even beyond the boundaries of Egypt. Backed by an estimated 500,000 sympathizers, Hassan el-Banna proved to be not only an inspired preacher but also an excellent or-

[10] William J. Handley, "The Labor Movement in Egypt," *Middle East Journal*, July 1949.

[11] A thorough treatment of this movement may be found in James Heyworth-Dunne, *Religious and Political Trends in Modern Egypt* (Washington, 1950).

ganizer, who definitely aimed at the assumption of political power in Egypt. Appealing first to underprivileged lower classes, the movement eventually spread to educated classes as well, enlisting the co-operation of some influential leaders. The tactics of Hassan el-Banna were tortuous: in 1942–1944, when Nahas was prime minister, he worked in close association with the Wafd; in 1944 he gave temporary support to the Saadist Party; but in 1945 he reverted to an independent course, starting a prolonged campaign of terrorism against all those whom he accused of collaboration with the British. It is asserted that part of his success has been due to subsidies received from King Farouk. The latter reportedly favored the Brotherhood as a counterweight to the Wafd.

The anti-Wafd, Saadist-dominated cabinets that governed Egypt from 1944 to 1949 faced a most difficult situation. Opposed by both the Wafd and the extremist groups, they had little appeal for the masses. At the same time they had to curb repeated outbreaks of violence, strikes, and antigovernment or antiforeign demonstrations, and calm down public excitement over the Palestinian issue. The war left a sad heritage of inflation and unbalanced agricultural production, deepened the gap between the fixed-income groups and the profiteers (predominantly Levantines, who made fortunes on contracts with the Allied forces), and caused fantastic fluctuations in the cotton market and—after the withdrawal of foreign armies—large-scale unemployment among workers. Thus, although Egypt did not suffer serious war devastation [12] and even emerged as a creditor with large sterling balances, her financial status—always socially inadequate—was seriously disturbed.

Trying to maintain order, the government took measures first against the Communists. As an alien-inspired group advocating radical revolution, the Communist Party became a natural target for government reprisals. In July 1946, following a wave of strikes and demonstrations, the government seized a number of leading Communists; in October and November the Egyptian police and army rounded up many Communist agitators at Fuad and El-Azhar Universities in Cairo and at Farouk University in Alexandria; and in January 1947 the government opened its prosecution case against Curiel and his nineteen associates. The majority of them were given jail sentences.

Governmental action against the Moslem Brotherhood did not

[12] Axis bombing of Alexandria and the Suez Canal was negligible.

follow immediately. There was considerable hesitation as to what course to follow, mixed, no doubt, with thoughts that an alliance with the Brotherhood might be politically valuable. But by late 1948 it became clear that Hassan el-Banna was determined to pursue an independent policy which brooked no compromise. There were a series of terrorist acts, and on December 4 General Salim Zaki Pasha, the Cairo chief of police, was killed by a student during a Brotherhood-inspired demonstration. Four days later the government outlawed the Brotherhood. On December 28 a student member of the Brotherhood assassinated Prime Minister Mahmud Fahmi Nokrashi Pasha in the building of the Ministry of Interior. The murder was conceived as a punishment for Nokrashi's anti-Brotherhood reprisals and for his allegedly conciliatory policy toward Britain. The drama reached its climax when, on February 12, 1949, Hassan el-Banna was shot and killed in broad daylight by a group of young men passing in an automobile. The assassins were not discovered, and the government did not seem to show much enthusiasm in pursuing the search. The death of its leader was a severe blow to the Brotherhood, and its activities slowed down perceptibly.

At this juncture King Farouk issued an appeal for national unity and asked the Wafd to enter the government under a neutral leadership. The move was dictated partly by the deteriorating internal situation and partly by the desire to avoid another Wafdist boycott of the elections, which were due in early 1950. The Wafd replied by presenting certain conditions, and in July 1949 a coalition cabinet including several Wafdist ministers was created. The cabinet's life was short, and in November it was replaced by a caretaker pre-electoral government of obscure officials.

In the January 1950 elections the Wafd obtained a resounding victory, securing 228 out of 319 seats in the Chamber. The outcome was interpreted as a rebuke to the Saadists for their incompetent conduct of the Palestinian war in 1948. Seventy-one-year-old Nahas Pasha again assumed the premiership, and in June 1950 he induced the King to remove seventeen appointed senators and replace them by Wafdist nominees. By this move the Wafd secured an absolute majority in both chambers.

Problem of Treaty Revision

Against this turbulent background Egypt conducted her postwar foreign policies. As usual, Anglo-Egyptian relations dominated.

Egypt emerged from the war determined to revise the treaty of 1936. The two points of special grievance were the continuing presence of British troops in Egypt and the problem of the Sudan. Egyptians demanded that even the limited British forces allowed by the treaty for the defense of the Canal Zone should be withdrawn. As for the Sudan, Egypt claimed that the condominium was a screen for complete British supremacy, and insisted on the "Unity of the Nile Valley."

The Egyptian claim for reunion with the Sudan was based on historical, ethnic, cultural, economic, and strategic considerations. From the historical point of view, Egypt had a strong case. So did she when she claimed common ethnic and cultural links with the Sudanese, although these links existed only with northern Sudan. The northern part of this huge territory is inhabited by people with a strong admixture of Arab blood who speak Arabic and are Mohammedan. The southern population is predominantly negroid and pagan and uses various non-Arabic languages. The economic argument ran as follows: The British have harnessed the economy of the Sudan to their own interests. Laying down a fine irrigation network, they have expanded Sudanese cotton plantations, especially in the Gezira province. Sudanese cotton competes with Egyptian cotton on world markets, and the Sudanese economy is competitive instead of complementary to the Egyptian. In regaining control of the Sudan Egypt would relieve her own population pressure (the Egyptian population has increased from around two million in 1800 to nearly twenty million in 1950), would help the Sudan solve her labor shortage, and would encourage the Sudanese to cultivate staple food crops which could be consumed on the spot or exported to Egypt.

The strategic argument was the most important. Egypt maintained that she could never feel completely secure so long as her water supply was controlled by a foreign nation. Egyptian publicists were not slow to quote from various British authors in support of this thesis. They also recalled the British ultimatum of 1924, which had arbitrarily announced an unlimited increase in the Gezira irrigation area as a reprisal for Sir Lee Stack's murder.

Egyptians were also irritated by the way the British handled internal Sudanese politics. There were two major political parties in the Sudan: the *Umma* (Nationalists) and the *Ashigga* (Cousins). The Umma, headed by Abdur Rahman Pasha, son of the Mahdi, stood for complete independence and separation from Egypt. Its press indulged in anti-Egyptian propaganda, and in the winter of 1946–1947 Abdur Rahman went to London to plead his party's case. The British quite obviously favored this movement.

The Ashigga Party advocated a dual monarchy, which would provide for full Sudanese autonomy under the Egyptian crown. It believed in the unity of the Nile valley as necessary to both nations. Ashigga, supported by the intelligentsia of mixed Sudanese-Egyptian stock and headed by the powerful religious leader, Sheikh Ali el-Marghani Pasha, gained a considerably larger following among the Sudanese masses than did Umma. Egyptians strongly objected to the favoritism shown by the British to Umma and feared that any postponement of the solution in the Sudan would merely give the British more time to spread antiunity propaganda. The dismissal by the British governor-general of the Egyptian chief religious judge from his post in the Sudan in 1947 added considerably to Egyptians' discontent.[13]

Such, then, were the main grievances of Egypt concerning the treaty of 1936. Demands for revision had been made by Nahas Pasha as Wafd leader as early as 1942 and by the Egyptian government, then headed by Ahmed Maher Pasha, in 1945. At both times the British expressed their willingness to discuss revision after the end of the war.

Sidki Pasha, prime minister in 1946, eventually conducted the negotiations with the British government. He had decided against a large multi-party delegation and, after months of preliminary discussions, went to London alone, where, in October 1946, he concluded an agreement with Ernest Bevin, Britain's foreign secretary. The Sidki-Bevin agreement provided for the withdrawal of British forces from the Canal Zone and contained a formula concerning the Sudan. British troop protection for the Zone was to be replaced by definite Anglo-Egyptian defense arrangements which would include maintenance by Egypt of certain workshops and installations ready to be turned over to the British army in case of war. As to the Sudan, the formula adopted was as follows:

The policy which the high contracting parties undertake to follow in the Sudan within the framework of the unity between the Sudan and

[13] For two views of the Sudanese problem, see Douglas D. Crary, "Geography and Politics in the Nile Valley," *Middle East Journal*, July 1949; and Mohamed Awad, "Egypt, Great Britain, and the Sudan: An Egyptian View," *Middle East Journal*, July 1947.

Egypt under the common Crown of Egypt will have for its essential objectives to assure the well-being of the Sudanese, the development of their interests, and their active preparation for self-government and consequently the exercise of the right to choose the future status of the Sudan. Until the high contracting parties can in full common agreement realize this latter objective after consultation with the Sudanese, the agreement of 1899 will continue and Article 11 of the treaty of 1936, together with its annex and paragraphs 14 to 16 of the agreed minute annexed to the same treaty, will remain in force not withstanding the first article of the present treaty.[14]

The gist of this formula was that, for the time being, the *status quo* in the Sudan would continue. When the time was ripe for a change, the Sudanese would decide for themselves what form of government they desired, even if it meant complete separation from Egypt. Such at least was the British interpretation of the agreement. The Egyptians, however, interpreted it differently, believing that the words "within the framework of unity . . . under the common Crown" definitely limited Sudanese freedom of choice. This difference of interpretations led to a protracted exchange of notes, which ended in a deadlock early in 1947. It may be pointed out that the first part of the Bevin-Sidki agreement, concerning the Suez Canal Zone, was quite acceptable to the Egyptians, but they refused to ratify the agreement on account of the Sudanese question.

Egypt's Open Defiance of Britain

In December 1946 Sidki had resigned. His successor, the Saadist leader Nokrashi Pasha, decided to apply double pressure on Great Britain to obtain a solution satisfactory to the Egyptians. It is noteworthy that neither Sidki, an Independent, nor Nokrashi, a Saadist, was an extremist and that, given complete freedom of action, they probably would have agreed to a realistic compromise solution. But the pressure of inflamed public opinion and a wave of anti-British riots made it impossible for any Egyptian statesman publicly to express moderation. If the non-Wafdist coalition which was then in power had succeeded in securing a diplomatic victory over Britain, its popularity would have been greatly increased and it might have wrested the monopoly of mass appeal from the Wafd. Added to this was the feeling that, if ever, this was the time to compel war-weary and empire-losing Britain to grant concessions.

The double pressure, previously referred to, consisted of two

[14] The text is in the *Middle East Journal*, April 1947, p. 207.

specific actions. One was to exploit the growing American interest in the Middle East, as evidenced by the expansion of oil business and air communications in the area, so as to supplant British supremacy by American co-operation. On June 15, 1946, the United States and Egypt had concluded a civilian air pact. In April 1947 the Egyptian chief of staff, General Ibrahim Atallah Pasha, visited the United States to sound out the American government as to its willingness to give advisory and technical assistance to the Egyptian army. At the same time it became known that Egypt was seeking an $88,000,000 loan from the United States. On March 12, 1947, President Truman had pledged American assistance to Greece and Turkey in view of the inability of weakened Britain to continue her burdens in those countries, and in May an American fleet composed of the aircraft carrier *Leyte* and three other warships paid a courtesy call in Alexandria. Both actions were indicative of definite American interest in the security of the eastern Mediterranean. Consequently, Egyptians hoped that by skillful manipulation they might induce the United States to show more interest in Egypt and thus render the Anglo-Egyptian defense arrangements unnecessary. In September 1947 Premier Nokrashi went in person to Washington to invite the United States to send a military mission to Egypt in order to fill the gap created by the withdrawal of the British mission. He met with poor success. The American government refused to compete with Britain in what was believed to be a British preserve. It was reluctant, moreover, to create a precedent which might affect its own position in Panama.[15]

Another method of pressure was to bring the Anglo-Egyptian dispute to the attention of the United Nations. On July 8, 1947, Nokrashi Pasha accused Great Britain before the Security Council on two counts: (1) Britain was guilty of maintaining her troops in Egyptian territory against the will of the people. The presence of these troops, Nokrashi asserted, offended the dignity of Egypt, hindered her normal development, infringed upon the fundamental principle of sovereign equality, and, therefore, violated the United Nations Charter. (2) Britain's occupation of the Nile valley and the pursuance of a hostile policy in the Sudan had given rise to a dispute, the continuance of which was likely to endanger international peace and security.

For these reasons Egypt was compelled, according to Nokrashi, to

[15] Halford L. Hoskins, "The Guardianship of the Suez Canal," *Middle East Journal*, April 1950, p. 143.

request the Security Council to direct the total and immediate evacuation of British troops from Egypt, including the Sudan, and the termination of the administrative regime in the latter area. Britain's reply was that the treaty of 1936 was still valid and that there was no evidence of a threat to international peace. There the matter rested, neither country receiving definite majority support. An American motion (which failed of acceptance) that both parties should be directed to reopen negotiations met with resentment in Egypt. In the meantime the British, anxious to observe the treaty scrupulously, evacuated their forces from Kom el-Dik citadel in Alexandria and liquidated their naval base there. In March the last British troops left the famous Kasr el-Nil barracks in Cairo. A new headquarters was established in Fayid, in the Canal Zone.

As an eminent French writer, Paul Morand, once wrote, England and Egypt are like an old married couple: they may quarrel, but they never break their bond. This adage seemed to be proved when Egypt became involved, in 1948, in the Palestinian war. Mass feeling reached a high pitch in the delta of the Nile. Thousands of men volunteered for military service, the regular army was sent to southern Palestine, and Hassan el-Banna's desperadoes simultaneously invaded Israel in guerrilla bands. Jewish residents of Egypt, a wealthy and generally loyal community, were attacked, their property damaged, and their status endangered. What mattered, however, was the shocking exposure of the weakness of the Egyptian state. Egypt, a country of twenty million inhabitants, could send only a small and totally inadequate army to Palestine. This army, after reaching Hebron in the east and the outskirts of Jaffa in the west, suffered severe defeats and barely managed to retain a narrow Gaza strip and a small bulge around Auja on the Negeb-Egyptian border. Jewish units went so far as to make an incursion into purely Egyptian territory toward El-Arish in Sinai. At this moment the British government intervened, warning Israel that any invasion of Egypt might compel it to abide by the treaty of 1936 and take appropriate measures for the defense of Egypt. This desire to stress the validity of the treaty led Great Britain, as soon as she was free from limitations imposed by the Palestinian truce agreements, to renew shipments of arms to Egypt.

The subsiding of the Palestinian furor and the return of the Wafd to power in 1950 resulted in a reopening of the negotiations for treaty revision. Talks to this effect between the two govern-

ments began in the winter of 1950–1951, but there was little likelihood of a successful conclusion. In the first place, the Palestinian
issue produced a kind of permanent tension between Britain and
Egypt, which was not alleviated by Britain's desire to appear pro-
Arab or at least neutral. Egypt, more humiliated than any other
Arab country by the outcome of the war, was determined to prevent
any oil-carrying tankers from reaching Israel, and for this reason
imposed irksome restrictions upon maritime traffic in the Suez
Canal.[16] In the second place, the British, who were willing to give
up their installations in the Canal Zone in 1946 (a year of high hopes
for peaceful co-operation between Russia and the West), were
definitely reluctant to abandon them in 1950.

In British opinion it would have been suicidal to withdraw from
Egypt when Russia threatened with invasion the whole European
and Asiatic area south of her borders. It was realized, not only in
London but also in Washington, that effectively to defend Greece
and Turkey, Iraq and Iran, the Western democracies must possess
an adequate base in the Middle Eastern hinterland, and Egypt was
believed to be the only one available. Apart from her strategic position as a link between the Indian Ocean and the Mediterranean,
Egypt was the only country in the Middle East possessing adequate
technical facilities (stores, workshops, harbors, aerodromes, and factories) and an ample labor force and food supply so that she could
be easily converted into a powerful military base. In this respect
the experience of both World Wars could not be overlooked. Thus
the problem of British withdrawal transcended the narrow limits
of Anglo-Egyptian relations and became a truly international problem with the United States and its North Atlantic allies having a
vital stake in the solution.

Under the circumstances it was, indeed, hard to see how a compromise solution could be reached. Egypt continued to insist on
total British evacuation. This anti-British mood was a manifestation
of a general anti-Western trend in Egyptian foreign and domestic
politics, a trend that became obvious after the Palestinian war.
Because of its pro-Israeli policy the United States became, for the
first time in Egyptian history, a target of voluble criticism and
denunciation.

On the outbreak of war in Korea the Egyptian government de-

[16] These restrictions led Israel, in mid-summer 1951, to bring the case to the
United Nations. For details, see pp. 495–496 below.

415

clared that it would not support the United Nations effort and would not send troops to Korea. On July 21, 1950, Egyptian Foreign Minister Saleh ed-Din Bey told a press conference that Egypt was maintaining neutrality in the conflict. His statement was corroborated on April 14, 1951, by Abdul Salam Fahmi Gamaa Pasha, president of the Chamber of Deputies and one of the leading Wafdists, who declared that in case of a general war Egypt would be neutral and at the proper time would simply abrogate her 1936 treaty with Britain.[17] These statements could not be interpreted as evidence of any agreement between Cairo and Moscow, and only a few observers were inclined to deduce from such acts as the Egyptian-Soviet trade agreements of February 1948 and July 1951 that Egypt was about to slip into the Soviet orbit. Yet there is no doubt that Egypt's neutral orientation was inconvenient to the West at a time when the West was trying hard to organize the defenses of the Free World against Soviet imperialism.

Egypt's anti-British campaign, intensified by the repercussions of the Anglo-Iranian crisis, reached its peak when, on October 8, 1951, Premier Mustafa Nahas Pasha presented to the parliament a series of decrees unilaterally abrogating the 1936 Anglo-Egyptian treaty, providing for the eviction of British troops from the Canal Zone, reuniting the Sudan with Egypt, and proclaiming Farouk "King of Egypt and the Sudan." On October 15 these decrees were unanimously approved by the parliament. A wave of anti-British riots, following these decisions, failed to induce the British to leave the Canal Zone. Britain declared Egypt's step illegal and reinforced her garrison in the Canal Zone, determined not to bend to intimidation. At the same time (October 13) in an effort to break the deadlock, the governments of the United States, Great Britain, France, and Turkey submitted to Egypt a long-contemplated proposal to establish an Allied Middle East Command to assure the defense of Egypt and the adjacent area. Egypt was invited to participate on a basis of equality in the proposed Command, with the understanding that the British garrison in the Canal Zone would be replaced by an allied force composed of troops of the participating nations. On October 15 the Egyptian government rejected these proposals. Two days later United States Secretary of State Dean Acheson publicly

[17] See the *New York Times*, April 15, 1951. Paradoxically enough, the Egyptian navy was at the same time carrying out joint maneuvers with the British Mediterranean fleet, "to gain experience," as was explained in official Egyptian quarters.

declared full American support of Britain's position and condemned Egypt's disregard of international obligations. In the ensuing few weeks it became known that proposals to join in a Middle Eastern defense pact were addressed to other Arab states and Israel as well and that the Western powers intended to go ahead with their plans even if the Arab states failed to respond favorably to these proposals.

Egypt's Middle Eastern Policy

Egypt's Middle Eastern policy has revolved around the fact that she is the most advanced and wealthiest of the Arab states. Her statesmen played a leading part in the formation of the Arab League, whose pact was signed on Egyptian soil in 1945. An Egyptian, Abdur Rahman Azzam Pasha, became secretary general of the League. Many observers felt that Egypt was trying to use the League as an instrument of her own policy and that Azzam Pasha mainly served Egyptian interests.

Owing, among other things, to the existence of El-Azhar University, the highest seat of Moslem learning, Egypt has always aspired to spiritual and political leadership in the Arab world. One of King Farouk's tutors and closest advisers has been Sheikh El-Maraghi, president of El-Azhar, and it is known that the King, in contrast to Mustafa Kemal of Turkey, believes in stressing Egypt's Arab and Mohammedan character as well as her links to the past. Cherishing the role of protector of the Arabs, King Farouk has extended his hospitality in postwar years to such rebellious Arab leaders as Haj Amin el-Husseini, the mufti of Jerusalem; Abdul Krim, leader of the Riff tribes in Morocco; and Fawzi el-Kawukji, Syrian independence fighter.

Jealous of her leading position among the Arab states, Egypt has consistently opposed the Greater Syria scheme as likely to create a rival center of power and influence. This opposition has led to political friendship with Ibn Saud of Arabia, whose fear of the Hashimi house of Iraq and Jordan has made him co-operate with Egypt. In pursuance of this policy Egypt courted the short-lived dictator of Syria, Husni Zaim, in 1949.

In the spring of 1951 Egypt endeavored to bring about the conclusion of a regional Middle East defense pact that would include Turkey in addition to the Arab states. League Secretary General Azzam Pasha visited Ankara in June 1951 to sound out official

417

Turkish opinion. Egypt's idea was to create a neutral Middle Eastern bloc, predominantly Arab, but strengthened by the inclusion of Turkey. Although no details of these talks were revealed, it was certain that such proposals could not evoke enthusiasm in Ankara because at that very time Turkey was working hard to gain admission to the North Atlantic Treaty Organization. Azzam's visit did not result in any agreements or declarations and, consequently, its results could be considered as negative. Turkey's reluctance to join the Arab bloc did not stem from the lack of interest in the regional security of the Middle East. Turkey favored regional defense arrangements and she proved it by cosponsoring, four months later, a joint Western proposal to establish a Middle East Command, to which we have referred earlier. But she was unwilling to compromise her status as a pro-Western state by adhering to a bloc dominated by a neutralist and largely anti-Western Egypt.

Prelude to Revolution: The Cairo Riots

The excitement produced by the denunciation of the Anglo-Egyptian Treaty led to an ever-increasing number of incidents between the British forces and the Egyptians in the Canal Zone. British troops, collectively and individually, became a favorite target of sniping, assaults, and, sometimes, attacks by guerrillas organized for that purpose by the Socialist Party [18] or other extreme groups. The British countered with a policy of reprisals, which only increased the tension. On January 19, 1952, Ismailia, an important town and base on the canal, became the scene of mass fighting, which ended six days later in British occupation of the town. The Egyptian auxiliary police (*Buluk Nizam*) were evicted from their barracks, and sixty-four lost their lives in the course of the battle.

The Ismailia incident inspired major riots in Cairo the following day, January 26. The mobs, instigated partly by Ahmed Hussein's Socialist Party and partly by the Communists, attacked and put to fire seven hundred commercial, social, and cultural establishments, mostly foreign-owned but including also a number of Egyptian-owned firms and institutions. Such well-known landmarks as the Shepheard Hotel, Barclay's Bank, the Turf Club, Groppi restaurants, and the Cicurel and Chemla department stores were either partly

18 The formerly fascist Young Egypt organization (also known as Green Shirts) founded in 1933 by Ahmed Hussein, a lawyer. In 1940 the group changed its name to the Nationalist Islamic Party, and finally after the war it adopted the name Socialist.

or totally destroyed with attendant loss of life. The toll was 552 wounded and 26 killed after a day of rioting. The attitude of the Wafdist-controlled government during this display of violence was enigmatic. For the greater part of the day the police did not intervene to any appreciable degree, letting the rioters have their way. Only toward the close of the day did the army appear on the scene —at a time when the energy of the mobs was waning.

This was, indeed, a black day in Cairo, not only for the British and other foreigners, but for all Egyptians who had a stake in the preservation of order and authority. Foremost among the latter was none other than King Farouk himself. Traditionally hostile to the Wafd, he seized this opportunity summarily to dismiss Nahas Pasha and his cabinet on January 27 and to appoint in his place a veteran statesman, Ali Maher Pasha. The subsequent six months saw considerable turbulence, and the Palace-appointed anti-Wafdist cabinets [19] had to face either a hostile Wafd-dominated parliament or, after its dissolution on March 29, a dangerous political vacuum.

THE JULY REVOLUTION

This vacuum was abruptly filled by a new dynamic force when at the dawn of July 23 a "Committee of Free Officers," a secret group formed in 1947, overthrew the government. A Revolutionary Command Council, composed of eleven young officers, assumed supreme authority in the country. The ostensible leader, Major-General Mohammed Naguib, became commander-in-chief of the armed forces, while Ali Maher Pasha was made premier. On July 26 Naguib handed to King Farouk an ultimatum to renounce the throne and leave the country forthwith. Farouk signed an act of abdication in favor of his infant son Ahmed Fuad II and on the same day left Egypt for Italy. On August 2 a Regency Council was formed. It consisted of three men: Prince Mohammed Abdul Moneim, Bahieddin Barakat, and Lieutenant-Colonel Mohammed Rashad Mehanna, the latter representing the Revolutionary Command Council (R.C.C.).

In the proclamations and statements that followed General Naguib and his fellow officers made it known that in effecting this revolution they were animated by the unselfish desire to see Egypt emancipated from imperialism and feudalism and served by an honest government that would ensure social justice, economic progress,

[19] Of Ali Maher (Jan. 27–March 1); of Naguib el-Hilali (March 1–June 28); of Hussein Sirri (July 2–20); and of Naguib el-Hilali (July 22–23).

and dignity to all citizens of the country. They emphasized the middle-class composition of their Council and in their actions laid stress on rapid and radical reform. Their government, they claimed, was the first in the long history of Egypt to serve the people rather than foreign or dynastic interests.

In conformity with these utterances the military junta launched a number of reforms which, if fully implemented, were indeed likely to bring about considerable improvement in Egypt. Within a few weeks after the coup the R.C.C. abolished honorary and hereditary titles and created purge commissions in government departments. On September 8, 1952—a memorable date in the annals of the revolution—it issued a decree on agrarian reform which limited individual holdings to a maximum of 200 feddans (about 208 acres) and provided for the distribution of surplus properties to needy peasants. This was followed by the abolition of family trust estates (*ahli waqfs*), the floating of a £E 200,000,000 loan to finance land reform, the passing of three labor laws, and the inauguration of studies to increase the cultivable area of land in Egypt. The latter point claimed special attention by the R.C.C., which concentrated on two specific projects. The first, launched in 1953, embraced ambitious irrigation, reclamation, and development schemes in a hitherto-neglected area in the western part of the Delta, since called the Liberation (*Tahrir*) Province. The second was the study and planning of a new high dam south of Aswan, which might add some three million feddans to the cultivable area, thus increasing it by about 40 per cent. In its solicitude for industrialization the new regime passed a notable decree on July 30, 1952, amending the company law of 1947 to permit foreigners to own 51 instead of 49 per cent of the stock of corporations. This decree was followed by another, more comprehensive, on April 1, 1953, which in a number of ways encouraged the investment of foreign capital in business enterprises in Egypt.

These steps represented what one might call constructive reform. But, as with any revolution, this one had its repressive side as well. The latter was expressed by a number of measures designed to punish abuses committed by former rulers, to discredit them in the eyes of the public, and to eradicate all traces of their influence in the administration and public life of Egypt. For the purpose of accomplishing these objectives the R.C.C. instituted two special kinds of courts: the graft courts to deal with cases of corruption (December

420

1952) and the Treason Court (*Mahkamat el-Ghadr;* later renamed Tribunal of the Revolution) to deal with major crimes against the state (January 1953).

With regard to the legal framework of its existence the new regime was more effective in destroying the old forms than in creating new ones. On December 10, 1952, the R.C.C. abrogated the 1923 constitution, and on January 12, 1953, it appointed a fifty-man committee to redraft the constitution. Four days later, following the discovery of a plot against the regime, all political parties were dissolved and their funds confiscated. Their place was henceforth to be filled by the Liberation Movement, a body launched during the mass rallies held on January 23 in commemoration of the first six months of the revolution. At the same time the R.C.C. announced a three-year transitional period within which a "healthy democratic and constitutional regime" would be formed. February 10 saw the promulgation of a provisional constitution of eleven articles, which enunciated the principles of government to apply during the period of transition. The gist of this document was expressed in Article 8, which said: "The Leader of the Revolution, presiding over the Revolutionary Command Council, shall assume full sovereign powers, particularly in regard to measures deemed necessary to protect the Revolution, the system on which it is based to achieve its objectives, as well as the right to appoint and dismiss Ministers." Article 9 declared that "the Council of Ministers shall exercise legislative powers," and Article 11 provided for a "Congress," to be composed of the R.C.C. and the Council of Ministers, the role of which would be to "consider the general policy of the State and subjects connected with it."

In the next three years the new government made several announcements of an impending restoration of the constitutional regime, committing itself, in some cases, to a definite date. These promises were not kept, usually because of some internal emergency that made their fulfillment impracticable. Ultimately, on January 16, 1956, exactly three years after the proclamation of the transitional period, a new constitution was announced. It was subject to approval by a plebiscite scheduled to take place on June 23, 1956, on the fourth anniversary of the revolution. The new constitution provided for the election of a National Assembly, the members of which would be nominated by a single party, "the National Union." It also proclaimed Egypt to be an Islamic, Arab state under a republican and democratic form of government headed by a president whose term of office would be six years. Among the more significant provisions was the one which provided for a referendum, at the discretion of the president, on any "major issues bearing on the country's higher interests." [20]

Basically, this document, as is often the case under similar circumstances, introduced little new beyond confirming the existing pattern of power in Egypt. All authority centered in the Revolutionary Command Council, which in its first three years managed to eliminate its political rivals and adversaries. The latter were numerous and rather formidable. In the first place, a "grand old party" such as the Wafd could not be expected to give up without a struggle. Fortunately for the R.C.C., the Wafd was headed by a septuagenarian, Nahas Pasha, whose vigor was declining, and its master brain, Fuad Serag ed-Din, had been subjected to violent criticism and considerably discredited before the coup of 1952, partly as a result of his responsibility for the Cairo riots of January 26. Furthermore, long years of corruption were not conducive to the breeding of heroes among the Wafdist rank and file. Consequently, when the test of strength came, especially in the first six months of the revolutionary era, the Wafd did not dare to resist the military junta openly. Other parties presented a less difficult problem. Owing their origin, for the most part, to personal rivalries or palace intrigue, they lost their ground as organized forces with the passing of the monarchy. The revolutionary government did not differentiate to any appreciable degree between them and the Wafd, considering both as representative of the old regime and applying equally stern measures to those of their leaders whom it deemed guilty of graft or treason.

No less severe was the policy of the R.C.C. toward the Communists and Ahmed Hussein's Socialists. Both movements were banned and, inasmuch as the junta operated with the double weapon of police repression and revolutionary propaganda, it succeeded in dealing a powerful blow to these extremist forces.

Ultimately the Moslem Brotherhood remained as the only major organized group with which the R.C.C. had to contend. The latter was very dangerous as an adversary because it had an effective organization, possessed a persuasive ideology, and had a tradition of resistance to the old regime. In fact, in the initial period of the rev-

[20] Art. 145. The text is in *Middle Eastern Affairs*, Feb. 1956.

olution mutual toleration if not friendship prevailed between the R.C.C. and the Brotherhood. Because it could claim that it was not a political party, the latter escaped dissolution and continued its activities long after the other parties were legislated out of existence. But in the long run the political objectives and ideology of the two movements were incompatible. Preaching the need for an Islamic state based on the Koran as the only source of law, the Brotherhood clearly aspired for power. The "Free Officers" did not intend to abdicate authority and refused to accept the idea of a theocratic state as a guiding principle. As early as November 1952 Mohammed Naguib, while visiting El-Azhar University, said that the army movement was based on "religion, union, and order" but warned that "those who speak of the religious government have but one aim—to divide the nation." [21] The proclamation of the republic at the historical meeting of June 18, 1953, which was attended by two members of the Brotherhood, was the last occasion for co-operation between the junta and the Brotherhood. From that time on the two movements diverged until in January 1954 the R.C.C. finally turned against the Brotherhood on the ground that its character was that of a political party and not a religious association. In the course of the month 450 Brethren were put under arrest, including Hassan Hodeibi, their "Supreme Guide," and six out of fourteen members of their Central Committee. Explaining this radical measure to a press correspondent, Colonel Anwar es-Sadat, a member of the R.C.C. in charge of Islamic affairs, declared:

Immediately after the revolution, Sheikh Hassan el-Hodeibi demanded that the Koranic law be applied in all its severity, i.e., that the thief have his hand cut off, that the cinema be forbidden, that the banks be closed to prevent lending at an interest, and that foreign companies be expelled. This gives you an idea of the mentality and logic of the Supreme Guide of Moslem Brethren. . . . We have tried in vain to convince the Sheikh that the struggle against feudalism, injustice, misery, and British imperialism was inspired by the very essence of the *sharia* and of all the divine laws.[22]

Lieutenant-Colonel Gamal Abdul Nasser, a leading member of the Council, added in another interview:

The Moslem Brotherhood has finished by installing a state within the state. Their chief, Hodeibi, who has not shunned collaboration with

[21] *Cahiers,* 1952, 2.   [22] *Ibid.,* 1954, 1.

Farouk, wanted to take the Koran as the sole rule of behavior. So far as I am concerned, I have not yet understood how one can govern according to the Koran only. One may draw from it all sorts of interpretations, and mine at any rate is not that of those fanatics.[23]

The doom of the Brotherhood was not decreed, however, until the end of 1954. The immediate causes of the final stern action by the R.C.C. were the campaign of criticism that the Brotherhood had launched against the ruling group after the conclusion of a new treaty with Britain (of which more later) and the attempt on the life of Colonel Abdul Nasser, by then premier of Egypt, which had taken place on October 26. This time the Brotherhood was not only outlawed but its leaders were indicted on charges of conspiracy and treason. The sensational trial revealed the existence of the Brotherhood's military arm, whose task was to seize power in the state by terrorism and assassinations. The verdicts of the revolutionary tribunal included a number of death sentences and long prison terms. Moslem Brethren thus became the first victims of the hitherto bloodless revolution.

The R.C.C., however, stressed the fact that, far from being atheistic, it cherished and protected religion as such. Its leading members frequently displayed their piety by attending Friday prayers and performing the *hajj* to Mecca. In November 1954 the R.C.C. obtained a public condemnation of the Brotherhood's terrorism by the ulema of El-Azhar. And, finally, R.C.C.'s fast-traveling Colonel Anwar es-Sadat did major work in promoting an Islamic conference that met in Mecca in 1955 and became thereafter a permanent organization, with Sadat himself as its secretary-general.[24]

The destruction of the Brotherhood put an end to the process of eliminating the junta's organized rivals and left it as sole arbiter of Egypt's destiny. Yet even the strongest government cannot operate in a vacuum, and it is legitimate to ask whether, apart from the army, the R.C.C. has any social support and, if so, among what groups. It is difficult to give a simple answer to this question inas-

[23] *L'Orient* (Beirut), Jan. 31, 1954.

[24] The new regime emphasized religious tolerance and during General Naguib's leadership gave considerable publicity to the good-will visits paid by him to the religious heads of Christian and Jewish communities in Egypt. The regime's basic objective seemed to be the elimination of undue influence by Islam upon Egypt's public life. A major step in this direction was the decree of September 24, 1955, abolishing, as of January 1, 1956, the entire system of Sharia and non-Moslem religious courts.

much as the situation in Egypt, ever since July 1952, has been undergoing a rapid evolution. In the beginning the officers' movement enjoyed great popularity among both the urban and the rural masses in Egypt. The sincerity of its leaders, the charismatic qualities of a fatherly and benevolent Mohammed Naguib (son of a mixed Egyptian-Sudanese marriage), and the deep urge for change in the country as a whole combined to produce enthusiasm sometimes bordering on frenzy among the emotionally starved multitudes of Egypt. In those early days certain moderate statesmen of the pre-revolutionary period (such as the generally respected Ali Maher) went along with younger intellectuals, students, and trade unionists in giving the benefit of the doubt to the R.C.C. As time went on, the enthusiasm of the masses began to abate and the inevitable restrictions on civil freedoms and economic activity gradually estranged the new rulers from the liberal-minded intelligentsia. In the beginning the R.C.C. was content to leave the cabinet posts to civilians while reserving for itself the role of a sort of Politbureau, the task of which was to guide and supervise the cabinet's activity. Later civilians began to be replaced by members of the R.C.C., who thus assumed the dual role of policy makers and head executives. This gradual elimination of civilians at the highest level marked a trend toward complete monopoly of power by the military.

Simultaneously, the R.C.C. underwent a number of internal readjustments, some of a very dramatic character. As was later revealed, General Naguib had not belonged to the original group of officers. He was merely "adopted" to serve as a front for the men of the R.C.C., who were both younger and more radical than he. The real leader of the movement from its very inception, Lieutenant-Colonel Gamal Abdul Nasser, resented the gradual usurpation of power by Naguib. In the ensuing contest Nasser emerged victorious, having shorn Naguib of power in three successive stages. In the first stage (February 25–March 8, 1954) the R.C.C. deprived Naguib of all his functions but, following popular demonstrations and a near mutiny of the cavalry corps in his favor, reinstated him in all three of the highest positions in the state (see p. 421). In the second stage (April 18–May 31) Nasser replaced Naguib as prime minister and president of the R.C.C., leaving him in the rather nominal position of president of the Republic. In the third stage (November 14) the R.C.C. deprived Naguib of the presidency and, accusing him of complicity with certain enemies of the revolution, placed him under virtual house arrest. The presidency remained vacant, with Nasser becoming its most likely incumbent once the new constitution began to operate.

In addition to this major shift, the R.C.C. experienced a few other disaffections within its midst, most notable of which were the attempted usurpation of power by Colonel Rashad Mehanna (representing the artillery and one of the three regents for Ahmed Fuad II) in January 1953 and the above-mentioned near mutiny of the cavalry led by Major Khalil Muhi ed-Din. Both Mehanna and Muhi ed-Din were removed from the Council, the first receiving a prison term, the second being sent on a mission abroad. Similarly, after a stormy career Major Saleh Salem, minister of guidance and Sudan affairs, incurred the displeasure of the R.C.C. toward the end of 1955. He was removed from both his cabinet and his Council position.

The New Regime's Foreign Policy

In foreign policy the new government could boast of a number of achievements. Although it inherited from the previous regime two major unsettled issues—those of Suez and the Sudan—it succeeded in resolving them within two years after its advent to power. It will be recalled that Britain and Egypt had reached agreement on the Canal question in 1947 but they failed to find a formula for the Sudan, as a result of which both problems were left unsolved. After the July revolution the process was reversed: the parties managed to solve the Sudan tangle considerably in advance of their final agreement on the Canal. That this was so was due, in the main, to the willingness of the new Egyptian rulers to compromise. Instead of blindly insisting on the "Nile Valley Unity" formula, they agreed to a second-best solution, which consisted in giving the Sudan the right to decide whether it desired union with Egypt or independence. According to the agreement signed with Britain or February 12, 1953, the Sudan was to pass through a transitional period of three years, during which it would develop institutions of self-government preparatory to its final emancipation. At the close of this period the Anglo-Egyptian occupation would end, and the Sudanese Constituent Assembly would decide the fate of the nation. In agreeing to this formula the Egyptians believed that the Sudanese would ultimately choose union in view of the strong position of those elements in the Sudan that favored amalgamation with

426

Egypt. Their optimism seemed to be vindicated when, in the first elections in Sudan's history, the National Unionist Party (pro-Egyptian) scored a signal victory over its opponents, securing fifty out of ninety-seven seats in the Constituent Assembly.[25] Both before and after the elections Egyptian propaganda pervaded the Sudan, Egypt's position being enhanced by the popularity of General Naguib among the Sudanese. With the passage of time the Unionist-dominated government of Ismail el-Azhari began to veer from the formula of union toward that of independence. Heroic efforts on the part of Major Saleh Salem, Egypt's minister of Sudanese affairs, to instill prounion sentiment in the Sudan began to meet with increasing failure. Salem's aggressive zeal clashed with Azhari's second thoughts on the benefits of the union. By the summer of 1955 relations between Khartum and Cairo had deteriorated to the point of a personal quarrel between Azhari and Salem, and the likelihood of union appeared remote. It seemed to be buried for the forseeable future, when, in a unilateral move, the Sudanese Chamber proclaimed independence on December 19, 1955. Egypt and Britain, also the Soviet Union and the United States, promptly recognized this decision.

The Suez Canal base was the next point at issue in Anglo-Egyptian relations. Following long and frequently interrupted negotiations, the "Heads of Agreement" were signed on July 27, 1954, followed by the conclusion of a final Agreement on October 19. The new pact provided for the abrogation of the Anglo-Egyptian Treaty of 1936, evacuation of British troops within twenty months from the date of signature, continuous maintenance of the Canal base by British civilian technicians under the sovereign control of Egypt, and Britain's right to re-enter Egyptian territory "in the event of an armed attack by an outside power on Egypt or any country which at the date of signature of the present agreement [is] a party to the treaty of joint defense between Arab League states [26] or on Turkey." The Convention of 1888 guaranteeing freedom of navigation in the Canal was reaffirmed along with recognition that the Canal was "an integral part of Egypt." Valid for seven years, this agreement

[25] The elections were held on November 25, 1953. The returns were as follows: National-Unionist Party, 50; El-Umma (a party advocating separation from Egypt), 23; Independents, 11; Party of the South, 9; Republican-Socialist Party, 3; Anti-Imperialist Front, 1; total 97.

[26] Egypt, Syria, Lebanon, Saudi Arabia, Yemen, Jordan, Iraq, Libya. The text of the Arab Defense Pact is in the *Middle East Journal*, Spring, 1952.

was accompanied by two annexes and seventeen exchanges of notes elaborating the details.[27]

By concluding this agreement Colonel Nasser's government achieved a notable diplomatic success. Yet this was not victory pure and simple inasmuch as (1) Egypt allowed the re-entry of British troops within a specified period and (2) she linked her security to that of Turkey and thus, however indirectly, became involved with Western strategy. On the other hand, she made sure that any out-break of hostilities between herself and Israel (which was not an "outside power") would not serve as a pretext for Britain's return to the base.

The Agreement had, moreover, international significance tran-scending the limits of Anglo-Egyptian relations. It removed an im-portant stumbling block in the way of possible Egyptian-Western co-operation and made Egypt more eligible than before for Ameri-can economic and military assistance. The optimism prevailing in Washington and London after the conclusion of the "Heads of Agreement" was strengthened when in policy statements on August 13 and September 2 Colonel Nasser declared that Egypt was bas-ically inclined toward the West and that Russia and communism represented the only conceivable danger to Egypt's security. Both statements, however, made a serious plea that the West postpone the negotiation of any regional security pacts in the Middle East. "It is only by a period of complete independence during which mu-tual trust is built up between Egypt and the Western powers that Egyptians will be able to look without suspicion on any closer ties between this country and other powers," said the statement of Sep-tember 2. "Co-operation based on trust and friendship, even though it is not specified by any written agreement, is better than a treaty that is regarded suspiciously by the average Egyptian." "Left alone, the Arabs will naturally turn toward the West to ask it for arms and assistance," added the statement.[28]

These friendly warnings were not, however, heeded by the West, anxious as it was to promote regional security schemes. By the end of 1954 Egypt's relations with the Western powers had suffered marked deterioration, principally on account of the impending con-clusion of the Baghdad Pact. Though enjoying dictatorial powers, Gamal Abdul Nasser and his associates could not safely disregard

[27] The text is in *Middle Eastern Affairs*, Nov. 1954.
[28] Compiled from the *New York Times*, Sept. 3, 1954, and *Cahiers*, 1954, 2.

public opinion, which was so opposed to any "foreign pacts" as to question the wisdom of the recent Anglo-Egyptian agreement. Consequently, if only for the sake of his position at home, Nasser emerged as the principal champion of a "no pacts" policy on behalf of the Arabs, leading a frontal attack on Iraq for betraying Arab solidarity and linking her fate with that of Turkey and the West. The Egyptian premier gave forceful expression to these views at the Arab League meetings in December 1954 and January 1955, the latter actually convoked at his request to consider the Turko-Iraqi alliance. He and his delegation also stood in the forefront of the neutralist group that dominated the proceedings of the Bandung conference of Asian and African nations in April 1955. His policy of ever-increasing opposition to Western security projects led him eventually to conclude two important military agreements, one with Saudi Arabia (October 27, 1955) and another with Syria (October 20, 1955), each of which placed the signatories' armed forces under a joint command headed by Egyptian generals.[29]

Egyptian-Israeli hostility was the most important factor vitiating the chances of improving Cairo's relations with the West. After a strong and successful Israeli attack on Egyptian positions at Gaza on February 28, 1955, Egypt began paying closer attention to her military preparedness even, as Nasser admitted later, at the expense of domestic reform. The premier endeavored to purchase arms from Britain and the United States in the summer of 1955. Meeting with a virtual refusal, he turned toward the Soviet bloc and in September 1955 concluded a barter deal with Communist Czechoslovakia whereby Egyptian cotton was to be exchanged for an undisclosed quantity of heavy military equipment and munitions.

This sensational transaction, symptomatic as it was of the worsening of Arab-Western relations, led the American government to send to Cairo forthwith George V. Allen, assistant secretary of state in charge of Middle Eastern affairs, on a fact-finding and good-will mission. Whatever arguments Allen was authorized to use did not prevent the Egyptian premier from consummating his deal with the Czechs and receiving, shortly afterward, Soviet jet bombers, tanks and, reportedly, submarines.

This notable Soviet success was promptly followed by a Russian offer to build the High Aswan Dam—a cherished project of the R.C.C.—at a competitive price. This time the Egyptians delayed

[29] The texts are in the *Middle East Journal*, Winter, 1956.

their reply, no doubt aware of the difference between the two transactions and the implications of the presence of numerous Soviet
personnel on Egyptian soil should such an offer be accepted. Egypt's
delay gave an opportunity to both the United States and the World
Bank to accelerate their long-pending study of the Aswan project
and to indicate their willingness to help the Egyptians despite the
cost involved.

In the tough game of power politics the new leaders of Egypt
are playing their hand boldly and skillfully. In essence they are
repaying the West for the latter's as-yet-unrepented assumption of
Arab inferiority and for its disregard of Arab wishes regarding Palestine. While engaged in a gamble fraught with many dangers,
Egypt's revolutionary rulers have alerted the West to the gravity of
the situation in the Arab East and to the need for a new policy to
counteract Soviet diplomatic and psychological successes.

Saudi Arabia

SINCE the eighteenth century the central province of the Arabian peninsula, the Nejd, has been the home of a militant puritanical sect, the Wahhabis. Their ruler was expelled by the rival clan of Rashids from Riyadh, the capital of the Nejd, to Kuwait in the latter part of the nineteenth century. The exile's son, Abdul Aziz ibn Saud, born in 1880, reconquered Riyadh in 1901, thereby establishing his own rule over the Nejd. During the next decade he waged constant warfare with foreign and domestic enemies. By 1913 Ibn Saud had succeeded not only in consolidating his rule in the Nejd but also in conquering El-Hasa, the easternmost province of Arabia.[1]

POWER AND PRESTIGE OF IBN SAUD

As a ruler whose domains extended to the Persian Gulf, Ibn Saud had attracted the attention of the government of India. The outbreak of the First World War intensified this interest, and, as we know, on December 26, 1915, Britain and Ibn Saud signed a treaty that secured the latter's benevolent neutrality. One of the consequences of this treaty was that Ibn Saud refrained from attacking his neighbor and Britain's ally, King Hussein of the Hejaz. Ibn Saud's restraint, however, was only temporary. There were enough points of friction between the Nejd and the Hejaz to produce deep hostility. A quarrel over the border oasis of Khurma led to an armed clash in the summer of 1918. The British, allied to both rulers, were

[1] Ibn Saud's personal history has been narrated by H. C. Armstrong, in *Lord of Arabia, Ibn Saud* (London, 1934), and by K. Williams, *Ibn Saud: The Puritan King of Arabia* (London, 1933).

at that time too hard pressed in the West to do anything about the gathering storm in Arabia.

Once started, the conflict between the Nejd and the Hejaz grew in intensity. In May 1919 the Wahhabis met the Hejazi forces commanded by Emir Abdullah at Turaba and in a fierce battle inflicted upon them a severe defeat which seriously shook the morale of King Hussein's warriors. During the next five years the adversaries lived in a state of uneasy truce while the problem of border settlements remained unsolved.

Meanwhile King Hussein's power and prestige were following a downward curve. It will be recalled that, aided by an annual British subsidy of £2,400,000, Sherif (and since 1916 King) Hussein had raised a desert army which, under Faisal and Lawrence, fought the Turks during the First World War. Hussein's willingness to cooperate stemmed, as we know, from an exchange of letters with Britain's high commissioner in Egypt, Sir Henry McMahon. In this correspondence Britain promised to support Arab independence, presumably under Hussein's rule. As soon as the war was over, however, the British and Hussein began to differ in their interpretation of the pledge. This led to a considerable cooling off of their mutual relationship. The British subsidy to Hussein ceased in 1920, causing him immediate difficulties. Militarily Hussein's position was far from reassuring: the bulk of his army had gone with Faisal to Damascus, where in the summer of 1920 it suffered defeat at the hands of the French. With his army dispersed and no subsidy to reassemble it, Hussein had to rely on voluntary tribal co-operation. And that, as events were to prove, was too little to match the disciplined and fanatical forces of Ibn Saud.

Similarly, Hussein's diplomatic position became very precarious. This was the result of a number of political mistakes, which may be summed up as follows:

1) Hussein did not avail himself of his opportunity during the war to conclude a formal treaty with Britain which would eliminate the ambiguities contained in the McMahon correspondence. Nor did he profit from Lawrence's visit in the Hejaz in 1921 to conclude a definite alliance with Britain, which was then proffered. Lacking such an alliance he had no legal claim for British support in time of crisis.

2) He made the mistake of not ratifying the Treaty of Versailles, offended as he was by the establishment of the mandatory system

in Palestine and Syria. Thus he did not become a member of the League of Nations and could not count on the collective security system when subjected to outside aggression.

3) He absented himself from the Lausanne conference in 1923 where basic questions of the Middle Eastern settlement were decided.

4) He neglected to cultivate the good opinion of the Moslem world by mismanaging the annual pilgrimages to Mecca. He allowed the essential services, including sanitary arrangements, to deteriorate to the chagrin of more liberal Moslem communities and foolishly picked a quarrel with Egypt over the memorial processions.[2]

5) He did nothing to improve relations with the large and powerful Indian Moslem community. The Indian Khilafat Committee was strongly critical of his war on Turkey as a betrayal of Islamic solidarity, and he should have tried to placate the Indian Moslems. His relations with Turkey and France were equally bad.

6) His ambition twice triumphed over sober judgment. On October 29, 1916, he had proclaimed himself "King of the Arab Countries," a title which provoked his numerous rivals in Arabia and which was much too pretentious considering the limited area under his jurisdiction. And on March 7, 1924, he made an even greater blunder by assuming the title of caliph after the expulsion of the last incumbent by the Kemalists.

This last action precipitated the crisis. Protests were heard in Moslem communities the world over. To his neighbor Ibn Saud of the Nejd this was the last straw. On August 24, 1924, the Wahhabis attacked Taif in the Hejaz and launched an offensive against Mecca. On October 3 Hussein abdicated, and eleven days later Mecca surrendered to Ibn Saud. Hussein's oldest son, Ali, who succeeded him, withdrew to Jidda, where he remained for over a year. On December 8, 1925, however, facing a renewed attack of Saudi forces, he also abdicated and later sought refuge in Iraq. On December 23 the Wahhabis took Jidda. Ibn Saud was in effective control of the whole area. On January 8, 1926, he was proclaimed King of the Hejaz and Sultan of the Nejd and Dependencies, thus uniting into a single state the major part of the Arabian peninsula.[3] Ex-King Hussein went into exile to Cyprus. He died in 1931 when on a visit to Amman.

[2] For similar difficulties encountered later by Ibn Saud, see below, p. 434.
[3] On September 18, 1932, Ibn Saud assumed the title of king of Saudi Arabia.

Ibn Saud and the Islamic World

Ibn Saud's first task was to consolidate his power. Inasmuch as the revenue and prosperity of Arabia derived largely from the pilgrim traffic, he gave high priority to the recognition of his rule by the Moslem world. On June 7, 1926, he convoked an Islamic Congress in Mecca. This was the second congress of this kind, the first having been held a few months before in Cairo to consider the perplexing question of the caliphate. In contrast to the Cairo gathering, which had been poorly attended and which had ended inconclusively, the meeting at Mecca proved a success. Ibn Saud made it clear to the sixty assembled delegates [4] that his conquest of the Hejaz was definite and that temporal matters were to be excluded from discussion. At the same time he declared the Holy Land (meaning the Hejaz) to be the trust of Islam as a whole and asked for advice as to the best way to serve the religious needs of the faithful. The Indian Khilafat delegation, one of the most influential in the Congress, wholeheartedly supported his expulsion of the "traitor" Hussein. Nevertheless the conquest of Mecca and Medina by his "heretical" sect of Wahhabis, whose fanaticism was well known, was something of a shock to the Moslem world. It was hard to conceive of this puritanical and iconoclastic group guarding and managing the holiest places of Islam. The question of the worship of saints and of their tombs and shrines proved especially controversial, the Wahhabis opposing such worship as idolatry. This primitive strictness contrasted with Indian and Egyptian liberalism, making mutual trust difficult to achieve. To add to the difficulties a new incident connected with the Egyptian *Mahmal* occurred while the Congress was in session. The *Mahmal* is a holy litter covered by an ornate carpet, a relic of royal pilgrimages of the thirteenth century. Egypt sends it, properly escorted, to Mecca every year. To the Egyptians this is a traditional ceremony which calls for pomp, color, and music. The very idea of it, i.e., the veneration of an inanimate object, together with its colorful character, is highly offensive to the Wahhabis. Although the Egyptian government had agreed in advance to eliminate the musicians from the *Mahmal* procession, the escort when

---

[4] These delegates represented unofficial religious organizations and not the governments, and they included a delegation of Moslems from the Soviet Union. For a thorough treatment of this congress, see A. J. Toynbee, *The Islamic World since the Peace Settlement* (*Survey of International Affairs, 1925*, vol. I; London, 1927), pp. 311 ff.

approaching Mecca made the mistake of playing bugle calls. This infuriated the Nejdis who, believing it a sacrilege, attacked the Egyptians. In the ensuing fight twenty-five Nejdis were killed. Only Ibn Saud's personal intervention restored order. But the Egyptian government ordered the *Mahmal* procession to return home without completing the pilgrimage. As a result of this incident the *Mahmal* ceremonies were suspended for the next ten years and only in 1936 did Egypt agree to their resumption.

While the *Mahmal* incident was indicative of the difficulties in the path of reconciliation between Wahhabism and the more liberal branches of Islam, these controversial issues did not prevent the Congress from achieving a good deal of harmony, especially in the practical matters of pilgrim traffic. The Congress adjourned in July after having adopted statutes that made it a permanent body to be convoked at regular intervals. Actually it never met again in Mecca, and an Islamic Congress which was called in 1931 in Jerusalem was held under different circumstances and with different terms of reference.[5] From Ibn Saud's point of view the Mecca Congress had achieved its purpose by bringing him implicit or explicit recognition from many Moslem states and by producing a friendly *modus vivendi* with the world of Islam.

Settlement with Britain

Equally important was the task of internal consolidation and of the tracing of the boundaries of his enlarged kingdom. The two problems were interrelated because internal consolidation frequently meant the elimination of some powerful tribal chieftain and the conquest of his borderland territory. We have already recounted Ibn Saud's conquest of El-Hasa in 1913. In 1920, after a brief struggle, he annexed Asir, a border principality between the Hejaz and Yemen. In 1921 he took Hail, the capital of the northern Shammar province, putting an end to the rule of his long-time rivals, the Rashids. In 1922 he extended his authority to Jauf, eliminating the Shalan dynasty. And in the same year he concluded border agreements with

---

[5] It was called under the joint sponsorship of Haj Amin el-Husseini, grand mufti of Jerusalem, and Shawkat Ali, the leader of the Indian Khilafat Committee, mainly for the purpose of cementing an alliance between the Arabs and the Indian Moslems and of securing general Moslem support for Arab claims in Palestine. A number of other politico-religious issues were also on the agenda. (For a detailed study of this congress, see H. A. R. Gibb, "The Islamic Congress at Jerusalem in December 1931," in *Survey of International Affairs*, 1934, pp. 99 ff.)

Iraq (at a conference at Uqair) and with Kuwait. Both agreements were negotiated with active British participation and both provided for those diamond-shaped neutral border zones which have since become a peculiarity of the maps of the area.

A major difficulty occurred in connection with the Transjordanian boundary. Transjordan was a new political entity devised, as we know, to give satisfaction to King Hussein's son, Emir Abdullah. As a geographical unit it was highly artificial, with no firm historical precedent to look to for guidance. At the time of the peace settlement Transjordan's borders had been traced in such a way as to embrace Maan and Akaba and to secure a junction with Iraq. Ibn Saud laid claims to both these towns, asserting that they formed an integral part of the Hejaz. Moreover, he insisted on a direct boundary between his kingdom and Syria. Such a change would have meant the transfer of a sizable desert rectangle, the so-called Transjordanian Corridor, from Abdullah's to Ibn Saud's sovereignty. It could be accomplished only at the expense of Transjordan's connection with Iraq. Neither Great Britain nor Emir Abdullah liked these suggestions. Britain, exercising as she did the mandatory authority over both Transjordan and Iraq, did not want to sever her imperial land route between the Mediterranean and the Persian Gulf. Emir Abdullah was anxious to keep the permanent connection with his brother Faisal's kingdom of Iraq.

These differences were eventually composed by two instruments. The first, the so-called Hadda agreement, which was concluded on November 2, 1925, by Sir Gilbert Clayton and Ibn Saud, reaffirmed with slight modifications the postwar *status quo* as to the Transjordanian Corridor. But it left the question of Maan and Akaba untouched.[6] The second was a general British–Saudi Arabian treaty signed at Jidda on May 20, 1927. Negotiated also by Clayton, the treaty reaffirmed Britain's recognition of Ibn Saud's "complete and absolute independence," provided for nonaggression and friendly relations, for Ibn Saud's acknowledgment of the special British position in Bahrein and in the Gulf sheikhdoms, and for co-operation in suppressing the slave trade. In an annexed note Ibn Saud agreed to the temporary possession of Maan and Akaba by Transjordan but reserved his right to claim these districts at the time of the final settlement. No British subsidy was stipulated.

The treaty of Jidda made no radical change in the traditionally

[6] For an exhaustive treatment of the boundary questions, see Toynbee, *Islamic World*, pp. 324–345.

good British-Saudi relations but by eliminating some causes of friction it placed them on a solid footing. Britain did not ask for and did not obtain any bases or political privileges in Ibn Saud's kingdom, but her position remained pre-eminent. British business establishments in Jidda, such as trading, insurance, shipping, and banking, were more numerous than those of other countries. And there was a cordial personal relationship between Ibn Saud and H. St. John B. Philby, a prominent British Arabist, who had gone on his first mission to the Nejd in 1917 and who had remained ever since in close touch with the King. In 1926 Philby settled in Jidda and in 1930, having adopted Islam, accepted appointment to the King's privy council.

The first test of the treaty came in the winter of 1927–1928 when one of the warlike Nejdi tribes, the Duwaish, raided the territory of Iraq and Kuwait. The Duwaish, strict in their adherence to pure Wahhabi faith, blamed Ibn Saud for his acceptance of Western innovations, defying his orders to respect international boundaries. Their insurrection was suppressed by the combined efforts of Ibn Saud and of the British Air Force, which bombed the tribe when it crossed the Iraqi frontier. Other border incidents between the British-held territories and Arabia, which occurred as a result of tribal feuds and migrations, were subsequently settled in a spirit of friendly co-operation.

This co-operation with Britain, which was based on mutual acceptance of the territorial and political *status quo* in the Arab Middle East, no doubt enhanced Ibn Saud's feeling of security. But it did not completely remove his fear of the Hashimites. In fact, apprehension that one day the sons of the expelled King Hussein might decide on a war of revenge always influenced Saudi foreign policy. And as the Hashimite brothers, Abdullah and Faisal, were both subject to British control, Ibn Saud was anxious to maintain friendship with Britain and to benefit from her restraining influence. In his search for stability he was glad, therefore, to conclude treaties of friendship with the Hashimite states, Iraq and Transjordan, in 1930 and 1933, respectively. The same fear of revenge caused him to pursue cautious policies toward other Arab rulers of the peninsula so as to avoid encirclement by enemies.

War with Yemen

In this respect his statesmanship was exposed to an acute test in 1934. In the spring of that year a conflict broke out between him and Imam Yehya of Yemen over the borderland of Asir. The conflict had been caused by a rebellion which had occurred in Asir a year earlier against the Saudi rule. Ibn Saud had successfully quelled it by forcing Asir's ruler, Hassan el-Idrisi, to flee to Yemen. Idrisi did not remain idle and from his safe base in Yemen, with the Imam's connivance, carried out a number of raids into his old principality. Deciding to strike at the root of the intrigue, Ibn Saud declared war on the Imam in March 1934, invaded Yemen, and inflicted severe defeats on Yehya's forces. The Imam sued for peace. In a treaty signed on June 23 Ibn Saud agreed to the restoration of the *status quo ante,* without insisting on territorial changes or reparations. This generous and statesmanlike behavior did not fail to impress the Imam, who ever after did his best to refrain from hostile actions. Ibn Saud's relations with the Hashimites were further improved by the conclusion, on April 2, 1936, of a treaty of nonaggression and Arab brotherhood with Iraq. Yemen, now quite friendly, adhered to it in 1937.

This sober and nonadventurous foreign policy made it possible for Ibn Saud to devote increasing attention to domestic improvements. Here his record was very commendable. At the time of his conquest of the Hejaz, banditry, assaults on pilgrims and trading caravans, and tribal raids were rife in the country. Within less than a decade the King effectively curbed lawlessness so that travel in Saudi Arabia ceased to be a hazardous venture. The King took full advantage of the Islamic institution of polygamy to marry daughters of tribal chieftains thus establishing inner political alliances. He settled considerable numbers of his own unruly Wahhabi *Ikhwan* (Brethren) in agricultural colonies. He also did much to raise economic standards and to introduce modern technical improvements. To cite an example, in 1926 there were twelve motor cars in the whole kingdom, but in 1930 there were 1,500 motor vehicles circulating between Jidda and Mecca alone.

DISCOVERY OF OIL

Of momentous significance to Saudi Arabia was the discovery of oil. On May 29, 1933, the Standard Oil Company of California obtained a sixty-year concession covering a huge area in the eastern part of the country. An operating company known as the California Arabian Standard Oil Company was established. When the Texas Company joined in the enterprise in 1934, its name was changed to the Arabian American Oil Company (Aramco). One of the first steps

438

of the concessionaire was to give a loan of £30,000 in gold sovereigns to the Saudi Arabian government.[7] The loan came in the nick of time, when Saudi Arabia was suffering from a decrease in pilgrim traffic, caused by the world depression. The American company did it entirely at its own risk, which, considering the strangeness and remoteness of Arabia and the lack of official American interest, was considerable. Yet it paid handsome dividends in good will and soon proved economically justifiable as well. Oil wells were drilled in Dhahran, Dammam, Abqaiq, and Abu-Hadriya in the province of Hasa, and both proven and estimated reserves surpassed the boldest expectations. Oil in commercial quantities began to be extracted in the late thirties, and a new concession agreement was signed between Aramco and Saudi Arabia on May 31, 1939. It is noteworthy that in 1937 Ibn Saud had received a very advantageous offer from Japan, but believing it to be motivated by political considerations he rejected it. Germany also had designs on Saudi oil, and in the same year Dr. Fritz Grobba, German minister to Iraq and Saudi Arabia, who was stationed in Baghdad, visited Jidda. Nevertheless, Ibn Saud preferred to continue his association with the Americans: it had the advantage of assuring the economic development of the country without incurring political liabilities.

Late in 1934 another step was taken toward the development of the natural resources of the country by the creation of the Saudi Arabian Mining Syndicate. Incorporated in the Bahamas, the Syndicate represented British and American capital. It undertook to exploit various minerals.

THE SECOND WORLD WAR

At the outbreak of World War II Ibn Saud adopted a policy of neutrality. Although the majority of his advisers were inclined to believe in an Axis victory, he was convinced that the Allies would ultimately prevail. As a result his policy was markedly benevolent toward the West. Ibn Saud was highly critical of Rashid Ali's coup in Iraq and did not fail to say as much to Naji Pasha es-Suweidi whom Rashid had sent on a mission to Riyadh. The King's friendly neutrality was by no means a negligible asset to the Allies, especially to Great Britain. Had he succumbed like some Arab extremists to

[7] According to K. S. Twitchell, *Saudi Arabia* (Princeton, N.J., 1947), p. 151. The amount of the loan is mentioned as £35,000 by M. Childs in "All the King's Oil," *Collier's*, Aug. 18, 1945.

439

pro-Axis temptations, he might have preached a holy war on the West. Such a call coming from the guardian of the holy places might have caused much embarrassment to the British, both in the Middle East and in India. Actually the King not only refrained from hostility but rendered Britain a signal service by sending his son, Emir Mansur, to address Indian troops in Egypt on the eve of the decisive battle of El-Alamein in 1942.

The most significant political development affecting Saudi Arabia in wartime was, however, the growth of close co-operation with the United States. It was revolutionary in its consequences for both countries: for Saudi Arabia, because it led this medieval country into an entirely new path of progress; for the United States, because in no other area of the world had American policy undergone such a radical change as in the arid Arabian peninsula. Until 1940 the American government had practically ignored Saudi Arabia. There was no diplomatic representation in Jidda and there were no consular offices. For seven years American oil companies had carried out vast operations in eastern Arabia without the benefit of official government protection. The war changed all that.

American oil investments provided the starting point. When the war broke out, the operations of the Arabian American Oil Company were seriously curtailed owing to wartime necessities and priorities. At the same time pilgrim traffic to Mecca and Medina suffered a severe reduction. These two factors placed Ibn Saud in a very difficult position. Some way had to be found to make up for the deficit, and this could only mean foreign—Ally or Axis—assistance. In the spring of 1941 the Axis position was very strong: Germany had just completed her conquest of Yugoslavia and Greece and was about to invade Crete; the pro-Axis coup had taken place in Baghdad; Axis forces in Africa were getting ready for an onslaught on Egypt; and Japan was enviously eyeing the oil riches of the Persian Gulf. The United States still clung to its neutrality and Russia was not yet at war with Germany. Britain stood alone facing one of the gravest crises in her history, and the odds seemed overwhelmingly in favor of the Axis. Yet Ibn Saud refused to treat with Berlin or Tokyo. Instead he appealed to the Arabian American Oil Company and to the British and American governments to help him out. He pointed out that by adopting their wartime priorities Britain and the United States had deprived him of expected oil royalties and asked for a $30,000,000 loan to be delivered in five yearly installments. His financial plight was so desperate that he threatened to cancel the concession if he failed to obtain the required funds. The company which had advanced the King £30,000 in 1933, was not in a position to satisfy his new demand. Yet the stake was too high to let the matter go by default. Consequently, the company appealed to the United States government for action. To speed up matters, Aramco's representative, James A. Moffett, saw President Roosevelt in April 1941, trying to obtain his approval for a government loan to the King. The loan would be guaranteed by the company's oil production. The President was at first hesitant, lacking the necessary legislative authority for such a transaction. Eventually, however, it was decided that the United States would request Great Britain to make funds available to Saudi Arabia out of a $425,000,000 loan which had just been granted to her. Thus, in a somewhat roundabout fashion Saudi Arabia obtained the financial aid which made it possible for her to avoid bankruptcy. Great Britain gave the Saudi government £400,000 for one year, and these payments increased progressively until, in 1945, they reached about £2,500,000. These grants were supplemented by American lend lease, which was extended to Saudi Arabia in April 1943.

By accepting financial assistance, Ibn Saud to some extent compromised his neutrality. But this was just the beginning of a longer process which eventually brought his country into the bosom of the United Nations. This process was accelerated in 1943 when the American joint chiefs of staff reached a decision to secure a good air base in the Middle East which would link Cairo with Karachi and thus facilitate the prosecution of the war against Japan. It may be added that in the meantime Americans had constructed an impressive air base in Abadan, on the Iranian coast. This base had been used both as a transit station to Russia and as a stopover to India. Inasmuch, however, as the Abadan airfield would have to be abandoned at the end of the war with Germany, it was deemed wise to secure another base in the Persian Gulf area. The choice fell on Dhahran in Saudi Arabia, where Aramco had its wells and installations. Negotiations to obtain Saudi Arabian permission were conducted in greatest secrecy both as a safeguard against enemy sabotage, as well as a protection for Ibn Saud, whose neutrality would be openly compromised, with the attendant risks of enemy reprisals. Even to this day the Department of State has not released the details of these negotiations or the exact date when the agreement was concluded.

441

It is known, however, that in December 1943 Major General Ralph Royce, commanding United States forces in the Middle East, made a trip from Cairo to Riyadh where he was received by the King. He was followed the next year by a special envoy, Lieutenant Colonel Harold Hoskins, who performed numerous assignments for the United States in the Middle East. To what extent, if any, these visits were connected with the air base negotiations has not been revealed. The agreement itself was concluded by an exchange of correspondence between the Saudi Arabian government and the American legation in Jidda, which, in 1943, had just been established on a permanent basis. It provided for a three-year use of the air base by American military authorities, after which period the base was to be handed over to the Saudi Arabians. The construction of the base began in 1944 (with the use of military personnel and Italian prisoners of war) and was completed in 1946.

The Dhahran air base replaced not only the Abadan base in Iran but also the Payne Field base in Cairo. It proved to be the largest and best-equipped American air base abroad outside enemy-occupied areas. And it could be easily extended over the flat desert area around Dhahran. The acquisition of this base emphasizes the long way the United States has covered from its initially isolationist position. To some Americans it was a shock to realize how far-flung their country's interests had become. In November 1945 Representative Philip I. Philbin of Massachusetts and Senator Owen Brewster of Maine voiced their surprise and criticism over what they called a government investment in a "quasi private" airfield and the use of military labor in this venture.[8]

Simultaneously other important developments in Saudi-American relations were taking place. In 1942 at the request of the King an American agricultural mission headed by K. S. Twitchell arrived in Saudi Arabia to advise on irrigation and related problems with a view to improving and extending the El-Kharj oasis. In 1943, at the time of General Royce's visit, an American military mission came to Riyadh for a few months to undertake the training of the Saudi Arabian army. This mission shared the task with the British mission whom the King had also invited. In the same year two of the King's sons, Emir Faisal and Emir Khalid, paid a visit to the United States.

By 1945 relations between the two countries had reached such a

[8] *New York Times,* Nov. 12, 1945 and March 29, 1946.

level of cordiality that it was deemed appropriate to arrange a meeting between the King and the President. While on his way back from Yalta President Roosevelt received Ibn Saud in February 1945 on board an American warship in the Great Bitter Lake in Egypt. It was the first trip abroad Ibn Saud had ever made. He took this opportunity to impress upon the President his concern over Palestine and—according to unconfirmed reports from Arab sources—received assurances of friendly support.[9] Two weeks later in his report to Congress the President referred to this meeting in the following words: "Of the problems of Arabia I learned more about that whole problem, the Moslem problem, the Jewish problem, by talking with Ibn Saud for five minutes than I could have learned in exchange of two or three dozen letters." [10] Afterward Ibn Saud frequently referred to Roosevelt in terms of highest praise, and the gift of a luxurious airplane no doubt deepened his friendly feelings. On March 1, 1945, Saudi Arabia declared war on Germany, and subsequently her representatives took part in the United Nations Conference at San Francisco.

[9] In a subsequent letter to King Ibn Saud, dated April 5, 1945, President Roosevelt referred to "the memorable conversation which we had not so long ago" and stated as follows:

"Your Majesty will recall that on previous occasions I communicated to you the attitude of the American Government toward Palestine and made clear our desire that no decision be taken with respect to the basic situation in that country without full consultation with both Arabs and Jews. Your Majesty will also doubtless recall that during our recent conversation I assured you that I would take no action in my capacity as Chief of the Executive Branch of this Government, which might prove hostile to the Arab people.

"It gives me pleasure to renew to Your Majesty the assurances which you have previously received regarding the attitude of my Government and my own, as Chief Executive, with regard to the question of Palestine and to inform you that the policy of this Government in this respect is unchanged" (*Department of State Bulletin*, Oct. 21, 1945, p. 623).

On May 17, 1946, under the Truman administration, Acting Secretary of State Dean Acheson sent identical notes to the diplomatic representatives of five Arab states, accredited in Washington, confirming his oral assurance to them on May 10 that before the United States reached any decision concerning the report of the Anglo-American Committee of Inquiry, it would consult with Arabs and Jews (*New York Times*, May 18, 1946).

In a letter addressed to King Ibn Saud by President Truman and released to the press on October 28, 1946, the President reiterated the official American assurance that "there should be no decision with respect to the basic situation in Palestine without consultation with both Arabs and Jews" (text in *New York Times*, Oct. 29, 1946).

[10] Robert E. Sherwood, *Roosevelt and Hopkins: An Intimate History* (New York, 1948), pp. 871–872.

SAUDI-AMERICAN FRIENDSHIP

What followed could be described as a multiple increase of diplomatic, military, technical, and economic contacts between the United States and Saudi Arabia. It was an interesting process with no trace of compulsion on the part of the United States and with full respect for the sovereign rights and the strict Moslem character of the Arab kingdom. To Soviet critics these new methods looked like wholesale American penetration of Arabia, and they did not hesitate to use the term "dollar diplomacy." These cordial relations were marred by one problem only, the problem of Zionism. In the fall of 1946 Ibn Saud strongly objected to President Truman's appeal for the admission of 100,000 Jews to Palestine.[11] In a letter made public in the American press the King reminded the President of the statement made by the United States government on August 16, 1945, to the effect that no proposals concerning Palestine would be made by the United States without taking into account the wishes of the Arab states,[12] and he deplored the President's departure from this course. The United Nations partition resolution of 1947 and the American pro-Israeli policy produced some tension, which was temporarily reflected in the negotiations concerning the extension of the Dhahran air base lease. But these matters never caused a break in relations.

In 1946 the Export-Import Bank granted Saudi Arabia a $10,000,000 loan. A year later Crown Prince Emir Saud visited the United States, receiving from the President the order of the Legion of Merit and a citation for meritorious services to the Allies during the war. In 1948 the United States navy, entering the Persian Gulf for the first time, paid a courtesy visit in Dammam, and the next year the American legation in Jidda was raised to the status of an embassy. In the spring of 1951 by a special agreement the United States made available to Saudi Arabia technical aid under the Point Four program. Finally, the two countries moved closer to each other by signing, in Jidda on June 18, 1951, a defense agreement that extended for the next five years the lease of the Dhahran air base, enabled the Saudi Arabian government to buy military equipment in the United States, and provided for the military training of the Saudi Arabian army

[11] This appeal was made on October 4, 1946.

[12] The text of Ibn Saud's letter to President Truman is in the *New York Times*, Oct. 18, 1946.

444

by American instructors. The new agreement contained a provision for renewal for the same period. It grew out of the fact that Saudi Arabia had qualified for assistance under the Mutual Defense Assistance Program as a nation "whose ability to defend itself or to participate in the defense of the area is important to the security of the United States."

There is little doubt that the growth of Saudi-American friendship hinged to a pronounced degree upon the spectacular development of the Arabian oil resources by Aramco. Commercial production began only in 1945, but by 1950 it reached the imposing figure of over 25,000,000 tons a year. Thus Saudi Arabia emerged as the second largest producer in the Middle East—right after Iran with her 30,000,000-ton output. The generous royalties made it possible, consequently, to raise Saudi Arabia's revenue from a meager $300,000 in 1917 to about $90,000,000 in 1950. At an estimated total population of six million, this meant an income of $15 per head, a rather imposing figure if we compare it with the £30 per head of social service funds in one of the most advanced countries—Great Britain.[13]

This sudden acquisition of wealth had a revolutionizing effect on the internal situation of the country. On July 17, 1947, Fuad Bey Hamza, minister of development, announced that Saudi Arabia intended to spend $270,000,000 on the technological development of the country in the fields of transportation, electrification, agriculture and water supply, schools, and hospitals. Following this announcement the government, with American assistance, launched large-scale plans of land reclamation. An irrigation network, artificial reservoirs and catchments, water pipelines, and artesian wells were constructed. Paved roads were built between Jidda, Mecca, Medina, and other larger centers. A Saudi Arabian air service linking the Red Sea with the Persian Gulf was established under a contract with Trans World Airlines. American engineers erected a huge pier in Jidda making its hitherto dangerous harbor easily accessible to the largest ships. Furthermore, entirely new harbors were built at Dammam and at Ras Tanura. The latter had become a terminal point for local pipelines from Aramco's oil fields and the site of an oil refinery.

The King's cherished project was to construct a railway which would link the capital with the eastern and western coasts. With this in view he sought, in 1947, an additional $100,000,000 loan from the United States, of which he secured $15,000,000 from the Import-

[13] For some interesting remarks on this subject, see *R.C.A.J.*, April 1950, p. 121.

Export Bank. Between 1949 and 1951 American technicians constructed a standard-gauge railroad between Dammam and Riyadh by way of the oasis of El-Kharj. Upon its completion the government announced its intention to reconstruct the old Damascus-Medina railway which was destroyed by Lawrence's irregulars during the First World War.

Anxious to promote unity in his vast country, Ibn Saud has put special stress on telephone and radio communications. To this end he entrusted the American Mackay corporation with the job of erecting a powerful radio station in Jidda. To raise health standards in the country, his government after the war purchased four packaged surplus hospitals from the American army. It also invited representatives of the American University in Beirut to make a study and present recommendations concerning public education facilities.[14]

This partnership with America and the attendant growth in wealth greatly enhanced Ibn Saud's prestige among the Arab states of the Middle East. Moreover, by his championship of the Palestinian Arabs the King added new laurels to his growing popularity. Even the relatively advanced and sophisticated Egyptians began to pay attention to the deeds and words emanating from the desert capital of Riyadh. And Farouk and his ministers were glad to have Ibn Saud's support in their opposition to the Greater Syria scheme. In 1947 Cairo was pleasantly flattered when Ibn Saud came to Egypt on the first state visit he ever paid to a foreign capital. The trip of King Abdullah of Transjordan to Riyadh in 1948 in the midst of the Palestinian crisis further accentuated Ibn Saud's growing stature in Arab affairs. Saudi Arabia ceased to be an isolated island in the Arab world and began to assert her weight in the politics of the region. This was perhaps best illustrated during the Syrian crisis of 1949 when Saudi Arabia not only played an important role in bringing about Husni Zaim's reorientation, but also made full use of her new economic power by granting Syria a substantial loan for development.

With all these changes there was a paradox in Saudi Arabia's position. On the one hand, she was growing in strength and influence and she was undergoing, with American assistance, a real technological revolution. On the other hand, her government and her social system

[14] An interesting first-hand account of Saudi Arabian accomplishments may be found in H. St. John B. Philby, "Golden Jubilee in Sa'udi Arabia," *R.C.A.J.*, April 1950. For more recent plans and developments, consult Richard H. Sanger, "Ibn Saud's Program for Arabia," *Middle East Journal*, April 1947.

were stationary, and both the King and his associates tenaciously clung to the old traditions. Ibn Saud remained an absolute monarch subject only to the limitations of Islamic laws. His government continued along strictly patriarchal lines. The kingdom was divided into two parts: the Nejd and the Hejaz, with his sons Saud and Faisal acting as viceroys of these provinces. Emir Saud was the heir-apparent and the commander-in-chief of the army. Emir Faisal, residing in Mecca, was also foreign minister of the kingdom. Because of the ban on infidels in the holy cities, he had to transact business with foreign diplomatic representatives through Sheikh Yasin, his under-secretary. Foreign legations and embassies were not located in Riyadh, but in Jidda, which rendered all negotiations slow and cumbersome. The government continued to frown upon the entry of aliens into the land, and frequently foreigners with legitimate business in Saudi Arabia found it difficult to obtain visas.

The King seemed to be much more interested in technological improvements than, for example, in the spread of education among his subjects, of whom 95 per cent remained illiterate. In fact, the shortage of properly trained talent among Saudi Arabians was such that a large number of positions in the government have had to be entrusted to citizens of more advanced Arab countries. Such were Yusuf Yasin, vice-minister of foreign affairs, a native of Lattakia; Fuad Hamza, ambassador in Paris, a Druze from Lebanon; and Hafez Wahba, minister in London, an Egyptian of Nejdi ancestry.

Despite all this, the technological progress of the country had affected social relationships. There had been a growth in urban population. The country was rapidly acquiring a class of industrial workers, skilled and unskilled, and of artisans conversant with modern mechanics. The electrification of certain towns had modified the pattern of daily life. A small "white collar" class of industrial and government employees was gradually forming. Contacts with the outside world through association with American technicians were being broadened. And the increasing prosperity of the country was not without effect on the standard of living and habits of the population.

Thus, in the mid-twentieth century change had come even to the heart of *Arabia Deserta*. It had come mainly as the result of the discovery of oil and ensuing American activity. By the old standards one might say that Saudi Arabia had become an American sphere of influence. This might be so, but there was nothing exclusive in the Saudi-American relationship to make it comparable to British treaty

447

arrangements with Egypt, Iraq, or Jordan. Obviously it was unrealistic to underestimate the power of the American dollar and its ability to compete with other influences. But despite her dependence on the United States Saudi Arabia retained full freedom to treat with other countries and to follow policies not always compatible with American objectives in this part of the world.

INTERNAL DEVELOPMENTS IN THE 1950'S

The internal changes which began in the Saudi kingdom with the discovery of oil in its subsoil became even more pronounced in the 1950's. On December 30, 1950, the Saudi government and Aramco concluded an agreement establishing a 50-50 profit formula, thus increasing substantially the government's revenue from oil operations. The amounts paid by the company to the King's treasury rose steadily from around $150,000,000 a year—a sum obtained after the new agreement—to well over $250,000,000 by 1956. This sudden influx of money brought a number of new problems to this underdeveloped and conservative country. Owing to the patriarchal character of its system, no division traditionally existed between the King's purse and the public treasury. But with the growing need for an orderly financial administration the Saudi government began in 1951–1952 to publish annual budgets. The next logical step was to establish a central bank of issue. The latter took the form of the Saudi Arabian Monetary Agency, which, nevertheless, was barred from engaging in normal banking activities by Koranic injunctions. Among other steps toward modernization could be listed the creation of a Council of Ministers in October 1953 and of a number of new Ministries, such as Education, Agriculture, and Commerce, which testified to growing governmental responsibilities in various sectors of the national life.

The basic problem, however, revolves not around changes in administrative structure but around proper utilization of revenues from oil for the public benefit. Improvements have occurred in the field of transportation (the Dammam-Riyadh Railroad was completed in 1952), in harbor development, and in an increase in hospital and school facilities. But critics maintain that an undue proportion of funds has been diverted to unproductive channels and that the high standards of probity respected in old Arabia are rapidly vanishing under the nefarious influence of easily acquired wealth. While these criticisms cannot be easily dismissed, a few points may be advanced to keep the problem of Saudi finances in proper perspective. In the first place, the kingdom faces a situation without precedent in its history. The change from a pastoral economy whose chronic deficits had to be supplemented by pilgrim fees and spending to an economy based on a steady influx of nearly astronomical revenue from one giant industry has been so abrupt that no human being used to the old way of life can fairly be blamed for experiencing a measure of confusion and indecision. In the second place, no government operates in a political vacuum. The Saudi political system has this peculiarity that in order to keep powerful tribes out of mischief the King has to pay them steady subsidies. This item has always accounted for a considerable portion of Saudi expenditures. Even with the gradual diminution of the tribes' importance and a shift of the locus of power toward the urban centers, money still had to be spent to keep the countryside quiet, either by direct donations or by the upkeep of irregular forces which supplement—and counterbalance—the strength of the regular army. Moreover, the death on November 9, 1953, of King Ibn Saud and the ascension of his oldest surviving son, Saud ibn Abdul Aziz, introduced new factors into the power relationships in the country, and these are likely to affect the financial structure as well.

Fortunately for the stability and security of the kingdom, the succession was without incident. Upon the old King's death, Saud was promptly proclaimed king by those members of his family and notables who were around him at the time. His numerous brothers and relatives, tribal chieftains, the leading ulema, the big merchants, and the governors subsequently paid him homage assuring him of their unswerving loyalty. At the same time his younger brother, Emir Faisal, was proclaimed crown prince. This appointment is indicative of the basically unsettled question of the succession. According to accepted Western patterns in hereditary monarchies the new King's eldest son should have been appointed crown prince. That this did not occur in Saudi Arabia was due primarily to the dispositions of Ibn Saud in this respect. But it also reflected the lack of a firm institutional framework and, by the same token, the power of a strong individual in matters of succession.

In contrast to his father, the new King from the very beginning was bound by arrangements not his own. Nor could he disregard his brothers and uncles or the early comrades-in-arms of his father,

449

especially the leading Wahhabi ulema. He also inherited from Ibn Saud a body of royal advisors, mostly of foreign, though Arab, origin who, by virtue of their superior education and greater international experience, had assumed a position of influence in the kingdom. These are the traditionalist forces, and the new King, brought up as he was in a traditionalist environment, finds it wise and proper to heed their advice.

At the same time he cannot ignore the rise of new forces and trends, the inevitable outcome of changing economic conditions. These new forces can be listed as industrial labor (Aramco had its first major strike a month before the new King's ascension, the workers demanding the right to form trade unions); the white-collar class, substantially reinforced by Palestinian refugees; the growing merchant and entrepreneurial class, sometimes of obscure social origins, which owes its position to the opportunities presented by the expanding oil industry and the influx of wealth; the Western-trained college graduates who are beginning to staff Saudi government departments; and the regular army, whose young officers are not only receiving professional military training but are also exposed to new ideas about the government and society as a result of their foreign contacts.

Most of these groups, both the old and the new, have to be catered to in some degree either by direct outlays of cash or by political behavior to obtain their approval. Inasmuch as the center of power is still located in the conservative camp, the King definitely leans toward the latter. On numerous occasions he has proclaimed his attachment to religion and to the Sharia as the only basis of legal order in the kingdom; he has fully upheld the complete ban on liquor introduced shortly before the death of his father; he has maintained the existing injunctions against movie theaters, music halls, and similar kinds of entertainment; he has shown special interest in pilgrimage matters and in the upkeep of the holy places; and he has promulgated rigorous laws forbidding Saudi youth to be educated abroad in other than academic institutions and prohibiting investment of Saudi capital in foreign countries.

The newer groups are inarticulately reformist and also nationalist. In this they conform to the general pattern in the rest of the Middle East. However, as yet they lack an organization or even a strong link with any specific social stratum. Western-educated Saudis often belong to the leading families of the kingdom and consequently they do not lack opportunities for advancement in this conservative society. Hence, though fully aware of the shortcomings of the older generation, they are too well off to become iconoclastic. However, humbler elements are also getting an education, and not to be dismissed is the influence of Egyptian school teachers and military instructors and of Palestinian and Levantine clerks and officials upon the shaping of the social consciousness of the country. In the eastern part of the kingdom the proximity of Bahrein with its more sophisticated elements has added another potentially disturbing factor.

In the spring of 1955 there were rumblings in the Middle East about some disaffection in Saudi Arabia, and Levantine newspapers published accounts of repressive measures taken against the troublemakers. Saudi missions abroad staunchly denied these stories, claiming that they had originated in the minds of enemies. As a close check on the veracity of such reports is extremely difficult, one can only speculate about the significance of some personnel shifts (and disappearances), the expulsion of certain Levantine elements,[15] and concentrations of irregular forces in a number of strategic points of the kingdom. It may not be inaccurate to say that if there is any question of reformism, the latter represents a mental attitude rather than an organized movement. Under the conditions prevailing in Saudi Arabia, the challenge to stability would come not from the newer strata but from rivalries, should such occur, in the royal family itself. The events that shook Yemen in the spring of 1955 (see p. 463 below) might serve as a pattern in this respect. Up to the present, there have been no outward signs of disharmony within the royal clan, King Saud's authority being publicly acknowledged by his brothers.

With regard to nationalism, to which reference has already been made, it has not only gone hand in hand with the awakening of the new social groups in the kingdom but it has infected conservative circles as well. Whether the latter are genuinely nationalistic or whether they regard nationalism as another device to strengthen their position of power is an open question. At any rate Saudi Arabia, formerly free of other than tribal and religious loyalties, is

[15] In the spring of 1955 a large number of Palestinians, with a few Lebanese and Syrians, mostly employed by Aramco, were expelled from Saudi Arabia. It was understood that this measure was directed in part against the Syrian National-Social Party (P.P.S.), which allegedly had found recruits among those expelled.

451

beginning to acquire the nationalist pattern characteristic of more advanced, formerly colonial peoples.

SAUDI FOREIGN RELATIONS IN THE 1950'S

Ever since the accession of King Saud, Saudi foreign policy has emphasized national sovereignty and the kingdom's role as a leading Arab and Islamic power. No doubt this conforms to the spirit of the times, but it also reflects the new King's position, which is different from that of his father. While the late Ibn Saud did his best to maintain friendly relations with the United States and accepted as a *fait accompli* Britain's pre-eminent status on the southern and eastern fringes of the Arabian Peninsula, his successor has developed a new approach to these problems. Drawing ever closer to Egypt, despite a radical difference in their internal systems, King Saud soon emerged as a proponent of neutralism, a champion of Arab Palestine and North Africa, an advocate of Yemen's claims to the disputed areas in the Aden borderland, and an archenemy of the Baghdad Pact. To most of these matters, of course, his father was not indifferent, but he never allowed any of them to overshadow the vital interests of his country, as he conceived them in his untutored yet realistic way. Consequently he played down such minor difficulties as might have arisen between him and the British concerning the unsettled boundaries, and he referred to the Americans of Aramco as his "partners."

Shortly before his death a dispute arose between his government and Britain concerning the Buraimi oasis situated at the junction of Saudi Arabia, Muscat-Oman, and the Trucial Coast. Reportedly rich in oil, this cluster of desert villages was claimed both by the British-protected coastal rulers and by Saudi Arabia. Following Saud's advent to the throne, the matter re-emerged as the cause of mutual recriminations between London and Riyadh. Here is a typical example of a dispute in which the alleged existence of oil in the oasis seems to have played a secondary role to national prestige, at least from the Saudi standpoint. In July 1954 Britain and Saudi Arabia agreed to submit the quarrel to international arbitration. Eventually, after thorough preparation of the case by the lawyers and experts of both parties, it was solved in a dramatic and unexpected way. Accusing Saudi Arabia of a campaign of bribery in the oasis to bring about a solution favorable to herself, the British member of the arbitration tribunal resigned in October 1955 shortly before the expected rendering of the verdict. Unable to reassemble the tribunal in its full strength, its president, a Belgian jurist, followed suit, thus bringing the proceedings to an end. To the accusations leveled at them the Saudis retorted that Britain had scuttled the arbitration proceedings in anticipation of an adverse decision. Shortly afterward British-officered troops of the Sultan of Muscat and the Sheikh of Abu Dhabi occupied the oasis, forcibly removing a Saudi police detachment. Saudi Arabia protested and threatened to bring a complaint to the United Nations.

The Buraimi dispute is symptomatic of the generally deteriorating relations with Britain. These relations embrace other questions too, foremost of which are Britain's support for the Hashimites in Iraq and Jordan and her sponsorship of the Baghdad alliance. King Saud's stand against the latter is claimed to stem from his concern for the welfare of the Arab League and the cause of Arab unity. This provides, however, only a partial clue to behavior the motives of which are much more complex. It is highly probable that a desire to obtain prestige and to cater to popular preferences in the Arab world and also, possibly, fear of Hashimite retribution for the defeat of thirty years earlier figured prominently among the reasons that prompted him to oppose the pact so vehemently. Amply provided with funds, King Saud freely used his new economic power to back up his foreign policy. The loan of $10,000,000 to Syria in the fall of 1955 seemed to prove this point.[16] It was publicly asserted abroad that Saudi influence was largely instrumental in bringing about the riots that shook Jordan and its monarchy in the winter of 1955–1956.[17] The upheaval followed reports that the Jordanian government planned to adhere to the Baghdad Pact.

To sum up, British-Saudi relations by the end of 1955 had reached their lowest level in a half-century, and the freely circulated rumors that a British-protected Persian Gulf federation was to be established under a Hashimite prince did nothing to restore mutual trust and friendship.

As for Saudi-American relations, they also suffered some decline, but not as much as did Saudi relations with Britain. Thanks to the tact and foresight of Aramco's management, the company was spared the tribulations which other less fortunate corporations ex-

[16] By virtue of a treaty of economic co-operation, concluded on November 9, 1955. See p. 311 above.
[17] See p. 385 above.

perienced in some neighboring countries. The one major issue that beclouded Saudi-Aramco relations was a controversy about the tankers. In February 1954 the Saudi Arabian government concluded an agreement with Aristotle Onassis, a Greek shipping magnate, concerning transport of oil in his tankers. This was contested by Aramco as violating its concession. Because the parties were unable to resolve the dispute by negotiation, they presented it to arbitration, which is still pending. However much the King may have been encouraged by his nationalist counselors to follow an anti-American line, it seems unlikely that he will follow an extremist policy reminiscent of Mossadegh. The basic American asset in the Arabian Peninsula is probably secure.

Another tangible point of interest is the Dhahran air base, leased to the United States for five years on June 18, 1951. In view of the fact that the leasehold agreement contained promises of arms supplies, which, according to the Saudis, have not been kept by the United States, the question has arisen as to Saudi willingness to prolong the agreement. It should be pointed out, however, that the United States is not the only beneficiary in this deal, inasmuch as Saudi Arabia, in addition to being paid for the use of the base, receives training for the officers of her air force under American instructors. Moreover, no matter how critical of anti-Soviet alliances the Saudis may be, they cannot ignore the fact that the presence of this base on their territory constitutes one of the strongest deterrents to a possible Soviet thrust toward the oil-rich Persian Gulf area. Thus it is by no means certain that Saudi Arabia would willfully reject such a safeguard to her independence. It was, perhaps, considerations of this sort which caused the Saudi government to go slow when Russia offered arms in the late summer of 1955. It is true that, after a period of silence and secrecy, it was the Saudis themselves who publicized the offer, but this appeared more like a bargaining device in their relations with the West than a serious intention to accept the proposal.

In the case of less vital interests, however, the Riyadh government has been much more intractable. In August 1954 it rather abruptly dismissed the American Point Four mission after three years of operation. Time and again it has gone on record as highly critical of America's preferential treatment of Israel, an issue which never ceases to supply fuel to Arab grievances against the West.

454

CHAPTER XIII

Yemen

IN CONTRAST to Saudi Arabia, the ancient land of Yemen does not have much political history to record. Known in antiquity as *Arabia Felix*, this mountainous country is fortunate in having more rainfall and more fertile soil than the rest of Arabia and, as a consequence, is able to support a relatively dense population of about three and one-half million. Dominated by the Zaidi sect of the Shia branch of Islam, Yemen has also a considerable proportion of Sunnis, as well as—until recently—about 90,000 Jews.[1] Until 1918 Yemen formed a part of the Ottoman Empire, the ruler of its highland Zaidi region, Imam Yehya, enjoying local autonomy under Turkish sovereignty. Yehya remained faithful to Turkey during the First World War, but his anti-Ally stand had no practical influence on the conduct of the war in the Middle East. The Turkish garrison in Yemen was for the most part isolated from the rest of the Ottoman forces, and Yehya's pro-Turkish policy was to a great extent neutralized by the pro-Ally attitude of his northern neighbors, the Idrisi princes of Asir.

After World War I

After the war Imam Yehya emerged as an independent ruler, largely by default, inasmuch as there was no power ready and willing to assume imperial responsibilities in the area. No official proclamation

[1] On September 10, 1950, Edward M. M. Warburg, chairman of the Joint Distribution Committee, announced that it was expected that by September 19 virtually all of Yemen's 50,000 Jews would have emigrated to Israel. This migration was popularly known as "Operation Flying Carpet" and resulted from the growing tension that had developed between the Arab and Jewish communities of Yemen after the Palestinian war.

455

of independence was ever issued in Sana, but Yehya quite obviously did not consider himself bound either by the Mudros armistice provisions or by the earlier British-Ottoman agreements regarding the boundaries in Arabia.

Following the armistice British troops landed on a few points of the Yemen coast and helped evacuate the wartime Turkish garrison. Having accomplished this task, they handed over the port of Loheia to their Idrisi allies while retaining temporarily the port of Hodeida. These actions greatly irked Imam Yehya, who claimed historical title to the whole of Yemen (and not to only the Zaidi-inhabited highlands). Consequently, at the end of 1919 he invaded Dala and a few other frontier districts of the British Aden Protectorate hoping thereby to compel the British to evacuate Hodeida. This they did in January 1921, but instead of giving it to Yemen they turned it over to Asir. Yehya thus found himself cut off from two valuable Red Sea ports. For over five years the Idrisis were in possession of the coastal plain, known as the Tihama, but the rise of Ibn Saud seriously undermined their position. Profiting from their weakness, Yehya, in March 1925, launched an attack and, following a brief campaign, captured Hodeida and Loheia. By this act he extended his dominions to the coastal lowland, gaining secure access to the Red Sea and acquiring control of the trade routes between the above-mentioned ports and Sana, the capital. The international repercussions of this development were twofold: on the one hand, the hitherto independent Asir principality was partitioned between Yemen and the Hejaz, Asir's Idrisi rulers accepting Ibn Saud's suzerainty in October 1926; on the other, British-controlled Aden suffered economically because of the diversion of trade with the Yemen interior from Aden to Hodeida. This, in turn, suited Italian interests in the region. Italy, already in control of Eritrea on the opposite side of the Red Sea, viewed Yemen as an area for commercial and political expansion. By securing a foothold in Yemen she might find herself sitting astride the southern reaches of the Red Sea, thus threatening the British life line.

Such a development, were it to occur, was definitely not in the British interest. Moreover, Britain had come to regard the whole of the Arabian peninsula as her exclusive sphere to which something like a British Monroe doctrine should apply. Britain's attitude was not so much dictated by imperial rapaciousness (she derived no direct profit from her dealings with Arab chieftains whom she usually had to subsidize) as by the desire to keep other powers away from the approaches to India. Yet while it was relatively easy for Britain to establish her supremacy over the small sheikhdoms and sultanates of the eastern and southern coast of Arabia, it was more difficult to extend it to the inaccessible highland fastness of Yemen. Being unprepared to establish her control by outright conquest (as she had done in Aden in the nineteenth century) Britain had to rely on diplomacy.

British-Italian Rivalry

In the diplomatic duel with Italy Britain suffered defeats. Between January and February 1925 Sir Gilbert Clayton spent nearly a month in Sana trying to reach some agreement with the Imam, especially in view of the latter's continued occupation of the border areas in the Aden Protectorate. But his mission ended in failure. By contrast, on September 2, 1926, Italy succeeded in concluding with Yemen a ten-year treaty of friendship and commerce by which she recognized Yemen's "full and absolute independence," a step which Britain so far had failed to take. In June 1927 a Yemeni mission headed by Yehya's second son paid a state visit to Italy. The Yemenites were received by Victor Emmanuel and Mussolini and were shown Italian industrial establishments. As a result both parties signed an additional agreement providing for the purchase of arms by the Yemen government.

In the meantime, British-Yemeni relations had taken a turn for the worse. Imam Yehya had not only not evacuated the Aden districts occupied in 1919 but had renewed his aggressive tactics by repeatedly raiding the Protectorate in 1927 and 1928. In the latter year he concluded a treaty with the Soviet Union, permitting the establishment of a Soviet commercial mission in Sana. Coming as it did in the year of the Sixth Congress of the Comintern and of pronounced Anglo-Soviet tension, this treaty was indicative of the Imam's growing defiance. The British retaliated by using the Royal Air Force, which drove the Yemenites back to the original boundaries and forced them to sue for a truce. Imam Yehya was still unwilling to repudiate his claim to the Aden territory, but by 1931 he decided not to press it any further and agreed to enter into negotiations with the British. His change of heart was due in part to the rise of the Wahhabi power to the north of his boundaries and in part to fear lest the British exploit his differences with the Sunni tribes of the Tihama plain and induce them to rise in open rebellion. The protracted negotiations led

457

to the conclusion, on February 11, 1934, of the British-Yemeni Treaty of Sana which provided for friendship, mutual co-operation, and the recognition of the *status quo* on the Aden boundary for the next forty years. The British failed to get from the Imam a definite renunciation of his territorial claims, the explanation being that the Imam was prevented by religious restrictions from changing the God-ordained boundaries of his country. Yemen's complete independence was given express recognition.

The next month Yemen fought a war with Saudi Arabia. Defeated, Imam Yehya adopted a much more cautious policy toward his formidable northern neighbor.

Yehya's gradual reconciliation with Britain did not deflect him, however, from his basic policy of opposing British penetration and of favoring contacts with other powers. His was the only Arab country in which no British representative was permitted to reside. Relations with Sana were handled for Britain by the British governor of Aden, and the only Britishers living in Yemen were a medical missionary with his wife and two assistants.

Anxious to preserve complete freedom of action the Imam in 1933 concluded treaties with Holland and France, but it was Italy that remained his principal partner. In 1936 the Italo-Yemeni treaty of a decade before was renewed for one year. Next year an Italian mission visited Sana and on October 15, with impressive ceremonies, signed a new twenty-five-year treaty with the Imam. A number of Italian doctors and engineers were invited to establish themselves in the country, and a quantity of arms was supplied by Italy.

The treaty of 1937 constituted the apogee of the Italian influence in Yemen. We must not forget, however, that in their essence Italo-Yemeni relations were no more than a function of Italo-British relations. Therefore any improvement in the latter was bound to be reflected in a lessening of the Italian penetration of Yemen. By an agreement signed on April 16, 1938, Britain and Italy temporarily composed their differences, regulating their respective positions in the Middle East. In the annexes to the agreement both parties undertook not to acquire "a privileged position of a political character" in Saudi Arabia or Yemen but to prevent other powers from doing so, not to intervene in the internal matters of this region, and to refrain from mutually hostile propaganda.[2] The last provision stemmed mainly from British objections to the Italian broadcasts beamed to the Arab world from Bari.

[2] Text in Cmd. 5726 of 1938.

The Second World War and Its Effects

As for the Imam, he continued to show his preference for the Axis. In 1938 he sent one of his sons to Tokyo to attend the inauguration of a new mosque. During the Second World War he remained neutral. The full story of the pressures that the belligerents brought to bear upon him has not yet been revealed, but it is known that a few British emissaries including the well-known Arabist Miss Freya Stark visited Sana in that period.[3] The British victory at El-Alamein undoubtedly had a cooling effect on Yehya's pro-Axis proclivities, and soon afterward, on February 26, 1943, the Imam ordered the arrest of forty Italians and two Germans, thus silencing two pro-Axis radio stations operating in his territory. This action was accompanied by the severence of diplomatic relations with the Axis powers. In March 1945 Yemen joined the Arab League but, in contrast to other Arab states, she did not declare war on Germany and Japan and did not qualify for participation in the San Francisco conference. Yemen was admitted to the United Nations in 1947 as a result of a later application.

After the war Yemen gradually abandoned her traditional isolation and, like some other countries in the Middle East, sought to replace former Axis links by economic and political bonds with the United States. First contacts with Americans had been made as early as 1930 when Charles Crane and K. S. Twitchell visited Sana to help Yemen in the exploitation of natural resources. In April 1946 the first American diplomatic mission headed by Colonel William Eddy concluded a treaty of commerce and friendship with the Imam, followed by the establishment on May 11 of regular diplomatic relations. A year later, on May 24, both countries signed an agreement granting Yemen credit up to $1,000,000 for the purchase of American surplus property, and in the following July one of Yehya's sons, Prince Seif el-Islam Abdullah made a trip to the United States, where he saw President Truman and held conversations with various American industrialists.

Internal Crisis of 1948

Early in 1948 Yemen was the scene of dramatic events which focused upon her, temporarily, the attention of the outside world. On February 17 of that year Sayid Abdullah ibn Ahmed el-Wazir, former

---

[3] See Harold Ingrams, "A Journey in the Yemen," *R.C.A.J.*, Jan. 1946; also Freya M. Stark, *The Arab Island, The Middle East, 1939–1943* (New York, 1945), ch. on Yemen.

governor of Hodeida and minister of state, executed a *coup d'état,* in the course of which Imam Yehya, his prime minister, Qadi Abdullah el-Omari, Yehya's two sons, Hussein and Moshin, and a few other persons close to the Imam were assassinated.[4] Sayid Abdullah proclaimed himself Imam and appointed Yehya's sixth son, Emir Seif el-Haqq Ibrahim, his prime minister. Ibrahim was a leader of the Free Yemeni Party, a group representing the commercial and landowning "bourgeoisie" of Yemen, who had grown increasingly restive under Yehya's old-fashioned and despotic rule. In 1946 Ibrahim had escaped to Aden, whence he came when the rebellion broke out. As to Sayid Abdullah, he belonged to a prominent family whose members had ruled Yemen in the past.

A few days after the coup a civil war broke out. The crown prince, Emir Seif el-Islam Ahmed, governor of Taiz, defied the new rulers, proclaimed himself Imam, and, gathering a force of loyal followers, launched an attack on Sana. In the meantime the Arab League, which met to consider the problem of recognition, decided to send a special commission to Yemen to study the situation. This commission never reached its destination, having spent considerable time in Riyadh before proceeding southward. On March 13 Crown Prince Ahmed succeeded in conquering Sana. Sayid Abdullah and his principal associates were captured and after a summary trial executed. A new government was formed. It included Mohammed Raghib Bey, Yehya's foreign minister, who resumed his old position. The Arab League was thus faced with a new situation. Opinions varied, but in the end Ibn Saud's view prevailed. The Wahhabi ruler condemned the regicide and at one moment appeared ready to intervene in Emir Ahmed's favor. Deferring to his views, the Arab League decided to uphold the principle of legitimacy and at a meeting in Beirut on March 21 granted its recognition to Seif el-Ahmed as the Imam of Yemen. Recognitions from other countries soon followed.

Yemen's International Position in the 1950's

On March 10, 1951, Yemen and Britain signed a new treaty designed to improve their mutual relations. Its principal innovation was a clause providing for the exchange of diplomatic representatives, Yemen having been reluctant to permit British diplomats to reside in the country. The treaty also provided for co-operation in

---

[4] For a detailed account of this crisis, see Eric Macro, "Yemen: A Brief Survey," *R.C.A.J.,* Jan. 1949.

the development of Yemen, should the latter so request; the creation of a mixed committee to deal with frontier problems; a mutual pledge not to change the *status quo* in the border regions until the committee finishes its work; and a promise to curb hostile propaganda against each other.

Despite this treaty Yemeni-British relations suffered a marked deterioration almost immediately afterward. The main cause was the unsettled territorial question and, in particular, the widely divergent attitudes of the parties toward the area situated between Yemen proper and Aden Colony, i.e., the Aden Protectorate. Composed of a number of petty principalities, this large stretch of land equivalent in size to Britain, Scotland, Wales, and Northern Ireland had at one time or another belonged to the dominion of the Zaidi imams of Sana, who were never reconciled to its subjection to British rule. Moreover, even as late as 1934—the time of the first Anglo-Yemeni treaty—British interests in this whole area were represented by no more than two officials: a political secretary and a political officer, whose main function, perforce, was to maintain liaison with Protectorate chiefs rather than to conduct a regular administration. As a result, the chiefs were largely left to their own devices, and the looseness of British control tended to emphasize their almost independent status. So long as this was the case, Yemen tolerated if she did not fully accept the *status quo*.

But Britain's restrained policy underwent considerable change, especially after World War II. In contrast to other areas in her Empire where she gradually reduced her responsibilities, in the Aden Protectorate Britain began to assert her dominance. This came about principally in two ways. In the first place, she embarked upon a policy aiming at improvement of the social and economic conditions in the protected principalities. This led to an increase in her administrative personnel of 3,000 per cent as compared to the number in 1934, naturally creating uneasiness in Yemen, which was always isolationist and suspicious of foreigners in close proximity. In the second place, in the early 1950's the British launched a project to unite the sultans, emirs, and sheikhs of the Protectorate in a federation. More precisely, the scheme was expected to comprise eighteen principalities of the West Aden Protectorate. Its principal objective, politically, would be to consolidate the British position in the area. Yemen rather naturally took a strong dislike to this plan inasmuch as she was loath to witness a gradual amalgamation of the separate petty states into a strong political unit under an aegis other than her own.

Added to this were two other considerations, both related to the internal situation in Yemen. The first and perhaps more important of the two was linked to the composition of Yemen's population. This was comprised of two principal groups: the Shafii and the Zaidi, representing two-thirds and one-third of the total, respectively. The Zaidis, inhabiting the mountainous interior, held a dominant position, the kings, nobles, and principal officeholders always being of Zaidi faith. The lowlands were peopled mostly by Shafiis as were the petty states of the Aden Protectorate. Consequently, the establishment of a predominantly Shafii federation implied the possibility that this new political center might compete with the imams of Sana for the loyalty of their Shafii subjects and thus endanger Zaidi supremacy in Yemen. The second consideration was that the markedly conservative government of Yemen could not remain oblivious to actual or contemplated changes in the economic and social life of the Aden Protectorate, inasmuch as any obvious contrast between the two areas was apt to prove disruptive to Yemen's internal stability.

For these reasons the Yemen government fought the Aden federation plan, resorting to a variety of methods to achieve its objective. For instance, it reverted to rather truculent behavior with regard to border areas. As a result, border incidents increased in number, sometimes assuming the proportions of a major Yemeni incursion into the Aden Protectorate. A Yemeni siege of Fort Mukheiras in December 1954 exemplified this tendency. The Aden authorities, on their part, reacted to these infiltrations by reinforcing the British-officered levies and policing the troubled areas with the Royal Air Force. Yemen's tactics did not stop there. The Imam's government resorted to propaganda and other inducements to win over a number of disaffected chiefs in the Aden Protectorate. In this respect Yemen profited from the general attitude of mistrust shown by the petty rulers in the Protectorate toward the British-sponsored federation plan. These rulers saw few, if any, advantages for themselves in a unification plan under British tutelage and consequently often leaned toward Yemen in this controversy.

Not content with this political action, Yemen raised certain legal points. She claimed that Britain was guilty of violating her agreements, especially the treaty of 1934, which provided for the *status quo* in the existing frontiers. By "frontiers" the Yemenis meant not only the rather vague demarcation line between their territory and the Aden Protectorate but also the borders between the principalities *within* the Protectorate itself. They based this claim on the plural employed in the text of the treaty when referring to the frontiers (*hudud*) and opposed the federation as likely to affect these inland border lines. In pursuance of her policy of opposition, Yemen also lodged protests against Britain's actions before the United Nations, once in July and again in October 1954. Charging Britain with "aggression," the Yemeni delegation protested against the proposed federation of what it termed Yemeni territory and in addition challenged Britain's sovereignty in the Aden Colony itself. The latter, it asserted in the Trusteeship Council, was Yemen's property which Britain had annexed by force.

While considerable doubts existed as to the legal validity of Yemen's contentions, the fact remained that it was Britain's forward policy in this hitherto fairly quiet region which lay at the root of the difficulties. Yemen's rulers could hardly be blamed for their negative reaction to moves and schemes which were apt to upset the existing political balance. By the same token, it was not illogical for Yemen in her foreign policy to line up with those states in the Arab League which, like herself, had had difficulties with Britain and leaned toward neutralism. On all major issues posed before the League, Yemen stood staunchly by the Cairo-Riyadh axis.

Internal Upheaval in 1955

Reference has already been made to Yemen's nervousness about the effect improvements in the Aden Protectorate might have on her own stability. Imam Seif el-Islam Ahmed owed his throne to the victory of conservative forces over the reformists and consequently viewed with uneasiness any movement within or without Yemen that was likely to threaten his and his allies' hold on the country. The ringleaders of the 1948 coup had all been executed, imprisoned, or exiled, but the real causes of rebellion remained, and important elements within the country had not been reconciled to Ahmed's rule. The Imam virtually acknowledged the unrest when he chose to make Taizz his "temporary" capital, ostensibly because he would not honor the people of Sana, a regicidal city, with his presence. The truth was that the people of Sana could not forget the ruthless behavior and plundering in 1948 by the tribesmen who had helped

Ahmed defeat Abdullah el-Wazir and his reformist government. Settled, industrious, and relatively prosperous, the inhabitants of the capital resented the supremacy of the backward tribal elements to whom Ahmed owed his elevation. To be sure, the Imam took steps to develop the country, mostly by inviting a few foreign experts to carry out certain limited technical projects. But he did not adopt any comprehensive plan of development and reform, and his policy continued, by and large, to follow the traditional isolationist pattern. In the meantime, however, Yemen's participation in the United Nations and the Arab League, the growing number of Yemeni students in Cairo and other foreign centers, and increasing trade contacts with the outside world tended to counter this isolationist tendency, exposing a good many people to foreign influences and ideas. Consequently the tension already existing between the conservative and the reformist forces was increasing. In the spring of 1955 it erupted in the form of a new coup that shook the kingdom profoundly.

Toward the end of March 1955 the leaders of a new conspiracy against Imam Ahmed made common cause with disaffected army units. After having presented inacceptable demands to Ahmed, the latter struck at the royal guards in Taizz, compelling the Imam to flee the palace and seek refuge in the El-Udi fortress. Mediation attempted by religious notables brought no results. Instead, the religious and the military leaders reached agreement on March 31 to depose Ahmed and to proclaim as imam his brother and minister of foreign affairs, Seif el-Islam Abdullah. The latter was reputed to be a man of more liberal tendencies, having traveled widely and absorbed a good deal of Western culture.

Imam Ahmed's deposition was challenged, however, by his son and crown prince, Seif el-Islam Mohammed el-Badr. Badr escaped from Taizz and reached the northern stronghold of Hajja, where he appealed for aid to the Hashid and Bakin tribes whose friendship he and his father had consistently cultivated. These were, in fact, the same tribes that had restored Imam Ahmed to the throne in 1948 and subsequently sacked Sana. Badr's dramatic appeal—he reportedly threw down his turban and dagger in a gesture of humiliation —did not go unheeded. The tribesmen offered him a force of eight thousand men, who promptly set out to relieve Ahmed, the latter still besieged in El-Udi. In the fierce battle that ensued between the army and the tribesmen, the army was handicapped by a shortage of munitions and gasoline, the main depot of which was in the fortress. As a result, the tribal force emerged victorious, capturing or putting to flight the rebel leaders. On April 4 Imam Ahmed regained his throne. Fifteen leaders of the coup were promptly executed, the list including Ahmed's two brothers, Seif el-Islam Abdullah, the would-be imam, and Seif el-Islam el-Abbas, governor of the province of Sana, as well as Ahmed Yehya Salayah, instructor-general of the army. Among those arrested but later released were four sons of Yemen's prime minister, Emir Seif el-Islam el-Hassan, who at the time of the coup was on a visit to Cairo. He was subsequently removed from his position but no other steps against him were reported.

On April 17 Imam Ahmed appointed Badr head of the government and simultaneously asked him to form a study commission to modernize Yemen's administration. Soon afterward Ahmed ordered the opening of the coffers containing the treasures of the late Imam Yehya. This fortune has been variously estimated at between $56,000,000 and $280,000,000. According to Yemeni declarations, the government intends to use it for development purposes. On his part, Prince Badr declared during a visit in Cairo early in May that his father "ardently desired to establish a democratic government" which would adopt a program of reforms and that it was to be "the government of the people for the people." [5]

The subsequent granting of an oil concession to an American firm can perhaps be taken as an indication that Imam Ahmed has decided to embark upon a path of development by ending the virtual ban upon foreign penetration of the country. Signed in October 1955 between Yemen's government and Walter S. Gabler, president of the Yemen Development Corporation, the thirty-year concession provides for the exploration and development of oil and mineral resources. Simultaneously Yemen was conducting negotiations with the Soviet Union, which on October 31 resulted in the renewal of the friendship treaty originally concluded in 1928. Early in 1956 a Yemeni spokesman in Cairo declared that Russia had offered to erect factories and supply agricultural machinery and road-building equipment to his country and that this offer was linked with the recently concluded treaty. Unconfirmed reports declare that the Soviet Union also offered arms to Yemen, as it did to other Arab states.

To sum up, in the decade between the end of World War II and

[5] *Cahiers*, 1955, 1.

the mid-1950's Yemen experienced two internal upheavals that were more than mere palace revolutions. They testified to the gradual awakening of a people long dormant under conditions of rigid isolation. Although the conservative forces preserved their supremacy in both tests of power, they realized that the old system could no longer be maintained in full force. Consequently, they have begun to make gradual concessions to the widely felt need for reform by encouraging technological developments in the country. This policy has foreign implications inasmuch as it is bound to open the country to greater numbers of alien specialists. Anxious to preserve her neutrality and resentful toward Britain, Yemen looked to both the United States and Russia as states that might help her speed up her technical progress. Whether this kind of development will be sufficient to satisfy the reformist elements in the country is a question.

PART FIVE

PROBLEMS OF WAR AND PEACE

CHAPTER XIV

World War II and the
Middle East

THERE was a considerable difference between the two World Wars in the Middle East. At the beginning of the first war most of the area formed part of the Ottoman Empire and the Allies had to conquer it in at least four military campaigns. When the second war broke out the Middle East was under the effective control of Great Britain and France either through mandates or through treaty arrangements with such semiemancipated countries as Egypt and Iraq. In two neutral states, Iran and Afghanistan, the Allies, using different methods in the two countries, succeeded in eliminating enemy influence. Turkey was the only truly independent major country in the Middle East, and she was the only one to preserve her neutrality.

Thus the Allies aimed at the preservation of the *status quo* in the Middle East and by virtue of their control of the area found their task easier than it had been during the First World War. The defense of the Middle East against the Axis received high priority in Britain, and this attitude found its reflection in the over-all Allied war strategy. At one critical moment of the war, in the summer of 1942, the United States had to deplete its own reserves to rush more tanks to the Middle East.[1]

[1] Winston Churchill, *The Second World War* (Boston, 1950), IV, 388. This and other volumes by Britain's wartime prime minister contain many revealing chapters on the war in the Middle East.

Military Operations

Because the Allies were in a relatively strong military position in the Middle East, actual fighting never occurred in the heart of the area but was relegated to its fringes.[2] During World War I the Allies had fought campaigns in the Dardanelles, Mesopotamia, Palestine and Sinai, eastern Anatolia, and the Arab interior. During World War II the Axis attempted to conquer the Middle East by a pincer movement, with one arm stretching across Libya and another enveloping the area via the Caucasus. In both regions it came very close to success, but failed to reach the goal.

The Soviet campaign in the Caucasus was a separate affair, with no other Allies participating directly. Russia, of course, was receiving lend-lease aid and, moreover, the British formed a rear defense line in northern Iraq with the aid of a Polish army corps in case the Caucasus was pierced by the Germans. The latter reached the farthest point of their offensive on November 19, 1942, occupying the north Caucasian oil areas up to Grozny, with only fifty miles between their front and the Caspian Sea. From that time onward they were in steady retreat.

Allied operations in the Libyan-Egyptian borderland were conducted by the British based on Egypt. It was a very mobile war, waged in three stages. In the winter of 1940–1941 (December to January) General Sir Archibald Wavell launched a rapid offensive against the Italians, who were in occupation of some border localities on the Egyptian coast, and succeeded in a brief and spectacular campaign in pushing the enemy back to El-Agheila, west of Benghazi. The British and Imperial troops captured 114,000 prisoners at a cost of 3,000 casualties. Wavell, however, overextended his lines of communication, which made it possible for combined Italo-German forces to mount a counteroffensive. Commanded by the able desert tactician General Erwin Rommel, the Axis troops drove the British all the way back to the Egyptian frontier. The British, weakened by the dispatch of 60,000 men to Greece, retreated without many casualties and

[2] To the author's knowledge no complete history of the Middle Eastern operations during the Second World War has as yet appeared. Churchill's memoirs are probably the most authoritative source on various phases of the war in the Middle East. A number of books have been written by soldiers and newspapermen alike, but none of them is exhaustive on this subject. See the section on the Second World War in the Bibliography.

470

managed to retain the Libyan fortress of Tobruk, which was encircled by the Axis.

Between May 29 and December 11, 1941, there was a lull in the operations, both parties preparing for a winter offensive. In December the British troops, commanded by General Sir Claude Auchinleck, launched their second offensive, during which they relieved Tobruk, captured Benghazi for the second time, but stopped short of El-Agheila (January 18, 1942). The German setbacks were largely due to a temporary depletion of their forces for the campaign in Russia. Reinforced, Rommel began a new drive into Egypt on May 27, 1942. In rather mysterious circumstances 25,000 South African troops quickly surrendered to him in Tobruk. The Germans shattered British armored formations at the battle of Knightsbridge, overcame valiant French resistance at Bir-Hakim, and drove deeply into Egyptian territory, reaching El-Alamein, only seventy miles from Alexandria.

A four months' lull followed during which Britain made her supreme effort to build up a powerful striking force between the seacoast and the Qattara depression. On October 23 the British Eighth Army under General Sir Bernard L. Montgomery began the third offensive, smashed the German line at El-Alamein, and drove Rommel back to Libya. Two weeks later, on November 8, 1942, an Anglo-American force commanded by General Dwight D. Eisenhower, made a successful landing in French North Africa. Later the Allied forces began relentlessly to pound at the Italo-German army from both east and west. On March 30, 1943, the British Eighth Army broke through the Mareth line into southern Tunisia, where it met the advanced detachments of the American Second Army Corps. By May 12 Axis resistance in North Africa had ended. Previous to that, between January and December 1941, British Imperial forces had liberated all Italian East African possessions (Ethiopia, Eritrea, and Somaliland).

Enemy air action over the British-held Middle East was not considerable, because the Axis tried not to antagonize the local population. The Axis concentrated on bombing Allied shipping and military objectives such as harbors, especially Alexandria, and the Suez Canal. Technically, the Canal was out of commission for only seventy-six days [3] during the entire war. But navigation in the Mediterranean

[3] H. L. Hoskins, "The Guardianship of the Suez Canal," *Middle East Journal*, April 1950, p. 148.

and the Canal was very dangerous, and many convoys had to be directed by the roundabout route of the Cape. As to the other strategic waterway—the Turkish Straits—Turkey as a neutral kept them closed to Allied and Axis navies for the greater part of the war. This was one of the reasons why Russia and Britain were compelled to occupy Iran to secure a route for military supplies. But even assuming a pro-Ally stand by Turkey, the Straits would not have been too useful on account of Axis air bases in the Balkans.

Psychological Warfare

While the Allies were militarily supreme in the Middle East, their psychological position was much weaker. There was considerable anti-British feeling in a number of Arab countries, partly resulting from unfulfilled promises of independence and partly stimulated by skillful Axis propaganda.[4] This propaganda harped on the theme of liberation from British control, and it had many willing listeners. By contrast, British propaganda sounded rather unconvincing. British broadcasts depicting the horrors of the Nazi occupation in Europe with its attendant cruelties against the Jews left the Arabs skeptical and indifferent. Middle East experience with the Germans had generally been most satisfactory, and even educated Arabs or Iranians could not conceive of the Germans as anything but cultured, efficient and frequently more courteous than the colonial British. On the other hand, stories of cruelty were not likely to frighten the lower-class audience, which was apt to applaud German strength and the anti-Jewish exploits. If we add the fact that Axis propaganda was devoid of scruples and freely used the most fantastic lies as a weapon, while the Allies were restricted by certain inhibitions, we can clearly see that in this duel the Axis was able to score considerable success.

Despite all its efforts the Axis could not change the fact that British rule was not really oppressive—that, indeed, it was much more indirect and humane than any foreign rule the Arabs had known in the past. Every informed person knew that Britain did not levy tributes from the Arab states but often paid them subsidies; that she did not make requisitions but purchases for which she paid in cash; and that instead of exploiting the Middle Eastern states she enabled them to accumulate sizable sterling balances in London. Moreover, Britain

[4] See Seth Arsenian, "Wartime Propaganda in the Middle East," *Middle East Journal*, Oct. 1948; and Nevill Barbour, "Broadcasting to the Arab World: Arabic Transmissions from the B.B.C. and Other Non-Arab Stations," *Middle East Journal*, Winter 1951.

and the United States assisted the Middle East to overcome wartime shortages through the Middle East Supply Center in Cairo. The Center, by its well-planned policy of allocations, averted many shortages and inconveniences.

The Arabs therefore did not have the same stake in the Second World War that they had in the First. Then they were trying to overthrow oppressive Ottoman rule, and to this end they were ready for many sacrifices. Now there was no such incentive, and all that the Arab governments really wanted was to reaffirm their independence, which they had to a considerable degree achieved prior to World War II. Arab public opinion between 1939 and 1945 presented a combination of pro-German and neutral attitudes. There was, moreover, a widespread belief that the war was a conflict of the big powers and as such of no direct concern to the Arabs. This explains why there was relatively little anti-Ally unrest in the Middle East during the war. There were, true enough, three exceptions to this rule: the Rashid Ali rebellion in Iraq; the recalcitrant attitude of Iran prior to August 1941; and minor difficulties in Egypt resulting in the arrests of Aziz el-Masri and Ali Maher Pasha. But these manifestations could not be compared in their magnitude to the Arab Revolt of 1916. In this connection we may observe that Germany made a serious blunder by concentrating on the Arabs instead of on the Moslem peoples of the Soviet Union. There the ground was much more fertile for a popular uprising. The German Foreign Office knew it, and it tried to use the services of Haj Amin el-Husseini and of some Turkish Pan-Turanians, but its efforts were frustrated by the arrogant self-confidence of Nazi careerists from Rosenberg's *Ostministerium*.

Well-informed Arab statesmen realized the difference between British humanitarianism and Nazi brutality. But, precisely because of this, they were more anxious to ingratiate themselves with the Axis in case of an Axis victory than to prove their loyalty to the British. By the same token, Arab governments did not make their troops available to the Allies. The only exception was Emir Abdullah's Arab Legion of Transjordan. And much as the Arab leaders may have congratulated themselves on smartly staying out of the battlefields, they surely must have regretted that their armies were not stronger and more experienced when they had to face a test in Palestine in 1948.

Because the Allies had to defend the Middle East and not conquer it, they did not have the same opportunity as in World War I to incite subversion behind enemy lines. In the only area where such

473

subversion was feasible, i.e., in Libya, the British made full use of the enmity existing between the Senussis and the Italian authorities. Exiled chiefs of the Senussis residing in Cairo were contacted, and assurances were given them that, in return for their aid to the Allies, Britain would support their independence and oppose the return of Italian rule.

The impact of the war on the Middle East was considerable. Politically the war accelerated the process of Arab emancipation which had begun a quarter of a century earlier. Syria and Lebanon gained full independence, while Iraq and Egypt secured Britain's consent to treaty revision. Indeed, one might say that as a result of the Second World War the Middle East changed position with eastern Europe. While the latter came under alien domination, the former won freedom. This is well reflected in the United Nations. Eastern European states are either not represented in the new world organization or, if represented, they act as mouthpieces of the Kremlin. By contrast, all the Middle Eastern states except Jordan have joined the organization and do not hesitate to use it as a platform for independent action, frequently in opposition to the big powers.

From the economic and social point of view the war had an unsettling effect. Allied spending, war contracts, profiteering, and hoarding made some people rich, but they also caused inflation and resultant suffering on the part of the masses. Young members of the intelligentsia could not help comparing their own poverty and impotence with Western wealth and strength as exemplified by the Allied war effort. The prolonged presence of Allied armies on their soil added an element of antiforeign resentment to the already pronounced discontent and frustration. These pent-up feelings found their outlet in a powerful wave of nationalism as soon as the war was over. The intensity of these emotions made many nationalists reckless and blind to the hard strategic realities which make their part of the world vitally important to the big powers.

474

CHAPTER XV

The Middle East's

Strategic Waterways

THE strategic importance of the Middle East is due, to a considerable extent, to the fact that this region possesses two major international waterways: the Turkish Straits and the Suez Canal. Most of the political struggles of the area have revolved around these narrow stretches of water. In fact, the Near Eastern question in the nineteenth century (see Chapter I) was essentially a rivalry on the part of the big powers for control of the Turkish Straits until the Isthmus of Suez was pierced by a canal in the latter part of the century. The canal put an end to the relative isolation of Egypt and inexorably linked that country with major world politics.

The economic significance of these waterways is obvious. Since time immemorial the Turkish Straits have been a vital trade route between the Black Sea shores and the Mediterranean. The prosperity of many a Mediterranean state, such as Genoa or Greece, has been largely dependent upon its ability to trade with the Black Sea hinterland. And, conversely, the Straits have played an increasingly important role in the foreign trade of Russia ever since the latter obtained an outlet to the Black Sea. The commercial significance of the opening of the Suez Canal, which replaced the old Cape route, is so obvious that it does not require elaboration.

The military importance of these waterways has always been considerable, and much military and naval planning of both World Wars revolved around these narrow passages. During World War II Germany and Italy made a major effort to seize the Suez Canal, as their repeated offensives toward Egypt proved; and Britain was ready to make sacrifices in other war theaters to defend the canal. Meanwhile, the task of supplying the USSR with arms and equipment was complicated for the Allies by the closure of the Straits by Turkey and by German air bases in the Balkans. Today one may ask whether the development of aviation and modern weapons has not rendered these old plans and calculations obsolete. The ultimate answer must be reserved for the future, but the Second World War has demonstrated that nations could not be indifferent as to who was in actual control of the Turkish Straits and of the Suez Canal. And as for peacetime, it may safely be asserted that control of these waterways may prove decisive so far as the political independence of Turkey and the diplomatic alignment of Egypt are concerned.

The following two sections will review in a concise manner pertinent facts of political interest concerning the Middle East's waterways, summing up what has been said in this volume and supplementing it with such information as may be necessary to present a unified picture of the problem.

THE TURKISH STRAITS

The Turkish Straits are composed of the Bosphorus in the northeast, the Dardanelles in the southwest, and the Sea of Marmara between them. Turkey's old capital and largest commercial center, Istanbul, is situated astride the Bosphorus. The economic significance of the Straits for Turkey can be measured by the fact that, in 1939, 76 per cent of her imports and 35 per cent of her exports were channeled through Istanbul and that, in the same year, Turkey accounted for 30 per cent of the total registered tonnage passing the Straits (see Table I).

Table I. Shipping of various countries passing through the Straits in 1939, in percentages of the total registered tonnage

Turkey	30.0	*Non-Black Sea powers:*	
		France	2.7
		Great Britain	14.0
		Greece	8.5
Black Sea powers:		Italy	14.7
Soviet Union	3.0	United States	2.8
Bulgaria	1.7	Yugoslavia	0.7
Rumania	7.7	Others	14.2

Despite the small percentage of Soviet tonnage registered in 1939, the Straits have generally played an important role in Russia's foreign trade. Thus, in 1936 and 1937 Soviet exports from Black Sea ports clearing through the Straits accounted for 30 per cent by value of the total USSR exports, and such products as grain, coal, manganese, petroleum, and its derivatives were shipped almost entirely through the Straits.[1]

The strategic importance of the Straits to Russia matches their economic importance. Eleven hundred miles of Black Sea coast form part of Russia's southern boundary. It would be much easier for the Soviets to defend this boundary against external aggression if they were in control of the narrow bottleneck of the Turkish Straits leading into the Black Sea. And, conversely, should Russia have expansionist ambitions in the Mediterranean and the Middle East, control of the Straits would greatly enhance her chances of success.

Period of Undisputed Turkish Sovereignty

The problem of who should control the Straits has never been settled with absolute finality. The political history of the Straits abounds in "rules" and "principles" considered sacrosanct and called "universal" by those states which were able to force their acceptance under certain circumstances and which had a vested interest in maintaining the *status quo*. But wars and changes in power relationships often produced a change of rules and a reversal of attitudes.[2] Like any other political institution, the status of the Straits has been and continues to be dependent upon the will and the ability of the states directly concerned to support it.

For three hundred years, from 1475 to 1774, the Black Sea was a Turkish lake, all its shores being under the full control of the Ottoman Empire. During that period the Ottoman government had an absolute monopoly of navigation in the Black Sea. Capitulatory rights granted to France and other countries frequently included freedom of passage through the Strait of Dardanelles so that foreign ships could reach Constantinople, but, with a brief exception in favor of Venice, none

---

[1] These statistics are reproduced from *The Problem of the Dardanelles, A Summary of Background Information* (Office of Public Affairs, Department of State, November 1946).

[2] For a historical treatment of the subject, see James T. Shotwell and Francis Deák, *Turkey at the Straits, A Short History* (New York, 1941).

477

of these treaties ever extended this freedom to the Bosphorus and the Black Sea.

Russia's First Gains

The first major change in this situation occurred in 1774, when, at Kuchuk Kainardji, the Straits were opened to Russian merchant ships in time of peace. This coincided with the acquisition by Russia of a direct outlet to the Black Sea. Despite this major concession, freedom of shipping in the Straits, so far as other countries were concerned, still remained within Turkey's discretionary power. By a series of bilateral agreements Turkey eventually extended the freedom of passage to merchant ships of other countries, but this freedom was not yet accepted as a general principle of the public law of nations. As to foreign warships, no exception and no compromise were admitted as it was the "ancient rule of the Ottoman Empire" to exclude warships of every nation from entering the Straits. This rule, true enough, was time and again violated during the Napoleonic era, yet its validity remained unquestioned.

Russia's southward expansion throughout the nineteenth century was expressed, so far as the Straits were concerned, in attempts to obtain complete control of this waterway. To occupy and annex the region of the Straits would have been an ideal solution for Russia. Such an annexation would have meant partition and probably destruction of the Ottoman Empire, and Russia was aware that she could not obtain it short of a major war with other interested powers. The history of the Eastern question in the nineteenth century eloquently proves that, whenever Russia was on the threshold of fulfilling this ideal objective, she invariably ran into stiff opposition from Britain and other European powers, who, by concerted action, prevented her from attaining her goal.

From Unkiar Iskelessi to the First World War

Unable to solve the problem of the Straits to her best liking, Russia had to content herself with alternatives that could be achieved by diplomacy. Denied outright possession, Russia was interested in such regulation of the Straits as would most favor her needs. If the Straits were to remain outside her physical control, the second-best solution for Russia was to have a formal pledge that the guardian of the Straits (i.e., Turkey) would always keep the Straits open to Russian merchant and war vessels but that she would close them to non-Black Sea

478

powers at Russia's will. This second-best solution Russia secured in the greatest triumph of her Near Eastern diplomacy, the Treaty of Unkiar Iskelessi in 1833. This arrangement was, needless to say, most undesirable from the British standpoint, and Britain lost no time or opportunity to effect a change in the control of the Straits. Such an opportunity came with the second act of Mohammed Ali's drama in 1839–1840. The resulting Treaty of London of 1840 and the Straits Convention of 1841 scrapped the preferential Unkiar Iskelessi arrangement and restored "the ancient rule of the Ottoman Empire" that the Straits must always be closed to foreign warships. The Straits Convention remained in force for the next eighty years as a basic law for the Straits and was raised to the dignity of the public law of Europe. It was confirmed by the Treaties of Paris in 1856, of London in 1871, and of Berlin in 1878. Its only minor modification occurred in 1871 when, by the above-mentioned Treaty of London, the sultan, hitherto obliged to keep the Straits closed to foreign warships, was given the right to open them in certain circumstances.

Thus, from 1841 until 1920, the principle of the closure of the Straits prevailed. This principle fitted well with the interests of Great Britain and certain other European powers, but not with those of Russia. It constituted an obvious obstacle to Russia's expansionist policy in the Near East, while, by the same token, it protected Britain's interests and communications in the eastern Mediterranean. There was, of course, nothing permanent in this situation. A strong Russia found the closure of the Straits a nuisance, but a weak Russia might find it beneficial. As things stood, however, in the nineteenth century Russia was or believed herself to be strong enough to prefer the open to the closed Straits. Rather naturally, her diplomacy reverted time and again to the precedent of Unkiar Iskelessi as the best solution short of actual domination of the Straits. This revisionism was particularly noticeable in the decade preceding the First World War, during which Russia made several attempts to secure a regime more to her liking. Yet, weakened as she was by the Japanese war and the revolution of 1905, she had to rely exclusively on diplomacy as she was unable in the twentieth century, in contrast to the nineteenth, to back up her demands by force. Negotiations with Britain in 1907, Austria in 1908, and Italy in 1909 aiming at the recognition of a preferential Russian position in the Straits did not bring the hoped-for results.

The Great War and the Peace Settlement

The so-called Constantinople agreement of 1915 by which the Entente powers agreed to Russian annexation of the Straits in case of victory in the war has already been discussed (Chapter II). This concession constituted a dramatic change in British and French policies, but its effects were nullified by the Bolshevik revolution and by the solemn renunciation by the Soviet government of the secret agreements.

The problem of the Straits came up at the time of the peace settlement, with a radical reversal in British (and Western) policy. Britain and her Western allies were then in a position to impose a solution independent of Russia's and Turkey's will because these two countries were kept out of the European councils in 1920. And the solution Britain chose was to declare, in the Treaty of Sèvres, the Straits open in time of peace and war to merchant and war shipping alike. This reversal stemmed from the radical change in power relationships. The new Russia was weak and, in British eyes, did not threaten the security of the eastern Mediterranean. Hence there was no point in insisting on the closure of the Straits. On the contrary, in view of increased British strength, it was advantageous to keep the Straits permanently open for the penetration of British and other Western fleets into the Black Sea, from which they could watch the movements of the new Soviet state and nip the danger in the bud should this state try to embark upon a revolutionary crusade beyond its borders.

True enough, the Treaty of Sèvres proved abortive owing to Turkey's nationalist resistance. But the new principle underlying control of the Straits remained valid in the postwar years and supplied the basis for the new regulations inscribed in the Treaty of Lausanne. Yet it was characteristic of the change in the political atmosphere between 1920 and 1923 that instead of being informed of the decisions taken in their absence, both Turkey and Soviet Russia were invited to take part in the discussions. The political configuration at the Lausanne conference was such that Britain and Russia appeared as the two main protagonists so far as the Straits were concerned. Russia desired to see the Straits closed, no doubt as a measure of protection against renewed Western intervention, and her chief delegate, Commissar Chicherin, desperately fought against the proposed international control of the Straits, defending the rights of Turkish sovereignty. Britain, by contrast, insisted on freedom of navigation and on international control (both principles incorporated in the Treaty of Sèvres), but she was willing to make concessions that would, to some extent, recognize Soviet security requirements and Turkish sensitivities.

Despite her friendship with Soviet Russia, Turkey did not entirely take the former's side. The Turks, who were very determined to have their way on many other points, were ready to accept emasculated international management of the Straits and, as to the problem whether the Straits should remain closed or open, they preferred to leave the matter to the big powers to fight over between themselves. To the Russians this Turkish halfheartedness was disappointing and, had Russia been stronger, Soviet-Turkish relations might have cooled appreciably. Because the weak Soviet state was interested in cultivating the good will of the guardian of the Straits, Turkey was spared Russian recriminations.

The Lausanne Convention

The result of these deliberations was new regulations adopted in the "Convention relating to the Straits" on July 24, 1923, the day of the signature of the principal Treaty of Lausanne. The main provisions were as follows:

Merchant ships. The principle of freedom of passage was affirmed in time of peace and war alike. The only exception applied when Turkey was at war: Turkey was then permitted to stop enemy ships but was not allowed to interfere with the free passage of neutral ships.

Warships. In peacetime, warships were allowed freedom of transit provided that the maximum force any *one* non-Black Sea power sent into the Black Sea did not exceed the most powerful Black Sea fleet. In any case, the nonriparian powers were each allowed to send into the Black Sea a force of not more than three ships, none to exceed 10,000 tons. In wartime, if Turkey remained neutral or nonbelligerent, the same principles were to apply as in time of peace. If Turkey was a belligerent, freedom of passage would apply to neutral ships only.

In addition, the region of the Straits was to be demilitarized and the Straits were to be subjected to the supervision (but not actual management) of the International Commission of the Straits composed of Turkey (president), France, Great Britain, Italy, Japan, Bulgaria, Greece, Rumania, Russia, Yugoslavia, and the United States (on adherence to the convention).[3]

[3] The Lausanne Convention, which had no termination date, was signed by

481

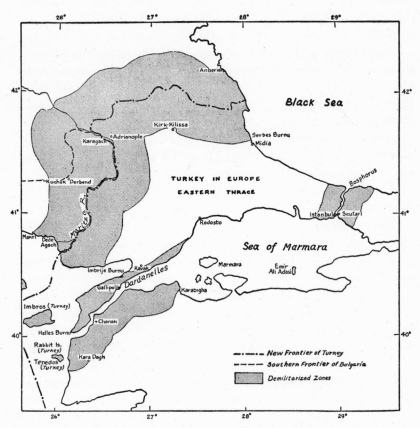

Map 6. The Turkish Straits. The boundaries and demilitarized zones follow the provisions of the Treaty of Lausanne, 1923.

The Montreux Convention

The Lausanne Straits Convention remained in force for thirteen years. On July 20, 1936, it was replaced by the Montreux Convention, which is still (1952) in force. The participants in the Montreux conference included the Soviet Union, which, as before, endeavored to reduce the freedom of the nonriparian states to enter the Black Sea. As at Lausanne, her main opponent was Britain, but the whole atmosphere was perceptibly changed. Because of the rising German danger to European peace, Britain and France were willing to go rather far to accommodate Turkey and not to antagonize Russia, with whom rapprochement was being sought. As a result, both Turkey and Russia came out of the conference with tangible gains. Russia's gain consisted in a reduction in the maximum tonnage allowed in the Black Sea to nonriparian powers. This greater security was conditioned, however, on Turkey's good will inasmuch as Turkey was given much greater freedom of action in the Straits.

The Montreux Convention contained the following main provisions:

Merchant ships. In peacetime, the principle of freedom of passage was reaffirmed without a time limit. In wartime, if Turkey was neutral or nonbelligerent, complete freedom of passage was to apply. If Turkey was a belligerent, merchant vessels of countries not at war with Turkey were to enjoy freedom of passage on condition of not assisting the enemy. Should Turkey be threatened by war, freedom of passage was to apply as in peace except that ships must enter the Straits in daytime and follow the route prescribed by Turkish authorities.

Warships. In peacetime, the maximum tonnage of all foreign warships, whether riparian or nonriparian, in transit through the Straits was limited to 15,000 tons. The Black Sea powers, however, were permitted to send capital ships displacing more than 15,000 tons, provided they passed singly and were escorted by not more than two destroyers. In general, the aggregate tonnage of nonriparian powers in the Black Sea was not to exceed 30,000 tons, but this figure could be increased to 45,000 tons if the Soviet navy were to exceed by at

---

the British Empire, France, Italy, Japan, Bulgaria, Greece, Rumania, Russia, Yugoslavia, and Turkey. Russia signed it on August 14, 1924, but did not ratify it. Its text may be found in *The Problem of the Turkish Straits* (Department of State, Pub. 2752, Near Eastern ser. 5, Washington, 1947).

least 10,000 tons its tonnage at the time of the signature of the convention. Warships of nonriparian powers must not stay longer than twenty-one days in the Black Sea.

In wartime, if Turkey remained neutral or nonbelligerent, freedom of passage as in peace was to apply to nonbelligerents only. Belligerents were not to pass the Straits except in cases of assistance rendered to a victim of aggression in virtue of a mutual assistance pact binding Turkey. Should Turkey become belligerent, she would acquire complete discretion as to the passage of warships through the Straits. Under a threat of war, Turkey was given the right to stop or let pass foreign warships at her discretion. Her decisions, however, were to be communicated to the signatories of the convention and to the Council of the League of Nations. A two-thirds majority of the Council, if upheld by a majority of the signatories, was permitted to reverse Turkey's decisions.

In addition to these main provisions the Montreux Convention abolished the International Straits Commission, restoring the jurisdiction to the Turkish government, and gave Turkey the right to remilitarize the Straits.[4]

The Situation during World War II

Turkey's nonbelligerency during the Second World War led her to pursue a cautious policy with regard to the Straits. Between 1939 and 1944 the Allies did not use the Straits for their supplies to Russia because unprotected merchant shipping would have been exposed to annihilation by the enemy, and naval escorts were not practical inasmuch as Turkey would surely have prevented their passage. By the same token, the German and satellite navies were denied the use of the Straits except for a few fraudulent passages of minor importance.

All in all, Russia had no basis to complain about Turkey's attitude because Turkey proved a reliable and—as far as circumstances permitted—impartial guardian of the Straits. Earlier, in 1936–1938, Russia had used the Straits freely to send agents and supplies to Spain. During World War II, even in the darkest moments of Stalingrad, Turkey did not let Axis naval forces enter the Black Sea.[5] As soon

[4] For the text, see *ibid.* The Montreux Convention was for twenty years. It was signed by Bulgaria, France, Great Britain, Greece, Japan, Rumania, Turkey, USSR, and Yugoslavia. Italy refused to participate in the discussions but acceded to the convention on May 2, 1938.

[5] For an evaluation of Turkey's attitude, see Norman J. Padelford, "Solutions

as it was practically possible, i.e., in the fall of 1944, Turkey permitted the use of the Straits to armed or escorted ships carrying lend-lease supplies to Russia.

In the Soviet view, this dependence on Turkey did not square with the new Soviet concepts of security. These concepts, which led Russia to demand outright control of strategic approaches to her territory instead of leaving them in the hands of smaller sovereign nations, dictated a new policy toward the Straits. The first official demand for a revision of the Montreux Convention was made by the Soviet government in June 1943, and the matter was discussed at the Potsdam conference in the summer of 1945. There Russia obtained American and British consent to changing the convention, without specification, however, of the changes. It was also decided at Potsdam that the question of revision should first be explored through diplomatic channels with the Turkish government.

Postwar Attempts at Revision

The United States made the first constructive proposals concerning the contemplated revision. In a note to the Turkish government on November 2, 1945, the United States set forth the following principles for future control of the Straits: (1) the Straits were to be open to the merchant vessels of all nations at all times; (2) the Straits were to be open to the transit of the warships of Black Sea powers at all times; (3) save for an agreed tonnage in time of peace, passage through the Straits was to be denied to the warships of non-Black Sea powers at all times, except with the specific consent of the Black Sea powers or except when acting under the authority of the United Nations; and (4) certain changes were to be made to modernize the Montreux Convention, such as the substitution of the United Nations system for that of the League of Nations and the elimination of Japan as a signatory.

The contents of this note were communicated to the British and Soviet governments also. Soon afterward the British and Turkish governments expressed their agreement in principle with the American proposals. The Soviet government delayed its reply for about ten months. On August 7, 1946, it finally presented a detailed note to Ankara, transmitting copies to Washington and London. In the first

---

to the Problem of the Turkish Straits, A Brief Appraisal," *Middle East Journal*, April 1948. For a Turkish view of the problem, see Ahmed Sükrü Esmer, "The Straits: Crux of World Politics," *Foreign Affairs*, January 1947.

part of the note Russia reminded Turkey of a number of incidents that had occurred in the Straits during the Second World War, namely, the passage through the Straits, in 1941, of the German patrol boat *Seefalke* and of the Italian auxiliary warship *Tarvisio;* the intended passage, in 1942, of 140,000 tons of auxiliary German warships into the Black Sea; and the passage, in 1944, of eight German auxiliary warships of the *Ems* type and of five vessels of the *Kriegstransport* type. For this reason Russia believed that the Montreux Convention had not prevented the use of the Straits by hostile powers, that Turkey could not escape responsibility for these acts, and that the convention should be revised so as to "conform to present conditions." In the second part of the note the Soviet government proposed five principles to govern the Straits. Of the five, the first three were a virtual repetition of the first three principles suggested the previous year by the United States. The last two, however, were far beyond anything contemplated by the Western powers. In the fourth principle Russia proposed that "the establishment of a regime of the Straits . . . should come under the competence of Turkey and other Black Sea Powers," and in the fifth she asked that defense of the Straits should be shared jointly by Turkey and the Soviet Union.

The Soviet note set off a series of diplomatic communications among Moscow, Ankara, Washington, and London. In lengthy and detailed notes Turkey contested Soviet allegations concerning the passage of Axis war vessels through the Straits; admitted fraudulent passage of a few minor units under the guise of merchant vessels; and declared herself unable to accept Soviet proposals concerning the future administration and defense of the Straits. Russia replied in equally exhaustive statements, trying to prove Turkey's ill will or reprehensible negligence in handling these wartime incidents and insisting on her own proposals as the only solution capable of guaranteeing Soviet security. In her notes Russia more than once referred to the Black Sea as a *closed* sea. In this exchange of views Washington and London took Turkey's side, likewise refusing to accept the fourth and fifth Soviet proposals.[6]

Appraisal of the Latest Proposals

In order fully to understand this Turko-Soviet duel, we must realize that, in setting forth its own suggestions in November 1945, the United States had gone far to meet the Soviet craving for increased security. A close analysis of the American proposals will show that,

[6] For the relevant texts, see *The Problem of the Turkish Straits.*

in their essence, they give Russia something very similar to the conspicuously preferential treatment she received in the Treaty of Unkiar Iskelessi, back in 1833. In both cases Russia was to have complete freedom to send her warships into the Mediterranean, while this freedom was to be denied the Western powers. The Unkiar Iskelessi deal had aroused much furor and hostility in the security-conscious Britain of the 1830's. And yet, in 1945, when Russia was emerging as a military and industrial colossus dominating two-thirds of Europe and the whole of northern Asia, Washington and London, anxious for and trustful of Soviet friendship, were ready, on their own initiative, to give Moscow what a hundred years earlier had brought Russia and the West to the brink of war. Seldom, indeed, have the annals of diplomacy revealed a greater desire for peace almost at any price on the part of powerful and victorious nations. The American proposal was made essentially in the spirit of Yalta, with the obvious intention of satisfying and accommodating the Soviet Union and with little regard to strategic considerations of Western security. But, as at Yalta, this was not enough for Russia, who, rejecting compromises, renewed the ancient tsarist claim for the possession or military domination of the Straits. This was, in reality, what the Soviet demand for the "joint defense" of the Straits meant. But to the West, in the awakened political realism of 1946, this solution was inacceptable. A continuation of diplomatic exchanges among the four capitals added little to the basic positions taken in late 1946. In fact, Russia's insistence on acceptance of her demands, coupled as it was with other expansionist moves all along her periphery, produced results opposite to those expected by Moscow. By 1950 it was clear not only that the fourth and fifth of the original Soviet proposals stood no chance of acceptance by the West, but that it would be hard to expect the West to stick to its own original principles in view of the deterioration of international security. Under these circumstances no surprise was registered in the West when, on April, 27, 1950, Turkey "finally and conclusively" rejected Moscow proposals for joint Soviet-Turkish control of the Straits. With this act any further debate on revision of the Montreux Convention seemed to be closed for the foreseeable future.

THE SUEZ CANAL

The Suez Canal is another strategic waterway in the Middle East, which though much younger than the Turkish Straits has equaled, if not actually surpassed, them in international importance.

The Canal was opened in 1869. Its construction took a full ten years. The technical problems attending this construction were numerous and diverse though not so difficult as those attending the digging of the Panama Canal. They were definitely overshadowed by the political problems, which from the very beginning made the canal an object of intense international rivalry.[7]

The Concession

The canal owed its inception to a former French consular official in Egypt, Ferdinand de Lesseps, who turning to his advantage an old friendship with Mohammed Said Pasha, viceroy of Egypt, obtained from him on November 30, 1854, a concession to construct a canal that would link the Mediterranean with the Red Sea, and to create an international company to administer it. The concession was to be valid for ninety-nine years from the date of the opening of the canal, after which time the canal would become the property of the Egyptian government. The latter would then pay the company an indemnity for its mobile properties, to be fixed by friendly negotiations or, lacking an agreement, by arbitration. The Egyptian government was to receive from the company 15 per cent of the net annual profits apart from the dividends that might accrue to it as owner of a number of the company's shares. Navigation in the canal was to be based on the principle of equality of all nations. This concession was succeeded on January 5, 1856, by a new one which contained more detailed provisions concerning the rights and obligations of Egypt and the company toward each other. Thus, for example, the company was exempted from Egyptian customs duties when importing necessary materials, was authorized freely to use the mines and quarries situated along the projected canal route, and was obliged to construct a sweet-water canal from the delta of the Nile to cater to the needs of the workers. A clause in this new concession provided that four-fifths of the workers on the construction were to be Egyptian. This clause proved to be a double-edged weapon. While seemingly protecting the rights of the Egyptians, in practice it evolved into an obligation of the Egyptian government to supply the company with an adequate labor force. A viceregal decree of July 20, 1856, subsequently determined the conditions of use of Egyptian

[7] For a thorough treatment of these rivalries, see Arnold T. Wilson, *The Suez Canal, Its Past, Present, and Future* (London, 1933); Halford L. Hoskins, *British Routes to India* (New York, 1928); André Siegfried, *Suez and Panama* (New York, 1940).

labor. When the company began its construction work, large numbers of the Egyptian workers were actually conscripted as forced labor, and it was only in 1866 that a new convention between Egypt and the company released the Egyptian government from this obligation on the payment of a considerable indemnity to the company.

Political Difficulties and British Intervention

The concessions granted to De Lesseps required ratification by the Ottoman sultan, and here the real difficulties began. Since the time of Mohammed Ali, France had enjoyed considerable influence in Egypt. England, although having important commercial interests there, could not boast of a similar position. But the situation in Constantinople was just the reverse. There British influence was paramount, especially after the beginning of the Russo-Turkish crisis of 1853, which led to the Crimean War. To obtain ratification for a firman granted by the viceroy of Egypt in favor of France or of a French citizen meant in practice to secure Britain's good will toward the project in question. As things stood then, Britain was definitely unwilling to show good will in this matter, and her government, headed by Palmerston, was opposed to the digging of the canal. This British opposition accounted for more than a decade of delay in ratification. Undaunted by these diplomatic reverses, De Lesseps went ahead with his plans. In 1858 he formed the Compagnie Universelle du Canal Maritime de Suez, the shares of which were subscribed for in a large part by the French public and by the Egyptian government, but with an understanding that an adequate part of the stock would be available to other nationalities. Then, still lacking ratification, De Lesseps launched construction work in the Isthmus in 1859. The next seven years constituted a period of nerve-racking activity for the originator of the company, who devoted his time to solving the technical, financial, and diplomatic problems, all strictly intertwined. In the meantime his good friend, Said Pasha died and was succeeded by a new viceroy, Ismail Pasha, an event which greatly complicated De Lesseps' task. Finally, having overcome most of the difficulties and, especially, having neutralized British opposition, De Lesseps secured a new convention with Ismail on January 30, 1866. This convention was ratified on March 19, 1866, by the sultan. The convention confirmed the former viceregal firman, adding some new provisions. Noteworthy among them was Article 16, which stated that the Compagnie Universelle was an Egyptian corporation

489

and as such was to be subject to the laws and customs of the country. It provided, however, for the application of French law on corporations to the company.

The inauguration of the canal three years later, celebrated in the presence of many crowned heads of Europe and the elite of European statesmen, was a moment of great personal triumph for De Lesseps. By that time the British attitude toward the canal had radically changed. Instead of opposing it, Britain became very much interested in the canal as a commercial and strategic route. As a result of the financial difficulties of his treasury, Khedive [8] Ismail in 1875 decided to sell his stock in the company. This amounted to 172,602 shares, which were placed on the European market. Disraeli, prime minister of Britain, promptly decided to purchase them. Lacking parliamentary authorization (Parliament was then in recess), he borrowed 100,000,000 francs from the banking house of Rothschild, instructing the latter to effect the purchase. Thus one of the boldest financial and political transactions in the world's history was made.

The purchase of Egypt's shares made Britain an important shareholder, although a majority of the shares still belonged to the French and politically the canal was under Turkish-Egyptian sovereignty. This situation underwent a radical change when Britain occupied Egypt in 1882. While Arabi Pasha's revolt supplied an excuse for this move, the occupation was largely due to Britain's desire to control the Suez Canal, this new strategic link in her imperial communications.

The Constantinople Convention

In 1888 nine major powers—France, Germany, Austria-Hungary, Spain, Britain, Italy, the Netherlands, Russia, and Turkey—concluded a convention in Constantinople defining the international status of the Suez Canal. Article 1 of the convention decreed that the Suez Canal must remain free and open to merchant and war vessels in time of war as well as in time of peace. The signatories pledged not to violate this provision and never to subject the canal to a blockade. According to further articles, hostilities in the canal were definitely forbidden, and this provision extended to the Canal's entrance ports and the waters within three maritime miles around the latter. Belligerents were not forbidden to use the canal for transit purposes but were to be subject to various restrictions in order to avert hostilities in canal waters. Article 10 of the convention gave Turkey and Egypt

[8] A new title accorded the viceroys of Egypt by the sultan in 1867.

the right to take measures as might be necessary for their defense and for the maintenance of public order. This provision was hedged with the reservation, expressly stated in Article 11, that these measures must not obstruct the free use of the canal. No fortifications were allowed in the Canal Zone. Article 14 made it clear that the principle of free navigation should be permanent and not limited to the duration of the concession.[9] Thus the Constantinople Convention proclaimed the principle of free navigation in the canal for all nations, without, however, providing for the neutrality of either the Canal Zone or of Egypt as a proprietary power. This explains why there seemed to be no legal incompatibility between the British occupation of Egypt and the principle of free passage. In practice, however, it meant that henceforth Britain had become a guardian of the Suez Canal and that in case of war with other powers she would close the canal to their ships, regardless of the legal aspects of such a move.

Experience of Two World Wars

The First World War supplied evidence that such was the case, and the same can be said of the Second World War. Britain's enemies were refused access to the canal on both occasions. Whereas during the First World War Britain freely used the canal for her own purposes, during the Second enemy aviation and submarine activity in the Mediterranean and south of the Red Sea made navigation in the canal a hazardous affair for the Allied navies. This was true despite the fact that the canal was closed as a result of enemy air activity only seventy-six days throughout the whole of the Second World War. It is worth noting that during both World Wars Britain initially attempted to comply with the provisions of free passage and non-blockade of the canal by seizing enemy ships or searching neutral ships suspected of carrying contraband cargo, not in the canal proper but in the open sea just beyond the convention-provided three-mile limit. For the purpose of search these ships were usually escorted to Alexandria, whence—if neutral—they were permitted to sail freely to their destinations after having satisfied the British authorities. Eventually this practice was abandoned as inconvenient to both parties concerned. The neutral ships preferred to be subject to search

[9] This and other relevant texts concerning the Suez Canal may be found in Moustapha el-Hefnaoui, *Les Problèmes Contemporains Posés par le Canal de Suez* (Paris, 1951). This is a serious and exhaustive study, strongly tinged with Egyptian nationalism.

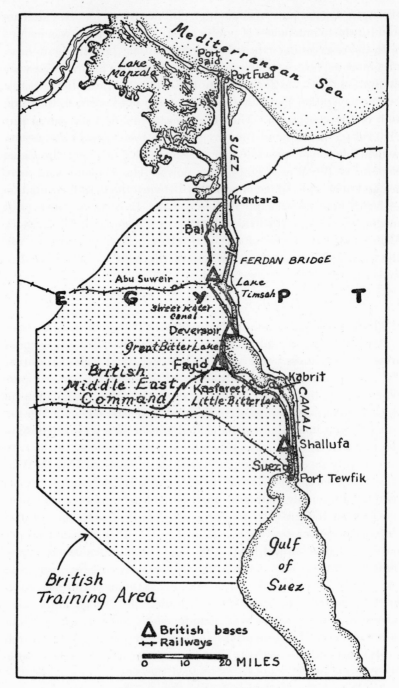

Map 7. The Suez Canal Zone.

at Suez or Port Said rather than to go off their course to Alexandria and thus delay their schedule.

Britain's *de facto* control of the Suez Canal obtained juridical confirmation by the Anglo-Egyptian Treaty of 1936. The treaty in Article 8 stated that the canal was "an integral part of Egypt," but that Britain was entrusted with the task of its defense, pending the mutually agreed upon ability of the Egyptian army to perform the task. It will be recalled from Chapter XI that Britain was authorized to keep 10,000 soldiers and 400 pilots in the Canal Zone apart from technical and administrative civilian personnel. Egypt undertook to build barracks for these troops and to supply them with water. At the time of this treaty, no one raised the problem of its compatibility with the Constantinople Convention of 1888, and it was generally assumed that the convention remained in force. It should be pointed out that at no time did the British assume direct responsibility for the administration of the canal traffic, which was left entirely to the company, and at no time did they deprive Egypt of her traditional right as the sovereign power to exercise police, customs, and sanitary controls over the canal and the adjacent area.

After the Second World War Egypt asked for a revision of the treaty of 1936 and for this purpose embarked upon negotiations with Britain, negotiations which failed and which in 1947 led to the placing of the Anglo-Egyptian dispute before the United Nations Security Council (see Chapter XI). Inasmuch as the Security Council was unable to reach any decision in the matter, the legal status of the canal remained unchanged.

Repercussions of the War in Palestine

The Palestinian war of 1948 brought the Suez Canal once again to the fore in international affairs. Egypt, as a belligerent, applied various restrictive measures against enemy ships and against neutral ships carrying contraband of war. These measures were based on Military Proclamation No. 5, issued by the Egyptian government in the early summer of 1948 and instituting a regime of inspection of ships in Alexandria, Port Said, and Suez. This proclamation, soon followed by further regulations concerning customs inspection and prize courts, did not differ from similar decrees issued, with the full approval of Egypt's British ally, between 1939–1945, which were designed to control enemy and neutral shipping during the Second World War. Although these measures interfered with normal naviga-

493

tion through the Suez Canal, no protests were raised by foreign maritime powers. It was silently admitted that Egypt, at war with Israel, was within her rights to adopt measures of self-defense and did not violate the Suez Canal Convention of 1888.

The Egyptian-Israeli armistice concluded at Rhodes on February 24, 1949, put an end to the hostilities and ushered in a new era of peaceful coexistence for the two states. By two regulations—of July 21 and of September 14, 1949—Egypt relaxed her controls over canal shipping but did not abolish them altogether. The September regulation, confirmed by a royal decree of February 6, 1950, limited the list of merchandise destined for Israel and liable to seizure by the Egyptian authorities. This list included the following six items: (1) arms and war materials; (2) chemical and pharmaceutical materials, which might be utilized in chemical warfare; (3) fuel in all forms; (4) airplanes and their spare parts; (5) tractors and motor vehicles for military use; and (6) currencies, gold, silver, and materials necessary to manufacture money.[10]

All ships, regardless of their flags, which were found to carry the above-mentioned cargo with Israel as the direct or indirect destination, risked the danger of confiscation of the forbidden items by Egyptian prize courts. Search and inspection could be applied to all ships passing through the canal even if their destination was clearly not Israel. The Egyptian government suspected certain vessels and shipping lines of directing their cargo to Israel by a roundabout route. For this reason, Egyptian authorities drew up a list of suspect ships, shipping companies, and ports and applied to the ships in question sterner measures of search. This interference with international shipping had no parallel in peacetime. It was applied with particular thoroughness to the tankers carrying crude or refined oil from the region east of the Red Sea to Mediterranean ports and greatly affected the supply of oil to Israel. As a result, the predominantly British-owned Haifa refinery remained idle, and after considerable delay could be put back into partial operation only by supplies of crude oil from Venezuela. Britain protested in Cairo against this Egyptian interference, pointing out that not only Israel's but also other countries' interests were involved, and that the Egyptian action had harmful effects on the economic development of states in no way connected with the Egyptian-Israeli dispute. Britain was not the only country to voice disapproval. Nine other important maritime nations,

[10] *Ibid.*, p. 203.

namely, Australia, Denmark, France, Italy, the Netherlands, Norway, South Africa, Sweden, and the United States, also lodged formal protests with the Egyptian government. British annoyance over the Egyptian behavior considerably increased when on July 1, 1951, an Egyptian corvette detained and boarded a British freighter, *Empire Roach*, in the Gulf of Akaba, not far from the Sinai coast. According to the British version the Egyptians behaved in a conspicuously un-ceremonious way, ordered the British crew to stay below the decks for thirteen hours, looted the ship's stores, stole £200 worth of goods, and wrecked the ship's radio. The ship was carrying supplies to the Jordanian port of Akaba at the head of the Gulf. Egypt maintained that she was within her rights in searching the British vessel because of the suspicion that the latter was heading toward the new Israeli harbor, Port Elat, situated very near Akaba, and because the search was made in Egyptian territorial waters.[11]

The Suez Canal Issue before the United Nations

Although not directly connected with Suez Canal traffic, this incident contributed to the deterioration of the already strained relations between Egypt and the major maritime powers and proved to be a turning point in their attitudes. Profiting from this state of mind, Israel on July 12, 1951, brought a complaint against Egypt before the United Nations Security Council. Israel's complaint included three counts. According to Israel, Egypt had violated (1) international law by exercising the rights of belligerency in time of peace; (2) the armistice of February 24, 1949; and (3) the Suez Canal Convention of 1888. The Security Council considered the matter between July 26 and September 1. The Egyptian delegate defended his country's behavior by repudiating each of the three contentions. First, he argued that the armistice was not yet a peace treaty and that Egypt was therefore still technically at war with Israel. Consequently, she was entitled to exercise the rights of a belligerent. Secondly, he claimed that the armistice put an end only to active military hostilities

[11] In subsequent years other incidents of this sort occurred, one of them involving Egyptian firing on an American vessel carrying a cargo of grain to Jordan. The difficulty stemmed from the fact that the only navigable channel leading into the Gulf of Akaba was located between Tiran Island and the Sinai coast, within Egyptian territorial waters. Whether or not such a channel should be considered as an international waterway, free of any restrictions that Egypt as a sovereign riparian state might want to impose, remained a moot question. There seemed to be no precedent, except for the general rules of international law, which could serve as a guide with regard to traffic in this disputed waterway.

but did not forbid the parties to apply economic measures. Moreover, the Egyptian delegate asserted that Israel had violated the armistice by expelling peaceful Arab populations across the Egyptian border, by raiding certain localities in the neutral frontier zone, and by illegally attacking Egyptian territory. He also pointed to the still unresolved problem of the Arab refugees, which in his opinion could hardly permit the existing Arab-Israeli relations to be considered as a peace. Thirdly, he asserted that the convention of 1888 specifically allowed Egypt to take self-protective measures in the Canal Zone, and that despite these measures freedom of navigation through the canal remained unimpaired, the volume of traffic actually increasing by leaps and bounds.

In the ensuing debate, representatives of Britain, France, and the United States supported Israel, at the same time attempting to reach some amicable settlement with Egypt. Owing to the latter's intransigence, however, the three above-mentioned powers felt compelled to submit a resolution condemning Egypt for her restrictions imposed on the passage of ships through the Suez Canal. During most of the debate (i.e., for six weeks) the Soviet delegate remained enigmatically silent; just before the vote was to be taken, he requested a week's delay in order to consult his government. This was accorded to him. On September 1, 1951, the resolution was submitted to a vote, which resulted in eight affirmative ballots (Brazil, Ecuador, France, the Netherlands, Turkey, the United States, the United Kingdom, and Yugoslavia) and three abstentions (China, India, and the USSR). Thus the resolution was adopted.[12] Specifically the resolution said that the armistice agreement contemplated "the return of permanent peace in Palestine," and that no party could reasonably assert that it was actively a belligerent two and one-half years after the armistice; invoked the opinions of Dr. Ralph Bunche and General Riley, chief of staff of the Truce Supervision Organization, in support of this thesis; found the Egyptian practices unjustified; and called "upon Egypt to terminate the restrictions on the passage of international commercial shipping and goods through the Suez Canal wherever bound, and to cease all interference with such shipping beyond that essential to the safety of shipping in the Canal itself and to the observance of the international conventions in force." [13]

[12] For a verbatim record of these proceedings, see *United Nations, Security Council, General,* S/PV. 549–558, July 26–Sept. 1, 1951.
[13] The full text is quoted in *Middle Eastern Affairs,* Aug.–Sept., 1951.

Despite this resolution Egypt persisted in her policy of interference, as a result of which the matter was repeatedly brought to the attention of the United Nations in subsequent years. In an apparent attempt to force the issue Israel in September 1954 sent her merchant vessel *Bat Galim* through the Canal via the Suez Gulf. In due course the ship was seized by the Egyptians and her crew detained. After a few months first the crew and then the ship were released, but the seizure once again underlined Egypt's contention that she was technically at war with Israel and that she would not relax her restrictive regulations with respect to maritime traffic with an enemy.

Relations between Egypt and the Suez Canal Company

The relations between the government and the company had been regulated by the original acts of concession. These acts were modified subsequently by numerous conventions of which there were over seventy between 1866 and 1937. Among them, three were of particular importance:

1) By a convention of March 21, 1880, the Egyptian government ceded its right to 15 per cent of the company's net profits to Crédit Foncier de France, which in turn founded a special company to distribute the shares. This cession was due to the disastrous state of Egyptian finances.

2) By a convention of 1920, it was agreed to include the living quarters of personnel in the position described as material and machines in the original acts of the concession. This meant an increase in the future indemnity to be paid by the Egyptian government to the Suez Canal Company at the time of the expiration of the concession.

3) Following the Anglo-Egyptian treaty and the abolition of the capitulations, the government and the company in 1936–1937 concluded a convention regulating a number of items such as customs exemptions, the maintenance of Ismailia Municipality and the use of fresh water. This convention provided, moreover, for the annual payment of £E300,000 by the company to Egypt, thus giving the latter a financial stake in the Suez Canal for the first time since 1880.

In 1947 the Egyptian parliament passed a law on corporations operating in Egypt. The law provided that at least 40 per cent of the members of the boards of directors of such corporations must be

497

Egyptians; also the personnel of corporations must be 75 per cent Egyptian and receive at least 65 per cent of the total payroll. In special cases, the law gave discretionary power to the minister of commerce and industry to allow exceptions to this rule. The law was to go into force within the next three years. Inasmuch as the Suez Canal Company enjoyed a special status, the company and the government opened negotiations in order to reconcile the provisions of the law with the company's interests. After several months' negotiations the parties reached an agreement which, on March 7, 1949, was formally embodied in a convention ratified by the Egyptian parliament. This convention introduced three main modifications into the company's status:

1) The company was gradually to "Egyptianize" its personnel. The administrative employees, except pilots and the maritime personnel, were to conform to the 1947 law before the end of the concession. As regards the board of directors, its number had been thirty-two prior to 1949, and it was composed of nineteen Frenchmen, ten Britons, one Dutchman, and two Egyptians. Their terms of office extended for eight years and they were eligible for reappointment. The new convention provided for an immediate additional appointment of two Egyptians, thus raising their number to four, with the understanding that it should be raised to seven by 1964. The number of foreign members of the board was to be thirty, and was to include eighteen Frenchmen, ten Britons, one Dutchman, and—an innovation—one American.

2) The company agreed to pay the Egyptian government 7 per cent of its gross annual profit, in any case not less than £E350,000. (This amounted to £E805,000 for the year 1948 alone.) By this arrangement, the Egyptian government has again become a partner, having an interest in the success of the enterprise.

3) The company also agreed to exempt from the canal toll charges small-scale shipping (mostly low-tonnage barges and other craft flying the Egyptian flag). This concession was estimated as being worth £E50,000 per year to Egypt.

The 1949 convention laid a new basis for the relationship between the government and the company with every likelihood that it would remain in force until November 17, 1968, the date of the expiration of the concession. The convention was not greeted in Egypt with unanimous enthusiasm despite the new profits accruing to the Egyptian treasury. Fuad Serag ed-Din Pasha, secretary general of the

Wafd Party, and later minister of interior in the Nahas cabinet, voiced profound criticism of the convention in the parliament. He complained that the convention practically disregarded the Egyptian law on corporations and said that the government instead of negotiating should have simply demanded that the company comply with that law. He pointed out that the number of the company's employees as of December 31, 1948, was 640, of which the foreigners constituted about 75 per cent and the Egyptians barely 25 per cent. Moreover, these Egyptians received only 15 per cent of the total payroll. He also stressed that the 25 per cent were not native Egyptians but naturalized foreigners who, after the abolition of capitulations, hastily acquired Egyptian citizenship as a protective measure. Fuad Serag ed-Din criticized also the government's weakness in agreeing to four instead of thirteen Egyptian members of the board, the latter number corresponding to the provisions of the law on corporations.

These criticisms elicited a reply from François Charles-Roux, chairman of the board of the company, in a statement made at a meeting of the shareholders in Paris. The chairman stated that the company had always had an exceptional character and that it had always operated under a convention. He pointed out that the preceding convention, concluded in 1936–1937, bore witness to the recognition by the Egyptian government of this special status. Hence it was logical for both parties to negotiate a new agreement in 1949. He stressed that the new convention had the virtue of slow adaptation to the new conditions, which would avert any upsets in the smooth functioning of the Suez Canal service. Provisions for the "Egyptianization" of personnel would apply only to future personnel and not to employees already on the job.

By ratifying the 1949 convention, Egypt committed herself to its terms until the end of the concession. This was the legal situation. Yet it would be unwise to underestimate such criticism as that mentioned above, which emanated from a prominent leader of the most powerful nationalist party in Egypt. It meant that Egyptian nationalists were eager to find fault with the new settlement and, granted an opportunity, might be tempted to give forceful expression to their views.

From the economic standpoint business in the canal was excellent after the Second World War. After the end of hostilities, traffic in the canal steadily increased until in 1950 it reached an all-time high of nearly 82,000,000 net tons, of which the tankers, light and loaded,

499

accounted for over 52,000,000 tons. This was a considerable increase over the nearly 69,000,000 tons in 1949, which in turn represented a 25 per cent increase over the preceding years.[14] The Palestinian war and the opening in 1950 of the Trans-Arabian pipeline across the desert introduced some complicating factors into the company's business, but did not deter it from steady expansion.

The conclusion in 1954 of a new Anglo-Egyptian agreement regarding the Suez Canal base and the expected expiration of the Suez Canal Company concession in 1968 were likely to pose major problems of a political and economic nature to Egypt and other powers. By virtue of the new Suez base agreement Egypt was to regain military control of the Canal by June 19, 1956, and thus become the sole guardian of the world's major strategic waterway. In view of the difference between the strength of Britain and of Egypt as well as because of the hostility prevailing in Egyptian-Israeli relations, this was bound to create an entirely new international situation. On the other hand, from 1968 on, Egypt was to become the only operator of the canal traffic. She would thus assume a responsibility for rather delicate technical operations, which hitherto had been performed by a body of specially trained and competent Westerners. These new political and technical arrangements, if allowed to materialize without major complications, such as, for example, a possible third world war, would certainly correspond to the deep aspirations of the Egyptian people and would remove a serious element of friction between Egypt and the Western democracies. How they might be reconciled with the strategic interests of the American-led coalition of non-Communist nations, only the future could tell.

[14] Periodic statistics of the traffic in the canal may be found in the *Bulletin de la Compagnie Universelle du Canal Maritime de Suez,* published regularly in Paris.

CHAPTER XVI

The Arab League

O N MARCH 22, 1945, in Cairo, seven Arab states (Egypt, Saudi Arabia, Iraq, Syria, Lebanon, Yemen, and Transjordan) signed the pact of the Arab League.[1] The League was born as the result of two influences: one was the desire for greater unity and strength, very popular among the Arabs; the other was British encouragement.

The time-tested device of all imperial governments has traditionally been to "divide and rule." How, then, could Britain reconcile her continuing supremacy over the Middle East with simultaneous support of an Arab movement for unity? This seemingly puzzling question can be answered only in the light of events that have occurred since 1914.

BACKGROUND FOR THE LEAGUE

It will be recalled that with the outbreak of the First World War basic British concepts regarding the Middle East underwent a radical change. Britain abandoned her policy of maintaining the integrity of the Ottoman Empire and replaced it with a plan to build up an Arab kingdom or federation. This Arab state would then inherit the

---

[1] On the origins and activities of the Arab League, consult Vernon McKay, "The Arab League in World Politics," *Foreign Policy Reports,* Nov. 15, 1946; C. A. Hourani, "The Arab League in Perspective," *Middle East Journal,* April 1947; G. E. K., "Cross-Currents within the Arab League: The Greater Syria Plan," *World Today,* Jan. 1948; "Arab Post-Mortem," *The Economist,* March 5, 1949; Maurice Moyal, "Post-Mortem on the Arab League," *World Affairs,* April 1949; A. D., "The Arab League: Development and Difficulties," *World Today,* May 1951; G. E. Kirk, "Independent Syria and Lebanon," *R.C.A.J.,* July–Oct. 1948; also Jean Lugol, *Le Panarabisme* (Cairo, 1946).

double function of the defunct Empire, namely, to serve as a friendly guardian of the British route to India and to act as a buffer against southward Russian expansion. With this end in view the British reached an agreement with Sherif Hussein that contained an explicit promise of Arab independence and an implicit recognition of the Hashimites as a ruling house. This agreement, however, was never fully implemented on account of Britain's wartime deals with the French and the Zionists. Moreover, the rise of Ibn Saud prevented its consummation in the Arabian peninsula. As a result, instead of achieving unity and independence the Arabs saw their lands divided and their freedom restricted. The Hashimites suffered grievous disappointments: King Hussein was ejected from his country by Ibn Saud; Faisal suffered a similar fate in Damascus at the hands of the French; and Abdullah, ready to assume the rule of Iraq, saw his hopes dashed and had to content himself with a barren tract of desert east of the Jordan River.

The peace settlement petrified the division of the Arab lands. In the interwar period Britain could implement her scheme of Arab unity only at the expense of France or the Zionists. This she was unwilling to do. Between 1939 and 1941, however, under the impact of the Nazi menace Britain regained her freedom of action. Finding it imperative to gain Arab good will Britain, early in 1939, sponsored the London conference of Arab states to consider the problem of Palestine. She thus set a pattern and a precedent for united Arab action under her protective wing. Moreover, soon after the conference and in response to Arab wishes, Britain issued the White Paper which was a blow to further Jewish immigration and expansion in Palestine. Britain took these measures with relative impunity because the Jews were unable to bargain with the two opposing camps. This time, due to Nazi policy, they had no choice but to stand by the democracies.

The second opportunity came in 1941 when the British conquered Syria and Lebanon from the Vichy French. Materially the British found themselves in a position to manipulate Arab politics throughout the Middle East because they were once again in military occupation of all Arab lands except Saudi Arabia and Yemen. Morally they felt no special inhibitions because of the French. France had not only failed them as an ally by surrendering and signing a separate peace with Germany but had gone so far as to permit Syria to be used as a base for enemy activities in the Middle East.

The conquest of Syria was the result of the dangerous situation which had developed in the Arab East in the spring of 1941. Axis influence was at its peak, and Britain felt an urgent need to make a bold bid for Arab friendship. At the end of action against pro-Nazi elements in Iraq, Foreign Secretary Eden declared, on May 29, 1941:

The Arab World has made great strides since the settlement reached at the end of the last war, and many Arab thinkers desire for the Arab peoples a greater degree of unity than they now enjoy. In reaching out toward this unity, they hope for support. No such appeal from our friends should go unanswered. It seems to me both natural and right that the cultural and economic ties, too, should be strengthened. His Majesty's Government for their part will give their full support to any scheme that commands general approval.[2]

Barely a week later British and Free French troops invaded Syria. With Vichy capitulation a stage was set for the next move on the political chessboard. British diplomatic action centered henceforth on two strictly related tasks: (1) to free Syria and Lebanon from French control, and (2) to encourage the union of the Fertile Crescent[3] under the leadership of the Hashimites. The achievement of these aims would fulfill the original British concept of 1915—at least in major part: the Syrians and the Lebanese would be friendly to Britain for their liberation, the people of the whole area would welcome the elimination of artificial political barriers, and Britain would enhance her position by supporting the dynastic interests of the Hashimites. She would, moreover, give an opportunity to such trusted friends as Nuri es-Said of Iraq to play a major role as empire builders and unifiers of the Arab world.

From 1941 onward British action was consistent and purposeful, and it was well synchronized with the action of the Arabs themselves. In this work British interests were well served by a powerful team of experienced Arabists such as Sir Kinahan Cornwallis, ambassador to Iraq; Brigadier E. H. Clayton, brother of the late Sir Gilbert Clayton, and a man who over a quarter of a century had come to know more living Arab statesmen than any other Westerner; Brigadier Glubb Pasha, commander of the Arab Legion; Sir Walter Smart, oriental secretary (and later minister) at the British embassy in Cairo, who was married to an Egyptian lady of a prominent family; Lord Moyne, British minister of state for the Middle East who replaced Richard Casey in 1944; and General Edward Spears, chief of the British

[2] *The Times* (London), May 30, 1941.
[3] Iraq, Syria, Lebanon, Palestine, and Transjordan.

503

mission to the Levant. General Spears in particular did his best to remove French influence from Syria and to establish friendly relations with Shukri el-Quwatli's National Bloc Party. Neither the De Gaulle-Lyttelton agreement nor official British denials could conceal the fact that, having to choose between Free French or Arab friendship, the British had chosen the latter. The situation was somewhat analogous to that prevailing in British-Zionist relations; the French, like the Zionists, could not bargain; they could only protest.

As to Arab action, the first steps were taken, as could be expected, by Nuri es-Said Pasha, prime minister of Iraq. In 1942 Nuri prepared a Blue Book in which he drew a plan of Arab union. It provided for an enlarged Syria which would include Lebanon, Palestine, and Transjordan and which would be linked with Iraq by a federative agreement. The whole would thus constitute a Fertile Crescent union. Such a union would have the merit of bringing together the countries that were near and similar to each other; it would be relatively small and therefore cohesive; and by its very modesty it would be a realistic first step in the gradual evolution toward a larger all-Arab entity. Nuri sent his plan to Richard Casey, British minister of state for the Middle East, and in 1943 circulated it privately among Arab leaders.[4] Nuri's action had Britain's full endorsement, and on February 24, 1943, Eden reiterated British support for a scheme of Arab unity. He added, however, that "the initiative in any scheme would have to come from the Arabs themselves" and that so far as he was aware "no such scheme which commands general approval has yet been worked out." [5] He thus referred to the fact that Nuri's proposals were not universally accepted. The truth was that they met considerable opposition in three distinct quarters. The first was Egypt, which feared that by the rise of a large united state in northern Arabia her own position of pre-eminence might be threatened. The second was Saudi Arabia, whose ruler was definitely opposed to any unification under the aegis of the rival Hashimite clan. And the third was Syria and Lebanon, whose "forty ruling families," prominent in the movement of the Arab awakening, preferred their republican oligarchy to a merger into a larger kingdom.

Thus Nuri's scheme suffered a setback and the initiative was taken over by Prime Minister Nahas Pasha of Egypt. Five weeks after

[4] It was printed in Baghdad in 1943 under the title *Arab Independence and Unity* by the government press but not released to the public.

[5] Quoted in Majid Khadduri, "Towards an Arab Union," *American Political Science Review*, Feb. 1946, p. 90.

Eden's statement Nahas presented tentative proposals for an Arab League to the Egyptian parliament. Nahas was motivated by three considerations: (1) he could not reject Nuri's plan without incurring the blame of opposing Arab unity; hence he had to come forward with some positive alternative; (2) he believed that an Egyptian-dominated Arab League might aid Egypt in achieving her national aspirations; (3) he was not devoid of personal ambition.

During the following eighteen months Nahas held conferences with the prime ministers or foreign ministers of all Arab states, who one by one visited Egypt. Nahas' concept of a loose league of sovereign Arab states gained wider acceptance than did Nuri's plan. Yet despite the nonradical character of Nahas' proposals, Saudi Arabia and Lebanon were very reluctant to commit themselves to any scheme of Arab unity. Lord Moyne's intervention finally convinced Ibn Saud that he had nothing to lose by joining the League, and Lebanon agreed to join under specific safeguards for her sovereignty.

Provisions of the Agreement

On October 7, 1944, in Alexandria, the seven Arab states of the Middle East signed a protocol in which they undertook, in the near future, to establish an Arab League according to a set of accepted principles. The protocol rejected earlier proposals for a full union, providing instead for an association of sovereign states, yet it stressed Arab unity in terms likely to evoke popular approval. Lebanon was reassured by a specific declaration guaranteeing her national sovereignty. The protocol, contained moreover, two significant provisions. One of them forbade the members to conduct policies detrimental to the League. And the other proclaimed the principle of nonintervention in the domestic affairs of the members. These two provisions were interpreted as a victory for British and Egyptian policies, respectively. The first meant that Syria and Lebanon would be prevented from concluding special treaties with France, thus confirming the gradual ouster—by British efforts—of France from the Levant. The second, by stressing the sanctity of the members' internal systems, was a rebuke to and a ban on the proroyalist unification propaganda hitherto conducted in Syria by the Hashimites. The latter was a diplomatic success for Egypt, and Azzam Pasha, future secretary of the League, hastened to remove all doubts on this point by declaring soon afterward that this provision had effectively shelved the Greater Syria plan.

When the Arab League came into being half a year later on the conclusion of the pact in Cairo, it was an even looser association than had been contemplated in Alexandria. The pact laid greater stress on the sovereignty of individual members and removed the ban on policies detrimental to the League. It provided for machinery composed of a Council and six committees, and it introduced the principle of majority decisions which would be binding upon those who accepted them. The Council was to convene twice a year, in March and in October, and also in extraordinary sessions upon the request of two member states. The League was to have a secretary-general, the first incumbent being named in the annex as Abdur Rahman Azzam Bey (later Pasha). Cairo was to be the seat of the League. The pact contained provisions concerning the pacific settlement of disputes but did not set up a collective security system. The main stress was laid on voluntary co-operation and consultation. Article 8 reaffirmed that "each member state shall respect the systems of government established in the other member states and regard them as exclusive concerns of those states. Each shall pledge to abstain from any action calculated to change established systems of government." But this provision was somewhat watered down in Article 9, which stated that "states of the League which desire to establish closer cooperation and stronger bonds than are provided by this Pact may conclude agreements to that end." There was no specific guarantee of Lebanon's independence inasmuch as the general principle of sovereignty covered this situation. In an annex Palestine, though not a member, was granted representation on the Council, and in another annex the League expressed its interest in the destiny and aspirations of those Arab countries that remained outside of it. Thus, the pact provided for a framework of Arab unity and co-operation. But in reality the League was created with a divided purpose. No real reconciliation was achieved between the Hashimite and Egyptian programs, and although the wording of the pact seemed to favor the Egyptian concept, neither party had renounced its ultimate ambitions.

THE LEAGUE AT WORK

A definite line can be drawn between the political and nonpolitical achievements of the League. In the nonpolitical field the League could pride itself on considerable accomplishments in the fields of cultural and technical co-operation. It sponsored exchanges of scholars and the conservation of ancient Arabic manuscripts; it called conferences of Arab engineers, doctors, archaeologists, and social scientists; it set up an Arab news agency; it prepared draft aviation agreements and other model treaties. It also reached decisions in the field of economic co-operation, especially pertaining to the boy-cott of Jewish goods, although in practice the latter measure fell short of expectations. But, as usual, the economic and social aspects were not decisive. It was the political action that really counted. It alone could determine whether or not the social and economic co-operation was in vain.

Politically there were two unifying factors: the problem of Pales-tine and the problem of the liberation of Arab peoples from foreign domination. Such points as the union of the Sudan with Egypt, the emancipation of Libya, and the freeing of Morocco could and did provide a platform for united political action and harmonious agree-ment.

Quarrel over Palestine

As to Palestine, she proved a double-edged weapon. So long as the League was not expected to do more than pass resolutions and make diplomatic representations the problem of Palestine elicited nothing but solidarity. But as soon as the League was called upon to act, Palestine proved a stumbling block, which almost destroyed the League.

The differences over action in Palestine in 1948 stemmed from the basic conflict of ideas between the Hashimites and Egypt to which we have already referred when describing Nuri Pasha's initiative. We must remember, however, that the chief standard-bearer of the Greater Syria plan was not Nuri but Emir Abdullah, who after Faisal's death had become the recognized head of the house of Hashim. In contrast to Nuri, Abdullah was impetuous and impatient. In July 1941, right after the ouster of the Vichy French from the Levant, Abdullah declared that the union of Arab lands was the official aim of his policy. Such an open avowal of his ambitions proved somewhat embarrassing to the British, who believed it to be premature and who preferred to prepare ground by Nuri's cautious action and by slow spadework in Syria herself. Soon after this declaration Britain's minister of state for the Middle East, Oliver Lyttelton, hurried to Amman to restrain Abdullah from further hasty actions. This action was not intended to deflect Abdullah from his objective as a long-range policy. Consequently, Abdullah sent his agents to Damascus and lost no opportunity to advocate his Greater Syria plan. On two occasions, in 1943 and 1947, when the Syrians were going to the polls, Abdullah made direct appeals to them for a union under his crown. The second of these appeals provoked serious protests in Egypt and Saudi Arabia, Ibn Saud threatening to revive his claims to Maan and Akaba. But the greatest deterrent to Abdullah's ambitions was the emergence in Syria of Quwatli's National Bloc, which was definitely resolved to preserve its monopoly of power.

Temporarily thwarted in Syria, Abdullah set his eyes on Palestine, where the impending changes seemed to offer an opportunity for aggrandizement. If he succeeded in securing control of the lands west of Jordan, he would make the first step toward the union of Arab countries and, as king of Palestine, increase his chances in Syria. Abdullah's position was strong: his Arab Legion was ready for action and a number of units were actually stationed in Palestine during the last phase of the British mandatory regime. In addition to this, Abdullah could count on the friendly co-operation of Musa Alami, representative of Palestinian Arabs in the Arab League, who during Haj Amin's absence had come to wield considerable influence in Palestine and who was known to favor the Fertile Crescent scheme.

Needless to say, such prospects were definitely distasteful to Egypt. Egypt decided that Transjordan's union with Palestine must be prevented at all costs and that the best way to achieve this was by encouraging the creation of a separate Arab state in Palestine. Saudi Arabia, Syria, and Lebanon wholeheartedly concurred. The next move was to bring the mufti of Jerusalem back from exile. Haj Amin had spent the war years in Germany and Italy. At the end of the war he was captured by the French, who placed him under house arrest in a villa near Paris. There was some talk in Allied circles of trying him as a war criminal, and Tito's Yugoslavia did list him as such for his aid in creating the Bosnian Moslem S.S. formations. But, before any such action could be taken, Haj Amin escaped from detention on board a Dutch plane and soon was welcomed by King Farouk in Egypt. His escape was engineered by the Syrian consul in Paris, Maaruf Dawalibi, who later, as a cabinet minister, went on record as favoring a pro-Soviet policy and neutrality in the East-West conflict. The role the French authorities played in this machination was not fully clarified, but they must have had a moment of gleeful satisfaction by thus embarrassing the British. In fact, it looked like a belated revenge for their ouster from Syria. The mufti had a vested interest in keeping Palestine a separate entity. He could muster a considerable following among Palestinian Arabs. By liberally providing him with funds and arms, Egypt reintroduced him into the Palestinian scene as a counterweight to Abdullah. The struggle for the spoils began long before Palestine was secured.

These rivalries and suspicions were reflected both during the arming of the Arab guerrilla forces and later during the war with Israel. Iraqi officers in charge of the Damascus training center did not want to issue arms to those Palestinian guerrilla leaders whom they believed to be the mufti's henchmen. On the other hand, Egypt and the mufti supplied arms to Kawukji's Liberation Army because Kawukji was anti-Hashimite, and they refused to arm those whom they suspected of connivance with Abdullah. As a result, the Arab population of Palestine was seriously short of weapons, and some of the larger centers such as Jaffa or Tiberias remained practically defenseless in the face of the total Jewish mobilization.

Likewise during the actual hostilities, co-operation between the Arab armies failed completely. Abdullah suspected that his rivals wanted his Arab Legion to take the brunt of the fighting and then, having bled it white, they would occupy Palestine with their own troops. For this reason he acted prudently, relying on his own strength and refusing to overextend his lines of communication by an advance toward the sea. By the same token Egypt instead of concentrating her troops in the coastal sector divided them into two groups, one advancing toward Tel-Aviv and the other toward Jerusalem. This division proved fatal. The Jerusalem force was badly defeated by Israel, and the Tel-Aviv force barely managed to maintain itself in a narrow strip near Gaza. Abdullah did nothing to relieve the hard-pressed Egyptians.

The breakdown of inter-Arab co-operation and the resulting defeat in Palestine could also be ascribed, in some measure, to the withdrawal of British support. For at least a decade Britain had conducted a pro-Arab policy in Palestine. The White Paper of 1939 and her attitude between 1945 and 1947 proved it. But this policy did not bring the expected returns, mainly due to Egypt's policies. By assuming leadership in the Arab League, Egypt not only threw out of gear the initial British-Hashimite plan of Arab unity but actually began to use the League as an instrument of her own policy. Contributing 42 per cent of the League's budget and securing a dominant voice through Azzam Pasha, Egypt exploited the League to foster her own anti-British tactics. When the matter of Palestine came before the United Nations in 1947, Britain was in a position to give substantial support to the Arab cause and, in fact, she did much to help the Arabs against the Zionists during the last phase of her administration in the Holy Land.[6] But, instead of reciprocating, Egypt chose this moment for anti-British intrigue by launching the inveterate foe of Britain, Haj Amin el-Husseini, into the Palestinian fray. The cup overflowed when Egypt, in an outburst of nationalist frenzy, brought the matter of British troops in Egypt and of the Sudanese regime to the United Nations. Premier Nokrashi's visit to Washington, in an attempt to replace Britain by the United States in Egyptian affairs, climaxed his anti-British campaign.

Under those circumstances British incentive to defend the general Arab cause in Palestine ceased to exist. Britain could help the Arabs in many ways. She could supply them with arms under the pretext that the Jews had violated the UN-proclaimed arms embargo. She could also, as a permanent member of the Security Council, prevent or delay the decision to impose the first truce on the belligerents. By halting the first bold thrust of the Arab armies the truce relieved certain hard-pressed sectors of Jewish defense and materially contributed to later Jewish victory. Moreover, her officers commanded the Arab Legion and, had they decided to rescue the Egyptian and Syro-Lebanese armies from their dire predicament, they probably could have done so. But the result would have been that large portions of Palestine would have fallen into the hands of the rabidly anti-British Egyptians, who would have hastened to install, with the Arab League's blessing, the mufti as the head of the new Arab state. Thus the anti-British camp in the League would only have been strengthened. This being so, the British thought it preferable to slow down the anti-Israel offensive and to secure some *modus vivendi* between Abdullah and the Jews. This meant that the only Arab-held part of Palestine would be the part occupied by the Arab Legion.

Such a policy, of course, hastened the defeat of the Arab armies other than the Legion, but it brought a sort of negative success to Britain. It demonstrated to the Arabs that the only Arab army capable of waging war was a British-trained force. It drove home to the Egyptians that without Britain's aid and advice their loudly advertised power was a hollow sword. It taught a stern lesson to the Quwatli Bloc in Syria, who, instead of being grateful for liberation, had

[6] See footnote to p. 336 above.

510

chosen to betray Britain and conspire with Egypt. In fact, the defeat shook the Syrian regime so profoundly as to make its continuance in power highly questionable, thus opening new vistas to British-backed Abdullah. This policy also greatly enhanced Abdullah's position: his Legion not only succeeded in the limited objectives it had proposed to attain but also proved its ability to march on Damascus and wipe out the Quwatli clique should Abdullah and the British decide to do so.

The split thus produced in the ranks of the Arab League was further deepened by the formation in Gaza, on September 20, 1948, of the All-Palestine government under Egyptian auspices; by the annexation of eastern Palestine by Jordan; and by the Syrian crisis of 1949. These three events were closely interrelated, but it was the latter which particularly threatened to upset Egyptian supremacy in the League.

The Hashimite-Egyptian Feud

We dealt at some length with General Husni Zaim's coup in Chapter VIII. The downfall of the Quwatli regime, which had always stood for Syrian independence, gave Abdullah a new opportunity to press his claim for a Greater Syria. The coup was apparently made by the army with the connivance of some younger groups from Aleppo. It would not be surprising if future revelations proved that Abdullah's agents had a hand in engineering it. It is significant that Zaim's first moves were for a closer union with Iraq and Jordan. Unfortunately for the Hashimites Zaim soon changed his mind and turned toward Egypt and Saudi Arabia. His abrupt aboutface was ascribed to clumsy handling of the affair by Nuri es-Said, who, during his visit in Damascus soon after the coup, treated Zaim too patronizingly.

With Zaim deserting Iraq and Jordan, Abdullah's star suffered an eclipse. But fate (or was it only fate?) came to his aid when, a few months later, Zaim was overthrown by Colonel Hinnawi, who, with Nazem el-Qudsi's People's Party, made the Fertile Crescent union his official plank. By the middle of December 1949, it looked as if the long-cherished plan of union were finally to be implemented, because the Syrian Constituent Assembly gave this matter high priority on its agenda. Colonel Shishakli's coup again frustrated these schemes. Shishakli's intervention did not settle Syria's destiny definitely. He had to share power with the Pan-Arab People's Party, and despite his attempts to keep Nazem el-Qudsi out of office the latter took advantage of his brief tour of duty as premier to submit to the Arab League, in January 1951, his scheme for a closer Arab union.

As a result of all these events Abdullah's relations with the Egyptian-dominated majority in the League reached such a low point that he decided to boycott the spring meeting of the League Council in 1950. The absence of the Jordanian delegation was promptly exploited by Nahas Pasha, who moved that Ahmed Hilmi Pasha, prime minister of the Gaza government, be invited to attend the session. Nahas' motion was adopted, but this led Abdullah to change his mind and order his minister in Cairo, Baha ed-Din Bey Tuqan, to appear at the meeting. Baha ed-Din was instructed, however, to abstain from participation in case the Council decided to discuss territorial dispositions in Palestine.

The minister's appearance at the meeting did not heal the breach, and Egypt actually proposed that Jordan should be expelled from the League because of King Abdullah's negotiations with Israel. Such negotiations had, indeed, been conducted in 1949 and early 1950 with a view to obtaining a five-year nonaggression pact, transit facilities through Israeli territory, and a free zone in Haifa for Jordan. They had, moreover, been preceded by the so-called Shuna agreement, secretly concluded late in March 1949 (prior to the Israel-Jordan armistice), whereby the Arab Legion had conceded to the Israeli army a belt of land five miles deep along the front line. Faced with this drastic action by the League, Jordan abruptly stopped the negotiations and on April 1, 1950, joined all the other Arab states in voting to exclude from the League any member making a separate peace with Israel. Even this concession to the majority did not save Jordan from further difficulties. On May 15 she was condemned by the League's Political Committee for her unilateral annexation of eastern Palestine. A new Egyptian motion to expel her won the support of Saudi Arabia, Syria, and Lebanon. The opposition of Iraq and Yemen [7] prevented this measure from materializing.

Furthermore, on Egypt's initiative the League drafted an Arab collective security pact. First adopted on April 9, 1950, by the Political Committee, the pact stated that aggression against any one of the signatories would be regarded as aggression against all. The signatories would then take all measures to repulse the aggression by

[7] The new Imam, Seif Ahmed, was grateful to Abdullah for endorsing the principle of legitimacy at the time of the crisis in Yemen. Abdullah was the first Arab ruler to send him a telegram supporting his right of succession.

armed forces, first notifying the United Nations Security Council and the Arab League Council. It also provided for a Joint Defense Council to be composed of defense and foreign ministers of member states and for a permanent committee of the chiefs of staff. On June 17, 1950, five out of seven Arab League members initialed the pact. Iraq refused to adhere because Jordan had not been present at the session. It was clear that Egypt treated the pact as an additional safeguard against possible Jordanian expansion in the direction of Syria and that, in order to preserve the *status quo,* she tried to transform the League from a consultative into a collective security body. This explained the reluctance of the Hashimite states to commit themselves to this new project. Eventually, on February 2, 1951, Nuri es-Said in the name of Iraq signed a revised pact after the more automatic features of collective security had been removed from the original draft. Jordan remained the only country outside the new system.

Abdullah's death at the hands of one of Haj Amin's henchmen in the summer of 1951 added a new complicating element to the already tangled picture. The removal of the main proponent of the Greater Syria plan was bound to produce far-reaching repercussions. The murder, true enough, redounded to the immediate benefit of Egypt and of other enemies of the Hashimites. But it was doubtful whether the plan of north-Arabian unity as such would be definitely buried.

In 1954–1955 Western attempts to build up a regional defense alliance led to further disagreements within the League. This time the spotlight shifted from Jordan to Iraq, whose premier, Nuri Said, was determined to link his country with Britain, Turkey, Iran, and Pakistan in what was to become the Baghdad Pact. Egypt, despite the change in her internal regime, strongly opposed this alliance. At an ordinary session of the Arab League Council, November 29–December 12, 1954, the general problem of Arab relations with the West came up for discussion. According to the premier of Lebanon (on whose testimony we have to rely in the absence of an official League communiqué), the following resolution was adopted: (1) The foreign policy of the Arab countries should be based on the Arab League Charter, the inter-Arab collective security and economic co-operation pact, and the United Nations Charter. This foreign policy does not admit any other pacts. (2) Co-operation between Arab states and the West should be subject to two basic conditions: (a) the West must help solve Arab problems equitably; (b) the West must help the Arab states to acquire the strength needed to defend their security and integrity against all aggression, such aid not to be prejudicial to their sovereignty. It was understood from other sources that Iraq made "clear and absolute" reservations to this resolution. In fact, her foreign minister, Musa Shahbandar, went so far as to declare in Damascus on December 22, 1954, that all the current agitation about Arab-Western collaboration did not make sense inasmuch as the Arabs had had, and continued to have, many ties with the West. In an attempt to prevent Iraq from joining the Western-sponsored alliance Egypt called an extraordinary meeting of the Arab League Council in late January 1955. Yet despite Egypt's insistence on censuring Iraq, the conferees came to no agreement, and the session broke up with opportunities abounding for further mutual recrimination. The latter has gained in intensity, especially after an abortive visit to Baghdad following the Cairo meeting by a subcommittee of three Arab premiers. Egypt argued that, by joining the Baghdad Pact, Iraq had violated the Arab League Charter, that she had broken Arab solidarity and become the tool of imperialism, thus ultimately serving the interests of Israel. Iraq's rejoinder was that she had kept other League members informed of her intentions, that the Charter did not prohibit alliances in self-defense, that her proximity to Russia and the existence of the borderland Kurdish minority required her to seek special safeguards, and that her partnership with Turkey and eligibility for Western arms supplies made the Arab camp stronger vis-à-vis Israel. Moreover, while criticizing the Baghdad Pact, Egypt herself had entered into a Suez base agreement with Britain, permitting the latter to re-enter her territory during the next seven years, without bothering to consult with sister nations. As for Saudi Arabia, argued the Iraqis, she had signed the Dhahran Air Base agreement with the United States, thus opening her territory to Western armed forces and forfeiting her moral right to criticize Iraq. The latter, stressed the spokesmen, instead of admitting foreign forces to her lands, had actually caused the evacuation of the two remaining air bases by the British.

Failing to secure a general censure of Iraq, Egypt concentrated on building a tripartite military alliance between herself, Saudi Arabia, and Syria, and by the beginning of 1956 she had succeeded in subordinating to her command the Syrian and Saudi Arabian military forces. With Saudi Arabia she countered a British attempt to bring Jordan into the Baghdad Pact by vigorous action aiming at the severance of such links as existed between Jordan and Britain in the political, military, and economic spheres. Her efforts were crowned with considerable but not full success. As a result of strong Saudi-Egyptian agitation and pressure Jordan was brought to the brink of revolution, and early in 1956 her new government promised not to join the Baghdad Pact. The abrupt dismissal and expulsion of General Glubb by King Hussein of Jordan constituted another signal victory for the Cairo-Riyadh axis. But Egypt and Saudi Arabia found it more difficult to persuade Jordan to give up British subsidies, despite formal offers of subsidies by them and Syria. By 1956 the League had experienced its second major crisis and to all practical purposes had ceased to function as an instrument of Arab solidarity. While Iraq found herself in a minority of one, Egypt had not succeeded in isolating her completely, such states as Lebanon, Jordan, and even Syria being unwilling to go on record as condemning Iraq for her action.

Thus, despite the imposing front, the Arab League was far from achieving the unity initially contemplated. The Palestine and the Baghdad Pact affairs clearly demonstrated how slender was the base of Arab co-operation and how the ruling groups permitted their selfish aims to overshadow the common interests of the Arab world. They also underscored the discrepancy between the aroused nationalist ambitions of individual states and their ability—or lack of it— to perform the minimum tasks for which a state is responsible.

The history of the League further demonstrated that no matter how much Britain was responsible for its birth, it soon ceased to be an instrument of British policy. In fact, by succumbing to Egyptian influence the League brought more embarrassment than benefit to Britain. It was not surprising, therefore, to hear London voices seriously questioning further continuation of the League in its present form. Suggestions were made to re-form the League on purely Asiatic lines. "The withdrawal of Egypt into Africa need cause no regrets," wrote *The Economist*. "From the purely Arab standpoint, it would produce a group far more homogeneous than that formed in 1945. . . . From Britain's angle, it would remove from a group of states that is not fundamentally anti-British, a leading member that has spread much ill-will toward Britain." [8]

On the other hand, Egypt in her self-confidence seemed to overstrain the cord: when, in 1950, she attempted to sway the League to

[8] "Arab Post-Mortem," *The Economist*, March 5, 1949, p. 422.

her own policy of neutrality in the Korean question, other members refused to go along. By her vituperative opposition to Iraq's policy of self-defense, Egypt seems to have made almost unbridgeable the rift that already existed within the Arab League. Under those circumstances, the admission to the League of two newly created Arab states, Libya (March 28, 1953) and the Sudan (January 19, 1956), made no perceptible change in the situation and could in no way be interpreted as strengthening the already moribund organism. In fact, each of the newcomers possesses her own political physiognomy, Libya being allied with, and subsidized by, Britain by virtue of a treaty of July 29, 1953, and the Sudan achieving independence in spite of the strong pressure by Egypt to merge with her in a single state. Much in Egypt's anti-Iraqi (and anti-Western) policy can be explained by the fact that her rulers, both old and new, must keep an eye on public opinion at home, the same being true of Saudi Arabia and Syria despite differences in their internal structures. But this is only further proof of the obstacles that lie in the path of Arab unity.

CHAPTER XVII

The Great Powers
and the Middle East

GREAT BRITAIN

OF ALL the great powers Britain alone had a tradition of supremacy in the Middle East. In establishing this tradition she encountered opposition and competition, but overcame both successfully. For a century and a half she waged a "cold war" with Russia, managing to keep her away from the Turkish Straits and the Persian Gulf. She eliminated French influence. And in two world wars she effectively frustrated German designs in the area.

Dictated by the necessity of protecting her imperial lifeline, Britain's supremacy had been exercised since 1918 by economic, military, and political means. Her trade with the Middle East and her share in the traffic in the Suez Canal were larger than those of any other country. British banks, shipping and insurance companies, chambers of commerce, tourist bureaus, and air lines held a predominant position. The currencies of Egypt, Iraq, Palestine, and Transjordan were based on the sterling. And Britain's control of a substantial share in the production and refining of oil accentuated this economic supremacy. In the course of the Second World War Britain became a debtor of the Middle Eastern countries to the sum of £600,000,000. These sterling balances contributed to further expansion of British exports to the area.

From the military standpoint Britain's control of the Middle East was almost complete in 1918 and during the Second World War.

In the interwar period she held certain areas directly as mandated territories. After relinquishing her last mandates in Transjordan (1946) and Palestine (1948), Britain continued her military predominance through a variety of means. There were treaty arrangements with Iraq, Egypt, and Jordan, the ownership of Malta, Cyprus, and Aden, postwar occupation of Libya, and naval control of the Persian Gulf. By virtue of her treaties with the above-mentioned Arab states Britain was entitled to keep 10,000 troops in the Suez Canal Zone, to enjoy priority in the training and equipping of the native armies, and to hold five major air bases: Amman and Mafraq in Jordan, Habbaniya and Shaiba in Iraq, and Fayid in Egypt. To this could be added virtual control of Jordan's Arab Legion, whose effectiveness had been considerably increased during and after the last war. A British military mission to Saudi Arabia completed this picture.

There was a period, in 1946–1947, when the British made a thorough re-examination of their imperial strategy and when new concepts seemed to be gaining ground. This was caused by two factors, namely, the lessons of the Second World War and the upsurge of nationalism in Egypt and Iraq. The war experience pointed to the great vulnerability of the Suez Canal and the sea lanes in the Mediterranean. It was only with supreme effort and many losses that British naval convoys could reach Alexandria from Gibraltar or Malta. Troops and equipment for the Middle Eastern campaign had to be convoyed around Africa. On the other hand, political ferment in Egypt and Iraq led some strategists to suggest that the preservation of British bases in these countries was not worth the popular hostility they engendered. The British General Staff seems to have given serious consideration to the transfer of British bases and installations to East Africa, where in the comparative security of Kenya, Tanganyika, and Uganda one could establish a powerful military center, not too distant from the areas of potential trouble and free of the political excitement of the Arab countries.[1]

This trend of thought found its reflection in Secretary Bevin's willingness to reduce Britain's military privileges when he discussed treaty revision with Egypt and Iraq in the postwar period. By 1948, however, these new concepts were definitely rejected, and Britain reverted to her old policy of maintaining military predominance in

[1] See Clifton Daniel, "British Seek New Bases to Defend Middle East," *New York Times*, Oct. 13, 1946.

the Middle East. This change was due to renewed manifestations of Soviet imperialism.

While Britain continued to think and act in terms of supremacy,[2] she realized that her ability to preserve it had shrunk considerably. At the end of the war her armies and her navy were supreme all over the eastern Mediterranean. But barely eighteen months later she abruptly acknowledged her inability to defend Greece and Turkey and invited the United States to take over this burden. Within a brief period a revolutionary change occurred: the United States began not only to share with Britain the defense of the Middle East, assuming as it did responsibility for its most vulnerable northern sector, but the American navy soon outstripped the Royal navy in its Mediterranean tonnage.

The mid-1950's witnessed a further evolution in British policy. Its principal feature was Britain's withdrawal from Suez and the Sudan and the shifting of emphasis to Iraq and the Persian Gulf. The transfer of her military base from the Canal Zone to Cyprus marked the virtual end of Britain's predominant position on the mainland southeast of the Mediterranean. Britain's role in shaping the Baghdad Pact as well as her forward movement in Buraimi and Oman indicated her renewed interest in the Persian Gulf, whose oil riches brought it again into a world prominence somewhat reminiscent of the situation in the beginning of the century. By this policy Britain seemed to divide the Middle East into western and eastern parts, with Jordan sitting astride the dividing line and gradually losing her character as a firm British stronghold.

British Political Action

Such, then, were the features of British economic and military supremacy in the area. But they would have been of little value if they had not been accompanied by political action. We have already

[2] Thus, for example, commenting on the conclusion of the revised Anglo-Iraqi Treaty of Portsmouth, *The Economist* of January 17, 1948, stated: "It remains important to remember that the orderly framework of British supremacy in the Middle East depends far more on mutual goodwill and interest than on any documents. British relations with the Middle East have just so much stability as the regimes which sustain them. In an opposition attack on the government of the day, Britain, the paramount power, is bound to be the first, as it is the most convenient, target. In Iraq opposition criticism of the new treaty is already loud on nationalist grounds. But this is a normal feature of relations between a great Power and a smaller ally. It need alarm no one provided the fact is kept constantly in view that Britain has a direct responsibility for the security, social advancement, and prosperity of the peoples of the Middle East."

described the role assigned to the Arab East in the British imperial strategy, and we have followed in some detail the vicissitudes of its implementation. Whatever else may be said about British policy, it is undeniable that it possessed three virtues that could not easily be brushed aside: it had a general imaginative concept, it was consistent and free of selfish partisan considerations, and it was ably executed by a fine team of experts.

It was characteristic of British policy that in relation to the native peoples it was devoid of crusading spirit and reforming zeal. Coming across an established social and economic order, the British rarely attempted to change it. Today they are often criticized in certain circles of the West for their allegedly reactionary practices and blamed for the backward structure of Middle Eastern society. But to be fair, those critics should remember British respect for the national culture and dignity of the peoples concerned. Whenever they had direct responsibility for the administration of an area, the British invariably gave it three things: (1) greater internal and external security, (2) sound finances, and (3) good roads and communications.

Yet, granting these truths, we must add that the British were much luckier in their dealings with backward than with advanced countries. Whenever their policy required contacts with patriarchal rulers or tribal potentates, it was invariably successful. But as soon as it faced a country with the trappings of Western democracy such as a parliament, a press, or a political party, it encountered considerable difficulties.

The deterioration of Britain's position in Jordan was a case in point. As long as this little country preserved its unspoiled desert character under the benevolent despotism of Abdullah, Britain enjoyed therein undisputed pre-eminence. But the addition of the west bank of the Jordan to its territory and the passing of Abdullah introduced new and disturbing factors, which by 1956 had resulted in serious eclipse of Britain's prestige in this newly awakened state.

Weaknesses of British Policy

This brings us to certain weaknesses of British conduct. It seems that the British government suffered from a somewhat artificial compartmentalization of its policies. It appeared to possess one policy for Europe, another policy for Asia, and still another policy for the Western Hemisphere. And while each might be good and commendable per se, they were not co-ordinated enough. The British-French relationship in the Middle East is a case in point. Britain's European policy during both World Wars demanded an alliance with France. In the name of this alliance Britain concluded the Sykes-Picot agreement in 1916 and the De Gaulle–Lyttelton agreement in 1941 to guarantee France's rights in Syria. But these deals did not fit well into Britain's Arab policy, and they were strongly resented by those responsible for its implementation.

A similar discrepancy, though less obvious, developed in British-American relations. The spirit of adolescent nationalism, so evident in the Arab societies in the last decade, largely owed its inspiration to American sources. The doctrine of self-determination, sweepingly proclaimed and making no distinction between degrees of national maturity, and the doctrine of democracy preached by American educational institutions in the Middle East were bound to produce a ferment which sooner or later had to find expression in politics. Yet for a long time the United States was not inclined to assume the attendant responsibilities, and Britain, jealous of her monopolistic position, did nothing to co-ordinate her own with American policies.

It was this adolescent nationalism of otherwise very ancient and cultured peoples that upset many British plans and that by 1949 posed the problem of whether or not the basic concepts and methods employed by Britain could stand the test of practice.

Britain's objective in 1945 had been to defend the Middle East from external aggression and to consolidate its strength under her own leadership. She tried to achieve these objectives by backing up the Arab League, by supporting the scheme of north-Arabian unity, by keeping her military bases, and by relinquishing her rule in Palestine. But by 1949, i.e., right after the Arab-Israeli war, it became clear that few of these objectives were attained. Thanks to the United States the Arab core of the Middle East found a protective though imperfect shield in the governments and armies of Turkey and Greece. But behind this shield there was a picture of shocking disintegration. The Arab League broke down under the impact of the Palestinian war, Arab rivalries, and the Baghdad Pact. Moreover, from its inception it hampered rather than promoted Britain's interests in the area. Egypt and Iraq suffered acute fits of xenophobia, refusing to accept revised treaties with Britain and eventually getting rid of the British bases in their territories. The British-sponsored Greater Syria plan suffered a series of setbacks as the result of Egyptian hostility, dictatorships in Syria, and the general distrust of the Arab masses. Abdullah's alliance with Britain became one of the reasons for his isolation, and the traditional British-Hashimite friendship has undergone a severe strain during the rule of his grandson, Hussein. By the mid-50's Saudi Arabia, a country formerly friendly to Britain, had definitely joined the anti-British camp, and her new king marked his hostility by banishing his late father's trusted friend, H. St. John B. Philby, and quarreling over the eastern borderlands. In Iran, under Mossadegh, Britain's position reached an all-time low, and it was only after tremendous exertions, in which other international elements were involved, that Britain was allowed to resume, in part only and under a different legal dispensation, her role in the Iranian oil industry. Israel, moreover, did not make a secret of her bitterness toward the nation that started her twenty-five years earlier on the path of statehood.

This was a sad record, and Britain's press and parliamentary circles did not conceal their disappointment. As early as 1949 a leading British periodical made an appeal for a re-examination of British policy and for a new approach toward the complex problems of the Middle East. Acknowledging Britain's inability to act alone in the defense of the area, it averred that

the physical resources that are required if the popular basis of non-Communist Governments in the Middle East is to be strengthened can only come, in the main, from the United States. . . . The new starting point of British interest in the Middle East must be a close Anglo-American understanding. No attempt to achieve such agreement was made in 1945, since understanding with America was not at that time the first objective of British policy in the Middle East. On the contrary there was an undercurrent of feeling in favour of excluding America from an area in which Britain had been dominant for the last eighty years. But the results have hardly been auspicious. The attempt, avoided in 1945, must be made today.[3]

What was said in 1949 could certainly be applied, with even greater emphasis, to the situation in the mid-1950's.

RUSSIA

During the past century and a half Russia had been the most persistent of Britain's rivals in Asia. The Soviet revolution did not change this basic pattern of rivalry; it only added a new ideological

[3] "New Start in the Middle East?" *The Economist,* July 16, 1949.

flavor to it. This Russian position differed from the British in this important respect: that while Britain was *in* the Middle East, especially after 1918, Russia remained *outside* it. What Russia strove for was to exchange these roles; hence her policy was a policy of change.

Trying to penetrate the Middle East and to dislodge Britain (as well as France), Russia used diplomatic, military, economic, and ideological weapons according to the need of the moment. Her first attempts after the revolution were both diplomatic and ideological. At the Congress of the Peoples of the East, held in Baku in September 1920 under the auspices of the Communist International, Russia put forward the slogan of liberation of the colonial and semicolonial peoples from the imperialist yoke.[4] The Comintern continuously harped on this theme, and at its Sixth Congress of 1928 prepared blueprints dealing with the doctrinal and tactical aspects of the revolution in the East. Their sharp edge was directed against the colony-owning Western powers, and no line of these "Theses" was repudiated even at the time of the Popular Front policy in the middle 1930's or during the actual alliance with the West in World War II.

The diplomatic action of the Soviet Union was synchronized with this ideological offensive and was designed to capture public opinion in the Middle Eastern countries and to secure the co-operation of their governments. The first round came in 1921 when Russia concluded treaties with Turkey, Iran, and Afghanistan. These treaties were well timed because their conclusion corresponded to the postwar deterioration in relations between Britain and the three countries in question. Turkey was then fighting her War of Liberation against British-supported Greeks, Iran was experiencing one of those paroxysms of xenophobia so characteristic of her emotional instability, and Afghanistan was frantically seeking to assert her newly won independence after the Third Afghan War. These treaties were all alike in that they used anti-imperialist phraseology calculated to impress the awakening masses of the East.

When it came, however, to their actual implementation, Russia's southern neighbors soon discovered that while the Kremlin was anxious to stir anti-Western moods, it was definitely reluctant to abandon the traditional objectives of tsarist imperialism. From the economic standpoint the new Russia was as eager to dominate the

---

[4] An account of the Baku Congress may be found in George Lenczowski, *Russia and the West in Iran, 1918–1948* (Ithaca, N.Y.), pp. 6 ff.

northern provinces of Iran and Afghanistan as was the old one. From the territorial angle the Soviets did not hesitate to use force to dislodge the Kemalists from Batum, to occupy Gilan in 1920, and to indulge in petty but aggressive bickering about the Atrek and Oxus boundaries with Iran and Afghanistan, respectively. Moreover, their much-vaunted support of self-determination proved to be no more than an anti-Western propaganda device that did not stand the test of reality when the Soviets brutally crushed national independence movements in the Caucasus and Central Asia. Finally, Soviet support of separatist tendencies among the Turkic-speaking groups across their southern border and the subversive activities of local Communist parties were not conducive to mutual cordiality. As time went on, relations between the Soviets and their southern neighbors cooled. This trend is perhaps best symbolized by the fact that, whereas between 1926 and 1928 Iran, Turkey, and Afghanistan had concluded a series of mutual friendship treaties under Soviet auspices and prodding, ten years later, in 1937, these same countries plus Iraq, signed the Saadabad Entente, implicitly directed against Soviet infiltration of the area. And this process of estrangement was far advanced in 1939 when Iran and Afghanistan entered into cordial relationships with Nazi Germany while Turkey veered toward an alliance with Britain and France.

There was practically no direct relationship between the Soviets and the Arab countries in the interwar period. The Arab East at that time was under the direct or indirect control of Britain and France, and there was no reason why these two powers should facilitate any contacts between revolutionary Russia and their colonial wards. Only with Saudi Arabia and Yemen, two states really independent after the First World War, did the Soviets establish diplomatic relations (in 1926 and 1928, respectively), and a Soviet commercial mission operated for a brief period in Sana. But to foment proletarian revolution in these isolated and remote regions where there was no proletariat and no strong anti-Western feeling was a losing proposition, and after some time Russia gave up her attempt to establish a foothold there.

Thus deprived of direct diplomatic relations, the Soviets acted through the Comintern and through the small and rather inefficient Communist parties in Arab lands and in Palestine. The official party line was to favor Arab nationalism and to side with it against Zionism. The latter, officially described as a petty-bourgeois capitalist ideology,[5] was considered an instrument of British imperialism and as such it was vigorously opposed both in Palestine and in Russia herself. This, however, did not prevent the Russians from sponsoring a Communist Party among the Jews of Palestine.[6] But care was taken to keep it separate from the Arab Communists in the same country.

Generally speaking, Communist influence in the Middle East in the interwar period was not great. Turkey, homogeneous, reformed, and nationalist, had her own ideals and definitely rejected the ideology so alien to her spirit. Iran and Afghanistan, with their conservative societies and their knowledge of Soviet intrigue among borderland groups, could not be expected to fall an easy prey to foreign ideological innovations. And the Arab peoples, physically isolated from Russia, conscious of the naval power which Russia did not possess, largely uninformed and devotedly Islamic, were not likely to become excited by the new Communist gospel.

Russian Activities during and after World War II

This situation underwent a radical change as the result of the Second World War. Britain's wartime pro-Soviet policy resulted in the lifting of the ban on Soviet diplomatic missions in Arab capitals, and from 1942–1943 Cairo, Baghdad, Beirut, and Damascus witnessed a real invasion of Soviet diplomats as well as commercial and cultural representatives. Once established behind the cloak of diplomatic immunity, these Soviet agents displayed considerable energy and versatility in their multifarious activities. They established contact with existing trade unions and helped to organize new ones. The Soviet-dominated World Federation of Trade Unions took an active interest in the Arab and Iranian labor movement and lost no opportunity to send visiting missions and to enhance the prestige of such Communist labor leaders as Reza Rusta in Iran or Mustafa el-Aris in Lebanon. A number of pro-Soviet dailies and periodicals sprang into existence in Teheran and the Arab capitals. The Middle East experienced a sudden growth of Soviet friendship societies and other front organizations ostensibly dedicated to the cause of culture, peace, or female emancipation. "Houses of culture," bookstores carrying Communist literature, exhibits of Soviet art, concerts and shows

---

[5] J. Stalin, *Marxism and the National and Colonial Question* (Marxist Library, n.d.), p. 289.

[6] See Martin Ebon, "Communist Tactics in Palestine," *Middle East Journal*, July 1948.

of Soviet artists, lectures of Soviet scholars, and Soviet motion pictures constituted just so many examples of Soviet infiltration. Iranian and Arab intellectuals and artists were conducted on free tours of Asiatic centers in the Soviet Union and lavishly entertained. And the co-operation of some "unemployed millionaires"—usually idle and frustrated heirs of large fortunes in Teheran or Cairo—was skillfully secured.

Soviet propaganda was like a good taxation system: it assumed various forms, sometimes open and sometimes well concealed but always pursuing its main objective. Of special interest was the encouragement given to national minorities and compact borderland groups. The Turkish-speaking population of Iranian Azerbaijan was an object of special solicitude, but other groups in a similar geographical position were equally subjected to Soviet blandishments. The Turkomans of the Iranian and Afghan northern plains, the Afghan Uzbeks and Tajiks, and above all the Kurds were consistently encouraged in their national aspirations. The creation in 1945 of a Soviet-sponsored Kurdish republic at Mahabad bore eloquent testimony to Soviet ambitions and tactics.

Courting as they did national minorities, the Soviets scored considerable success with the Armenians. This unfortunate nation, scattered all over the Middle East and unpopular with Arabs, Iranians, and Turks alike, successfully preserved its identity and culture on the basis of its loyalty to the Armenian Orthodox Church. The fact that the headquarters of its leader, the *catholicos,* was situated in Echmiadzin in Soviet Armenia gave Russia a chance to influence Armenian public opinion abroad. Moreover, the structure of Armenian society, which contains large numbers of skilled workers, mechanics, and intellectuals, all somewhat frustrated by discrimination and lack of opportunity in their foster countries, facilitated the spread of Communist ideology among their rank and file. Soviet propaganda among them was so ingenious that it even succeeded in causing the Dashnak Party to falter in its anti-Soviet stand.

In 1946 the Soviet Union loudly advertised and carried out the "repatriation" to Soviet Armenia of many thousands of Armenians living in the Middle East and elsewhere.[7] In performing this feat the Soviets turned to their benefit the peculiar psychological complexes of a race both persecuted and scattered. Hope for greater social

[7] For an account of this exodus, see Bertold Spuler, "Moskaus kirchenpolitische Offensive im Vorderen Orient," *Ost-Probleme,* June 2, 1951.

justice under the Communist system (enhanced by a somewhat naïve conviction that in the Armenian SSR things might look much brighter than in other parts of the Soviet Union), inner rebellion against the hostility of their adopted countries, belief in the myth of Russian invincibility, and a mystical longing to die in the shadow of Ararat—all combined to give this exodus the semblance of a mass pilgrimage. As to Russia, she scored a diplomatic success by proving that there were people willing to accept the Soviet system with enthusiasm; she enlarged her contacts with the Armenian community as a whole, using them when necessary for anti-Turkish propaganda; and through the new settlers she gained a lever of pressure on their relatives who remained abroad.

The many-faced character of Soviet political activity was well illustrated by the frequent recourse to religious propaganda. Ever since 1941 Soviet publications and broadcasts had laid great stress on the alleged freedom of religion in the Soviet Union and on the good will of the government toward Islam. In the later stages of the war and in the postwar period delegations of Soviet Moslems made pilgrimages to Mecca and paid visits to Iran. Care was taken to staff Soviet legations and embassies in the Middle East with a certain number of Soviet Moslems, sometimes of high diplomatic rank. These officials skillfully displayed their piety by making their Friday prayers in the most-frequented mosques. The degree of Soviet support to fanatical religious societies, such as the Moslem Brotherhood in Egypt or *Fadayan Islam* in Iran, remains a matter of speculation, but in view of their inherently anti-Western character, it would not be surprising if we should learn some day that Soviet money was at least partly responsible for some of their actions.[8] In Britain, at any rate, opinions were voiced that the trouble-making Fakir of Ipi on the Afghan-Pakistan frontier had been a steady recipient of Soviet subsidies.

The Soviets did not hesitate also to use the Russian Orthodox Church as an instrument of their policy.[9] Special efforts were made to bring to Moscow Orthodox bishops from the Middle East to attend the Holy Synods, whose business it was to elect the patriarchs. The aim of these tactics was to subordinate the Orthodox hierarchies in Turkey, Greece, Syria, Palestine, and other parts of the Middle

[8] Philip W. Ireland, "Islam, Democracy, and Communism," in *Islam in the Modern World,* a symposium edited by D. S. Franck (Washington, 1951), p. 65.

[9] Albion Ross, "Soviet Revives Tie to Levant Church," *New York Times,* July 17, 1950; see also Spuler, *op. cit.*

East to the supremacy of the Russian Church. In some cases these tactics failed, but in some—notably in Jewish-held Jerusalem—they succeeded.

The action of Soviet diplomatic missions was obviously well coordinated with that of local Communist parties. For some time, especially during the Western-Soviet alliance during the war, these parties enjoyed immunity from official molestation. In Iran the Tudeh Party grew in numbers and influence and so did the Communist parties in Iraq and Egypt. This artificial truce did not last long, however, and in 1947–1949 stern measures were taken against the Communists in Iran, Iraq, Egypt, and Syria. As a result, in some countries the parties went underground, but as events in Iran proved in 1951, they did not cease to be active.

Over and above these indirect activities were various manifestations of direct Soviet pressure. Apparently encouraged by the easy manner in which the West had surrendered eastern Europe to her mercy, Russia, right after the war, made a bold bid for the control of Iran and Turkey and for an opening in the Mediterranean. The chapters on Iran and Turkey have described in some detail how Russia engineered a rebellion in Azerbaijan and how she intimidated the Iranian premier to grant her an oil concession, and what demands she presented with regard to the Turkish Straits and the east-Anatolian border areas. We may add that at the inter-Allied Potsdam conference of 1945 the Russians requested a trusteeship over Tripolitania or Eritrea. Early in 1947 Soviet pressure, through Communist guerrillas, had become so dangerous in Greece that the President of the United States found it necessary to proclaim what amounted to a new doctrine in American foreign policy.

Although Soviet schemes against Greece, Turkey, and Iran had suffered setbacks as a result of Western countermeasures, Russia did not relent in her efforts to frustrate their defense plans and to exploit to the full the political difficulties arising between the West and the Arabs on account of the Palestinian question. The year 1955 witnessed a renewed Soviet offensive in the area—this time essentially diplomatic and psychological—aimed at penetrating the Arab East and nullifying Western benefits from the Baghdad Pact. The acute manifestations of anti-Westernism in Egypt, Jordan, Syria, and—to some extent—Saudi Arabia seemed to indicate that Russia had made impressive gains over her Western rivals.

THE UNITED STATES

Relations between the United States and the Middle East may be divided into three distinct periods: the first, ending with the year 1941; the second, embracing the war period, 1941–1945; and the third, after 1945.

In the first period, the United States displayed no steady political interest in the area. For a long time Protestant missionaries and educators were the only Americans to pay serious attention to the Middle East. Such institutions as the American University of Beirut (founded as Syrian Protestant College in 1866), the American University at Cairo, and Robert College and the American Women's College in Istanbul, as well as the secondary schools known as "colleges" in Teheran and Baghdad, bore testimony to the cultural links established between the New World and the ancient Bible lands. There were, in addition, American Presbyterian missions in a number of Middle Eastern countries which combined religious with charitable and medical work. All these institutions made America popular in the eyes of the peoples who had come into contact with them, and the fact that the American government had no political axe to grind in connection with their activities only strengthened the general good will toward American democracy.

The first instance of American political intervention occurred in 1918–1919 at the time of the Peace Settlement. Point Twelve of Wilson's Fourteen Points specifically dealt with the disposition of the Ottoman Empire, and the general principle of national self-determination enunciated therein made a profound impression on the literate public of the Middle East. Judging by their reaction to these statements, one might assert that the American crusade for a just and honorable world order evoked more hopeful expectations than the simultaneous social radicalism beamed from revolutionary Russia. Anxious to implement his principles, President Wilson sent two missions to the Middle East to ascertain the will of the people directly concerned: the King-Crane mission to Syria and Palestine and the Harbord mission to Armenia. But the play of power politics in Paris largely frustrated Wilson's designs and resulted in the compromises which only thinly disguised traditional European imperialism. Following Wilson's death and the repudiation of the Versailles Treaty, the United States withdrew altogether from world politics, thereby leaving the Middle East to its own devices.

Subsequent American interest in the area was of sporadic nature. The United States, in its concentration on economic issues as the only ones which seemed to matter, insisted on and defended the principle of the Open Door, especially with regard to the areas mandated by Britain. In 1924 this solicitude led to an Anglo-American agreement concerning equality of opportunity in Palestine. The discovery of oil in Iraq, on the other hand, led to a temporary controversy between the interested American companies and Britain over the spoils of pre-war Turkish Petroleum Company. This controversy was complicated by the fact that at the same time another American group, known as the Ottoman-American Development Company, headed by Admiral Chester, sought to ratify in Turkey its old (1909) concession which had failed in 1913 because of British and German opposition. On April 9, 1923, Turkey awarded Chester an exclusive mineral, railway, and oil concession which covered "twenty kilometers on either side of a 2,400 mile right-of-way, beginning at Ankara and going, by way of Sivas, Kharput, and Diarbekir, on straight through Mosul to the border of Persia." [10] The inclusion, shortly before the Lausanne treaty, of the controversial Mosul territory in this concession meant that the interests of the Chester group were bound to clash with Britain's claim to Mosul in her capacity of a mandatory power for Iraq. Somewhat earlier, in 1922, the Standard Oil Company of New Jersey had reached an agreement with Britain whereby it secured a 25 per cent share in Iraq's oil resources, thus acquiring a vested interest in Britain's control of Mosul. Both industrial groups looked, of course, toward their government for support, and for a moment it appeared that the United States might be drawn into an unpleasant political controversy. The whole affair remained in abeyance for two more years inasmuch as the Lausanne Treaty did not definitely dispose of the Mosul question. But with the award, in 1925, of the contested area to Iraq by the Council of the League of Nations, Chester's rights were automatically repudiated. This opened the way for a definite agreement between the American oil group and the British government, an agreement which had the blessing of the Department of State because it implemented the Open Door principle.

Apart from these economic issues the attention of the United States government was drawn to the Middle East in connection with the

[10] Benjamin Gerig, *The Open Door and the Mandates System* (London, 1930), p. 146.

Palestinian problem.[11] The Balfour Declaration of 1917, as we know, owed its birth to the influence of American Jews, supported by the friendly attitude of their government. But with the establishment of the mandate, which explicitly provided for the fulfillment of the Declaration, official American interest in Palestine somewhat slackened, it being taken for granted that the mandate had basically satisfied Zionist aspirations. Two other factors accounted for diminished American interest: one was the fact that the leadership of World Zionism rested in the hands of British (and not American) Jews, who were anxious to work with Britain; and the other was the fact that, until 1939, Britain had not drastically limited Jewish immigration into Palestine, thus allowing the Jewish national home to grow.

All in all, the political approach of the United States toward the Middle East up to 1941 could be described as one of indifference, good will, and a conviction that the area was a British preserve where no major American interests were involved. Even the entry of the American oil business into the scene, with its concessions in Iraq, Bahrein, and Saudi Arabia, did not materially change this aloof attitude.

During the War

During the second period (1941–1945) the United States suddenly developed multiple contacts with the Middle East as a result of the war emergency. The conduct of the war in this area ceased to be a purely British affair. American troops appeared in Iran to handle the supplies to Russia; they also came to Egypt and Palestine, mainly to accomplish various technical tasks connected with the American armor with which the British army was being equipped. The American navy and merchant marine played a vital role in conveying supplies to the Middle East theater. And the United States air force established a chain of bases linking North Africa with the India-Burma-China theater. This military tie with the area was strengthened by several economic measures: the United States extended lend lease to most of the Middle Eastern countries, gave active support and guidance to the Middle East Supply Center, and took an active interest in the interim arrangements concerning oil production.

[11] See Carl J. Friedrich, *American Policy toward Palestine* (Washington, 1944); for a general American policy toward the area, see Walter Batsell, *United States and the System of Mandates* (New York, 1925), and Harvey P. Hall, *American Interests in the Middle East* (Headline Series, No. 72, Nov.–Dec. 1948).

Mainly to serve American strategic needs in the Far East, the Anglo-Iranian Oil Company adjusted its facilities to produce high-octane aviation gasoline. And in 1943 Harold Ickes, administrator of the American petroleum authority, suggested active government participation in the projected pipeline through the Arabian desert. American responsibilities in this respect grew to such an extent that in 1944 the government found it necessary to appoint a high-ranking official, James Landis, as United States economic minister to the Middle East. It was significant that at the same time the government created the post of petroleum attaché for the whole region, attached to the American embassy in Cairo.

The government also grew more alert to the political problems of the Middle East. Colonel Donovan, director of the Office of Strategic Services; Wendell Willkie, acting as the President's personal representative; Ambassador Harriman; and a number of other highly placed persons visited the area during the war. Even President Roosevelt, although mortally tired after the Yalta conference, found time to devote a few days to a conference with Arab rulers in the Suez Canal Zone. The United States had shown friendly helpfulness to Saudi Arabia at the time of her economic crisis, and to Syria and Lebanon in their struggle for emancipation.

After the War

In the postwar period this increased interest in the Middle East expanded. Oil, Palestine, and the Soviet menace provided three avenues of approach. The spectacular development of oil production in Saudi Arabia and Kuwait, with American holdings in Bahrein, Iraq, and Egypt, brought home to American leaders the strategic importance of the region. The virtual repudiation by Britain of the Balfour Declaration, through the White Paper of 1939, and the attendant renewal of strife in Palestine placed before the United States the necessity of defining its position, the necessity being made more urgent by the fate of Jews in Europe and by the transfer of Zionist leadership to American Jewry. And, last but not least, growing Soviet expansionism compelled Washington in 1947 to take a clear stand on its political and military commitments in the northern belt of the Middle East and thus to define a new frontier of American security. The growing importance of the area found its eloquent expression in the inauguration, in 1949, of annual conferences of American diplomatic representatives in the Middle East, held in one of the area's capital cities and as a rule presided over by an Assistant Secretary of State. Similarly, the Middle East began to be mentioned with increasing frequency in postwar statements on foreign policy made by the President or the Secretary of State.[12]

While the United States could claim a considerable measure of success in lining up on its side Greece, Turkey, Iraq, Iran, and Pakistan, i.e., the countries of the Northern Tier of Middle East defense, it certainly had made little headway in the Arab world. Here American policy was not free from baffling dilemmas. In the first

[12] In presenting the Mutual Security Program for 1952 to Congress, the State Department made the following statement regarding the Middle East:

"The Near Eastern area is important to the security of the United States and of the free world. It lies athwart the principal lines of sea and air communication in the eastern Hemisphere. It is a land bridge between Asia and Africa, Soviet control of which would expose the African continent. It is a source of a prime strategic material, oil, the continuing supply of which is essential to friendly nations in Europe and Asia. It supplies three-fourths of the petroleum requirements of western Europe." (Quoted by *The Economist,* Aug. 4, 1951.)

In his foreign aid message to Congress on May 24, 1951, President Truman similarly stressed the great importance of the Middle East to the entire free world, adding:

"No part of the world is more directly exposed to Soviet pressure. The Kremlin has lost no opportunity to stir these troubled waters, as the post-war record amply demonstrates. Civil war in Greece; pressure for Turkish concessions on the Dardanelles; sponsorship of the rebellious Tudeh party in Iran; furthering of factional strife in the Arab states and Israel—all reflect a concerted design for the extension of Soviet domination for this vital area.

"There is no simple formula for increasing stability and security in the Middle East. With the help of American military and economic assistance, Soviet pressure has already been firmly resisted in Turkey and the Soviet-inspired guerrilla war has been decisively defeated in Greece. But the pressure against the Middle East is unremitting. It can be overcome only by a continued build-up of armed defenses and the fostering of economic development. Only through such measures can these peoples advance toward stability and improved living conditions, and be assured that their aims can best be achieved through strengthening their associations in the free world.

"To these ends, I am recommending $415,000,000 in military aid for Greece, Turkey, and Iran; a portion of this aid will be available for other Middle Eastern nations if necessary. I am also recommending $125,000,000 in economic aid for Middle Eastern countries, exclusive of Greece and Turkey for whom economic aid is provided as part of the program for Europe. This amount also includes programs of technical assistance to Libya, Liberia and Ethiopia, three independent states of Africa whose economic problems are similar to those of the Middle Eastern countries" (*New York Times,* May 25, 1951).

On his part, Secretary of State Acheson, in a major foreign policy speech delivered on April 18, 1951, warned that the Korean conflict must not "blind us to the less obvious, but no less critical, realities of the Near East" (*New York Times,* April 19, 1951).

533

place there was an incompatibility between the frequent declarations and deeds in favor of Israel, on the one hand, and the necessity of cultivating the good will of the Arabs, on the other. In fact, this incompatibility led to sudden shifts and contradictory moves. The White House, with an eye to internal politics, seemed to ignore the interests of Arab policy, while the Department of State was reputed to favor the Arabs as against Israel. These hesitations and fluctuations did nothing to increase American prestige. Indeed, much of the capital of good will, laboriously accumulated through decades of missionary and educational work, seemed to be wasted. As one observer phrased it, "The United States succeeded in four years to do what it took Britain thirty years, namely to antagonize the Middle East." There was, of course, exaggeration in this remark, but no doubt it reflected the dangers inherent in a policy which refused to follow a consistent line.

By the mid-1950's it was time for the American government and the American public to take stock of their achievements and failures, to reflect, and to adjust their policy both to the needs of the moment and to the realities of the Middle Eastern scene. That area has lost none of its importance in recent years, and it has apparently received high priority in the strategy of Soviet and Communist expansion. The nonexistence of satellite buffer states in this region makes localization of a war, such as occurred in Korea, highly unlikely. In fact, the Middle East is the only area directly adjacent to Russia which has not yet fallen prey to Communist imperialism. It is vital for the United States and its partners to defend the Middle East against aggression so as to keep it within the limits of the free world. While it is relatively easy to agree on this objective, the implementation is certain to encounter serious obstacles. To maximize defense possibilities in this area it is necessary to obtain the military as well as the political co-operation of all countries. The promotion of security arrangements, such as the inclusion of Greece and Turkey in NATO or the signing of the Baghdad Pact, undoubtedly points to the right military solutions.

In the political area, it is imperative to obtain, on the one hand, true co-ordination of Western policies and, on the other, the friendship or, at least, the friendly neutrality of the various states. It is in this sector that American policy has suffered its greatest defeats. For too long a time has the United States taken it for granted that certain areas of the world are to be considered integral parts of the

British or French Empire or spheres under their influence. Such a view might be justified if supported by two conditions: (1) that the areas in question accept their subordinate position without protest and (2) that the British and the French are able to maintain their control without major upheavals. The history of the Middle East from the First World War onward clearly proves that neither of these two conditions has obtained. The Middle East has been swept by a powerful wave of nationalism demanding freedom and equality and backing up these demands by struggle and sacrifice. Neither the French nor the British have been able to maintain control in this part of the world. One by one the Middle Eastern countries have gained statehood and independence, and the sad thing about it is that, almost without exception, British and French withdrawals have lacked grace and dignity. To continue, under these circumstances, to speak of "supremacy," as some British sources have done, is to be anachronistic, and there is no necessity for the United States to endorse this antiquated thinking. One can, of course, defend the Franco-British position by pointing to the existence of vital military bases in the areas in question, bases which have served the interests of American security. While their usefulness has been obvious, it still does not follow that they could have been secured only through imperial domination. It is conceivable, though not certain, that the same results might have been obtained through bilateral agreements between independent countries. In fact, American experience with Turkey and Saudi Arabia, two very different states but both independent, proves that a new approach might be successful. In contrast, the British base in the Suez Canal Zone ultimately became an almost self-defeating arrangement. The base was originally planned to defend Egypt against foreign aggression and according to the treaty of 1936 was not to contain more than 10,000 troops. In the last years of its existence it had to be manned by not less than 80,000 men, brought there to defend it against the Egyptians.

The increase in the number of British troops required in the Canal Zone points to another aspect of the situation, namely, the inadvisability of disregarding the attitudes of native governments and peoples. In the United States voices are sometimes heard to declare that we should write off most of the Middle Eastern peoples as politically unreliable and militarily weak. Reliability, however, is obviously linked to the over-all question of political loyalty. There

535

is no reason to expect loyalty from a group which feels that it has been treated disloyally by the West. The problem here seems to be to remove the resentments and create a basis for loyalty. The West has long acted on the assumption that certain nations possess military prowess and others do not. The performance of the well-armed and indoctrinated Chinese in Korea and of the Communist Viet-Namese indicates that our ideas about the martial qualities of certain ethnic groups require revision. Instead of rigidly classifying nations in this respect, it would perhaps be wiser to admit that high morale, superior weapons, and good organization are the real ingredients of military prowess and that none of these are beyond the reach of any group.

In conclusion, it may be suggested that, while the United States has a vital interest in preserving its partnership with the major members of the North Atlantic Community and in maintaining the network of bases that this partnership helps provide, it need not subscribe to the outmoded notions that have often characterized the policies of these powers. One may well ask whether the American ideals of democracy and self-determination have not too often been subordinated to expediency, thus robbing American policy of the moral advantage that it once possessed and that it might well try to regain in the present revolutionary era in the non-Western world.

APPENDIX TABLES,

BIBLIOGRAPHY, AND INDEX

Appendix Tables

I. Area and population of the countries of the Middle East

	Area in sq. km.	Population	Density per sq. km.
Afghanistan	650,000	12,000,000 [a]	18
Egypt [b]	1,000,000	21,935,000 [c]	22
Gaza Strip	202	300,000 [c]	1,485
Iran	1,630,000	20,253,000 [c]	12
Iraq	435,415	4,871,000 [d]	11
Israel	20,678	1,688,000 [e]	80
Jordan	96,513	1,360,000 [c]	14
Lebanon	10,400	1,353,000 [c, f]	130
Saudi Arabia	1,600,000	7,000,000 [d]	4
Syria	181,337	3,535,000 [c, g]	19
Turkey	767,119 [h]	22,949,000 [e]	29
Yemen	195,000	4,500,000 [a]	23

Sources: United Nations, Statistical Office, *Demographic Yearbook, 1954* (New York, 1954); *Review of Economic Conditions in the Middle East,* Supplement to *World Economic Report, 1949–50,* United Nations, Department of Economic Affairs (New York, March 1951).

[a] 1949 estimate.

[b] The area of inhabited and cultivated territory is 34,815 sq. km.; the corresponding density is 630.

[c] 1953 estimate.   [d] 1952 estimate.

[e] 1954 estimate.   [f] Lebanese nationals only.

[g] Excluding nomads and seminomads, estimated at 288,400 in 1945.

[h] Excludes swamps and lakes with an area of 9,861 sq. km.

II. Middle Eastern Petroleum Concessions [a] (Explanation of Abbreviations Follows Table)

Country and owner of concession	Date granted and/or revised [b]	Expiration date	Area in sq. miles	Per cent of total area	Year of first production
Aden Protectorate:					
Petroleum Concessions, Ltd. (I.P.C.)	Jan. 12, 1938 [c]		Mainland area of Protectorate except Amirate of Beihan		
D'Arcy Exploration Co., Ltd. (B.P.)	Feb. 1956		Kamaran Islands		
Bahrein:					
Bahrein Petroleum Co., Ltd. (SOCAL, 100%; after 1936, SOCAL, 50%; Texas, 50%)	1930 / June 19, 1940	1989 / 2024	100,000 acres / entire area	73.7 / 100.0	1933
Egypt:					
Sahara Petroleum Co. (U.S.)					
Anglo-Egyptian Oilfields, Ltd. (Egyptian, British-Dutch)					
Egyptian Oil Exploration Co. (U.S.)					
Gewerkschaft Vereinigte Borgholzhausen (Ger.)					
Société Cooperative des Petroles (Eg.)					
International Egyptian Oil Co., Inc. (international)					
Mobil Oil Egypt, Inc. (U.S.)					

Iran:					
William Knox D'Arcy	May 28, 1901	1961	480,000	76.4	1913
Anglo-Iranian Oil Co., Ltd.	April 29, 1933	1993	100,000	15.9	1913
(United Kingdom govt., 52.5%; Burmah Oil Co., Ltd., 25%; individuals, 22.5%)					
Iranian Oil Participants, Ltd.[d]	Oct. 29, 1954	1979 [e]	100,000	15.9	1954
(B.P., 40%; Shell, 14%; C.F.P., 6%; SONJ, 7%; Socony, 7%; SOCAL, 7%; Gulf, 7%; Texas, 7%; Iricon Agency, Ltd. [9 Amer. independent companies], 5%)					
Iraq:					
Iraq Petroleum Co., Ltd.	March 24, 1925	2000	32,000	20.5	1927
(B.P., 23.75%; Shell, 23.75%; C.F.P., 23.75%; SONJ, 11.875%; Socony, 11.875%; C. S. Gulbenkian, 5%)					
Mosul Petroleum Co., Ltd. (I.P.C.)	May 25, 1932	2007	46,000	29.5	1927
Basrah Petroleum Co., Ltd. (I.P.C.)	Nov. 13, 1938	2013	Remaining portion of Iraq except Khanaqin field	49.6	
All three companies of I.P.C. group	Feb. 3, 1952 [f] March 24,1955 [g]				
Khanaqin Oil Co., Ltd. (B.P.)	Aug. 30, 1925	1995	684	0.4	
Israel:					
Lapidoth-Israel Oil Co.	Dec. 25, 1951				

541

II. Middle Eastern Petroleum Concessions (*continued*)

Country and owner of concession	Date granted and/or revised	Expiration date	Area in sq. miles	Per cent of total area	Year of first production
Jordan:					
Transjordan Petroleum Co., Ltd. (I.P.C.)		1954			
Edwin W. Pauley Co.	Oct. 30, 1955	2010		33.3	
Kuwait:					
Kuwait Oil Co., Ltd.	Dec. 23, 1934	2009 [h]	6,000	100.00	1946
(Gulf, 50%; D'Arcy Kuwait Co., Ltd. [B.P.], 50%)	Dec. 1, 1951 [i]				
Kuwait-Saudi Arabian Neutral Zone:					
American Independent Oil Co. [j]	June 28, 1948	2008	Undivided half of Zone	50.0	1953
Pacific Western Oil Corporation [k]	Feb. 20, 1949	2009	Undivided half of Zone	50.0	1953
Muscat-Oman:					
Petroleum Development (Oman), Ltd. (I.P.C.)	June 24, 1937	2012	52,000 [l]	63.4	
Dhofar Cities Service Co. (Cities Service Oil Co. and Richfield Oil Co.)	July, 1953		Dhofar area		
Qatar:					
Petroleum Development (Qatar), Ltd. (I.P.C.)	May 17, 1935 Sept. 1, 1952 [m]	2010	Entire peninsula	100.00	1949

					1936
Saudi Arabia:					
Standard Oil Co. of Calif.[n]	May 25, 1933	1993	360,000	60.6	
Arabian American Oil Co.[o]	July 21, 1939	1999	440,000	74.1	
(SOCAL, 30%; SONJ, 30%; Texas, 30%; Socony, 10%)	Oct. 1, 1948	1999	Offshore area		
	Dec. 30, 1950 [p]				
	Oct. 2, 1951 [q]				
Syria:					
Syria Petroleum Co., Ltd. (I.P.C.)	March 26, 1940	2015	41,700	40.4	
	Dec. 6, 1955 [r]				
Syrian-American Oil and Gas. Co. (J. W. Menhall)	Early 1949	2019	Remaining portion of Syria 28 tracts in the north		
	May 16, 1955 [s]				
Trucial Coast:					
Petroleum Development (Trucial Coast), Ltd. (I.P.C.)	1939	2014	Abu Dhabi and Fujaira		
Petroleum Concessions, Lt., (I.P.C.)	1937	2012	Remaining portion of territory [t]		
	1951	2026			
Yemen:					
C. Deilman Bergbau, G.m.b.H.[u]	Oct. 9, 1953	1973			
Yemen Development Corp.	Nov. 22, 1955	1985	40,000 [v]		

Source: Data up to 1949 are largely based on *Review of Economic Conditions in the Middle East*, Supplement to *World Economic Report*, 1949–50, United Nations, Department of Economic Affairs, New York, March 1951. Data after 1949 have been compiled from a variety of sources, such as published company reports, the press, and professional journals as well as information supplied to the author by certain companies.

Abbreviations:

A.I.O.C.—Anglo-Iranian Oil Co., Ltd.

B.P.—British Petroleum Co., Ltd. (formerly Anglo-Iranian Oil Co., Ltd.).

C.F.P.—Compagnie Française des Petroles.

Gulf—Gulf Oil Co. or its subsidiaries, such as Gulf Exploration Co.

I.P.C.—Iraq Petroleum Co.

Shell—Royal Dutch-Shell Group.

SOCAL—Standard Oil Co. of California.

SONJ—Standard Oil Co. (New Jersey).

Socony—Socony Mobil Oil Co. (formerly Socony Vacuum Oil Co.).

Texas—Texas Oil Co.

a Includes exploration permits, agreements other than concessions, and major revisions.

b Only major revisions included.

c Exploration permit, periodically renewable.

d Signatory of an agreement which replaces the concession of the A.I.O.C. The latter's properties in Iran were nationalized in March 1951, and the operation of the oil industry was entrusted to the National Iranian Oil Company (N.I.O.C.), a government agency. The N.I.O.C. operates the Naft-i-Shah field and the Kermanshah refinery, leaving the operation of the Khuzistan fields and the Abadan refinery to Iranian Oil Participants, Ltd.

e With three possible five-year renewals.

f Profit-sharing agreement.

g Further financial revision.

h On Dec. 31, 1951, extended to 2026.

i Profit-sharing agreement.

j Concession obtained from the ruler of Kuwait.

k Concession obtained from the government of Saudi Arabia.

l Subsequently reduced to 40,000 due to the exclusion of Dhofar from the original area.

m Profit-sharing agreement.

n In 1936 the Texas Oil Co. acquired a 50% interest in Arabian operations and organized, together with its partner, Standard Oil Co. of California, the California Arabian Standard Oil Co. On January 31, 1944, the name was changed to Arabian American Oil Co. (Aramco).

o In the revised agreement the supplemental area included the undivided half-interest of Saudi Arabia in the Iraq and Kuwait Neutral Zones and the area under preferential rights in Saudi Arabia, amounting to 177,000 square miles. In 1948 the concessionaire relinquished its rights over the Kuwait-Saudi Arabian Neutral Zone and that part of Saudi Arabia lying west of 46° east longitude. The lease of preferential rights is to expire on July 21, 2005. As of 1956 the area under the Company's concession is understood to cover 400,000 square miles, excluding the offshore areas.

p Profit-sharing agreement (after U.S. taxes).

q Further financial revision (profit-sharing before U.S. taxes).

r Agreement to terminate the concession.

s Exploration permit, replacing earlier agreement, for 4 years, renewable for 4 additional years.

t Covers the Sheikhdoms of Ajman, Dubai, Kalbah, Ras el-Khaimah, Sharjah, and Umm el-Quwain.

u Partnership with the Yemen Government.

v Approximate figure. Concession covers northern two-thirds of the country, except the Tihama plain.

III. Estimated oil reserves and production of crude petroleum in the Middle East and certain other countries
(thousands of barrels)

Country	Reserves				Production in 1954		Ratio of 1955 reserves to 1954 production
	End of 1945	Mid-year 1955	% of world in 1955	Change since 1945	Amount	% of world	
Bahrein	250,000	235,000	0.15	15,000	10,991	0.22	21.4
Egypt	75,000	100,000	0.07	25,000	13,760	0.28	7.3
Iran	6,000,000	13,000,000	8.41	7,000,000	21,316	0.43	609.9
Iraq	4,750,000	14,500,000	9.38	9,750,000	228,468	4.56	63.5
Kuwait	4,000,000	27,500,000	17.80	23,500,000	347,557	6.93	79.1
Neutral Zone	. . . .	400,000	0.26	400,000	5,991	0.12	66.8
Qatar	500,000	1,500,000	0.97	1,000,000	36,732	0.73	40.8
Saudi Arabia	3,000,000	36,000,000	23.29	33,000,000	347,844	6.94	103.5
Trucial Coast	. . . .	50,000	0.03	50,000			
Turkey	. . . .	80,000	0.06	80,000	413	0.01	193.7
Middle East total	18,575,000	93,365,000	60.42	74,790,000	1,013,072	20.22	92.1
United States	19,941,846	30,060,000	19.46	10,118,154	2,316,323	46.21	13.0
U.S.S.R.	8,000,000	10,000,000	6.48	2,000,000	423,000	8.44	23.6
Venezuela	7,000,000	10,919,000	7.07	3,919,000	691,786	13.80	15.8
World total	58,026,846	154,539,200	100.00	96,512,354	5,013,163	100.00	30.8

Source: *World Oil*, Aug. 15, 1955.

IV. Oil revenue of three major countries in the Middle East [a]

Year	Iraq [b] (in pounds sterling)	Iran [b] (in pounds sterling)	Saudi Arabia [c] (in U.S. dollars)
1950	5,600,859	16,031,735	107,193,000
1951	13,901,532	8,326,446	164,009,000
1952	40,197,025	—	211,228,000
1953	51,446,466	—	223,393,000
1954	68,497,161	—	275,264,000
1955	73,742,886	31,971,616 [d]	270,929,000

[a] Representing total of financial obligations of the companies to the governments.

[b] Official figures.

[c] Unofficial figures, compiled from a variety of sources, including the press.

[d] Estimate.

V. Dollar value of imports and exports [a] excluding gold, 1951–1954
(In millions of United States dollars)

Country	1951 Imports	1951 Exports	1952 Imports	1952 Exports	1953 Imports	1953 Exports	1954 [b] Imports	1954 [b] Exports
Aden Colony [c]	141	125	158	128	172	116	140	87
Cyprus [c]	54	43	57	51	59	43	46	33
Egypt [d]	667	583	628	417	502	394	320	296
Iran [e]	212	134	155	178	164	95	. .	. .
Iraq [f]	142	81	173	56	192	56	146	32
Israel	380	47	321	44	282	60	218	70
Jordan [g]	36	4	40	4	39	6	. .	. .
Lebanon [h]	136	41	141	35	143	40	123	29
Syria [h]	133	126	138	146	131	170	73 [i]	72 [i]
Turkey	402	314	556	363	532	396	361	221
Total [j]	2,303	1,498	2,367	1,422	2,216	1,376	1,354	768

Source: *Economic Developments in the Middle East, 1945 to 1964,* Supplement to *World Economic Report, 1953–54* (United Nations, 1955).

[a] Special trade unless otherwise indicated.

[b] First nine months.

[c] General trade.

[d] Excluding trade with the Sudan.

[e] Figures for Iran exclude imports and exports of the petroleum company and other concessionaires; figures refer to the Iranian year beginning 21 or 22 March; for technical reasons, the rate of 3.101 cents U.S. per Iranian rial is used for conversion while the actual rates (including exchange certificates) for most imports and exports fluctuated between 2.5 and 0.966 cents U.S. per rial during 1950 to 1953.

[f] Excluding pipeline exports of crude petroleum.

[g] Excluding trade of concessionaires.

[h] Excluding trade of the petroleum companies.

[i] January to June only.

[j] Totals include figures for Iran without adjustment for overlapping months of the fiscal year.

VI. Growth of population of Palestine, 1922–1944

Year	Total	Moslems	Jews	Christians	Others
1922	752,048	589,177	83,790	71,464	7,617
1927	917,315	680,725	149,789	77,880	8,921
1932	1,052,872	771,174	180,793	90,624	10,281
1937	1,401,794	883,446	395,836	110,869	11,643
1938	1,435,285	900,250	411,222	111,974	11,839
1939	1,501,698	927,133	445,457	116,958	12,150
1940	1,544,530	947,846	463,535	120,587	12,562
1941	1,585,500	973,104	474,102	125,413	12,881
1942	1,620,005	995,292	484,408	127,184	13,121
1943	1,676,571	1,028,715	502,912	131,281	13,663
1944	1,739,624	1,061,277	528,702	135,547	14,098

Source: *Great Britain and Palestine 1915–1945.*

VII. Estimated population of Israel, 1949–1954

Year	Total	Jews	Non-Jews	Immigrants	Emigrants
1949	1,066,000	910,000	156,000	239,424	
1950	1,258,000	1,094,000	164,000	169,720	
1951	1,516,000	1,346,000	170,000	174,014	7,647
1952	1,607,000	1,430,000	177,000	23,408	11,128
1953	1,650,000	1,468,000	182,000	10,388	828
1954	1,688,000	1,499,000	189,000		

Source: United Nations, Statistical Office, *Demographic Yearbook, 1954* (New York, 1954).

Bibliography

THE AREA IN GENERAL

Adamiyat, Fereydoun. Bahrein Islands: A Legal and Diplomatic Study of the British-Iranian Controversy. New York: Praeger, 1955.

Arnold, Sir Thomas W. The Caliphate. Oxford: Clarendon Press, 1924.

Baker, Robert L. Oil, Blood and Sand. New York: Appleton-Century, 1942.

Barazi, Mouhsine. Islamisme et Socialisme. Paris: Geuthner, 1929.

Batsell, Walter R. The United States and the System of Mandates. New York: Carnegie Endowment for International Peace, 1925.

Beaujeu-Garnier, J. L'Economie du Moyen-Orient. Paris: Presses Universitaires, 1951.

Belot, Raymond de. The Struggle for the Mediterranean, 1939–1945. Princeton: Princeton University Press, 1951.

Ben-Horin, Eliahu. The Middle East: Crossroads of History. New York: Norton, 1943.

Bentwich, Norman. The Mandates System. London, New York: Longmans, 1930.

Berger, Rabbi Elmer. Who Knows Better Must Say So! New York: American Council for Judaism, 1955.

Bonné, Alfred. The Economic Development of the Middle East. London: Kegan Paul, Trench, Trubner and Co., 1945.

Bonné, Alfred. State and Economics in the Middle East: A Society in Transition. Rev. ed. London: Routledge and Kegan Paul, 1955.

Boutros-Ghali, B. Y. The Arab League, 1945–1955. (International Conciliation, no. 498.) New York: Carnegie Endowment for International Peace, 1955.

Brockelmann, Carl. History of the Islamic Peoples. New York: Putnam, 1947.

Brooks, Michael. Oil and Foreign Policy. London: Lawrence and Wishart, 1949.

Bullard, Sir Reader. Britain and the Middle East. New York: Longmans, 1951.

Carlson, John R. Cairo to Damascus. New York: Knopf, 1951.

Caroe, Sir Olaf K. Wells of Power, the Oilfields of South-West Asia: A Regional and Global Study. New York: Macmillan, 1951.

Cooke, Hedley V. Challenge and Response in the Middle East: The Quest for Prosperity, 1919–1951. New York: Harper, 1952.

Cumming, Henry H. Franco-British Rivalry in the Post-War Near East. New York: Oxford University Press, 1938.

Davis, Helen Miller, comp. Constitutions, Electoral Laws, Treaties of States in the Near and Middle East. 2d ed. Durham, N.C.: Duke University Press, 1953.

Douglas, William O. Strange Lands and Friendly People. New York: Harper, 1951.

The Encyclopaedia of Islam. Ed. M. Th. Houtsma and others. London: Luzac, 1913–1934. Suppl., 1938.

Fernau, F. W. Moslems on the March. Tr. from the German by E. W. Dickes. New York: Knopf, 1954.

Fielding, George E. Hate, Hope and High Explosives: A Report on the Middle East. Indianapolis: Bobbs-Merrill, 1948.

Fisher, Sydney N., ed. Social Forces in the Middle East. Ithaca, N.Y.: Cornell University Press, 1955.

Fisher, W. B. The Middle East: A Physical, Social and Regional Geography. London: Meuthen; New York: Dutton, 1950.

Frye, Richard N., ed. The Near East and the Great Powers. Cambridge: Harvard University Press, 1951.

Gerig, Benjamin. The Open Door and the Mandates System. London: Allen and Unwin, 1930.

Gibb, H. A. R. The Arabs. New York: Oxford University Press, 1940.

Hall, H. Duncan. Mandates, Dependencies and Trusteeship. Washington: Carnegie Endowment for International Peace, 1948.

Hindus, Maurice. In Search of a Future. New York: Doubleday, 1949.

Hitti, Philip K. The Arabs: A Short History. Princeton: Princeton University Press, 1943.

Hollingworth, Clare. The Arabs and the West. London: Methuen, 1952.

Hoskins, Halford L. The Middle East: Problem Area in World Politics. New York: Macmillan, 1954.

Hoskins, Halford L. Middle East Oil and United States Foreign Policy. Washington: Library of Congress, 1950.

Hurewitz, J. C. Middle East Dilemmas. New York: Harper, 1953.

Hurewitz, J. C. Unity and Disunity in the Middle East. New York: Carnegie Endowment for International Peace, 1952.

Hurewitz, J. C., ed. Documents of Near East Diplomatic History. New York: Columbia University School of International Affairs, 1951. (Mimeographed.)

Ireland, Philip Willard, ed. The Near East. Chicago: University of Chicago Press, 1942.

Izzeddin, Nejla. The Arab World: Past, Present, and Future. Chicago: Regnery, 1953.

Jackh, Ernest, ed. Background of the Middle East. Ithaca, N.Y.: Cornell University Press, 1952.

Kazemzadeh, Firuz. The Struggle for Transcaucasia (1917–1921). New York: Philosophical Library, 1952.

Kimche, Jon. Seven Fallen Pillars. Rev. ed. New York: Praeger, 1953.

Kirk, George. The Middle East, 1945–1950. New York: Oxford University Press, 1954.

Kirk, George. The Middle East in the War. London: Royal Institute of International Affairs, 1953.

Kirk, George E. A Short History of the Middle East: From the Rise of Islam to Modern Times. Rev. ed. New York: Praeger, 1955.

Knatchbull-Hugessen, Sir Hughe. Diplomat in Peace and War. London: J. Murray, 1949.

Kohn, Hans. Nationalism and Imperialism in the Hither East. London: Routledge, 1932.

Kohn, Hans. Western Civilization in the Near East. New York: Columbia University Press, 1936.

Lacoste, Raymond. La Russie Soviétique et la Question d'Orient. Paris: Editions Internationales, 1946.

Laissy, Michel. Du Panarabisme à la Ligue Arabe. Paris: Maisonneuve, 1949.

Lawrence, Thomas E. Seven Pillars of Wisdom. London: J. Cape, 1935.

Longrigg, Stephen Hensley. Oil in the Middle East. New York: Oxford University Press, 1954.

McFadden, Tom J. Daily Journalism in the Arab States. Columbus, O.: Ohio State University Press, 1953.

Mandelstam, André N. La Politique Russe d'Accès à la Mediterrannée au XXᵉ Siècle. (In Hague, Academy of International Law. Recueil des Cours, 1934, I.) Paris: Hachette, 1935.

Marriott, J. A. R. The Eastern Question. Oxford: Clarendon Press, 1917.

Mattison, Frances C. A Survey of American Interests in the Middle East. Washington: Middle East Institute, 1953.

The Middle East. London: Europa Publications, 1948–.

Mikesell, Raymond F., and Chenery, Hollis B. Arabian Oil, America's

Stake in the Middle East. Chapel Hill, N.C.: University of North Carolina Press, 1949.

Montagne, Robert, Rondot, Pierre, and Colombe, Marcel. Evolution Politique des Pays de l'Islam Méditerranéen. Paris: Peyronnet, 1953.

Reitzel, William. The Mediterranean: Its Role in America's Foreign Policy. New York: Harcourt, Brace, 1948.

Review of Middle East Oil. London: Petroleum Times, 1948.

Romainville, François de. L'Islam et l'U.R.S.S. Paris: Hermès, 1947.

Roosevelt, Kermit. Arabs, Oil and History: The Story of the Middle East. New York: Harper, 1949.

Royal Institute of International Affairs. The Middle East: A Political and Economic Survey. 2d ed. London and New York: The Institute, 1954.

The Security of the Middle East: A Problem Paper. Washington: Brookings, 1950.

Seton-Williams, M. N. Britain and the Arab States: A Survey of Anglo-Arab Relations, 1920–1948. London, Luzac, 1948.

Shwadran, Benjamin. The Middle East, Oil and the Great Powers. New York: Praeger, 1955.

Speiser, Ephraim. The United States and the Near East. Cambridge: Harvard University Press, 1947.

Stark, Freya M. The Arab Island. New York: Knopf, 1945.

Stoddard, Lothrop. The New World of Islam. New York: Scribner, 1921.

Storrs, Sir Ronald. Memoirs. New York: Putnam, 1937.

Strany Blizhnevo i Srednevo Vostoka. Gosudarstvenny Nauchny Institut "Sovietskaya Entsiklopedia," Ogiz: 1944.

Thicknesse, S. G. Arab Refugees: A Survey of Resettlement Possibilities. London: Royal Institute of International Affairs, 1949.

Topf, Erich. Die Staatenbildungen in den Arabischen Teilen der Türkei seit dem Weltkriege. Hamburg: De Gruyter, 1929.

Warriner, Doreen. Land and Poverty in the Middle East. London: Royal Institute of International Affairs, 1948.

Webster, Sir Charles. The Foreign Policy of Palmerston, 1830–1841: Britain, the Liberal Movement and the Eastern Question. London: G. Bell and Sons, 1951.

Who's Who in Egypt and the Middle East. Cairo: Imprimerie Française, 1950.

Williams-Thompson, Richard. Progress or the Pashas? London: Frederick Muller, 1952.

Wilson, Sir Arnold. The Persian Gulf. London: George Allen and Unwin, 1928.

Woodward, E. L., and Butler, Rohan, eds. Documents on British Foreign

551

Policy, 1919–39. 1st ser., vol. IV, 1919. London: H.M. Stationery Office, 1952.

Wright, Quincy. Mandates under the League of Nations. Chicago: University of Chicago Press, 1930.

Young, T. Cuyler, ed. Near Eastern Culture and Society. Princeton: Princeton University Press, 1951.

The First World War and the Peace Settlement

Adamov, Evgenii A. Die Europäischen Mächte und die Türkei während des Weltkrieges. Dresden: C. Reissner, 1932.

Antonius, George. The Arab Awakening. New York, London: H. Hamilton, 1938.

Bowman-Manifold, Sir Michael G. E. An Outline of the Egyptian and Palestine Campaigns, 1914 to 1918. Chatham, Mackay, 1922.

Dane, Edmund. British Campaigns in the Nearer East, 1914–1918. London: Hodder and Stoughton, 1917–19. 2 v.

Emin, Ahmed. Turkey in the World War. New Haven, Conn.: Yale University Press, 1930.

Howard, Harry N. The Partition of Turkey. Norman, Okla.: University of Oklahoma Press, 1931.

Larcher, Maurice. La Guerre Turque dans la Guerre Mondiale. Paris: Berger-Levrault, 1926.

Lawrence, Thomas E. Revolt in the Desert. New York: Doran, 1927.

Storrs, Sir Ronald. Orientations. London: Nicholson and Watson, 1937.

Survey of International Affairs, 1925. London: Oxford University Press, 1927.

Temperley, H. W. V., ed. A History of the Peace Conference of Paris. London: Henry Frowde and Hodder and Stoughton, 1924. Vol. VI.

Townshend, Charles V. My Campaign in Mesopotamia. London: T. Butterworth, 1920.

The Second World War

Australia. Active Service: With Australia in the Middle East. Canberra: Australian War Memorial, 1941.

Beaton, Cecil. Near East. London: Batsford, 1943.

Churchill, Winston S. The Second World War. Vol. III: The Grand Alliance; Vol. IV: The Hinge of Fate. Boston: Houghton Mifflin, 1949–1950.

Cowie, Donald. The Campaigns of Wavell: The Inner Story of the Empire in Action. London: Chapman, 1942.

De Guingand, Maj.-Gen. Sir Francis. Operation Victory. London: Hodder and Stoughton, 1947.

Hill, Russell. Desert Conquest. New York: Knopf, 1943.

Moorehead, Alan. Don't Blame the Generals. New York: Harper, 1943.

552

Moorehead, Alan. Mediterranean Front. New York: Whittlesey, 1942.

Paiforce: The Official Story of the Persia and Iraq Command, 1941–1946. London: H.M. Stationery Office, 1948.

Talbot, Godfrey. Speaking from the Desert. London: Hutchinson, 1944.

Young, Desmond. Rommel, the Desert Fox. New York: Harper, 1950.

Minorities

Bouron, Narcisse. Les Druzes. Paris: Berger-Levrault, 1930.

Fany, Messoud. La Nation Kurde et Son Evolution Sociale. Paris: Rodstein, 1933.

Hamilton, Archibald M. Road through Kurdistan. London: Faber, 1939.

Hourani, Albert H. Minorities in the Arab World. New York: Oxford University Press, 1947.

Landshut, S. Jewish Communities in the Muslim Countries of the Middle East. London: Jewish Chronicle, 1950.

Luke, Harry C. Mosul and Its Minorities. London: Hopkinson, 1925.

Malek, Yusuf. The British Betrayal of the Assyrians. Chicago: Assyrian National Federation and the Assyrian National League of America, 1935.

Rambout, L. Les Kurdes et le Droit. Paris: Editions du Cerf, 1947.

Rondot, Pierre. Les Chrétiens d'Orient. Paris: Peyronnet, 1955.

Safrastian, Arshak. Kurds and Kurdistan. London: Harvill Press, 1948.

Soane, E. B. To Mesopotamia and Kurdistan in Disguise. London: J. Murray, 1926.

Stafford, Ronald S. The Tragedy of the Assyrians. London: Allen and Unwin, 1935.

Vratzian, Simon. Armenia and the Armenian Question. Boston: Hairenik Publishing Co., 1943.

Strategic Waterways

Hallberg, Charles W. The Suez Canal. New York: Columbia University Press, 1931.

Hefnaoui, Moustapha el-. Les Problèmes Contemporains Posés par le Canal de Suez. Paris: Guillemot et de Lamothe, 1951.

Hoskins, Halford L. British Routes to India. New York: Longmans, 1928.

Reinhard, Ernst. Kampf um Suez. Dresden: Kaden, 1930.

Schonfield, Hugh J. The Suez Canal. New York: Penguin, 1939.

Schonfield, Hugh J. The Suez Canal in World Affairs. London: Constellation Books, 1952. New York: Philosophical Library, 1953.

Shotwell, James T., and Deák, Francis. Turkey at the Straits. New York: Macmillan, 1940.

Siegfried, André. Suez and Panama. New York: Harcourt, Brace, 1940.

Wilson, Sir Arnold T. The Suez Canal. London: Oxford University Press, 1939.

COUNTRIES OF THE MIDDLE EAST

Afghanistan

Dollot, René. L'Afghanistan. Paris: Payot, 1937.

Fouchet, Maurice. Notes sur l'Afghanistan. Paris: Maisonneuve, 1932.

Fraser-Tytler, W. K. Afghanistan: A Study of Political Developments in Central and Southern Asia. Rev. ed. London: Oxford University Press, 1953.

Ik'bal, 'Ali Shah, Sirdar. The Tragedy of Amanullah. London: Alexander-Onseley, 1933.

Pakhtunistan: The Khyber Pass as the Focus of the New State of Pakhtunistan. London: Embassy of Afghanistan, 1952.

Pazhwak, A. Rahman. Afghanistan (Ancient Aryana). London: Key Press, 1954.

Rybitschka, Emil. Im Gottengegebenen Afghanistan. Leipzig: Brockhaus, 1927.

Snesarev, A. E. Afghanistan. Moscow: Gosizdat, 1921.

Sykes, Sir Percy M. A History of Afghanistan. London: Macmillan, 1940. 2 v.

Ziemke, Kurt. Als Deutscher Gesandter in Afghanistan. Stuttgart: Deutsche Verlagsanstalt, 1939.

Egypt

Abbas, Mekki. The Sudan Question: The Dispute over the Anglo-Egyptian Condominium, 1884–1951. London: Faber, 1952.

Adams, Charles C. Islam and Modernism in Egypt. New York: Oxford University Press, 1933.

Barawy, Rashed el-. The Military Coup in Egypt: An Analytic Study. Cairo: Renaissance Book Shop, 1952.

Christophe, Leon R. L'Egypte et le Régime des Capitulations. Paris: Pedone, 1938.

Cleland, William W. The Population Problem in Egypt. Lancaster, Pa.: Science Press, 1936.

Colombe, Marcel. L'Evolution de l'Egypte, 1924–1950. Paris: Maisonneuve, 1951.

Cromer, Evelyn B., First Earl of. Modern Egypt. New York: Macmillan, 1916.

Crouchley, Arthur E. The Economic Development of Modern Egypt. New York: Longmans, 1938.

Cumberbatch, A. N. Egypt: Economic and Commercial Conditions in Egypt, October, 1951. London: H.M. Stationery Office, 1952.

Elgood, Percival G. The Transit of Egypt. New York: Longmans, 1928.

Galatoli, Anthony M. Egypt in Midpassage. Cairo: Urwand & Sons Press, 1950.

Heyworth-Dunne, James. Religious and Political Trends in Modern Egypt. Washington: The author, 1950.

Howell, Joseph M. Egypt's Past, Present and Future. Dayton: Service, 1929.

Issawi, Charles. Egypt at Mid-century: An Economic Survey. New York: Oxford University Press, 1954.

Kabil, Ibrahim H. Le Commerce Extérieur de l'Egypte. Paris: Pedone, 1935.

Kitaigorodskii, P. Egipet v Bor'be za Nezavisimost'. Moscow: 1925.

Landau, Jacob M. Parliaments and Parties in Egypt. Tel-Aviv: Israel Oriental Society, 1953.

Lloyd, George Ambrose, 1st Baron. Egypt since Cromer. New York: Macmillan, 1933–34. 2 v.

Lugol, Jean. Egypt and World War II. Cairo: Société Orientale de Publicité, 1945.

Marlow, John. A History of Modern Egypt and Anglo-Egyptian Relations, 1800–1953. London: Cresset, 1954. New York: Praeger, 1954.

Moore, Austin L. Farewell Farouk. Chicago: Scholars' Press, 1954.

Nasser, Gamal Abd el-. The Philosophy of the Revolution. Cairo: Dar el-Maaref, 1954. Washington, D.C.: Public Affairs Press, 1955, under title *Egypt's Liberation.*

Neguib, Mohammed. Egypt's Destiny. London: Victor Gollancz, 1955. New York: Doubleday, 1955.

Newman, Edward W. P. Great Britain in Egypt. London: Cassell, 1928.

Rifaat, Mohammed, Bey. The Awakening of Modern Egypt. London: Longmans, 1947.

Royal Institute of International Affairs. Great Britain and Egypt, 1914–1951. London and New York: The Institute, 1952.

Schmitz-Kairo, Paul. Ägyptens Weg zur Freiheit. Leipzig: Goldmann, 1937.

The Unity of the Nile Valley: Its Geographical Bases and Its Manifestations in History. Cairo: Government Press, 1947.

Wavell, Archibald P., Viscount. Allenby in Egypt. New York: Oxford University Press, 1944.

Young, George, Egypt. New York: Scribner, 1927.

Youssef, Amine, Bey. Independent Egypt. London: J. Murray, 1940.

Iran

Afschar, Mahmoud. La Politique Européenne en Perse. Berlin: Nay, 1921.

Alavi, Ebrahim-Khelil. Le Redressement Economique de l'Iran. Paris: Imprimerie Artistique Moderne, 1939.

Amini, Ali. l'Institution du Monopole de Commerce Extérieur en Perse. Paris: Rousseau, 1932.

Balfour, James M. Recent Happenings in Persia. London: Blackwood, 1922.

Blücher, Wipert von. Zeitenwende in Iran, Erlebnisse und Beobachtungen. Biberach an der Riss: Koehler and Voigtländer, 1949.

Curzon, George N., Earl of Kedleston. Persia and the Persian Question. London: Longmans, 1892.

Elwell-Sutton, Lawrence P. Modern Iran. London: Routledge, 1941.

Elwell-Sutton, Lawrence P. Persian Oil: A Study in Power Politics. London: Lawrence and Wishart, 1955.

Emelianov, A. G. Persidskii Front. Berlin: Gamaiun, 1923.

Fatemi, Nasrollah S. Diplomatic History of Persia, 1917–1923: Anglo-Russian Power Politics in Iran. New York: R. F. Moore Co., 1952.

Fatemi, Nasrollah S. Oil Diplomacy: Powderkeg in Iran. New York: Whittier Books, 1954.

Filmer, Henry. Pageant of Persia. Indianapolis, Ind.: Bobbs-Merrill, 1936.

Ford, Alan W. The Anglo-Iranian Oil Dispute of 1951–1952. Berkeley, Calif.: University of California Press, 1954.

Frye, Richard N. Iran. New York: Henry Holt, 1953.

Furon, Raymond. L'Iran. Paris: Payot, 1952.

Groseclose, Elgin E. Introduction to Iran. New York: Oxford University Press, 1947.

Gupta, Raj Narain. Iran: An Economic Study. New Delhi: Indian Institute of International Affairs, 1947.

Haas, William S. Iran. New York: Columbia University Press, 1946.

Hamzavi, A. H. Persia and the Powers: An Account of Diplomatic Relations, 1941–1946. London, New York: Hutchinson, 1946.

Kemp, Norman. Abadan: A First-Hand Account of the Persian Oil Crisis. London: Allan Wingate, 1953.

Khalatbary, Abbas. L'Iran et le Pacte Oriental. Paris: Pedone, 1938.

Kościalkowski, Stanislaw. L'Iran et la Pologne à travers les Siècles. Teheran: Société Polonaise des Etudes Iraniennes, 1943.

Lenczowski, George. Russia and the West in Iran, 1918–1948. Ithaca, N.Y.: Cornell University Press, 1949.

Melzig, Herbert. Resa Shah, der Aufstieg Irans und die Grossmächte. Stuttgart: Unison, 1936.

Millspaugh, Arthur C. Americans in Persia. Washington: Brookings, 1946.

Moazzami, Abdollah. Essai sur la Condition des Etrangers en Iran. Paris: Sirey, 1937.

Motter, T. H. Vail. The Persian Corridor and Aid to Russia. Washington: Department of the Army, 1952.

Nakhai, M. L'Evolution Politique de l'Iran. Brussels: J. Felix, 1938.

Niedermayer, Oskar von. Under der Glutsonne Iran's. Munich: Einhorn, 1925.

Pavlovich, M. (*pseud.* of Mikhail Vel'tman) and Iranskii, S. Persiia v Bor'be za Nezavisimost'. Moscow: Nauchnaia Assotsiatsiia Vostoko-vedenia, 1925.

Poidebard, A. Au Carrefour des Routes de Perse. Paris: Cres, 1923.

Rajput, A. B. Iran Today. New Delhi: Lion Press, 1953.

Roberts, Norman S. Iran, Economic and Commercial Conditions. London: H.M. Stationery Office, 1948.

Saba, M. Bibliographie de l'Iran: Domât-Montchrestien, 1936.

Sayre, Joel. Persian Gulf Command: Some Marvels on the Road to Kazvin. New York: Random House, 1945.

Schulze-Holthus, Bernhardt. Daybreak in Iran: A Story of the German Intelligence Service. Tr. by M. Savill. London: Staples Press, 1954.

Shuster, William M. The Strangling of Persia. New York: Century, 1912.

Siassi, Ali A. La Perse au Contact de l'Occident. Paris: Leroux, 1931.

Stark, Freya M. The Valleys of the Assassins. New York: Dutton, 1934.

Steppat, Fritz. Iran zwischen den Grossmächten, 1941–1948. Oberursel: Verlag Europa-Archiv, 1948.

Sykes, Christopher. Wassmuss, "the German Lawrence." London: Longmans, 1936.

Sykes, Sir Percy M. A History of Persia. London: Macmillan, 1930. 2 v.

Thomas, Lewis V., and Frye, Richard N. The United States and Turkey and Iran. Cambridge: Harvard University Press, 1951.

Van Wagenen, Richard W. The Iranian Case, 1946. New York: Carnegie Endowment for International Peace, 1952.

Wilber, Donald N. Iran: Past and Present. 3d ed. Princeton: Princeton University Press, 1955.

Wilson, Sir Arnold T. Persia. New York: Scribner, 1933.

Wilson, Sir Arnold T. South-West Persia: A Political Officer's Diary, 1907–1914. London: Oxford University Press, 1941.

Zanguehneh, Azami. Le Petrole en Perse. Paris: Domât-Montchrestien, 1933.

Zavriev, D. S. Torgovo-Politichesky Kurs Persii. Tiflis: Zakkniga, 1934.

Iraq

Bell, Gertrude L. Letters. Ed. Lady Florence Bell. New York: Boni and Liveright, 1927. 2 v.

Burne, Alfred H. Mesopotamia: The Last Phase. Aldershot: Gale, 1936.

Coke, Richard. The Heart of the Middle East. London: T. Butterworth, 1925.

Crutiansky, Leon. La Question de Mossoul. Paris: Presses Modernes, 1927.

Erskine, Beatrice (Strong). King Faisal of Iraq. London: Hutchinson, 1933.

Foster, Henry A. The Making of Modern Iraq. Norman, Okla.: University of Oklahoma Press, 1935.

Haldane, Sir Aylmer L. The Insurrection in Mesopotamia, 1920. London: Blackwood, 1922.

Iraq. Statistical Abstract, 1944–5. Baghdad: Government Printer, 1946.

Ireland, Philip W. Iraq: A Study in Political Development. London: J. Cape, 1937.

Khadduri, Majid. Independent Iraq: A Study in Iraqi Politics since 1932. London: Oxford University Press, 1951.

Lloyd, Seton. Iraq. New York: Oxford University Press, 1944.

Longrigg, Stephen Hemsley. Iraq, 1900 to 1950: A Political, Social, and Economic History. London: Oxford University Press, 1953.

Macdonald, Alan David. Euphrates Exile. London: Bell, 1936.

Main, Ernest. Iraq from Mandate to Independence. London: Allen and Unwin, 1935.

Van Ess, John. Meet the Arab. New York: John Day, 1943.

Wilson, Sir Arnold T. Loyalties; Mesopotamia, 1914–1917. London: Oxford University Press, 1930.

Wilson, Sir Arnold T. Mesopotamia 1917–1920: A Clash of Loyalties. London: Oxford University Press, 1931.

Israel

Abcarius, M. F. Palestine through the Fog of Propaganda. London: Hutchinson, 1946.

Andrews, Fanny F. The Holy Land under Mandate. New York: Houghton Mifflin, 1931.

Balfour, Arthur J. Speeches on Zionism. London: Arrowsmith, 1928.

Barbour, Nevill. Palestine: Star or Crescent? New York: Odyssey Press, 1947.

Barer, Shlomo. The Magic Carpet. New York: Harper, 1952.

Begin, Menachem. The Revolt: Story of the Irgun. New York: Schuman, 1951.

Ben-Gurion, David. Rebirth and Destiny of Israel. New York: Philosophical Library, 1953.

Ben-Jacob, Jeremiah. The Rise of Israel. New York: Grosby House, 1949.

Bentwich, Norman. Israel. New York: McGraw-Hill, 1953.

Bernadotte, Folke. To Jerusalem. London: Hodder and Stoughton, 1951.

Bernfeld, Marcel. Le Sionisme. Paris: Jouve, 1920.

Bilby, Kenneth W. New Star in the Near East. Garden City: Doubleday, 1950.

Brandeis, Louis D. Brandeis on Zionism. Washington: Zionist Organization of America, 1942.

Burrows, Millar. Palestine Is Our Business. Philadelphia: Westminster Press, 1949.

Cohen, Israel. The Zionist Movement. New York: Zionist Organization of America, 1946.

Crossman, Richard. Palestine Mission: A Personal Record. New York: Harper, 1947.

Crum, Bartley C. Behind the Silken Curtain. New York: Simon and Schuster, 1947.

De Haas, Jacob. History of Palestine: The Last Two Thousand Years. New York: Macmillan, 1934.

Dunner, Joseph. The Republic of Israel. New York: Whittlesey House, 1950.

Esco Foundation for Palestine. Palestine: A Study of Jewish, Arab, and British Policies. New Haven, Conn.: Yale University Press, 1947.

Fink, Reuben. America and Palestine: The Attitude of Official America and of the American People toward the Rebuilding of Palestine as a Free and Democratic Jewish Commonwealth. New York: Herald Square Press, 1945.

Friedrich, Carl J. American Policy toward Palestine. Washington: Public Affairs Press, 1944.

Garcia-Granados, Jorge. The Birth of Israel: The Drama As I Saw It. New York: Knopf, 1948.

Gaury, Gerald de. The New State of Israel. London: Derek Verschoyle, 1952. New York: Praeger, 1952.

Granovsky, Abraham. Land Policy in Palestine. New York: Bloch, 1940.

Graves, R. M. Experiment in Anarchy. London: Gollancz, 1949.

Hanna, Paul L. British Policy in Palestine. Washington: American Council on Public Affairs, 1942.

Herzl, Theodor. The Jewish State. New York: Scopus, 1943.

Horowitz, David. State in the Making. New York: Knopf, 1953.

Hurewitz, J. C. The Struggle for Palestine. New York: Norton, 1950.

Infield, Henrik F. Cooperative Living in Palestine. New York: Dryden Press, 1944.

Jabotinsky, Vladimir. The Story of the Jewish Legion. New York: Ackerman, 1946.

Jeffries, Joseph M. N. Palestine: The Reality. New York: Longmans, 1939.

Joseph, Bernard. British Rule in Palestine. Washington: Public Affairs Press, 1948.

Kimche, Jon and David. The Secret Roads: The "Illegal" Migration of a People, 1938–1948. London: Secker and Warburg, 1955.

Kisch, Frederick H. Palestine Diary. London: Gollancz, 1938.

Koestler, Arthur. Promise and Fulfillment; Palestine, 1917–1949. New York: Macmillan, 1949.

Lehrman, Hal. Israel: The Beginning and Tomorrow. New York: William Sloane, 1951.

Leonard, L. Larry. The United Nations and Palestine. New York: Carnegie Foundation for International Peace, 1949.

Lilienthal, Alfred M. What Price Israel. Chicago: Regnery, 1953.

Lowdermilk, Walter C. Palestine, Land of Promise. New York: Harper, 1944.

McDonald, James G. My Mission in Israel. New York: Simon and Schuster, 1951.

Magil, Abraham B. Israel in Crisis. New York: International Publishers, 1950.

Main, Ernest. Palestine at the Crossroads. London: G. Allen, 1937.

Manuel, Frank E. The Realities of American-Palestine Relations. Washington: Public Affairs Press, 1949.

Muenzer, Gerhard. Labor Enterprise in Palestine. New York: Sharon Books, 1947.

Parkes, James. End of an Exile. London: Vallentine, Mitchell, 1954.

Parkinson, Sir Cosmo. The Colonial Office from Within, 1909–1945. London: Faber, 1947.

Patai, Raphael. Israel between East and West. Philadelphia: Jewish Publication Society of America, 1953.

Pearlman, Maurice. Collective Adventure. London: Heinemann, 1938.

Pearlman, Lt. Col. Moshe. The Army of Israel. New York: Philosophical Library, 1950.

Rabinowicz, Oskar K. Fifty Years of Zionism. London: Robert Anscome, 1950.

Rackman, Emanuel. Israel's Emerging Constitution, 1948–51. New York: Columbia University Press, 1955.

Royal Institute of International Affairs. Great Britain and Palestine, 1915–1945. (Information Paper No. 20.) London: The Institute, 1946.

Sacher, Harry. Israel: The Establishment of a State. New York: British Book Centre, 1952.

Sakran, Frank C. Palestine Dilemma; Arab Rights versus Zionist Aspirations. Washington: Public Affairs Press, 1948.

Sayegh, Fayez A. The Palestine Refugees. Washington: Amara Press, 1952.

Schechtman, Joseph B. The Arab Refugee Problem. New York: Philosophical Library, 1952.

Sokolow, Nahum. History of Zionism, 1600–1918. New York: Longmans, 1919. 2 v.

Sykes, Christopher. Two Studies in Virtue. New York: Knopf, 1953.

Vlavianos, Basil J., and Gross, Feliks, eds. Struggle for Tomorrow: Modern Political Ideologies of the Jewish People. New York: Arts, Inc., 1954.

Weizmann, Chaim. Trial and Error: The Autobiography of Chaim Weizmann. New York: Harper, 1949.

Welles, Sumner. We Need Not Fail. Boston: Houghton Mifflin, 1948.

Zaar, Isaac. Rescue and Liberation: America's Part in the Birth of Israel. New York: Bloch Publishing Co., 1954.

Zander, Walter. Soviet Jewry, Palestine and the West. London: Gollancz, 1947.

Jordan

Abdallah, King of Jordan. My Memoirs Completed. Tr. by Harold Glidden. Washington, D.C.: American Council of Learned Societies, 1954.

Glubb, John Bagot. The Story of the Arab Legion. London: Hodder and Stoughton, 1948.

Graves, Philip, ed. Memoirs of King Abdullah of Transjordan. New York: Philosophical Library, 1950.

Jarvis, Major Claude Scudamore. Arab Command: The Biography of Lt. Col. F. W. Peake Pasha. London: Hutchinson, 1942.

Konikoff, A. Transjordan: An Economic Survey. Jerusalem: Economic Research Institute of the Jewish Agency for Palestine, 1946.

Luke, Harry C., and Keith-Roach, Edward. The Handbook of Palestine and Trans-Jordan. London: Macmillan, 1930.

Toukan, Baha Uddin. A Short History of Trans-Jordan. London: Luzac, 1945.

Saudi Arabia

Aldington, Richard. Lawrence of Arabia: A Biographical Enquiry. London: Collins, 1955.

Armstrong, Harold C. Lord of Arabia, Ibn Saud: An Intimate Study of a King. London: Barker, 1934.

Bassi, Ugo. L'Italia e l'Arabia Centrale. Modena: Bassi, 1932.

Benoist-Méchin, Baron. Le Loup et le Léopard: Ibn Séoud. Paris: Albin Michel, 1955.

Brémond, Edouard. Yémen et Saoudia: L'Arabie Actuelle. Paris: Lavauzelle, 1937.

Donkan, Rupert. Die Auferstehung Arabiens. Vienna: Goldmann, 1935.

Eddy, William A. F. D. R. Meets Ibn Saud. New York: American Friends of the Middle East, 1954.

Graves, Robert. Lawrence and the Arabian Adventure. New York: Doubleday, 1928.

Ingrams, William H. Arabia and the Isles. London: J. Murray, 1942.

Kheirallah, George. Arabia Reborn. Albuquerque: University of New Mexico Press, 1952.

Lebkicher, Roy, Rentz, George, and Steineke, Max. The Arabia of Ibn Saud. New York: Russell F. Moore, 1952.

Nallino, Carlo A. L'Arabia Sa'udiana. Rome: Istituto per l'Oriente, 1939.

Philby, H. St. John B. Arabia. New York: Scribner, 1930.

Philby, H. St. John B. Arabia of the Wahhabis. London: Constable, 1928.

Philby, H. St. John B. Arabian Days. London: Robert Hale, 1948.

Philby, H. St. John B. Arabian Highlands. Ithaca, N.Y.: Cornell University Press, 1952.

Philby, H. St. John B. Arabian Jubilee. London: Robert Hale, 1951. New York: John Day, 1953.

Philby, H. St. John B. A Pilgrim in Arabia. London: Robert Hale, 1946.

Philby, H. St. John B. Saudi Arabia. London: Ernest Benn, 1955. New York: Praeger, 1955.

Rihani, Ameen. Makers of Modern Arabia. New York: Houghton Mifflin, 1928.

Sanger, Richard H. The Arabian Peninsula. Ithaca, N.Y.: Cornell University Press, 1954.

Thomas, Bertram. Alarms and Excursions in Arabia. Indianapolis, Ind.: Bobbs-Merrill, 1931.

Thomas, Lowell. With Lawrence in Arabia. New York: Grosset, 1955.

Twitchell, K. S. Saudi Arabia. 2d ed. Princeton: Princeton University Press, 1953.

Syria and Lebanon

Abouchid, Eugenie Elie. Thirty Years of Lebanon and Syria (1917–1947). Beirut: Sader Rihani Printing Co., 1948.

Achkar, J. Evolution Politique de la Syrie et du Liban, de la Palestine et de l'Iraq. Paris: 1935.

Catroux, General Georges. Dans la Bataille de Méditerranée. Paris: Julliard, 1949.

David, Philippe. Un Gouvernement Arabe à Damas: Le Congrès Syrien. Paris: Marcel Girard, 1923.

Du Véou, Paul. Le Désastre d'Alexandrette, 1934–1938. Paris: Baudinière, 1938.

Haddad, George. Fifty Years of Modern Syria and Lebanon. Beirut: Dar-al-Hayat, 1950.

Hitti, Philip K. History of Syria. New York: Macmillan, 1951.

Hornet, Marcel. Syrie, Terre Irredente. Paris: Peyronnet, 1938.

Hourani, Albert H. Syria and Lebanon: A Political Essay. London: Oxford University Press, 1946.

Lammens, R. P. Petite Histoire de Syrie et du Liban. Beirut: Imprimerie Catholique, 1924.

MacCallum, Elizabeth P. The Nationalist Crusade in Syria. New York: Foreign Policy Assn., 1928.

Morgan Jones, John. La Fin du Mandat Français en Syrie et au Liban. Paris: Pedone, 1938.

O'Zoux, Raymond. Les Etats du Levant sous Mandat Français. Paris: Larousse, 1931.

Pearse, Richard. Three Years in the Levant. London: Macmillan, 1949.

Puaux, Gabriel. Deux Années au Levant: Souvenirs de Syrie et du Liban, 1939–1940. Paris: Hachette, 1952.

Puryear, Vernon J. France and the Levant. Berkeley, Calif.: University of California Press, 1941.

Rabbath, Edmond. Unité Syrienne et Devenir Arabe. Paris: Rivière, 1937.

Schultz-Esteves, Christoph. Syriens Freiheitskampf. Leipzig: Goldmann, 1939.

Stark, Freya M. Letters from Syria. London: J. Murray, 1942.

Weygand, Maxime. Recalled to Service: The Memoirs of General Maxime Weygand of the Académie Française. Tr. by E. W. Dickes. Garden City: Doubleday, 1952.

Turkey

Allen, Henry E. The Turkish Transformation. Chicago: University of Chicago Press, 1935.

Armstrong, Harold C. Grey Wolf, Mustafa Kemal: an Intimate Study of a Dictator. London: Barker, 1932.

Bisbee, Eleanor. The New Turks: Pioneers of the Republic, 1920–1950. Philadelphia: University of Pennsylvania Press, 1951.

Bisbee, Eleanor. People of Turkey. New York: East and West Assn., 1946.

Conker, Orhan, and Witmeur, Emile. Redressement Economique et Industrialisation de la Nouvelle Turquie. Paris: Sirey, 1937.

Djemal, Ahmad, Pasha. Memories of a Turkish Statesman, 1913–1919. New York: Doran, 1922.

Du Véou, Paul. La Passion de la Cilicie, 1919–1922. Paris: Geuthner, 1938.

Ekrem, Selma. Turkey: Old and New. New York: Scribner, 1947.

Germanskaia Politika v Turtsii, 1941–1943. Moscow: 1946. (Available in French translation: La Politique Allemande, 1941–1943. Turquie. Documents Secrets du Ministère des Affaires Etrangères d'Allemagne. Paris: 1946.)

Gordon, Leland J. American Relations with Turkey, 1830–1930. Philadelphia: University of Pennsylvania Press, 1932.

Graves, Philip P. Briton and Turk. London: Hutchinson, 1941.

Gurko-Kriazhin, V. A. Istoriia Revoliutsii v Turtsii. Moscow: Mir, 1923.

BIBLIOGRAPHY

Halidah Adib, Khanum. Memoirs. New York: Century, 1926.

Halidah Adib, Khanum. The Turkish Ordeal. New York: Century, 1928.

Heyd, Uriel. Foundations of Turkish Nationalism: The Life and Teachings of Ziya Gökalp. London: Harvill Press, 1950.

Jackh, Ernest. The Rising Crescent. New York: Farrar and Rinehart, 1944

Jäschke, G. Die Türkei in den Jahren 1942–51. Wiesbaden: Harrassowitz, 1954.

Johnson, Walter. Turbulent Era: A Diplomatic Record of Forty Years, 1904–1945. Cambridge, Mass.: Houghton Mifflin, 1952.

Kinross, Patrick Balfour, Lord. Within the Taurus. London: John Murray, 1955.

Kral, August, Ritter von. Kamâl Atatürk's Land: The Evolution of Modern Turkey. London: King, 1938.

Levonian, Lutfy, ed. The Turkish Press. Athens, School of Religion, 1932.

Lingeman, E. R. Turkey: Economic and Commercial Conditions in Turkey. London: H.M. Stationery Office, 1948.

Luke, Sir Harry Charles Joseph. The Making of Modern Turkey. London: Macmillan, 1936.

Mears, Eliot Grinnell. Modern Turkey. New York: Macmillan, 1924.

Mikusch, Dagobert von. Mustapha Kemal. New York: Doubleday, 1931.

Moyzisch, L. C. Operation Cicero. New York: Coward-McCann, 1950.

Okay, Kurt. Enver Pascha, der Grosse Freund Deutschlands. Berlin: Verlag für Kulturpolitik, 1935.

Ostroróg, Leon, Hrabia. The Angora Reform. London: University of London Press, 1927.

Papen, Franz von. Memoirs. London: Andre Deutch, 1952.

Pavlovich, M. (pseud. of Mikhail Vel'tman), Gurko-Kriazhin, V. A., and Raskolnikov, F. Turtsiia v Bor'be za Nezavisimost'. Moscow: Nauchnaia Assotsiatsiia Vostokovedeniia, 1925.

Thomas, Lewis V., and Frye, Richard N. The United States and Turkey and Iran. Cambridge: Harvard University Press, 1951.

Thornburg, Max, Spry, George, and Soule, George. Turkey: An Economic Appraisal. New York: Twentieth Century Fund, 1949.

Toynbee, Arnold J. The Western Question in Greece and Turkey. London: Constable, 1922.

Turkey. La Guerre de l'Indépendance Turque. Istanbul: Imprimerie d'Etat, 1937.

Vere-Hodge, Edward R. Turkish Foreign Policy, 1918–1948. Ambilly-Annemasse: Imprimerie Franco-Suisse, 1950.

Ward, Barbara. Turkey. New York: Oxford University Press, 1942.

Waugh, Sir Telford. Turkey: Yesterday, Today, and Tomorrow. London: Chapman and Hall, 1930.

564

Webster, Donald E. Turkey of Ataturk. Philadelphia: American Academy of Political and Social Science, 1939.

Ziemke, Kurt. Die Neue Türkei (1914–1928). Stuttgart: Deutsche Verlagsanstalt, 1930.

Yemen

Faroughy, A. Introducing Yemen. New York: Orientalia, 1947.

Scott, Hugh. In the High Yemen. London: J. Murray, 1942.

Tritton, Arthur S. Rise of the Imams of Sanaa. London: Oxford University Press, 1925.

Index

566

Arms agreement, Anglo-American-French, 352
Arslan, Emir Adil, 270
Asads, the, 289
Ashkhabad, government of, 112
Asir, 435, 456
Askari, Jafar el-, 239, 243ff.
Assali, Sabri el-, 303, 306, 309
Assyrians, 50, 131, 236f.
Atallah Pasha, Gen. Ibrahim, 413
Atassi, Faidi el-, 303, 306
Atassi, Hashim el-, 270, 272, 296f., 300, 303, 309
Atilhan, Rifat, 150
Atrash, Sultan Pasha el-, 303
Attlee, Clement, 330
Auchinleck, Gen. Sir Claude, 471
Austria, 8ff.
    see also Habsburgs
Azem, Haqqi el-, 271
Azem, Khalid el-, 293, 297ff., 306, 309f.
Azerbaijan (Iranian), 43, 181ff., 190
Azerbaijan (Russian), 164
    see also Transcaucasia
Azhari, Ismail el-, 427
Aziz Khan, 218
Azzam Pasha, Abdur Rahman, 417, 505

Bacha-i-Sakao, 216ff.
Badr, Seif el-Islam Mohammed el-, 46
Baghdad Pact, 159, 205f., 229f., 260ff., 291f., 305ff., 363, 385ff., 428f., 452f., 513f.
Bahais, 205, 374
Bahrein, 171, 174, 197
Bailey, Lt. Col. F. M., 112
Baker, Newton D., 80
Bakhtiyaris, the, 34, 40
Baku, 112, 145
Baku Congress, 162, 523
Balfour, Lord A. J., 78ff.
Balfour Declaration, 80ff., 86, 531f.
Balkan Entente Pact (1934), 132
Balkan Pact (1953), 157, 159
Bandung conference, 429
Banna, Sheikh Hassan el-, 407ff.
Barakat, Bahieddin, 419
Barazi, Muhsin el-, 296
Barkatullah, 43, 210
Barrett, Gen., 59
Bat Galim, 497
Batum, Treaty of, 62f.
Bayar, Celal, 151, 156, 205f.
Begin, Menachem, 346, 354
Bell, Gertrude, 96, 233

Ben Gurion, David, 318, 327, 343f., 353, 355, 360
Bennike, Major-Gen. Vagn, 360f.
Berenger-Long agreement, 92
Berlin, Treaty of, 19f., 479
Berlin-Baghdad railway, 24
Bernadotte, Count Folke, 338f.
Bernadotte plan, 349f.
Bevin, Ernest, 250, 332, 518
Beynet, Gen., 281
Biltmore Program, 327
Bitar, Salah el-, 302
Blum, Léon, 273
Brandeis, Louis D., 78ff., 315
Brest-Litovsk, Treaty of, 62f., 65
Britain, British, see Great Britain
Bryan, William J., 80
Bucharest, Treaty of, 13
Bukhara, see Central Asia
Bulganin, Nikolai A., 227
Bulgaria, 3, 19, 26, 131, 132
Bunche, Ralph, 496
Buraimi oasis, 452, 519
Bushnaq, Mustafa, 380
Bustani, Emile, 286
Buzu, Ali, 303, 310
Byrnes, James, 183
Byroade, Henry A., 366f.
Byzantine Empire, 3, 9

Cairo conference (1943), 144
Cairo riots, 418f.
Cakmak, Marshal Fevzi, 122, 142
Capitulations:
    granted to France, 5
    repudiated by Ottoman Empire, 45
    in Turkey, 102, 108
    abolished in Iran, 167
    abolished in Egypt, 401
Carlowitz, Treaty of, 9
Casey, Richard, 403, 504
Catherine the Great, 10
Catroux, Gen. Georges, 277ff.
Caucasus, 55, 142
    see also Transcaucasia
Cecil, Lord, 80
Central Asia, 32, 110ff., 208, 212f., 222
Chadirchi, Kamil, 243, 254
Charles-Roux, François, 499
Chiang Kai-shek, 403f.
Churchill, Sir Winston S., 56, 96, 97, 144, 180, 281, 403
Churchill Memorandum, 317, 322
Clark-Kerr, Sir Archibald, 245
Clayton, Brig. E. H., 503
Clayton, Sir Gilbert, 96, 241, 436
Clemenceau, Georges, 91

567

Kashani, Mullah Ayatollah Abol Ghassem, 184, 199ff.
Kavtaradze, Sergei, 178
Kawukji, Fawzi el-, 283, 337, 417, 509
Kazim Bey, 43
Kemal, Mustafa (Atatürk), 57, 59, 103ff., 117ff., 154
Kenna, Khalil, 253
Khadduri, Rabbi Sassoon, 251
Khalid, Emir, 442
Khalid, Mohammed, 286
Khalidi, Awni, 264
Khalifa, Mohammed Abdur Rahman, 380, 382
Khatib, Anwar el-, 382, 384
Khazal, Sheikh, 166, 174
Khiva, see Central Asia
Khrushchev, Nikita S., 227, 364
Khuri, Bishara el-, 269, 279, 283f., 287f.
Khuri, Faris el-, 270, 272, 279, 305f.
Kianuri, Nur ed-Din, 186
Kiazim Kara Bekir, Gen., 105
Kibya raid, 360f., 384
Kikhya, Rushdi el-, 297
King-Crane Commission, 88ff., 529
Kitchener, Lord, 23, 75, 394
Kokand, see Central Asia
Köprülü, Fuat, 151
Köprülü family, 8
Korean war, 150, 299, 352, 415f.
Kressenstein, Col. Kress von, 63
Krim, Abdul, 417
Kubbah, Mohammed Mehdi, 254
Kuchik Khan, 164, 166
Kuchuk Kainardji, Treaty of, 10f., 478
Kumar Mahendra Pratap, 43, 210
Kurds and Kurdistan:
  loyalty to Turkey in Great War, 47
  to be autonomous, 101
  and Treaty of Lausanne, 108
  general inspectorate for, 123, 126
  revolts in Turkey, 126
  independence favored, 131
  Republic of Mahabad, 181
  rebellion in Iran (1950), 185
  in Iraq, 235f., 249
  encouraged by Russia, 526
Kuwait, 198
Kuzbari, Maamun, 302f.

Laidoner, Gen. Johan, 130
Lake Tiberias village incident, 362f.
Lampson, Sir Miles, 277, 400, 405
Landau, Hanna, 355
Landis, James, 532
Lansing, Robert, 80

Lausanne, Treaty of (1912), 24f.
Lausanne, Treaty of (1923), 107-109, 129
Lausanne Straits Convention, 481ff.
Lawrence, Col. T. E., 58, 96f.
League of Nations:
  and Mosul, 130
  and Alexandretta, 133, 273
  and Iran oil dispute, 175
  and Iraq, 240f.
  and White Paper on Palestine, 325
  and Egypt, 401
  see also Mandates
Lebanon, 22, 283ff.
  see also Syria
Lepanto, battle of, 7
Lesseps, Ferdinand de, 21, 488ff.
Libya, 24f., 47, 474, 507, 516, 518
Lie, Trygve, 182
Lindenblatt, Dr., 169
Livshitz, David, 355
Lloyd George, David, 79, 86, 91, 98, 107
London conference on Palestine, 323f., 502
London, secret Treaty of, 69f.
London, Treaty of (1840), 17, 479
London, Treaty of (1871), 479
London Straits Convention, 479
Lossow, Gen. von, 39, 63
Lowdermilk, Walter C., 349
Lyttelton, Oliver, 277, 403, 507

Macartney, Sir George, 112
McDonald, James G., 331, 349
McGhee, George, 194
Mack, Julian W., 78
McMahon, Sir Henry, 75
MacMichael, Sir Harold, 328
Madfai, Jamil el-, 243, 246, 248, 253, 256f.
Mahabad, Republic of, 249
Mahdi Mohammed Ahmed, 23, 393
Maher Pasha, Ahmed, 398, 406
Maher Pasha, Ali, 404, 406, 419, 425
Mahmud II, 25
Mahmud, Sheikh of Suleimaniya, 235
Mahmud, Gen. Nur el-Din, 255f.
Mahmud Pasha, Mohammed, 397f., 402
Mahmud Shah Khan, 218, 221, 224
Majali, Hazzah el-, 385f.
Makki, Hussein, 201
Malche, Dr., 123
Malcolm Treaty, Anglo-Persian, 29
Malik, Charles, 285
Malki, Lt.-Col. Adnan, 308f.
Malleson, Gen. Sir Wilfrid, 112

571

Wahba, Hafez, 447
Wahhabi tribes and faith, 16, 434ff.
Wassmuss, Consul, 40, 42
Wavell, Gen. Sir Archibald, 470
Wazir, Sayid Abdullah ibn Ahmed el-, 459f., 464
Weizmann, Chaim, 77ff., 314ff.
Weygand, Gen. Maxime, 276
White Paper on Palestine (1939), 324f., 327
Wiley, John, 190
William II, of Germany, 23, 35, 53, 313
Willkie, Wendell, 532
Wilson, Sir Arnold T., 95, 234
Wilson, Sir Henry Maitland, 277
Wilson, Woodrow, 79ff., 87f., 90, 98, 529
Wingate, Sir Reginald, 75, 395
Wise, Stephen S., 78, 80

Yadin, Col. Yigal, 338
Yafi, Abdullah, 284
Yakub, Emir, 208

Yalçin, Husein Cahit, 155
Yalman, Ahmet Emin, 153
Yalta, agreement of, 487
Yasin, Sheikh Yusuf, 447
Yazdi, Morteza, 186
Yeghen Pasha, Adly, 398
Yehya, Imam, 51, 437, 455ff., 465
Yemen, 47, 60f., 437f., 455ff.
Yilderim, 56f., 125
Young Turks, 26f., 37, 45, 127
Yugoslavia, 157ff.

Zaghlul Pasha, Saad, 394ff.
Zahedi, Gen. Fazlollah, 202ff.
Zahir Shah, Mohammed, 219
Zaim, Gen. Husni, 293ff., 417, 511
Zaki Pasha, Gen. Salim, 409
Zeki Pasha, 61
Zhabotinsky, Vladimir, 80, 318
Zia ed-Din Taba-Tabai, Sayid, 165f., 179
Zionism and the Zionists, 77ff., 85f., 251, 312ff., 444, 524f., 531
Ziwar Pasha, 397

88455